European Union

■ Power and policy-making

Second edition

Edited by Jeremy Richardson

ROUTLEDGE
Taylor & Francis Group

London and New York

First edition published 1996
by Routledge

Second edition published 2001
by Routledge
11 New Fetter Lane, London EC4P 4EE

Simultaneously published in the USA
and Canada
by Routledge
29 West 35th Street, New York, NY 10001

*Routledge is an imprint of the Taylor
& Francis Group*

Selection and editorial matter © 2001
Jeremy Richardson; individual chapters
© the contributors

Typeset in Century Old Style by
Taylor & Francis Books Ltd

Printed and bound in Great Britain by
TJ International Ltd, Padstow, Cornwall

*British Library Cataloguing in Publication
Data*
A catalogue record for this book is available
from the British Library

*Library of Congress Cataloging in
Publication Data*
European Union : power & policy-making /
edited by Jeremy Richardson.–2nd ed.
p. cm.
Includes bibliographical references and index.
1. European Union. 2. European Union
countries–Politics and government.
I. Richardson, J. J. (Jeremy John)
JN30 .E942 2001
341.242'2–dc21   00–051746

ISBN 0–415–22164–1 (hbk)
ISBN 0–415–22165–X (pbk)

Contents

CONTENTS

3 Integration theory and the study of the European policy process: towards a synthesis of approaches   51

Laura Cram

CONTENTS

16 European Monetary Union: developments, implications and prospects 321

VALERIO LINTNER

17 Implementing EU public policy 335

DIONYSSIS DIMITRAKOPOULOS AND JEREMY RICHARDSON

Contributors

Torbjörn Bergman, University of Umeå, Sweden
Thomas Christiansen, University of Wales, Aberyswyth, UK
Laura Cram, University of Sheffield, UK
Dionyssis Dimitrakopoulos, Centre for European Politics, Economics and Society, Oxford, UK
Gerda Falkner, Max-Planck Institute, Germany
Mark Franklin, Trinity College, Hertford, USA
Liesbet Hooghe, University of Toronto, Canada
Michael Keating, European University Institute, Florence, Italy
Valerio Lintner, London Guildhall University, UK
Sonia Mazey, Hertford College, Oxford, UK
Michael Nentwich, Austrian Academy of Sciences, Austria
Michael Newman, University of North London, UK
B. Guy Peters, University of Pittsburgh, USA
Tapio Raunio, University of Helsinki, Finland
Jeremy Richardson, Centre for European Politics, Economics and Society, and Nuffield College, Oxford, UK
Michael Smith, University of Loughborough, UK
Mark Thatcher, London School of Economics and Political Science, UK
Daniel Wincott, University of Birmingham, UK
The late **Vincent Wright,** formerly Nuffield College, Oxford

Preface

The first edition of this volume was published in 1996. That year brought the start of another Intergovernmental Conference (IGC) dominated by many of the familiar debates which have dogged the European Community and the European Union since the first steps towards integration were taken in 1951. Issues on the agenda included the powers and organisational rules of the main European institutions; relationships between those institutions; the difficult problems presented by the possibility of further enlargement; the role of non-governmental actors such as interest groups and citizens in addressing the democratic deficit, and above all, the fundamental question of whether the gradual erosion of national sovereignty should continue or, indeed, whether it might actually be reversed. Most of these issues were still on the agenda in the 2000 IGC, and problems such as the weakness of the euro in the first phase of monetary union were added complications. These fundamental questions were discussed in the context of strong globalisation tendencies and increased pressures for transnational regulation, which force all policy actors, public or private, to recognise the benefits of collective action beyond national borders.

Cries of 'Europe in crisis', of Europe 'having lost its way', of 'Europe entering another period of Euro-sclerosis' were as familiar in the year 2000 as they were in 1996. However, the doomsters are almost certainly exaggerating the current difficulties of the EU and failing to appreciate just how resilient most political systems are. It usually takes long-term and fundamental trends, as developed in the old Soviet bloc, for systems to fail. This is because modern, pluralistic systems are dynamic learning organisations, capable of change. The key institutions and individuals operating those systems have enough intelligence to know when to draw back, when to change tack, and when to lie low and let issues stew. The more cautious and humdrum period through which the EU is passing currently can be seen, therefore, as a natural response by governing elites to a more difficult climate of public opinion. In a sense, nervousness about public opinion within the EU is no bad thing. Indeed, it might suggest that the Union's democratic deficit might not be quite as bad as is often suggested. Despite a much more cautious approach to further integration, the ruling elites in the EU still have a keen sense of the risks of moving away from a process that has been underway for decades. Perhaps it is foolish to make political predictions, but I suspect that the now quite long period of self-doubt and criticism will be just one more phase in what has been a fairly continuous process of Europeanisation.

This should not blind us to the busy 'low politics' of European integration which seem-ingly marches on. That the pace of integration, in terms of the production of new directives and regulations, has slowed down is unarguable, yet policy innovation continues in new ways and 'integration via policy-making' is the norm.

If this assertion is correct, what is the main purpose of this book? Its task is straight-forward, albeit difficult to fulfil adequately in one reasonably short volume. It is to explain to students of European integration (and to some degree to students of the politics of individual states which are now embedded in the EU policy process) the ways in which power is exercised within the EU today. Our focus is on the policy-making process, as that ultimate arena of power in society. What role do institutions and other actors play in deciding what European policy is about and in determining the content of the enormous mass of European legislation now in place? Thus, whatever labels we might attach to the EU – federal or intergovernmental for example – they are not the main focus of this volume. Suffice for our purposes that the Union still constitutes a very 'productive' and maturing system of public policy-making within which an increasing number of different types of policy actor are involved. There is long-running a 'policy-making engine' at work which seems to push along Euro-sceptics and enthusiasts alike. Our efforts should be judged by whether or not we have assisted students in developing their understanding of the institutions and processes involved in this dynamic – from the ways in which the rather fluid policy agenda is set in the European Union, to the ways in which policy is implemented or (often) not in the member states which have signed up to collective policy decisions.

As editor of this volume, which is part of the Routledge European Public Policy Series, I have an overriding debt. The volume could not have been produced without the enthusiasm of the many contributors and their considerable expertise in the European policy process and its development. Their professionalism made my editorial task pleas-antly light. I also owe a debt to Carol Phillips of Nuffield College, for her help in preparing the manuscript for publication and to the Nuffield Foundation for supporting my work on policy styles. Finally, I owe a great debt to my wife Sonia Mazey who introduced me to the importance of studying Europeanisation and remains my mentor in all things European.

The first edition was dedicated to my daughter Tessa, born as the volume was being completed. This new edition is dedicated to my friend and former Nuffield colleague Vincent Wright who died in Oxford in July 1999. He was a true European and a great supporter to all who studied Europe.

Jeremy Richardson
Oxford, April 2001

Part I

THEORETICAL AND HISTORICAL PERSPECTIVES

Chapter 1

Policy-making in the EU

Interests, ideas and garbage cans of primeval soup

Jeremy Richardson

> Many people have proposals they would like to see considered seriously, alternatives they would like to see become part of the set from which choices are eventually made. They try out their ideas on others in the policy community. Some proposals are rapidly discarded as somehow kooky; others are taken more seriously and survive, perhaps in some altered form. But in the policy primeval soup, quite a wide range of ideas is possible and is considered to some extent. The range at this stage is considerably more inclusive than the set of alternatives that are actually weighed during a shorter period of final decision-making. Many, many things are possible here.
>
> (Kingdon 1984: 128)

The EU as a policy-making state: the importance of multiple policy stakeholders in the exercise of 'loose-jointed' power play

One of the main attributes of the nation state is the ability to make 'authoritative alloca-tions' for society. In practice this means an ability to formulate and implement public policy programmes governing the operation of society. Whether the European Union (EU) can be considered a fully fledged state is debatable. For example, Hix, drawing on Almond's (1956) and Easton's (1957) characterisations of political systems, concludes that the EU is certainly a political system in that it exhibits most of the characteristics that those writers attribute to political systems. However, he concludes that it is not a state as it lacks a monopoly on the legitimate use of coercion that characterises a state (Hix 1999: 2–5). Even so, it is beyond dispute that the EU has acquired for itself at least the *policy-making* attributes of a modern state across an increasingly wide range of policy sectors and has quite a degree of coercive power in order to enforce policy decisions. Indeed, much of the criticism of the EU during the Maastricht and Amsterdam debates was centred upon the alleged 'excessive' policy-making role of the EU in general and of the Commission in particular (see Mazey in this volume). The argument now is that the EU has become a 'nanny' state, over-regulating the economic and social life of member states. Increasing Euroscepticism appears to be causing some of the key stakeholders, particu-larly the member states, to apply the brakes to the seemingly inexorable extension of the EU's policy-making competence. As Radaelli (1999) suggests, things began to change in the 1990s. Not just the quantity of EU legislation has been subject to challenge, but also its quality and the processes by which it is made. As he notes, the Amsterdam Treaty contains an entire title on the quality of EU legislation. Thus, 'good legislation requires consulta-tion, regulatory impact assessment, and systematic evaluation of the results achieved by European public policies. But it also requires transparency' (Radaelli 1999: 5). In practice, the erosion of national sovereignty means the erosion of the power of the member states exclusively to decide much of their public policy via domestic policy-making processes and institutions. Empirically, it is beyond dispute that the EU level is now the level at which a high proportion of what used to be regarded as purely domestic policy-making takes place. Hix suggests that the EU sets over 80 per cent of the rules governing the exchange of goods, services and capital in the member states' markets (Hix 1999: 3). The locus of decision-making – and therefore power – has shifted. A more complex structure of policy-making has developed, encompassing a much wider range of public and private policy actors. All of these actors – especially national governments – are having to adjust to the empirical reality of this situation. They have all 'lost' some power in a common pooling of policy-making sovereignty. For those European nations who are members of the EU (and for many who are not), at least two policy-making systems now cohabit – domestic and EU policy systems. As Laffan *et al.* suggest, the defining characteristic of the Union is the enmeshing of the national and the European, or the embedding of the national in the European (Laffan *et al.* 2000: 74–8). This has led to what they term a system of 'international governance', with the EU, as an arena of public policy, presenting 'a challenge to national political systems because they are confronted with the need to adapt to a normative and strategic environment that escapes total control' (Laffan *et al.* 2000: 84–7).

Though state-like in at least this key attribute, the EU is, of course, a complex and unique policy-making system. Its multinational and neo-federal nature, the extreme openness of decision-making to lobbyists, and the considerable weight of national politico-administrative elites within the process, create an unpredictable and multi-level policy-making environment. Even the relationships between key institutions – such as the Commission, the European Parliament (EP), the Council of Ministers (CM) and the European Court of Justice (ECJ) – are still in a considerable state of flux, as many of the chapters in this volume demonstrate. Although clearly a very *productive* policy process, the EU political system cannot be said to be a stable one, as the basic constitutional architecture is still very much in dispute. At best the EU policy process might exhibit some stable patterns of cross-national coalition-building; at worst it may exhibit some of the extreme aspects of a garbage can (Cohen *et al.* 1972) model of decision-making. It is no surprise, therefore, that the EU regulatory system has been described as a 'patchwork of different national regulatory styles' (Héritier 1996).

At this relatively early stage in the development of the EU policy process it is difficult to formulate reliable descriptions – let alone theoretical models – which will capture more than a few aspects of the policy process as a whole. The objective of this chapter is limited, therefore, to an analysis of the possible utility of what has become the dominant 'model' for analysing the policy process in Western Europe – the so-called policy community/policy network model. Fortuitously, approaching EU policy-making via this perspective also enables us to utilise related approaches to the study of policy-making which emphasise the importance of ideas, knowledge and expertise, rather than pure 'interest'. It will be argued that there are inherent similarities in these two 'actor-based' approaches, even though they originate from quite different academic perspectives. Essentially they both focus on sets of actors as *stakeholders* in the policy process. Elsewhere in this volume, contributors analyse the roles of 'official' or 'public' stakeholders (e.g. national governments, the Commission, the EP, the ECJ). However, all of these actors are influenced by ideas, knowledge and private interests. Thus, over thirty years ago E. E. Schattschneider reminded us that the supreme instrument of political power was the ability to determine what politics was about (Schattschneider 1960). Although this is a neglected aspect of the workings of the EU (see Peters in this volume), evidence does suggest that the EU agenda-setting process is especially problematic because of its transnational nature and because of the wide range of state and non-state actors involved in the EU policy process (Mazey and Richardson 1993). Moreover, as with nation states, the EU's policy agenda is permeable to extra-territorial influences – from non-EU states such as the USA and Japan, but also from international standard-setting bodies and organisations such as the World Health Organisation (WHO) (Richardson 1994a). and via the EU's participation in global regulatory agencies such as the World Trade Organisation (WTO). Thus, the EU is not only a form of 'supranational' system of policy-making in its own right, it is also part of a higher level of supranational policy-making, beyond the regional level. Such complex policy-making arrangements privilege the role of experts and technocrats who are increasingly transnational in their focus and activities. Thus, analysis of the role of 'communities' of experts – so-called epistemic communities (see below) – is important in the EU because they so often transcend national boundaries. The policy community/policy network approach, in contrast, appears to have some utility in assisting our understanding of the ways in which agenda issues are translated or 'processed' into technical and workable EU legislative proposals – especially in technical areas of 'low politics' (Hoffmann 1966). Other related concepts from public policy, which attempt to integrate analyses of ideas and interests – such as Sabatier's 'advocacy coalitions' and Kingdon's 'policy streams' – may also be useful in assisting our understanding of the policy dynamics of the EU, especially if we view the EU policy process as essentially a multi-level, multi-arena game. They may enable us to better understand how all decision-makers in the EU, public or private, national or supranational, come to 'frame' public policy problems (Rein and Schön 1991).

The 'level of analysis' question is, of course, important. Thus, it may be a mistake to look for only *one* model of the EU policy process. Within the EU, policy can be determined at a number of levels and the policy process goes through a number of stages. Also, particular policy areas may themselves be episodic, exhibiting different characteristics at different times. Different models of analysis may be useful at different levels within the EU and at different stages of the policy process. For example, if we were to conceptualise the EU policy process into four stages – agenda-setting, policy formulation, policy decision, and policy implementation – we might need to utilise rather different conceptual tools in order to understand fully the nature of the processes in each stage. The epistemic communities approach might be particularly useful in understanding stage one, the policy community/network model for stage two, institutional analysis for stage three, and interorganisational behaviour and implementation analysis for stage four. Even then, reality is likely to be much more messy, suggesting that we need a fairly eclectic use of concepts and models. 'Grand theory' must await a much stronger empirical base, bearing in mind that there are major cross-sectoral variations in EU policy styles. For example, some policy areas may be highly pluralistic (e.g. environmental policy) and others may exhibit some corporatist tendencies (e.g. agriculture).

It is also important to note that the EU policy-making system as a whole might vary over time. Thus, just as the pace and nature of the integration process is not constant (see Mazey in this volume), so the nature of the policy process within it can vary over time. It is now conventional wisdom that the EU policy style is less clearly a *regulatory* style, reflecting the increased resistance to further Europeanisation and the weakened position of the Commission as the motor of integration (see Christiansen chapter in this volume). The annual output of directives has declined; there is said to be less 'old-style' regulation; and there is an alleged shift towards new policy instruments that emphasise co-operation, voluntary action, demonstration projects, good practice, benchmarking, etc. The greater emphasis on 'softer' policy instruments (which may actually disguise the continuation of old-style regulation – see Richardson and Rittberger 2001) has been accompanied by an intensification of consultation of stakeholders (see Mazey and Richardson in this volume). The more the policy-making legitimacy of the EU has been challenged, the more the Commission has mobilised stakeholder participation in the process.

In searching for useful theories and concepts, the notion of the EU as a policy-making 'state', backed by the legal co-operation of the ECJ, is important. Our central argument here is that the 'stuff' of European integration is as much about detailed, often technical, Euro-legislation (a mixture of Euro-regulation and softer policy instruments) as it is about high politics issues such as monetary union or the creation of a European superstate. While these issues are, of course, crucial, and certainly absorb the interest of national governments, the 'European policy game' continues to be played at the detailed policy level and continues to attract the attention and efforts of a plethora of interest groups and others in the manner predicted by the neo-functionalists. Low politics this may be, in the Hoffmann terminology (Hoffmann 1966), but it is probably the nine-tenths of the EU 'policy iceberg' that is below the water line. There is an increasing amount of political activity at this level within the EU and some means has to be found of analysing and conceptualising it. Moreover, this policy-making activity is not simply a question of intergovernmental relations – if only because such a wide range of non-governmental actors is so obviously involved, at both the national, EU and extra-EU levels. EU policies are not simply the outcome of interstate bargaining, even if the policy process usually appears to culminate in this way. It is a complex process involving different types of actors – institutional and non-institutional, governmental and non-governmental – with all actors involved in what Tsebelis terms 'nested games' (Tsebelis 1990) and in serial coalition-building.

Regardless of the way that problems and issues arrive on the political agenda, it is a phenomenon of modern government that procedural mechanisms (formal and informal institutions, formal and informal rules) are devised to bring the various stakeholders together in order to thrash out a solution which is ultimately acceptable. Hence, modern government is not just characterised by *ad hoc* and permanent committees, but by a 'procedural logic' which brings policy actors together in some kind of relationship – hence the popularity in public policy analysis of approaches utilising variants of the 'policy network' approach. Even in past periods of so-called 'Euro-sclerosis' or in the current phase of Euro-scepticism, the Union (especially in the form of the European Commission) finds ways of 'legislating in hard times'. The very fact that it is currently more difficult to generate and pass European legislation merely intensifies the logic of actor mobilisation. For 'the European project' to move forward, the many stakeholders need to be given more incentives to participate at the Euro-level and their participation needs to be structured and institutionalised. As Laffan *et al.* suggest, 'enhanced policy responsibility has led to an expansion of policy networks and communities around the core of the Union institutions' (Laffan *et al.* 2000: 85). A central aspect of the Jacques Santer dictum 'doing less but doing it better' (European Commission 1995: 6) is even greater effort to involve the many stakeholders having a recognised interest in any given policy area.

Policy communities, policy networks and issue networks

It is worth remembering that the term 'policy community' was originally used (at least in Britain) with a quite deliberate emphasis on *community*, and at a time when policy stability rather than policy change seemed more common. Moreover, it was developed as a counterweight to more traditional analyses of the British policy process. For example, the subtitle of *Governing under Pressure* (first published in 1979) was provocative in claiming that Britain was a *post-parliamentary* democracy: the focus of the analysis was on the informal relationships between different policy actors rather than on the roles of formal institutions. Thus:

> In describing the tendency for boundaries between government and groups to become less distinct through a whole range of pragmatic developments, we see policies being made (and administered) between a myriad of interconnecting, interpenetrating organisations. It is the relationship involved in committees, the policy community of departments and groups, the practices of co-option and the consensual style, that perhaps better account for policy outcomes than do examinations of party stances, of manifestos or of parliamentary influence.
>
> (Richardson and Jordan 1979: 73–4)

Interestingly, Anderson and Burns use the post-parliamentary label in their 1996 characterisation of the EU system of governance. Instead of parliamentary governance, they
emphasise the role of experts, organisations and networks of public and private actors
(Andersen and Burns 1996: 224). The term policy community was meant to convey a very
close and stable relationship between policy actors – somewhat close to the dictionary
definition of community: 'joint ownership of goods, identity of character, fellowship (... of
interest)'. Use of the word community also implied some notions regarding *level of
analysis*. If policy actors could be brought together in a long-term and stable relationship
which presented the prospect of an *exchange relationship*, then this was most likely at the
sub-sectoral or even micro level. There was also an implication of stable policies as well
as stable relationships and a stable membership. Thus, it was argued that:

> The logic of negotiation also suggests that policy-makers in both government and groups will
> share an interest in the avoidance of sudden policy change. Working together they will learn
> what kind of change is feasible and what would so embarrass other members of the 'system'
> as to be unproductive. Members of the system will begin to debate in the same language (if not
> with the same values), and arguments will be treated seriously only if discussed in these
> common criteria. There is a role diffusion in that all members – government officials, academic
> experts and group officials – become policy professionals.
>
> (Jordan and Richardson 1982: 93–4)

In fact, there was a considerable note of caution in these early formulations of the policy
communities concept. The implication was that it had its greatest utility when analysing a
particular level of (often technical) decisions – almost exactly the thrust of the argument
in this chapter in terms of the EU policy process. Thus, the current vogue for the use of
network analysis at this supranational level needs tempering by reference to what its original proponents claimed and to the unusual degree of complexity in the EU policy
process. Compared with most national policy-making systems in Europe, the EU is characterised by very large numbers of actors, bringing extremely diverse policy frames to
the negotiating tables, and facing an array of policy-making venues (see below) at which
they can influence EU policy. The policy game is qualitatively different (Richardson 2000).

A further reason for caution in characterising the EU policy process simply in terms of
policy communities and organised networks is that there is some evidence that the sectori-
sation of policy-making, on which policy communities, particularly, are based, is being
eroded. Indeed, Jordan and Richardson had themselves begun, as early as 1982, to emphasise the linkages between policy communities, both within policy sectors and between
policy sectors. They argued that 'there will be many linkages between various policy
communities in each sector (for example, between branches of medicine, social services
and social policy) ... but there will also be some linkages between sectors ... what
evidence we have suggests that consultation of various types is more extensive than
formerly' (Jordan and Richardson 1982: 89–90).

Put simply, the pattern appears to be an increase in the number of stakeholders
demanding and getting participation in EU policy-making, and an extension of the range
of policy sectors from which they are drawn, for each particular example of consultation.
This gradual shift in emphasis – from a world of policy-making characterised by tightly
knit policy communities, to a more loosely organised and therefore less predictable policy
process – is very familiar in the US. The seminal work (on either side of the Atlantic) is
still Heclo's 1978 analysis, which began to re-direct us towards policy *dynamics* rather
than policy stability. Just as many authors (including this one!) were emphasising *stable*

policy communities, Heclo had observed a trend which appears to be still running strongly at both the national and international levels – namely that policy problems often eventually escape the confined and exclusive 'worlds' of professionals and are resolved in a much looser configuration (if indeed such a structured term can be used) of participants in the policy process. Heclo argued that the nature of power in Washington had begun to change – exercising power was not as much fun as it used to be in the 'clubby' days of Washington politics (Heclo 1978: 94). Politics was less 'clubbable' because more and more groups had entered the policy process. Thus 'as proliferating groups have claimed a stake and clamoured for a place in the policy process, they have helped diffuse the focus of political and administrative leadership' (Heclo 1978: 94–5). The process had gone so far, he argued, that:

> With more public policies, more groups are being mobilized and there are more complex relationships among them. Since very few policies ever seem to drop off the public agenda as more are added, congestion among those interested in various issues grows, the chances for accidental collisions increase, and the interaction tends to take on a distinctive group-life of its own in the Washington community. One scene in a recent Jacques Tati film pictures a Paris traffic circle so dense with traffic that no one can get in or out; instead, drivers spend their time socializing with each other as they drive in endless circles. Group politics in Washington may be becoming such a merry-go-round.
>
> (Heclo 1978: 97)

In the context of the EU, all we need do is substitute for Washington the traffic circle in front of the Commission's Berlaymont building – or the professional and social networks in Kitty O'Shea's bar just off the traffic circle. Correctly, Heclo argued that we needed to rethink our notions of political power, existing conceptions of power and control were not well suited to the 'loose-jointed' power play of influence that was emerging. In a now classic formulation, he argued that:

> Obviously questions of power are still important. But for a host of policy initiatives undertaken in the last twenty years it is all but impossible to identify clearly who the dominant actors are. Who is controlling those actions that go to make up our national policy on abortions, or on income redistribution, or consumer protection, or energy? Looking for the few who are powerful we tend to overlook the many whose webs of influence provoke and guide the exercise of power. These webs, or what I will call 'issue networks', are particularly relevant to the highly intricate and confusing welfare policies that have been undertaken in recent years.
>
> (Heclo 1978: 102)

Again one is reminded of the EU policy process, where interest groups and national governments often feel that policies come from 'nowhere' (Mazey and Richardson 1993). Indeed, Dyson borrows a term from Heinz *et al.* (1993) to describe the policy processes relating to European Monetary Union (EMU). Conventional wisdom might suggest that the German state, and especially the Bundesbank, has such 'state strength' (Krasner 1978: 55) as to secure their desired pay-offs, but the policy process seems much more messy and complex. Dyson observes, 'there is little evidence that a single actor – whether the Commission or Ecofin or the Bundesbank – occupies the central policy-brokering role within the EMU process in any continuous sense, capable in a more or less autonomous way of promoting compromise or imposing settlements. In this sense, the EMU policy process has a "hollow core"' (Dyson 1994: 332).

The primary causes of the increasing 'messiness' of the EU policy process are twofold.

First, the very act of adding more countries increases complexity enormously. In formu-lating what he terms an 'EU law of physics', Pascal Lamoy, the EU's Trade Commissioner, has suggested that 'complexity is an exponential and not proportional function of the number of members of the EU' (*Financial Times* 3 Aug. 2000). Second, the addition of new members significantly adds to the number and range of interest groups who demand participation at the European level. There are simply too many players with too many diverse interests for the policy community (or, indeed, corporatist) model to become the dominant paradigm within the EU.

Even Heclo, however, was reluctant to accept a total-disorder thesis, making at least two important qualifications to the model of confusion, diffuse power, and lack of accountability. He pointed out a paradox of disorder and order when he argued that there was a second tendency cutting in the opposite direction to the widening group participa-tion in public policy. In the midst of the emergence of the loose issue networks cited above we could also see what he called 'policy as intramural activity'. Thus:

> Expanding welfare policies and Washington's reliance on indirect administration have encour-aged the development of specialized subcultures composed of highly knowledgeable policy-watchers. Some of these people have advanced professional degrees, some do not. What they all have in common is the detailed understanding of specialized issues that comes from sustained attention to a given policy debate.
>
> (Heclo 1978: 49)

In a less quoted passage, he deftly links the two apparently contradictory trends, as follows:

> Whatever the participants' motivation, it is the issue network that ties together what would otherwise be the contradictory tendencies of, on the one hand, more widespread organizational participation in public policy and, on the other, more narrow technocratic specialization in complex modern policies. Such networks need to be distinguished from three other more familiar terms used in connection with political administration. An issue network is a shared-knowledge group having to do with some aspect (or, as defined by the network, some problem) of public policy. It is therefore more well-defined than, first, a shared-attention group or 'public', those in the networks are likely to have a common base of information and under-standing of how one knows about policy and identifies its problems. But knowledge does not necessarily produce agreement. Issue networks may or may not, therefore, be mobilized into, second, a shared-action group (creating a coalition) or, third, a shared-belief group (becoming a conventional interest organization). Increasingly, it is through networks of people who regard each other as knowledgeable, or at least as needing to be answered, that public policy issues tend to be refined, evidence debated, and alternative options worked out – though rarely in any controlled, well-organized way.
>
> (Heclo 1978: 103–4)

So, how can sense be made of these contrasting images of the policy process? On the one hand, we have the policy community concept. On the other hand, there is the rather 'disor-derly' issue network concept. The suggestion by Rhodes that policy communities and issue networks are part of a continuum – and that policy networks should be used as a *generic* term – is a sensible reminder that there is no *one* model of policy-making. He draws on Benson's 1982 definition of a network as 'a cluster or complex of organizations connected to each other by resource dependencies and distinguished from other clusters or complexes by breaks in the structure of resource dependencies' (Benson 1982: 148). However, he goes on to distinguish five types of networks 'ranging along a continuum from highly integrated policy communities to loosely integrated issue networks' (Rhodes 1990: 304).

Recognising the network concept as a continuum does enable us to focus on the possibility of changes in the nature of the policy process over time and from sector to sector. Thus, it may be that at any given time several types of policy networks (in the generic sense) are in operation within the EU. If so, we need to analyse the interrelationships (if any) between these and the conditions under which they emerge. Also, over time, the policy process might change its characteristics quite significantly, along the continuum; and, of course, it may often be unhelpful to use the network analogy at all for the analysis of some EU policy decisions.

Describing certain stages of the policy process in network terms can be useful and illuminating, but we must not neglect the role of institutions. For example, in the EU the role of the Council of Ministers is obviously crucial, yet it is difficult to see analysis of policy networks as being central to an analysis of the Council. No doubt ministers will to some degree reflect the power of national networks in the manner suggested by Putnam (Putnam 1988), but, clearly, they do not follow their national interest group systems slavishly. Similarly, the Commission, as an institutional actor in its own right, is enormously powerful in the EU policy process. Again it can be seen as a broker of interests, or a *bourse* of ideas and interests (Mazey and Richardson 1994), but it is much more than that and has its own institutional interest to protect and expand (see Christiansen, and Mazey and Richardson, in this volume). Moreover, we must not neglect the role of ideas, of ideology, or the special powers of state actors in setting the agenda for policy change at both the national and international levels; in many instances policy networks, where they exist, are responding to rather than creating policy change.

What then is the utility of the policy network approach and what is its potential for EU level analysis? Two modest but sensible claims might be made. First, by trying to identify networks of policy actors we at least focus on what might be called the *stakeholders* in the EU policy processes. If EU politics is about who gets what, how and when (as surely it is?), then identifying the range of actors involved and trying to see if they can realistically be described as networks is at least the starting point for understanding how the system of making EU policies works. Sensible research questions are: 'Who has an *interest* in this policy problem? How are they mobilised and organised? What is the timing and nature of their involvement in the policy process? How are their preferences determined, and are they really fixed? Do they develop stable relationships with each other?' We also need to ask who is likely to gain and who is likely to lose from different policy outcomes. In addressing these questions within the EU, we need to be cautious in transposing some of the (alleged) characteristics of various types of policy network. For example, many groups involved in the EC policy process have little or no formal involvement in policy delivery, nor are they necessarily involved in any direct resource dependencies with other decision-makers except in a general sense. Similarly, they may have quite different value systems and often exhibit very contrasting and conflicting views of the policy problem and of possible solutions. The basis of the relationship between these different actors is threefold: (1) recognition of each other as legitimate stakeholders in the policy area/problem; (2) a recognition that collaboration may be the best means of extending the Pareto boundary to mutual advantage; (3) they desire negotiated and stable policy environments in preference to instability and uncertainty. In other words, co-operation within various types of policy network is sensible for Pareto maximisers; there are mutual gains to be had. This is rather different from direct resource dependency or a shared direct involvement in service delivery, or from shared values. Focusing on networks of stake-holders may, therefore, help us to analyse the detailed process by which new knowledge and policy ideas (which may well originate elsewhere, see Reich 1988; Radaelli 1995; Braun and Busch 1999) are translated into specific policy proposals via the involvement of the wide variety and large number of stakeholders that can be identified.

Here, the *institutional* context of the EU is crucial. Thus the Commission is both an adolescent and a promiscuous bureaucracy (Mazey and Richardson 1995). At the stage of translating ideas into detailed and workable public policies (in now fifteen member states), the resource dependencies identified by Rhodes and Marsh at the national level may begin to emerge (Rhodes and Marsh 1992). At the detailed and technical stage, Commission offi-cials, in particular, need the expertise of other policy actors. If the devil is in the detail, then policy networks – and indeed policy communities – may come into their own as concepts for advancing our understanding of the EU as a policy-making state. (For a debate on the utility of network analysis in understanding EU policy-making, see Kassim 1994; Peterson 1995a; Peterson 1995b; for a general discussion of networks, see Atkinson and Coleman 1989; Dowding 1995; Thatcher 1998; Coleman and Perl 1999; Richardson 2000.)

Policy-making under uncertainty: knowledge and mutual gains

If one were to be unkind one might see much work on policy networks (and especially on policy communities) as the 'politics of the piddling', i.e. policy communities may play a key role only in the *processing* of issues at the technical and detailed level once key agenda decisions have been reached. Again, the British case post-1979 is illustrative. The Thatcherite revolution was not so much about excluding pressure groups in an attempt to govern without consensus, it was more about determining the new agenda for each policy sector and then consulting the affected interests about how best to implement the new policies for health, education, the legal profession, etc. (Richardson 1994b). Most of the radical policy change which took place did not *emanate* from policy communities or policy networks – they reacted to exogenous changes. Policy-making within the EU may bear some similarities to this policy style. The EU is faced with fifteen different policy systems, each reflecting national power structures (and national policy networks) and national compromises in determining the 'national interest'. If European integration is to take place, these national policy arrangements must be challenged in some way and new policy settlements agreed. Aspects of an impositional policy style (Richardson 1982) can be seen, ultimately, in the way ECJ decisions affect the nation states, in the pressure for more effective national implementation of EU laws, and of course in the increased use of qualified majority voting within the Council of Ministers, further extended at the Nice IGC in 2000. In the end, both national policy-making styles and national policy frame-works are challenged by EU legislation. Whilst the EU lacks the state attribute of the monopoly of force, it does possess great power in the form of legal (and now financial) sanctions and the power to exact retribution on recalcitrant players in policy 'games'. It is not surprising therefore that the range of potential actors in this change process is enor-mous and the patterns of interaction are sometimes unpredictable.

Garbage can politics

How, then, does policy change take place within the EU in the absence of a European government and of a stable governing coalition? In a key passage, Adler and Haas argue that it is useful to turn the study of the political process into a question about who learns what, when, to whose benefit and why (Adler and Haas 1992: 370). Perceiving the policy process as centrally concerned with ideas, knowledge and their use is both helpful and consistent with our concern with actor-based models of the policy process. The work by Peter Haas and his colleagues is of particular relevance to the workings of the EU. Although concerned with international co-operation (and therefore approaching the EU from an international relations perspective) Haas's comment that 'a related question/debate is the extent to which state actors fully recognise and appreciate the anarchic nature of the system and, consequently, *whether rational choice, deductive-type approaches or interpretative approaches are most appropriate ...*' (emphasis added) is very apposite to our own task here. Thus, virtually all interest group respondents (and most national officials) who were interviewed in our study of the role of interest groups in the EU policy process emphasised the fluidity and unpredictability of the process (see Mazey and Richardson in this volume). Adopting the rational actor model was difficult for them in situations of high uncertainty and in the absence of crucial information about the policy positions and behaviour of other stakeholders. Indeed, they may be totally unaware of other key actors in the process, let alone of the policy preferences and strategies of those actors! In such situations, the term 'network' should be used with great caution. Literally, 'network' should mean that the various actors do interconnect in some way. Empirically, this is sometimes difficult to determine and, rather like the puzzle relating to the existence of life elsewhere in the universe, policy actors are often uncertain as to the identity of other actors elsewhere in the 'system'. Again, this is as true for national governments as it is true for, say, firms or associations. Actors often operate under a huge degree of uncertainty in what are often very long-running games, with uncertain pay-offs. The total 'system' is large and amorphous, with numbers of part-time participants and a range of ideas floating around in some ethereal fashion. In these situations the policy process may resemble the 'garbage can' model of decision-making developed by Cohen *et al.* in 1972 and elaborated by Kingdon (Cohen *et al.* 1972; Kingdon 1984). The central feature of the original garbage can model is that 'decision situations' (or what Cohen *et al.* termed 'organized anarchies') are characterised by three general properties. First, there are *problematic preferences*. The organisation operates on the basis of a variety of inconsistent and ill-defined preferences (Cohen *et al.* 1972: 1). Their description of organisational life fits well with what we already know about some aspects of the EU – namely, that 'it (the organisation) can be described better as a loose collection of ideas than as a coherent structure, it discovers preferences through action more than it acts on the basis of preferences' (Cohen *et al.* 1972: 1). The second characteristic of decision situations is *unclear technology*. Thus, although the organisation manages to survive and even produce, its own processes are not understood by its members. In the EU, both the Maastricht and Amsterdam IGCs saw demands for the *simplification* of the EU policy process and for greater predictability of decision pathways. Similarly, the Nice IGC in 2000 was concerned with the likely increased complexity of the EU policy process which would result from enlargement (see Falkner and Nentwitch in this volume). Organisations operate 'on the basis of simple trial-and-error procedures, the residue of learning from the incident of past experience, and pragmatic inventions of necessity' (Cohen *et al.* 1972: 1). Finally, there is *fluid participation* in that participants vary in the amount of time and effort they devote to different domains. In practice, it is useful to view an organisation as 'a *collection of choices looking for problems, issues and feelings looking for decision*

13

situations in which they might be aired, solutions looking for issues to which they might be the answer, and decision-makers looking for work' (Cohen *et al.* 1972: 2, emphasis added).

The Haas argument is, centrally, that the politics of uncertainty lead to a certain mode of behaviour – namely that policy-makers, when faced with 'the uncertainties associated with many modern responsibilities of international governance turn to new and different channels of advice, often with the result that international policy co-ordination is advanced' (Haas 1992: 12).

As he argues, the concept of uncertainty is important for two reasons:

> First, in the face of uncertainty … many of the conditions facilitating a focus on power are absent. It is difficult for leaders to identify their potential political allies and to be sure of what strategies are most likely to help them retain power. And, second, poorly understood conditions may create enough turbulence that established operating procedures may break down, making institutions unworkable. Neither power nor institutional cues to behavior would be available, and new patterns of action may ensue.
>
> (Haas 1992: 14)

However, as Sebenius points out, uncertainty and power do go hand in hand, as uncertainty presents opportunities for power to be exercised if individuals or institutions are sufficiently alert to the opportunities. He therefore argues that we need to emphasise the interplay of power and knowledge in influencing outcomes (Sebenius 1992: 325). Alongside uncertainty in the policy process there are opportunities for mutual learning and joint problem-solving – especially when issues involve technical uncertainties in such areas as scientific, environmental, economic and security affairs. By combing the politics of uncertainty and the politics of learning, Sebenius in fact captures the core meaning of 'policy community' as a concept. Thus he states that 'beyond understanding technical uncertainties, finding joint gains also requires that each party learn about the other's priorities in order to craft mutually beneficial trades' (Sebenius 1992: 329). Co-operation, therefore, can produce what Walton and McKersie term 'integrated bargaining' as opposed to 'distributive bargaining'. In the former the effort is directed towards expanding the pie, whereas in the latter it is a more adversarial process of dividing the pie (Walton and McKersie 1965). Sebenius goes on to quote Howard Raiffa as follows:

> In complicated negotiations where uncertainties loom large, there may be contracts that are far better for each negotiating party than the non-contract alternative, but it may take considerable skill and joint problem solving to discover these possibilities. *Without the right atmosphere and without some reasonably trustful communication of values, such jointly acceptable contracts might never by discerned.*
>
> (Raiffa quoted by Sebenius 1992: 329, emphasis added by this author)

This is not too dissimilar to our original formulation of the policy communities concept suggested in *Governing under Pressure* in 1979. This emphasised the development of a common understanding of each other's problems and a recognition that beneficial bargains could be struck over time. Logically, this does not imply consensus on values or on outcomes – but it does imply a consensus that collaboration can produce efficiency gains all round. There may be considerable and bitter disputation, yet the game continues to be played in order to secure mutual gains or to avoid individual losses. This seems to fit what we know about the EU policy process. Lax and Sebenius have emphasised that the bargaining process indeed exhibits both conflict and consensus. Thus:

the competitive and co-operative elements are inextricably entwined. In practice they cannot be separated. This bonding is fundamentally important to the analysis, structuring the conduct of negotiation. There is a central, inescapable tension between co-operative moves to create value jointly and competitive moves to gain individual advantage. This tension affects virtually all tactical and strategic choice. Analysts must come to grips with it; negotiators must manage it.

(Lax and Sebenius 1986: 30)

Participating in joint policy-making activity therefore has the potential to maximise benefits to the parties involved. Using concepts from negotiation analysis, Sebenius points out that outcomes can be influenced by favourably affecting the zone of possible agreement between the parties. The 'zone of possible agreement' means 'a set of possible agreements that are better for each potential party than the non-co-operative alternatives to an agreement' (Sebenius 1992: 333).

Expertise and epistemic communities

The value of these approaches is that they remind us that policy actors, such as those participating in the EU policy process, are often operating under considerable degrees of uncertainty and are prepared to engage in a negotiative process even when there is considerable disagreement over basic goals or core beliefs. The key role of epistemic communities in this process relates directly to the principle that policy-makers are operating under conditions of uncertainty. Thus:

> Given the technical uncertainties regarding an issue and the legitimacy of claims to expertise of members of an epistemic community, especially those placed close to the decision-making process, their influence may cause the perceived interests of key players in different countries to grow closer together, along with their understanding of underlying causal relationships. In this situation, the epistemic community members may come to act as a coordinated set of common interpretative filters.

(Sebenius 1992: 354)

It is the knowledge-based (or at least *perceived* knowledge-based) nature of epistemic communities that provides these networks of actors with the potential to influence the policy process. Authoritativeness, and therefore legitimacy, are the key currencies of these types of networks, and they are central to the definition of epistemic communities formulated by Peter Haas, as follows:

> An epistemic community is a network of professionals with recognised expertise and competence in a particular domain and an authoritative claim to policy-relevant knowledge within that domain or issue-area. Although an epistemic community may consist of professionals from a variety of disciplines and backgrounds, they have (1) a shared set of normative and principled beliefs, which provide a value-based rationale for the social action of community members; (2) shared causal beliefs, which are derived from their analysis of practices leading or contributing to a central set of problems in their domain and which then serve as the basis for elucidating the multiple linkages between possible policy actions and desired outcomes; (3) shared notions of validity – that is, intersubjective, internally defined criteria for weighing and validating knowledge in the domain of their expertise; and (4) a common policy enterprise – that is, a set of common practices associated with a set of problems to which their professional competence is directed, presumably out of the conviction that human welfare will be enhanced as a consequence.

(Haas 1992: 3)

As with the policy network concept, epistemic communities as a concept is also subject to refinement and redefinition. In a useful footnote, Haas reveals that other characterisations of epistemic communities were discussed during the preparation of the special issue of *International Organization* in which his seminal paper appears. Some of the additional notions used were as follows:

> members of an epistemic community share intersubjective understandings; have a shared way of knowing; have shared patterns of reasoning; have a policy project drawing on shared values, share causal beliefs, and the use of shared discursive practices; and have a shared commitment to the application and production of knowledge.
>
> (Haas 1992: 3)

Interestingly, Haas sees some kind of logic in this process of policy co-ordination via epistemic communities. The situation in which policy-makers find themselves leads almost naturally to the use of experts of various kinds. Just as it has been argued in Britain that there is a 'logic of negotiation' (Jordan and Richardson 1982: see also Mazey and Richardson in this volume), so the dynamics of uncertainty, interpretation and institutionalisation at the international level drive policy-makers towards the use of epistemic communities. Haas argues that 'in international policy co-ordination, the forms of uncertainty that tend to stimulate demands for information are those which arise from the strong dependence of states on each other's policy choices for success in obtaining goals and those which involve multiple and only partly estimable consequences of action' (Haas 1992: 3–54). Uncertainty gives rise to demands for information – particularly about 'social or physical processes, their interrelationship with other processes, and the likely consequences of actions that require considerable scientific or technical expertise' (Haas 1992: 4).

Haas goes on to suggest that state actors are 'uncertainty reducers' as well as power and wealth pursuers. In conditions of high uncertainty, it becomes difficult for national governments to define clearly just what the national interest is. They are not only engaged on a two-level game as suggested by Putnam, they are also involved in a multi-dimensional international game where strategies consistent with the national interest in one sector may be inconsistent with the national interest being pursued in another sector. It is not surprising that state actors look for ways of reducing uncertainty. They recognise that changing the world is going to be very difficult and that they may have to settle, therefore, for minimising their surprises. Again, this is consistent with what we know about national policy-making – many policy-makers are risk-averse and one way of reducing risk to them is to *share* it. For example, Henderson's now classic study of a series of British policy decisions describes risk-sharing behaviour through consultation, as follows:

> making sure that, at every stage of the policy process, the right chairs have been warmed at the right committee tables by the appropriate institutions, everything possible has been done and no one could possibly be blamed if things go wrong.
>
> (Henderson 1977: 189)

Bearing in mind just how large the EU is, it would be surprising if Commission officials did not engage in similar behaviour. By drawing other policy actors into the policy process, the Commission may be able to build coalitions in favour of its own notions of desirable policy change. By assisting the formation of networks of 'relevant' state and non-state actors, and by 'massaging' the way that these networks operate, the

Commission can maintain its position as an 'independent' policy-making institution and can increase its leverage with the Council of Ministers and the European Parliament. Information and ideas are important building blocks in this process.

In a key passage, Haas argues that epistemic communities play a central role in providing much-needed information and ideas.

> Epistemic communities are one possible provider of this sort of information and advice. As demands for such information arise, networks or communities of specialists capable of producing and providing the information emerge and proliferate. The members of a prevailing community become strong actors at the national and transnational level as decision-makers solicit their information and delegate responsibility to them. A community's advice, though, is informed by its own broader world view. To the extent to which an epistemic community consolidates bureaucratic power within national administrations and international secretariats, it stands to institutionalise its influence and insinuate its view into broader international politics.
>
> Members of transnational epistemic communities can influence state interests either by directly identifying them for decision-makers or by illuminating the salient dimensions of an issue from which the decision-makers may then deduce their interests. The decision-makers in one state may, in turn, influence the interests and behaviour of other states, thereby increasing the likelihood of convergent state behaviour and international policy coordination, informed by the causal beliefs and policy preferences of the epistemic community. Similarly, epistemic communities may contribute to the creation and maintenance of social institutions that guide international behaviour. As a consequence of the continued influence of these institutions, established patterns of cooperation in a given issue-area may persist even though systematic power concentrations may no longer be sufficient to compel countries to coordinate their behaviour.
>
> (Haas 1992: 5)

His suggestion that 'systemic power concentrations' can also *prevent* policy co-ordination is an important qualification to the epistemic communities concept. Thus, no-one is arguing that epistemic communities explain everything about the policy process. The advocates of the concept have been notably more cautious than current 'network' supporters in making claims for its explanatory power. Haas cites Ikenberry's analysis of post-war economic management as illustrating the *limitations* on the effects of the consensual views of specialists. The influence of epistemic communities is over the form of policy choices – 'the extent to which state behaviour reflects the preferences of these networks remains strongly conditioned by the distribution of power internationally' (Haas 1992: 7).

We should add that not only is the power of epistemic communities constrained by the realities of the distribution of power internationally, it is also constrained by the need for policy-makers – at both EU and national levels – to involve other forms of actors, particularly conventional interest groups. Not only are there rival epistemic communities, but they get caught up in conventional interest group politics. For example, telecoms is often cited as a classic example of epistemic communities at work (Cowhey 1990). The argument that much of the deregulatory trend can be traced to epistemic communities in the telecoms field looks convincing, yet national interests are directly affected, as are the interests of individual firms in the telecoms sector. Thus, one should not go overboard in emphasising the importance of knowledge and ideas. As Jacobsen argues, the pervasive flaw in 'power of ideas' arguments is their failure to take account of the fact that ideas and interests cannot be separated (Jacobsen 1995: 309). As Campbell emphasises, '... arguing that ideational conditions affect policy-making outcomes does not mean that interests are unimportant' (Campbell 1998: 400). Like Jacobsen, he suggests that it is the *interaction* of ideas and interests that is crucial. For example, this is very evident in the field of EU environmental policy-making, where the environmentalists often act as a 'megaphone for science'; policy has to be mediated in some way, via these powerful political actors. It is here, perhaps, that the policy community/policy network concept comes back into its own. Thus, a Commission official may place considerable emphasis on the knowledge-based influence of an epistemic community – the threat posed to the ozone layer by CFCs for example – but practical action has to involve the close co-operation of the industries involved – such as refrigeration equipment or foam manufacturers. In practice, the Commission did indeed set up various working parties to 'process' the CFC problem, and it is at this stage that familiar policy networks – indeed *policy communities* in the sense defined earlier – emerged to process the CFC issue (Mazey and Richardson 1992).

The 'primeval soup' of the EU and the importance of advocacy coalitions

This later 'processing' stage in the EU policy process is possibly less problematic in terms of finding useful models – some combination of network, institutional and intergovernmental bargaining models seems reasonable. It is the *emergence* of problems, issues and policy proposals which seems much more problematic in terms of available models of analysis – hence the attractiveness of the epistemic communities approach. As Kingdon suggests, the phrase 'an idea whose time has come, captures a fundamental reality about an irresistible movement that sweeps over our politics and our society pushing aside everything that might stand in its path' (Kingdon 1984: 1). He identifies a number of possible actors in the agenda-setting process, including the mobilisation of relevant publics by leaders, the diffusion of ideas in professional circles among policy elites, particularly bureaucrats, changes in party control or in intra-party ideological balances brought about by elections. The processes involved in agenda-setting are identified as being of three kinds – problems, policies, politics (Kingdon 1984: 17). His objective is to move the analysis from the usual political science preoccupation with pressure and influence (possibly a criticism of network analysis) and instead to explore the world of ideas. Using a revised version of the Cohen *et al.* garbage can model (1972), he analyses three 'process streams' flowing through the system – streams of problems, policies and politics, largely independent of each other. He likens the generation of policy proposals to a process of biological natural selection. Thus:

> many ideas are possible in principle and float around in a 'policy soup' in which specialists try out their ideas in a variety of ways … proposals are floated, come into contact with one another, are revised and combined with one another, and floated again … the proposals that survive to the status of serious consideration meet several criteria, including their technical feasibility, their fit with dominant values and the current national mood, their budgetary workability, and the political support or opposition they might experience. Thus the selection system narrows the set of conceivable proposals and selects from that large set a short list of proposals that is actually available for serious consideration.
>
> (Kingdon 1984: 21)

He argues that the separate streams of problems, policies and politics come together at certain critical times. Solutions are joined to problems, and both of them are joined to favourable political forces. The timing of this coupling is influenced by the appearance of 'policy windows'; these windows are opened either by the appearance of compelling problems or by happenings in the political stream (Kingdon 1984: 21). Again, this seems to fit the EU rather well.

He cites one of his (US) respondents as saying that it is almost impossible to trace the origin of a proposal. 'This is not like a river. There is no point of origin' (Kingdon 1984: 77). There is an almost uncanny resemblance between this description of US policy-making and the perceptions of key actors in the EU policy process. Identifying just where a policy 'started' in the EU is extremely difficult – hence the common response that 'policies seem to come from nowhere'. It is a characterisation which is very different from that produced in the policy communities model and indeed also from the generic network model. The relationship between these two apparently opposing models of policy-making is that even the garbage can model – which does indeed seem to capture much of what we know empirically about the EU agenda-setting process – might *eventually* result in a more structured network of policy actors concerned with detailed policy decisions. In this sense, some kind of 'resource dependency' as suggested by Rhodes might emerge at later stages in the EU policy process because successful implementation depends on the co-operation of many stakeholders. Even Kingdon is at pains to point out that the processes he describes are not entirely random, 'some degree of pattern is evident in these fundamental sources: processes within each stream, processes that structure couplings, and general constraints on the system' (Kingdon 1984: 216).

One reason why the process is not random is, of course, that policy problems and policy ideas both help determine preferences and attract coalitions of actors. The EU policy process is at least 'mature' in the sense that it has produced a mass of public policy so far and continues to generate (at best via a greater mix of policy instruments) yet more policy proposals and outputs. The institutional rules might still be uncertain and the balance between EU institutions still in a state of flux, but the policy game is certainly ongoing. Essentially, EU policy-making is institutionalised 'repeat social interaction'. As Busch argues, situations of repeat social interactions pose special problems for game theorists and rational choice analysts (Busch 1999: 36). He quotes Hechter as arguing that game theory 'must not be judged solely by the mathematical elegance of its solutions, but by its capacity to shed light on those real world collective action problems' (Hechter 1990: 248). Busch sees ideational factors as one way out of trying to explain repeated games. He cites work by Garrett and Weingast, arguing that ideas can play a potentially pivotal role as 'shared beliefs may act as "focal points" around which the behaviour of actors converges' (Garrett and Weingast 1993: 176). Sabatier also argues that (within a policy sub-system) 'actors can be aggregated into a number of advocacy coalitions composed of people from various organisations who share a set of normative and causal beliefs and who often act in concert. At any particular point in time, each coalition adopts a strategy(s) envisaging one or more institutional innovations which it feels will further its objectives' (Sabatier 1988: 133; Sabatier 1998). An advocacy coalition can include actors from a variety of positions (elected and agency officials, interest group leaders, researchers) who share a particular belief system, i.e. a set of basic values, causal assumptions and problem perceptions, and who show a non-trivial degree of co-ordinated activity over time. Sabatier developed the model partly in response to the complexity of policy sub-systems. Using the US air pollution control sub-system as an example, he found that it contained a large, diverse set of actors. Normally, he argues, the number of advocacy coalitions would be quite small – in a 'quiescent sub-system' there might be only a single coalition, in others between two and four (Sabatier 1988: 140). To Sabatier, it is shared beliefs which provide the principal 'glue' of politics. Indeed, he emphasises stability of belief systems as an important characteristic of policy sub-systems. Policy change within a sub-system can be understood as the product of two processes. First, the efforts of advocacy coalitions within the sub-system to translate the policy cores and the secondary aspects of their belief systems into governmental programmes. Second, *systemic* events – for example, changes in socio-economic coalitions, outputs from other sub-systems, and changes in the system-wide governing coalition – affect the resources and the constraints on the sub-system actors, i.e. policy change takes place when there are significant 'perturbations' external to the sub-system (Sabatier 1988: 148). One of his hypotheses seems especially relevant to more recent developments in the EU. Thus, his 'hypothesis seven' is that: 'Policy-orientated learning across belief systems is most likely when there exists a forum which is a) prestigious enough to force professionals from different coalitions to participate and b) dominated by professional norms' (Sabatier 1988: 156). There is some evidence that Commission officials are moving towards institution-alised structures which do just this, i.e. bring together groups of policy actors (be they epistemic communities, advocacy coalitions or different policy communities) in a forum – such as the Environmental Forum within DG Environment or the September 1993 confer-ence to discuss possible changes to the Drinking Water Directive (Richardson 1994a; see also Mazey and Richardson in this volume). As Sabatier suggests, the purpose of these structures:

> is to force debate among professionals from different belief systems in which their points of view must be aired before peers. Under such conditions, a desire for professional credibility and the norms of scientific debate *will* lead to a serious analysis of methodological assump-tions, to the gradual elimination of the more improbable causal assertions and invalid data, and thus probably to a greater convergence of views over time concerning the nature of the problem and the consequences of various policy alternatives.
>
> (Sabatier 1988: 156)

Again, we see a suggestion that policy-makers are intent on securing agreement and stability, and recognise that this process must involve the participation of the various types of 'stakeholders' in the policy area or policy sub-system. Indeed, the Commission itself uses the term 'stakeholder' in the consultation process. For example, when it published proposals in February 2001 to encourage 'greener' products, it announced that it would convene a 'stakeholder workshop' in order to discuss the proposals. A particu-larly acute problem for the EU, which can only be exacerbated by the next round of enlargement, is that the number of competing advocacy coalitions may well be signifi-cantly larger than the national (US) system from which Sabatier draws his evidence, reflecting the historically diverse nature of the fifteen member states. In the EU, stake-holders can be members of epistemic communities, conventional interest groups such as trade associations or environmental groups, firms, members of national administrations, other institutional actors such as MEPs and increasingly, national regulatory agencies. The trouble is that numbers are often very large and, hence, it is a difficult managerial task to construct coherent policy communities and the 'glue' holding coalitions together might be rather weak – hence the common feature of temporary, ad hoc, coalitions of actors *not* sharing a common intellectual base, policy frame, or belief system.

Multiple policy-making 'venues' and the erosion of national sovereignty

The very fact that EU policy-making is a collective exercise involving large numbers of participants, often in intermittent and unpredictable 'relationships', is likely to reinforce the processes by which national autonomy is being eroded, as well as the capacity for consistent EU-level political leadership. The likelihood of any one government or any one national system of policy actors (e.g. governments and interest groups combined) imposing their will on the rest is low. National governments know this. We can, therefore, expect to see the emergence of two apparently contradictory trends. First, the need to construct complex transnational coalitions of actors will force all actors to become less focused on the nation states as the 'venue' for policy-making. Just as many large firms have long since abandoned the notion of the nation state, so will other policy actors; they will seek to create and participate in a multi-layered system of transnational coalitions. Second, the 'politics of uncertainty' will lead national governments and national interest groups to try to co-ordinate their Euro-strategies (e.g. see DTI 1993; 1994). In that sense, Euro-policy-making may bring them closer together. (For a more detailed discussion of this paradox, see Mazey and Richardson in this volume.)

One reason for the difficulty in maintaining stable national coalitions is that membership of the EU presents all policy actors with a choice of venue for the resolution of policy conflicts. As Baumgartner and Jones argue, political actors are capable of strategic action by employing a dual strategy of controlling the prevailing image of the policy problem and also seeking out the most favourable venue for the consideration of issues (Baumgartner and Jones 1991: 1046). In this sense, the EU policy process represents a different order of multiple access points for policy actors when compared with many of the policy systems of the member states. Many of them, such as Britain and France, have traditionally operated rather centralised policy-making systems with, consequently, relatively few national 'venues' for exercising influence. The EU policy process is more akin to the US and German systems, where interests have a wide range of venues to engage in the policy process. Unified and centralised policy systems may encourage cohesion in policy communities in part because all of the players know that there are relatively few options for exercising influence elsewhere: this is not the case within the EU, where several 'venues' are available to actors who have lost out in any one of them. The tendency of the EU policy process to pass through periods of stability and periods of dramatic institutional change – in the episodic fashion suggested earlier – will also lead to instability in actor relationships. As Baumgartner and Jones suggest, changes in institutional structures (a feature of the EU) can also often lead to dramatic and long-lasting changes in policy outcomes (Baumgartner and Jones 1993: 12).

Conclusion: still muddling, not yet through?

Fundamentally, all of these models and concepts are concerned with the policy process as a collective enterprise – whether the models are concerned with the emergence of policy problems, new knowledge, policy ideas, or the processing of these into workable policies and programmes. Policy-making and policy-implementing are *collective* activities, and we need models which help characterise the process of problem-solving in a collective setting where the sovereignty of a range of actors – not just of nation states – is pooled. Earlier, we suggested caution in adopting any *one* model for analysing the EU policy process.

Clearly there is an ongoing and very 'productive' policy process, i.e., there is now an enormous mass of EU public policy in existence and a continuation of the flow of much technical and detailed EU legislation. Equally clearly there is a vast range of actors, institutions, problems and ideas from which EU policy finally emerges. It often seems like Kingdon's 'primeval soup' or the Cohen *et al.* 'garbage can'. Identifying the broad characteristics of this process is proving difficult, partly due to the disaggregated nature of much EU policy-making. The common problems of secularisation and segmentation – and hence of policy co-ordination – are writ large in the EU. Despite the erosion of sectoral boundaries, through such initiatives as gender mainstreaming, EU policy-making is often still sectoral or sub-sectoral in nature. In part the difficulty in making reliable generalisations is because the process is obviously exceedingly complex; in part it is because the process is changing in that the politics of the EU is also about constantly changing the 'decision-rules' of the system. And in part it is because analysing the EU tends to be approached from two rather different academic perspectives – models of national policy-making on the one hand and models of international policy-making on the other. The thrust of this chapter has been to suggest that we can make progress if we focus on policy actor behaviour – as well as on institutions and institutional relationships – in order to begin our search for a better understanding of the EU as a policy system or series of policy subsystems.

If we focus on actors as 'stakeholders' in the governance of the EU, we are able to survey a range of actor types and a range of relationships. Different types of actors and different types of relationship may emerge at different times. The policy process is both episodic and taking place in several venues at any one time, and analysis of the behaviour of each actor needs to recognise that actors may be involved in a series of 'nested games' (Tsebelis 1990) which they only partially understand. Actors are involved in a whole series of policy games and this might explain the fact that actors may appear to settle for sub-optimal choices. Tsebelis argues that it is vital for observers of policy-making to take into account contextual factors (i.e., the situation in other arenas) as these may lead actors to choose different strategies (Tsebelis 1990: 9). Here, we argue that an additional requirement is for *us* to understand that *they* do not always understand what they are doing and what the outcomes might be. The multiplicity of games in which national governments are involved inevitably affects their autonomy as policy actors. Moreover, the relationship between the EU and its member states is directly affected by the extremely complex nature of the EU policy process itself – hence our advocacy of multiple models. Clearly, intergovernmentalism is important. We still have nation states; national governments try to act in either the national interest or their own political interests; and these governments are accorded a strong institutional presence via the Council of Ministers. Yet two phenomena – largely the focus of this chapter – place significant limits on intergovernmentalisation as a model of analysis. First, we do see a proliferation of various types of policy network – more usually the loose, more dynamic issue-networks on the US model suggested by Heclo (1978), rather than the policy community model originally suggested in Britain by Richardson and Jordan (1979). Put simply, the traditional 'clients' of national governments have become transnationally promiscuous in their relationships (see also Mazey and Richardson in this volume). Second, the 'politics of expertise' and the 'politics of ideas' have become especially important in situations of loose networks and high uncertainty. This also weakens national sovereignty because of the increasingly cross-national nature of expertise and the more open market for policy ideas and frames.

The complexity of the EU policy process means that we must learn to live with multiple models and learn to utilise concepts from a range of models in order to help us describe it as accurately as possible. In practice, the EU policy process may be closer to a garbage can model than to any 'rational' policy process. We suggest this because the EU policy system appears to be a classic case of 'bounded rationality' – namely, '… because the cognitive and computational capacities of decision-makers are limited, decision-makers consider only a very small number of alternative solutions to organizational problems' (Heimer and Stinchcombe 1999: 28). As Heimer and Stinchcombe suggest, organisations that have attempted to function with a more open agenda are particularly good cases in which to study bounded rationality at work. Clearly, the EU institutions are classic examples of open agenda-setting (see Peters in this volume). Nevertheless, just as Heclo could detect the paradox of order and disorder, so, within the garbage can of the EU policy process, we can also detect a paradox. The process is not *entirely* random. As Heimer and Stinchcombe argue, correctly, in order to understand organisational decision-making 'we must look both at the randomness introduced by garbage can processes and the predictability introduced by participants' membership in occupational groups, the championing of solutions by professional bodies, legal constraints on choice opportunities, or outsiders' attempts to label difficulties as problems worthy of organizational attention' (Heimer and Stinchcombe 1999: 44). Translating their general analysis to the specific features of the EU we can see the emergence of something like occupational groups, in the form of interest groups, the championing of solutions by professional bodies, in the form of epistemic communities, the legal constraints on choice opportunities as exercised by the ECJ, and outsiders' attempts to pose problems as opportunities in the form of the advocacy of new ideas and policy frames.

The trajectory of European integration, and the construction of a dense European policy system, have certainly been uneven – and these processes might be facing new and possibly intractable problems, as Mazey suggests in this volume – but the remarkable thing about the EU is that both phenomena have continued over time. In its own way, the Union has become adept at what Lindblom saw as a key feature of modern policy-making, the so-called 'science of muddling through' (Lindblom 1959). That this muddling through has produced a complex and inconsistent pattern of public policies and a very 'messy' institutional structure, even including opt-outs for certain member states, should occasion no surprise. In effect, the EU has become a gigantic 'frame-reflection' machine – namely a set of rather fluid institutional arrangements for what Schön and Rein termed the 'resolution of intractable policy controversies'. As they suggest, '… when controversies are situated in messy and politically contentious policy arenas, they actually lend themselves, through design rationality [namely, policy-making as a dialectic within which policy-makers function as designers and exhibit … a particular kind of reflective practice] to pragmatic solution' (Schön and Rein 1994: xviii). Big institutional features – such as the three pillars and opt-outs within the EU – are good examples of pragmatic solutions via a process of frame reflection. Actors come to the table with hugely different policy frames, yet more or less workable (albeit untidy) solutions emerge. The most remarkable feature of the EU is not that it is institutionally messy or that EU public policy is a 'regulatory patchwork' (Héritier 1996), but that so much EU public policy is now in place, despite the multitude of interests and policy frames in play in the EU policy game. *Somehow*, the system works as a policy-making system. In part, this is because, as Mazey suggests in this volume, actors have, thus far, been able to focus on specific policy issues instead of being in deadlock over the fundamentals of the EU and its future. In part, the system works because of the use of subterfuge as a policy style. Thus, as Héritier argues, 'subterfuge is a typical pattern of European policy making in view of an imminent dead-lock ...' (Héritier 1999: 97). She emphasises the deep attachment to diversity in the EU and the inability of members to agree on the direction of the polity and sees the EU institu-tions as fragmented, with inherently ambiguous rules. As a consequence, the EU 'decisional processes are obstacle-ridden, cumbersome and ... prone to stalemate' (Héritier 1999: 97). Yet, despite this apparently unmanageable and chaotic situation, decisions do emerge. Essentially, she argues, actors find a variety of 'escape routes' with subterfuge being the only way to keep policy-making going (Héritier 1999: 97). In a sense, the EU is a rather good example, perhaps, of Hood's observation that 'elements of the garbage can model may at least in some circumstances be better viewed as a design recipe than an unintended condition' (Hood 1999: 77). Thus, we may conclude by borrowing the title of one of Charles Lindblom's articles on policy-making (Lindblom 1979) - namely, that the EU is 'still muddling, not yet through'!

References

Adler, Emanuel and Haas, Peter (1992) 'Conclusion: Epistemic Communities, World Order and the Creation of a Reflective Research Program', *International Organization*, 46/1, pp. 367–90.

Almond, Gabriel (1956) 'Comparing Political Systems', *Journal of Politics*, 18/2, pp. 391–409.

Andersen, S. S. and Burns, T. (1996) 'The European Union and the Erosion of Parliamentary Democracy: a Study of Post-parliamentary Governance', in Andersen, S. S. and Eliassen, K. A. (eds) *The European Union: How Democratic Is It?* (Sage: London).

Atkinson, M. and Coleman, W. (1989) 'Strong States and Weak States: Sectoral Policy Networks in Advanced Capitalist Economies', *British Journal of Political Science*, 19/1, pp. 47–67.

Baumgartner, F. R. and Jones, B. D. (1991) 'Agenda Dynamics and Policy Subsystems', *Journal of Politics*, 53/4, pp. 1044–74.

Baumgartner, F. R. and Jones, B. D. (1993) *Agendas and Instability in American Politics* (Chicago: Chicago University Press).

Benson, J. K. (1982) 'A Framework for Policy Analysis', in Rogers, D. and Whitten, D., *Interorganizational Coordination* (Ames: Iowa State University Press), pp. 137–76.

Braun, Dietmar and Busch, Andreas (eds) (1999) *Public Policy and Political Ideas* (Cheltenham: Edward Elgar).

Busch, Andreas (1999) 'From "Hooks" to "Focal Points": the Changing Role of Ideas in Rational Choice Theory', in Braun, Dietmar and Busch, Andreas (eds) *Public Policy and Political Ideas* (Cheltenham: Edward Elgar).

Campbell, John L. (1998) 'Institutional Analysis and the Role of Ideas in Political Economy', *Theory and Society*, 27, pp. 377–409.

Cohen, Michael, March, James and Olsen, Johan P. (1972) 'A Garbage Can Model of Organizational Choice', *Administrative Science Quarterly*, 17, pp. 1–25.

Coleman, W. D. and Perl, A. (1999) 'International Policy Environments and Policy Network Analysis', *Political Studies,* 47/4, pp. 691–709.

Cowhey, Peter F. (1990) 'The International Telecommunications Regime: The Political Roots of Regimes for High Technology', *International Organization*, 44/2, pp. 169–99.

DTI (1993) *Review of the Implementation and Enforcement of EC Law in the UK* (London: DTI).

DTI (1994) *Getting a Good Deal in Europe, Deregulatory Principles in Practice* (London: DTI).

Dowding, Keith (1995) 'Model or Metaphor? A Critical Review of the Network Approach', *Political Studies*, 43, pp. 136–58.

Dudley, Geoffrey and Richardson, Jeremy (1996) 'Why Does Policy Change over Time? Adversarial Policy Communities, Alternative Policy Arenas and British Trunk Roads Policy 1945–95', *Journal of European Public Policy*, 3/1, pp. 63–83.

Dyson, Kenneth (1994) *Elusive Union: The Process of Economic and Monetary Union in Europe* (London: Longman).

Easton, David (1957) 'An Approach to the Study of Political Systems', *World Politics*, 9/5, pp. 383–400.

European Commission (1995) *Commission's Work Programme for 1995*, OJC225, August, Brussels.

Garrett, G. and Weingast, G. (1993) 'Ideas, Interests and Institutions: Constructing the European Community's Internal Market', in Goldstein, Judith and Keohane, Robert (eds) *Ideas and Foreign Policy: Beliefs, Institutions and Political Change* (Ithaca: Cornell University Press).

Haas, Peter (1992) 'Introduction: Epistemic Communities and International Policy Co-ordination', *International Organization*, 46/1, pp. 1–35.

Hechter, Michael (1990) 'Comment: On the Inadequacy of Game Theory for the Solution of Real-world Collective Action Problems', in Cook, Karen Schweers and Levi, Margaret (eds) *The Limits of Rationality* (Chicago: University of Chicago Press).

Heclo, H. (1978) 'Issue Networks and the Executive Establishment', in King, Anthony (ed.) *The New American Political System* (Washington D.C.: American Enterprise Institute).

Heimer, Carol and Stinchcombe, Arthur L. (1999) 'Remodelling the Garbage Can: Implications of the Origin of Items in Decision Streams', in Egeberg, Morten and Laegreed, Per (eds) *Organizing Political Institutions: Essays for Johan P. Olsen* (Oslo: Scandinavian University Press).

Heinz, John P., Laumann, Edward O., Nelson, Robert L. and Salisbury, Robert H. (1993) *The Hollow Core* (Cambridge, MA: Harvard University Press).

Henderson, P. D. (1977) 'Two British Errors: Their Probable Size and Some Possible Lessons', *Oxford Economic Papers*, 29/2, pp. 159–205.

Héritier, Adrienne (1996) 'The Accommodation of Diversity in European Policy-Making: Regulatory Policy as Patchwork', *Journal of European Public Policy*, 3/3, pp. 149–67.

Héritier, Adrienne (1999) *Policy-Making and Diversity in Europe: Escape from Deadlock* (Cambridge: Cambridge University Press).

Hix, Simon (1999) *The Political System of the European Union* (Basingstoke: Macmillan).

Hoffmann, Stanley (1966) 'Obstinate or Obsolete: The Fate of the Nation State and the Case of Western Europe', *Daedalus*, 95/3, pp. 862–915.

Hood, Christopher (1999) 'The Garbage Can Model of Organization: Describing a Condition or a Prescriptive Design Principle?' in Egeberg, Morten and Laegreed, Per (eds), *Organizing Political Institutions: Essays for Johan P. Olsen* (Oslo: Scandinavian University Press).

Jacobsen, John Kurt (1995) 'Much Ado about Ideas: The Cognitive Factor in Economic Policy', *World Politics*, 47, pp. 283–310.

Jordan, Grant and Richardson, Jeremy (1982) 'The British Policy Style or the Logic of Negotiation?' in Richardson, Jeremy (ed.) *Policy Styles in Western Europe* (London: Allen and Unwin), pp. 80–110.

Judge, David and Earnshaw, David (1996) 'From Co-operation to Co-decision: The European Parliament's Path to Legislative Power', in Richardson, Jeremy (ed.) *Policy-Making in the European Union* (London: Routledge).

Kassim, Hussein (1994) 'Policy Networks and European Union Policy Making: A Sceptical View', *West European Politics*, 17/4, pp. 15–27.

Kingdon, John W. (1984) *Agendas, Alternatives and Public Policies* (New York: HarperCollins).

Krasner, Stephen D. (1978) 'United States Commercial and Monetary Policy: Unravelling the Paradox of External Strength and Internal Weakness', in Katzenstein, Peter (ed.) *Between Power and Plenty: Foreign Economic Politics of Advanced Industrial States* (Madison: University of Wisconsin Press), pp. 51–87.

Laffan, Brigid, O'Donnell, Rory and Smith, Michael (2000) *Europe's Experimental Union: Rethinking Integration* (London: Routledge).

Lax, David and Sebenius, James K. (1986) *The Manager as Negotiator* (New York: Free Press).

Lindblom, Charles (1959) 'The Science of Muddling Through', *Public Administration Review*, 19, pp. 79–88.

Lindblom, Charles (1979) 'Still muddling, not yet through', *Public Administration Review*, 39, pp. 517–26.

Maloney, William and Richardson, Jeremy (1995) *Managing Policy Change in Britain: The Politics of Water Policy* (Edinburgh: Edinburgh University Press).

Mazey, Sonia and Richardson, Jeremy (1992) 'Environmental Groups and the EC', *Environmental Politics*, 1/4, pp. 109–28.

Mazey, Sonia and Richardson, Jeremy (eds) (1993) *Lobbying in the European Community* (Oxford: Oxford University Press).

Mazey, Sonia and Richardson, Jeremy (1994) 'The Commission and the Lobby', in Edwards, Geoffrey and Spence, David (eds) *The European Commission* (London: Longman), pp. 169–201.

Mazey, Sonia and Richardson, Jeremy (1995) 'Promiscuous Policy-Making: The European Policy Style?', in Rhodes, Carolyn and Mazey, Sonia (eds) *The State of the European Union* (Boulder: Lynn Reinner and Longman).

Peterson, John (1995a) 'Policy Networks and European Union Policy Making: A Reply to Kassim', *West European Politics*, 18/2, pp. 389–407.

Peterson, John (1995b) 'Decision-Making in the European Union: Towards a Framework for Analysis', *Journal of European Public Policy*, 2/1, pp. 69–93.

Putnam, Robert, D. (1988) 'Diplomacy and Domestic Politics', *International Organization*, 42/3, pp. 427–60.

Radaelli, Claudio (1995) 'Knowledge Utilisation and Policy-Making', *Journal of European Public Policy*, 2/2, pp. 159–83.

Radaelli, Claudio (1999) *Technocracy in the European Union* (London: Longman).

Reich, Robert, B. (ed.) (1988) *The Power of Public Ideas* (Cambridge, MA: Harvard University Press).

Rein, H. and Schön, D. (1991) 'Frame-Reflective Policy Discourse', in Wagner, P., Weiss, C.H., Wittrock, B. and Wollman, H. (eds) *Social Sciences, Modern States: National Experiences and Theoretical Crossroad* (Cambridge: Cambridge University Press), pp. 262–89.

Rhodes, R. A. W. (1990) 'Policy Networks: A British Perspective', *Journal of Theoretical Politics*, 2/3, pp. 292–316.

Rhodes, R. A. W. and Marsh, D. (1992) 'New Direction in the Study of Policy Networks', *European Journal of Political Research*, 21/1, pp. 181–205.

Richardson, Jeremy (ed.) (1982) *Policy Styles in Western Europe* (London: Allen and Unwin).

Richardson, Jeremy (1994a) 'EU Water Policy-Making: Uncertain Agendas, Shifting Networks and Complex Coalitions', *Environmental Politics*, 4/4, pp. 139–67.

Richardson, Jeremy (1994b) 'Doing Less by Doing More? British Government 1979–1994', *West European Politics*, pp. 178–97.

Richardson, Jeremy (2000) 'Government, Interest Groups and Policy Change' *Political Studies*, 48/5, pp. 1006–25.

Richardson, Jeremy and Jordan, Grant (1979) *Governing under Pressure: The Policy Process in a Post-Parliamentary Democracy* (Oxford: Martin Robertson).

Richardson, Jeremy and Rittberger, Berthold (2001) 'The Ascendance of New Environmental Policy Instruments', paper presented to the European Community Studies Conference, 31 May–2 June 2001, Madison, Wisconsin, USA.

Sabatier, Paul (1988) 'An Advocacy Coalition Framework of Policy Change and the Role of Policy-Orientated Learning Therein', *Policy Sciences*, 21, pp. 128–68.

Sabatier, Paul (1998) 'An Advocacy Coalition Framework: Revision and Relevance for Europe' *Journal of European Public Policy*, 5/1, pp. 93–130.

Schattschneider, E. E. (1960) *The Semi-Sovereign People: A Realist's View of Democracy in America* (New York: Holt).

Schön, Donald A. and Rein, Martin (1994) *Frame Reflection: Toward the Resolution of Intractable Policy Controversies* (New York: Basic Books).

Sebenius, James K. (1992) 'Challenging Conventional Explanations of International Co-operation: Negotiation Analysis and the Case of Epistemic Communities', *International Organization*, 46/1, pp. 323–65.

Tsebelis, George (1990) *Nested Games: Rational Choice in Comparative Politics* (Berkeley: University of California Press).

Thatcher, Mark (1998) 'The Development of Policy Network Analysis. From Modest Origins to Overarching Frameworks', *Journal of Theoretical Politics*, 10/4, pp. 389–46.

Walton, Richard and McKersie, Robert (1965) *A Behavioral Theory of Labor Negotiations* (New York: McGraw Hill).

Chapter 2

European integration

Unfinished journey or journey without end?

Sonia Mazey

> We believed in starting with limited achievements, establishing a *de facto* solidarity from which a federation would gradually emerge. I have never believed that one fine day Europe would be created by some great political mutation … The pragmatic method we had adopted would … lead to a federation validated by the people's vote, but that federation would be the culmination of an existing economic and political reality.
>
> (Jean Monnet, *Memoirs*, London: Collins, 1978)

Introduction

The 'Community method' of functional integration advocated by Jean Monnet was an ingenuous device; crucially it enabled the (federalist inclined) founding fathers of European integration to side-step the politically intractable barrier of national sovereignty. Then, as now, there was no consensus over the precise form that European co-operation should take. The founding Treaties of the European Communities did not resolve this issue; rather they represented an ambiguous compromise between intergovernmentalists and European federalists involved in the post-war debate on European co-operation. The former viewed the European Coal and Steel Community (ECSC), the European Economic Community (EEC) and the European Atomic Energy Community (EURATOM) created by the Treaties, as functional agencies charged only with the co-ordination of national, economic strategies in designated sectors.[1] However, European federalists hoped that these agencies would, over time, provide the basis for a more comprehensive kind of political integration. The institutional arrangement created by the founding Treaties reflected this ambiguity. On the one hand, the European Commission and the European Court of Justice provided for a supranational European executive and legal authority. On the other hand, however, national governments, represented in the Community's Council of Ministers, enjoyed important legislative and executive powers with regard to the adoption and implementation of EC policies. This uncertainty regarding the proper status and ultimate objectives of European integration left open the question of the future development of the European Community.

In the absence of a clear blueprint or constitution, the process of European integration has been uneven and the institutional architecture of the Union has become increasingly cumbersome. Nationalism, economic recession, piecemeal EU enlargement, increasing Euro-scepticism and the growing importance of the Council of Ministers within the Union's decision-making system have at various times impeded European policy-making and the process of European integration. Nevertheless, since 1957, the legal basis, institutional framework and policy competence of the EC has gradually been consolidated and extended way beyond the provisions of the original Treaties. Three key turning points in this respect were the 1986 Single European Act (SEA), the 1992 Maastricht Treaty and the 1997 Amsterdam Treaty, each of which introduced significant amendments to the founding Treaties. The cumulative impact of these changes has been the creation of a unique system of European governance, albeit an incomplete one. As Weiler has observed:

> the originality of Europe has been in constructing a polity which to date has achieved a level of legal and material integration far exceeding that obtained by any historical confederation, and yet has managed to maintain the distinct political identity and essential sovereignty of its Member States and their nations in a manner which has defied the experience of all federations.
>
> (Weiler 2000: 219)

Precisely what kind of 'state' the EU is – or is likely to become – is, however, far from clear.[2] It would be naive to assume that the EU is an embryonic Westphalian state. Moreover, there may be no *single* answer to this question. In order to accommodate the increasingly diverse interests and needs of an expanding community, member states have accepted the need for compromise and adaptation. The abandonment in the 1992 TEU of the two 'holy cows' (Weiler 1997: 98) of European integration – preservation of the *acquis communautaire* and, within the *acquis*, the constitutional framework of the Community – was a watershed. These changes ushered in a new, era of 'flexible' integration, characterised by the resort to intergovernmental co-operation in certain areas and the acceptance of 'opt-outs' for some countries from particular Community obligations. In consequence, the EU now resembles the proverbial curate's egg: in certain areas it is a supranational, legal order; in other policy areas integration is – for the moment at least – based upon voluntary co-operation between sovereign states.

It is impossible to predict the future development of the European Union. What is clear, however, is that the integration process has now reached a critical juncture. As Michael Newman observes elsewhere in this volume, the 'permissive consensus' which facilitated the elite-driven process of European integration has now disappeared. The 1990s have witnessed increasing Euro-scepticism throughout the EU and growing public debate about the rationale for and nature of European integration. As Stevens (2000) observes, European publics have become increasingly instrumental in their attitude towards EU membership. Against this background, the planned accession of the ten central and eastern European countries (CEECs) (plus Cyprus, Malta and Turkey), scheduled to begin in 2003, will severely test the integrative capacity of the EU. In preparation for this test, the existing member states have already embarked upon the politically difficult process of EU policy adjustment and institutional reform. Yet, unlike previous enlargements, embracing the CEECs will require far more than merely marginal adjustments to existing policies and institutional arrangements. CEEC enlargement will also dramatically increase the political, cultural and economic heterogeneity of the EU and is thus likely to intensify pressures for flexible integration. In these circumstances, the member states – and European publics – may at last be forced to deliberate the *raison-d'être* of European integration.

This chapter highlights the historical development of the EU and seeks to explain how and why this process occurred. The central theme of the discussion is that there is no *single* dynamic of European integration and, therefore, no single theoretical framework can encapsulate the totality of European integration. Rather, it is argued that the process of European integration has been a 'multi-faceted, multi-actor and multi-speed' process. Thus, harmonisation of national laws and technical standards, increased educational and cultural exchanges within the EC, the mutual recognition of professional qualifications by member states and the growth of European regulations are as much part of the integration process as the high politics of intergovernmental conferences (IGCs) and Treaty reform. At different times in the community's history, different actors, institutions and pressures have been influential in either facilitating or limiting the further development of the EU. Thus, even when European integration seemed to have stalled at the so-called 'high politics' level (as appeared to be the case during the late 1970s), integration nevertheless continued to take place at the level of low politics and by means of policy implementation.

A 'multi-level' framework for analysis

As argued by intergovernmentalist models of integration, national interests and national governments have undoubtedly played a crucial role in determining the degree and pace of European integration. This dynamic is particularly apparent with regard to 'history-making' decisions (Peterson 1995) such as the initial establishment of the European Communities (Stirk and Weigall 1999; Milward 1992), subsequent renegotiation of the Treaties (Moravcsik 1991; 1998; Moravcsik and Nicolaïdis 1998) and the creation of European Monetary Union (Dyson and Featherstone 1999). In this context, interstate bargains conducted by national political leaders and administrative elites have been a very visible dynamic of integration. The EU policy preferences of national governments are informed in part by political ideology and 'core beliefs' (Sabatier 1988) – not least with regard to the principle of European integration. In consequence, the changing composition and ideological character of member governments have also played a role in determining the pace and direction of European integration. However, to confine our explanation of European integration to the motivations and actions of national governments would be to study only the tip of the iceberg. In addition, we need to evaluate the often less visible, but no less important role played by other actors and institutions involved in this process, broadly defined.

First, as Mazey and Richardson suggest in Chapter 11, organised interests have since the establishment of the ECSC played an important role in the European decision-making process (Haas 1958; Kirchner 1980; Mazey 1992). Corporatist interests have enjoyed formal representation at the European level from the outset, initially in the ECSC's Consultative Committee and subsequently in the Economic and Social Committee of the EC. Sectoral interests were also represented in the Expert Committees, set up by the High Authority in 1952 as a means of fostering collaboration with national experts on policy issues and problems. As the policy competence of the EC has expanded, increasing numbers and types of interests including local and regional authorities, professional associations and non-governmental organisations have been drawn into the policy-making process. This long-term trend has contributed to the process of European integration in two ways. First, it has resulted in the permeation of the European Commission (and, increasingly, the European Parliament) by an increasing range of interests, many of whom have become influential, albeit often discreet, Euro-lobbyists. Second, there is now a dense transnational interest-group system, centred upon Brussels. As we have argued elsewhere, (Mazey and Richardson 2001), organised interests have become institutionalised (albeit to varying degrees) in the 1,000 or so advisory groups (Van Schendelen 1998; Greenwood 1997) and other high-level working groups, *ad hoc* committees and consultative platforms and forums inside the Commission. Significantly, as predicted by neo-functionalist and transaction-based theories of European integration, recent studies have confirmed increasing levels of support since the mid-1980s among diverse interest groups for the Single European Market (SEM), European Monetary Union (EMU) and European regulation (Cowles 1995; Majone 1992; 1996; Mazey and Richardson 1993; 1999; 2001; Sandholtz 1993; Stone Sweet and Brunell 1998; Van Schendelen 1992). External threats, increasing competitive pressures and high transaction costs have persuaded many firms, for instance, of the benefits of further integration. Commercial interests are not, however, the only beneficiaries of European integration: the EU has also been an important, alternative policy-making arena for women, environmentalists and trade unions. Not surprisingly, such groups tend to favour further European integration as a means of imposing policy change upon recalcitrant national governments (Mazey 1998; Cichowski 1998). Organised interests are now important actors in both the low and high politics of the EU: they lobby for specific EU policy outcomes; and they are vocal participants in the wider debate over European integration. Witness, for instance, the involvement of interest groups in recent IGCs (Mazey and Richardson 1997).

Many groups (especially sectoral and producer groups) have increasingly developed their own European organisations in response to the growing importance of EC policies. The exact number of Euro-lobbyists is unknown. However, back in 1992 the Commission estimated that there were some 3,000 interest groups in Brussels, including more than 500 European associations, and that in total some 10,000 people were employed as lobbyists of one sort or another in Brussels (Commission of the European Communities 1992). By February 2000, the Commission's own directory of non-profitmaking European associations had expanded to include some 800 groups. Direct lobbying by firms has also increased: between 1985 and 1997 more than 350 firms established their own EU affairs office in Brussels (Coen 1999: 9). Of course, groups continue to lobby their national administrations, but increasingly, they enjoy direct access to European policy-makers. National governments may be privileged actors in the European decision-making process, but they are by no means the only ones.

Second, as revealed in other contributions to this volume, the EU institutions themselves have by means of both their own development and their actions contributed to the process of European integration. The incremental development of the European Parliament, for instance, highlights the way in which institutions can, under certain circumstances, acquire a sort of institutional momentum. The Parliament, having begun life as a rather insignificant consultative body has, over the years, consciously sought to strengthen its authority and has secured incremental increases in its budgetary and legislative powers. These developments, combined with the introduction in 1979 of direct elections to the European Parliament and the increasing cohesion of the transnational party groupings within the assembly, have significantly increased the democratic legitimacy of the European Parliament. Moreover, the European Parliament has since the 1970s actively campaigned for further European integration and appropriate EU institutional reform. The Parliament has not been the only EU institution which, in seeking to increase its own power, has effectively strengthened the supranational character of the EU. The entrepreneurial encroachment by the European Commission into new policy sectors since 1957 and the progressive 'constitutionalisation' of the EU Treaties by the European Court of Justice have also (often unobtrusively) increased the supranational authority of the EU. As Stone Sweet and Brunnell (1998) have argued, the growth of transnational trade has resulted in the expansion of supranational legal rules. Notwithstanding variations in the domestic impact of European legislation, its 'reach' is now extensive: by 1992 EU law included 22,445 EU regulations, 1,675 directives, 1,198 agreements and protocols, 185 Commission or Council recommendations, 291 Council resolutions and 678 communications. In France, the EU had become the largest source of new law, with 54% of all new laws originating in Brussels (*Conseil d'Etat. Rapport Public* 1992, cited in Alter 2000: 493). In principle, member states retain the authority to reverse these unanticipated institutional and policy developments. In reality, however, 'recapturing ground in previously institutionalized fields of activity ... will often be rather difficult. Decision rules hamper reform, and extensive adaptations to existing arrangements increase the associated costs' (Pierson 1996: 146). The key point – highlighted by historical institutionalist explanations of European integration – is that though member states play a central role in policy development within the European Union, 'the dead weight of previous institutional and policy decisions at the European level seriously limits their room for manoeuvre' (Pierson 1996: 147). In consequence, integration becomes 'path-dependent', characterised by piecemeal adaptation of existing arrangements.

Third, any satisfactory account of the historical development of the EC must examine the wider context of European integration. In particular, it should consider the extent to which external geopolitical and economic pressures as well as ideas have been influential in determining the pace of European integration and the EU policy agenda. In the immediate post-war period, for example, the threat of Soviet communism and the positive attitude of the US government towards European integration helped to focus the minds of European leaders upon the need for some form of European co-operation. Similarly, the dramatic collapse of the Soviet Union in 1989 was an important catalyst for further 'deepening' and 'widening' of the EU in the 1990s. Community initiatives such as the development of EC-wide research and technology policies and, more generally, the SEM project are in large part an attempt to counter the competitive challenge posed to European industries by US and Japanese firms and the so-called 'tiger economies' of East Asia. Finally, as Kingdon (1984) argues, prevailing ideas are also important in helping to frame and shape public policy outcomes. Thus, as indicated below, federalist ideas and aspirations were undoubtedly important in shaping the immediate post-war debate on the future organisation of European co-operation. These ideals were enthusiastically promoted by the European Federalist movements, and prominent individuals such as Jean Monnet, which together constituted an influential 'advocacy coalition' (Sabatier 1988), i.e. individuals with shared values and beliefs who are influential in setting the policy agenda. In contrast, the current preference among EU member states for economic liberalisation owes much to the present fashion for market solutions to problems, espoused by a new, influential advocacy coalition within the EU.

Interaction between these different variables makes it impossible to identify any single dynamic of European integration; rather the present constitutional and institutional arrangement of the EU is the culmination of a multi-level, multi-faceted process of change and adjustment. As the policy competence of the Union has expanded, so the community's constitutional and institutional basis has evolved. The transition from sectoral integration to political union has thus been accompanied by the piecemeal consolidation and *ad hoc* extension of the institutional capacities of the EU. One aspect of the European integration process has, however, been constant throughout the period under discussion, namely the deep-seated ideological divide between the commitment (at elite levels) of the original Six to some form of political union and the more sceptical attitude of some later entrants to the Community, notably the UK, Greece, Denmark and Sweden. The significance of this cleavage – not to mention other conflicts of interest – begs the question as to how the Union has not only survived, but also continued to evolve. Intergovernmentalist, neo-functionalist and historical institutionalist explanations of the integration provide different, but not mutually exclusive answers to this question. In part, however, the very ambiguity of the European project has facilitated its survival. This opaqueness has enabled different actors to redefine the nature and objectives of integration and to adapt EU constitutional and institutional arrangements to suit new needs. Thus, in many respects, the picture that emerges from the following discussion is one of European integration by muddling through.

Creating the European Community 1945–1965: the primacy of politics

The immediate origins of European unification lie in the economic and political problems confronting European countries, notably France and Germany, in the immediate aftermath of the Second World War. The war had devastated European economies, and national governments in 1945 were forced to address the task of economic reconstruction. The establishment of the three European Communities during the 1950s offered a solution to this problem. European integration was also a response to the political legacy of the Second World War. Of crucial importance in this respect was the urgent need – given the onset of the Cold War – to anchor West Germany into the Western alliance system. However, before this could be achieved, French fears about the threat posed to France by an economically powerful West Germany would have to be allayed. The Schuman Plan, which formed the basis of the ECSC, was specifically designed to reassure French policy-makers on this point. The post-war debate on the future of European co-operation was thus clearly an issue of 'high politics'. As such, it was dominated by intense, intergovernmental negotiations between national politico-administrative elites, whose support for (though, in the case of the UK, non-participation in) European integration can be explained primarily in terms of perceived national interest (Stirk and Weigall 1999; Milward 1992). However, the experience of war had also created widespread revulsion towards nationalism and given fresh impetus to federalist movements, which argued that the nation-state system was a primary cause of international conflict (Lipgens 1982). Between 1945 and 1955 European federalist movements constituted an important 'advocacy coalition' which pushed the issue of European integration to the forefront of political agendas throughout Western Europe, and whose vision of Europe inspired key policy-makers such as Jean Monnet and Robert Schuman.

The political impact of post-war European federalism

The basis of the post-war European federalist movement was the belief that the establishment of a federal European government would put an end to the long-established pattern of wars between European sovereign nation-states. The idea was not a new one. In the aftermath of the First World War the idea of a 'United States of Europe' had been propounded by the Austrian Count Koudenhove-Kalergi, founder of the Pan-Europa movement, established in 1923. Influential members of this early advocacy coalition had included the French Socialist leader, Léon Blum; the President of the German Reichstag, Paul Lobe; Aristide Briand, French Foreign Minister (1925–32); and Gustav Streseman, German Foreign Minister (1923–9). Despite the fact that by the end of the 1920s, this movement contained prominent economists, lawyers, educationalists, journalists and politicians, it had nevertheless failed to win the support of the general public, who remained wedded to the concept (and reality) of national sovereignty (Lipgens 1982: 40–1). However, the experience of the Second World War gave fresh impetus to the debate on federalism. After 1939, federalist movements and publications proliferated, especially within resistance movements throughout Europe. Particularly influential in this process was the Italian resistance leader, Altiero Spinelli, author of the 1941 federalist Ventotene Manifesto and founder in 1943 of the *Movimento Federalista Europeo*, which was influential in mobilising popular support for the federal idea after 1945.

The immediate post-war period witnessed a fresh upsurge of public opinion in favour of European integration. From the outset, however, the debate was ambiguous and vague with regard to detail: though the general idea of European co-operation attracted wide-spread support, no such consensus existed regarding the precise nature of any such arrangement. In September 1946, for instance, the former British Prime Minister, Winston Churchill, declared that 'We must build a kind of United States of Europe' to counter the Soviet threat. The impact of this speech was enormous. It gave important credibility to European federalist movements, despite the fact that Churchill was opposed to both feder-alism and British participation in any system of European co-operation. There were also important divisions between the plethora of 'European' movements established during this period. By far the largest and most prominent of these competing advocacy coalitions was the European Union of Federalists (UEF). This was established in 1946 and comprised some sixty, affiliated, national groups and over 100,000 members. Other 'European' movements established during this period included the International Committee for a Socialist United States of Europe, the French Committee for a United Europe, the United Europe Movement, the European League for Economic Co-operation and the European Parliamentary Union. Significantly, however, not all movements shared the federalist aspirations of the UEF. For example, the United Europe Movement, founded in 1947 by Winston Churchill, and the European League for Economic Co-operation, presided over by the Dutch ex-prime minister, Paul van Zeeland, advocated European co-operation rather than federalism.

The momentum created by the post-war advocacy coalition in favour of (some form of) European integration culminated in the European Congress held in The Hague in May 1948, organised jointly by the above associations. The Congress brought together 713 delegates from thirteen countries. Among those present were Konrad Adenauer, West German Chancellor 1949–63; some twenty ex-prime ministers including Winston Churchill, Paul Reynaud and Paul van Zeeland; famous writers and academics including Bertrand Russell; and leading federalists such as Hendrik Brugmans, Alexandre Marc and Denis de Rougemont (Vaughan 1979). On the key issue of what kind of European design should be created there emerged at the Hague Congress a clear divide between the federalist UEF and the more moderate United Europe Movement which, backed by other conservative groups, advocated a confederal association. In the event, the latter view prevailed. The Congress approved a vaguely worded communiqué demanding the creation of 'a United Europe throughout whose area the free movement of persons, ideas and goods is restored', a Charter of Human Rights, a Court of Justice and a 'European Assembly, where the live forces of all our nations shall be represented'. In October 1948 the broad-based European Movement was established to implement the recommendations of the Hague Congress. Subsequent negotiations were marked by a (now familiar) cleavage between the French, Italian and Belgian governments, who wanted to establish a supranational European organisation, and the British government (backed by the Scandinavian governments), who favoured an intergovernmental arrangement. The feder-alists were defeated. The Council of Europe, established in May 1949, provided a forum for voluntary co-operation between sovereign, national governments in the Committee of Ministers and between members of national parliaments in the Consultative Assembly.

Undeterred, the European federalists launched a further attempt in 1952 to establish a supranational European Political Community (EPC) as part of a proposal for a European Defence Community (EDC). The EDC idea was the French government's response to US demands that West Germany be permitted to rearm in order that it might contribute to the defence of Western Europe. Though it enjoyed the support of both the West German

Chancellor, Konrad Adenauer and the US government, the EDC project collapsed in August 1954 with the refusal of the French National Assembly to ratify the so-called Pleven Plan. The failure of the EDC project marked an important turning point within the post-war debate on European integration. In the immediate post-war period, the social, economic and political situation in Western Europe was so fluid, and external pressures so favourable, that it was just conceivable that the radical federalist strategy advocated by the UEF might just have succeeded. Yet, despite the popularity of the federal idea in European countries and the important 'policy entrepreneur' role (Peters 1994) played by the federalist movements, the resilience of nationalism and the structures of the nation-states constituted an insurmountable barrier to such a development.

The establishment of the European Communities: the Monnet method

Federalist ideas nevertheless continued to exert a powerful influence upon national policy-makers seeking political solutions to the economic and security problems facing Western Europe. The founding fathers of the European Community – Jean Monnet, the French Planning Commissariat, and Robert Schuman, French Foreign Minister – were essentially pragmatic federalists. Though they shared the ideals of the so-called radical federalists, they disagreed with their head-on approach, believing instead that the only way to achieve European integration was by small, incremental steps in sectors where the issue of national sovereignty was less contentious than in 'high politics' areas such as defence and foreign policy (Monnet 1978; Duchêne 1994). This 'Community method' of functional integration underpinned the Schuman Plan, drawn up in April 1950 by the French Foreign Minister, Robert Schuman, at the request of Jean Monnet. The Plan was presented to the French government as a European solution to the urgent need to find a new structure to contain the resurgent heavy industries of the Ruhr (Willis 1968). It proposed that French and German coal and steel production should be 'pooled' and placed under a common, supranational authority, the High Authority, which would be responsible for establishing a common market for coal and steel among the member states. European regulation of these industries would also facilitate economic reconstruction. Six countries – Belgium, The Netherlands, Italy, Luxemburg, West Germany and France – signed the Paris Treaty in April 1951, establishing the ECSC. Significantly, the British government refused to join the ECSC. Three reasons help to explain the British aloofness from Europe during this period. First, the British wartime experience had strengthened rather than weakened national sentiments. Second, as Churchill had made clear in his 1946 Zurich speech, the primary British obligation at this time was to another 'natural grouping', the Commonwealth. Hence his remark during this speech that 'We are with Europe, but not of it. We are linked, but not comprised. We are interested and associated, but not absorbed' (cited in Lipgens 1982: 318). Third, Labour and Conservative politicians alike were united in their ideological opposition to a supranational European authority which they believed would constrain national policy-makers and undermine the sovereignty of Parliament.

The ECSC Treaty provided for five main institutions which constitute the foundations of the present institutional framework of the EC: a Special Council of Ministers (subsequently, the Council of Ministers); a High Authority (prototype of the European Commission); a 78-member Common Assembly (which developed into the European Parliament); a corporatist Consultative Committee (which later became the Economic and Social Committee) and a Court of Justice for settlement of disputes. The organisation and internal power structure of the ECSC embodied several ambiguities and compromises. Monnet's personal commitment to European federalism and his own experience of working in international organisations had convinced him of the need for the High Authority to be a supranational executive, wholly independent of national governments. More specifically, he believed that only a truly supranational executive would be able to act as a catalyst for the development of European policies. Yet, the High Authority was far from being a sovereign body. It was paralleled as an executive by the Special Council of Ministers, insisted upon by the Benelux countries as a means of defending the national interests of the smaller countries (Urwin 1989). The ECSC was followed by the creation in 1957 of two new communities: the EURATOM, intended to faciliate co-operation between member states in the development of nuclear technology for peaceful purposes; and the EEC. The EEC proposal came from the Benelux governments (inspired by the Benelux customs union established in 1944) and was supported by the powerful Action Committee for the United States of Europe, a non-governmental organisation formed in 1955 by Monnet. The EEC marked an important departure in the sense that it was not another sectoral community. The integrative impact of the EEC was potentially far-reaching: it sought to establish both a customs union and a common market.[3] Moreover, the means by which the EEC was to achieve these aims, together with a precise timetable, were clearly specified in the Treaty. Finally, while the customs union lay at the heart of the EEC Treaty, it also provided for a number of common policies in areas such as agriculture, transport and competition policy. Social policy was also included, in the sense of policy relating to employment. A Social Fund and an Investment Bank were established and the policies were to be financed by a Community budget, whose income would eventually come from its 'own resources' (Pinder 1995). Once again, the British government remained aloof from the integration process. Indeed, the British government representative – a civil servant from the Board of Trade – to the Spaak Committee, set up in 1956 to prepare the details of the two new communities, had withdrawn from the negotiations at the first mention of supranational institutions.

Several factors facilitated the establishment of the European Communities: the pressing need to achieve Franco-German conciliation; the post-war economic situation and the wider political environment (notably the onset of the Cold War) all served to focus the minds of European policy-makers upon the problem of European co-operation. The particular solution adopted reflected the influence of competing advocacy coalitions (pro- and anti-European federalism), the pivotal role played by individuals such as Jean Monnet and Robert Schuman, and the political commitment of the six member governments to European integration. Thus, in Kingdon's terms, there had existed an important 'window of opportunity'. In the early 1960s, support for the EEC (which quickly established itself as the most important of the three Communities) increased among member governments, business and agricultural interests. Rapid economic growth rates in the EEC were attributed, in part at least, to the removal of internal tariffs. Meanwhile, the CET, far from provoking protectionism in the international economy, provided the catalyst for far-reaching multilateral tariff cuts, as reflected in the Kennedy Round of GATT negotiations in the mid-1960s.

De Gaulle and the empty-chair crisis: towards intergovernmentalism

The founders of the EC had intended that the European Commission would become a technocratic, supranational European executive, embodying the European General Will

(Featherstone 1994). Between 1957 and 1965 an assertive Commission, under the presidency of the German federalist Walter Hallstein, set about realising this aim. However, the Treaties were ambiguous in this respect and in 1965, the Commission's authority was seriously challenged by the French President, General de Gaulle. Elected in 1958, De Gaulle immediately made clear his opposition to European supranationalism, which contradicted his *certaine idée* of France, based upon a powerful sovereign state, nationalism and an independent foreign and defence policy. De Gaulle's election marked an important turning point in the development of the EC: the political consensus in favour of European integration disappeared, and with it the agreement on the existing institutional balance of power within the Community. In 1961, De Gaulle launched his intergovernmental alternative to the EC, the so-called Fouchet Plan which sought to establish a 'union of states' to coexist with the existing Community in a number of areas, most notably foreign policy, defence and culture. When this initiative failed, de Gaulle scorned the existing Community, declaring at a press conference in May 1961, that 'there is and can be no Europe other than a Europe of States – except of course a Europe of myths, fictions and pageants' (cited in Pinder 1995: 12). Thereafter, de Gaulle's strategy was to exploit the EC in defence of French national interests – a strategy reflected in the priority accorded by France to the establishment of the CAP.

De Gaulle's antagonism towards the Community culminated in the so-called 'empty chair' crisis, which lasted from July to December 1965. During this period French ministers refused to attend meetings of the Council of Ministers and the French permanent representative was withdrawn from Brussels. The crisis was triggered by French opposition to the Commission's proposals for financing the Common Agricultural Policy, the introduction of the Community's 'own resources', the granting of more extensive budgetary powers to the European Parliament and, in particular, the introduction of majority voting into the Council of Ministers. Such developments – wholly consistent with the neo-functionalist concept of 'spillover' – were anathema to de Gaulle. The crisis was resolved in January 1966 by the Luxemburg Compromise, which shifted the institutional balance of power away from the Commission in favour of the Council of Ministers. While the Commission's right to initiate policy was confirmed by this document, it was agreed that the Commission should, in future, consult more closely with member governments before issuing new proposals. Moreover, with regard to majority voting in the Council of Ministers, the Luxemburg Compromise stated that where 'issues very important to one or more member countries are at stake ministers will seek to reach solutions with which all can be comfortable'. The Luxemburg Compromise effectively confirmed the right of member states to veto EC legislative proposals, thereby reversing the federalist ambitions of the Commission.

1965–1984: European integration by other means

Conventional wisdom holds that the integration process stalled during the 1970s and early 1980s. Evidence cited in support of this view typically includes references to the Commission's increasing resort to 'package deals', recurrent 'crisis' EC summits, 'deadlocked' meetings of the Council of Ministers and the discordant relationship between the UK (which joined the EC in 1972) and the rest of the Community (George 1990). This apparent 'slowing down' of the European integration process at the high politics level is usually attributed to the Luxemburg Compromise, EC enlargement and the onset of worldwide recession in 1974. This view of the European Community during the 1970s has some validity. The Luxemburg Compromise *did* alter the European policy style: henceforth the Commission was forced to negotiate complex package-deals with the member states. EC enlargement from six to nine members inevitably increased the *'lourdeur'* (Dehousse and Majone 1994: 94) of EC decision-making, especially in the light of the Luxemburg Compromise and the opposition of two of the new member states (the UK and Denmark) to further political integration. The 'Community spirit' which had prevailed during the 1960s was thus eroded in the 1970s. Meanwhile, the onset of economic recession in Western Europe gave rise to protectionist temptations in some quarters as national governments struggled to control rising unemployment and domestic inflation levels.

Yet, notwithstanding these problems, European integration continued to take place in some form or another throughout the 1970s. Indeed, as Caporaso and Keeler argue 'the resilience of the EC during these troubled times looks even more impressive from the post 1989 perspective' (Caporaso and Keeler 1995: 37). Moreover, in many respects, the pressures and developments (both internal and external to the Community), that culminated in the 1986 SEA, originated in the 1970s. In terms of EC 'institution-building', for instance, the 1970s witnessed the introduction of European Political Cooperation (EPC), the establishment of regular meetings of the European Council and the introduction of direct elections to the European Parliament. The creation of EPC, which brought together the foreign ministers of the EC, was an intergovernmentalist development, but it marked the beginnings of European foreign policy co-ordination. The introduction of regular meetings of the EC heads of government was essentially a response by national governments to the difficulties highlighted above. It reflected their desire – despite the differences between them – to maintain a European dialogue. The European Council, though an intergovernmentalist body, has since its inception played an important agenda-setting role in the integration process. Indeed, several European Council meetings stand out as decisive turning points in the European unification process. Meanwhile, the incremental development of the European Parliament's budgetary powers in 1970 and 1975 gave the EP increased leverage over the Council of Ministers. This, in turn, provided the Parliament with new opportunities to seek allies among the member states in support of its longterm campaign for increased legislative powers. The introduction in 1979 of direct elections to the EP established the democratic legitimacy of the Parliament – another crucial step in this campaign.

Second, the capacity of the EC institutions to set and process the 'normal' policy agenda remained relatively unaffected by the public clashes between the heads of government. Thus, one study revealed that 'in 1975, the Council of Ministers considered 329 proposals from the Commission and adopted 75 per cent of these within 2 years'. The same study also showed that the annual volume of Commission proposals rose steadily from 1975, reaching 456 in 1979 (of which 77.4% were adopted by the Council) and 522 in 1984 with an 84.3% success rate. The average length of time taken to process legislation declined from 150 days in 1975 to 108 days in 1984 (Sloots and Verschuren 1990, cited in Wood and Yesilada 1996: 100). Moreover, during the 1970s, the policy-making competence of the EC continued to expand: existing policies were extended and new policies introduced – in some areas, beyond the parameters of the founding Treaties. EC enlargement in 1974, for instance, was accompanied by the introduction of an EC regional policy and European Regional Development Fund. The origins of EMU also lie in the 1971 Werner Plan and the 1979 launch of the first EMS (the snake). Less dramatically, a large corpus of EC environmental legislation was adopted during the 1970s (despite the absence of a

Treaty basis for such legislation), and the scope of EC social policy extended beyond the narrow confines of the Treaties. Two crucial consequences of the expansion of the EC's policy competence during this period were the increase in the size and complexity of the European Commission (further EC institution-building) and the progressive 'Europeanisation' of domestic policy-making. The latter development was reflected in the steady rise in the number of transnational Euro-groups and the progressive harmonisation of national legal and technical standards. ECJ rulings during this period quietly reinforced this trend.

The pace and direction of European unification during the 1970s was thus shaped by several interrelated dynamics. Within this process, individuals often played a key role. For example, the decision in 1978 to launch the original EMS owed much to the personal efforts of the UK Commissioner Roy Jenkins and the French President, Valéry Giscard d'Estaing. As in 1945, the EC external environment was also influential in persuading EC heads of government of the potential benefits of European co-operation. For example, international currency fluctuations following the collapse in 1971 of the Bretton Woods system, gave an important impetus to European monetary integration. Meanwhile, the development of EC social and environmental policies during the 1970s owed much to the mobilisation of interest groups – notably environmentalists and women – and the 'purposeful opportunism' (Cram 1993) of the European Commission.

Treaty reform and European integration

Since 1985, the EU has been in a constant state of flux. Piecemeal enlargement, combined with a series of intergovernmental conferences and Treaty reforms, have resulted in the simultaneous deepening and widening of the EU. These developments have been extensively analysed elsewhere and no attempt is made here to undertake such a task. Rather, the following (necessarily brief) review of the ongoing process of Treaty reform is used here to highlight three central themes of this chapter: the multi-faceted nature of European integration; the increasing 'democratisation' of the integration process; and the extent to which integration has been path-dependent. The impetus for reform has generally come from recognition of the need for EU adaptation. As such, the reform agendas have been to a large extent policy and problem driven. However, as the political salience of European integration has increased, other actors have increasingly come to assume an influential role in the reform process. Their impact, as highlighted by the Amsterdam Treaty provisions, has been to broaden the reform agenda to embrace more fundamental issues relating to citizenship, human rights and democracy. In keeping with historical institutionalist models of integration, the cumulative impact of incremental institutional adjustments to the EU have also been significant. Notwithstanding the increasing resort since 1992 by member states to subsidiarity and flexibility as mechanisms for accommodating diversity, the cumulative impact of successive reforms has been significant. The competence of the EU has been significantly extended and the powers of the 'supranational' European institutions considerably increased.

The 1986 Single European Act:
completing the Single European Market

The 1986 SEA marked a decisive turning point in the development of the EC. It committed the twelve EC member states to completing the Single European Market (SEM), i.e. a Common Market, by January 1993 and to establishing EMU. The SEA also committed the signatories to EC institutional reform, designed primarily to facilitate the establishment of the SEM. More specifically, the SEA extended qualified majority voting (QMV) in the Council of Ministers and introduced the 'co-operation procedure', which further increased the legislative powers of the EP with regard to SEM legislation. The SEA also strengthened the legal basis for EC environmental, social and regional policies, and gave formal recognition to the European Council and EPC. Explanations of the SEA abound. Intergovernmentalist interpretations emphasise the importance of national interests and intergovernmental bargaining (Moravcsik 1991; Keohane and Hoffmann 1991). According to this view, the convergence of national economic strategies in France, Germany and the UK after 1983 was a crucial catalyst in the creation of a new political consensus among European leaders in favour of the central policy issue, namely the SEM project (see also Pollack 2000). However, as Dehousse and Majone point out, this merely begs the question as to why, how and from where this consensus developed (Dehousse and Majone 1994: 100). Nor can this explanatory model wholly account for the linkage in the SEA between the SEM project and EC institutional reform, greater social and environmental protection, and economic and social cohesion – issues that seriously divided member states.

A more comprehensive explanation of the SEA also has to evaluate the impact of other pressures and actors involved in the negotiation of the Act. External pressures which contributed to the SEA included the increasing threat of international competition and the emergence during the early 1980s within the EC of a new, neo-liberal, economic orthodoxy. Moreover, while national governments were centrally involved in the negotiation and ratification of the SEA, they were certainly not the only actors involved in setting and processing this policy agenda. Considerable evidence exists, for instance, of the agenda-setting role played in the early 1980s by transnational business and financial interest groups in favour of the SEM, EMU and European regulation (Majone 1992; Mazey and Richardson 1993; Sandholtz 1993; Cowles 1995; Van Schendelen 1992). Within the EP, the Kangaroo Group, an all-party grouping, which had since 1980 campaigned for the removal of non-tariff barriers within the EC, was influential in providing the political impetus for the 1985 Single Market programme. The EP was also influential in maintaining the momentum for EC institutional reform. Back in 1980, the federalist MEP Altiero Spinelli had formed the Crocodile Club, which drew up the Draft Treaty establishing the European Union (DTEU). Adopted by the EP in 1984, the DTEU formed the basis for the IGC discussions, which culminated in the SEA. During the 1985 IGC, the Commission, headed by the dynamic Jacques Delors, played a crucial 'brokerage' role, linking market integration (the core, substantive policy choice embodied in the SEA) to institutional reform, social regulation and economic cohesion. Going one step further back, the SEM project rested largely upon the principle of mutual recognition, a principle established by the European Court of Justice in its landmark *Cassis de Dijon* ruling in 1979. The SEA was therefore the product of several interlinked institutional and systemic dynamics, which converged around the SEM project. As Dehousse and Majone argue, 'once the general idea of completing the internal market was accepted, it proved possible to convince even the most reluctant Member States that a shift towards more majority voting was necessary in several areas' (Dehousse and Majone 1994: 104). Even the Eurosceptic UK Prime Minister Mrs Thatcher became caught up in this process of *engrenage*.

The 1992 Maastricht Treaty on European Union: achieving European Monetary Union

The SEM project unleashed a fresh wave of 'low politics' integration in the form of harmonisation of national standards and regulations, and the abolition of non-tariff barriers. The dynamic for European integration was further maintained by the combined impact of the Commission and the advocacy coalition in favour of EMU. In keeping with the neo-functionalist concept of 'spillover', the Commission argued that EMU was a necessary corollary of the SEM. In June 1988, the Commission president, Jacques Delors, secured the European Council's support for his proposal to establish a high-level working party (chaired by himself and largely composed of the governors of member states' banks), to draw up proposals for achieving EMU. In 1989, the committee recommended the gradual establishment of a single currency and an IGC was convened to consider the Treaty amendments required in order to establish the EMU. This pragmatic integration strategy was, however, suddenly blown off course by international events. The dramatic collapse of the Soviet Union after 1989 and consequent unification of Germany in 1991 thrust upon the Community member states a much wider policy agenda. First, just as in 1945, France was again anxious to anchor a powerful Germany into the Community system. The German Chancellor, Helmut Kohl, was also anxious to demonstrate Germany's continuing commitment to European integration. Crucially, these objectives reinforced both countries' commitment to further deepening of the EU, and more specifically, to the realisation of EMU. Second, the disintegration of the Soviet system created new uncertainties about the future development of Western security. Doubts regarding the future European role of NATO gave further impetus to those member states, such as France, who wished to see a more powerful role for the WEU and the development of a common European security policy. Third, Eastern enlargement of the Community – and the financial and institutional implications of such a development – was also now an unavoidable issue. At the suggestion of the French President, François Mitterrand, and of Helmut Kohl, the European Council in June 1990 agreed to set up a second IGC on European political union. The outcome of the two IGCs was the TEU, adopted at the Maastricht meeting of the European Council in December 1991.

Again, there are numerous analyses of the Maastricht Treaty (see for example Duff *et al.* 1994; Laursen and Vanhoonacker 1992). The single most important achievement was the commitment by the signatories to create the EMU by 1 January 1999 at the latest.[4] Predictably, however, the IGC on political union had reopened, but failed to resolve, a bitter debate on the meaning and direction of European integration. In the absence of any underlying political consensus, the Treaty was a messy compromise between the federalist model of Europe supported by Germany, Italy and the Benelux countries, the more intergovernmental model upheld by France and the even looser co-operation advocated by the UK. The newly named 'European Union' established by the Treaty comprises three distinct institutional pillars: the European Community (EC), Common Foreign and Security Policy (CFSP); and Justice and Home Affairs (JHA). Of these, only the European Community has a supranational executive and legal authority. The CFSP and JHA pillars provide instead for intergovernmental co-operation in the fields of European foreign and security policy, and policing, asylum and immigration policies respectively. The Treaty also established a Franco-German defence corps and committed member states (albeit in vague terms) to the eventual establishment of a common foreign and security policy (CFSP) within the framework of the West European Union (WEU).

Within the EC pillar, member states acknowledged the need for faster decision-making. Thus, QMV was extended slightly to areas beyond the realm of the internal market including environmental policy, consumer protection and some aspects of social policy. For similar reasons (and in response to group and institutional lobbying), a new 'co-decision procedure' which gave the European Parliament a veto power in specified policy areas such as the internal market, the environment and consumer protection was introduced. In a feeble attempt to address the problem of the 'democratic deficit' within the EC, the TEU introduced the principle that a new Commission must enjoy the support of a majority of MEPs and included symbolic references to 'European citizenship'. Finally, a new, consultative, Committee of the Regions was also established (largely in response to demands from the German Länder) to represent local and regional authorities in EC decision-making. The Community's competence was further extended in the fields of education, vocational training, youth, social policy, public health, consumer protection, environment, culture, research and technology, and trans-European networks. At the same time, however, the principle of subsidiarity was affirmed, restricting the actions of the Community to those matters where the objectives 'cannot be sufficiently achieved by the Member States' (Article 3b TEU). In order to resolve the intractable divide beteen the British government and the other eleven member states, Protocols to the Treaty permitted the UK to opt out of the EMU[5] and the new Social Chapter, enhancing the rights of workers in the workplace.

Viewed as part of a much longer-term process, the Maastricht agreement marked yet another step in the process of European integration, bringing agreement on the EMU timetable, further extension of the EC's competence and more institution-building. The establishment of an institutional framework for foreign policy and defence co-operation is a potentially significant development, as is the concept of European citizenship, which was also introduced by the TEU. Thus, in certain respects, the Maastricht agreement carried the Community over an important threshold. However, the legal and institutional patchwork created by the Treaty heralded an important change in the *method* of the European integration. Hitherto, under the so-called 'Community method' all member states had been obliged to proceed at the same pace within a single Community. The Maastricht Treaty marked a departure from this pattern. The creation of the two intergovernmental pillars and the decision to allow the UK to opt out of key Treaty obligations (EMU and the Social Protocol to the Treaty) marked an important first move towards more flexible integration.

The Maastricht Treaty also marked the end of the 'permissive consensus' on the part of the European publics with regard to European integration. Whereas the SEA had prompted little public debate, ratification of the Maastricht Treaty provoked an unexpected upsurge of public opposition to European integration in general and the Community institutions in particular. Popular fears of mass immigration and strong nationalist sentiments were compounded by more specific concerns about the Community's 'democratic deficit' reflected in the unaccountability of the Commission, the weakness of the European Parliament, and the non-transparency of the EC decision-making process. Ratification of the Treaty proved problematic in several member states. In Denmark, the 1992 referendum on the TEU produced a negative vote (which was subsequently reversed in a second referendum in 1993) and the French referendum produced only a *petit oui* – 51 to 49% to the TEU. In the UK, the Conservative government, which was bitterly divided over Europe, was forced to make ratification of the Treaty an issue of confidence in order to obtain the necessary parliamentary majority. Meanwhile, in Germany, ratification of the Treaty was delayed because of a legal challenge by the Länder authorities to the constitutionality of the Treaty. Several factors – some specific to individual member states – help to explain this backlash against European integration. However, one important cause of this sentiment was the increasing impact of European integration, especially after 1986. The incremental expansion of EU legislation inevitably increased the political visibility of European integration. European policies were also beginning to constrain national policy-makers. In particular, completion of the SEM and member states' determination to meet the rigorous 'convergence criteria' for entry to the EMU had, by 1992, begun to have unpleasant economic consequences in several countries. For the first time, many people who had hitherto either benefited from or been unaffected by EU policies were reminded of the potential costs of membership. Euro-barometer polls confirm that public support for European integration has continued to decline. Whereas in 1991 72% of European people believed European integration was a 'good thing', this figure had fallen to 49% by 1999 (European Commission 1999: 25). Meanwhile, European integration has become an increasingly salient political cleavage in many member states, dividing mainstream parties and spawning a host of populist, anti-European movements and parties. Increasing Euro-scepticism has made further European integration a more difficult and more uncertain process. Witness, for example, the British Conservative government's last-ditch attempt in 1996 to bolster flagging domestic fortunes by obstructing the IGC negotiations and blocking the adoption of some seventy pieces of EU legislation (Sverdrup 2000: 261; see also Duff 1998). The emergence of a vigilant and critical public has rendered the Monnet method of integration both impractical and politically unacceptable. These developments were reflected in the nature of the 1996 Intergovernmental Conference and the provisions of the 1997 Amsterdam Treaty.

The 1997 Amsterdam Treaty: towards flexible integration

The IGC to review the 1992 TEU had been written into the Maastricht Treaty and began in March 1996. (On the 1996 IGC see Edwards and Pjipers 1997). Its official purpose was to revise the European Treaties 'with the aim of ensuring the effectiveness of the mechanisms and the institutions of the Community'. Though initially intended as an opportunity to review the workings of the pillar structure, the decision taken by the Madrid European Council in 1995, to push ahead with eastern enlargement, inevitably shifted the focus of this review. As Pollack notes, compared to previous IGCs, this one was an 'outlier' in the sense that 'it was convened not to advance any particular policy goal, but to … reform the institutions of the Union in preparation for its impending enlargement' (Pollack 2000: 279). The 1996 IGC was also novel in another respect. Previous IGCs had taken the form of diplomatic negotiations between national administrative officials and foreign ministers over a clearly defined number of issues. However, the changed political circumstances demanded that the 1996 IGC be conducted in a more open and democratic manner. Throughout 1996 an enormous number of regional, national and European institutions, parties and interest groups were invited to insert their ideas and interests into the proposals. The impact of this initiative was twofold. First, participation in the IGC by large numbers of NGOs in favour of a more democratic EU meant that the discourse of the IGC was characterized by normative and political debate rather than by legal reasoning (Sverdrup 2000: 260). Second, the openness of the IGC made it extremely difficult for national and EU level political and administrative elites to control the agenda. As one bureaucrat reflected: 'gone are the days when we had articles in square brackets, and the processes were purely technical; now decision-making in the IGC is open, unclear and democratic' (Michel Petite, European Commission, cited in Sverdrup 2000: 260).

Analyses of the 1997 Amsterdam Treaty (see Duff 1997; Westlake 1998; Neunreither and Wiener 2000) generally emphasise the modest nature of the Amsterdam Treaty. Yet, there were some important institutional developments – some of which reflected NGO concerns regarding human rights – which resulted in a further deepening of the EU. In particular, the European Parliament's legislative powers were significantly increased through substantial extension of the co-decision procedure. It is now the general rule both for matters where QMV applies[6] and for the new areas brought into the Treaty for the first time. The Council has also lost its right under the co-decision procedure to a 'third reading', whereby the Council could override the opinion of the Parliament. Thus, in many areas the EP is now a co-equal legislator with the Council. As a gesture towards those lobbying for greater Commission accountability, the EP also gained the right to approve the appointment of the Commission President. Turning to the Commission, the authority of the President was strengthened slightly within the College of Commissioners. The Commission's authority was strengthened by the creation of new community competences, by the (gradual) 'communitarisation' of immigration, visa and asylum policies[7] and by the introduction of a shared right of initiative between member states and the Commission for other third-pillar (JHA) policies. Meanwhile, the European Court of Justice's jurisdiction was extended to include immigration and visa issues (a development that is likely to provoke important ECJ rulings in this area). Finally, the Treaty extended slightly the use of QMV in the Council of Ministers in areas such as equal opportunities, social exclusion, public health and employment.

With respect to competence, the following developments are worthy of note. First, the Treaty introduced a new Employment Title (VIII), which makes 'a high level of employment' an EU objective and provides for co-ordination and monitoring of national employment policies. The inclusion of this new Title owed much to the alliance of social democratic governments, anxious to demonstrate their commitment (not least for domestic political reasons) to developing the social dimension of Europe. However, the voluntaristic policy approach adopted by the Treaty was triumph for Blairite, neo-liberal modernisers within the European Left (Pollack 2000). Second, a new title, headed 'Visas asylum immigration and other policies related to the free movement of persons', incorporates the Schengen agreement as well as visa, immigration and asylum policies into the first pillar. Third, the Treaty reiterates the Union's commitment to liberty, democracy, respect for human rights and fundamental freedoms, strengthens the legal basis for the promotion of sex equality (Article 12) and introduces a new anti-discrimination provision (Article 13). Fourth, in an attempt to make CFSP more effective, the Amsterdam Treaty incorporated the so-called 'Petersberg Tasks' into the Treaty. Meanwhile, the new Article 17 extended CFSP to include the progressive framing of a common defence policy and the possible integration of the WEU into the EU. The Treaty also introduced the principle of 'constructive abstention', which enables the Council to adopt CFSP policies relating to an agreed common strategy or joint action by QMV.

'Constructive abstention' constitutes one of the three forms of flexibility introduced in the Amsterdam Treaty; it enables a member state to refrain from voting on, and to formally declare that it will not apply, a decision which will nevertheless commit the Union. Pre-defined flexibility covers a specific field and is applicable as soon as the treaty comes into force. Examples of pre-defined flexibility include the (existing) British and Danish opt-outs from the EMU and the British (and by implication Irish) opt-out from the new Title IV of the Amsterdam Treaty relating to visas, asylum and immigration. Third, in acknowledgement of the increasing diversity within an enlarging EU, the Treaty introduced a general flexibility clause, which permits 'closer co-operation' among 'the most ambitious Member States to deepen co-operation between themselves', albeit subject to fairly stringent conditions[8] (Stubb 2000). Since 1997, both the concept and potential implications of flexibility have been the subject of considerable political and academic debate (see Stubb 2000; Wallace 2000; Junge 1999; Philippart and Sie Dhian Ho 2000). Precisely what form flexibility might take in the future and what the implications of such a development might be for European integration is unclear. Some models envisage flexibility merely as a temporary expedient permitting some states to proceed at a faster pace (multi-speed Europe). Other conceptions see flexibility as a means of allowing some states to co-operate in areas beyond a 'core' Europe (concentric circles), though in some cases the size of this core is either minimal or non-existent ('Europe à la carte') (Junge 1999). Whether or not flexibility will result in the emergence of a 'vanguard' group of federalist-inclined member states, or whether it will permanently divide the wealthy inner core of the EU against the poorer periphery is a moot point.

Integration beyond Amsterdam: the 2000 Intergovernmental Conference and the Treaty of Nice

The IGC 2000 started on 14 February 2000 and ended with the Nice European Council in December that year (on the IGC 2000 see Best, Gray and Stubb 2000). The immediate purpose of this IGC was to reform the EU decision-making process in preparation for enlargement. Key institutional issues to be resolved included the size of the European Parliament and the Commission, and the weighting of national votes within the Council. During the IGC, member states were generally reluctant to declare their position on these sensitive issues, preferring instead to postpone the hard bargaining until the December Council. At Nice, intergovernmental bargaining over institutional issues was acrimonious as member states fought to defend their institutional status. The Council was also overshadowed by a bitter row between France and Germany, sparked by France's refusal to grant the latter's request that its greater population be reflected in voting procedures in Brussels. Difficult decisions were nevertheless taken. With regard to the size of the Commission, the Nice Treaty established that from 2005 there should be one Commissioner per member state until the Union comprises 27 member states. Thereafter, the Council (without consulting either the Parliament or the Commission) will decide on the size of the Commission and choose its members according to a rotation system yet to be devised. The ceiling of 700 seats in the European Parliament established by the Amsterdam Treaty was breached at Nice, where member states fixed the maximum number of MEPs at 732 and agreed that each member state should have between 99 and 5 seats. With regard to the weighting of votes in the Council, member states finally agreed to increase the number of total votes from 87 now up to 345 (with 27 member states) and to reallocate the number of votes allotted to each country. From 2005, the threshold for a qualifying majority will be 258 votes out of 345 – thereby increasing the threshold to 74.8% from its longstanding threshold of 71.3%. A qualified majority must also comprise, when formally challenged for verification by any member state, 62% of the Union's population (compared to the previous informal requirement of 58%). Overall, the changes to the Council's voting rules favour the larger (and more populous) states. Moreover, in a backwards step (for an IGC that was supposed to streamline decision-making), the new arrangements raise the threshold for QMV at the same time as increasing the weight of votes. Though balance of power issues dominated the Nice Council, a number of other reforms were agreed by the member states, which, though incremental in nature, represent a further deepening of the Union. Such developments include: the further extension of QMV and co-decision to new policy areas; further increases in the powers of the Parliament; enlargement and reform of the European Court of Justice; the incorporation of WEU into the EU; and the establishment of Eurojust, a unit of public prosecutors to co-ordinate the fight against crime. Member states also redrafted the provisions of the Amsterdam Treaty relating to closer cooperation. Henceforth, closer cooperation will also be possible in the second pillar in order to implement a joint action or common position providing it does not have defence implications. Henceforth a minimum of eight member states is required to form closer cooperation in the three pillars and the national veto has been abolished.

Outside the formal IGC, the Commission, the Council and the Parliament also jointly proclaimed the EU Charter of Fundamental Rights at the Nice summit. The Charter had been prepared outside the IGC by an *ad hoc* 'Convention' composed of representatives of the heads of state and government, the Commission, the European Parliament and national parliaments. At the insistence of some member states (led by the British government) there is no reference to the Charter in the Nice Treaty. Nevertheless, this document represents an important landmark in the integration process. The Charter builds upon the concept of European citizenship introduced in the TEU and the Union's commitment to fundamental rights and freedoms as provided for in the Amsterdam Treaty. As such, the Charter marks the first attempt to give concrete meaning to the concept of European citizenship. Moreover, notwithstanding the relatively weak juridical status of the Charter, its political import will probably be considerable since it is unlikely to be ignored either by interest groups or the European Court of Justice. The status of the Charter will in any case form part of a much wider debate upon the future of the Union. In a declaration annexed to the Treaty of Nice, the member states called for a deeper and wider debate on the future of the European Union, culminating in another IGC in 2004. Issues singled out by the Nice Council for discussion during the next four years include the delineation of powers between the EU and member states, the status of the EU Charter of Fundamental Rights, simplification of the Treaties, and the role of national parliaments in the EU system.

Thus, the future of the European Union remains uncertain. The Nice treaty has yet to be ratified by the member states. Moreover, though these reforms may have prepared the EU for enlargement in a technical sense, there was little evidence at Nice of a wider vision of Europe. Indeed the Nice Council exposed sharp disagreements between the EU heads of government over the future direction of the EU. In particular, the Council highlighted the discord that now exists within the historically crucial 'motor of European integration', the Franco-German alliance. In part, this tension stems from the French refusal to acknowledge the dominant position of Germany within the EU and Germany's increasing reluctance to bow routinely to France. However, it also reflects the fact that the two countries are now in opposing camps on the key debate in the EU. France, led by President Jacques Chirac, appears to favour an intergovernmental Union. Meanwhile, the German Chancellor, Gerhard Schroeder, favours European federalism and has called for a European constitution. This debate will no doubt continue until – and probably beyond – 2004.

Conclusion: European integration: a journey without end?

The European Union did not spring from a single founding moment; it is the product of nearly fifty years of muddling through. As Marks writes, though 'notions of federalism, intergovernmentalism and so forth, have influenced the development of the EU ... they have not determined it. In practice, the institutions of the EU have been created to achieve discrete, diverse, contested and contingent goals' (Marks 1997: 27). At each stage, the final destination or *raison d'être* of the European Union has been fudged by the member states. Nevertheless, the integration process has continued, driven by national governments, self-interested individuals and groups, European institutions such as the Parliament, the Commission and the Court, and exogenous pressures. Since the 1980s, the Union has been in a constant state of constitutional and institutional flux. Successive reforms of the founding Treaties have incrementally brought about significant deepening of the EU, reflected in the creation of the 'Euroland' currency Union, the setting up of Europol, and the progressive Europeanisation of new policy areas such as defence and immigration. Moreover, recent reforms have constitutuionalised citizenship issues such as fundamental rights, sex equality and anti-discrimination.

The pressures for integration are unlikely to cease – and indeed may even increase. It would, however, be wrong to assume that European integration will lead inevitably to some form of federal European state. There is no agreement between the member states on the fundamental issue of the meaning and purpose of European integration. The endorsement of flexibility in the Amsterdam Treaty is a pragmatic acknowledgement of this fact. Flexibility opens up new opportunities for institutional pluralism within the EU, which in future years may result in more uneven and more shallow levels of co-operation, especially in an enlarged Union. Whether or not this proves to be the case will depend not only upon the actions of national political and socio-economic elites, but also upon the attitudes and inclinations of European publics. The increasing political salience of European integration since 1990 has rendered obsolete the elitist method of integration. There is now widespread acknowledgement on the part of national and EU politicians and administrative elites that integration cannot be agreed 'behind the backs of people' (Günter Verheugen, German Commissioner, cited in *Financial Times*, 28 June 2000). Democratisation of the European integration process, though politically necessary, is likely to make further European integration more difficult to achieve, both because of widespread Euro-scepticism and because people are beginning to debate the *raison d'être* of the European Union.

Notes

1   The ECSC was created by the 1951 Paris Treaty and the EEC and the EURATOM were both established by the 1957 Rome Treaty. The 1965 Merger Treaty created a common Council of Ministers and a common Commission serving all three European Communities. The 1957 'Convention on Certain Institutions Common to the European Communities', signed in parallel with the Treaty of Rome, stipulated that the European Parliament, the European Court of Justice and the Economic and Social Committee would serve all three Communities.

2   Attempts to conceptualise the EU system of governance abound. The *Westphalian model* regards the EU as an embryonic, transnational polity. Further integration through constitution-alisation is implied to create a fully-fledged, democratic state. In contrast, the *inter-governmentalist* conception of the EU is that of a 'structure to complement, co-ordinate, even in limited ways supplant the policies of nation-states, correcting for their manifest weaknesses; yet the EU has not, will not, and should not replace the nation-state' (Moravcsik and Nicolaïdis 1998: 17). European integration is the product of sequential intergovernmental bargains and is intended to further the self-interests of and thus strengthen the participating nation-states. The *regulatory model* envisages the EU as being primarily concerned with market integration and regulation. It advocates delegation to supranational institutions for those policy areas which, for

reasons of efficiency, have to be dealt with at the European level (Majone 1991; 1996). The *multi-level governance model* conceives of European integration as 'a process of diffusion of state authority; upward to supranational institutions and downward to sub-national regions' (Philippart and Sie Dhian Ho 2000: 311). Subnational actors are increasingly involved in national and supranational policy-making arenas and transnational networks. The allocation of tasks to different levels of government is to be determined by the (somewhat elusive) principle of subsidiarity.

3   Members of a customs union agree (1) to abolish all internal tariffs and other trade impediments; (2) to establish a common trade policy towards the rest of the world. In the EC this takes the form of the Common External Tariff (CET). A Common Market implies greater integration. Members agree in addition to promote the free movement of capital and labour within the customs union. Achievement of a European Common Market was the primary objective of the 1986 SEA and the 1992 project.

4   Eleven member states formed the EMU, which was established on 1 January 2000. The UK, Denmark and Sweden declined to join, while Greece failed to meet the convergence criteria for membership.

5   Following the negative, 1992 Danish referendum on the Maastricht Treaty, Denmark negotiated a similar opt-out from the EMU.

6   The one exception is agriculture, where the Council decides by QMV, but needs only to consult Parliament. The co-operation procedure is required only for certain decisions relating to EMU.

7   After a transitional period of five years, during which time the right of initative is shared between the Commission and the Council, asylum, immigration and visa policies, and judicial co-operation in civil matters, will come under the Community pillar.

8   According to the new Title VII of the Amsterdam Treaty (Articles 43–5), flexibility must further integration, maintain the single institutional framework, constitute a measure of last resort, involve the majority of the member states, preserve the *acquis communautaire*, protect outsiders, be open to all and comply with the additional criteria laid down in the pillar-specific enabling clauses.

References

Alter, K. (2000) 'The European Union's Legal System and Domestic Policy: Spillover or Backlash?', *International Organisation* 54/3: 489–518.

Best, E., Gray, M. and Stubb, A. (eds) (2000) *Rethinking the European Union: IGC 2000 and Beyond*, Maastricht: European Institute of Public Administration.

Caporaso, J. and Keeler, J. (1995) 'The EU and Regional Integration Theory', in C. Rhodes and S. Mazey (eds), *The State of the European Union*, vol. 3: *Building a European Polity?*, Boulder: Lynne Reinner, pp. 29–62.

Cichowski, R. (1998) 'Integrating the Environment: The European Court and the Construction of Supranational Policy', *Journal of European Public Policy* 5/3: 387–405.

Coen, D. (1999) 'Business Interests and European Integration'. Unpublished paper presented at a conference, 'Organised Interests in the European Union: Lobbying, Mobilisation and the European Public Area', at Nuffield College, Oxford, 1–2 October.

Commission of the European Communities (1992) *An Open and Structured Dialogue between the Commission and Interest Groups* (SEC (92) 2272 final), Brussels: Commission of the European Communities.

Cowles, M. (1995) 'Setting the Agenda for a New Europe: The ERT and EC 1992', *Journal of Common Market Studies* 33/4: 501–26.

Cram, L. (1993) 'Calling the Tune without Paying the Piper? Social Policy Regulation: The Role of the Commission as a Multi-Organization: Social Policy and IT Regulation in the EU', *Journal of European Public Policy* 1/2: 195–217.

Dehousse, R. and Majone, G. (1994) 'The Institutional Dynamics of European Integration', in S. Martin (ed.), *The Construction of Europe: Essays in Honour of Emile Noël*, Dordrecht: Kluwer Academic Publishers, pp. 91–112.

Duchêne, F. (1994) *Jean Monnet: The First Statesman of Interdependence*, New York: Norton.

Duff, A. (ed.) (1997) *The Treaty of Amsterdam: Text and Commentary*, London: Federal Trust.

Duff, A. (1998) 'Britain and Europe: The Different Relationship', in M. Westlake (ed.), *The European Union beyond Amsterdam: New Concepts of European Integration*, London: Routledge, pp. 34–46.

Duff, A., Pinder, J. and Pryce, R. (eds) (1994) *Maastricht and Beyond: Building the European Union*, London: Routledge.

Dyson, K. and Featherstone, K. (1999) *The Road to Maastricht: Negotiating Economic and Monetary Union*, Oxford: Oxford University Press.

Edwards, G. and Pijpers, A. (eds) (1997) *The Politics of European Treaty Reform*, London: Pinter.

European Commission (1999) *Eurobarometer* 51: 25.

Featherstone, K. (1994) 'Jean Monnet and the "Democratic Deficit" in the European Union', *Journal of Common Market Studies* 32/2: 149–70.

George, S. (1990) *An Awkward Partner: Britain in the European Community*, Oxford: Oxford University Press.

Greenwood, J. (1997) *Representing Interests in the European Union*, London: Macmillan.

Gustavsson, R. (1996) 'The European Union: 1996 and Beyond: A Personal View from the Sideline', in S. S. Andersen and K. A. Eliassen (eds), *The European Union: How Democratic Is It?*, London: Sage.

Haas, E. (1958) *The Uniting of Europe*, Stanford: Stanford University Press.

Junge, K. (1999) *Flexibility, Enhanced cooperation and the Treaty of Amsterdam*, European Dossier Series, London: Kogan Page.

Keohane, R. O. and Hoffmann, S. (eds) (1991) *The New European Community: Decisionmaking and Institutional change*, Boulder: Westview, pp. 177–94.

Kingdon, J. W. (1984) *Agendas, Alternatives and Public Policies*, New York: HarperCollins.

Kirchner, E. (1980) 'Interest Group Behaviour at the Community Level', in L. Hurwitz (ed.), *Contemporary Perspectives on European Integration: Attitudes, Non- governmental Behaviour and Collective Decision Making*, Westport: Greenwood Press, pp. 96–119.

Laursen, F. and Vanhoonacker, S. (1992) *The Intergovernmental Conference on Political Union: Institutional Reforms, New Policies and the International Identity of the European Community*, Maastricht: European Institute of Public Administration.

Lipgens, W. (1982) *A History of European Integration 1945–1947: The Formation of the European Unity Movement*, Oxford: Clarendon.

Majone, G. (1991) 'Cross-National Sources of Regulatory Policy-making in Europe and the United States', *Journal of Public Policy* 11/1: 79–106.

Majone, G. (1992) 'Regulatory Federalism in the European Community', *Government and Policy* 10: 299–316.

Majone, G. (ed.) (1996) *Regulating Europe*, London: Routledge.

Marks, G. (1997) 'A Third Lens: Comparing European Integration and State Building', in J. Klansen and L. Tilly (eds), *European Integration in Social and Historical Perspective*, Lanham, MD: Rowman and Littlefield, pp. 23–43.

Mazey, S. (1992) 'Conception and Evolution of the High Authority's Administrative Services (1952–1960): From Supranational Principles to Multinational Practices', in *Yearbook of European Administrative History*, Baden-Baden: Nomos Verlagsgesellschaft, pp. 31–48.

Mazey, S. (1998) 'The European Union and Women's Rights: From the Europeanization of National Agendas to the Nationalization of a European Agenda?', *Journal of European Public Policy* 5/1: 131–52

Mazey, S. and Richardson, J. (1993) *Lobbying in the European Community* Oxford: Oxford University Press.

Mazey, S. and Richardson, J. (1997) 'Policy Framing: Interest Groups and the 1996 IGC', in A. Pijpers, and G. Edwards (eds), *The European Union and the Agenda of 1996*, London: Pinter.

Mazey, S. and Richardson, J. (1999) 'Interests', in Laura Cram and Neill Nugent (eds), *Developments in the European Union*, London: Macmillan, pp. 105–29.

Mazey, S. and Richardson, J. (2001) 'Institutionalising Promiscuity: Groups and European Integration', in W. Sandholtz and A. Stone Sweet (eds), *The Institutionalisation of European Space*, Oxford: Oxford University Press.

Milward, A. (1992) *The European Rescue of the Nation-State* London: Routledge.

Monnet, J. (1978) *Memoirs*, London: Collins.

Moravcsik, A. (1991) 'Negotiating the Single European Act: National Interests and Conventional Statecraft', *International Organisation* 45: 19–56.

Moravcsik, A. (1998) *The Choice for Europe: Social Purpose and State Power from Messina to Maastricht*, Ithaca: Cornell University Press.

Moravcsik, A. and Nicolaïdis, K. (1998) 'Federal Ideals and Constitutional Realities', *Annual Review*, *Journal of Common Market Studies* 36.

Neunreither, K. and Wiener, A. (eds) (2000) *European Integration after Amsterdam: Institutional Dynamics and Prospects for Democracy*, Oxford: Oxford University Press.

Peters, G. (1994) 'Agenda-setting in the European Community', *Journal of European Public Policy* 1/1: 9–26.

Peterson, J. (1995) 'Decision-making in the European Union: Towards a Framework for Analysis', *Journal of European Public Policy* 2/1: 69–94.

Philippart, E. and Sie Dhian Ho, M. (2000) 'From Uniformity to Flexibility: The Management of Diversity and its Impact on the EU System of Governance', in G. De Burca and J. Scott (eds), *Constitutional Change in the EU: From Uniformity to Flexibility*, Oxford: Hart, pp. 299–336.

Pierson, P. (1996) 'The Path to European Integration: A Historical Institutionalist Analysis', *Comparative Politics* 29/2: 123–63.

Pinder, J. (1995) *European Community: The Building of a Union*, Oxford: Oxford University Press.

Pollack, M. (2000) 'A Blairite Treaty: Neo-liberalism and Regulated Capitalism in the Treaty of Amsterdam', in K. Neunreither and A. Wiener (eds), *European Integration After Amsterdam: Institutional Dynamics and Prospects for Democracy*, Oxford: Oxford University Press.

Richardson, J. J. and Jordan, G. (1979) *Governing under Pressure*, Oxford: Blackwell.

Sabatier, P. (1988) 'An Advocacy Coalition Framework of Policy Change and the Role of Policy Orientated Learning Therein', *International Organisation* 46: 1–35.

Sabatier, P. (1998) 'The Advocacy Coalition Framework: Revisions and Relevance for Europe', *Journal of European Public Policy* 5/1: 98–130.

Sandholtz, W. (1993) 'Choosing Union: Monetary Politics and Maastricht', *International Organisation* 47: 1–39.

Sloots, T. and Verschuren, P. (1990) 'Decision-making Speed in the European Community', *Journal of Common Market Studies* 29: 75–85.

Stevens, A. (2000) 'Ever-Closer Union: European Co-operation and the European Dimension', in R. Sakwa and A. Stevens (eds), *Contemporary Europe*, London: Macmillan, pp. 137–60.

Stirk, P. M. R. and Weigall, D. (eds) (1999) *The Origins and Development of European Integration: A Reader and a Commentary*, London: Pinter.

Stone Sweet, A. and Brunell, T. (1998) 'The European Court and the National Courts: A Statistical Analysis of Preliminary References 1961–95', *Journal of European Public Policy* 5/1: 66–97.

Stubb, A. (2000) 'Negotiating Flexible Integration in the Amsterdam Treaty', in K. Neunreither and A. Wiener (eds), *European Integration after Amsterdam: Institutional Dynamics and Prospects for Democracy*, Oxford: Oxford University Press, pp. 153–74.

Sverdrup, O. (2000) 'Precedents and Present Events in the European Union: An Institutional Perspective on Treaty Reform', in K. Neunreither and A. Wiener (eds), *European Integration after Amsterdam: Institutional Dynamics and Prospects for Democracy*, Oxford: Oxford University Press, pp. 241–65.

Urwin, D. (1989) *Western Europe since 1945: A Political History*, 4th edn, London: Longman.

Van Schendelen, M. P. C. M. (1998) *EU Committees as Influential Policymakers*, Aldershot: Ashgate.

Van Schendelen, R. (ed.) (1992) *National Public and Private Lobbying*, Aldershot: Dartmouth Press.

Vaughan, R. (1979) *Twentieth Century Europe*, London: Croom Helm.

Wallace, H. (2000) 'Flexibility: A Tool of Integration or a Restraint on Disintegration?', in K. Neunreither and A. Wiener (eds), *European Integration after Amsterdam: Institutional Dynamics and Prospects for Democracy*, Oxford: Oxford University Press, pp. 175–91.

Weiler, J. (1997) 'The Reformation of European Constitutionalism', *Journal of Common Market Studies* 35/1: 97–131.

Weiler, J. (2000) 'IGC 2000: The Constitutional Agenda', in E. Best, M. Gray and A. Stubb (eds), *Rethinking the European Union: IGC 2000 and Beyond*, Maastricht: European Institute of Public Administration, pp. 219–36.

Westlake, M. (ed.) (1998) *The European Union beyond Amsterdam: New Concepts of European Integration*, London: Routledge.

Willis, F. R. (1968) *France, Germany and the New Europe 1945–1967*, Stanford: Stanford University Press.

Wood, D. M. and Yesilada, B. A. (1996) *The Emerging European Union*, London: Longman.

Chapter 3

Integration theory and the study of the European policy process

Towards a synthesis of approaches

LAURA CRAM

Introduction

In this chapter the development of European integration theory is examined: its roots, development, and the current state of the debate. The chapter presents a critical overview of the key theoretical approaches to the study of European integration and examines how the study of the EU as a system of governance has enriched attempts to understand the integration process. It concludes with the argument that more attention now needs to be paid to the societal dimension of European integration and how the societal impact of the EU as a system of governance relates to the broader process of European integration.

The evolution of European integration theory: the theoretical roots

During the Second World War and in its immediate aftermath, many scholars sought to elaborate a new type of political system which would facilitate co-operation between states and the preservation of international (or at least Europe-wide) peace. Some theorists focused on the desirable *end product* of this co-operation (for example federalism and functionalism), while others focused on the *background conditions* which would be required for the establishment of a new transnational political community (for example, the transactionalist/communications school). Each, in their own way, contributed to the elaboration of later neo-functionalist attempts to explain the emerging *process* of European integration which had begun with the establishment of the European Coal and Steel Community in 1951.

Federalism

For many scholars and politicians the potential solution to the conflict between European states lay in the development of a European federation of states. Throughout the Second World War, there were many references to the peace-making potential of a European federal political structure. The federalist movement had strong roots in the European resistance movement, and even further back, for example, in the writings of Coudenhove-Kalergi (1923; 1938; 1943). The development of the post-war federalist movement was championed by committed federalists such as Jean Monnet, Walter Hallstein and Altiero Spinelli (1966), who were to be disillusioned by the slow progress in Europe and the virtual abandonment of any attempt to create a true European federation. European integration has, thus far, fallen far short of the ideals of these federalists. While remaining a popular vision today, the 'federalist approach is more a strategy for fulfilling a common purpose and common needs than a theory explaining how these integrative forces arise' (Hodges 1972: 13).

Transactionalism/communications school

In contrast, the work of Deutsch (1954; 1964; 1966; 1967), and other scholars working within the transactionalist/ communications tradition, focused on the *conditions* necessary for political integration to occur. Mutual transactions or communications were, for Deutsch, a necessary, but insufficient, prerequisite for the development of a political community. Thus, travel, trade, telecommunications and postal links might, in themselves, lead to *mutual relevance* but, without creating *mutual responsiveness*, would fail to generate a sense of community. For Deutsch (1966: 96), mutually responsive transactions resulted from a complex learning process from which shared symbols, identities, habits of co-operation, memories, values and norms would emerge. Deutsch's vision of political integration did not insist on the presence of any specified institutional structure but rather depended on a 'historical process of social learning in which individuals, usually over several generations, learn to become a people' (Deutsch 1966: 174).

This view of political integration presents affiliation or attachment in largely functional terms. Affiliation, whether to the national or EU level, is thus contingent upon the perceived benefits to be reaped. Deutsch *et al.* (1957: 87), for example, argued that 'The issue of political integration (thus) arose primarily when people demanded greater capabilities, greater performance, greater responsiveness, and more adequate services of some kind from the governments of the political units by which they had been governed before. Integration or amalgamation were first considered as possible means to further these ends, rather than as ends in themselves'.

The transactionalist/communication school approach was widely criticised, not least, for its methodological focus on transaction flow indices which did not provide an adequate picture of the multi-faceted integration process (Inglehart 1967 and Puchala 1970). However, Deutsch had highlighted the importance of the *socio-psychological* aspects of community formation (Hodges 1972: 19), which were to be highly influential on subsequent work in the field of European integration and, in particular, on Haas's neo-functionalism. More recently, Deutsch's focus on the key role played by transactions in the creation and maintenance of the governance regime within the EU has been recognised as crucial by Sandholtz and Stone Sweet (1998). Meanwhile, an extensive literature, drawing upon new institutionalist approaches, examining the role of institutions, institutionalisation, lock-in, path dependency and the question of preference formation (Armstrong and Bulmer 1998; Pierson 1996) also focuses on the learning process and the development of 'integrative habits' as a result of prior co-operation.

Functionalism

Perhaps the most influential work of this period, both upon the European integration process and upon subsequent attempts to conceptualise this process, was David Mitrany's functionalism. Yet, functionalism was not a theory of European integration. Indeed, Mitrany was directly opposed to the project of European regional integration. In his advocacy of a 'A Working Peace System', Mitrany (1943/1966: 68) proposed a *universal*, rather than a *regional*, solution to what he saw as the 'problem of our generation': 'how to weld together the common interest of all without interfering unduly with the particular ways of each'.

A central tenet of Mitrany's work was his opposition to nationalism, and the territorial organisation of power which, like his contemporaries, he saw as a threat to world peace. Mitrany (1943/1966: 82) was vehemently opposed to the divisive organisation of states in the international system, which he described as arbitrary 'political amputations'. Yet, while many of his fellow scholars were searching for *European* co-operative solutions to the problem of world conflict, Mitrany (1943/1966: 96) maintained that 'peace will not be secured if we organize the world by what divides it'. In the pursuit of peaceful, non-coercive community-building, nationalism at the nation-state level must not, Mitrany argued, simply be replaced by nationalism at the European level.

In his 1943 text Mitrany deals specifically with what he calls the 'perplexities of feder-alism'. Mitrany had a number of problems with this, the most frequently proposed, solution to the problem of conflict in Europe. First, he argued that the 'problems which now divide the national states would almost all crop up again in any territorial realign-ment; their dimensions would be different, but not their evil nature' (Mitrany 1943/1966: 46). Second, while he agreed with the federalists that, 'cooperation for the common good is the task' (Mitrany 1943/1966: 97–8), he argued that it would be 'senseless' to tie this co-operation to a territorial authority. The number of necessary co-operative activities for Mitrany (1943/1966: 98) would remain limited while, he argued, 'their range is the world'. Further, as all proposed federal solutions were limited, either territorially or ideologically, there was no guarantee that the necessary political consensus could be achieved to create the new constitutional framework which a federation would require. A federation, by its very nature, would prove divisive: 'federation like other political formations, carries a Janus head which frowns division on one side in the very act of smiling union on the other' (Mitrany 1943/1966: 93).

A key factor in understanding Mitrany's functionalist vision is the distinction which he draws between political/constitutional co-operation and technical/functional co-operation in his advocacy of a new international society. For Mitrany (1943/1966: 58), the task was clear: 'our aim must be to call forth to the highest possible degree the active forces and opportuni-ties for co-operation, while touching as little as possible the latent or active points of difference and opposition'. The political/constitutional route had clearly failed to rise to this challenge. Mitrany was all too aware of the failings of recent peace pacts, international treaties and of international organisations (which retained states as members) like the League of Nations. In contrast, Mitrany advocated the development of technical interna-tional organisations, structured on the basis of functional principles,[1] which would perform collective welfare tasks. Internal political conflict and interminable debates about the bound-aries of national sovereignty were to be side-stepped. The function to be carried out would determine the type of organisation best suited for its realisation. This 'technical self-determination' would, in turn, mean that there would be 'no need for any fixed constitutional division of authority and power, prescribed in advance' (Mitrany 1943/1966: 73). Indeeed, 'anything beyond the original formal definition of scope and purpose might embarrass the working of the practical arrangements' (Mitrany 1943/1966: 73).

For Mitrany, it was rules, experts and the principle of 'technical self-determination' (1943/1966: 72), rather than territorial structures or national politicians, which would facil-itate the decline of ideological conflict, the demise of nationalism, and would allow peaceful co-operation to develop on a world-wide scale. In Mitrany's words: 'It is no longer a question of defining relations between states but of merging them – the workday sense of the vague talk about the need to surrender some part of sovereignty' (Mitrany 1943/1966: 42). If the needs of society were revealed, Mitrany (1943/1966: 99) argued, 'quite starkly for what they are, practical household tasks' it would 'be more difficult to make them into the household idols of "national interest" and "national honor"'.

While not entirely opposed to some kind of formal international union in the future, Mitrany (1943/1966: 97) cautioned that, as yet, the 'political way was too ambitious'. Indeed Mitrany feared that the political/constitutional approach might even hamper progress towards a working international system. Only through co-operation in technical/functional organisations might it be possible to 'set going lasting instruments and habits of a common international life' (Mitrany 1943/1966: 58). Without these habits, political/constitutional action could not be contemplated, while with these learned habits of integration such political/constitutional action may ultimately prove superfluous (Mitrany 1943/1966: 97). Although somewhat vague on the processes by which functional action would lead to international society, Mitrany (1943/1966: 58) argued that the 'growth of new habits and interests', as a result of functional co-operation, would begin to dilute persisting or emergent ideological divisions. Ultimately, 'every activity organised in that way would be a layer of peaceful life; and a sufficient addition of them would create increasingly deep and wide strata of peace – not the forbidding peace of an alliance, but one that would suffuse the world with a fertile mingling of common endeavour and achievement' (Mitrany 1943/1966: 98). With the 'working peace system' up and running, nationalism could, at last, be replaced by allegiance to the world community.

In the context of European integration, Mitrany's functionalism remains important not least because of its influence on two of the key architects of the European Coal and Steel Community (ECSC): Jean Monnet and Robert Schuman. Monnet and Schuman, in creating the ECSC, borrowed key aspects of what might be termed the *functionalist method*, without adopting Mitrany's central goal: the dissolution of territorially based authorities. Thus Monnet and Schuman employed Mitrany's focus on technical, sector-specific integration, and his emphasis on avoiding political debates about the surrender of national sovereignty, in order to facilitate the incremental establishment of a territorially based organisation and the creation of a new regional authority structure. For Schuman, the pooling of resources in the European Coal and Steel Community, was 'a first step in the federation of Europe'.[2] Clearly, this was a very different end from that proposed by Mitrany!

In many ways this deracination of Mitrany's approach to international co-operation (later perpetuated in many respects by the (mis)categorisation of neo-functionalist theory as a direct descendant of functionalism)[3] has led to Mitrany's vision surfacing in the literature on European integration more often as a caricature of itself than as a true reflection of Mitrany's functionalist ideal of an international society.[4] Mitrany directly opposed the recreation of territorially based state structures at the European level except in so far as they represented unrelated responses to technical self-determination.

Neo-functionalism

Functionalism met with many criticisms: not least because of the rather naive belief that a neat division between technical/functional issues and political/constitutional issues could be sustained. Increasingly political scientists argued that the division between technical, non-controversial, economic issues, on the one hand, and political issues, on the other, was untenable: 'economic integration, however defined, may be based on political motives and frequently begets political consequences' (Haas 1958: 12). Likewise, while Mitrany had prescribed the necessary development of a new world community, quite how the transition from functional action to international society would take place was never clearly specified and relied on a rather organic process of expansion which was not consistently observable in practice. By the late 1950s Ernst Haas (1958: 4), in *The Uniting of Europe*, described Western Europe as a 'living laboratory' for the study of collective action between European states. A wide range of organisations, which required the collaboration of European governments, operated in Western Europe.[5] Yet, as Haas (1958: 4) noted, 'detailed data on how – if at all – cohesion is obtained through these processes is lacking'. It was this very *process* which Haas set out to investigate with the development of neo-functionalism.

In many ways the title neo-functionalism is something of a misnomer or 'a case of mistaken identity' (Groom 1978). Developed, in part, to address the gaps in existing functionalist theory and practice and, in part, as a pluralist critique of the realist school,[6] which had hitherto dominated the study of international relations, the neo-functionalist approach is of very mixed intellectual parentage. Neo-functionalism, as well as addressing some of the shortcomings of Mitrany's functionalism, also represents a clear divergence from some of the central tenets of Mitrany's functionalism in a number of important respects. Although incorporating many elements of the 'functionalist method', as practiced by Monnet and Schuman on the basis of their deracinated version of functionalist theory, neo-functionalism also draws upon some of the central tenets both of the communications school and of the federalist school of integration theory.

Focus on the process of developing a new political community in Europe

Neo-functionalism, in its early articulation, focused specifically upon the integration project in Europe. It sought to explain what was happening in Europe, and to provide a conceptual framework within which developments in Europe could be understood.[7] For Haas, it was not the necessary background *conditions* nor the *end product* of co-operation between the nation-states which were the focus of his study.[8] Rather, the focus of study for neo-functionalists was the *process* of political integration itself. For Haas (1958: 16):

> Political integration is the process whereby political actors in several distinct national settings are persuaded to shift their loyalties, expectations and political activities toward a new centre, whose institutions possess or demand jurisdiction over the pre-existing national states.

In terms of the relationship between Mitrany's functionalism and the neo-functionalism developed by Haas, it is important to note that for neo-functionalists the basic unit of analysis remained the territorially based state system so vehemently opposed by Mitrany (Groom 1978: 114). There was no concept in neo-functionalism of transcending the traditional territorial division of states: these were simply to be supplemented/replaced by new territorially based organisations at the European level.

The role of supranational institutions

In terms of the intellectual parentage of neo-functionalism, Haas viewed a central government as 'essential institutionally' and a national (in this case European) consciousness as 'essential socially' (Haas 1958: 8). The links with the federalist[9] and communications schools respectively are clear. Although recognising the importance of the insights developed by Deutsch, and in particular of the importance of an emergent European-centred belief system, for Haas (1958: 7), 'the existence of political institutions capable of translating ideologies into law [is] the cornerstone of the definition'. The contrast with Mitrany's functionalism is stark. Mitrany specifically warned against the creation of territorially based supranational authority structures: 'for an authority which had the title to do so would in effect be hardly less than a world government; and such a strong central organism would inevitably tend to take unto itself rather more authority than that originally allotted to it' (Mitrany 1943/1966: 75). In contrast, in Haas's neo-functionalist approach, the very propensity of organisations to maximise their powers is an important element of the process through which a political community is formed. Indeed, the supranational institutions are allotted a key role as potential 'agents of integration' (Haas 1958:

29). The supranational institutions were expected both to facilitate the transfer of elite loyalties to the European level and to play the role of 'honest broker', facilitating decision-making between recalcitrant national governments (Haas 1958: 524).

Interests, learning and authority-legitimacy transfers

The neo-functionalist approach shares with Mitrany's functionalism a focus on social actors and technical experts. However, Haas did not share Mitrany's vision of politically neutral actors carrying out technical/functional tasks unaffected by political conflict. Less idealistic, Haas's pluralist-based neo-functionalism recognised the continuing importance of national political elites, and emphasised the key role played by interest-based politics, in driving the process of political integration. National political elites might, for example, become more supportive of the process of European integration as they learned of the benefits which might ensue from its continuation.[10] In turn, a re-evaluation of the interests of the political elite (whether in favour of, or in opposition to, the European project) would result, ultimately, in the transformation of traditional nationally centred belief sytems:

> As the process of integration proceeds, it is assumed that values will undergo change, that interests will be redefined in terms of regional rather than a purely national orientation and that the erstwhile set of separate national group values will gradually be superseded by a new and geographically larger set of beliefs.
>
> (Haas 1958: 13)

In its focus upon the learning of integrative habits, as a result of prior co-operation, neo-functionalism displays a clear link with both the functionalist and communication schools. For Haas, however, this was not a one-way process. Although the attitudes of national political elites would influence the development of the integration process, supranational political elites also had a role to play in encouraging the process of integration. Thus, 'decision-makers in the new institutions may resist the effort to have their beliefs and policies dictated by the interested elites and advance their own prescription' (Haas 1958: 19). It was through a complex *interaction of belief systems* that Haas envisioned that the reorientation of the activities of national political elites, in response to European-centred interests and aspirations, would take place.[11] Ultimately, Haas argued that as 'beliefs and aspirations' were transformed, through the interaction of supranational and national belief systems, a 'proportional dimunition of loyalty to and expectations from the former separate national governments' could be expected (Haas 1958: 14). A shift in the focus of national loyalties and, importantly, of expectations towards the new supranational authority structure would similarly be expected.

The central importance of the transfer of loyalty in early neo-functionalist explanations of the process of political integration is undisputed. However, in his later work, Haas (1970: 633) recognised the difficulty of measuring this transferral and welcomed the contribution of Lindberg and Scheingold (1970), who stressed the importance of the extent to which authority for decision-making had been transferred to the European level. The degree to which *authority-legitimacy* transfers had taken place would, they argued, provide a measurable indicator of progress towards a new political community. The authority-legitimacy transfer was not, however, the sole defining criterion of political integration identified by Haas. Crucially, the process of political integration encompassed not only a change in the focus of the '*loyalties*' of the political elite but also in the focus of their '*expectations* and *political activities*' (Haas 1958: 16).[12]

The reorientation of the interests of the political elite, Haas argued, may result as much from their opposition to, as from their support for, the integration process. It is the reorientation of national expectations and political activities in response to supranational developments in Europe, or to the pull of the new centre, which are crucial for the process of political integration, not simply the extent to which the political actors are in support of the process of integration. Haas (1958: 288) considered that although elites with 'long-run negative expectations' of supranational activity might appear irreconcilable to the 'unification pattern', in fact, 'even the consistently negative-minded may be persuaded to adjust' (Haas 1958: 296). Meanwhile, groups with short-run negative expectations who mobilise in response to specific supranational policies which they oppose, 'may, in self defence, become a permanent institution with a common – albeit negative – body of expectations' (Haas 1958: 288).

Any shift in loyalties, in response to the activities of the new centre, need not be absolute or permanent. Multiple loyalties may continue to exist. Hence, for Haas (1958: 15–16), it was more likely to be the convergence of a very disparate set of interests which would drive the process of integration and result in the establishment of a new political community, than any mass conversion to the doctrine of 'Europeanism'. Ultimately, a self-interested shift in loyalty, or in the focus of political activities, by the political elite will increase the dynamic towards the development of the new political community, whether it results from positive or from negative long-term expectations of the integration process (Haas 1958: 297). It is this process which is usually referred to as *political spillover*.

Spillover v. technical self-determination

It is the process of political 'spillover' which is, perhaps, most closely associated with the neo-functionalist approach to the study of European integration and which represented the most significant advance upon Mitrany's functionalist method. Political spillover, in short, consists of a convergence of the expectations and interests of national elites in response to the activities of the supranational institutions. This, in turn, may result in a transfer of loyalties (authority-legitimacy transfers) or, at minimum, in a transformation in the political activities of national elites (for example, a rise in European lobbying) in favour of, or opposed to, new supranational policies. Crucially, political spillover could be positively or negatively inspired and was expected to increase as supranational policies were revealed to be of increasing relevance to national elites.

The concept of political spillover was a major advance upon Mitrany's functionalist focus on the notion of 'technical self-determination', and on Mitrany's reliance on a rather organic process in which successful co-operation in one area would encourage co-operation in another area. Haas, however, continued to recognise the importance of *functional* or *technical* spillover, which, he argued, was based on a quite different logic from that which drove political spillover: 'sector integration … begets its own impetus toward extension to the entire economy even in the absence of specific group demands and their attendant ideologies' (Haas 1958: 297). In neo-functionalist terms, the process of functional or sectoral spillover referred to the situation in which the attempt to achieve a goal agreed upon at the outset of co-operation, such as the harmonisation of coal and steel policy, becomes possible only if other (unanticipated) co-operative activities are also carried out, for example harmonisation of transport policy or economic policy. In this way co-operation in one sector would 'spill over' into co-operation in another, previously unrelated, sector.

Haas increasingly sought to refine his understanding of the dynamics of the process of functional or sectoral spillover and to move away from the automaticity inherent in the concept of 'technical self-determination'. In 1960, Haas argued that there was no 'dependable, cumulative process of precedent formation leading to ever more community-oriented organizational behaviour, unless the task assigned to the institutions is *inherently expansive*, thus capable of *overcoming the built-in autonomy of functional contexts* and of surviving changes in the policy aims of member states'.[13] With his focus on inherently expansive tasks, Haas clearly distinguished his neo-functionalism from Mitrany's functionalism. Far from focusing on the very separate demands of different functional tasks, Haas focused on the potential linkages between sectors. It was this focus on linkage politics which, in part, contributed to the image of the political integration as an inexorable process: a snowball, constantly gathering momentum as the process of integration rolled on.

Importantly, the snowball effect identified by neo-functionalism, was not limited only to political, or to functional/sectoral spillover, but also incorporated what Haas (1958: 317) referred to as *geographical spillover*. Haas recognised that co-operation between one group of member states was likely to have some effect upon excluded states: not least by altering existing patterns of trade. In turn, the responses of non-member states might, he argued, influence the process of integration. In this context, Haas (1958: 314–17), referred particularly to the integrative effects which UK participation in the European Free Trade Area had had upon the UK government's attitude towards European co-operative ventures. By 1957, the UK government had recognised that, at least, 'qualified association' with the EEC was necessary. Haas (1958: 317) noted that 'a geographical spill-over is clearly taking place'. This is an aspect of neo-functionalist spillover which is often overlooked but which has clear resonances today as the EU seeks to accommodate an increasing range of demands for membership.

The heyday of neo-functionalism

Initial evaluations of the neo-functionalist approach appeared favourable. As the ECSC 'spilled over' into the European Economic Community and Euratom, in many ways it seemed that neo-functionalism had rather neatly encapsulated the process of European integration.

> Economic integration – with its evident political implications and causes – then became almost a universal battlecry, making complete the 'spill-over' from ECSC to Euratom and its promise of independence from oil imports, from sector common markets to the General Common Market.
>
> (Haas 1958: 298)

Not only had the Rome Treaties been signed in 1957, providing a good example of *sectoral spillover*, but, by the early 1960s, a number of members of the competitor European Free Trade Association (EFTA) had begun to apply for membership of the EEC. Hence a type of *geographical spillover* had also begun.[14] *Political spillover*, was in clear evidence, as interest groups mobilised, for example, around the issue of the Common Agricultural Policy. Not least, the European Commission, with Walter Hallstein as President, had adopted an active constitutional role for itself and was a committed 'agent of integration'. As the goals of the first transition phase were achieved, it was decided that the second phase could be shortened. At the time it appeared that 'the spill-over may make a political community of Europe in fact even before the end of the transition period' (Haas 1958: 311).

Very shortly, however, it became clear that the picture was not so simple as neofunctionalism had painted it. Within a few short years: de Gaulle had vetoed the UK membership application (hence curtailing the process of geographical spillover); the French 'empty chair policy' of 1965 had put paid, at least in the short term, to any notion of Commission activism and its encouragement of political spillover; and, finally, the oil crisis and recession of the early 1970s had brought even the automaticity of sectoral spillover into question. Clearly, forces other than those identified by Haas were at play and now had to be explained.

The state-centred approaches: realism and intergovernmentalism

The study of international relations more generally had been dominated, in the post-war period, by the realist model of world politics. The most influential text in post-war international relations, *Politics Among Nations* (Morgenthau 1948), identified a world system in which the dominant actors were rational unitary states, prepared to use force to achieve their goals, and for whom the maintenance of military security lay at the apex of their hierarchy of goals.[15] From a realist perspective, the interaction between states in a conflictual international environment was central, and the balance of power was constantly shifting. From this perspective, co-operative ventures between nation-states were likely only to constitute a temporary equilibrium, from which the partners were at liberty to withdraw should they no longer feel that their interests were best served by membership.

While there have been many criticisms of the realist approach, it is perhaps unsurprising that one of the most powerful early critiques of the neo-functionalist approach to the study of European integration should have had roots in this tradition of thought. While acknowledging the shortcomings of the realist school, not least the fact that states could in no way be characterised as unitary actors, Stanley Hoffmann (1966), in his intergovernmentalist critique of the neo-functionalist approach, developed upon some of the insights of the realist school.

Hoffmann emphasised the importance of the international environment and the role which national governments played within the global system. The role of national governments was to promote the interests of their peoples to the best of their abilities within an adversarial world system. The implications of this for the study of regional politics (such as the process of European integration) were important. First, the importance of regional politics was, Hoffmann (1966: 865) argued, far less important to national governments than 'purely local or purely global' concerns. Within the global international system 'regional subsystems have only a reduced autonomy' (Hoffmann 1966: 865). Second, Hoffmann highlighted the contingent nature of any transnational co-operation. While 'extensive co-operation is not at all ruled out', there 'would be no assurance against a sudden and disastrous reversal' (Hoffmann 1966: 896). For Hoffmann, national governments were more 'obstinate' than 'obsolete' in the process of European integration. This was clearly a serious challenge to the snowball effect of co-operation proposed by the neofunctionalist approach.

Hoffmann (1966: 886) also drew attention to the 'limits of the functional method' or, as he referred to it, the 'Monnet method' (Hoffmann 1966: 885). Critically, Hoffmann criticised the logic of integration implicit in the 'Monnet method', and which Haas had incorporated into his neo-functionalist approach. Hoffmann argued that, in fact, it was the 'logic of diversity' which prevailed and which would set limits to the 'spillover' anticipated by the neo-functionalists (Hoffmann 1966: 882). In areas of vital national interest, Hoffmann argued, national governments were not willing to be compensated for their losses by gains in other areas. Crucially, some issues were more important than others. Instead, national governments would choose to minimise uncertainty and would maintain tight control over decision processes when vital interests were at stake.

> Russian roulette is fine only as long as the gun is filled with blanks … Functional integration's gamble could be won only if the method had sufficient potency to promise an excess of gains over losses, and of hopes over frustrations. Theoretically, this may be true of economic integration. It is not true of political integration (in the sense of 'high politics').
>
> (Hoffmann 1966: 882)

Hoffmann's distinction between issues of 'low politics' (economic and welfare policies) and matters of 'high politics' (foreign policy, security and defence) was central to his critique of the neo-functionalist approach. The ambiguity implicit in the neo-functionalist 'logic of integration' might appear acceptable to national governments when taking decisions about tariffs, and almost sufficed for discussions on the issue of agriculture. When it came to the discussion of matters of 'high politics', however, clear and consistent goals would be required (Hoffmann 1966: 883). National governments would not be persuaded to accept anything less.

Developing integration theory in the 1970s

There have been many attempts to reassess and revitalise neo-functionalism. Many of these resulted in important refinements to Haas's original work (see, for example, Lindberg 1963; Haas 1964; Lindberg and Scheingold 1970; Nye 1968; Schmitter 1970). Increasingly, it was recognised that integration was not an inexorable process, in which national governments found themselves caught up, but a process which might just as easily 'spill-back' or 'spill-around'. However, in the context of the late 1960s and early 1970s it was difficult to make a case for the neo-functionalist approach. Indeed, while in 1970 Haas was reflecting upon the 'Joy and Anguish of Pre-theorising', by 1975 he was declaring the *Obsolescence of Regional Integration Theory*. As the EEC faced a period of stagnation, shaken by international events and the actions of domestic leaders, the snowball of neo-functionalism seemed to have melted.

The study of European integration was clearly less fashionable in this 'doldrums period' (Caporaso and Keeler 1995: 13). For a number of years scholars of European integration, having observed the apparent stagnation of the integration process and the consignment of neo-functionalist and communication school approaches to the theoretical wastelands, were, understandably, somewhat hesitant to generate 'grand theories' of European integration. However, as Caporaso and Keeler (1995: 16) argue, the scholarship generated during this period deserves more attention and respect than it has received. As well as providing many important insights into the integration process, the studies of this period provided the foundations for later studies both of the integration process and of the functioning of the European Union as a polity or system of governance. Case studies of European policy-making proliferated, significantly enhancing understandings of how the European institutions and member states interacted. Scholars such as Wallace, Wallace and Webb (1977/1983) reminded observers of European integration that these everyday political activities, although less dramatic than major Treaty negotiations, still needed to be understood. Indeed, they argued that these low-profile, everyday activities might have important implications for the future of European integration. Meanwhile, a number of theoretically distinct developments were to play a significant role in facilitating a more synthetic approach to the study of European integration in the late 1980s and throughout the 1990s.

Domestic politics approaches

First, scholars recognised the importance of domestic politics and of the political concepts developed in the context of domestic politics in enhancing our understanding of European policy-making. In 1975, Puchala questioned the snowball effect of neo-functionalism and argued that national governments remained important determinants of the integration process. In 1977 Wallace, Wallace and Webb edited a detailed series of case-studies into the process of policy-making in the European Community. They concluded that national governments remained the central actors in the integration process and that an understanding of the internal domestic politics of the member states was crucial to any rounded understanding of the integration process. This approach was further developed in 1983 when Bulmer sought to move away from the 'supranationalism versus intergovernmentalism' debate and to explain the 'linkages between the domestic and EC tiers' (Bulmer 1983: 349). Bulmer criticised the persistent focus on the European Community solely as an international organisation and argued that the analytical tools usually applied to the study of national politics could usefully be applied to the study of the behaviour of member states in the European Community.

Interdependence/regime theory

Meanwhile, the study of international organisations more generally was undergoing some radical changes. Students of international relations, rejecting the realist model of international relations, began to attribute to international organisations a degree of dynamism, not solely attributable to the interests of nation-states (Keohane and Nye 1974; 1977). Interdependence theorists recognised the fragmented nature of the state, the importance of transnational actors (including for example multinational companies) and the effect on national governments of participating in international regimes. Co-operation between member states in an interdependent world is unavoidable, and membership in international regimes may help to minimise the uncertainties inherent for nation-states in international collaboration. Crucially, however, in this interdependent world, 'recurrent interactions can change official perceptions of their interests' (Keohane and Nye 1977: 130). Although the interdependence school did not focus specifically on the European Community, but more broadly on the creation of international regimes, this approach generated a number of important insights which have been incorporated into subsequent attempts to understand the process of European integration.

Law and integration

Finally, the study of European institutions was being presented with some new challenges. Increasingly, scholars argued that the study of European institutions needed to encompass an examination of the role of the Court of Justice and of the impact of European law in the process of European integration. During this period, Weiler (1982) and Stein (1981) began to draw attention to the relevance of the law to any study of the European integration process. While the other institutions might have been going through a doldrums period, this was hardly the case for the Court:

> Tucked away in the fairyland Duchy of Luxemburg and blessed, until recently, with benign neglect by the powers that be and the mass media, the Court of Justice of the European Communities has fashioned a constitutional framework for a federal-type structure in Europe.
>
> (Stein 1981: 1 cited in Wincott 1995a)

The relaunch of integration theory

Following the relaunch of the Community (now European Union), with the Single European Act (and subsequently the Maastricht, Amsterdam and Nice Treaties), the study of European integration enjoyed a renewed momentum. As Caporaso and Keeler (1995: 22) noted, 'to a striking extent, however, the new debates parallel the old': the central division remained – that between state-centric and non-state-centric approaches to the study of European integration. Scholars from both perspectives sought to incorporate the strengths of earlier approaches, while addressing their weaknesses and building upon some of the theoretical insights developed in the 1970s.

Some of the most ambitious studies initially emerged as an attempt to explain the negotiation of the Single European Act (SEA): a key constitutional event in the history of European integration. In '1992: Recasting the European Bargain', for example, Sandholtz and Zysman (1989) incorporated some of the key insights of the neo-functionalist approach. They argued that, in the run-up to the Single European Act, the European Commission played a crucial leadership role, acting as a 'policy entrepreneur'.[16] Aided by a transnational industry coalition which was in favour of the single market, they argued, the Commission was able to persuade an important coalition of national governments of the benefits of market unification (Sandholtz and Zysman 1989: 96).

Sandholtz and Zysman (1989) also addressed one of the most powerful critiques of the neo-functionalist approach: that it neglected the impact of the international environment. For Sandholtz and Zysman (1989: 100), changing international and domestic conditions – the rise of Japan, the relative decline of the US and the evident failure of existing national economic policies in Europe – were the very events which made 1992 possible: 'international and domestic situations provided a setting in which the Commission could exercise policy entrepreneurship, mobilizing a transnational coalition in favour of the unified internal market'. Thus, as well as drawing upon the insights of the neo-functionalist school, Sandholtz and Zysman incorporated aspects of the 'domestic politics' approach and recognised the vital catalytic role played by changes in the international environment.

In contrast to the revised neo-functionalist interpretation of the SEA advocated by Sandholtz and Zysman, Moravcsik (1991: 42), drawing on the insights of realist and intergovernmentalist approaches, argued that interstate bargains between Britain, France and Germany were the key determinants of the negotiation of the SEA. Moreover, the bargains struck represented the 'lowest common denominator solution', achievable only because of the convergence of national interests. Each government had closely guarded its national sovereignty and had placed strict limits on any future transfer of sovereignty (Moravcsik 1991: 46–8). While acknowledging the influence of the realist school of thought (states as the principal actors in the international system), and of the regime school of international relations (shaping interstate politics by providing a common framework which reduces transaction costs and minimises uncertainty), Moravcsik (1991: 48) differentiated his 'intergovernmental institutionalism' by stressing the importance of 'domestic politics' in influencing the changing interests of states.

Moravcsik (1993) further developed his argument in 'Preferences and Power in the European Community'. In this work on *liberal intergovernmentalism*, he argued that 'state behaviour reflects the rational actions of governments constrained at home by domestic societal pressures and abroad by their strategic environment' (Moravcsik 1993: 474). The preferences of national governments, which determine their positions in international negotiations, are determined, he argued, by domestic societal forces: 'the identity of important societal groups, the nature of their interests and their relative influence on domestic policy' (Moravcsik 1993: 483). Within the framework of liberal intergovernmentalism, however, Moravcsik (1993: 484, 488) allowed for a degree of what he termed 'agency slack'. Thus, within the principal–agent relationship, in which societal principals delegate power to governmental agents, there is occasionally some limited discretion allowed to those agents. Where the interests of societal groups are ambiguous or divided, the constraints upon government are loosened: allowing politicians 'a wider range of *de facto* choice in negotiating strategies and positions'.

National governments have not, he argued, simply passively enjoyed the benefits of the occasional discretion allowed to them by divided or unclear domestic pressures. They have actively sought to maximise their room for manoeuvre. Thus, Moravcsik (1993) has argued that national governments have used EU institutions as part of a two-level game (cf. Putnam 1988) to increase the policy autonomy of national governments in relation to domestic interests: 'particularly where domestic interests are weak or divided, EC institutions have been deliberately designed to assist national governments in overcoming domestic opposition' (Moravcsik 1993: 515). Thus, far from supranational elites tying member states into a process to which they are resistant, the European Union may in fact strengthen the state by allowing, for example, chief executives 'to manipulate their own domestic constituents into accepting common policies' (Moravcsik 1994: 47).

Moravcsik has refined and developed his liberal-intergovernmentalist perspective in his 1998 text *The Choice for Europe*. Central to his argument remains the tenet that European integration is best explained 'as a series of rational choices made by national leaders' (Moravcsik 1998: 18). In his analysis of five major bargains in the history of the EU, he set himself the task of explaining: What best explains national preferences?; What best explains the outcomes of the interstate bargains which are negotiated on the basis of these national preferences?; and, having negotiated these bargains, How and why is the decision to create EU institutions and delegate powers to them made? Moravcsik's tripartite explanation for the process of European integration concludes: that national preferences are best explained by economic interests; that the outcome of interstate bargains is best explained by the relative power of the states involved; and, finally, that the decision to delegate powers to EU institutions is taken because it is the most effective way of ensuring the credibility of commitments from other member states.

Understanding the European Union as a system of governance

Throughout the 1990s, attempts to understand major constitutional decisions, as landmarks in the integration process, were accompanied by a growing literature examining the functioning of the *EU as a system of governance*. Drawing on approaches from the areas of comparative politics and policy analysis (Armstrong and Bulmer 1998; Bulmer 1994a; 1994b; Cram 1997; Hix 1999; Majone 1993; Marks 1992; Mazey and Richardson 1993; Pierson 1996; Peterson 1995; Peterson and Bomberg 1999; Richardson 1996; Sbragia 1992; Scharpf 1988; Wallace and Wallace 1996 and 2000):

> increasingly scholars assume that some institutional structure is in place and examine what goes on inside these structures. Politics and policy-making within institutions have assumed an analytic place alongside the politics of institutional change.
>
> (Caporaso and Keeler 1995: 43)

It is now commonly recognised that it is important to focus, not simply on the process through which major institutional change takes place in the EU, but also on the 'day to day' functioning of the EU as a polity.

One of the early approaches to introduce the concept of governance to the study of the EU was Marks's (1992) formulation of multi-level governance. Initially developed through his examination of the structural policy of the EU, the concept of multi-level governance emphasizes the fluid and open-ended nature of the EU system within which a broad range of actors operating at different levels, from the local to the international, have the potential to play an influential role. Various studies, meanwhile, conducted in the early 1990s revealed the crucial role which interest groups have played in the EU policy process (Mazey and Richardson 1993; Greenwood *et al.* 1992). Other studies demonstrated how EU institutions have influenced the agenda-setting, policy formulation and implementation processes. Studies highlighted: the role of bureaucratic politics in the EU (Peters 1992); the role of the Commission as agenda-setter (Peters 1994; Pollack 1995); and the Commission's role in the promotion of the EU regulatory regime (Majone 1989; 1991a; 1991b; 1992a; 1992b; 1993; Dehousse 1993; Cram 1993; Bulmer 1994b). Likewise, the role of the European Parliament as 'conditional agenda-setter' has been examined (Tsebelis 1994; 1996). Increasingly, too, scholars began to assess the important political role played by the European Court of Justice (Weiler 1991; Garrett 1992; Shapiro 1992; Garrett and Weingast 1993; Burley and Mattli 1993; Wincott 1995a) and, importantly, to examine the critical interactions between the Court and other institutions within the policy process (Alter and Meunier-Aitsahalia 1994; Wincott 1995b). Scholars were, meanwhile, forced to recognise the complexity of the role played by EU institutions. Analysts have, for example, cautioned against over-generalisation concerning the role of 'the Commission', which is a highly differentiated structure (Cram 1994), or of the impact of the European Parliament, as its influence varies between policy sectors (Judge *et al.* 1994).

These policy-based studies had important implications for evaluations of the most appropriate 'conceptual lenses' (Allison 1971) through which to view the integration process. Peterson (1995: 71), for example,[17] conceptualised the European Union as a multi-tiered system of governance. He distinguished between the different types of decision taken, the different actors which dominate and the different types of rationality which inform their actions, at the various levels of analysis identified within the EU. Peterson concluded that no single theory could explain EU governance at all levels of analysis. Broad 'macro' approaches to the issue of integration (such as neo-functionalism or state-centred 'intergovernmentalist' approaches) were particularly useful for explaining the major 'history-making' decisions of the EU. When it came to explaining 'policy-setting' or 'policy-shaping' decisions, however, 'macro-theories tend to lose their explanatory power' (Peterson 1995: 84). Indeed, as our understanding of the EU policy process, and of the process of European integration more generally, became more sophisticated, it increasingly appeared to be the case that 'our explanatory goals are best served by specifying the analytic strengths – and limitations – of approaches that work better in combination than alone' (Sandholtz 1993: 39).

Towards a synthesis of approaches

While scholars have argued that it is necessary to distinguish between the *politics* of the EU policy process, and the process of European *integration* (Hix 1994), or between *history-making* and *day-to-day* decisions (Peterson 1995), it is important not to overstate the division between the two. It is clearly useful to distinguish between different levels of analysis for analytic purposes. It is important, however, to remember that this divide is not clear-cut. The relationship between the politics and processes which accompany 'day-to-day' decision-making, as opposed to 'constitutional' or 'history-making' decisions, is, in many respects, reciprocal. From this perspective, the studies of the 'normal politics' of the EU, identified by Caporaso and Keeler (1995: 42), might most usefully be viewed, not simply as occurring *alongside* the development of integration theory but, rather, as performing a crucial role by enhancing existing understandings of the process of European integration and of the various influences upon the environment in which major 'history-making' decisions are taken. The insights of these studies have been crucial in facilitating the development of a more rounded understanding of the integration process.

In 1993, Sandholtz criticised the presentation of the debate about European integration as a dichotomy between intergovernmentalist and institutionalist approaches. Although decisions are taken in intergovernmental institutions (therefore analysis of intergovernmental bargaining processes is important), he argued that the preferences on the basis of which national governments influence EC policies 'are themselves influenced by EC institutions and law' (Sandholtz 1993: 3). In emphasising the endogenous nature of preference-formation, Sandholtz not only recalled the insights of Haas, who argued that participation at the European level would alter the perceptions which national elites held of their own interests, but also emphasised the development of shared identity, norms and behaviour patterns developed within the context of an international regime (in this case, the European Monetary System). Examining the decision of the member states to commit themselves to monetary policy in the Maastricht Treaty, Sandholtz (1993: 3) argued that there is an important link between participation in the EU policy regime and the formation of government preferences:

> membership in the EC has become part of the interest calculation for governments and societal groups. In other words, the national interests of EC states do not have independent existence; they are not formed in a vacuum and then brought to Brussels. Those interests are defined and redefined in an international and institutional context that includes the EC.

Sandholtz went on to develop this theme in his later work with Stone Sweet (1998). In this work, a reassessment of the contribution made by Deutsch and the transactionalist school to the study of European integration is made by a number of scholars. Sandholtz and

Stone Sweet advance a theory of integration which takes into account exchange (or trans-actions) between transnational actors, the role of supranational organisations, and the institutionalisation of certain behaviours through the elaboration of rules (Sandholtz and Stone Sweet 1998). Thus, rather than simply examining the background conditions that are necessary for integration to occur – the main focus of Deutsch's work on the EU – Sandholtz and Stone Sweet also try to explain the process through which integration might be expected to take place. The focus in their work on interests, rules and suprana-tional institutions also draws upon the work of Haas and the neo-functionalists.

Also emerging within the Haasian tradition of institutional analysis is the considerable contribution made by scholars who have applied the historical institutionalist approach to the study of the EU. Drawing on the work of scholars such March and Olsen (1989) and Thelen and Steinmo (1992), the starting point for the insights provided by historical insti-tutionalism is that institutions at the EU level do not simply provide an arena within which EU politics are conducted, but themselves play an important role in shaping the norms, values and conventions shared by actors involved at the EU level (see, for example, Bulmer 1994a; Armstrong and Bulmer 1998). Although the national govern-ments of the member states are recognised by historical institutionalists as key actors, responsible for major EU decisions such as treaty revisions, it is argued that the basis on which governments make such decisions is affected by the history of their participation in the EU. This notion of the importance of the history of participation is a key feature of historical institutionalism. Employing terms such as 'lock in' and 'path dependency', Pierson (1996), for example, seeks to demonstrate the constraints which have emerged over time on EU actors, and especially upon the autonomous actions of member-state governments as a result of their involvement in the EU.

Interestingly, in his 1998 text, Moravcsik (1998: 494) also recognised that 'integration has politically significant consequences, notably shifts in the preferences and institutional environment in which future decisions are made'. However, he makes a crucial distinction between 'intended' and 'unintended' consequences. For Moravcsik, intended 'lock-in' effects may be an important secondary force behind integration, but he argues that only rarely are these lock-in effects undesired or unanticipated by national leaders. Moravcsik (1998) has also, however, begun to call for a move away from the dichotomising of inte-gration theory: 'rather than contrast two ideal types of historical and structural analysis, we might profitably direct more attention toward the possibilities for synthesis'.

Conclusion: beyond a system of governance: bringing the societal dimension back in

The importance of the societal dimension of European integration has long been recog-nised. As Jean Monnet said, when establishing the European Coal and Steel Community in 1951, 'we are uniting people, not forming coalitions of states' (Duchêne 1994: 363). Indeed, it has been argued that Monnet 'was interested less in perfected constitutional blue-prints than in shaping human patterns of response to induce a change of process' (Duchêne 1994: 367). For political scientists too, the extent to which the preferences of individuals involved in interactions at the EU level may be 'redefined in terms of regional rather than a purely national orientation' (Haas 1958: 45) has long been viewed as a crucial question for the study of European integration. Still, however, the question of 'how – if at all – cohesion is obtained' (Haas 1958: 4) remains unanswered.

The process of 'social learning' and the 're-evaluation of preferences' were central concerns for Deutsch and later Haas and, as has become clear, these are issues which are now recognised as central to scholars from both ends of the integration theory spectrum. Yet, the question of how societal actors relate to the EU is an aspect of the work of Deutsch and Haas which even some of their sympathisers have specifically sought to avoid. Sandholtz and Stone Sweet (1998: 5), for example, state that they 'acknowledge the insights of two of the founders of integration theory, Karl Deutsch and Ernst Haas' and believe that 'on crucial questions they got it right'. However, they choose to 'set aside Deutsch's concern with the formation of communities and identities *per se*, and the issue of whether or not identity formation precedes state-building' (Sandholtz and Stone Sweet 1998: 5). Deutsch (1966: 174) did not, of course, view this as a mono-linear process, but rather saw the two processes of identity formation and state-building as mutually rein-forcing: 'experience and complementarity may then continue to reproduce each other, like the proverbial chicken and egg, in a syndrome of ethnic learning'. Similarly, in borrowing from Haas, Sandholtz and Stone Sweet (1998: 6) nevertheless 'leave as an open question the extent to which the loyalties and identities of actors will shift from the national to the European level'.

Although there has been a recent rise in social constructivist approaches to the study of the EU (see, for example, Christiansen *et al.* 1999) which claim that ideas and identities are important in the construction of the EU, there is, as yet, little empirical evidence to back up these claims. Once again, broader debates in international relations have been mirrored in the study of the EU. Yet, as many have acknowledged, the EU is not simply an area of contestation between states, but a functioning polity or system of governance which impacts upon societal actors and which in turn is affected by the actions of these actors. In this context, it is surprising that there has been so little scholarly attempt to explore systematically the various perceptions or 'imaginings' (cf. Anderson 1991) of the Union which prevail amongst the European people(s), let alone how these have or have not changed and their implications for the process of integration or for the potential for disin-tegration. What is perhaps most surprising is how little systematic use has been made of the extensive literature on nationalism and national identity in the EU context.

Within the EU, being Scottish, English, French, German or Greek takes preference over being European. However, in addition, a measure of 'banal Europeanism' (Cram 2001) could be said to have become embedded. As EU politicians have increasingly high profiles at, for example, international summits or in trade negotiations, this has begun to become unremarkable. National media coverage is frequently taken up with issues relating to the EU, often expressing neither opposition or support, but simply reporting relevant infor-mation. To some extent, news about the EU has become 'home' news (cf. Billig 1995: 175). In addition, EU-level media sources, such as the *European Voice*, an Economist publica-tion, have begun to reinforce a sense of the existence of the EU as an entity which needs significant political coverage. Similarly, many national daily newspapers now employ a Europe correspondent. As individuals begin to take for granted the presence of the EU flag among other, national flags, signs indicating the support of EU funding and the fact that they must go through the EU nationals' channel at customs; as they find their EU driving licences and passports unremarkable, or say in relation to, for example, working hours, 'isn't there an EU ruling on that?', then it could be argued that membership of the EU has increasingly become the norm.

At a basic level, it is undeniable that a degree of 'banal Europeanism' (Cram 2001) exists within the EU. Thus, how this is, or is not, transmitted among the European people(s), and the role which societal actors play in European integration, may have long-term implications for national elites and for the process of European integration which have not yet been fully realised. Now what is required is a more nuanced political sociology of the European Union which acknowledges that the EU is more than simply a system of governance which can be viewed in isolation from its broader societal dimension.

Acknowledgement

I would like to thank James Mitchell for his helpful comments on this paper. This paper draws on research conducted with the help of ESRC Grant number L213252023.

Notes

1   In his advocacy of functionally organised international organisations Mitrany referred, for example, to the organisation of the International Labour Organisation (1943/1966: 83–5).
2   Schuman Declaration, 9 May 1990, reproduced in part in Weigall and Stirk (1992: 59).
3   See A. J. R. Groom (1978) on this point and also below.
4   For example, in a footnote to his 1965 article in the *Journal of Common Market Studies*, Mitrany notes one misplaced critique of 'functionalism': 'the experience of the European communities shows the unreality of the "functionalist" thesis that starting from small, autonomous specialized authorities one could build a complete state!' (M. J. Petot cited in Mitrany 1965/1966: 198). Yet, as Mitrany reminds us: 'A complete state and its introverted nature happens to be the very idea which functionalism seeks to overcome internationally' (Mitrany 1965/1966: 198). The critique, in fact, relates more closely to Monnet and Schuman's dcracinated version of functionalism than to Mitrany's functionalist thesis.
5   Haas notes in particular: The Organisation for European Economic Co-operation; the Council of Europe; the Western European Union; and the European Coal and Steel Community.
6   See below for a summary of the key aspects of the realist approach to international relations.
7   Later this was to result in the criticism that neo-functionalism, with its n of 1, did not travel well and, therefore, that its strengths as a generalisable theory of integration were diminished (see Caporaso and Keeler (1995) on this point).
8   Although both of these were recognised as crucial aspects of European integration.
9   Although Haas specifically points out that the central institutions need not be federal but could equally be unitary state structures (Haas 1958: 8).
10 Although they may equally, Haas recognised, become opposed to the integration process as they recognise its costs (Haas 1958: 287–8).
11 Interestingly, Haas had found the ECSC legislature rather wanting in this respect – it had clearly not lived up to the expectations Monnet had of a federal executive – Haas felt, however, that the Assembly might prove to be a more 'faithful prototype' of a federal parliament (Haas 1958: 311).
12 Emphasis added.
13 Emphasis added. Haas (1960: 376), quoted in Lindberg (1963: 10–11).
14 Applications for membership came from Denmark, Ireland and the UK in 1961 and from Norway in 1962.
15 See R. Keohane and J. Nye (1977) on Morgenthau.
16 Recall Haas's (1958: 29) emphasis on the important role of institutions as 'agents of integration'.
17 Later developed in Peterson and Bomberg 1999.

References

Allison, G. (1971) *Essence of Decision: Explaining the Cuban Missile Crisis*, Boston: Little, Brown and Company.

Alter, K. and Meunier-Aitsahalia, S. (1994) 'Judicial Politics in the European Union: European Integration and the Pathbreaking Cassis de Dijon Decision', *Comparative Political Studies* 26/4: 536–61.

Anderson, B. (1991) *Imagined Communities* (first publ. 1983), London: Verso.

Armstrong, K. and Bulmer, S. (1998) *The Governance of the Single European Market*, Manchester: Manchester University Press.

Billig, M. (1995) *Banal Nationalism*, London: Sage.

Bulmer, S. (1983) 'Domestic Politics and EC Policy-Making', *Journal of Common Market Studies* 21/4: 349–63.

Bulmer, S. (1994a) 'The Governance of the European Union: A New Institutionalist Approach', *Journal of Public Policy* 13/4: 351–80.

Bulmer, S. (1994b) 'Institutions and Policy Change in the European Communities: The Case of Merger Control', *Public Administration* 72: 423–44.

Burley, A. and Mattli, W. (1993) 'Europe Before the Court: A Political Theory of Legal Integration', *International Organisation* 47: 41–76.

Caporaso, J. and Keeler, J. (1995) 'The European Union and Regional Integration Theory', in S. Mazey and C. Rhodes (eds), *The State of the European Union*, vol. 3, Boulder: Lynne Reiner/Longman.

Christiansen, T., Jørgensen, K. and Wiener, A. (eds) (1999) *The Social Construction of Europe*, special issue, *Journal of European Public Policy* 6/4.

Coudenhove-Kalergi, R. N. (1923) *Pan-Europa*, Glarus: Pan-Europa.

Coudenhove-Kalergi, R. N. (1938) *Europe Must Unite*, Glarus: Pan-Europa.

Coudenhove-Kalergi, R. N. (1943) *Crusade for Pan-Europe*, New York: Putnam.

Cram, L. (1993) ' Calling the Tune Without Paying the Piper? Social Policy Regulation: The Role of the Commission in European Union Social Policy', *Policy and Politics* 21: 135–46.

Cram, L. (1994) 'The European Commission as a Multi-Organization: Social Policy and IT policy in the EU', *Journal of European Public Policy* 1/2: 195–217.

Cram, L. (1997) *Policy-Making in the EU: Conceptual Lenses and the Integration Process*, London: Routledge.

Cram, L. (2001) 'Imagining the Union: A Case of Banal Europeanism', in H. Wallace (ed.), *Whose Europe? Interlocking Dimensions of Integration*, London: Macmillan.

Dehousse, R. (1993) 'Integration v Regulation: On the Dynamics of Regulation in the European Community', *Journal of Common Market Studies* 330/4: 383–402.

Deutsch, K. (1954) *Political Community at the International Level: Problems of Definition and Management*, Garden City: Doubleday & Co.

Deutsch, K. (1964) 'Communication Theory and Political Integration', in P. Jacob and J. Toscano (eds), *The Integration of Political Communities*, Philadelphia: Lippincott.

Deutsch, K. (1966) *Nationalism and Social Communication*, 2nd edn, Cambridge, MA: MIT Press.

Deutsch, K. (1967) *Arms Control and Atlantic Community*, Chichester: Wiley.

Deutsch, K., Burrell, S. and Kann, R. (1957) *Political Community and the North Atlantic Area*, New York: Greenwood Press.

Duchêne, F. (1994) *Jean Monnet: The First Statesman of Interdependence*, London: Norton.

Garrett, G. (1992) 'International Cooperation and Institutional Choice: The European Community's Internal Market', *International Organisation* 46/2: 533–60.

Garrett, G. and Weingast, B. (1993) 'Ideas, Interests and Institutions: Constructing the European Community's Internal Market', in J. Goldstein and R. Keohane (eds), *Ideas and Foreign Policy: Beliefs, Institutions and Political Change*, London: Cornell University Press.

Green, M. (1995) 'Setting the Agenda for a New Europe: The ERT and EC 1992', *Journal of Common Market Studies* 33/4: 501–6.

Greenwood, J., Grote, J. and Ronit, K. (eds) (1992) *Organised Interests and the European Community*, London: Sage.

Groom, A. J. R. (1978) 'Neofunctionalism: A Case of Mistaken Identity', *Political Science* 30/1: 15–28.

Haas, E. (1958) *The Uniting of Europe*, Stanford: Stanford University Press.

Haas, E. (1960) 'International Integration: The European and the Universal Process', *International Organisation* 15: 366–92.

Haas, E. (1964) *Beyond the Nation-State: Functionalism and International Organisation*, Stanford: Stanford University Press.

Haas, E. (1970) 'The Study of Regional Integration: Reflections on the Joys and Anguish of Pre-Theorising', *International Organisation* 4: 607–46.

Haas, E. (1975) *The Obsolescence of Regional Integration Theory*, Berkeley: Institute of International Studies.

Hix, S. (1994) 'The study of the European Community: The Challenge to Comparative Politics', *West European Politics* 17/1: 1–30.

Hix, S. (1999) *The Political System of the European Union*, London: Macmillan.

Hodges, M. (ed.) (1972) 'Introduction', in *European Integration*, London: Penguin.

Hoffmann, S. (1966) 'Obstinate or Obsolete? The Fate of the Nation State and the Case of Western Europe', *Daedalus* 95: 892–908.

Inglehart, R. (1967) 'An End to European Integration', *American Political Science Review* 61: 91–105.

Judge, D., Earnshaw, D. and Cowan, N. (1994) 'Ripples or Waves: The European Parliament in the European Community Policy Process', *Journal of European Public Policy* 1/1: 27–52.

Keohane, R. and Nye, J. (1974) 'Transgovernmental Relations and the International Organisations', *World Politics* 26/1: 39–62.

Keohane, R. and Nye, J. (1977) *Power and Interdependence: World Politics in Transition*, Boston: Little, Brown.

Lindberg, L. (1963) *The Political Dynamics of European Economic Integration*, Stanford: Stanford University Press.

Lindberg, L. and Scheingold, S. (1970) *Europe's Would-Be Polity: Patterns of Change in the European Community*, Englewood Cliffs: Prentice-Hall.

Majone, G. (1989) 'Regulating Europe: Problems and Prospects', *Jarbuch zur Staats- und Verwaltungswissenschaft*, Baden-Baden.

Majone, G. (1991a) 'Cross-National Sources of Regulatory Policymaking in Europe and the United States', *Journal of Public Policy* 11/1: 79–106.

Majone G. (1991b) 'Market Integration and Regulation: Europe after 1992', *European University Institute Working Papers* SPS No. 91/10, Florence.

Majone, G. (1992a) 'Market Integration and Regulation: Europe after 1992', *Metroeconomica* 43: 131–56.

Majone, G. (1992b) 'Regulatory Federalism in the European Union', *Government and Policy* 10: 299–316.

Majone, G. (1993) 'The European Community: Between Social Policy and Social Regulation', *Journal of Common Market Studies* 31/2: 153–69.

March, J. and Olsen, J. (1989) *Rediscovering Institutions: The Organisational Basis of Politics*, New York: Free Press.

Marks, G. (1992) 'Structural Policy in the European Community', in A. Sbragia (ed.), *Euro-Politics: Institutions and Policy-Making in the 'New' European Union*, Washington: The Brookings Institution.

Mazey, S. and Richardson, J. J. (eds) (1993) *Lobbying in the European Union*, Oxford: Oxford University Press.

Mitrany, D. (1943/1966) *A Working Peace System*, Chicago: Quadrangle.

Mitrany, D. (1965/1966) 'The Prospect of European Integration: Federal or Functional', *Journal of Common Market Studies*, reprinted in *A Working Peace System*, Chicago: Quadrangle.

Moravcsik, A. (1991) 'Negotiating the Single European Act: National Interests and Conventional Statecraft in the European Community', *International Organisation* 45: 19–56.

Moravcsik, A. (1993) 'Preferences and Power in the European Community: A Liberal Intergovernmentalist Approach', *Journal of Common Market Studies* 31/4: 473–524.

Moravcsik, A. (1994) 'Why the European Community Strengthens the State: Domestic Politics and International cooperation', paper presented to the Conference of Europeanists, Chicago, April 1994.

Moravcsik, A. (1998) *The Choice for Europe: Social Purpose and State Power from Messina to Maastricht*, London: UCL Press; Ithaca, NY: Cornell University Press.

Morgenthau, H. (1948, 1954, 1960, 1967) *Politics Among Nations: the Struggle for Power and Peace*, New York: Knopf.

Nye, J. (1968) (ed.) *International Regionalism*, Boston: Little, Brown.

Peters, B. (1994) 'Agenda-Setting in the European Community', *Journal of European Public Policy* 1/1: 9–26.

Peters, G. (1992) 'Bureaucratic Politics and the Institutions of the European Union', in A. Sbragia (ed.), *Euro-Politics: Institutions and Policy-Making in the 'New' European Union*, Washington: The Brookings Institution.

Peterson, J. (1995) 'Decision-Making in the European Union: Towards a Framework for Analysis', *Journal of European Public Policy* 2/1: 69–93.

Peterson, J. and Bomberg, E. (1999) *Decision-making in the European Union*, London: Macmillan.

Pierson, P. (1996) 'The Path to European Integration: A Historical Institutionalist Perspective', *Comparative Political Studies* 29/2: 123–63.

Pollack, M. (1995) 'Creeping Competence: The Expanding Agenda of the European Community', *Journal of Public Policy* 14: 97–143.

Puchala, D. (1970) 'International Transactions and Regional Integration', *International Organisation* 24: 732–63.

Puchala, D. (1975) 'Domestic Politics and Regional Harmonisation in the EC', *World Politics* 27/4: 496–520.

Putnam, R. D. (1988) 'Diplomacy and Domestic Politics', *International Organisation* 42: 427–61.

Richardson, J. (ed.) (1996) *European Union: Power and Policy-Making*, London: Routledge.

Sandholtz, W. (1993) 'Choosing Union: Monetary Politics and Maastricht', *International Organisation* 47/1: 1–39.

Sandholtz, W. and Stone Sweet, A. (1998) *European Integration and Supranational Governance*, Oxford: Oxford University Press.

Sandholtz, W. and Zysman, J. (1989) '1992: Recasting the European Bargain', *World Politics* 42/1: 95–128.

Sbragia, A. (1992) 'Introduction', in A. Sbragia (ed.), *Euro-Politics: Institutions and Policy-Making in the 'New' European Union*, Washington: The Brookings Institution.

Scharpf, F. W. (1988) 'The Joint-Decision Trap: Lessons from German Federalism and European Integration', *Public Administration* 66/3: 239–78.

Schmitter, P. (1970) 'A Revised Theory of Regional Integration', *International Organisation* 24: 836–68.

Shapiro, M. (1992) 'The European Court of Justice', in A. Sbragia (ed.), *Euro-Politics: Institutions and Policy-Making in the 'New' European Union*, Washington: The Brookings Institution.

Spinelli, A. (1966) *The Eurocrats: Conflict and Crisis in the European Community*, New York: John Hopkins University Press.

Stein, E. (1981) 'Lawyers, Judges and the Making of a Transnational Constitution', *American Journal of International Law* 70: 1–27.

Thelen, K. and Steinmo, S. (1992) 'Historical Institutionalism in Comparative Politics', in K. Thelen, S. Steinmo and F. Longstreth (eds), *Structuring Politics: Historical Institutionalism in Comparative Analysis*, Cambridge: Cambridge University Press.

Tsebelis, G. (1994) 'The Power of the European Parliament as a Conditional Agenda-Setter', *American Political Science Review* 88/1: 128–42.

Tsebelis, G. (1996) 'More on the European Parliament as a Conditional Agenda-Setter', *American Political Science Review* 90/4: 839–43.

Wallace, H. and Wallace, W. (eds) (1996) *Policy-Making in the European Union*, 3rd edn, Oxford: Oxford University Press.

Wallace, H. and Wallace, W. (eds) (2000) *Policy-Making in the European Union*, 4th edn, Oxford: Oxford University Press.

Wallace, H., Wallace, W. and Webb, C. (1977/1983) *Policy-Making in the European Community*, Chichester: Wiley.

Weigall, D. and Stirk, P. (eds) (1992) *The Origins and Development of the European Community*, Leicester: Leicester University Press.

Weiler, J. (1982) 'Community, Member States and European Integration: Is the Law Relevant?', *Journal of Common Market Studies* 20/1–2.

Weiler, J. (1991) 'The Transformation of Europe', *Yale Law Journal* 100: 2403–83.

Wincott, D. (1995a) 'The Maastricht Treaty: An Adequate "Constitution" for the European Union?', *Public Administration* 72/4.

Wincott, D. (1995b) 'Institutional Interaction and European Integration: Towards an Everyday Critique of Liberal Intergovernmentalism', *Journal of Common Market Studies* 33/4: 597–609.

Part II

AGENDA-SETTING AND INSTITUTIONAL PROCESSING

Chapter 4

Agenda-setting in the European Union

B. GUY PETERS

Agenda-setting is a crucial stage in the policy process for any political system.[1] By definition, no policy can be made if the issue to which it is addressed can not first be placed onto the active agenda of a governmental institution. Having a new issue considered is not in general an easy task and almost always requires substantial political mobilisation, and often a good bit of luck as well. Therefore, agenda-setting is an initial crucial 'veto point' (Immergut 1992) in the policy process at which political and administrative leaders can exercise their power, either to have a policy intervention considered, or to prevent anything from happening that would diminish the well-being of their constituent group.

As (still) an emerging political system, agenda-setting is perhaps especially important for the European Union. The ability of European institutions to move issues onto its agenda, and to define those issues in ways that facilitate further integration, is crucial to the continued success of the policy-making system. Despite its numerous successes, the EU is not yet a fully institutionalized policy-making system, and remains far from a fully institutionalized polity (Peters 2000). Given those features, shaping the agenda is more important than it might be in more fully legitimated and institutionalised systems.

Agenda-setting as a political process

As we shall point out below in greater detail we should, in fact, conceptualise agenda-setting as having several components, rather than as being the rather simple decision whether to consider the issue or not. In particular, there is the prior question of just what the issue that may be considered actually is. The social and political construction of the issue is as important to the final determination of how the issue will be processed and decided as is the initial decision to consider it at all. A single issue can be conceptualised in different ways that will make it more or less attractive to policy-makers. Further, its construction will determine which set of decision-making institutions will process the issue, and therefore to some extent determine its fate.

Not all issues are equal in the agenda-setting process. Many issues seem to reappear almost automatically on government agendas, as they arise through the annual budget or they are components of programmes that must be re-authorised on a frequent basis (Walker 1977). For some programmes, however, this frequent attention by government decision-makers is not entirely welcome. Some programmes return to the agenda because they are unpopular with significant actors in the political system and they frequently must defend themselves against attempts to shut them down. Thus, the most desirable trajectory for a programme may be to go through the policy process once and then be able to hide from much subsequent attention unless it is intended to enhance the programme.

Crises can move some issues onto the agenda and through the entire policy process within days. The advocates of other policy changes, however, must strive for years in order to have their favourite concern be considered for the first time. Likewise, certain types of issues tend to be advantaged by political systems and others are disadvantaged, if not excluded outright. Issues that affect certain social groups, e.g. children, adversely can be placed on an active agenda readily, while those affecting traditional 'pariah groups', e.g. AIDS patients or drug-abusers, will take much longer (Rochefort and Cobb 1994). Therefore, one way to gain an analytic handle on the 'style' (Richardson 1982; Mazey and Richardson 1993b) and character of a political system is to examine how issues are first identified, how they are defined, and how they are then processed for further consideration through that system.

Most of the above discussion is based on a conception of agenda-setting as an incremental process of agenda *accretion* conducted within a political equilibrium. We should also remember that the European Union has also had instances in which issues have been placed on the agenda in large bundles. These bundles of issues have come at times from the initiative of the Commission, especially from the activist Jacques Delors (Sandholtz and Zysman 1989) and his proposals contained in the Single European Act. The subsequent Maastricht and Amsterdam Treaties added perhaps even more issues to the European agenda.

Other large spates of new agenda items have appeared during the semi-annual meetings of the prime ministers of member countries that often have been used to loosen up any rigidities in the system. This is especially true given that each president or prime minister wants to have major initiatives adopted while he or she is the host for this meeting. This observation points to the importance of agenda-setting as a political process. It is certainly true that at the national level politicians want to be identified with certain issues, and the same is true at the supranational level.

The conventional discussion of agenda-setting is also based on the idea that the pressure for policy change tends to be external, i.e. it emanates from societal interests seeking to utilise the state for their own benefit. This view certainly can be sustained for the European Union, as the growing literature on lobbying within the EU would indicate (Mazey and Richardson 1993a; 1993b). In all political systems, however, issues are a resource as well as a problem, and actors within formal institutions can utilise problems and issues to exert pressures toward achieving their own goals (personal and/or organisational). Organisations can attempt to seize on or create (conceptually if not in reality) problems in order to enhance their own power within the political system (Allison 1971; Donnelley 1993); in this process societal groups may become 'pressured' as well as exert 'pressure'.

The European Union has been conceptualised in a number of different ways (Sbragia 1992; Tugendhat 1988), but one important approach to this entity is to think of it as a political system not all that dissimilar to others. In that conceptualisation, the fundamental task of the political system is to make policy, and to do so issues must be placed on the agenda of the EU. This chapter will attempt to understand how this important stage of policy-making occurs within the EU, and the possible impacts that the rather peculiar structures and processes of the Union may have on agenda-setting. We will first explicate several of the aspects of the EU as a political entity that we believe have an impact on agenda-setting. We will then examine several possible ways to understand the processes of agenda-setting in the Union. Finally, we will look at the way in which the nature of institutions and agenda-setting processes will influence the range of possible policy outputs of the Union.

The fundamental argument of this chapter is that agenda-setting in the European Union is significantly different from that process as it is practised in most national political systems. In particular, we will argue that the existence of a number of points of access, of a large number of influential policy advocates, and of a wide range of policy options that have been legitimated in one or more of the constituent political systems, makes agenda-setting substantially easier than in most other settings. The other two classes of political systems which may share some of the same openness are presidential regimes and federal regimes. As Pierson and Weaver (1993: 145) have argued, fragmented, presidentialist political systems are characterised by an asymmetry between agenda-setting and policy adoption. On the one hand a fragmented, presidential-style system allows for much easier placement of issues on one or another active agenda. On the other hand, however, these systems make the effective resolution of those issues, and the implementation of any decisions that are reached, more problematic. Also, federal systems permit issues and solutions to be legitimated at one level and then moved onto the agenda of the central government.[2]

This relative openness to new ideas is also a function of the relative lack of institutionalisation of the European system, when compared to more established political systems; the EU has its own rigidities, but they are perhaps fewer than in longer-established systems. If other political systems are characterised by 'punctuated equilibria' (Baumgartner and Jones 1993), then the EU appears still to be searching for its initial policy equilibrium in most areas – agriculture with its clearly developed EU style and substance of intervention may be the exception (Butler 1993). Thus, a strategically minded policy advocate could go 'venue shopping' (Wendon 1998) to find the best locale for consideration of a favourite issue.

That systemic openness is not, however, an undivided benefit, and with it goes a great deal of indeterminacy and potential instability. The agenda is open to a variety of types of interventions, some of which may undermine the direction that the leadership is attempting to impose on the political system. Thus, from the perspective of the central political and administrative managers in the system, the loosely coupled, albeit fused (Wessels 1998), system may present a barrier to effective control (but see Hix 1998).

The other aspect of agenda-setting that is distinctive in the European Union is that the way in which an issue is defined in this process will have a greater effect upon how it is resolved than is true in other systems. While in most national systems problem definition may determine which ministries and which committees will process the issue, in the EU problem definition may determine whether the issue is one of 'high politics' or 'low politics' (see Wallace 1996; Eichner 1997). The former implies that the issue is defined as one involving more overt considerations of national interest, while the latter may be determined more by bureaucratic and technical considerations. Some issues naturally fall into one class or the other, but for many issues there appears to be some latitude for different constructions of the issue.

The nature of agendas

The agenda literature has pointed to the difference between systemic agendas, which are the sum of all issues which a political system has accepted as being legitimate items for concern, and more specific institutional agendas. The greater openness of the European Union is apparent for placing issues onto the systemic agenda (Cobb and Elder 1983), although there is no guarantee that those issues will then actually be moved onto an active institutional agenda. An issue may be able to gain active consideration on the agenda of a particular Directorate-General that has an interest in having a particular conception of a policy accepted as *the* official definition.

The absence of institutionalisation and the loosely articulated policy-making system, however, may make moving any one version of the issue any further through the European policy process difficult. What is more likely is that there will be several organisations (administrative and legislative) with alternative conceptualisations of the same issue, each vying to have its own view enacted. In such a relatively unstructured situation as exists within the EU there is an even more pronounced need for policy entrepreneurs than there is in other political settings (see Pollack 1997), although the literature has documented the importance of those entrepreneurs in a number of other settings as well (Hargrove 1987).

The above discussion points to several important distinctions to be made in this discussion. The most important is that between the placing of an issue on an agenda and its placement on that agenda in a particular form. Thus, in the political struggle for policy, having a favourite agenda item placed on the agenda, but in a form that is not acceptable, must be counted as a defeat for a policy entrepreneur. Indeed, in many instances a policy entrepreneur would probably prefer to have the issue not considered at all than to have it considered in an undesirable format. One of the most important powers for a political actor is to create non-decisions (Bachrach and Baratz 1962) when a decision might be inimical to his or her interests, and a policy activist within the EU would be no different in that respect.

Although placing an issue on the agenda in an undesirable (to one or another set of actors) form can be inimical to those interests, merely placing the issue on the agenda at all may be threatening to advocates of some issues. One strategy for opponents of a policy idea is to have it considered before the time is 'ripe', thus killing off the programme. As noted, policies that lack powerful constituencies or patrons are placed in jeopardy every time they come forward for consideration. This is often the case for means-related social programmes in individual countries. In the European Union there are also some programmes of this type. For example, the contemporary social agenda of the Union is also unpopular with a substantial number of influential actors, so that whenever it must be considered actively it runs the risk of being cut back, or even cut out.

Within the European Union there are, everything else being equal, even more alternative policy conceptualisations than might exist within a single country. The acceptance on one format or another of an issue may represent the victory of one national or professional perspective on the problem, and with that the need for other countries to adapt, or to attempt to defeat, the proposal.[3] The shift from harmonisation to mutual recognition as the mechanism for policy integration tends to attenuate the conflicts that might otherwise exist, but even then some national policy definitions may have serious negative impacts on others, so that there will be pressures for more uniform policies. This is especially true for policies that have clear spillover effects on other countries, e.g. environmental pollution or technical safety standards. Likewise labour and social policies that might make the workings of the single internal market more difficult are highly suspect.

The characteristics of lobbying within the European Union also tend to accentuate the number of alternatives available to decision-makers. Although they have been moving toward presenting more unified positions, Euro-organisations tend to function more as the clearing houses of national interests and organisations than as the aggregators of those interests. Therefore, an industry or a commodity group in agriculture or whatever often will not present a unified position but instead may provide a menu from which decision-makers can choose. The separate national organisations and individual firms may also continue to lobby for their own favourite policies. There are certainly attempts at co-ordinating the disparate views, but these tend to run into opposition based on national differences and differing perceptions of desirable outcomes. The result is a complex 'honeycomb' of interests (Mazey and Richardson 1993a: 199) and substantial indeterminacy of policies.

These differing national and professional (Eisner 1991) perspectives on policy point to the ideational aspects of policy, as distinct from the sheer political power necessary to motivate action in a political system. Very few issues are presented to government already neatly wrapped and identified. Rather, issues become defined through a complex process of contending ideas, advocacy, learning and ultimately either political domination or synthesis. In this political process information and ideas may be as important as power, and policy entrepreneurship becomes a process of marshalling evidence as well as counting votes (Krehbiel 1991).

The first stage of this process of agenda-setting is the social construction of the issue; what *is* the issue really? Interests (whether national or economic or bureaucratic) that can control this initial definition are likely to be successful at the end of the process. This is true whether they want to use the issue for substantive policy change or whether they are only attempting to use the issue as a means of gaining enhanced political power. Further, the proper selection of issues can be used as a means of advancing an agenda of integration (Pollack and Hafner-Burton 2000). The more the issue can proceed by stealth, without raising obvious flags of national interests, the more likely it will be to be processed quickly and in a manner that advances the broader European programme.

The political institutions of the European Union

We will not engage in any full-scale explication of the nature of the political institutions of the EU, that task having been done thoroughly in a number of other places (Peters 1992; Nugent 1999). Rather, we will point to several salient features of those institutions that influence the manner in which agendas are set, and therefore to some extent what issues will appear on the agenda and what their form might be. Some of these institutional features, e.g. fragmentation, are common to almost all political systems but appear in a somewhat exaggerated form in the EU. Therefore, the process here will be like all other agenda-setting processes but may again be a somewhat extreme version of that common process.

Fragmentation

The complexity and fragmentation of European Union institutions present at once a barrier and an opportunity for the potential agenda-setter. There appears at first glance to be a clear political domination by the Commission in the policy process of the Union, but in reality there are multiple avenues of potential influence, even within the Commission itself. Each of the Commissioners is a political actor with some independent authority, albeit presumably neutered to some extent by the pledge of allegiance to the Union as opposed to former national interests. Political leaders in some countries have utilised the Commission as a place to reward politicians in their declining years for previous service, or as a place to exile potential problems. However, the Commissioners themselves may consider the appointment an opportunity to advance their personal ambitions. They may believe that they can utilise policy activism within their portfolio as a means of reviving their political careers on either the national or the European stage.

Similarly the administrative structure of the Commission is divided into a number of Directorates-General (DGs), each headed by a powerful and (presumably) ambitious Director General. These DGs also have an incentive to capture potentially significant policy initiatives and shape them in a manner compatible with the assigned tasks of their organisation. It is important to note here that the issue boundaries of the DGs are not always clearly defined, and many significant issues logically may fall into more than one. This indeterminacy, in turn, generates a need for a social and political process to define the issue in a way that best suits one organisation or another. An emerging policy area such as biotechnology, for example, might be seen as falling either into agriculture (DG Agriculture), research science and technology (DG Research), or perhaps even competition policy (DG Competition) (Patterson 1998). The organisational outcome of this competitive process among the DGs will not only determine their relative political power but also influence the nature of the policy goals and instruments that will become operational in this area.

Environmental policy is another obvious example of the fragmentation in European institutions. The European role in the environment falls between DG Environment and the newer 'Euro-Quango' of the European Environmental Agency (Vogel 1993; Dehousse 1997). This policy area is also heavily impacted by other DGs that have complementary and competitive interests. For example, regional affairs (DG Regional Policy) has an interest in promoting economic development in the less economically developed portions of the Union, and may not be as concerned with the environmental impacts of their activities as other parts of the EU would like them to be. Similarly, DG Agriculture may well have interests that conflict with those of the environmental organisations. The absence of adequate co-ordination mechanisms may prevent making the allocative decisions (jobs versus the environment, for example) that should be expected from a more coherent governmental apparatus.

The existence of these options for the organisational placement of an issue provides the entrepreneurial agenda-setter with several opportunities, provided the issue being advocated is one that is attractive to at least one set of powerful interests. This relative lack of institutionalisation of the European bureaucracy led Mazey and Richardson (1993b) to refer to it as an 'adolescent bureaucracy' – and although it has matured it may not have emerged totally from adolescence. The range of opportunities available permits advocates of appealing issues not only to have the issue considered but also perhaps to have it considered in a particular format by the receptive DG. On the other hand, however, if the issue is politically unattractive, the prospective agenda-setter may be told that the issue is beyond the remit of the particular DG, and the poisoned chalice can be refused rather easily.

The legislative side of government in the EU has somewhat less opportunity to place issues on any official agenda, given that the formal right of policy initiation resides with the Commission. Still, these institutions (in this argument I include the Council as a legislative body rather than an executive body) do have some capacity to have issues brought up for consideration. First, the Council is composed of ministers from the member countries and as such is almost certainly able to have items placed on the agenda. This may not be done formally, but the informal process certainly provides them with substantial powers. Second, the differentiation of the European Parliament into functional committees that roughly shadow the DGs within the Commission enables it to bring issues to the attention of the relevant parts of the Commission, although not really to force active consideration within the Commission. Tsebelis (1994), for example, discusses the European Parliament as a 'conditional agenda-setter', given that, under the 'co-operation procedure', it can pass legislation that is more difficult for the Commission and Council to overturn than to adopt (Jacobs and Corbett 1990).

Finally, we should remember that the European Union has a more active court system than is found in many European countries (Burley and Mattli 1993), so that issues may be forced on to an active agenda simply through the ability of one or another actor to bring suit either against a member state or perhaps against some component of the EU itself. This makes agenda-setting for government in the European Union more open than it otherwise would be, and makes it more like the United States, in which some of the major issues decided by government (racial integration, abortion) have been initiated through the legal system. This capacity of societal interests to bypass legislative and executive institutions (nationally as well as supranationally) weakens those institutions but may also make them more responsive to potential issues in their relevant environments than they might otherwise have been. Rather than permitting an issue to come forward in an undesirable (to it) manner through the court system, a DG may choose to bring that forward itself.

The absence of effective policy co-ordination

Any complex political system encounters difficulties in ensuring adequate policy co-ordination among its numerous institutions, actors and policy sectors (Peters 1995; Peters and Wright, this volume). The European Union, we will argue, has an even greater problem than most political systems with co-ordination, given that it lacks one important tool that has been crucial to agenda management and policy linkages in other democratic political systems. This device is the political party, and even more specifically party government (Rose 1974; Katz 1987). The concept of party government is a familiar one in democracies: a party or coalition presents a set of policy ideas to the public which, if elected, they enact and then implement.[4]

Political parties can provide a mechanism for co-ordinating policies across institutions and even across levels of government. Given that the political systems of the member countries of the EU are parliamentary democracies,[5] their citizens are accustomed to having their executive and legislative branches co-ordinated through a party or a coalition of parties. The evidence is that the ability of political parties to provide that co-ordination is, however, less than perfect in these systems (Rose 1974). They do, however, offer the possibility of developing a set of priorities, a co-ordinated policy agenda and to constrain the range of alternatives considered at any one time. This is true even if that agenda is not always put into effect.

Political parties cannot perform the function of co-ordinating policy priorities in the EU. In the first place, the executive (the Commission) is appointed by the national governments and reflects the configuration of forces in these countries more than it does the distribution of partisan allegiances within the EU itself. There is an emerging form of parliamentary responsibility within the EU, but there is a very long way to go to forge the type of accountability linkage required to permit any party or coalition to co-ordinate those institutions. Further, the political parties within the European Parliament are themselves aggregations of national parties, so that the parties generally lack the unity required to produce a more coherent pattern of agenda-setting. There are efforts to enhance the coherence of parties and some successes, but there is still not the capacity for prioritisation that exists in many national systems.

Another aspect of the co-ordination problem within the EU is that there are separate national policy styles that are embodied in the individual commissioners, so that if a particular portfolio has an (e.g.) Irish Commissioner, then policy may take on an Irish flavour so long as that individual remains in office (see Van Waarden 1995). In this instance EU policy-making may look like policy-making in a coalition government with the member countries being the functional equivalent of the several parties in a coalition. This is likely to be true even if the Commissioners behave as required by their oath of office and do not attempt to serve national interests. The argument here is that their styles and cultures are as important in determining their behaviour as any specific calculations about national advantage they might be tempted to make.

To take this argument to an even lower level of aggregation, we can argue that the DGs themselves often are not integrated and co-ordinated entities. In part this lack of institutionalisation is a function of their relative newness. While organisations in national bureaucracies have had a number of decades or even centuries to develop their collective cultures, those of the European Union have had only a few decades. Even if that time might be enough to develop a strong culture in a stable environment, the instability both of the organisational formats and of personnel has minimised the capacity to create a common organisational perspective in the EU. This institutionalisation problem is exacerbated by the fact that the members of these organisations are drawn from the same wide variety of political and administrative cultures as are the members of the Commission. This heterogeneity might be overcome if there were other integrating factors, e.g. a common professional background, but in most instances the bureaucracy itself has remained internally inconsistent and relatively uncoordinated.

Finally, the interface between the political and civil service levels in Brussels is not very well developed, with conflict often prevailing over co-operation. A lack of common purpose between the civil service and their nominal masters is hardly peculiar to the EU, but it is perhaps exaggerated by the other complexities of the system. Perhaps because of the internal inconsistencies and national differences within any DG, the commissioners have at times utilised their personal *cabinets* almost as alternatives to the civil service. Those actions have created substantial tensions on the basis of both organisational and national differences (Barber 1993). These difficulties have generated demands for streamlining the Commission and for providing greater policy co-ordination through a strengthened president of the Commission and several vice-presidents (Gardner 1992). Until that happens, however, there will be substantial co-ordination problems in the 'executive branch' of the European Union.

In summary, there is the danger of an overload of demands within the European Union. The structure of interest groups has yet to become stabilised into well-defined networks, with the consequence that there are a large number of European and national groups contending for influence over policy decisions. Given that there are also a large number of points of access for this interest group activities, there is a significant volume of relatively unstructured interactions between the private sector and the formal institutions of the Union. Without adequate institutionalisation, or the co-optation of interest groups that characterises some national systems (Heisler with Kvavik 1974), all this activity is likely to generate unpredictability and rapidly shifting policy agendas.

Proto-federalism

As well as having divided institutions internally, the European Union also has a divided territorial structure that influences the pattern of agenda-setting. There is something of an emerging federal structure, with the acceptance of the Maastricht Treaty making Brussels all the more like the central government of a federal or confederal union. There is also a structure of regional government that is becoming more clearly articulated within the member countries, although those regional governments vary in the extent to which they can act autonomously *vis-à-vis* Union institutions (Keating 1993). Thus, there are a number of territorial bodies that can be used as points of access for socio-economic groups that want to press their own policy agendas on the wider European Union.

In particular, groups that are rarely successful at the national level may find that increasingly they have alternative routes of access available to achieve a favourable governmental decision. This is especially true for interests, e.g. ethno-regionalist groups, that traditionally have been excluded and frustrated at the national level. For example, several regions in France have been able to bypass Paris almost entirely as they press their demands on Brussels. In the United Kingdom, Scotland and Wales have both been successful in extracting resources from the EU, as much because of their relatively deprived economic status as their nationalistic ambitions, but still this appears to many to be greater success than they have enjoyed with London over several centuries.

On the one hand, regional groups may be able to obtain greater policy autonomy on their own, given pressures toward 'subsidiarity' at the EU level. Further, the regional aggregations, as well as non-territorial interests such as environmental groups, may be able to circumvent roadblocks at the national level and go directly to Brussels. There are no guarantees of success at influencing the agenda at any level of government, but there are certainly greater opportunities to gain access and to shape at least one agenda in the multi-level environment than there were prior to the emergence of the EU as a significant force in a range of policy areas.

It should be noted further that subnational groupings are not the only ones who may experience frustration at the national level. National governments themselves may feel that their options are constrained by traditional patterns of policy, or by the strength of entrenched social interests. For example, labour unions are perceived as a barrier to economic change in many countries, and the ability to go to the European level to circumvent restraints that might prevent policy innovation at the national level can be an important resource. Environmental activists (in and out of government) may also find it useful to utilise the Union as a means of pulling an 'end run' on entrenched business interests in their societies.

The proto-federal structure of the EU is seen perhaps most clearly in the implementation of programmes, and in this process the groups that may be able to win at the agenda stage may yet lose, or at least be faced with another political fight. While the group may have an issue defined as it wants when being processed in Brussels, the implementors of a programme also have some latitude in how they will define and administer the policy. The EU policy process attempts to limit that freedom, but any administrative system must permit its members some flexibility and some ability to deal with individual cases. Therefore, national patterns and priorities may reassert themselves through implementation.

The territorial structure of the EU may have an influence on policy that extends beyond simply whether an issue is being actively considered or not. Agenda-setting is not just about having an issue considered actively by government, it is also about how that issue will be defined once it makes it onto the agenda. Policy issues do not define themselves but rather are shaped through complex social and political processes (Best 1989; Hilgartner and Bosk 1988). One of the important features of agenda formulation in the EU is that the number of different national policy styles provides a number of ready-made alternatives for many policies considered by the European Union. For example, in environmental policy, does one accept the issue of acid-rain as formulated by the British or does one propose the more stringent conceptualisation of the Dutch and Germans (Zito 1999)? These differences may be less significant in areas now governed by mutual recognition rather than by harmonisation (Shapiro 1992: 134–6), but the presence of alternatives is an important characteristic of agenda-setting in the EU.

An additional advantage presented by the multiplicity of actors within the EU is that a wider variety of issues are already on the 'systemic agendas' (Cobb and Elder 1983) of these countries than there would be in any one political system. The systemic agenda is the sum of all issues that government has decided are worthy of public consideration, whether or not they are under active discussion in any institution at the time. The presence of fifteen different systemic agendas in the fifteen member countries presents policy entrepreneurs (Kingdon 1984) within the EU itself with the opportunity to select issues that have already been legitimated in one or more national contexts. These issues then can be used to advance European integration, and/or advance the interest of their particular institution (a DG for example) while still claiming some political source of legitimacy for the action. There are also instances in which the selection of one particular view of policy can advance a national interest, if for no other reason than that it prevents pressures for policy changes.

The process

The European Union institutional framework within which agenda-setting occurs has a decided influence over the process that emerges. The institutional framework we have described is characterised by a great deal of fragmentation and the existence of a number of complementary and potentially competitive actors. This fragmentation also implies that there is the danger of deadlock and mutual blockage, without the intervention of actors willing to make agenda-setting a major concern. James Christoph (1993), for example, describes EU policy-making as 'loosely knit, headless, porous, inefficient, often unpredictable and occasionally chaotic'. This process also encounters the risk of producing only incremental outcomes while more vigorous policy change may be needed. Therefore, the EU would appear to be a congenial environment for policy entrepreneurs (Riker 1980). Indeed, it has been argued that the environment is much better suited to policy entrepreneurship (and agenda-setting) than to actually achieving the policy goals. That policy-making environment is characterised by a great deal of indeterminacy, combined with the existence of a number of policy options that already have at least some legitimacy from their associations with national governments. What is needed is some means of breaking the institutional deadlock.

The above description is very much that of pluralist politics. The institutions of the EU create a number of arenas for the interplay of relatively autonomous groups. The existence of a number of arenas means that groups that lose in one can be successful in another. This represents then a marked departure from the format of governing in many of the constituent countries of the EU. In those systems relationships between state and society are marked by the rather formalised interactions associated with corporatism (Streeck and Schmitter 1991). In this case not only are the outcomes of the process less determined but the issue of access itself is problematic. In such a setting interests may be willing to trade specific policy interests in order to secure their long-term relationship with a DG or other part of the Union apparatus.

The process of determining agendas in almost any political system is a process of selection, but that characteristic is perhaps even more pronounced in the context of the European Union. In the first place, there are a large number of actors who want to participate in the process, each perhaps with its own conceptions of good and bad policy, and with a set of institutional interests to pursue through the process. Second, the number of policy options is perhaps even greater than within the conventional national political system (Wilsford 1994). There are usually a number of different and viable policy conceptions among the member countries that can offer a policy selector a range of choices to solve the same problem. Furthermore, the range of policies within the proper purview of the EU is not clearly defined, with the consequence that an active policy entrepreneur may be able to expand the range of issues under consideration and with it expand the scope of Union action.

The process of agenda-setting in the EU may therefore be conceptualised as something very much akin to the now classic model of 'garbage can' decision-making (Cohen *et al.* 1972). There is a multiplicity of actors and solutions combined through a loosely linked process, with solutions seeking problems as much as problems chasing solutions. Also, preferences are unstable and uncertain and the decision that something needs to be done often creates the preferences rather than vice versa. This model represents a reversal of the usual logic assumed in rationalist models of decision-making, and it may be particularly applicable to the question of agenda-setting and problem definition. Issues may come to the agenda simply because they were convenient and served some other organisational purpose rather than as a true reflection of the goals of the organisation. Once the process of moving an issue onto the agenda is settled, the questions of policy formulation may be resolved in a manner assumed in more conventional models.

This inversion of the usual rationalist model of the policy search procedure may be particularly applicable to the behaviour of the various Directorates-General of the Commission. These organisations tend to have a particular range of solutions and policy definitions available to them, e.g. competition policy, and may want to utilise those solutions as the means of gaining involvement in as great as possible a range of policy concerns. The DGs therefore may compete with one another to reduce the ambiguity in the policy area and to be able to define the agenda. Some students of agenda-setting (Baumgartner and Jones 1993) have argued that organisations seek to impose monopolies of problem definition over particular policy areas, and this competition among DGs would be a part of that process. As yet the definitions of policy within the EU appear sufficiently loose and unstructured that there will be few monopolies and a continuing pattern of competition and instability.

Imbalances within the European system

The institutional features described above have, to some degree, made the European Union the prospective agenda-setter's paradise. There is a loosely coupled political system with a number of independent points of access that will enable the energetic policy advocate to inveigle his or her way into the proceedings. There is also a wider range of policy options and different conceptions of 'good' policy than exist in most national governments. This range of options will enable the policy advocate to choose an acceptable option that will begin with familiarity and acceptance from at least a portion of the relevant decision-making elite. Finally, there are a number of political actors who may well believe that they have something to gain in terms of their careers by being involved with a successful policy initiative. All of these factors make the prospects for agenda-setting within the Union appear very positive for the policy advocate.

In fact, the prospects for agenda-setting appear to be almost the opposite of the rather gloomy scenario for policy implementation within the European Union advanced by Scharpf (1988) and others. Scharpf argued that because successful implementation in the EU (and other federal or quasi-federal arrangements) required the agreement of at least two independent actors, the likelihood was that only the lowest common denominator could ever emerge as policy. Further, given that there are some countries with relatively poorly developed policy regimens in issue areas such as the environment, the lowest common denominator is likely to appear very low indeed to the more advanced actors. Thus, it is argued, the progress of any European vision is likely to be thwarted by the inability to move a more progressive vision along rapidly, and with that there will be discontent among some important actors within the system.

Agenda-setting and the attendant formulation of specific policy interventions, on the other hand, is a more individualistic action over which the constituent members of the European Union are less likely to have a veto power. All that is required is that a very limited number of actors – perhaps only an individual commissioner or council member – agree that the issue is worthy of consideration. As noted above, this openness is by no means a guarantee of success, but it does present the opportunity for the policy activist to motivate the discussion in a particular direction. This structure then provides the EU with a very broad systemic agenda of issues, as well as numerous versions of most of those issues, with the consequent ability of decision-makers to pick and choose among them. Thus, an issue will not require any common denominators in order to reach an agenda but in fact it is often possible to address problems in ways that may be highly desirable and that can move the discussion well beyond the lowest common denominator.

One further factor that differentiates the agenda-setting stage from the implementation stage is that both sets of actors involved – societal interests and official actors (political or bureaucratic) – often can gain advantages from having the agenda defined in a particular way. Further, given that there is not a monopoly on either side, a quasi-market in ideas and policies can develop that can in the best circumstances move away from the rather dismal forecasts concerning implementation. There is no guarantee that this quasi-market will be successful in producing an optimal or even a desirable outcome, but its openness (see above) does appear to offer some opportunities for negotiation and dealing to move it away from the less desirable outcomes predicted by the implementation scenario.

In the case of implementation there is a hierarchical situation in which one actor is attempting to impose its will on other powerful actors. Implementation may be in part bargained within the European Union (Hancher *et al.* 1993), but at its heart there still is a hierarchical determination of priorities in Brussels, and hence a diminished ability to bargain subsequently over the acceptability of policies. In addition, implementation is a monopoly situation in which within each geographical entity there is a single actor responsible for implementation. The European Union can not shop around to find an implementor who is more interested in the goals of the Union (or the particular DG in question).[6] Since neither of those two restraints come into play in the case of agenda-setting, there is much more capacity to move the decision-making beyond the dismal outcomes that Scharpf has predicted for the other end of the policy-making cycle.

The quasi-market that can be, and has been, developed for policy ideas is very similar to the idea of the 'advocacy coalition' model for policy-learning (Sabatier 1988). The fundamental point is that, as well as being about political interests, conflicts over policy often are about ideas and about the technical content of policy. In these instances advocacy of ideas is the means by which the participants learn about their policy options and attempt to create a viable consensus over one policy option. Although this process can not alter the fundamental perspectives of the participants (their 'core values'), argumentation over these more technical issues can often identify a zone of agreement, and with that there emerges a possibility for effective policy.

Within the European Union there are potentially a number of alternative conceptualisations of policies, and with that the potential for conflicts over the definition of policy, and of course potentially over the necessity for any policy at all. There can be national styles of science, just as there are national styles of governing, and with those scientific differences can arise varying advice over desirable policies. Merely saying that an issue will be solved 'technically' or 'rationally' is no guarantee that there will be agreement. Making policy then becomes an exercise in the mobilisation of knowledge and political power to attempt to gain control over a policy area. In that exercise teaching and learning can be the mechanism for spreading a particular conceptualisation, with policy entrepreneurs being the advocates assumed to be important to the spread of those ideas (Kingdon 1984). Knowledge and ideas are, of course, put to the use of societal interests, but they also can have influence of their own. As noted above, policies need to be shaped and need to be shaped by activists and entrepreneurs who have the commitment to the ideas.

A similar set of ideas is contained in the growing literature on 'epistemic communities' in international politics (Adler 1992; Haas 1990). Again, this literature argues that policymaking in areas with a significant technical content is a function of the ideas created by the knowledge (epistemic) communities. These communities will be large and selfcontained and will have their own standards of proof and utility for their knowledge. What this body of literature does not do, that the advocacy coalition literature does do rather well, is to present an idea of how the potential (probable?) conflicts among different policy communities will be resolved. It appears that epistemic communities are conceptualised much as paradigms in the Kuhnian approach to the philosophy of science and lack any external standards of proof for justifying their claims.

This problem of conflict between epistemic communities is all the more a problem when different communities are associated with different national conceptions of science. It may at times be difficult to separate genuine disagreements over science from national styles, or even national self-interest, in these policy debates. For example, British scientists have used measurement techniques for acid rain that could help justify their government's opposition to stricter standards for emissions. Did the scientific standards provide the justification for the policy perspective or did the scientific approach grow out of a clear national perspective on policy? Those chicken-and-egg questions are always difficult to answer.

Winners and losers

Although the structure and process for agenda-setting may lead to greater optimism than those of implementation, certain types of policies are still advantaged, while others are disadvantaged. The principal advantage appears to lie with policies that can be used to distribute benefits across a wide range of countries, or regions, and therefore can provide political benefits to a wide range of actors (politicians as well as administrators). In this sense the system is not dissimilar to the policy outcomes in the United States, with its tendency toward parochial, 'pork barrel' politics. In this sense the outcomes may be somewhat like those predicted by Scharpf, in that the lowest common denominator is not to make decisions that demonstrably extract resources from one country or region and give them to another.

Another implication of the process of agenda-setting within the European Union, following from the above discussion, is that policies that do not create obvious winners and losers – even when they must and do exist – are advantaged. This is to some extent true in any political system but appears especially true for the European Union. The general policy approach of the Union tends to be regulatory, given that the major policy focus has been economic and that the principal instruments available have been regulatory (Majone 1992). One of the virtues of regulatory policy is that it tends to disguise the winners and losers in politics from casual observers, given that the ultimate impacts of policy tend to be manifested through market activities rather than through taxes and subsidies. In general, however, the argument can be made that the EU will adopt the instruments that will evoke the least opposition from national or industrial sources (Cram 1994).

Summary

All political systems must confront the need to develop and process a range of policy issues. The European Union is no different but it must process those issues in the context of a very complex and penetrable political system. The fragmentation of the institutions and the multiple points of access permit policy entrepreneurs within the EU to force the system to consider a range of alternatives. This characteristic makes the agenda-setting process within the EU the antithesis of the implementation process. Rather than moving toward a lowest common denominator, agenda-setting has the possibility of being innovative and moving the policy debate to a higher level of attainment, however that concept might be measured.

One implication of the above analysis is that the political system of the European Union could be destined to create dissatisfaction. On the one hand there is the possibility of being creative, or at least of selecting a high-quality policy alternative from a list of options that already have been legitimated in one or more of the member countries. On the other hand, there is ample reason to believe that even if such a policy is adopted it will be very difficult to have it implemented, given the co-ordination and implementation problems that exist between Brussels and the member countries. There are cycles of optimism and pessimism in EU politics, but this apparent imbalance at the two ends of the policy cycle may be a continuing policy-making problem.

Notes

1   This analysis is based on the rather conventional 'stages' view of the policy process often associated with the work of Charles O. Jones (1983). It assumes a linear process moving from agenda-setting through implementation and evaluation. Especially given the complexities of politics within the EC we should expect some aspects of the process to be decidedly non- linear.
2   This process has been evident in the United States, where social insurance was first adopted at the state level and then moved to the federal level.
3   The need to fight at this stage may be minimised because of the control which national governments retain over implementation (Siedentopf and Ziller 1988).
4   As Rose and others point out, this rarely works as smoothly in practice as it does in the theory.
5   The exception is France, which has been described as 'semi- presidential' (Duverger 1980) but which also has definite traits of a parliamentary regime.
6   The principle of subsidiarity tends to provide more opportunity for implementation through subnational governments. This is particularly true where those governments are well-developed and already powerful, as in Germany.

B. GUY PETERS

References

Adler, E. (1992) 'The Emergence of Cooperation: National Epistemic Communities and the International Evolution of the Idea of Nuclear Arms Control', *International Organisation* 46: 101–46.

Allison, G. T. (1971) *The Essence of Decision* (Boston: Little, Brown).

Bachrach, P. and Baratz, M. (1962) 'The Two Faces of Power', *American Political Science Review* 56: 947–52.

Barber, L. (1993) 'The Towering Bureaucracy', *Financial Times*, 21 June.

Baumgartner, F. R. and Jones, B. D. (1993) *Agendas and Instability in American Politics* (Chicago: University of Chicago Press).

Best, J. A. (1989) *Images of Issues* (Berlin: De Gruyter).

Burley, A.-M. and Mattli, W. (1993) 'Europe Before the Court: A Political Theory of Legal Integration', *International Organisation* 47: 41–76.

Butler, F. (1993) 'The EC's Common Agricultural Policy (CAP)', in J. Lodge, *The European Community and the Challenge of Europe* (New York: St Martin's).

Christoph, J. B. (1993) 'The Effects of Britons in Brussels: The European Community and the Culture of Whitehall', *Governance* 6: 518–37.

Cobb, R. W. and Elder, C. D. (1983) *Participation in American Politics* (Baltimore: Johns Hopkins University Press).

Cohen, M. D., March, J. G. and Olsen, J. P. (1972) 'A Garbage Can Model of Organizational Choice', *Administrative Science Quarterly* 17: 1–25.

Cram, L. (1994) 'The European Commission as a Multi-Organization: Social Policy and IT Policy in the EU', *Journal of European Public Policy* 1: 195–217.

Dehousse, R. (1997) 'Regulation by Networks in the European Community: The Role of European Agencies', *Journal of European Public Policy* 4: 246–61.

Donnelley, M. (1993) 'The Structure of the European Commission and the Policy Formulation Process', in S. Mazey and J. J. Richardson (eds), *Lobbying in the European Community* (Oxford: Oxford University Press).

Duverger, M. (1980) 'A New Political Systems Model: Semi-Presidential Government', *European Journal of Political Research* 8: 165–87.

Eichner, V. (1997) 'Effective European Problem-solving: Lessons from the Regulation of Occupational and Environmental Protection', *Journal of European Public Policy* 4: 591–608.

Eisner, M. A. (1991) *Antitrust and the Triumph of Economics: Institutions, Expertise and Policy Change* (Chapel Hill, NC: University of North Carolina Press).

Gardner, D. (1992) 'EC Commission Faces a Bruising Shake-up', *Financial Times*, 23 September.

Haas, E. B. (1990) *When Knowledge is Power* (Berkeley: University of California Press).

Hancher, L., Molle, W. T. M., Ter Kulle, B. H. and Van Schendelen, M. P. C. M. (1993) 'Bargained Administration in Europe', unpublished paper, Erasmus University, Rotterdam, November.

Hargrove, E. (1987) *Leadership and Innovation; A Biographical Perspective on Entrepreneurs in Government* (Baltimore: Johns Hopkins University Press).

Heisler, M. O. with Kvavik, R. (1974) 'Patterns of European Politics: The "European Polity" Model', in Heisler, M. O. (ed.), *Politics in Europe* (New York: David McKay).

Hilgartner, C. and Bosk, S. L. (1988) 'The Rise and Fall of Social Problems: A Public Arenas Model', *American Journal of Sociology* 94: 53–78.

Hix, S. (1998) 'The Study of the European Union II: The New Governance Agenda and its Rival', *Journal of European Public Policy* 5: 38–65.

Immergut, E. M. (1992) *Health Politics: Interests and Institutions in Western Europe* (Cambridge: Cambridge University Press).

Jacobs, F. and Corbett, R. (1990) *The European Parliament* (Boulder, CO: Westview).

Jones, C. O. (1983) *Introduction to the Study of Public Policy*, 2nd edn (Monterey, CA: Wadsworth).

Katz, R. S. (1987) *The Future of Party Government: European and American Experiences* (Berlin: De Gruyter).

Keating, M. (1993) 'Regional Governments in Western Europe', paper presented at the Conference on Regional Politics and Policy, University of Western Ontario, London, Ont., October.

Kingdon, J. W. (1984) *Agendas, Alternatives and Public Policies* (Boston: Little, Brown).

Krehbiel, K. (1991) *Information and Legislative Organization* (Ann Arbor: University of Michigan Press).

Majone, G. (1992) 'Regulatory Federalism in the European Community', *Government and Policy* 10: 299–316.

Mazey, S. and Richardson, J. J. (1993a) 'Interest Groups in the European Community', in Richardson (ed.), *Pressure Groups* (Oxford: Oxford University Press).

Mazey, S. and Richardson, J. J. (1993b) 'Policy Making Styles in the European Community: Consultation of Groups and the Process of European Integration', paper presented at 1993 meeting of the European Community Studies Association, Washington, DC, May.

Mazey, S. and Richardson, J. J. (1993c) 'Pressure Groups in the EC', in J. Lodge (ed.), *The EC and the Challenge of the Future* (London: Pinter).

Mazey, S. and Richardson, J. J. (1996) 'EU Policy-making: A Garbage Can or an Anticipatory and Consensual Policy Style?', in Y. Meny, P. Mueller and J.-L. Quermonne (eds), *Adjusting to Europe* (London: Routledge).

Nugent, N. (1999) *The Government and Politics of the European Community*, 3rd edn (Durham, NC: Duke University Press).

Patterson, L. A. (1998) 'Making Biotechnology Policy in the European Union', Ph.D. dissertation, Graduate School of Public and International Affairs, University of Pittsburgh.

Peters, B. G. (1992) 'Bureaucratic Politics and the Institutions of the European Community', in A. Sbragia (ed.), *Euro-Politics: Institutions and Policymaking in the 'New' European Community* (Washington, DC: The Brookings Institution).

Peters, B. G. (1995) 'Managing Horizontal Government: The Politics of Coordination', in *Searching for a New Paradigm for Public Administration* (Seoul: Korean Association for Public Administration).

Peters, B. G. (2000) 'Théorie institutionelle et décision publique européenne', paper presented at Colloque on L'intégration Européenne: Entre emergence institutionelle et recomposition de l'Etat, 26–7 May.

Pierson, P. D. and Weaver, R. K. (1993) 'Imposing Losses in Pension Policy', in R. K. Weaver and B. A. Rockman (eds), *Do Institutions Matter?* (Washington, DC: The Brookings Institution).

Pollack, M. (1997) 'The Commission as Agent', in N. Nugent (cd.), *At the Heart of the Union: Studies of the European Commission* (London: Macmillan).

Pollack, M. A. and Hafner-Burton, E. (2000) 'Mainstreaming Gender in the European Union', *Journal of European Public Policy* 7.3: 43–56.

Richardson, J. J. (1982) *Policy Styles in Western Europe* (London: Allen & Unwin).

Riker, W. (1980) 'Implications from the Disequilibrium of Majority Rule in Institutions', *American Political Science Review* 74: 432–46.

Rochefort, D. A. and Cobb, R. W. (1994) 'Instrumental Versus Expressive Definitions of AIDS Policymaking', in Rochefort and Cobb (eds), *The Politics of Problem Definition* (Lawrence, KS: University Press of Kansas).

Rose, R. (1974) *The Problem of Party Government* (London: Macmillan).

Sabatier, P. (1988) 'An Advocacy Coalition Framework of Policy Change and the Role of Policy Oriented Learning Therein', *Policy Sciences* 21: 129–68.

Sandholtz, W. and Zysman, J. (1989) '1992: Recasting the European Bargain', *World Politics* 42: 95–128.

Sbragia, A. (1992) 'Thinking About the European Future: The Uses of Comparison', in Sbragia (ed.), *Euro-Politics* (Washington, DC: The Brookings Institution).

Scharpf, F. W. (1988) 'The Joint Decision Trap: Lessons from German Federalism and European Integration', *Public Administration* 66: 239–68.

Shapiro, M. (1992) 'The European Court of Justice', in A. M. Sbragia (ed.), *Euro-Politics* (Washington, DC: The Brookings Institution).

Siedentopf, H. and Ziller, J. (1988) *Making European Policies Work: The Implementation of Community Legislation by Member Countries* (London: Sage).

Streeck, W. and Schmitter, P. C. (1991) 'From Corporatism to Transnational Pluralism: Organised Interests in the Single European Market', *Politics and Society* 19: 133–64.

Tsebelis, G. (1994) 'The Power of the European Parliament as a Conditional Agenda-Setter', *American Political Science Review* 88.1: 128-42.

Tugendhat, C. (1988) *Making Sense of Europe* (New York: Columbia University Press).

Van Waarden, F. (1995) 'Persistence of National Policy Styles: A Study of their Institutional Foundations', in B. Unger and F. Van Waarden (eds), *Convergence or Diversity?* (Aldershot: Avebury).

Vogel, D. (1993) 'The Making of EC Environmental Policy', in S. S. Andersen and K. A. Eliassen (eds), *Making Policy in Europe* (London: Sage).

Walker, J. L. (1977) 'Setting the Agenda in the U.S. Senate', *British Journal of Political Science* 7: 423–35.

Wallace, H. (1996) 'Politics and Policy in the EU: The Challenge of Governance', in H. Wallace and W. Wallace, *Policy-Making in the European Union* (Oxford: Oxford University Press).

Wendon, B. (1998) 'The Commission as an Image-venue Entrepreneur in EU Social Policy', *Journal of European Social Policy*, 339–53.

Wessels, W. (1998) 'Comitology: Fusion in Action', *Journal of European Public Policy* 5: 209–34.

Wilsford, D. (1994) 'That is the Question: Integrating and Harmonizing Health Services and Pharmaceuticals in the European Community', *Journal of Health Politics, Policy and Law*.

Zito, A. (1999) *Creating Environmental Policy in the European Union* (London: Macmillan).

Chapter 5

The European Commission

Administration in turbulent times

Thomas Christiansen

Introduction

National governments like to claim that their European policies place them at the heart of the European Union, but it may be more appropriate to place the European Commission at this prime location (Nugent 2000). From the outset, when Jean Monnet became the first president of the Commission's precursor, the High Authority of the European Coal and Steel Community (ECSC), the institution has been closely linked to, even identified with, the progress of the integration project.

The Commission is central to the integration process because in most areas of EU policy-making it carries the sole responsibility for proposing new legislation. The monopoly of initiative with respect to most first-pillar matters has made the Commission a pivotal actor in the EU policy-process, placing it in a privilged position in relation to national governments, organised interests and the European Parliament. It has allowed the Commission a part in framing the issues, setting the agenda and, in a wider sense, shaping the evolution of the European Union.

Beyond initiating EU legislation, the Commission's functions also include the mediation – even 'manipulation' – of member state positions during the decision-taking phase of the policy-process (Schmidt 2000), and control over compliance with EU legislation once this has been passed (Mendrinou 1996; Peters 2000). Furthermore, in a range of areas, the Commission itself is either the decision-taker (for example in competition policy) (McGowan 2000; Brent 1995) or policy-manager (for example in managing pre-accession assistance to the countries of Central and Eastern Europe) (Levy 2000; Laffan 1997). Finally, the Commission also has a role in informing citizens about EU policies (Mak 2000) and representing the EU's trade interests in international fora (Woolcock 2000).

The variety of tasks it has to perform within the system of European governance make the Commission a complex institution. It has to possess technical expertise in almost every area of government activity as well as an astute awareness of the politics of these issues, if it wants to see its policy proposals and other initiatives succeed. The need to handle the often contradictory demands of administrative expertise and political preference within the same institution can exacerbate tensions within the Commission. And pressure to meet an expanding range of tasks with often limited resources can create problems with administrative 'overload', which in turn may damage the efficiency and legitimacy of Commission actions.

The identification of administrative and political logics within the Commission make it essential to stress one fundamental point at the beginning of this chapter: the term 'Commission' is being used to denote a number of different 'animals': 'Commission' stands both for the college of 20 individual Commissioners constituting the political, quasi-ministerial level of the institution, as well as for the body of $c.20,000$ officials who make up its administrative services. In view of the tensions mentioned above, the relationship between these political and administrative levels of the Commission has been difficult.

In the early phase, Commissioners tended to be senior civil servants, but in the recent past have been recruited from among senior politicians in the member states (Donnelly and Ritchie 1994; MacMullen 2000). Commission staff are normally recruited through competitive examinations from across the European Union, but at the higher echelons of the administration appointments have traditionally involved an element of 'parachuting' – the appointment of senior officials according to national and party political patronage rather than by promotion through the ranks (Spence 1994) as well as the growing practice of filling Commission posts through secondment of officials from national administrations (Trondal, 2001).

While the need to reconcile administrative and political responsibility within the Commission can be dated back to the origins of the High Authority, the more recent phase of dynamic integration following the creation of the Single Market has brought new pressures. Given the direct or indirect relevance of Commission activities for governments, interest groups, businesses and consumers, the institution is now frequently in the spotlight of public attention. This higher profile has had two consequences which are essential to an understanding of recent developments concerning the Commission: on the one hand, there is now an often critical, if not hostile, scrutiny of Commission activity by the – predominantly national – media. In this respect, the focus is not only on potentially controversial policy proposals or decisions the Commission is preparing, say in areas of tax harmonisation or state aid control. Crucially, the focus is on the Commission itself, often with heavy emphasis on its arcane internal practices and its alleged propensity to mismanagement or even fraud (Grey 2000).

The second, related consequence is a lingering debate about the Commission's lack of public accountability. The twenty Commissioners are nominated and appointed by national governments, and while they are not 'faceless bureaucrats', as critics sometimes claim, they can legitimately be called 'unelected'. Reforms in the Maastricht and Amsterdam Treaties to enhance the role of the European Parliament in the confirmation of the Commission President and the College of Commissioners have not altered this basic fact, and the legitimacy of the Commission has been precarious as a result.

The combination of high political profile, administrative overload, media scrutiny and questionable public accountability has made for a heady brew in the 1990s. Jacques Delors, Commission President in 1984–94, had invigorated the institution after decades of 'eurosclerosis' by putting it into the driving seat of the successful and dynamic Single Market programme. But the next big project, the agreements on Economic and Monetary Union and on Political Union contained in the Maastricht Treaty, already saw the Commission's star wane. Delors' successor, Jacques Santer, assumed office with the motto 'Doing less, but doing it better', but towards the end of his term he became the victim of the volatile mix of political ambition, administrative mismanagement and fragile legitimacy which the Commission had developed in the 1990s. In response to criticism from within and outside the Commission, the European Parliament first instituted a Committee of Independent Experts to investigate fraud and mismanagement. When the EP then threatened to dismiss the Commission on the basis of the Committee's report (Committee 1999), emphasising the absence of either collective or individual responsibility in the Commission, the entire Santer Commission was forced to resign in March 1999.

The events at the end of the 1990s constituted a major crisis for the Commission, but it also constituted an opportunity to approach the first substantial reform of the Commission in twenty-five years (Spence 2000). The new Commission, headed by Romano Prodi, has had to embark on a wide-ranging process of reform which, if carried through, may imply significant changes for the institution, the individuals working within it, and its relations with other institutions, the member states and the wider public. For the time being, the 1999 crisis and ongoing reform process have certainly weakened, even traumatised, the Commission. It is not inconceivable, though, that in the long run the 'fresh start' afforded by these events may come to be seen as invigorating, and that ultimately a 'new Commission' will emerge as a stronger player in the policy process.

This chapter analyses the evolution of the European Commission against the background of these problems and opportunities. The next section charts the development of the Commission's role in the European policy process. Subsequent sections deal with the resulting pressures for the administrative and political levels of the Commission, before attention returns to the current internal and treaty-based reforms. By way of conclusion, the chapter discusses the key issues for the Commission in view of the challenges ahead.

Conflicting demands and internal tensions

The above comments have already indicated that the Commission is having to deal with internal tensions such as the political/administrative divide (Christiansen 1997). Another such contradiction is the Commission's dual role of providing both stability and dynamism for the European Union. To some extent, this balancing act between dynamism and continuity which the Commission has to perform matches a related conflict: from the beginnings of the High Authority, Jean Monnet, its first president, had been aware of what he regarded as the dangers of bureaucratisation (Mazey 1992). He had wanted the High Authority to remain an elitist body of policy-making experts, rather than risk becoming bogged down in the quagmire of parliamentary politics (Wallace and Smith 1995) or in the minutiae of sectoral integration (Mazey 1992). Walter Hallstein, the first EEC Commission President and former diplomat, chose a more explicitly political approach to conducting Commission business. When clashing with de Gaulle, he learned to his cost what the dangers of a 'political' Commission were. The '1965 crisis' – which had France withdrawing from the Council for almost a year after a dispute over the Common Agricultural Policy – was as much about the content of policy as it was about the power of the Commission. De Gaulle's concern at this juncture was not only to preserve French interests in a particular policy field. In a wider sense, the crisis was sparked by – and put an end to – Hallstein's ambition to turn the Commission into something like an internationally recognised 'European government'.

What followed the show-down between de Gaulle and Hallstein were two decades of a decidedly 'non-political' Commission: implementing treaty provisions where it was acceptable to member states, but remaining passive where there was opposition from national capitals. The initiative on institutional reform was definitely left to member states and the European Court.

But while the experience of the 1960s spelled an end to far-reaching federalist ambitions, it did not incapacitate the Commission in its more subtle policy-making role. In what remained a cumbersome institutional framework and an unfavourable overall climate, the Commission executed its assigned tasks and indeed sought to extend Community competences. The main aim of the Rome Treaty, the abolition of all custom tariffs within the Community and the creation of a Common External Tariff by 1969, was achieved ahead of schedule. But more than just the administration of agreed policies, and the successful management of two rounds of enlargement in the 1970s and early 1980s, this period also saw the Commission 'quietly' extending the limits of Community activity.

In fields such as education, research and development and the environment, on which the treaties were silent, the Commission developed, first, a Community agenda, and, subsequently, the policy tools to facilitate Community action. In regional policy the Commission sought to go beyond the straightforward budget bargain among member states and began to design policies such as the Integrated Mediterranean Programmes that actually had a substantial regional dimension. Progress in all of these cases was gradual, cumbersome and slow-moving, and yet these early advances were the essential foundations for the Commission's more ambitious and self-confident projects of the late 1980s.

The pattern of Commission activity in this period was to circumvent potential obstruction of national governments by involving a wide range of non-governmental groups and interests in deliberation about new policy initiatives. Such groups and organisations were regularly drawn into the ambit of the Commission by its comparative openness to outside views and representation (Mazey and Richardson 1994). They would then emerge favourable to the development of a European policy in the design of which they had participated. The advantage of such a strategy was that the emerging transnational network of interest groups and non-governmental organisations, supportive of a Community role in social regulation, would eventually put pressure on national administrations and governments to 'fall into line'. At the very least, the Commission could point to 'demand' from private interests in a given Community policy, and in this way legitimise its activity in the unchartered waters outside the treaty.

Simultaneously, the Commission built up a body of 'soft law': it oversaw the growth of frameworks of rules, recommendations, decisions and practices in novel policy sectors which were strong enough to structure social and economic interests – leading them to accept that 'Europe matters' – without having to seek explicit member state approval by sending formal proposals to the Council. This construction of soft law continued to be significant even when policy-making in the wide variety of sectors become codified later (Snyder 1993). It provided valuable experience in a novel system of administration and implementation – a system in which the Commission cannot rely on hierarchy or coercion, but where its power must be based on negotiation and persuasion.

In this way, although its political ambitions had run dry, the Commission's capacity to mould social and economic interests, to construct agendas for EC action and to develop the innovative practices necessary for European governance, meant that the 1970s and early 1980s were an important phase in its 'maturation process'. It was on the basis of this experience that, with Jacques Delors taking up the presidency in 1985, there was a return to a proactive, political leadership from the Berlaymont. A number of factors – and many of them external to the Commission and even the Community itself – came together in the success of the '1992' programme. But there was also Delors' ability to invigorate and lead an administration that had in many areas shown the kind of bureaucratic fatigue Monnet had feared from the outset. At the end of Delors' ten-year tenure at the helm of the Commission its potential for political leadership (Drake, 1995) had been demonstrated conclusively.

Jacques Santer may have tried to scale back the profile and politicisation of the Commission, concentrating instead on consolidation of policies and a series of modest reforms (Peterson 1999). But it was too late to return the genie to the bottle. Given the range of activities in which the Commission is now involved and the potential for any matter, however technical, to become a matter of controversy and thereby of 'high politics', the Commission could not shy away from publicity and exposure to public debate. The appointment of Romany Prodi – a former prime minister from one of the larger member states – to succeed the disgraced Santer in 1999 appeared as an acknowledgement of this state of affairs among national governments. Prodi did not shy away from either limelight or political controversy, although he soon had to confront a hostile media reception (*Financial Times*, 18 January 2000).

As a result of its increasing significance and high profile, the Commission has been facing a broad range of criticisms. It is castigated for being too bureaucratic or technocratic (for which read: insensitive to the political priorities of the day) as well as for too much political activism (for which read: too involved in deciding political priorities). Such criticisms of the Commission are contradictory, but not necessarily wrong. The fact of the matter is that there is an inherent contradiction in the Commission providing both political leadership and an impartial civil service to the EU system. The tension, if not contradiction, between the organisational modes underlying 'bureaucracy' and 'politics' were recognised early on as fundamental issues for the Commission (Coombes 1970; Scheinmann 1966). Insofar as there is a general problem of reconciling democracy and bureaucracy in liberal democratic systems (Pollit 1988), the problem for the Commission was simply the reproduction, perhaps exacerbation, of similar conflicts erupting in national administrative systems.

As already indicated at the outset, the Commission had been treading such a path between the scylla of bureaucratisation and charybdis of politicisation for some time. But by the mid-1990s the Commission was facing more than the traditional balancing act between political bargaining and technocratic rule. The pressures on the Commission appeared as a triangular force-field, in which the 'corners' were constituted by public accountability, attention to member state interests and a measure of independent expertise. This state of affairs reflects, for the Commission, the overall

> contradictions between intergovernmental bargaining, functional administration and democracy [which are] embedded in the treaties establishing the European Communities.
>
> (Wallace and Smith 1995: 140)

Such an observation leads us to concentrate on the study of the Commission's internal tensions. Studying the internal dynamics of the Commission is analytically useful because such a perspective avoids the pitfalls of envisaging the Commission as a single, unitary organisation, without having to abandon the idea of institutional self-interest. The institutional self-interest (or 'survival') argument, often advanced when it comes to explaining Commission activity (Moravcsik 1993; Fuchs 1995), while useful, is in itself not very profound. It does not tell us much about the precise content of that self-interest. As has been pointed out, in the making of public policy, a complex interaction is going on between individual bureaucrats' self-interest and their institutional environment (Egeberg 1995). Charting the Commission's activity in terms of the demands put on it by democratic, intergovernmental and technocratic pressures helps to fill the notion of institutional self-interest with content. Crucially, it allows us to account better for its change over time.

Second, studying its internal dynamics will lead us to an understanding of differences within the Commission. It is a complex and varied institution, where organisational logics are not always compatible with each other. The coexistence of a number of distinct administrative traditions and policy styles (Richardson 1982; Burnham and Maor 1995), the autonomy of individual administrative units (Schink 1992), the way in which sectoral policies engender differing organisational cultures (Cini 2000), the persistence of national allegiance within 'inter-national' organisations (Egeberg 1999; Macdonald 2000) – all these are important in generating a comprehensive understanding of the European Commission.

Expansion and functional specialisation of the Commission's services

The European Commission is the product of a functionalist path of integration. While often seen as the champion of a federalist cause for Europe, its organisational design has largely been determined by the tasks it has had to fulfil within the European Union. As these have grown over time, so the Commission has grown in size and administrative specialisation. Commission services are currently organised in some 23 Directorates-

General (DGs). These are predominantly sectoral in nature, that is, they provide for the specialised technical and administrative know-how in the various policy sectors in which the Union is active. In addition, there are 'horizontal' DGs which are dealing with cross-cutting concerns such as the budget, personnel or financial control. Specialised services, directly answerable to the President, are responsible for legal affairs, press relations, fraud control and the like (Nugent 1995, 2001).

As a result of this process of expansion and specialisation, it is probably fair to say that the Commission is now both too large and too small. It is too large considering Monnet's initial plans were for a moderate supranational agency with limited functional responsibility. It is too large also for those who want to see European integration as an intergovernmental affair that can do without expansive bureaucratisation at the centre. Yet, at the same time, the Commission's services are small in relation to both the size of national administrations and the size of the problems it has to address. It is also for these reasons of size, and because of constrained financial and administrative resources, that the Commission now operates largely regulatory policies.

Most of the Commission's competences relate to the regulation of the internal market. Creating and maintaining the 'four freedoms' – the free movement of capital, goods, services and persons – has precedence over the regulation of individual sectors. The Commission continues to spend considerable resources managing the coal and steel, agriculture and fisheries sectors, but the balance has been steadily tilting. With the implementation of the '1992' programme, overseeing deregulation on the national level and building up a corresponding European-wide regulatory framework has taken centre-stage inside the Commission. There are essentially three aspects to this issue: facilitating the abolition of national rules, policing the emerging single market, and developing minimum standards for those areas affected by deregulation.

The main task for the Commission here is in dealing with non-tariff barriers – the vast amount of national health, safety and trading standards inhibiting free trade and the free movement of production factors. In theory, there is a distinction to be made between the distortion of trade through illegitimate practices designed to benefit national producers, and the legitimate interests in social and environmental protection that member states may continue to undertake. In practice, member states had used taxes, technical and health standards for products and services, state subsidies and public procurement policies as subtle forms of protectionism, after tariffs and customs duties had been abolished.

A key tool in approaching this issue has been the mutual recognition principle, which the Commission first spelt out in its 1985 White Paper on the Single Market. Forcing all member states to allow trade in products once they have been licensed for trade in one member state, and the resulting process of regulatory competition, the introduction of this principle has allowed the Commission to concentrate on designing the minimum requirements that all products still have to fulfil, and on policing the market that is emerging (Majone 1993).

In this way, the Commission could leave the cumbersome process of harmonisation, which had bogged down Community activity in the decades before the Single Act, to market-led competition between member states' regulatory systems. It could then concentrate on the creation of the policy tools necessary to police the emerging market, and to devise auxiliary policies to provide for minimum standards in fields affected by deregulation. Yet even this was in many cases decentralised to bodies such as CEN and CENELEC – European-wide industry-based standardisation organisations seeking to develop non-binding standards for product safety and electrical appliances, respectively. Consensus on standards emerging from these private organisations would, once endorsed by the

Commission, become *de facto* EU standards for the single market. Essentially, the Commission developed a policy of merely overseeing what became in many sectors market self-regulation.

Policing the internal market – which for the Commission has mainly meant the definition and application of rules for merger control and state aid control – has also become increasingly important. The Commission's Competition DG is widely seen as one of the most powerful sections of the administration. The direct, wide-ranging and open-ended powers given to the Commission in this field justify the observation that this is 'the first supranational policy of the Union' (McGowan and Wilks 1995). A legal scholar even likens the Commission, combining the roles of prosecutor and of judge in this policy field, to that of a 'leviathan' that must be 'bound' in the future (Brent 1995).

If the policing of the internal market has not been an uncontroversial process, then the same is true for the regulatory framework the Commission is building up to ameliorate its effects and provide for minimum social, environmental and health standards. Arguably, the Commission has often used the 'free movement' argument on a tenuous legal basis to build up additional competences. A result of this, and of subsequent treaty changes, are extensive policy competences in the education, environmental and social field, and policies which constitute more than simply a combat against non-tariff barriers (Pollack 1994; Eichener 1992; Mazey 1995).

The often uncertain legal basis, its limited financial resources and the sometimes hostile attitude of member states have forced the Commission to be innovative in going about the creation of such policy competences. The presence of a 'health and safety at work' clause in the Single Act, requiring only a qualified majority vote in the Council, has resulted in the Commission basing a whole host of social policies on this article rather than facing the national veto in the Social Chapter procedures (Cram 1993).

There is, however, more to the Commission's work than just the more or less extensive definition of the internal market programme. The Single Act had introduced, next to the 'four freedoms', Community competences in environmental policy and made the achievement of economic and social cohesion a goal of the integration process. The latter, in turn led to the reform and extension of structural funds for regional policy, the development of 'Trans-European Networks' and of a 'European Spatial Development Perspective' as well as the creation of the Cohesion Fund.

The reformed structural funds and the associated process of implementation and lobbying, in particular, brought state actors in direct contact with the Commission (Marks *et al.* 1996). The Commission actively assisted this 'partnership' by establishing an advisory committee composed of local and regional decision-makers (Hooghe 2000). The combined effect of these developments was, for the EU, the establishment of the Committee of the Regions in the TEU and for the Commission an involvement in European territorial politics.

Periodically expanding framework programmes for environment and research and development policy did much the same in these fields. Here, too, the Commission established direct links with affected actors in domestic systems: national administrations, business firms, universities, research institutes, interest and pressure groups. Again, the DGs involved increased in size and significance, but also had to resort to policy innovation and indeed experimentation in order to find a way of co-operating with often hesitant or reluctant national administrations.

After Maastricht, the Commission had accumulated competences in most fields that national administrations have traditionally controlled. In some areas, such as state aid control or the management of aid for Eastern Europe, the Commission's responsibilities are, in fact, unique even by national standards. In the hangover mood following the Maastricht ratification it came as little surprise, therefore, that questions should be asked about the 'limits' (Dehousse 1994) of this 'creeping' (Pollack 1994) extension of competences. In a variety of policy areas there were demands for 'decentralisation' – often little-disguised attempts at repatriation of Commission powers back to national administrations. At the same time, the Commission has had to accept the imposition of limitations set on its role even in areas like trade where its dominance had been long-established (Meunier and Nicolaides 1999). In other areas in which the Commission had begun to acquire a recognised role – in particular CFSP/external relations (Nuttall 1996; Bruter 1999) and Treaty reform (Christiansen and Jørgensen 1998; Dinan 2000) – it has to contend with the established role of the Council Secretariat.

Member states had already been attempting to regain some control over policy management and implementation through increased use of 'comitology' (Chapter 7, this volume). In addition, a number of 'Decentralised Community Agencies' were established in the early 1990s. The more prominent among these are the European Environmental Agency in Copenhagen, the European Monitoring Centre for Drugs and Drug Addiction in Lisbon, the European Agency for the Evaluation of Medicinal Products in London. Decentralised agencies are meant to facilitate the exchange of information and to prepare the harmonisation of national provisions in areas requiring detailed technical expertise. The creation of such agencies first appeared like an intrusion into what would otherwise have been the territory of the Commission, but now looks more like a sensible 'outsourcing' of specialised knowledge, allowing the Commission to concentrate on core tasks.

With respect to the impact of institutional changes elsewhere, it is worth mentioning the way in which the Council Secretariat has increased in significance as a result of recent Treaty changes. The 'triple-hatting' of the Council's Secretary-General as 'Mr CFSP' and WEU Secretary-General, the establishment of a CFSP policy unit in the Secretariat and its partial merger with the WEU secretariat have turned the Secretariat into an important institution in its own right (see Chapter 7 in this volume).

The challenge of policy co-ordination

But it would be misleading to look just at the conflict between the Commission and the member states without also recognising the incidence of conflicts and bureaucratic politics within the Commission. The dual aim of the Union, to provide for an internal market and for economic and social cohesion – reminiscent of the earlier distinction between negative and positive integration – has also led to conflicts between the DGs in the Commission championing different objectives. Internal disputes between the environment and the internal market DGs about the stringency of environmental protection, or between the Competition and Regional Policy DGs about the degree of public support for poorer regions (Wishlade 1993), are prime examples in this respect. The point to be made is a straightforward one: far from being a unitary actor, the Commission is an internally much-fragmented organisation. The term 'multi-organisation' has been coined to capture the way in which different logics are being followed by different parts of the administration (Cram 1994).

Consequently, there are dangers of fragmentation: inter-institutional contacts and relations proliferate in specific sectoral areas, so that ultimately each DG has regular contact with 'its' working groups in the Council, with 'its' committee in Parliament, and, indeed, with 'its' specific policy 'constituency of interests' in European society or market-place. The emergence of 'epistemic communities' – the development of and emergence of shared values among dedicated policy-makers, -recipients, -advisors, and experts in a given field – is a recognisable phenomenon (Richardson 1996). The extent to which the Commission not only participates but actively encourages such transnational policy communities is only one side of the coin. The other side is the increasing difficulty of uniting the policy-making strands of various DGs behind a formal 'Commission line'. More significantly, perhaps, in addition to inter-institutional wrangles, deadlock *within* the Commission may be becoming an obstacle to Union decision-making.

Such intra-Commission conflict is not simply an issue for technocratic co-ordination. It affects the cohesion among Commissioners and, given the increasingly politicised nature of their work, leads to cabinet-style instances of 'bureaucratic politics' under the motto 'where you stand depends on where you sit' (Peters 1992; Page and Wouters 1994). It might well be a sign that it is because more power and significance now go with the job, that it has become difficult for the Commissioners to avoid turf-battles and political differences. But, whatever the underlying reasons, this has not made it any easier for the Commission to carry out its mission.

If the Commission has matured from a small agency to an extended bureaucracy, then individual DGs have turned from organisational sub-sections into quasi-ministries in their own right. Consequently, insofar as the Commission has been able, also on behalf of the EC/EU as a whole, to project the image of 'corporate actor' (Kenis and Schneider 1987; Fuchs 1995), and indeed to continue functioning as a unified institution, it is important to look at the institutional arrangements which bind it together. There are a variety of procedures to counter such centrifugal trends.

First of all, there are various bureaucratic mechanisms to provide for the harmonisation of Commission business. Most of these involve the Secretariat-General (SG), which is designed to co-ordinate the work of the various DGs. Its responsibility of co-ordinating the drafting of legislative texts within the Commission makes the SG the nerve-centre of the institution. The increasing difficulties of such horizontal co-ordination have led to suggestions for the development of the SG into something like a 'clearing-house' for the Commission's legislative proposals (Dehousse *et al.* 1992). Monitoring legislation, chairing the regular meetings of Directors-General, and representing the Commission in inter-institutional negotiations, the SG is the gatekeeper between internal and external relations of the Commission.

In addition, the SG organises the weekly meetings of Directors-General, *chefs des cabinets* and deputy *chefs des cabinets*, respectively. The *cabinets*, the personal advisory staffs of each Commissioner, are primarily responsible for relaying information back and forth between the Commissioner's desk and the Directorate-General under his or her responsibility. In this sense they play a crucial part in the vertical integration of political and administrative spheres within the Commission. But in the post-1992 phase their role in the conduct of the Commission's horizontal co-ordination has become equally, if not more, important. In pursuing policies conducted by other Commissioners and DGs, the *cabinet* members provide their Commissioner with the ability to keep track of the whole range of business at the weekly Commission meeting (Donnelly and Ritchie 1994; Ross 1994). This function is more than merely supportive of policy co-ordination: each Commissioner's capacity to follow and accept the whole of the Commission agenda is the necessary basis for the principle of collegiality – the acceptance that Commission decisions will be supported and defended collectively *vis-à-vis* other institutions and the general public.

The elaborate efforts the Commission undertakes, especially at the Director-General and *chef de cabinet* level, to co-ordinate its policy-making activity have already been mentioned. Yet the very need for such extensive co-ordination indicates the ways in which the Commission is different from ordinary bureaucracies. It lacks, in this context, a full-blown hierarchical structure: while the individual DGs provide the 'chain of command' which is traditionally associated with bureaucracies, the Commission – the college of 20 Commissioners – is essentially a non-hierarchical body. Its members are equals, and their president a *primus inter pares*. Individual Commissioners, unlike national ministers in some member states, are not meant to run their portfolio autonomously. The collegiality principle means that a common Commission policy must be supported by all Commissioners and that, in turn, all Commissioners take an interest in every portfolio.

The co-ordination imperative places considerable strain on Commissioners' *cabinets* and on the Secretariat-General. Their work to co-ordinate policy is not only directed at identifying overlap, closing gaps and avoiding inconsistency, but also at bringing the principle underlying the Commission's work – that the Commissioners speak with a collective voice – closer to becoming reality. The officials involved have to look as much sideways as they have to look up and down. Procedural delays and inter-departmental differences within the Commission are a result of this basic requirement for co-ordination. But there is also the positive effect of a culture of compromise and bargaining, which prepares the Commission well for the inter-institutional negotiations that follow. The internal process of policy co-ordination will probably have brought out the sensitive issues of a policy proposal, and the result is something that is less likely to offend Council and Parliament than any directive that might be the product of a single DG.

Problems of accountability and legitimacy

The re-emergence of a proactive and 'political' Commission from the late 1980s onwards, together with the more general critique of the Union's 'democratic deficit', meant that there has been increasing focus on the democratic credentials of the Commissioners and of the Commission President (Haaland Matlary 1997). The most immediate response has been a redefinition of the Parliament's powers of supervision *vis-à-vis* the Commission. Until Maastricht, parliamentary powers over the Commission were purely negative: the EP could, with a two-thirds majority, force the entire Commission to resign – a provision potentially so damaging that the Santer Commission chose to resign voluntarily rather than face such a vote in the EP.

The EP had no say in the more 'positive' process of appointing the Commission. A number of reforms have since changed this situation. First, the change in the Commission's term of office – extending it to five years and making it run parallel to the parliamentary term – enhanced the potential for linking the Union's party politics and the appointment for the Commission. This linkage was not very strong during the 1994 European elections, and the 1999 election was overshadowed by the wider crisis of the Commission. However, the potential for a more dynamic relationship in the future is certainly there, especially as parties become more involved in the legitimation of Union politics (Hix 1995).

One important development in this respect has been the investiture procedure, which was revised at Amsterdam. Put into action after the nomination of the new Commission, it requires the Commissioners-designate not just to undergo lengthy hearings in front of the respective committees of the European Parliament, but also to complete extensive questionnaires about their competence and their European credentials. The new investiture procedure may, in itself, not do much about the EU's 'democratic deficit' as long as the Parliament lacks a stronger link to the electorate (Hix 2000), but it is a reform that strengthens further the hand of the Parliament vis-à-vis the Commission. The revised procedure is part of an emerging model of appointments in the EU which provides the Parliament with considerable leverage *vis-à-vis* the EU's 'executive' (Jacobs 1999).

This turns the discussion to the more general area of the Commission's inter-institutional relations. Above we discussed the explosion of the Commission's contacts with interest groups and other non-governmental organisations during the past ten years. During the same time, the nature of inter-institutional relations between Commission, Council and Parliament has changed fundamentally. As we have seen, the Commission's relationship with the Parliament has become more adversarial as the EP's influence and self-confidence have increased – the traditional partners in the integration project are now also rivals (Westlake 1994).

The Commission's relations with the Council of Ministers have also become more structured, despite the balance between autonomy from national interference and dependence on member state support. One aspect of this has been the allocation of executive tasks to the Council Secretariat, as mentioned above. Another feature is the growth of what is now generally referred to as 'comitology'. Council and Commission share the executive function in the Union, and the preferred method of conducting the execution of policies is through the creation of specialised committees (Docksey and Williams 1994). With the expansion of Union competences, the 'comitology' structure has been greatly expanded: there are hundreds of these committees now, and their supervision – not to mention legitimation – has become increasingly difficult (Buitendijk and van Schendelen 1995). In a wider sense, the expansive layer of committees dealing with consultation, co-ordination, management and implementation can be seen as a form of joint governance of EU policies by Commission, Council and member states (Christiansen and Kirchner 2000).

Institutional reform: beyond the fall of the Commission

The driving forces for the current phase of reforming the Commission are derived from a mixture of external and internal pressures on the Union. Externally, the prospect of enlargement has demanded institutional changes for almost a decade. Minor changes to the Commission were included in the Amsterdam Treaty, while further changes are expected from the IGC 2000. Beyond the IGC, reforms have become necessary because of the circumstances of the Santer Commission's resignation in 1999. The new Prodi Commission took office on a platform of reform, and a raft of proposals for internal reforms is now on the table in the form of a White Paper (European Commission 2000b).

But internal reforms had already been initiated during Santer's Presidency (Peterson 1999), and to a limited extent the current reform programme is a continuation of earlier reforms. In the light of the events in 1999, there is now much greater impetus and political will to change the workings of the Commission. But at the more technical level, there are definite signs of continuity: for example, the DECODE exercise – a kind of internal census and survey of Commission staff and their occupation – was launched in October 1997, and its results now inform Kinnock's reform programme (European Commission 1999b).

But further and far-reaching changes have become necessary in response to the report into mismanagement and corruption by the Committee of Independent Experts (Committee 1999) mentioned at the outset. These concern a number of issues both at the micro-level – in terms of internal auditing and accounting – as well as at the macro-level – in terms of the redefinition of the relationship between Commission and Parliament. The former issues have been tied into the catalogue of reforms contained in the White Paper. The latter have in part been addressed by *ad hoc* arrangements between the new Commission President, the new Commissioners and the European Parliament, and are in part on the agenda of treaty reform and a wider-ranging White Paper on European Governance.

A final source of change is the mere fact that a new Commission, under a new Commission President, has taken office. Even if everything else remained unchanged, one would expect some movement in the internal organisation and the external representation of the Commission. But as a result of these combined pressures for reform, the Commission is at an important juncture in its development. The mismatch between inadequate resources and structures on the one hand, and demands placed on the Commission on the other hand, has become too large to ignore. The choice facing decision-makers has been whether to increase resources and reform the structures, or else to reduce the role of the Commission in the policy process.

The 1999 crisis, in particular, could be seen to point in two quite different directions for the Commission: it could either be used to support the argument that the Commission is too unprofessional, badly organised and mismanaged to be entrusted with the high politics tasks with which it now deals on a daily basis – a rolling back of its competences and a greater degree of oversight by the member states would have been the logical response based on this reasoning. But the opposing view seems to have won out: that the Commission needs to be fundamentally reformed in order to be equipped for the tasks assigned to it by the member states. In a way, the appointment of Prodi as Commission President – a politician having carried highest political office in one of the larger member states and made a success of reform there – was already a statement that the Commission needs stronger leadership than was provided by Santer. The anticipation then was that, if the reform of the Commission was successful, the Commission would emerge stronger rather than weaker from the nadir of 1999.

In looking at the direction of these ongoing changes, three trends can be identified: the search for greater public accountability, a strengthening of internal hierarchy and an enhanced institutional independence for the Commission. These are, to some extent, interrelated developments, but reforms feed into each of these individually, making distinct trends discernible. There are further reform issues not captured by these trends, but they are of lesser significance in this context. The remainder of the section will discuss the direction of reforms in some more detail.

One reflection of this emerging balance was the undertaking which the European Parliament extracted from Prodi, and which Prodi extracted from each individual Commissioner, that he or she would resign their post if the Commission President or the Parliament requested it. Essentially, Parliament and Commission Presidency had found a way around the absence of any Treaty provision that would allow the Parliament to vote individual Commissioners out of office. This appears to strengthen both the principle of individual responsibility and, by giving greater power to the President, the principle of internal hierarchy. These powers have now been formalised by the Nice Treaty.

In line with greater accountability to the public, the Commission is heading for a more hierarchical internal organisation. In part, the latter is a result of the former: if individual action is more clearly identifiable (thanks to greater transparency) and more likely to be subject to sanction (thanks to greater accountability), then the dynamics of command and control are more likely to respond. But there are also reform trends directly aiming at making the Commission more hierarchical and strengthening the role of the Commission President.

Beyond its aim of addressing the Commission's inherent need for co-ordination, the above-mentioned principle of collegiality has an important consequence: providing sustained leadership and giving direction to Commission affairs are extremely difficult to achieve. Traditionally, the lack of formal powers to 'govern' the Commission have been very challenging for successive holders of this office. The Commission President has to oversee an increasingly large administration and a diverse group of Commissioners. To advance, in this context, the course of European integration against at times sceptical national governments and an uncertain public takes special qualities. In retrospect it is perhaps fair to say that some of the previous Presidents failed in their task of actively promoting European integration. Much of what the Commission does and can do depends on the willingness of national governments to proceed with European integration. But the Commission President can exercise political leadership and thereby exert significant influence on the course of integration. Jacques Delors' two and a half terms in office are the best manifestation of this potential (Drake 1995).

What is important, in this respect, is that an effective Commission President's qualities must include not only a determination to advance the course of European integration, and an awareness of what is politically feasible, but also a relatively tight control over the institution itself. As is now well documented (Ross 1994; Grant 1994), Delors' success as Commission President hinged also on his ability to 'run' the Commission itself. Towards this aim, the presence of a group of dedicated staff, in particular Delors' *chef de cabinet* Lamy, and Secretary-General Williamson, was critical in allowing Delors to streamline policy-making, to promote forcefully his strategy for a 'relaunch' of the Community and, ultimately, to enhance greatly the institutional standing of the Commission. A leadership role for the Commission depends therefore much on the individual choices made by the President in office – it is a capacity for leadership that depends on the utilisation of the Commission's resources (Nugent 1995).

The Amsterdam Treaty provided for two further changes here: first, that the designated Commission President now has to agree to the nominations of the other members of the Commissioners (Art. 158) and, second, that the Commission shall work under the 'political guidance' of the President (Art. 163). The President now also has a greater say in the allocations of portfolios to individual Commissioners. In different political circumstances, these provisions may be regarded as feeble, especially in the light of the needs of enlargement. But in the current political climate these changes constitute substantial advances.

Prodi has already made use of his new power of 'political guidance' by appointing a number of new 'Commissioners' Groups', bringing a number of Commissioners together in order to oversee developments in a particular area (Reform, Inter-institutional Relations, External Relations, etc.). As these Groups are tasked with overseeing the co-ordination of Commission policy in a particular area, and since the Commission President reserves the right to attend and chair these Groups, they can be seen as a means not only of improved horizontal linkage of policy, but also of greater control of the college by the President. And to the extent to which the President does *not* take charge of these groups, they put the relevant Commissioners chairing the Groups in a position more senior than their fellow Commissioners – a development that could be seen as an early form of the division of the Commission into senior and junior Commissioners that is often discussed – and rejected – as a solution to the eventual problems of the size of the post-enlargement commission.

Prodi has also sought to reform the *cabinets*, with mixed results: what was first a demand to appoint a *chef de cabinet* of a different nationality was then downgraded to *chef* or deputy *chef* and eventually became a minimum requirement of three nationalities to be represented among the members in the *cabinet*. Allowing for the nationality of the Commissioner, this has meant the appointment of at least two non-nationals – which is one more than was required previously. The size of *cabinets* was also reduced to six members.

Similar changes are required at the top of the administrative level of the Commission. While a new rule that Directors-Generals may not be of the same nationality as their Commissioner has led to some movement among the top grades (Peterson 2000), Kinnock has also stated on more than one occasion that the practice of 'flags on posts' (Spence 1994) will come to an end (European Commission 1999a). Given what was said earlier about the nature of appointments in the Commission, this development can be regarded as the beginning of a 'cultural revolution' (*European Voice* 1999). The effort to maintain broad geographical representation will remain, but it will be a matter for the Commission to decide who gets which job. Prodi himself demonstrated a willingness to go down this route when he appointed a new Commission secretary-general and spokesman in June 2000 unilaterally rather than going through the normal arrangement relying on informal consultation of, and lobbying by, representatives of national governments (*European Voice* 2000).

For the duration of the reform process, and most likely for the future thereafter, the Commission's Secretariat-General will become more important as the nerve-centre of the Commission (European Commission 2000b). With much emphasis on improved internal co-ordination under the supervision of the SG, there are additional channels of executive control over the operation of the Commission. The reform White Paper, while talking the language of new public management, may yet make the Commission a more traditionally bureaucratic organisation, with greater central control over the activities of its various parts. At the same time, treaty changes and secular developments promise to make the college of Commissioners more like a traditional cabinet, with the ability of the President to direct, and dismiss, individual members. The sum product would be a more hierarchical institution.

A final comment on this aspect is due in relation to the IGC 2000, which had Commission reform on its agenda (Dinan and Vanhoonacker 2000). The Commission, in its own submission to the IGC, provided a choice of two models for the reform in preparation for enlargement (European Commission 2000a). One option for reform is the limitation of the number of Commissioners to 20 and the loss of the second Commissioner for the larger member states, once new members join the Union (Bar Céndon 2000). Such a decision was already foreshadowed by the Declaration annexed to the Amsterdam Treaty. It remained a sensitive issue, given that it raises fundamental issues about the relationship between member states and Commissioners and about the equality – or lack of it – among member states (Presidency of the European Union 2000).

In the event, the European Council at Nice in December 2000, took decisions with regard to changes both in the size of the Commission and the appointment of its President and its members. The question of the size of the Commission has been resolved in the following manner: from 2005 the Commission will include only one national from each member state. Implying the loss of a second Commissioner for the larger member states, this concession contributed to their demand to increase their relative voting power in the Council and the Parliament. As such, this reform of the Commission was part of the wider confrontation between smaller and larger member states at Nice.

While this solution removes the immediate 'threat' of the creation of a so-called *directoire* – a Commission composed of two levels of seniority in which nationals from larger member states would occupy the higher echelon – it may only be a postponement of such a system. A further decision at Nice was that when the EU's membership reaches 27 states, there will be fewer Commissioners than there are member states. The Council will then choose members of the Commission according to a rotation system which is to be adopted unanimously. While the prospect of a Union of 27 member states may be far off, smaller member states have nevertheless been concerned that this will introduce a two-class system within a college of Commissioners in which some nationalities will have to rotate more frequently than others.

Finally, Nice also contained changes in the appointment procedure of the Commission President and Commissioners. The European Council is to select the Commission President, and the Council is to adopt the list of Commissioners, by qualified majority vote – a departure from the previous provision where these decisions required unanimity. President and Commissioners will be formally appointed by the Council by QMV, after they have received the approval by the European Parliament. This is a reform that may be seen to reduce the hold of individual member states over members of the Commission; the clear link between Commissioner and member state has, however, been reinforced through the new provisions mentioned above.

Dependence on support from the European Parliament has become more significant, whereas the Commission President now has greater freedom to act independently. It is important, however, to remember that, in the main, formal changes have been outlined here, and that informal influence from the member states is, if at all, only indirectly affected. But the formal changes are already quite significant, in that member states are increasingly bound to lose control over the appointment procedures, both at the Commissioner level and at the level of senior officials. The Treaty changes giving the Commission President new powers while making him (or her) more directly accountable to the EP ought to marginalise the role of member states – *once* the President has been nominated. As regards senior officials, it will have to be seen whether, after the turmoil of the initial changes, a new *modus vivendi* develops, or whether member states and/or informal networks based on nationality find a way to play the new system in a fashion similar to the old one.

Conclusion

The 1990s have been a turbulent decade for the European Commission. At the outset was the ambitious and largely successful project by Jacques Delors to reposition the Commission within the system of EU governance. But the advances the Commission had made had been bought with credit, on the assumption that the Commission would in due course deliver efficient and accountable decision-making. At the end of the decade, the bills kept coming in, and the modest reforms offered by Jacques Santer were not enough to cover the debt. The year 1999 was a nadir for the European Commission, but it has also opened the door for a unique opportunity to overhaul the institution and restructure its place within the Union's architecture.

The wide-ranging plans of Prodi and Kinnock to modernise and 'streamline' the institution will have to confront bureaucratic inertia, staff unions and the vested interests of national governments. The latter are bound to lose their privileged access to

Commissioners and officials, if the Commission as a whole is to operate in a more transparent, accountable and 'consumer-oriented' fashion. But while direct access for member states may be waning, co-operation and co-ordination between Commission and Council Secretariat is becoming more important. More important still will be the Commission's relationship with the Parliament, not only in the extraordinary circumstances of investiture or potential dismissal, but also with respect to routine decision-making.

The outcomes of Nice – the linkage of the Commission's size to the number of member states as well as the launching of a 'post-Nice process' of constitutional review – spell further changes for the Commission. In any case, the next round of enlargement will affect the Commission's work not only through constitutional changes, but also through the import of new administrative cultures, languages and work practices. The pressure to adapt to changing circumstances will therefore remain, even after the Kinnock reforms have run their course. The turbulent times for the European administration are here to stay.

References

Bar Céndon, A. (2000) 'The Number of Members of the Commission: A Possible Reform', in E. Best, M. Gray, and A. Stubb (eds), *Rethinking the European Union* (Maastricht: European Institute of Public Administration), pp. 77–104.

Brent, R. (1995) 'The Binding of Leviathan: The Changing Role of the European Commission in Competition Cases', *International and Comparative Law Quarterly* 44/2: 255–79.

Bruter, M. (1999) 'Diplomacy without a State: The External Delegations of the European Commission', *Journal of European Public Policy* 6/2: 183–205.

Buitendijk, G. and van Schendelen, M. P. C. M. (1995) 'Brussels Advisory Committees: A Channel of Influence?', *European Law Review* 20/1: 37–58.

Burnham, J. and Maor, M. (1995) 'Converging Administrative Systems: Recruitment and Training in EU Member States', *Journal of European Public Policy* 2/2: 185–204.

Christiansen, T. (1997) 'Tensions of European Governance: Politicised Bureaucracy and Multiple Accountability in the European Commission', *Journal of European Public Policy* 4/1: 73–90.

Christiansen, T. and Jørgensen, K. E. (1998) 'Negotiating Treaty Reform in the European Union: The Role of the European Commission', *International Negotiation* 3/4: 435–52.

Christiansen, T. and Kirchner, E. (eds) (2000) *Committee Governance in the European Union* (Manchester: Manchester University Press).

Cini, M. (2000) 'Administrative Culture in the European Commission', in N. Nugent (ed.), *At the Heart of the Union: Studies of the European Commission*, 2nd edn (Basingstoke: Macmillan), pp. 73–90.

Committee of Independent Experts (1999) *First Report into Allegations regarding Fraud, Mismanagement and Nepotism in the European Commission* (Brussels).

Coombes, D. (1970) *Politics and Bureaucracy in the European Community: A Portrait of the European Commission*, London: George Allen and Unwin.

Cram, L. (1993) 'Calling the Tune without Paying the Piper? Social Policy Regulation: The Role of the Commission in European Community Social Policy', *Politics and Policy* 21/3: 135–46.

Cram, L. (1994) 'The European Commission as a Multi-organization: Social Policy and IT Policy in the EU', *Journal of European Public Policy* 1/2: 194–217.

Dehousse, R. (1994) 'Community Competences: Are there Limits to Growth?', in R. Dehousse (ed.), *Europe After Maastricht: An Ever Closer Union?* (Munich: Law Books in Europe/C. H. Beck), pp. 103–25.

Dehousse, R., Joerges, C., Majone, G. and Snyder, F. (1992) *Europe after 1992: New Regulatory Strategies (EUI Working Paper LAW No. 92/31)* (Florence: European University Institute).

Dinan, D. (1997) 'The Commission and Enlargement', in J. Redmond and G. Rosenthal (eds), *The Expanding European Union: Past, Present, Future* (Boulder, CO: Lynne Rienner), pp. 17–40.

Dinan, D. (2000) 'The European Commission and the Intergovernmental Conference', in N. Nugent (ed.), *At the Heart of the Union: Studies of the European Commission*, 2nd edn (Basingstoke: Macmillan), pp. 250–69.

Dinan, D. and Vanhoonacker, S. (2000) 'IGC 2000 Watch', *ECSA Review* 13/3: pp. 1–9.

Docksey, C. and Williams, K. (1994) 'The Commission and the Execution of Community Policy', in D. Edwards and G. Spence (eds), *The European Commission* (London: Longman), pp. 117–45.

Donnelly, M. and Ritchie, E. (1994) 'The College of Commissioners and their Cabinets', in D. Edwards and G. Spence (eds), *The European Commission* (London: Longman), pp. 31–61.

Drake, H. (1995) 'Political Leadership and European Integration: The Case of Jacques Delors', *West European Politics* 18/1: 140–60.

Egeberg, M. (1995) 'Bureaucrats as Public Policy-Makers and their Self-Interest', *Journal of Theoretical Politics* 7/2: 157–67.

Egeberg, M. (1999) 'Transcending Intergovernmentalism? Identity and Role Perceptions of National Officials in EU Decision-making', *Journal of European Public Policy* 6/3: 456–74.

Eichener, V. (1992) *Social Dumping or Innovative Regulation? (EUI Working Paper SPS No. 92/28)*, paper prepared for the European University Institute, Florence.

European Commission (1999a) *Communication from Neil Kinnock to the European Commission: Some Strategic Reform Issues (SEC (99) 1917/2)* (Brussels).

European Commission (1999b) *Designing Tomorrow's Commission: A Review of the Commission's Organisation and Operation* (Brussels).

European Commission (2000a) *Adapting the Institutions to Make a Success of Enlargement (COM (2000) 034)* (Brussels).

European Commission (2000b) *Reforming the Commission*, White Paper (Brussels).

European Voice (1999) 'Commission Needs a "Cultural Revolution"', 29 July, p. 5.

European Voice (2000) 'Levi Forced out of Limelight as Prodi Reshuffles Jobs', 4 May, p. 1.

Financial Times (2000) 'Prodi's Progress', 18 January, p. 9.

Fuchs, G. (1995) 'The European Commission as a Corporate Actor? European Telecommunications Policy After Maastricht', in S. Rhodes and C. Mazey (eds), *The State of the European Union*, vol. 3 (Boulder, CO: Lynne Rienner), pp. 413–30.

Grant, C. (1994) *Delors: Inside the House that Jacques Built* (London: Brealey).

Grey, S. (2000) *Tackling Fraud and Mismanagement in the European Union*, paper prepared for the Centre for European Reform, London.

Haaland Matlary, J. (1997) 'Democratic Legitimacy and the Role of the Commission', in P. Koslowski and A. Foellesdal (eds), *Democracy and the EU* (Berlin: Springer).

Hix, S. (1995) 'Parties at the European Level as an Alternative Source of Legitimacy: The Party Federations and the EU Socio-Economic Agenda', *Journal of Common Market Studies* 33/4: 527–54.

Hix, S. (2000) 'Executive Selection in the European Union: Does the Commission President Investiture Procedure Reduce the Democratic Deficit', in K. Neunreithner and A. Wiener (eds), *European Integration after Amsterdam* (London: Routledge), pp. 95–111.

Hooghe, L. (2000) 'A House with Differing Views: The European Commission and Cohesion Policy', in N. Nugent (ed.), *At the Heart of the Union: Studies of the European Commission*, 2nd edn (Basingstoke: Macmillan), pp. 91–110.

Jacobs, F. (1999) *Nominations and Appointments: An Evolving EU Model*, paper prepared for the Biennial ECSA Conference, Pittsburgh.

Kenis, P. and Schneider, V. (1987) 'The EC as an International Corporate Actor: Two Case Studies in Economic Diplomacy', *European Journal of Political Research* 15/4: 437–57.

Laffan, B. (1997) 'From Policy-Entrepreneur to Policy-Manager: The Challenge Facing the European Commission', *Journal of European Public Policy* 4/3: 422–38.

Levy, R. (2000) 'Managing the Managers: The Commission's Role in the Implementation of Spending Programmes', in N. Nugent (ed.), *At the Heart of the Union: Studies of the European Commission*, 2nd edn (Basingstoke: Macmillan), pp. 206–29.

Macdonald, M. (2000) 'Identities in the European Commission', in N. Nugent (ed.), *At the Heart of the Union: Studies of the European Commission*, 2nd edn (Basingstoke: Macmillan), pp. 51–72.

MacMullen, A. (2000) 'European Commissioners: National Routes to a European Elite', in N. Nugent (ed.), *At the Heart of the Union: Studies of the European Commission*, 2nd edn (Basingstoke: Macmillan), pp. 28–50.

Majone, G. (1993) 'The European Community between Social Policy and Social Regulation', *Journal of Common Market Studies* 31/2: 153–70.

Mak, J. (2000) *Dialogue and Deliberation as Informal Ways to Enhance Legitimacy of the EU?*, paper prepared for the ECPR Joint Session, Copenhagen.

Marks, G., Nielsen, F., Ray, L. and Salk, J. E. (1996) 'Competencies, Cracks, and Conflicts: Regional Mobilization in the European Union', *Comparative Political Studies* 29/2: 164–91.

Mazey, S. (1992) 'Conception and Evolution of the High Authority's Administrative Services (1952–1956): From Supranational Principles to Multinational Practices', in E. Heyen with G. Melis, J.-L. Mestre, V. Wright and B. Wunder (eds), *Jahrbuch der Europäischen Verwaltungsgeschichte*, 4: *Die Anfänge der Verwaltung der Europäischen Gemeinschaft* (Baden-Baden: Nomos), pp. 31–47.

Mazey, S. (1995) 'The Development of EU Equality Policies: Bureaucratic Expansion on behalf of Women?', *Public Administration* 73/4: 591–610.

Mazey, S. and Richardson, J. (1994) 'The Commission and the Lobby', in D. Edwards and G. Spence (eds), *The European Commission* (London: Longman), pp. 169–201.

McGowan, L. (2000) 'Safeguarding the Economic Constitution: The Commission and Competition Policy', in N. Nugent (ed.), *At the Heart of the Union: Studies of the European Commission*, 2nd edn (Basingstoke: Macmillan), pp. 147–69.

McGowan, L. and Wilks, S. (1995) 'The First Supranational Policy of the European Union: Competition Policy', *European Journal of Political Research* 28/2: 141–69.

Mendrinou, M. (1996) 'Non-compliance and the European Commission's Role in Integration', *Journal of European Public Policy* 3/1: 1–22.

Meunier, S. and Nicolaides, K. (1999) 'Who Speaks for Europe? The Delegation of Trade Authority in the EU', *Journal of Common Market Studies* 37/3: 477–501.

Moravcsik, A. (1993) 'Preferences and Power in the European Community: A Liberal Intergovernmentalist Approach', *Journal of Common Market Studies* 31/4: 473–523.

Nugent, N. (1995) 'The Leadership Capacity of the European Commission', *Journal of European Public Policy* 2/4: 603–23.

Nugent, N. (2000) *At the Heart of the Union: Studies of the European Commission*, 2nd edn (Basingstoke: Macmillan).

Nugent, N. (2001) *The European Commission*, Basingstoke: Palgrave.

Nuttall, S. (1996) 'The Commission: The Struggle for Legitimacy', in C. Hill (ed.), *The Actors in Europe's Foreign Policy* (London: Routledge), pp. 130–47.

Page, E. and Wouters, L. (1994) 'Bureaucratic Politics and Political Leadership in Brussels', *Public Administration* 72/3: 445–59.

Peters, G. (1992) 'Bureaucratic Politics in the European Community', in A. Sbragia (ed.), *Euro-politics: Institutions and Policymaking in the 'New' European Community* (Washington, DC: Brookings Institution).

Peters, G. (2000) 'The Commission and Implementation in the European Union', in N. Nugent (ed.), *At the Heart of the Union: Studies of the European Commission*, 2nd edn (Basingstoke: Macmillan), pp. 190–205.

Peterson, J. (1999) 'The Santer Era: The European Commission in Normative, Historical and Theoretical Perspective', *Journal of European Public Policy* 6/1: 46–65.

Peterson, J. (2000) 'Romano Prodi: Another Delors?', *ECSA Review* 13/1: 1–8.

Pollack, M. (1994) 'Creeping Competence: The Expanding Agenda of the European Community', *Journal of Public Policy* 14/2: 95–145.

Pollit, C. (1988) 'Bureaucracy and Democracy', in D. Held and C. Pollit (eds), *New Forms of Democracy* (London: Sage), pp. 158–91.

Presidency of the European Union (2000) *Presidency Report on the IGC to the Feira European Council* (Brussels).

Richardson, J. (1982) *Policy Styles in Western Europe* (London: Allen & Unwin).

Richardson, J. (1996) 'Actor Based Models of National and EC Policy-Making: Policy Communities, Issue Networks and Advocacy Coalitions', in H. Kassim and A. Menon (eds), *The EU and National Industrial Policy* (London: Routledge).

Ross, G. (1994) *Jacques Delors and European Integration* (Cambridge: Polity Press).

Scheinmann, L. (1966) 'Some Preliminary Notes on Bureaucratic Relationships in the European Economic Community', *International Organisation* 20/4: 750–73.

Schink, G. (1992) 'Kompetenzerweiterung im Handlungsystem der Europäischen Gemeinschaft: Eigendynamik und "policy-entrepreneure"', unpublished Ph.D. thesis, Florence.

Schmidt, S. (2000) 'Only an Agenda-Setter?', *European Union Politics* 1/1: 37–61.

Snyder, F. (1993) *Soft Law and Institutional Practice in the European Community (EUI Working Paper LAW No. 93/5)* (Florence: European University Institute).

Spence, D. (1994) 'Structure, Functions and Procedures in the Commission', in D. Edwards and G. Spence (eds), *The European Commission* (London: Longman), pp. 97–114.

Spence, D. (2000) 'Plus ça change, plus ça même chose? Attempting to reform the European Commission', *Journal of European Public Policy* 7/1: 1–25.

Trondal, J. (2001) *The 'Parallel Administration' of the European Commission*, Paper presented at the ECPR Joint Sessions of Workshops, Grenoble, April 2001.

Wallace, W. and Smith, J. (1995) 'Democracy or Technocracy? European Integration and the Problem of Popular Consent', *West European Politics* 18/3: 137–57.

Westlake, M. (1994) *The Commission and the Parliament: Partners and Rivals in the European Policy-making Process* (London: Butterworth).

Wishlade, F. (1993) 'Competition Policy, Cohesion and the Coordination of Regional Aids in the European Community', *European Competition Law Review* 14/4: 143–50.

Woolcock, S. (2000) 'European Trade Policy', in H. Wallace and W. Wallace (eds), *Policy-making in the European Union*, 4th edn (Oxford: Oxford University Press), pp. 373–400.

Chapter 6

Parliaments and policy-making in the European Union

Torbjörn Bergman and Tapio Raunio

Introduction

Freely elected parliaments are the building-blocks upon which representative democracy is built. When studying EU democracy, Andersen and Eliassen (1996: 3) state that the 'core of every representative system is its parliamentary institutions'. Katz and Wessels (1999: 10) concur and argue that 'in the European tradition, parliaments are the central institutions for political legitimacy'. The idea that parliament is at the core of democracy has long been intertwined with the existence of the independent nation-state (Blondel *et al.* 1998: 1). While international organisations often also have assemblies of national representatives, these are not directly elected and their main purpose is to act as something of a 'talking shop'.

The European Parliament (EP) is directly elected and has considerable influence over policy-making. By these standards, the EP is a genuine parliament.[1] It does not, however, have some of the powers that have traditionally been the prerogative of the parliaments in the EU member states. The proper role of the European Parliament and the nation-state parliaments within the EU is hotly debated.[2] One of the two main camps in this debate argues in favour of transforming the EP into something of a 'national' (or federal) parliament, but at the level of the European Union. This would in their view help reduce the EU democratic deficit and address the lack of democratic legitimacy which has been demonstrated by decreasing turnout in European elections. For others, the main democratic link is and should be one in which national parliaments control their governments, who, in turn, represent the member states in the Council (on this debate, see the analyses in Chryssochoou 1998; Lodge 1996; Newman 1996: 173–200). More recently, however, academics have begun to argue that solutions to the democratic deficit will have to consider the roles of both the EP and the parliaments of the member states (Katz and Wessels 1999; Newman 1996: 194–200; Schmitt and Thomassen 1999). From this perspective, the problem is not only the proper role of the EP, nor is it only the role of the (currently) fifteen national parliaments, the challenge is to find a better mix of roles for all sixteen parliaments.

This chapter examines the influence of parliaments in the EU policy process. Our primary objective is to investigate the changing role of the European Parliament, but we also discuss the role of domestic legislatures. The main argument is that while the EP is still far from enjoying many of the powers that are usually associated with domestic parliaments, the institutional set-up of the Union allows the EP to have a significant influence over the EU legislative process. The strong policy influence is in turn facilitated by a quite effective and innovative parliamentary organisation. The chapter is organised as follows. In the next section we discuss legislative procedures and the powers of the European Parliament and compare the EP with national legislatures. The following section analyses the internal organisation of the EP, focusing on committees and party groups. In the fourth section we briefly analyse the input of national parliaments. We conclude with a summary and a discussion of the future of the European Parliament and other European legislatures.

The European Parliament in EU politics

An important truism that sometimes gets lost in the debate over the EP's role and functions is that the Union's procedures for making policy vary considerably across policy areas. The member states have ceded decision-making authority to EU institutions in areas such as external trade, the internal market, and the Common Agricultural Policy (CAP). When the EU decides new legislation in these areas, it is binding on the member states. EU legislation is also binding in other policy areas, such as environment, health policy and regional policies, but in these matters the member states also have legislation of their own. There are also policy areas, such as education and culture, in which the Union primarily complements national legislation and tries to facilitate co-operation among member states. In yet other policy areas, for example civil law, income tax, and social-moral issues such as religion and abortion, decision-making authority remains outside the scope of the Union institutions, including the Parliament.

There are many other differences between the roles and influence of the EP and the national parliaments of the member states. For one thing, almost all public spending and social transfers are controlled by the member states and their parliaments. The European Union spends less than 2% of the GDP of the whole EU area. In contrast, in 1995 the member states spent an average of about 53% of their own GDP on public spending (Hix 1999b: 241–2). Moreover, constitutional questions, such as those concerning the balance of power between Union institutions, must be approved by the parliaments of the member states, but not by the EP. In several important policy areas within the EU, the EP is limited to indirect forms of influence. These include important parts of the Economic and Monetary Union (EMU), Common Foreign and Security Policy (the second pillar), and parts of Justice and Home Affairs (i.e. what is left of the third pillar). In addition, with a few exceptions, such as rules governing the duties of Members of the European Parliament (MEPs) and the possible approval of a unified electoral system for electing its own members, the EP does not have the formal right to initiate legislation. Moreover, as regards executive accountability, there is no single executive (of the type that exists in the member states) that the Parliament can overthrow. Instead, the Commission, the Council and the European Council (the summits of the national leaders) share the role of 'executive'.

But the EP is nonetheless important. The Parliament has enjoyed the right to dismiss the whole Commission since the European Coal and Steel Community, provided that an absolute majority of members and two-thirds of the votes cast support a no-confidence motion. While the Parliament has never sacked the Commission, the voluntary resignation of the Santer Commission in March 1999 was in fact initiated and caused by pressure exerted upon the Commission by the MEPs. The Maastricht Treaty also gave the Parliament the right to approve the whole Commission with a simple majority of votes cast. Testing its new powers after the 1994 elections, the chamber first held a vote on Jacques Santer, the European Council's candidate for the Commission President, who only narrowly escaped defeat. The Parliament then subjected the prospective commissioners to detailed hearings in the EP committees. Finally, the Parliament gave its approval to the whole Commission. In this way the Parliament itself established the practice formally introduced by the Amsterdam Treaty, according to which any future Commission President must receive the support of the EP before putting together his or her team of commissioners (Westlake 1998).

There are also other ways in which MEPs exercise influence. The Commission is legally bound to answer written and oral questions tabled by MEPs (Raunio 1996), and commissioners and Commission civil servants appear regularly in the EP committees. The Parliament is also consulted in the appointment of the members of the Court of Auditors and the President and the Board of the European Central Bank (ECB). In 1998 the latter were subjected to hearings similar to those that the EP conducts with the commissioners prior to their appointment. The ECB president also appears regularly before the economic and monetary affairs committee of the Parliament. Other inter-institutional contacts have also increased considerably since the 1980s, with MEPs and parliamentary staff frequently consulting the Commission and the Council, particularly about forthcoming EU legislation and the preferences of member states on legislative matters.

The EP is also important in deciding how the Union will spend its money. If it can muster the necessary majorities, the EP can both change (amend) and block (veto) the Union's budget proposal. Its budgetary amendment rights are restricted to the so-called non-compulsory expenditure, which excludes the CAP and thus 45% of the budget in 1999 (Hix 1999b: 247). However, the Parliament has repeatedly challenged the distinction between the compulsory and non-compulsory parts of the budget and it has used its powers to add new budget lines within the non-compulsory part. For example, the Parliament has forced the Council to accept increases in funding for education, training, culture, and social and employment policies (Maurer 1999).

The legislative influence of the Parliament is significant, but, again, its influence varies considerably between policy areas, which are themselves linked to four main decision-making procedures. One procedure applies only to a small but important number of issues such as the incorporation of new member states into the Union and certain other international agreements. This is the assent procedure under which the EP cannot change the proposal, but which requires that the EP must support the proposal for it to be adopted. The decision rule under the assent procedure is usually simple majority, but accession of new members, adoption of a uniform electoral system for EP elections and sanctions in the event of a breach of human rights must be approved by an absolute majority of all MEPs (Corbett *et al.* 2000: 203), currently 314 votes out of a total of 626 MEPs. Under this procedure, a major source of EP influence stems from its potential to act as a veto player. This means that even if it cannot propose anything on its own, it can block Commission and Council proposals, which does give it some leverage over the other two institutions.

Adding to the complexity, there are three other main decision-making procedures that directly involve the EP. These are consultation, co-operation and co-decision procedures. The consultation procedure is the oldest and existed before the first direct elections to the EP, which were held in 1979. Under this procedure, the role of the EP is advisory, i.e. it must be heard but its opinions are not binding on the Commission or the Council. The procedure is now used mainly for agricultural policy and police and judicial co-operation. A Commission proposal becomes law if a qualified majority vote (QMV) of the Council accepts it. Alternatively, a unanimous Council can decide to amend a Commission proposal.

The Single European Act (SEA), which went into effect on 1 July 1987, introduced the co-operation procedure. From 1987 to 1999 it covered a broad set of policy areas, including much of the internal market legislation. The procedure provides the EP with a limited ability to veto Commission proposals. If the EP rejects a Commission proposal, the proposal can only be implemented if the Commission and a unanimous Council agree to pass the legislation. It is referred to as a procedure of co-operation because a majority of MEPs (more than half of MEPs actually voting on the matter) can propose amendments to Commission proposals. If the Commission supports these amendments, it is up to the Council to decide to accept the proposal by QMV. After this, there is a second round of scrutiny and negotiation. If the Council has made changes to the original proposal, then an absolute majority of MEPs can once again submit amendments. If the Commission accepts these, they go to the Council for final decision. The Council can either accept the proposal by QMV or alter the proposal, which requires unanimity among the governments of the member states.

The fourth main procedure went into effect with the 'birth' of the European Union on 1 November 1993. The new treaty, commonly known as the Maastricht Treaty, introduced the co-decision procedure. Co-decision is basically an extension of the co-operation procedure. Of symbolic importance is the fact that under this procedure legislation is made in the name of both the EP and the Council, while under consultation and co-operation procedures it is made in the name of the Council. In addition, under this procedure, after the second round, if the Council is unwilling to accept EP amendments, it has to refer the matter to a Conciliation Committee composed of an equal number of Council and EP representatives (15 each). Between 1 November 1993 and 1 May 1999, if the Conciliation Committee could not agree on a common solution that was supported by a majority of EP representatives and a qualified majority of Council members, a unanimous Council could offer the EP a final proposal. This proposal became law unless an absolute majority of all MEPs vetoed it.

Between the entry into force of the Maastricht Treaty (1 November 1993) and the end of the 1994–99 legislative term, the EP was involved in 379 co-decision procedures, 116 co-operation procedures, 87 assent procedures, 1,113 consultation procedures and 102 budgetary procedures (Maurer 1999). The Amsterdam Treaty, which entered into force on 1 May 1999, radically changed the relative distribution among these procedures and practically eliminated the co-operation procedure. It is now used only for a few rather technical areas of the EMU.

The Amsterdam Treaty also changed the co-decision procedure. The most important change concerns the role of the Conciliation Committee. If the EP and the Council continue to disagree in the Conciliation Committee, the Council can no longer offer its position as a 'take it or leave it' proposal. Instead, new legislation is simply not passed. If, on the other hand, the Conciliation Committee does agree on a text, it becomes law provided both an absolute majority of MEPs and a qualified majority of the Council support it. The new co-decision procedure also reduces the importance of the Commission. If the EP and the Council agree, approval by the Commission is no longer necessary (Tsebelis and Garrett 2000). In addition, the Amsterdam version of the co-decision procedure is now the one that is used in most policy areas. The long list of policy areas to which it applies includes the internal market, employment policy, social policy, equal opportunities, broad aspects of environmental policy and Union efforts to combat fraud (Hix 1999b: 60–5, 366–75). The Treaty of Nice makes the list even longer.

Why do these procedures matter? For one thing, they matter because they show that over the last two decades, MEPs have become increasingly influential. In fact, one can probably not fully understand the evolution of the Parliament unless one considers that it has been something of an underdog fighting for recognition. Indeed, the top priority and pet subject of most MEPs has been increasing the powers of the EP in the EU decision-making process, especially vis-à-vis the Council (Corbett 1998). However, the precise role and influence of the EP is difficult to pinpoint. A particularly controversial debate concerns the argument by George Tsebelis that the Parliament is in fact less powerful under the (Maastricht) co-decision procedure than under the co-operation procedure.

The basis for the discussion was an article by Tsebelis (1994) in which he argued that the EP is quite influential under the co-operation procedure. According to Tsebelis, this is because EP amendments, if accepted by the Commission, are more difficult for the Council to amend than to accept. At this stage, Council unanimity is required for amendments, qualified majority for acceptance. When the Maastricht Treaty entered into force, the new legislative procedure of co-decision was generally saluted as a major new step forward for the Parliament. However, Tsebelis and Garrett (1997) maintained that the co-operation procedure is more favourable to the EP than the (Maastricht) co-decision procedure. This is because the co-decision procedure allows the Council to offer the EP a final 'take it or leave it' proposal. And because the EP is almost always willing to accept a marginally better policy than no policy at all, the Parliament is unlikely to turn down a Council proposal. There are, however, at least two major problems with their thesis.[3]

The first is that the thesis that the EP is more influential under co-operation than under co-decision squares badly with the knowledge and expertise of most analysts familiar with how the EP and the EU actually works (see for example Crombez 1996; Earnshaw and Judge 1996; Moser 1996; Scully 1997; Wurzel 1999). According to MEPs and most analysts, the Maastricht version of the co-decision procedure was a significant step forward for the EP in its institutional power-struggle with the Council over EU legislation. By using model assumptions that allow for variations in the impatience (discount rates) of the institutional actors and the number of relevant dimensions, it is also possible to show why the EP sometimes actually vetoed Council proposals under the Maastricht co-decision procedure (Rittberger 2000). Thus, the models that emphasise EP power under the co-operation procedure might have been built on assumptions too restrictive to generate an empirically correct understanding of the EP role under different procedures.[4]

The second problem is a practical one, and it is that the rules have changed. This has created a new bargaining environment in which the old debate is less relevant. The Amsterdam Treaty modified the co-decision procedure so that it no longer ends with the Council presenting the EP with a final proposal that the Parliament has to accept or reject. Under the current rules, neither institution completely dominates the other. In fact, on largely theoretical grounds Tsebelis and Garrett (2000) argue that under the co-decision procedure, the EP is on an equal footing with the Council as a legislator. However, because the procedure is so new, that argument has not yet been subject to systematic empirical testing.

In the absence of stricter tests of the new co-decision procedure and studies of how the role and influence of the EP measure up to that of national parliaments, a comparative discussion of available indicators can still be useful. Comparisons between member state legislatures and the European Parliament are notoriously difficult to make.[5] Nonetheless, three useful cross-national indicators of the role and influence of the parliament in a political system are its impact on policy, the degree to which it independently sets its own agenda and the extent to which interests outside of the formal decision-making institutions work to influence it. Let us briefly compare the EP to national legislatures on these three dimensions.

A modern classic on the relationship between the legislature and the executive branch is a chapter by Nelson Polsby (1975) in which he makes a useful distinction between parliaments as 'arenas' and parliaments as 'policy transformers'. Drawing on this distinction, Philip Norton (1998: 196–7) argues that on the national level, the Italian parliament is probably the most influential of the EU member state parliaments. Table 6.1 illustrates Norton's ranking. In descending order of parliamentary policy influence relative to the executive, the Italian parliament is followed by the Scandinavian parliaments and the Dutch parliament. The German *Bundestag* occupies the middle position, followed by the parliaments of Belgium and the UK. Furthest from the Italian parliament are the parliaments of France and Ireland.

Table 6.1 Ranking of parliaments on a 'transformer–arena' scale (based on Norton 1998: 197), an 'agenda–power' scale (Döring 1995: 225) and a 'lobby attractiveness' scale (Liebert 1995: 430–3)

Transformer	Sets its own agenda	Attracts lobbyists
US Congress	US Congress	US Congress
Italy (5)	The Netherlands (7)	Austria (3)
Denmark (4)	Italy (6)	European Parliament (3)
Finland (4)	European Parliament	Finland (3)
Sweden (4)	Denmark (5)	Germany (3)
The Netherlands (4)	Finland (5)	Italy (3)
European Parliament (under co-decision)	Sweden (5)	The Netherlands (3)
Germany (3)	Austria (4)	Belgium (2)
Belgium (2)	Belgium (4)	Denmark (2)
UK (2)	Germany (4)	Greece (2)
France (1)	Spain (4)	Luxemburg (2)
Ireland (1)	Luxemburg (3)	Sweden (2)
	Portugal (3)	UK (2)
	France (2)	France (1)
	Greece (2)	Ireland (1)
	Ireland (1)	Portugal (1)
	UK (1)	Spain (1)
Arena	Government sets the agenda	Ignored by lobbyists

Note:

In the columns for transformation of policy and agenda-setting, we are responsible for the ranking of the European Parliament. As a comparative suggestion, we have placed the US Congress at the top of each column. Norton places some of the parliaments in the same category. For example, he does not distinguish between the three Scandinavian and the Dutch parliaments. The number in the parenthesis refers to the category that a specific parliament is placed in by Norton. Within each category, the member states are placed in alphabetical order. Norton does not discuss the parliaments of Austria, Greece, Luxemburg, Portugal and Spain. Döring places the respective legislatures in one of seven different groups. Liebert places the parliaments in one of three categories. She is also the only one of the three experts that includes the European Parliament in her analysis. Norton, Döring and Liebert all base their rankings on reports by country experts.

How does the EP measure up when compared with national parliaments on this indicator? While we draw on available information, the placement of the EP is entirely our own tentative and suggestive evaluation (but see also Scully 2000). For the EP, the answer to this question depends on which decision-making procedure one studies. Under the consultation procedure, the EP ranks low, with the Parliament possessing only the right to issue non-binding opinions. The placement in Table 6.1 refers to the influence of the Parliament under the current version of the co-decision procedure and is based on the following assessment. With regard to the co-decision procedure, the Parliament ranks high: it is an equal partner with the Council, it can block legislation, and it has proved successful in getting its amendments accepted by the Council (see also Scully 2000; Nugent 1999: 241). At the same time, however, it lacks the formal right to initiate legislation on its own and it does not effectively control a single executive. In terms of the arena versus policy-transformer distinction, we therefore place the EP under the co-decision procedure just below the Scandinavian and Dutch parliaments as a legislature that is able to shape policy.

On the other two indicators, the ranking is not confined to the co-decision procedure but instead it refers to more general assessments of how the EP stands in a comparison with the member states' parliaments and the US Congress. An authoritative account of the difference between the member state parliaments is Herbert Döring's (1995) ranking of their agenda power. This ranking is illustrated in the middle column of Table 6.1. The scale captures the extent to which the parliament's agenda is determined by the cabinet as opposed to when the parliament sets its own agenda. We have placed the US Congress at the top, indicating that it has the most agenda-setting power. Among the member states, the Dutch parliament, followed by the Italian, are the most independent agenda-setters. They are followed by the Scandinavian parliaments, with Austria, Belgium, Germany and Spain in the next group. Luxemburg and Portugal have below average agenda control, followed by France and Greece. The work of the Irish and UK parliaments tends to be most dominated by their respective cabinets (Döring 1995: 224–5).

As for the agenda-setting powers of the EP, again the placement is our own. It is based on the following reasoning. On the one hand, the EP formally controls its own proceedings and internal rules. On the other hand, the policy content of the agendas of committees and the plenary is largely determined by the inter-institutional legislative procedures, especially since the coming into force of the Amsterdam Treaty. The Treaty greatly extended the application of the co-decision procedure, and it also set strict time limits for both the Council and the Parliament. Again, however, the European Parliament also has extensive amendment rights and it uses them effectively. In addition, the committees and the whole chamber can debate topics of their own choice, and the Parliament has in the past made active use of this right, often discussing politically sensitive matters which have been neglected by the member states, the Council or the Commission. The BSE ('mad-cow disease') crisis and financial mismanagement inside the Commission are two well-known examples. Weighing these aspects together, we place the EP high on this indicator, on a par with the Italian parliament and above the Scandinavian parliaments.

Another indicator of the role of a parliament is the way in which lobbyists, pressure groups and other organised interests try to influence members of parliament. This is true for the member states as well as at the level of the European Union. In the United States much of the agenda-setting and *de facto* decision-making takes place in Congress, which is also famous for being surrounded by powerful lobbyists (Rush 1998). In a cross-national comparison of how lobbying and other interest-group activities relate to European parliaments, Liebert (1995: 429–33) finds that the French, Irish, Portuguese and Spanish parliaments tend to be the least attractive targets for outside interests. In a second category she places Belgium, Denmark, Greece, Luxemburg, Sweden and the UK. As for the parliaments of Austria, Finland, Germany, Italy, the Netherlands and the European Parliament, the pattern is that a large range of interest groups monitor and influence parliamentary processes. There is no question that lobbyists find the EP attractive. While the bulk of pressure group efforts are directed at the Commission, the Parliament has been the target of increased lobbying activity since the SEA. The Parliament has recently also begun to pay more attention to the consequences of lobbying, drawing up stricter rules to regulate lobbying activity (Shephard 1999). (With regard to lobbying in the EU system, see the chapter by Sonia Mazey and Jeremy Richardson, this volume.)

In sum, because it functions in an EU political system that is partly supranational and partly intergovernmental, there are important constraints on the EP's powers. It is not as influential as the US Congress, which also operates in a separation-of-powers system. But the EP has a significant influence over the budget and over the appointment and removal of the Commission. It is also involved in appointments to other institutions and it scrutinises both the Commission and other institutions. Not least, it is an important co-legislator in most policy areas, it has considerable agenda-setting powers and it is attractive to outside interest groups (another sign of an influential parliament). Thus, the MEPs probably have a more direct impact on policy output at the EU level than many national MPs have on national-level policy. MEPs also use the internal organisation of the Parliament and the party groups to facilitate an effective use of the powers of the EP, a subject which we discuss in the next section.

Decision-making in the European Parliament

The previous section charted the development of the Parliament from a 'talking shop' to a policy-shaping assembly with considerable legislative powers. The inter-institutional dimension is also reflected in the internal organisation of the Parliament, with the MEPs structuring their work so as to maximise their policy influence vis-à-vis the Council and the Commission. Again a comparison with the House of Representatives of the US Congress is a good point of departure. The work of both legislatures, especially the processing of legislative bills, is structured around committees, and individual representatives enjoy considerable freedom of manoeuvre. Three organisational and behavioural aspects are of particular interest in this respect: committee work, division of labour within party groups, and majority building between the groups.

During the past decades, committees have become increasingly powerful within European national legislatures, in terms both of legislative work and of control of the executive. This development is primarily explained by the need to acquire policy expertise through sectoral specialisation (Damgaard 1995; Mattson and Strøm 1995; Norton 1998). EP committees are very important. The 1999–2004 EP has seventeen permanent committees. The Parliament can also establish temporary committees or temporary committees of inquiry to investigate administrative malpractice or breaches of EC law (Corbett et al. 2000: 261–4; Shackleton 1998).

In 1996 the Parliament established a temporary committee of inquiry to examine the Community transit system. In its report Parliament criticised the way in which member states used the money allocated for this purpose. The second temporary committee of inquiry, also set up in 1996, dealt with the BSE crisis. The Parliament's actions had a profound impact on EU consumer protection policy. In a resolution adopted on 19 February 1997, the Parliament warned the Commission that if it did not follow its recommendations, a motion of censure would be introduced, thus threatening to dismiss the entire Commission. In the Amsterdam Treaty public health matters (including veterinary medicine) were subsequently moved to the co-decision procedure (Maurer 1999). Both inquiries showed that the EP is able to use existing instruments in innovative ways to increase its leverage within the EU system.

Committees process all legislative initiatives considered by the EP. In addition – with the exception of resolutions adopted at the end of topical and urgent debates, oral questions or question time – plenary deliberation is almost always based on committee reports. When a bill arrives in the assembly, the legislative co-ordination unit normally decides which committee is responsible for producing a report on the issue and designates one or more committees as opinion-giving committees. The Conference of Committee Chairmen is also involved in allocating legislative work. When there is dispute between two or more committees, the matter can be taken to the Conference of Presidents. However, the allocation of bills is usually unproblematic. Once assigned, the responsible committee chooses a *rapporteur* from among its membership, whose task is to produce a draft report on the proposal.[6]

When drafting a report, the rapporteur must be prepared to compromise in order to accommodate views of other groups. Compromising is necessary to facilitate smooth passage of the report through the committee and later in the plenary. This is especially true for legislative reports dealing with matters that fall under the absolute majority requirement. Rapporteurs, and particularly the committee staff who often carry out the background work, normally consult a variety of actors when preparing draft reports, including party groups, external experts, interest groups and civil servants in the Commission and Council. The committee then votes on the draft report and amendments to it. When adopted, the report is then sent to the plenary. Before the final debate and vote, party groups decide on their positions, including what amendments to propose, and whether or not to support the report. National party delegations, especially the larger ones, often hold their own discussions prior to the group meetings. Finally, the report and tabled amendments are voted on in the plenary.[7]

The number of committees and their policy jurisdictions have been changed on a regular basis to improve the scrutiny of legislation and to achieve a more efficient division of labour among the MEPs. The committee system also facilitates log-rolling (i.e. 'vote trading' among individual members to win favours from each other) and the development of policy expertise. The latter is particularly important given the superior administrative resources of the Council and the Commission. The party groups have reacted to this committee-based specialisation by strengthening their own position in the chamber, both through procedural changes and through closer control of committee work (Bowler and Farrell 1995).

In practice, party groups control both the EP's agenda and its internal organisation, primarily through the Conference of Presidents, the Bureau, and the Presidency. The Conference of Presidents consists of the EP President and party group chairmen. Decisions are based on consensus, or failing this, voting, with votes weighted according to the sizes of the groups. The Conference decides on parliamentary organisation and legislative planning. It determines the composition and competence of permanent committees, temporary committees of inquiry, of joint parliamentary committees, standing delegations and *ad hoc* delegations. It also draws up the draft agenda of the plenary and authorises the drawing-up of own-initiative reports by committees. The Bureau is composed of the President and the fourteen Vice-Presidents of the EP and is primarily responsible for internal administrative and financial matters.[8]

Party groups control the appointment of committee seats and chairs. Committee seats are reallocated halfway through the electoral term. The majority of representatives are full members of one committee and substitutes in another. Committee chairs are prestigious and influential positions and heavily contested by individual members. The d'Hondt system is used to allocate chairs and vice-chairs between the groups. Chairmanships are reallocated at mid-term. Party group co-ordinators are responsible for leading and co-ordinating the work of their groups in the committees. While there is great variation between individual issues, group positions are often strongly influenced by the group co-ordinator and committee members.

Table 6.2 Party groups in the European Parliament, 1979–2000

Groups	Date 1979	1981	1984	1987	1989	1993	1994	1995	1997	2000
PES	113	123	130	165	180	198	198	221	214	180
EPP	107	117	110	115	121	162	157	173	181	233
ELDR	40	39	31	44	49	46	43	52	41	51
EDG	64	63	50	66	34					
EDA	22	22	29	29	20	20	26	26		
COM	44	48	41	48						
CDI	11	11								
RB			20	20	13	16				
ER			16	16	17	14				
V					30	28	23	25	28	48
EUL					28					
LU					14	13				
GUE-NGL							28	31	33	42
EN							19	19		
FE							27	29		
ERA							19	19	20	
UPE									55	
UEN										30
EDD										16
NA	9	11	7	15	12	21	27	31	54	26
Total	410	434	434	518	518	518	567	626	626	626

Notes:

Party group abbreviations: PES = Party of European Socialists; EPP = European People's Party; ELDR = European Liberal, Democrat and Reform Party; EDA = European Democratic Alliance; COM = Communist and Allies Group; CDI = Technical Group of Co-ordination and Defence of Independent MEPs; RB = Rainbow Group; ER = European Right; V = The Green Group; EUL = European United Left; LU = Left Unity; GUE-NGL = Confederal Group of the European United Left (since 1995 the group has had the sub-group Nordic Green Left added to it); EN = Europe of Nations; ERA = European Radical Alliance; FE = Forza Europa; UPE = Union for Europe; UEN = Union for Europe of the Nations; EDD = Europe of Democracies and Diversities; NA = Non-attached.

Dates: 1979 = after the European elections (EE); 1981 = following the first EP elections in Greece on 18 October 1981; 1984 = after the second EE; 1987 = situation 31.12.1987. First European elections in Spain were on 10 June 1987, and in Portugal on 19 July 1987; 1989 = after the third EE; 1993 = situation in January 1993 following the mergers between EPP and the EDG in May 1992 and between the EUL and PES in January 1993; 1994 = after the fourth EE; 1995 = situation in January 1995 after the latest EU enlargement; 1997 = situation in March 1997; 2000 = situation in April 2000.

Group formation is regulated in the standing orders of the Parliament, and groups with representatives from only one country are no longer permitted.[9] Further incentives for group formation are provided in the form of material and procedural benefits. Material benefits include office space, staff, and money for organising meetings and distributing information. Procedural rights include committee and intra-parliamentary leadership appointments and the allocation of reports and plenary speaking time, which are all based on the rule of proportionality between the groups.[10] While the availability of such benefits explains the emergence of almost purely technical groups like the CDI in the 1979–84 EP and the Rainbow Group in the 1984–94 EP, the material incentives and procedural rights facilitate party group co-operation among members. Non-attached MEPs are largely marginalised in the chamber.

Table 6.2 shows the distribution of seats between party groups in the period 1979–2000. The EP party system is primarily based on the familiar left–right dimension. The main groups are officially the parliamentary groups of their Europarties: social democrats (PES), conservatives/Christian democrats (EPP), liberals (ELDR), and the greens (V) (see Bell and Lord 1998; Hix and Lord 1997). The number of political groups has remained rather stable since the first Euroelections. PES and EPP have been the two dominant groups, controlling more than half of the seats after each election. The third core group is the liberals. The communists, or the radical left, have formed a group since 1973, and the greens have done so since their electoral breakthrough in 1989. The conservative party family has been represented by both the EDG, a group formed around the British Conservatives, which joined the EPP in May 1992, and the Gaullist EDA, which was founded back in 1965. The extreme right parties were also able to form a group after the 1984 and 1989 elections. However, there is notable discontinuity among the smaller groups, which have tended to be rather loose coalitions. The composition of the smaller groups often undergoes quite substantial changes during a five-year electoral term. For example, in the 1994–99 Parliament the EPP made substantial gains, first in November 1996 when the Portuguese PSD joined the group (coming from the ELDR), and then in June 1998 when Forza Italia MEPs left the UPE to enter the EPP group.[11]

The internal organisation of party groups is broadly similar to the structure of party groups in national legislatures (Raunio 2000b). The group is led by a chairman, who normally serves the whole five-year legislative term. A number of vice-chairmen assist the chair. The party group bureau – composed of the chair, vice-chairmen, the heads (and perhaps additional members) of national party delegations, and the treasurer – is primarily responsible for organisational and administrative issues, but also prepares policy decisions for group meetings. Meetings of the whole group are held in Brussels prior to the plenary week, as well as during the plenaries. When MEPs feel they cannot follow the group position, they can use the group meetings to explain their decision (Bay Brzinski 1995). Party groups also set up working groups to deal with specific policy questions (see Hix and Lord 1997: 77–166; Raunio 1997).

The MEPs represent over a hundred national parties and fifteen member states. This heterogeneity has led observers to question the logic of group formation and the stability and cohesion of the party groups (see Andeweg 1995). And indeed, while voting behaviour in the directly elected Parliament indicates that the majority of groups are rather cohesive (Attinà 1990; Hix and Lord 1997; Kreppel 2000; Raunio 1997), national parties are the key components of party groups, and MEPs depend on their national parties for re-election. Since the EP group leadership is, in practice, excluded from candidate selection, this also precludes group leaders from using the threat of hindering re-election against troublesome representatives.[12]

The inter-institutional ambitions of the EP and its decision rules provide strong incentives both for cohesive party groups and for coalition formation among these groups. The decision rules require that the Parliament muster absolute majorities to amend or reject legislation. In an effort to put pressure on the Council and the Commission, party groups and MEPs manufacture broad majorities for both legislative and non-legislative resolutions. Co-operation among MEPs and party groups is a prerequisite for influence. Indeed, analysing over 500 amendments under the co-operation procedure, Kreppel (1999: 533) concludes that 'the EP is more successful when it is able to present a united front to the other EU institutions independent of the type of amendment being made'. Until the 1999 elections the manufacturing of winning coalitions was mainly based on informal co-operation between PES and EPP, with both major groups generally preferring new EU legislation to the status quo and with both groups in broad agreement over integration.[13] Coalition formation is also facilitated by ideological convergence between the Europarties, which in turn reflects overall partisan policy moderation across Europe (Hix 1999a).

In sum, the Parliament has adapted its own internal modes of operation to meet the demands of the EU decision-making system (see also Hix 1999b: 74–98). The EP has its own Rules of Procedure, a set of written rules which are frequently updated and designed to make the most of the assembly's hard-won legislative powers. Formal rules are probably of particular importance for the EP, given its multinational membership and high turnover rates at elections (Bowler and Farrell 1999). The thrust of legislative work is done in the committees, where individual rapporteurs engage in coalition-building in order to gain the support of the committee and the plenary majority for their reports. These ideological compromises inside the assembly help the Parliament get its amendments and resolutions accepted by the Council. The Parliament also invests resources in creating policy expertise. To that end, party groups, committees and individual representatives have staff whose main function is to gather information and maintain contacts with outside actors. Such information-gathering is essential for legislative success (Wurzel 1999).

The European Parliament and the national parliaments

The trend toward greater power for the European Parliament does not, however, overshadow the fact that national governments are still the principal actors in the EU political system. While the Maastricht and Amsterdam Treaties considerably increased the status of the EP, the Treaty of Nice does not mark a new major power shift in favour of the European Parliament. In terms both of legislative powers and of power to appoint and control the Commission, the Council remains the main legislative body of the Union. Heads of government meeting at the summits of the European Council also decide key personnel choices, including the Presidents of the Commission and the European Central Bank, and map out long-term EU policies.

Moreover, when assessing the role and influence of the EP, it should not be forgotten that the EU controls only a fraction of the total public spending in the EU area. Member states – and ultimately their parliaments – control the purse strings in European politics. Early in the twentieth century, parliamentary politics was predominantly about lawmaking. At the beginning of this century, however, parliamentary politics is very much about control over public spending. In the EU, this remains largely in the hands of the member states.

But European integration has certainly had an impact on member state parliaments. While the decision-making process has been gradually parliamentarised at the EU level, there is broad agreement among both integration scholars and legislative experts that the political dynamics of European integration tend to weaken the ability of national parliaments to control the executive branch. This occurs in two ways. First, the prevailing institutional democratic deficit favours the Council against national legislatures. The increased application of QMV in the Council weakens the ability of individual national parliaments to force governments to make *ex ante* commitments before making decisions at the European level. Second, the extensive involvement of national ministers and civil servants in drafting and implementing EU legislation insulates or marginalises national parliaments. The resulting information deficit reduces the ability of domestic MPs to control their governments in European matters. Not surprisingly, the overwhelming majority of both MPs from member state legislatures and MEPs think that national parliamentary control of EU legislation is weak and needs to be strengthened (Katz 1999a).

However, not all is gloom and doom for democracy in the member states. National legislatures have adapted strategically to European developments. All domestic parliaments now have European Affairs Committees for consulting and scrutinising the government in these matters (Bergman 1997; Raunio 1999). Because of this, in some policy areas, such as foreign policy and agriculture, at least some national parliamentarians now receive more information than they did when these issues were an exclusive matter for the member states (see for example Bergman and Damgaard 2000). However, not all member state parliaments are the same or have the same level of ambition with regard to institutionalising relations with the EP and the EU. For example, there is considerable variation in how domestic legislatures scrutinise what the government ministers do at Council meetings. Parliaments of the northern member countries subject their governments to tighter scrutiny than their southern counterparts. This variation is at least partly explained by public and party opinion on integration, but it also reflects traditional patterns of policy-making and implementation that vary considerably among the member states. The northern European member states tend to have a much larger share of EU critics, and they have national parliaments that are more inclined and better prepared to scrutinise EU proposals. This, in turn, is also associated with cross-national differences in member states' records as regards the implementation of EU legislation (Bergman 2000).[14]

Attempts have been made to create general and encompassing links between the EP and national parliaments. One such avenue is regular meetings between the Presidents/Speakers of all sixteen parliaments. Another is co-operation between the EP and the national EU Affairs Committees (within a framework known as COSAC). However, the lack of decision-making powers granted to these bodies and the vast differences in the status and roles of national parliaments effectively limits the impact of these arenas to symbolic value and the promotion of general networking. More importantly, some countries (such as Belgium and Germany) allow MEPs to be present when MPs in the European Affairs Committees deliberate on EU matters (Bergman 1997). This can be seen as an indication of how EU issues are beginning to transcend the traditional distinction between domestic issues and foreign policy in the minds of European politicians. It also points to the important role of political parties.

Political parties are often criticised for being out of touch with voters and for basing their existence on public subsidies (see for example Katz and Mair 1995). At the same time, they integrate the different steps of the constitutionally mandated chain of authority from voters to implementation. In Western Europe, political parties have been particularly important for linking voters to top-level decision-making (Müller 2000).

Despite this, the EP party groups and the umbrella organisations of political parties that exist on the European level have so far played only a marginal role in integrating European politics vertically. That is, they do not serve as a link connecting European voters to decision-making in Parliament. Instead, elections to the EP are still of 'second-order' to European voters (see the chapter by Mark Franklin in this volume), and political allegiances still rest predominately with national politics. Nevertheless, policy co-ordination and co-operation between MEPs and their national parties is likely to increase as a result of the EP's post-Amsterdam powers (Raunio 2000a). In fact, surveys carried out in 1990 and 1996 showed that MEPs are deeply embedded in their national political systems, with frequent contacts with voters, domestic party organisations and interest groups (Bowler and Farrell 1993; Katz 1999b). When asked about the influence of various actors on their decisions in the Parliament, MEPs viewed national parties as almost as influential as their EP group leadership (Katz 1999b).

Conclusion

The rapid constitutional evolution of the integration process has brought the EU closer to a system in which legislation is decided jointly by the Parliament, representing the people(s), and the Council, representing the member states. The Amsterdam Treaty made the co-decision procedure, in which the Council and the EP are equal partners, the main procedure for passing European legislation. The Parliament can now be categorised as a strong policy-influencing legislature. Free from the imperative of opposing or supporting the executive, one main function of the Parliament is to influence the content of EU legislation. The EP's policy-shaping nature is, in turn, reflected in the internal politics of the assembly, with emphasis on detailed legislative work and inter-group bargaining. The Parliament also actively tries to shape the EU policy agenda using both debates and resolutions.

Another of the EP's main functions, and one often stressed by the MEPs themselves, is to shape the future institutional solutions of the EU. MEPs have learned to play the game of institutional rule-setting quite well, and they try to create new practices that strengthen their position even without formal Treaty amendments. Unfortunately for the MEPs, the Parliament has no formal say over its position. National governments and parliaments are still the final gatekeepers with regard to decisions about the future of integration. This is something that most MEPs want to change. During the IGC held in 2000, the EP argued in favour of strengthening its role 'as the representatives of the peoples' in contrast to the Council that is said to represent 'the States' (European Parliament 2000). Items included on the EP's wish-list were, (a) that a small number of MEPs could be elected at the European level from an EU-wide constituency; (b) that the EP would get to pick the Commission President from a pool of Council candidates; (c) that the distinction between compulsory and non-compulsory expenditures be abolished; (d) that the Council use only qualified majority voting (i.e. never unanimity) under the co-decision procedure; and (e) that approval by the EP should be required for Treaty amendments. While the Treaty of Nice provided little in this direction, the EP is likely to try again at the next round of treaty negotiations.

Why have the member states been willing to grant the EP more powers? One reason is that member states in the Council have been more concerned with achieving other objectives than with trying to prevent an enhanced role for the Parliament. The member states have wanted to avoid getting bogged down in institutional power struggles that, in the worst case, would delay progress on other important objectives such as eastern enlargement. The EP agenda of streamlining decision-making procedures is also compatible with the Council's own ambition to secure efficient legislative procedures that function even after further EU enlargement. Moreover, having already granted the EP significant powers, it is increasingly difficult for the Council to ignore the EP's views with regard to reforming the EU institutional balance. Thus, the Parliament has found the necessary support from national governments to win new powers. The majority of member state governments have allied with the Parliament, either because they are ideologically in favour of supranational democracy and (EP) parliamentary accountability, or because the role of the EP has been a relatively minor issue on the IGC agenda.

In the long run, however, the negotiating position of the Parliament can be undermined by its failure to link with the peoples. Average turnout in Euro-elections has steadily fallen since the first elections held in 1979, and various public opinion surveys testify that only a small minority of EU citizens possesses even an elementary understanding of the powers and work of the Parliament. Another downside is that the work of the Parliament is arguably dominated by minor technical details. Electorates throughout the Union may find it hard to understand why well-paid MEPs spend valuable plenary time discussing the length of lorries and the size of strawberries. As a remedy, the future Parliament is perhaps likely to be characterised by more public position-taking and party competition than before. MEPs will probably continue to subject the internal proceedings of the Commission to tighter scrutiny than before, an issue that never fails to interest national media. Increased party competition is also something that *could* possibly be a remedy against the EU citizens' general lack of interest in the EP. Thus, paradoxically, at a time when political parties are often criticised domestically for being out of touch with voters, they are still the best hope for linking MEPs both to national parliamentary democracy and directly to the voters.

Acknowledgements

The authors gratefully acknowledge the Bank of Sweden Tercentenary Foundation's support to Torbjörn Bergman and the research programme on 'Constitutional Change and Parliamentary Democracy' (1996: 0801) which allowed us to work jointly on this chapter. We thank Magnus Blomgren, Camilla Sandström and Jeremy Richardson for very useful comments on a draft of this chapter. We are also thankful to Cynthia Kite for her help with language editing. Bergman wants to thank the Department of Political Science, University of California, San Diego for the Visiting Researcher program (1999/2000) during which this chapter was written.

Notes

1   The EP is therefore more than a 'quasi-parliament', which puts it in stark contrast to assemblies in other treaty-based international organisations. For example, Finkelstein (1998: 864) argues that the United Nations General Assembly is a quasi-parliament because it does not live up to the usual definition of a parliament, namely that it is not 'a body designed or empowered to enact laws for its constituents'.
2   In this chapter we use the terms 'nation-state', 'national' and 'domestic' parliament interchangeably. We also use 'parliaments' and 'legislatures' as synonyms.
3   A third problem is that it is also theoretically unclear what should be inferred from the general 'failure' of the EP to exercise its veto. The problem is sometimes referred to as the problem of observational equivalence (see for example Narud and Strøm 2000: 149). On the one hand, the

Parliament's failure to exercise its veto might signal its impotence. On the other hand, a priori, it could equally well represent a situation in which the Council did not make a decision contrary to the EP's interests because it is common knowledge that such a decision would be vetoed. This is a well-known problem in the analysis of parliaments and decision-making. Is the fact that parliamentary committees and parliaments almost always support government proposals a sign that they are weak relative to the government? After all, one could also argue that the parliament controls the government to such an extent that the cabinet proposes only what the parliament can accept in the first place.

4   Responding to critics who argue that Tsebelis overestimated the influence of the EP under the co-operation procedure and underestimated the influence of the Council, Tsebelis and Kalandrakis (1999) found that, empirically, the EP was successful in getting more than half of all its amendments passed in the environmental policy area. And contrary to what Tsebelis (1994) first assumed, amendments were accepted even more frequently in the first round of the legislative co-operation procedure than in the second round.

5   In fact, Tsebelis and Kalandrakis (1999: 145) argue that a comparison between the EP and the parliaments of the member states 'indicates a confusion too often present in both official EU texts as well as scholarly work'. This is because in many respects the role of the EP resembles a parliament in a separation-of-powers system (of the US type) more than a parliament in a parliamentary system (on this point see for example Coultrap 1999; Tsebelis and Garrett 1997). The analysis below also supports this thesis, but this does not preclude careful comparison with both types of systems.

6   The distribution of rapporteurships between political groups is a well-established bargaining process. For individual MEPs, rapporteurships offer the opportunity to gain recognition as policy experts, and certain representatives have managed during their tenure in the Parliament to almost monopolise reports on a particular issue area. The rapporteur system means that individual members, and not for example committee chairs, are key persons in the passage of individual pieces of legislation, especially as the rapporteur often has considerable informational advantage over the other members. Indeed, several MEPs with experience from national parliaments have argued that individual representatives wield more influence on legislation in the EP than in domestic parliaments. For example, Alan Donnelly, the former leader of the UK Labour Party's delegation, argued that 'individual members of the assembly now have considerably more power in terms of their direct legislative responsibilities than any member of a national parliament who does not hold a ministerial position.' (Alan Donnelly, 'Parliament Needs One Home to Win Respect It Deserves', *European Voice*, 27 January–2 February 2000, p. 14).

7   For detailed information on the passage of legislation in the Parliament under the various legislative procedures, see Corbett *et al.* (2000: 176–232).

8   The President of the EP is elected for two and a half years. In the 1989–99 Parliament the PES and EPP shared the Presidency. In the 1994–99 legislature, for example, the first President was Klaus Hänsch, a German social democrat, with José María Gil-Robles Gil-Delgado, a Spanish conservative, replacing him at mid-term in January 1997. Therefore it came as quite a surprise, at least for the social democrats, when a centre-right coalition elected Nicole Fontaine (EPP) as the new President in July 1999. Imitating the deals between EPP and PES, the EPP and ELDR came to an agreement, according to which the liberals would support Fontaine and the EPP would in turn back the candidacy of ELDR group leader Pat Cox at mid-term in January 2002.

9   The EP Rules of Procedure (14th edn, June 1999, Rule 29(2)) explicitly forbids the establishment of mono-national groups: 'A political group must comprise Members from more than one Member State. The minimum number of Members required to form a political group shall be twenty-three if they come from two Member States, eighteen if they come from three Member States and fourteen if they come from four or more Member States.'

10 For detailed information on such material and procedural rights, see the EP Rules of Procedure and Corbett *et al.* (2000: 81–6).

11 Such lack of stability is common, with whole national party delegations or individual MEPs switching from one group to another during the legislative term much more frequently than occurs at the national level. European elections are also difficult hurdles for the smaller groups, as a group may fail to meet the numerical criteria needed to gain group status should a key national party lose all or most of its seats (Bardi 1996).

12 Interestingly, MEPs are content with the present candidate selection mechanism. While about two-thirds of representatives favoured in 1996 a common electoral system, only just over 10% of MEPs supported transferring the right of candidate selection to Europarties (Wessels 1999).

13 MEPs are often accused of 'going native', that is, taking positions that are more pro-integrationist than those held by their constituents and national parties. However, while survey data confirms that MEPs are indeed more pro-European than the electorate, the same also applies to national MPs, and thus the problem is that the whole political elite, not just MEPs, are unrepresentative of their voters (see the chapters in Schmitt and Thomassen 1999). Moreover, survey data and voting behaviour analysis indicate that the impact of attitudinal socialisation, i.e. members adopting more pro-European postures through their work in the Parliament, seems to be limited (Franklin and Scarrow 1999; Scully 1998; Westlake 1994).

14 For more detailed information on parliamentary control of European legislation at the national level and links between the national parliaments and the EP, see for example the country chapters in Bergman and Damgaard (2000) and Norton (1996).

References

Andersen, S. and Eliasson, K. (1996) 'Introduction: Dilemmas, Contradictions and the Future of European Democracy', in S. Andersen and K. Eliasson (eds), *The European Union: How Democratic Is It?*, London: Sage, pp. 1–11.

Andeweg, R. (1995) 'The Reshaping of National Party Systems', *West European Politics* 18/3: 58–78.

Attinà, F. (1990) 'The Voting Behaviour of the European Parliament Members and the Problem of Europarties', *European Journal of Political Research* 18/4: 557–79.

Bardi, L. (1996) 'Transnational Trends in European Parties and the 1994 European Elections of the European Parliament', *Party Politics* 2/1: 99–113.

Bay Brzinski, J. (1995) 'Political Group Cohesion in the European Parliament, 1989–1994', in C. Rhodes and S. Mazey (eds), *The State of the European Union*, vol. 3: *Building a European Polity?*, Boulder: Lynne Rienner, pp. 135–58.

Bell, D. S. and Lord, C. (eds) (1998) *Transnational Parties in the European Union*, Aldershot: Ashgate.

Bergman, T. (1997) 'National Parliaments and EU Affairs Committees: Notes on Empirical Variation and Competing Explanations', *Journal of European Public Policy* 4/3: 373–87.

Bergman, T. (2000) 'The European Union as the Next Step of Delegation and Accountability', *European Journal of Political Research* 37/3: 415–29.

Bergman, T. and Damgaard, E. (eds) (2000) *Delegation and Accountability in European Integration: The Nordic Parliamentary Democracies and the European Union*, Journal of Legislative Studies 6/1 (special issue also available as a book, London: Frank Cass).

Blondel, J., Sinnott, R. and Svensson, P. (1998) *People and Parliament in the European Union: Participation, Democracy, and Legitimacy*, Oxford: Clarendon Press.

Bowler, S. and Farrell, D. M. (1993) 'Legislator Shirking and Voter Monitoring: Impacts of European Parliament Electoral Systems upon Legislator–Voter Relationships', *Journal of Common Market Studies* 31/1: 45–69.

Bowler, S. and Farrell, D. M. (1995) 'The Organising of the European Parliament: Committees, Specialisation and Co-ordination', *British Journal of Political Science* 25/2: 219–43.

Bowler, S. and Farrell, D. M. (1999) 'Parties and Party Discipline within the European Parliament: A Norms-Based Approach', in S. Bowler, D. M. Farrell and R. S. Katz (eds), *Party Discipline and Parliamentary Government*, Columbus: Ohio State University Press, pp. 208–22.

Chryssochoou, D. (1998) *Democracy in the European Union*, London: Tauris Academic Studies.

Corbett, R. (1998) *The European Parliament's Role in Closer EU Integration*, Basingstoke: Macmillan.

Corbett, R., Jacobs, F. and Shackleton, M. (2000) *The European Parliament*, 4th edn, London: John Harper.

Coultrap, J. (1999) 'From Parliamentarism to Pluralism: Models of Democracy and the European Union's "Democratic Deficit"', *Journal of Theoretical Politics* 11/1: 107–35.

Crombez, C. (1996) 'Legislative Procedures in the European Community', *British Journal of Political Science* 26/2: 199–228.

Damgaard, E. (1995) 'How Parties Control Committee Members', in H. Döring (ed.), *Parliaments and Majority Rule in Western Europe*, Frankfurt and New York: Campus and St Martin's Press, pp. 308–25.

Döring, H. (1995) 'Time as a Scarce Resource: Government Control of the Agenda', in H. Döring (ed.), *Parliaments and Majority Rule in Western Europe*, Frankfurt and New York: Campus and St Martin's Press, pp. 223–46.

Earnshaw, D. and Judge, D. (1996) 'From Co-operation to Co-decision: The European Parliament's Path to Legislative Power', in J. Richardson (ed.), *European Union: Power and Policy-making*, London: Routledge, pp. 96–126.

European Parliament (2000) *European Parliament Resolution containing the European Parliament's Proposals for the Intergovernmental Conference* (Minutes of 13/04/2000 – Provisional Edition), www2.europarl.eu.int/igc2000/offdoc/en/offdoc0_0.htm (accessed 15 May 2000).

Finkelstein, L. (1998) 'The United Nations General Assembly', in G. Kurian (ed.), *The World Encyclopedia of Parliaments and Legislatures*, vol. 2, Washington, DC: Congressional Quarterly Inc., pp. 864–72.

Franklin, M. N. and Scarrow, S. E. (1999) 'Making Europeans? The Socializing Power of the European Parliament', in R. S. Katz and B. Wessels (eds), *The European Parliament, the National Parliaments, and European Integration*, Oxford: Oxford University Press, pp. 45–60.

Hix, S. (1999a) 'Dimensions and Alignments in European Union Politics: Cognitive Constraints and Partisan Responses', *European Journal of Political Research* 35/1: 69–106.

Hix, S. (1999b) *The Political System of the European Union*, Basingstoke: Macmillan.

Hix, S. and Lord, C. (1997) *Political Parties in the European Union*, London: Macmillan.

Katz, R. S. (1999a) 'Representation, the Locus of Democratic Legitimation and the Role of the National Parliaments in the European Union', in R. S. Katz and B. Wessels, *The European Parliament, the National Parliaments, and European Integration*, Oxford: Oxford University Press, pp. 21–44.

Katz, R. S. (1999b) 'Role Orientations in Parliaments', in R. S. Katz and B. Wessels (eds), *The European Parliament, the National Parliaments, and European Integration*, Oxford: Oxford University Press, pp. 61–85.

Katz, R. S. and Mair, P. (1995) 'Changing Models of Party Organisation and Party Democracy', *Party Politics* 1/1: 5–28.

Katz, R. S. and Wessels, B. (eds) (1999) *The European Parliament, the National Parliaments, and European Integration*, Oxford: Oxford University Press.

Kreppel, A. (1999) 'What Affects the European Parliament's Legislative Influence? An Analysis of the Success of EP Amendments', *Journal of Common Market Studies* 37/3: 521–37.

Kreppel, A. (2000) 'Rules, Ideology and Coalition Formation in the European Parliament: Past, Present and Future', *European Union Politics* 1/3: 340–62.

Liebert, U. (1995) 'Parliamentary Lobby Regimes', in H. Döring (ed.), *Parliaments and Majority Rule in Western Europe*, Frankfurt and New York: Campus and St Martin's Press, pp. 407–47.

Lodge, J. (1996) 'The European Parliament', in S. Andersen and K. Eliasson (eds), *The European Union: How Democratic Is It?*, London: Sage, pp. 187–214.

Mattson, I. and Strøm, K. (1995) 'Parliamentary – Committees', in H. Döring (ed.), *Parliaments and Majority Rule in Western Europe*, Frankfurt and New York: Campus and St Martin's Press, pp. 249–307.

Maurer, A. (1999) *(Co-)Governing After Maastricht: The European Parliament's Institutional Performance 1994–1999*, study for the European Parliament, DG for Research.

Moser, P. (1996) 'The European Parliament as a Conditional Agenda Setter: What are the Conditions? A Critique of Tsebelis (1994)', *American Political Science Review* 90/4: 834–8.

Müller, W. C. (2000) 'Political Parties in Parliamentary Democracies: Making Delegation and Accountability Work', *European Journal of Political Research* 37/3: 309–33.

Narud, H. and Strøm, K. (2000) 'Adaptation without EU Membership: Norway and the European Economic Area', in T. Bergman and E. Damgaard (eds), *Delegation and Accountability in European Integration: The Nordic Parliamentary Democracies and the European Union*, *Journal of Legislative Studies* 6/1: 125–50 (special issue also available as a book, London: Frank Cass).

Newman, M. (1996) *Democracy, Sovereignty and the European Union*, New York: St Martin's Press.

Norton, P. (ed.) (1996) *National Parliaments and the European Union*, London: Frank Cass.

Norton, P. (ed.) (1998) *Parliaments and Governments in Western Europe*, London: Frank Cass.

Nugent, N. (1999) *The Government and Politics of the European Union*, 4th edn, Durham: Duke University Press.

Polsby, N. (1975) 'Legislatures', in N. Polsby and F. Greenstein (eds), *Handbook of Political Science: Governmental Institutions and Processes*, vol. 5, Reading, MA: Addison-Wesley, pp. 257–319.

Raunio, T. (1996) 'Parliamentary Questions in the European Parliament: Representation, Information, and Control', *Journal of Legislative Studies* 2/4: 356–82.

Raunio, T. (1997) *The European Perspective: Transnational Party Groups in the 1989–1994 European Parliament*, Aldershot: Ashgate.

Raunio, T. (1999) 'Always One Step Behind? National Legislatures and the European Union', *Government and Opposition* 34/2: 180–202.

Raunio, T. (2000a) 'Losing Independence or Finally Gaining Recognition? Contacts Between MEPs and National Parties', *Party Politics* 6/2: 211–23.

Raunio, T. (2000b) 'Second-rate Parties: Towards a Better Understanding of European Parliament's Party Groups', in K. Heidar and R. Koole (eds), *Parliamentary Party Groups in European Democracies: Political Parties Behind Closed Doors*, London: Routledge, pp. 231–47.

Rittberger, B. (2000) 'Impatient Legislators and New Issue Dimensions: A Critique of Garrett and Tsebelis' "Standard Version" of Legislative Politics', *Journal of European Public Policy* 7/4: 554–75.

Rush, M. (1998) 'Lobbying', in G. Kurian (ed.), *The World Encyclopedia of Parliaments and Legislatures*, Washington, DC: Congressional Quarterly Inc., vol. 2, pp. 810–14.

Schmitt, H. and Thomassen, J. (eds) (1999) *Political Representation and Legitimacy in the European Union*, Oxford: Oxford University Press.

Scully, R. M. (1997) 'The European Parliament and the Co-Decision Procedure: A Reassessment', *Journal of Legislative Studies* 3/3: 58–73.

Scully, R. M. (1998) 'MEPs and the Building of a "Parliamentary Europe"', *Journal of Legislative Studies* 4/3: 92–108.

Scully, R. M. (2000) 'Democracy, Legitimacy and the European Parliament', in M. G. Cowles and M. Smith (eds), *The State of the European Union*, vol. 5, Oxford: Oxford University Press, pp. 228–45.

Shackleton, M. (1998) 'The European Parliament's New Committees of Inquiry: Tiger or Paper Tiger', *Journal of Common Market Studies* 36/1: 115–30.

Shephard, M. P. (1999) 'The European Parliament: Getting the House in Order', in P. Norton (ed.), *Parliaments and Pressure Groups in Western Europe*, London: Frank Cass, pp. 145–66.

Tsebelis, G. (1994) 'The Power of the European Parliament as a Conditional Agenda Setter', *American Political Science Review* 88/1: 128–42.

Tsebelis, G. and Garrett, G. (1997) 'Agenda Setting, Vetoes, and the European Union's Co-decision Procedure', *Journal of Legislative Studies* 3/3: 74–92.

Tsebelis, G. and Garrett, G. (2000) 'Legislative Politics in the European Union', *European Union Politics* 1/1: 9–36.

Tsebelis, G. and Kalandrakis, A. (1999) 'The European Parliament and Environmental Legislation: The Case of Chemicals', *European Journal of Political Research* 36/1: 119–54.

Wessels, B. (1999) 'Institutional Change and the Future Political Order', in R. S. Katz and B. Wessels (eds), *The European Parliament, the National Parliaments, and European Integration*, Oxford: Oxford University Press, pp. 213–28.

Westlake, M. (1994) *Britain's Emerging Euro-Elite? The British in the Directly-Elected European Parliament, 1979–1992*, Aldershot: Dartmouth.

Westlake, M. (1998) 'The European Parliament's Emerging Powers of Appointment', *Journal of Common Market Studies* 36/3: 431–44.

Wurzel, R. (1999) 'The Role of the European Parliament: Interview with Ken Collins MEP', *Journal of Legislative Studies* 5/2: 1–23.

Chapter 7

The Council of Ministers

The politics of institutionalised intergovernmentalism

THOMAS CHRISTIANSEN

Introduction

Given its prominence in the decision-making process of the European Union, the Council of Ministers is strangely elusive: it is both a permanent institution and the frequent gathering of national ministers, representatives or officials. It is part of the EU's executive (with the European Commission) and part of the EU's legislature (with the European Parliament). The Council occupies the impressive Justus Lipsius buildings in the heart of the Brussels Euro-district, yet every other month ministerial meetings take place in Luxemburg. And while traditionally the Council has had the ultimate say on EU policies, it has also remained the most inscrutable: compared to either Commission or Parliament, the Council not only lacks transparency, but has positively embraced secrecy as part of its routine work practice. All this may make it difficult to generalise about the Council, but it also makes for an interesting institution.

At the most basic level, the Council provides for the formal representation of member states in the European Union. National ministers, attending Council meetings, arrive with positions derived from domestic preferences regarding the issues under consideration. Yet this almost immediately leads to one fundamental tension in the work of the Council: given that member state positions on policy-proposals are rarely ever identical, the Council is not simply an – or even *the* – decision-making organ of the Union, but also the main forum for negotiation in the EU.

The idea that a *single* institution should be the channel of the *multiplicity* of national interests is a subset of the wider 'unity in diversity' paradox of the European Union. The Council is generally regarded as an intergovernmental institution, making it the focus of those who regard the member states as being in ultimate control of the integration process. Yet – in part precisely because member states have sought to maintain a close hand in the running of the integration process – the Council itself has become increasingly institutionalised. By the end of the 1990s, the Council's Secretary-General was also acting as the EU's High Representative for Foreign Policy, and the Council Secretariat was becoming the hub of the EU's common foreign policy and military security bodies. Thus there has been increasing emphasis on what is *common* rather than on what is *intergovernmental* in the work of the Council – reinforcing a trend that had already been identified at the beginning of the 1990s (Wessels 1991). The Council may not (yet) be a supranational institution in its own right, but it certainly has moved on from being purely a site of decision-taking and the forum for bargaining among representatives of national governments for which it was originally conceived.

This chapter will examine the institutional evolution of the Council. In doing so it will look at the variety of institutional forms that together constitute the Council. The following sections discuss the politics of the Council as a meeting place of national and sectoral interests respectively. Given the expansion of the EU's agenda and the subsequent growth in the number of Councils, a special focus here will be the concerns about coherence and co-ordination in the Council's work. The next section looks at the role of the Presidency – an important institutional device which was, in part, a response to the problem of co-ordination – before turning to the European Council, which has become an increasingly important part of any Presidency's work programme. After this excursion into the Council's 'superstructure' follows a discussion of its 'underbelly' of committees and working groups, where much of the routine matter of Council decision-making takes place. A further section charts the role of the Council Secretariat, with particular emphasis on its recent rise to institutional prominence. The conclusion assesses the increasing institutionalisation of intergovernmentalism and the issues that this raises for the future evolution of the Council, and of the EU in general.

The Council of Ministers: institutionalising intergovernmentalism

The Council is the main, formal point for the representation of national interests in the EU policy process. There are, of course, numerous ways in which member states influence EU business informally, whether this is through the lobbying of the Commission in the pre-proposal stage of the legislative process, the impact of domestic party hierarchies on voting in the European Parliament (EP) or the use of comitology committees to oversee the implementation of policies. But in a formal, constitutional sense, the Council provides for the systematic involvement of member state representatives in almost any aspect of European integration.

Before going further in discussing the nature of the politics of the Council, it may be useful to distinguish between three different levels on which this interest representation occurs:

- Ministerial level: national ministers (or their representatives) meeting in the composition of different sectoral Councils.
- Heads of State and Government level: prime ministers and/or presidents meeting as the European Council.
- Administrative level: national officials and/or experts meeting in committees and working groups.

While subsequent sections will look at the latter two of these categories, this section will concentrate on the role played by national ministers in the Council. Nevertheless, it is important to recognise from the outset that the work of the Council is embedded within this wider institutional structure.

National ministers attend Council meetings in order to take decisions on the legislative proposals from the European Commission or amendments proposed by the EP. As implied above, they do so in a wide range of different sectoral Councils. What was initially the preserve of foreign ministers soon involved also ministers of agriculture and, with the widening of the EU's competences, an ever-wider range of national ministers. Indeed, given the particular nature of EU policies, there may well be more Councils than there are ministers in some national cabinets, requiring ministers to attend more than one type of Council. There is also a particular EU nomenclature for some of these meetings, including the two politically most significant ones: the General Affairs Council (composed of national foreign ministers) and the ECOFIN Council (composed of national economics and finance ministers).

Member states have two rather different, even opposing, rationales for representing their interests in the Council: on the one hand, individual governments will seek to see their policy preferences realised in decisions about EU policies, if necessary (and possible) against the opposition of other governments. In this respect one can distinguish between various 'cleavages' separating national governments (Hix 1999), including the Left/Right split, differences about the speed and reach of European integration and, with respect to the EU budget, the divide between net-contributors and net-recipients.

On the other hand, the Council also serves the collectivity of governments to advance a common interest in the intergovernmental aspects of European integration. This refers less to the substance of policy, and more to the structure of the Union and to questions like inter-institutional relations and the use of decision-making procedures. Even in this area, though, there is scope for disagreement among national positions, since some member states, in particular some of the smaller ones, may prefer more supranational solutions (like a strengthened role of the European Commission) to the more intergovernmentalist positions of others. Much of the defence of member states' structural interests takes place in the European Council and in Intergovernmental Conferences, but it also plays a part in routine policy-making. This has contributed to some of the particularities of the EU system of governance like the decentralised implementation of policies, the creation of independent agencies or the growth of comitology.

When looking at the politics of the Council, much depends on the decision-making procedure at force in any given area. The main distinction here is between 'unanimity' and 'qualified majority vote' (QMV). Unanimity requires all member states to agree on a single position in order to arrive at a decision – or else fail to move beyond the status quo. Here, a single member state can block a decision, which is why unanimity is the decisional mechanism applied to policy areas or issues which are sensitive and where some member state would not accept to be overruled.

The application of QMV, on the other hand, provides opportunities for coalition-building, confrontations between different camps and decision-taking against the votes of one or more member states, as long as the required majority agrees. The majority is 'qualified', because it is more than the simple or absolute majority of member states. Instead, in areas in which QMV applies, each member state has a weighted vote recognising its relative size. In 2000, the qualified majority required 62 votes out of a total of 87, and states' voting weights range from 10 for the four larger member states to 2 for Luxemburg – but these figures will change with the ratification of the Nice Treaty (see below) and with subsequent enlargements. This also goes to show that Council votes are hardly proportional to the population size of the member states: proportionality would give Germany 160 times – rather than five times – as much weight as Luxemburg, to point just to the most obvious discrepancy.

Despite this lack of proportionality: QMV is of fundamental significance as it constitutes the departure from the principle of 'one state, one vote' which characterises the nature of decision-making in traditional intergovernmental institutions. More important still is the acceptance of member states that legally binding decisions can be taken against their will, which is what giving up the national veto implies. That is why QMV can be seen as one of the defining features of the European Union. But it is also for this reason that the application of QMV has been highly controversial. While it had been written into the Rome Treaties, it was challenged by President de Gaulle when what he saw as core interests of France were being threatened by the integration process. Temporarily suspended by the 'Luxemburg Compromise' in 1966, the non-application of QMV has been blamed for its part in the decades of 'eurosclerosis' that followed. But QMV survived, not only in terms of a gradual return to the actual treaty provisions, but also through the expansion of its application in every instance of treaty reform since the Single European Act.

With the increased use of QMV, the weighting of votes has become more important, both in terms of member states' individual votes and in terms of the threshold for the achievement of a qualified majority. The matter is particularly thorny in the context of enlargements, as the arrival of new member states inevitably opens the issues of the relative weights not only of the new members, but also of the existing ones. This had already been a bone of contention in the preparation for the last enlargement and was only resolved through the so-called Ioannina compromise, in March 1994 – just before the EFTA enlargement (Hayes-Renshaw and Wallace 1997). But the issue of Council voting weights has required a more fundamental reform in view of the eastward expansion of the EU. During the negotiations of the Amsterdam Treaty the issue was tackled, but proved to be too divisive for agreement. In the process, it also became entangled with a different issue – the number of Commissioners – as the larger member states were holding out for compensation in the form of voting weights for agreeing to give up their second Commissioner post. In the event, solutions to both questions were postponed until the next round of treaty reform.

At the Intergovernmental Conference (IGC) in 2000, which was called explicitly to deal with these issues, discussions were again very difficult and initially very little progress was made. Given that the majority of countries seeking to join would be regarded as smaller member states, coming after the EFTA enlargement with countries of a similar population profile, the existing mechanism for allocating voting weights would exacerbate the disproportionality with respect to population numbers. Consequently, the pressure for re-weighting had become strong, especially from the larger member states (Best 2000). Some proposals even went further, suggesting the replacement of QMV with a system of 'double simple majorities', i.e. decisions would be adopted if the simple majority of countries and of their combined population numbers could be gathered in support (European Commission 2000). In the Treaty agreed at Nice in December 2000 the issue was resolved only after lengthy and highly acrimonious discussions.

In the end, member states agreed to revise the weighting of votes in the Council rather than introduce a completely new voting system. From 2005 onwards the total number of votes has been increased, allowing for a greater range of individual countries' voting weights. The effect, indeed the purpose, of this exercise has been to give greater weight to the larger member states. For the smaller countries, the resultant reduction in their voting weight was cause for considerable concern. This was especially true in cases where the pre-existing parity in voting power has been of symbolic as well as of material value in the proceedings of the Council. Thus it took long and hard negotiations until Belgium would agree to accept having one vote less than the Netherlands in the future. At the same time, there was insistence from France, in particular, that Germany should maintain a voting weight in line with the other 'big Four' states, despite the significant disparity in their respective population sizes. This position ultimately prevailed, but only after Germany succeeded in getting a further provision – or 'safety net' – accepted: according to the new rule QMV in the Council requires not only the threshold number of weighted votes (now 170 out of a total of 237 for current members), but also the support of member states totalling at least 62% of the EU population (Conference 2000). This additional 'population element' to Council voting privileges larger member states over smaller ones further, but it benefits Germany, with more than a quarter of the current EU population, in particular.

In a 'Declaration on the Enlargement of the EU' annexed to the Nice Treaty the rules for QMV have already been set for a Union of up to 27 members, including a table with the designated votes for all current accession states except Turkey. While this does provide for a greater degree of certainty and may help to smooth subsequent enlargement discussions, it also constitutes a *fait accompli* for the accession states. Given that the sliding scale of Council votes is skewed in favour of the existing member states, the legitimacy of these decisions may be questioned, especially in the applicant countries.

In its submission to the IGC 2000, the Commission had also argued for a 'simplification' of the decision-making procedure. The perceived need for simplification arises from the fact that the legislative process has been much more complex than the distinction between unanimity and QMV in Council voting implies. The number of different decision-making mechanisms has grown over time, as every instance of treaty reform added further procedures. Within the Council alone, there are also provisions for taking decisions by simple majorities and by two-thirds majorities, although these are used more rarely. Some decisions also require the simple majority of member states in addition to the qualified majority of Council votes. Waters are further muddied by the specific arrangements that have had to be found because of flexibility – opt-outs or instances of closer co-operation – where decisions are taken by a reduced number of member states, as is the case with respect to the single currency (Edwards and Philippart 1999).

Taking also into the account the different ways in which Council and EP interact in the legislative process – the consultation, co-operation, co-decision and assent procedures as well as the fact that the EP is *not* involved in some areas – the number of possible permutations had grown to some 14 different procedures pre-Nice (Hayes-Renshaw and Wallace 1997). It has been a situation that has certainly not aided the search for more transparency in the Council, and the general desire to bring the integration process closer to 'the people'. If it becomes impossible for anyone but the experts involved to understand the way in which the EU arrives at its decisions, then such a multiplicity of procedures becomes a normative concern and practical liability.

The proposal for simplification centred on harmonising the use of QMV and the co-decision procedure, so that all instances of QMV in the Council would imply co-decision with the EP, and vice versa. The implication of such a reform would have been a substantial expansion of both co-decision and QMV, and was therefore regarded as more than just simplification – it would strengthen the Parliament *vis-à-vis* the Council, and the collectivity of member states *vis-à-vis* individual states that may seek to block decisions (Kaila 2000). Inevitably, the discussions about the expansion of QMV turned out to be one of the most contentious issues in the IGC 2000, and the result was, in the light of the French presidency's ambitions, quite limited. QMV was extended mainly to procedural matters such as appointments of the President and members of the Commission, the Council Secretary-General, or members of the Court of Auditors, rather than to substantive policy areas. In the areas of taxation and social policy, where the French Presidency was pushing hard to make advances, member states maintained their veto. Revealingly, the rules for structural and cohesion fund decisions will only change to QMV in 2007, i.e. *after* the decisions about the next 5-year programme have been adopted. In this way, the member states currently benefiting from EU regional policy have managed to hold on to their veto in this sensitive area for funding up to 2012 – again a decision that has invited cynical comments from observers who are concerned about the equal treatment of existing and future member states.

In any case, the Nice decisions hardly amount to a 'simplification' of EU decision-making. If anything, matters have become even more complex and, for the general public, more obscure. Thus, member states have dutifully placed the demand for simplification of the treaties and greater transparency of EU decision-making on the agenda of the next IGC, envisaged for 2004. This IGC, and the 'post-Nice' process leading up to it, will also deal with a clearer delimitation of competences between member states and the Union, the role of national parliaments in the EU structure and the future status of the Charter of Fundamental Rights.

Beyond interstate relations: bureaucratic politics in the Council

The debates about re-weighting of votes and the extension of QMV reflect the expectation that the politics of the Council pitch member states against member states. Given the nature of the Council as the main forum for the representation of member state interests, that is justified. But the politics of the Council go beyond the confrontation between different member state positions. Indeed, the development of the Council – the expansion in the number of sectoral Councils – is a powerful illustration of the way in which the concept of 'national interest' needs to be unpacked when studying the politics of the European Union. Looking at the relationship between the various Councils reveals the differences in opinion not just between, but also within countries.

As mentioned above, the initial Council was composed of foreign ministers, whose meeting is termed the General Affairs Council. As the extension of Community competences has progressed, other Councils dealing with more specialised matters have been created. The more prominent among these are the Agriculture Council, the ECOFIN Council and the Internal Market Council, but there are now sectoral Councils in practically all areas of government activity, from civil protection to culture and education. Each of these Councils brings together the national ministers (or their representatives) who have domestic competence in the respective area. The frequency of their meetings differs according to the volume of EU decision-making in that sector. For example, foreign ministers or agriculture ministers hold monthly meetings, whereas transport ministers meet only four times a year.

The sectoral Councils provide a forum for the representation of diverse national interests in their respective areas, but they also have a wider significance as an arena for the socialisation of ministers who share a common interest in the management of the sector for which they are responsible domestically. This is a major departure from domestic politics, where meetings at ministerial level – usually in the cabinet – will pitch the ministers from different departments against one another. In a domestic cabinet meeting, the positions of, say, the transport, environment and budget ministers are bound to reflect the different sectoral and bureaucratic interests at play. The emergence of such interdepartmental differences would be expected from a bureaucratic politics perspective (Peters 1992).

In the Council, sectoral ministers, who 'at home' have to fight lonely battles in cabinet meetings, will find themselves in the company of colleagues from the other member states with often similar experiences from their domestic background. In addition, they all will share the knowledge of the subject-matter, are used to the lobbying from organised interests in the field and are familiar with the political and administrative problems in the area. It is on the basis of such a common background, that they meet in the context of the Council. If the right conditions are present, an *esprit de corps* may grow among them – participation in, for example, the Agriculture Council, will emphasise identification as the UK *Agriculture* Secretary as well as the *UK* Agriculture Secretary. In that sense, the Council fulfils a function not only in terms of the representation of national interests, but also in terms of the creation of transnational policy communities at the highest political level. This 'reverse dynamic' is even stronger at lower administrative levels, where bureaucratic interaction is more frequent, and where much of the routine decision-making takes place – a subject to which we will return below.

The development of a transnational sense of community in the Council will depend on numerous factors, including the length of time individual ministers spend in their jobs, the frequency and intensity of their meetings, the contentiousness of issues under discussion and the antagonism of domestically determined positions to be represented (Egeberg 1999). Socialisation is actively encouraged through the increasingly frequent recourse to 'informal' Councils – Council meetings which are organised by, and held in, the country holding the Presidency, rather than in the usual meeting rooms in Brussels or Luxembourg. It is a practice that originated among foreign ministers, who started in the mid-1970s to hold 'Gymnich-type meetings' in the context of European Political Co-operation. Foreign ministers extended this practice to the General Affairs Council, and it is now practised by all Councils, though with differing frequency. The rationale for holding such meetings is the expectation that a meeting conducted in an informal atmos-phere and without the pressure to take routine decisions permits a more relaxed discussion of the broader strategic issues and the general direction of policy. Initially conceived as meetings without a set agenda, they now provide an opportunity to address a specific issue in greater depth (Council of the European Union 1999). Often informal Councils conclude by espousing a certain vision for the development of EU policy in a given area.

The point to be made here is that the Council has to be regarded as more than simply the meeting place of national interests. It is also the meeting place of different sectoral and bureaucratic interests and thus exposes the complexity – and potential contradictions – subsumed by the concept of a 'national interest' (Lewis 2000). But if individual Councils do develop an *esprit de corps*, dividing lines between the various Councils are likely to emerge, in line with the observation about domestic bureaucratic politics made above. In institutional terms this means that there is also the potential for internal fragmentation and that co-ordination across the various sectoral Councils becomes an issue (Lipsius 1995). It is in this respect that the role of the General Affairs Council has been elevated, so that it stands above the sectoral Councils. If issues cannot be resolved, they can be referred to the GAC, though the crowded agenda there means that the potential for the resolution of the often highly technical issues of other Councils may be limited (Lipsius 1995). There are other mechanisms for co-ordinating the activity of the sprawling complex of Councils. These include the Presidency, the European Council, the work of contributory committees, in particular the Committee of Permanent Representatives, and the Council Secretariat. The following sections will look in more detail at the role these institutions play in the structure of the Council.

Member states as agenda-setters: the role of the Presidency

The Council's position as the key legislative institution of the Union implies a reactive role: it has to respond to the proposals made by the Commission and, increasingly, to the amendments proposed by the Parliament. That is why traditionally the Commission, and more recently the Parliament, rather than the Council, are regarded as the agenda-setters in the EU policy process. But there are a number of ways in which national governments have sought to regain control of, or at least play a part in, the setting of the Union's agenda. The most important mechanisms to be discussed here are developments linked to the Council: the EU Presidency and the European Council.

The Presidency started off as a seemingly functional innovation in the Council: to share among national administrations the task of organising Council business and chairing the various ministerial meetings and working groups (Westlake 1995). Every six months, one member state takes over this role, and ministers and officials chair any of the meetings that are convened during that period. Apart from allowing individual meetings at any level to run more smoothly, this also facilitates the continuity of negotiation and decision-making over time. The institution of the Presidency also permits a greater degree of both horizontal co-ordination (across the various sectoral Councils) and vertical co-ordination (between meetings of ministers, permanent representatives and national officials). The growing number of sectoral Councils is one reason why the Presidency has become more important over time: as more EU business is being debated and decided in a larger number of fora, there is greater potential for inconsistency and therefore greater demand for effective co-ordination (Wallace 1985).

Yet the Presidency is anything but an innocent functional creation. The institution of the Presidency is political not only because it affects the relationship between the individual member state, the collectivity of states and the EU institutions, but also because it is closely linked to the management of the EU's external affairs – arguably a key area of 'high politics', and one from which member states have long sought to exclude the more supranational institutions. Starting in the 1970s with the establishment of European Political Co-ordination and now in the context of the Common Foreign and Security Policy, the Presidency is responsible for the external representation of the EU's foreign policy positions. This is a delicate task, given the increasing visibility of the EU in world politics, and considering that it requires the state in question to handle foreign policy in a manner that is different from the execution of its national foreign policy. Both the nature of the issues, and the way in which these are handled, will be different from that country's conventional national foreign policy.

The nature of European foreign policy means that there is bound to be a tension between, on the one hand, the need to respond quickly to issues or crises as they happen, and, on the other, to maintain a process of inclusive consultation with all member states. Similar demands are present in other policy areas, putting great pressure on the government holding the Presidency. Therefore the Presidency not only constitutes a substantial administrative responsibility, but also involves high political profile and carries with it the accompanying risks and opportunities.

The establishment of a rotating Presidency among member states also reaffirms the role of national governments in the EU structure. In fact, in terms of the distinction of different types of interest representation made earlier, it emphasises the role of the *individual* country rather than the collectivity of member states. In that sense, the Presidency has become an important, albeit limited, counterweight to the loss of national autonomy in the EU generally, and in the Council in particular. Holding the Presidency permits the respective national government to prioritise certain issues during its term and to manage the agenda accordingly. For example, if the country holding the agenda is a southern or northern member state, it may want to push a specific geographical concern such as, respectively, the Euro-Mediterranean Partnership or the Northern Dimension. On the other hand, if the country holding the Presidency is a net contributor to the EU's budget, then it has a stronger interest in privileging budget reform in the setting of the agenda.

But this is no simple game of preferences. At any one time, the EU's agenda is influenced by numerous factors. Some are structurally or externally determined, especially since much of EU business is conducted through multi-annual programmes. This is true both for spending programmes like the structural funds and for regulatory programmes, for example in environmental or social policy. When such programmes need to be renegotiated, any Presidency will have to address these accordingly during its term.

Developments that are 'external' to the EU, for example the need to respond to the changes in Central and Eastern Europe through an accession strategy, will also impose themselves on the agenda of any country holding the Presidency. Other member states or actors like the Commission or foreign countries will also raise issues that the Presidency may be unable to ignore. Crucially, the Presidency is expected to act as an honest broker with regard to issues raised by other member states and will have to take these into account when constructing the agenda.

It is only within these limitations that the Presidency can emphasise – rather than impose – its own priorities in the setting of the agenda. In fact, the Presidency is very much a double-edged sword, precisely because of these limitations and the requirement to appear as an objective keeper of the common good (Wallace 1993). A Presidency which is seen to be abusing its agenda-setting role and its chairmanship in the pursuit of its own national interest will be ineffectual, and it may even be that it is easier to defend a certain position or push a specific interest when *not* holding the Presidency. In any case, holding the Presidency requires the member state in question to strike a fine balance between, on the one hand, the pursuit of a national agenda – which may have built up over a considerable period of time – and, on the other hand, the necessities of effective decision-making and agenda-management – which may override the national interest.

Beyond the rational calculation of interests, the Presidency also performs a powerful symbolic function: it confers upon the incumbent country a special role which permits the government to emphasise its specific understanding of the goals and the direction of the integration process. The Presidency unifies the European and the national identity of the state, enabling the government to pursue a discourse (and perhaps a European policy) which may at other times prove elusive. For domestic consumption, the image of a country holding the Presidency removes the potentially antagonistic perception which often regards the state as pitched against an external 'Europe'. In its place governments seek to put the image of a country that, while asserting its role and identity within the Union, works for the common good – an imagery that is accompanied by symbols, logos and slogans specifically designed for the occasion. In a wider sense, the Presidency also serves as a powerful symbol externally that European integration is driven by states, rather than being a process happening to them.

The term of the Presidency begins formally with the identification of a number of key themes at the outset of the term. These themes are part of a communication to the Council, European Parliament and the Commission – and the wider public – in the first week of the term, and form the basis of a more detailed work programme involving the various sectoral Councils over the coming six months. In addition to the prepared programme, the Presidency will be expected to lead the EU response to unexpected developments and crises, whether these are internal to the EU or part of its foreign policy. An effective Presidency therefore needs both a clear vision of what it seeks to achieve during its term and an ability to respond rapidly to the changing political circumstances of the day. Again, there is a balance to be struck between strong leadership and intensive consultation in order to ensure that all member states agree to, comply with and, if necessary, contribute to the policy that emerges from the deliberations in the Council.

In practical terms, the Presidency raises substantial resource issues for the country concerned. Setting the agenda and co-ordinating EU business across the range of sectoral Councils and administrative levels requires much preparation before, and constant attention during, the term. The greatest part of the pressure will be on the relevant sections in foreign ministries, prime ministers' offices and any other ministries that would usually perform a co-ordinating role in the domestic EU process. Staff in these departments will now be required also to relate regularly and systematically to their counterparts in other member states. Also the EU sections in sectoral ministries will be affected by their country holding the Presidency, as they will have to co-ordinate the discussions or negotiations with regard to dossiers falling into their area of competence. Another resource issue is the need to chair meetings of working groups, committees of Councils in Brussels: given that these meetings number in the hundreds over the term of any Presidency and imply preparation as well as physical presence, there is much demand on staff time at both ministerial and official level as well as a greater reliance on the assistance of the Council Secretariat (see below).

The resources of any country are stretched by the demands of the Presidency, but this has been an issue particularly for the smaller member states. For them, the combination of greater political responsibility and extraordinary demands on resources are especially challenging. On the other hand, more used to compromising national positions in the context of EU negotiations, smaller countries are more likely to avoid the temptation of overlaying the formal responsibilities of the Presidency with their own political priorities – something which has been a more obvious problem for the larger member states. In either case, the size of a member state matters for the conduct of the Presidency, both in terms of the resources of the administration and in terms of the political weight of the incumbent. That is one reason why in the determination of the sequence of countries holding the Presidency there has been a departure from the simple alphabetical rule that was in place until the accession of Spain and Portugal. A new sequence has been specifically written into the Treaty, in order to ensure a balance between larger and smaller member states (Westlake 1995).

Leadership from the top? The evolution of the European Council

It is also the responsibility of the Presidency to organise meetings away from hubs of Brussels and Luxembourg. Above, reference has already been made to informal Council meetings, but the Presidency is also responsible for running ministerial meetings with representatives of third countries, for example from the accession countries, or landmark conferences on topical aspects of the integration process. But the 'highlight' of any Presidency is the organisation of a summit meeting that originally was not contained in the founding treaties but has become one of the pivotal institutions of the EU: the European Council. What began in the 1970s first as extraordinary summits of prime ministers eventually became normalised as regular meetings of heads of state and government, hosted by the Presidency. With the passage of the Single European Act in 1985 the new institution, by then recognised as the European Council, was formally incorporated into the Treaty. At least twice a year, the European Council brings together the heads of state and of government – i.e. all prime ministers and the presidents of France and Finland – as well as the President of the Commission. While the European Council does not have a formal role in the legislative process, it plays an important part in the wider decision-making process of the Union.

Each Presidency holds at least one European Council meeting at the end of its term, in June or in December. Also because of this timing, but mainly due to the inherent significance of a meeting at the highest political level, the European Council functions as a stocktaking exercise for the Presidency – an opportunity for decision-makers as well as observers to see how much progress has been achieved with respect to the Presidency's work programme. Beyond stocktaking, the European Council has become a focal point of the decision-making process. Particularly in cases where there has been deadlock in the sectoral Council, and where the foreign ministers in the General Affairs Council have been equally unable to reach agreement. In this situation, the European Council can function as the arbiter of the last resort.

In contrast to the ministerial Council meetings, which have become routine matters in the EU policy process, the European Council remains a high profile event that can concentrate the minds of the decision-makers. The meeting in a unique geographical setting – frequently European Council meetings are held away from national capitals – the limited time-frame (usually only 48 hours) and the extraordinary attention from the international media all contribute to an atmosphere of expectation and a desire on the parts of governments to deliver results. The Presidency, in particular, will want to see *their* European Council meeting regarded as a success – which means prime ministers need to be seen taking decisions on the major issues. It is because of these particular dynamics of the European Council that it has on occasion given fresh impetus to specific issues or to the integration process at large. Especially with respect to the 'big issues', such as budget reform or enlargement, the European Council, rather than the Council of Ministers, has been the forum in which landmark decisions have been taken (Bulmer and Wessels 1987). Decision-making in the European Council has always required a consensus among member states; it will be interesting to see after Nice what effect the introduction of QMV for certain decisions will have for the dynamics of the European Council.

This is an interesting reversal of roles, since critics originally expected the European Council to be the more conservative player in the integration process (Sasse 1975; Wessels 1980). The initial expectation was that the meeting of heads of state and government would reassert national interests and reign in ministers who, in the course of frequent meetings in the Council, had been socialised into compromising too quickly domestically agreed positions in the search of EU-wide agreement. This may well be the case in certain instances, but the European Council has also seen vested sectoral interests being overridden at the highest political level. After all, it is at this level that package deals and trade-offs, these quintessential features of EU policy-making, are best constructed. And as it has become more difficult to strike such deals in the fragmented world of ministerial Councils, the European Council has increasingly performed this role.

In the 1990s, there has been a marked increase in the frequency of treaty reform, with three major revisions of the founding treaties contained in the Maastricht (1991), Amsterdam (1997) and Nice (2000) Treaties. Each of these treaties takes its name from the place at which the respective European Council met in order to take the final decisions and to sign the final act. This symbolises the significance of the Presidency for running – and concluding – the negotiation of Treaty reform. IGCs are mainly conducted at the level of senior officials representing the member states in weekly meetings, with participation also from the Commission and the European Parliament. There are regular meetings also of foreign ministers in order to provide political guidance, and any European Council meeting held during an IGC constitutes a forum to review the state of the negotiations. The European Council meeting which is to conclude the IGC and agree the draft treaty will largely be taken over by the need to reach agreement on the last remaining – often most controversial – aspects of that round of treaty reform.

The Presidency and the European Council are key institutions in the European Union: they reaffirm the role of individual countries and of the highest political level in the integration progress. As such, they have proved to be an integral part of a Euro-polity that is being constructed with, and by – not against – the member states. In practical terms, they both constitute mechanisms for co-ordination across the various areas of EU activity and provide the political leadership that may otherwise be missing in a Union of fifteen (or more) member states. And they offer opportunities for national governments, and for the collectivity of states, to influence the setting of the EU's agenda and to maintain control over the direction of EU policy. In that sense, they are aspects of the institutional structure which assists member states to balance the agenda-setting powers of the supranational institutions, in particular those of the European Commission.

Administrative integration: the committees and working groups of the Council

The Council's relationship with the Commission is often characterised as one of rivalry, with the Commission pushing for further integration, with the Council holding back and providing member states with a mechanism to hold the Commission in check. In reality, the situation is more complex, not only because the European Parliament is an increasingly potent player in a tripartite relationship, but also because both the Commission and the Council are internally more differentiated than these one-dimensional images suggest. Chapter 5 in this volume demonstrates the degree to which intergovernmental dynamics impinge on the work of the Commission (Christiansen 2001). The reverse can be said of the Council, where we can witness an accelerating trend towards a greater degree of institutionalisation.

The previous sections have emphasised the fluidity of Council business, with different ministers meeting in different places, guided by a Presidency that changes hands every six months. But the Council is a central institution of the European Union, with a physical presence in Brussels, an expanding number of permanent staff and a certain capacity for independent action. The building blocks of this institutionalisation of intergovernmentalism are, on the one hand, the structure of committee and working groups which do the preparatory work for the ministerial meetings, and, on the other hand, the Council Secretariat, which provides organisational, logistical and legal backup for the meetings of ministers and officials. This section and the next will look at each of these aspects of institutionalised intergovernmentalism in turn.

The institution 'Council of Ministers' extends well beyond the regular meetings of ministers. In fact, much of the legislative decision-making of the Council is done in committees and working groups which 'prepare' the ministerial meetings. With the expansion of the number of ministerial Councils, the number of committees and working groups has grown exponentially, as there will be numerous specialised committees and working groups working for each individual Council. It is at this administrative level that the bulk of the routine work of the Council is done. Council working groups are the first port of call for Commission proposals and, if applicable, EP amendments. Here, national officials who are familiar with the technical detail of the measure in question vet Commission proposals, EP amendments and the various opinions of representatives emerging in the meeting with a view to their respective domestic preferences.

At the heart of the Council's committee structure stands COREPER, the standing committee of permanent representatives. Its members are the member states' ambassadors to the EU, heading their countries' permanent representations in Brussels. As such, they fulfil a dual role which perfectly characterises the function of the Council's committee structure as the 'hinge' between member state and European Union more generally (Christiansen and Kirchner 2000). Permanent representatives are an important part of the individual countries' system of interest representation as well as being an integral part of the EU's decision-making process. Wearing the 'national hat', permanent representatives are gatekeepers of information and interests, working across the range of issues and regularly committing their member state to decisions in the process. Wearing their 'EU hat', they help to co-ordinate the work of the sectoral Councils and of more specialised working groups by preparing the agendas of Council and of European Council meetings (de Zwann 1995). Indeed, permanent representatives help to keep the agendas of ministers free for sensitive questions or the debate of politically contested issues, as COREPER itself takes decisions on matters which are considered routine business or on which member states can more easily find agreement.

COREPER stands at the top of a hierarchy of the numerous committees which form part of the Council of Ministers (Hayes-Renshaw and Wallace 1997). In fact, a distinction needs to be made between the committee of permanent representatives, who meet as COREPER II, and the meeting of their deputies, which is known as COREPER I. In addition, there are a number of specialised committees – for example, the Standing Committee on Agriculture – which are directly established by the Treaties, and which consist of senior officials from the ministries in the member states. Like the two COREPERs, these committees receive their workload from working groups made up of officials or experts from national or regional administrations, who have been evaluating and searching for agreement on the detailed policy proposals issued by the Commission. Within the allotted period, the working groups or specialised committees either reach agreement on the measure in question or else notify the permanent representatives of the need for further discussions. It is at this stage that administrative issues start to be overtaken by political considerations (Westlake 1995).

As items move up through the Council hierarchy, from working group to COREPER and eventually to ministerial meetings, they are being designated as either 'A' or 'B' points on the agendas of the respective meetings. An 'A' point implies that the issue has been settled at a lower level, and it will usually be passed as a matter of course at the higher level, with no further discussion required. Ministers, when meeting in the Council, will therefore concentrate on the 'B' points of the agenda, indicating the – much smaller – number of items on which officials or permanent representatives have not been able to reach agreement in their preparatory meetings.

A look at the committee structure of the Council demonstrates the degree of 'administrative interaction' between national and European levels (Wessels 1990). Every month, Council working groups and committees bring together thousands of officials from the ministries and regulatory authorities of the member states in Brussels. Here they interact not only with representatives from other member states, but also with officials from the Commission and the Council Secretariat who also participate in their meetings. In addition, they are likely to be the object of attention from lobbyists and organised interests who will seek to influence the decision-making process in one or the other direction. The volume and the intensity of these bureaucratic interactions has a number of significant consequences for European governance. First, it does establish a strong and permanent presence of member state administrations at the European level. This deserves emphasis, also because frequent references to the 'Brussels bureaucracy' in the media and in the political debate tend to imply that the corridors in Brussels are only populated by Commission officials. This is obviously misleading, as the number of national officials travelling to, or living in, Brussels in order to attend Council, committee and working group meetings is probably greater that the number of A-level officials in the Commission.

Second, in terms of the decision-making process, it is important to recognise administrative interaction in the Council as a two-way process. Interests are channelled from the national to the European level, but in the process officials are also becoming aware of the positions taken by other countries and will communicate these back to their superiors 'at home'. On the one hand, there are opportunities here for genuine problem-solving and the search for best practice, making the Council's committee structure an important site for the transnational integration of member state administrations (Lewis 2000). On the other hand, the participants in working group meetings will recognise the limits of any emerging consensus and – if politically acceptable – will adjust their negotiating position accordingly. At times, this can mean that negotiators, rather than receiving orders from the national capital as to what position they *should* take, end up telling their masters what position in a shifting debate they *can* take.

This recognition of the nature of the Council as an arena for two-way exchange, rather than a site of one-directional representation of national interests, is related to a further point about socialisation. This was already mentioned in the context of ministerial Councils. If anything, this dynamic effect of frequent interaction in transnational meetings is even more important at the administrative level. With party politics and media attention (normally) taken out of the equation, officials can concentrate on the technical necessities of the issue at hand. They will have to work within the confines of a politically circumscribed negotiating space, but within these limits there is much potential for collegiality and group dynamics. This includes not only the potential development of a common identity or the growth of an epistemic community, but also the opportunity for individual participants to influence the proceedings based on their knowledge, the strength of their argument or negotiating skills rather than purely on the political weight of their member state (Lewis 1998). That is why it is justified to look for the supranational rather than only the intergovernmental features in the system of Council working groups (Beyers and Dierckx 1998).

Towards 'actorness': the elevation of the Council Secretariat and the Secretary-General

Administrative interaction within the structure of the Council already demonstrates the difficulty in clearly distinguishing between supranational and intergovernmental dynamics of the European institutions. The picture becomes even more blurred if the Secretariat-General of the Council is entered into the equation. Here we have an institution whose original purpose was simply the logistical assistance of regular meetings of ministers and officials from the member states, but which has gone a long way towards developing into a political institution in its own right.

The core function of the Secretariat-General remains the support of the meetings of working groups, committees and ministers in the Council. This ranges from the provision of meeting space, via the taking of minutes and dissemination of agendas, supporting papers and minutes, to assistance through legal advice and research services. The Secretariat is the institutional memory of the Council, and as such is the ultimate guide to working methods, internal procedures and past practice. It is the legal and procedural know-how, in particular, which has helped the Secretariat to become a distinct player in the Council. In advising member states on the procedures by which decisions are taken, and on legal questions arising from the drafting of legislation, the Secretariat makes an important, albeit hidden, contribution to the decision-making process.

Beyond assistance to the Council generally, the Secretariat works in particular for, and with, the Presidency. In the preparation of meetings, but in particular in the drafting of joint opinions or legal documents afterwards, the Secretariat will assist the Presidency (Sherrington 2000). It is here that demands on the administrative resources of the member states, especially of smaller countries, are being counterbalanced by administrative support from the Secretariat. In such cases, when the member state holding the Presidency relies heavily on the services of the Secretariat, the two operate closely together, with the Secretariat rather than the national capital taking on an influential role in drafting minutes, agendas and legislation.

The Secretariat's role of assisting the Presidency with legal and procedural advice before, during and after meetings of national representatives is of political significance in the context of any important decision taken in the Council, but even more so in the course of an Intergovernmental Conference (Christiansen and Jørgensen 1998). Given the legal implications of any treaty change and the complexity of the existing constitutional arrangements, the expertise present in the Secretariat's legal service provides it with an important role in the process of negotiations (Hayes-Renshaw and Wallace 1997). Crucially, though, it depends on the attitude of the Presidency whether that potential is being realised or not: a strong Presidency with clear goals and an ability to manage the demands of the role effectively may not defer to the Secretariat's opinions. A weaker Presidency, on the other hand, may leave much of the work – and the opportunity to influence the direction of negotiations – in the hands of Secretariat officials.

If the Secretariat has a role in the EU's decision-making process, it may be worth asking what its interests are. A simple answer would point to the institutional interests of the Council, as the Secretariat is bound to benefit, or suffer, from any change in the Council's institutional standing. But the Secretariat's attitude to institutional reform may differ from one issue to another, and would also depend on (the nationality of) the officials involved. In general, though, it makes most sense to look at the Secretariat in relation to the European Commission. In the past, both institutions have been keen to take over wider responsibilities as the competences of the EU were being enlarged.

Against this background, the Secretariat has been remarkably successful to gain an executive role in the more intergovernmental policy areas of the Union, and in particular with respect to the development of the EU's common foreign, security and defence policies (Presidency of the European Union 1999). In doing so, the Secretariat has acquired new competences in representing the EU abroad. The European Commission, whose responsibilities in areas such as trade, development and humanitarian aid make it an important player in the management of the Union's external relations, is 'fully associated' with the CFSP. Through its President, the Commission also represents the EU at G8 summit meetings of major industrial powers. But the central institutions of EU diplomacy are now firmly located in the Secretariat, turning it into a new actor in the conduct of the EU's external relations.

The process began with the EPC Secretariat, which had been established outside the existing institutional framework of the Community, being integrated into the Council Secretariat through the Maastricht Treaty. After the addition of a 'Policy Planning Unit', the Secretariat also contains 'task forces' on the different geographical areas of CFSP activity as well as a Situation Centre for crisis management. Also attached to the Secretariat are the EU's observer mission in the former Yugoslavia and the growing number of Special Envoys appointed to co-ordinate EU policy to troubled regions like South-Eastern Europe, the Middle East and the African Central Lakes region.

Compared to the foreign policy machinery of states, this is still a very small administration, but through co-operation with the member states' diplomatic services and the Commission's network of representations in third countries there would be growing potential for effective joint action (*Financial Times* 2000). For much of its history, there has been a search for 'actorness' in the intergovernmental nature of CFSP, and the use of the Secretariat as the home of an emerging EU foreign policy bureaucracy is one answer to this aspiration. A further, far-reaching step has been the creation of the post of High Representative of the CFSP through the Amsterdam Treaty. This role of 'Mr CFSP' (or, as the case may be, 'Ms CFSP') has been added to the existing post of the Secretary-General, who heads the Secretariat.

Past Secretaries-General of the Council Secretariat were senior diplomats in one of the member states before taking up their job in Brussels, but the political significance of the post experienced a quantum leap with the appointment, in 1999, of Javier Solana. Before joining the Secretariat, Solana had been Foreign Minister in Spain and Secretary-General of NATO, and as such is regarded as a political 'heavyweight'. His responsibilities were further extended when, later in 1999, he was also appointed as Secretary-General of the Western European Union, signalling the strengthening links and the partial merger of this organisation with the Council. Solana's seniority together with his experience in foreign affairs and defence matters adds substantially to the actorness of the CFSP: now there is a central authority to communicate common positions, negotiate on the EU's behalf with third countries and oversee the growing number of EU missions and interventions in crisis regions. Nevertheless, the emphasis in judging the significance of this new post must be on the *potential* for enhancing the EU's foreign policy capabilities. Much still depends on the political will among member states – often lacking in the past – to agree to common positions and subsequently to comply with these.

Javier Solana's experience as NATO Secretary-General is significant also in the context of efforts to develop a dedicated EU role in defence matters. For decades, the 'security' aspect of CFSP had been treated sensitively in order to ensure that military issues would not appear on the agenda of the EU. This was in response both to internal constraints – the sensitivities of neutral or non-aligned member states – as well as to external relationships – the desire among most EU members to maintain a strong link with the USA in the framework of NATO. But in the late 1990s, in response to an Anglo-French initiative and in the wake of the Kosovo war, consensus was emerging among member states that the EU ought to have a military capability to conduct so-called 'Petersberg tasks' – military intervention in crisis areas for the purposes of peace-keeping, peace-enforcement or humanitarian assistance. The Helsinki Council in December 1999 spelt out the vision and the needs of such a military dimension of the EU. It implies not only the designation of up to 120,000 troops in the member states for use in EU-led operations, but also the build-up of military expertise in the EU's central institutions (Presidency of the European Union 1999). In order to achieve this, a number of political and military bodies have been convened within the Council (Presidency of the European Union 2000). In the future, the Council Secretariat will be the home not only of the EU's diplomatic centre, but also of its military staff – a development that raises new questions about the balance between transparency and secrecy (*The Guardian* 2000).

The emergence of the Council Secretariat as a political institution and the transformation of the Secretary-General into a significant player in the development of CFSP could be expected to exacerbate existing rivalries with the Commission, given that institution's own role in the area of external relations. In this context it is worth mentioning that the relationship between Chris Patten, the EU Commissioner for External Relations in the

Prodi Commission, and Javier Solana has, on the whole, been amiable and co-operative. Clearly, in the search for a coherent and effective conduct of the EU's foreign relations, encompassing external economic relations, humanitarian aid, CFSP and military intervention, co-operation between Commission and Council – both Secretariat and foreign ministers – is more important than ever. In this respect, there has only been limited experience since the changes effected by the Amsterdam Treaty. Their mutual dependence in managing the EU's external relations is encouraging and points to a stronger foreign policy partnership between Council Secretariat and Commission in the future – not quite the result that was to be expected from the long-standing efforts of member states to keep foreign policy matters out of the hands of supranational institutions.

Conclusions

The Council of Ministers operates on a number of different levels, and is embedded within a wider context of intergovernmental institutions. Its role remains central to European governance as the key channel for the representation of national and sectoral interests from the member states to the European Union. Interest representation has become more complex as the number of member states has grown, the range of issues has expanded and the negotiations involve questions of greater technical detail. In response to these developments, the number of sectoral Councils has multiplied and an extensive network of committees and working groups has evolved around the original meeting of foreign ministers which remains at the heart of the Council structure.

The expansion of competences and the growing number of arenas for deliberation in turn require greater co-ordination of Council business. In this respect, the Presidency and the European Council have become more important, but beyond co-ordination they have also provided welcome opportunities for member states to regain the initiative and a greater degree of control over the integration process.

But, as this chapter has sought to show, the evolution of the Council is also marked by some unexpected and arguably unintended consequences. Negotiations among ministers and officials is not just a one-way street of interest representation: frequent meetings and continuous deliberation among member state representatives also provide an environment for policy-learning, cultural exchange, socialisation and even the transformation of allegiances. As such, the Council structure constitutes an important site for the establishment or growth of policy networks and other channels of interest representation which cut across the member states.

Most recently, the Council Secretariat has witnessed a boost, as new foreign policy and military bodies have been created and its head has also been appointed as the EU's High Representative for the CFSP. In addition, the appointment of a senior politician from one of the larger member states to this new role confirms it as one of high political standing. The combined effect of these developments is that the Secretariat is being recognised as the core of the EU's ambitions in the diplomatic and security field. If these ambitions are being turned into reality, the Secretariat and the High Representative stand much to gain, but, given the past record of the EU in this field, there is also a case for caution. These are still very early days in the long-term endeavour to provide the EU with effective institutions for foreign policy and military intervention. From an institutional point of view it remains to be seen, in particular, whether the relationship between the Council Secretariat and the Commission evolves as one of partnership or rivalry in the management of the Union's external relations.

The strengthening of the Secretariat illustrates the trend towards a greater degree of institutionalisation in the Council more generally. It demonstrates the dilemma national governments face as they ask the EU to perform additional tasks while also seeking to maintain close control over their execution. It may be that, by transferring powers to the Secretariat and the committee structure, governments have prevented the Commission from gaining further powers. Yet, in the process the Council itself has become more of a supranational body and the conglomerate of institutions now involved in the making of EU policy has become ever more difficult to hold to account.

During the 1990s, institutionalised intergovernmentalism has found new ways of responding to the dilemmas of European governance. The prospect of enlargement and further treaty reform will interact with this long-term trend towards greater institutionalisation and demands a more serious effort at institutional reform than has been under-taken so far. Internal changes such as the reduction of the national veto and the external challenges of an enlarged European Union will test the effectiveness and the legitimacy of these institutions. There may be testing times ahead, but the experience so far shows that member states are willing and able to adapt the Council to the changing demands of its environment.

References

Best, E. (2000) 'The Debate about the Weighting of Votes: The Mis-Presentation of Representation?', in E. Best, M. Gray and A. Stubb (eds), *Rethinking the European Union* (Maastricht: European Institute of Public Administration), pp. 105–30.

Beyers, J. and Dierckx, G. (1998) 'The Working Groups of the Council of the European Union: Supranational or Integovernmental Negotiations', *Journal of Common Market Studies* 36/3: 289–319.

Bulmer, S. and Wessels, W. (1987) *The European Council: Decision-making in European Politics* (Basingstoke: Macmillan).

Christiansen, T. (2001) 'The European Commission: Administration in Turbulent Times', in J. J. Richardson (ed.), *The European Union: Power and Policy-making*, 2nd edn (London: Routledge), pp. 93–111.

Christiansen, T. and Jørgensen, K. E. (1998) 'Negotiating Treaty Reform in the European Union: The Role of the European Commission', *International Negotiation* 3/4: 435–52.

Christiansen, T. and Kirchner, E. (eds) (2000) *Committee Governance in the European Union* (Manchester: Manchester University Press).

Conference of the Representatives of the Governments of the Member States (2000), *Treaty of Nice* (Brussels).

Council of the European Union (1999) *An Effective Council for an Enlarged Union: Guidelines for Reform and Operational Recommendations* (Brussels).

de Zwann, J. (1995) *The Permanent Representatives Committee: Its Role in European Union Decision-Making* (Amsterdam: Elsevier).

Edwards, G. and Philippart, E. (1999) 'The Provisions on Closer Co-operation in the Treaty of Amsterdam', *Journal of Common Market Studies* 37/1: 87–108.

Egeberg, M. (1999) 'Transcending Intergovernmentalism: Identity and Role Perceptions of National Officials in EU Decision-making', *Journal of European Public Policy* 6/3: 456–74.

European Commission (2000) *Adapting the Institutions to Make a Success of Enlargement (COM(2000) 034)* (Brussels).

Financial Times (2000) 'EU Prepares to Streamline its Failing Diplomacy"', 4 September, p. 2.

Hayes-Renshaw, F. and Wallace, H. (1997) *The Council of Ministers* (London: Macmillan).

Hix, S. (1999) *The Political System of the European Union* (Basingstoke: Macmillan).

Kaila, H. (2000) 'Qualified-Majority Voting: The Key to Efficient Decision-making in the European Union', in E. Best, M. Gray, and A. Stubb (eds), *Rethinking the European Union* (Maastricht: European Institute of Public Administration), pp. 131–44.

Lewis, J. (1998) 'Is the Hard Bargaining Image of the Council Misleading? The Committee of Permanent Representatives and the Local Election Directive', *Journal of Common Market Studies* 36/4: 479–504.

Lewis, J. (2000) 'The Methods of Community in EU Decision-making and Adminstrative Rivalry in the Council's Infrastructure', *Journal of European Public Policy* 7/2: 261–89.

Lipsius, J. (1995) 'The 1996 IGC', *European Law Review* 20/3: 235–57.

Peters, G. (1992) 'Bureaucratic Politics in the European Community', in A. Sbragia (ed.), *Euro-Politics* (Washington, DC: The Brookings Institution).

Presidency of the European Union (1999) *Presidency Conclusions of the Helsinki European Council* (Brussels).

Presidency of the European Union (2000) *Presidency Report on Strengthening the Common European Security and Defence Policy to the Lisbon European Council* (Brussels).

Sasse, C. (1975) *Regierungen, Parlamente, Ministerrat: Entscheidungsprozesse in der Europäischen Gemeinschaft* (Bonn: Europa Union Verlag).

Sherrington, P. (2000) *The Council of Ministers: Political Authority in the European Union* (London: Pinter).

The Guardian (2000) 'Security Lapses in Brussels HQ Cast Doubt on EU Defence Plans', 19 February.

Wallace, H. (1985) 'The Presidency of the Council of Ministers of the European Community: Tasks and Evolution', in C. O. Nuallain (ed.), *The Presidency of the European Council of Ministers: Impacts and Implications for National Governments* (London: Croom Helm), pp. 1–21.

Wallace, H. (1993) 'A Critical Assessment of the Styles, Strategies and Achievements of the Two Presidencies', in E. Kirchner and A. Tsagkari (eds), *The EC Council Presidency: The Dutch and Luxembourg Presidencies* (London: UACES), pp. 45–51.

Wessels, W. (1980) *Der Europäische Rat* (Bonn: Europa Union Verlag).

Wessels, W. (1990) 'Administrative Interaction', in W. Wallace (ed.), *The Dynamics of European Integration* (London: Pinter), pp. 229–41.

Wessels, W. (1991) 'The EC Council: The Community's Decisionmaking Center', in R. O. Keohane and S. Hoffmann (eds), *The New European Community: Decisionmaking and Institutional Change* (Boulder, CO: Westview), pp. 133–54.

Westlake, M. (1995) *The Council of the European Union* (London: Catermill).

Chapter 8

The national co-ordination of European policy-making

Negotiating the quagmire

B. Guy Peters and Vincent Wright

Co-ordinating European Union policy-making confronts national governments with numerous and particularly difficult and distinctive problems. Some of these challenges are familiar to any government, given that co-ordination is a universal problem in government. All governments are attempting to reduce waste, improve services and ensure that there are no gaps in services. Membership in the European Union, however, places even greater demands on governments, and presents a range of new demands for policy coherence.

The purpose of this chapter is to examine the nature of co-ordination problems (in the first section); then, second, the apparatus which has been established at both the national and EU level to deal with co-ordinating; and, in the third section, the effectiveness of that apparatus. The argument of the chapter may be summarised brutally: (1) member states are acutely aware of co-ordination problems; (2) different mechanisms have been established to deal with those problems; (3) the effectiveness of those mechanisms differs widely both across the member states and according to the level (EU or national) and issue involved; (4) effectiveness cannot be divorced from the ambitions of, and the constraints upon, the member states; and (5) policy effectiveness does not necessarily flow from co-ordination effectiveness, and weaknesses of co-ordination may even be highly functional.

The quagmire: EU co-ordination policy

Co-ordinating any form of policy-making at national level is already problem-ridden. At the EU level those problems become acute. The first problem lies in the very concept of co-ordination. The public policy literature distinguishes between anticipatory, active and reactive, between formal and informal, between vertical and horizontal, between negative and positive and between policy and procedural (ensuring the respect for due process) forms of co-ordination, while recognising that the distinctions are singularly blurred in practice. The literature also generally fails to provide a framework which links the various forms of co-ordination. In fact, nation-states have an entire repertoire of co-ordinating activities available to them, with the mix varying according to the member state, and these can be applied to EU co-ordination as readily as to other policy concerns.

More importantly, it is not always clear what outcomes are being sought by attempts at policy co-ordination. At a minimum this activity may imply an attempt to avoid particular mishaps or fiascos, or a wish 'not to impede, frustrate or negate one another's activities' (Metcalfe 1987). At the other end of the spectrum, co-ordination involves a desire for overall steering for government and, as such, is persistent, generalised and purposeful. However, most co-ordination activities fall between these two extremes. Selznick, in a classic work (Selznick 1957), identifies four functions of institutional leadership which provide a useful clue about the goals of co-ordination. These functions are:

- the definition of an institutional mission and role (the 'creative task of setting goals');
- the institutional embodiment of purpose (the capacity 'to build policy into an organisation's social structure');
- the defence of institutional integrity ('maintaining values and institutional identity');
- the ordering of internal conflict ('reconciling the struggle between competing interests').

Clearly, the co-ordination objectives of the member states of the Union vary considerably, depending on the mix of ideological ambition, institutional capacity and political constraints – a point to which we will return.

The second set of complications relates to the EU policy chain which stretches considerably co-ordination requirements. In the first place, the EU is distinctive among international organisations in locking its members into a continuous policy-making process of both an active and reactive nature. The co-ordination chain extends from that existing within each ministry to interministerial co-ordination (of both a vertical and horizontal nature) at the domestic level, to co-ordinating the domestic–EU interface, to co-ordinating within Brussels (Kassim *et al.* 2000). Success depends on a country's capacity to co-ordinate across the extended policy chain (the case of Britain for the 1986 subsidies to shipbuilding directive) (Siedentopf and Ziller 1988: 198).

Second, the various levels of co-ordination may be usefully distinguished for analytical purposes but, in practice, they intertwine in constant fashion, creating a highly unstable policy environment. The impact of this interaction among levels of co-ordination may be seen in a number of ways. Thus, the administration of Brussels bears the imprint of the structures and their functioning in several member states, but these latter administrations have been forced into reforming personnel management and into organisational modernisation, experimentation and innovation by membership of the Union (Debbasch 1988; Gomez Fuentes 1986): institutions are created and then sometimes disbanded (the Irish cabinet subcommittee of 1973 to 1977 is an example), or they have their competencies expanded or contracted (the history of the French SGCI, the centralising body responsible for co-ordinating EU policy, is revealing in this respect (Menon 2000)); the balance of power may shift (often between the Economics or Finance Ministry and the Foreign Office, with the Ministry or Junior Ministry for European Affairs being squeezed between the two, depending on the prevailing political climate). The ricochet effect between national and EU levels is constant, and means that EU policy-making takes place in an unsettled environment – and one which is further destabilised by internationalisation, technological change, privatisation, liberalisation and new public management reform programmes (Wright 1994).

The second impact of the constant interaction of domestic and EU policy-making may be seen in the need to be sensitive to the co-ordinating requirements at *both* levels and those requirements may be conflicting. As will be noted later, a first-class integrated national machine – such as that of the British – may suffer from inflexibility and occasional aversion to accommodation and coalition-building, which may lead to miscalculations and policy failures in Brussels (Ludlow 1993). A third indication of the intimate and complex relationship between national and EU policy-making is well known: constraints at one level may be transformed into opportunities at the other. National bargaining positions in Brussels may be reinforced, by invoking 'problems back home' while essential but unpalatable politics (notably in the area of industrial restructuring) are imposed on domestic constituencies by governments which readily finger Brussels as the real culprit.[1] The Maastricht convergence criteria have been crucial in strengthening national governments against interest groups favouring spending. Finally, the impact for co-ordinators of the national–EU interaction may be seen in the changes it has brought about in the leverage of individual actors (powerful regions, courts, central banks, legislatures) and in the reshaping of policy networks linking interests, Brussels and the state (Goetz 1995; Mazey and Richardson 1993; Schmidt 1995).

The third major set of complications springs from the nature of the European Union, which presents distinctive difficulties for national co-ordinators. It might be argued that some of these difficulties are present at national level and are merely accentuated at EU level. Thus, managing the problems of fragmentation, sectoralisation, and policy interdependencies is not peculiar to Brussels, but the extent and nature of these problems in Brussels is of a different order from that prevailing in the member states. Thus, the degree of sectoralisation is such that it is often difficult to discern a clear national interest (Snyder 1990: 60), or the sectoral requirements of national actors may clash with their stated preferences (Peterson 1991: 271; Paterson and Whilson 1987). Similarly, co-ordinators at both national and EU level are confronted with different forms of co-ordination – negative and positive – and also with different policy types. It may be agreed that both national and EU-level co-ordinators have to contend with regulatory, redistributive and distributive policy types, involving different actors, different institutional procedures and different bargaining requirements (Pollack 1994). Both levels also deal with routine as well as emergency situations. Both levels, finally, are involved in 'history-making' as well as low policy-making. However, the differences lie in the periodic bursts at EU level of 'polity-level bargaining' over major systemic and constitutional issues – which is not the case in the majority of member states – and, perhaps more important – in the fact that discussions over low politics are sometimes highly emotional and politicised when systemic or constitutional implications issues are suspected to exist within these seemingly mundane issues.

There are several other distinctive features of the EU regime which singularly complicate the life of national co-ordinators. They may be summarised as follows:

The structural ambivalence of EU decision-making. The EU combines elements of an incipient federation, a supranational body, an intergovernmental bargaining arena and an international regime (Sbragia 1994). It is treaty-based yet displays the features of a putative constitutionalism. Depending on the pillar involved, negotiations may be closed and secret, based on non-public bargaining principles rooted in concepts of classical international law between states, or they may be pluralistic and transparent as the result of the development of the Union into an arena of interest articulation and aggregation. Decisions are both international treaties and contracts and normal binding legislative acts. To understand the Union we need the tools of both international relations and comparative politics (Hix 1998). The ambivalence of the Union touches all aspects of its institutions – the lack of separation of powers between the legislature and executive functions, which has important legal ramifications; the role of the Commission, which oscillates between policy entrepreneurship and leadership (Cram 1993) and passive spectatorship, and which combines a capacity to control the agenda with managerial weakness and inadequate expertise (Sutherland 1993; Hay 1989); the constant interpenetration of national officials, elected officials (at EU, national and local levels) and Commission officials, leading to the blurring of identities, loyalties and responsibilities.

The changing size of the Union with successive enlargements, which has an immediate and radical impact on the task of co-ordinators. These problems in co-ordination may be exacerbated as countries of Eastern and Central Europe become members, bringing with them different political traditions and economic circumstances.

The evolving agenda of the EU, which, for a variety of reasons (intergovernmental bargains, functional spillover, side payments) has expanded in scope, variety, depth and political saliency. Co-ordination was clearly much easier when the agenda was restricted to customs union, parts of energy policy, competition policy, agriculture and commercial policy. Matters are further complicated by the fact that some countries have opted out (although generally not entirely) of some areas, and that the political saliency of a particular issue may differ widely across the member states: witness, for instance, the anger of the British at proposals to increase the minimum meat content in sausages to a level that any self-respecting Frenchman or Italian would have found unacceptably low, or the ironic fury of the British, who had tolerated years of travel with British Rail but who amaze their continental partners by organising mass pickets against the 'inhuman' transport of live animals.

The constantly changing nature of the EU means not only that more sectors involving more actors must be co-ordinated, it also deprives national co-ordinators of two powerful weapons of public policy. The first is a reasonably settled 'assumptive world' – a set of historically rooted operational codes and assumptions about the conception of 'good' or appropriate policy; good policy within Europe may be very different from that in the national tradition. The second is path dependency based on policy continuity over a long period of time. Both introduce essential elements of predictability and constraint into national policy-making, thus reducing the requirements of co-ordination (Dror 1975).

The lack of control over large areas of agenda-setting: Brussels is a highly fragmented universe, characterised by a proliferation of policy advocates and policy entrepreneurs. It is penetrated by lobbies and interests of a territorial as well as sectoral nature whose links with their nation-state are being loosened or redefined (if not entirely cut) (Grant 1993; Peterson 1992; McLaughlin *et al.* 1992; Sandholtz and Zysman 1989; Peters, this volume); the market for policy ideas is wider and more dynamic than in the member states. Managing policy initiatives and innovations is difficult because of the lack of 'negotiated order' structured around well-established and reasonably stable policy networks (Mazey and Richardson 1993: 22–3). This does not mean, of course, that member states are powerless in agenda-setting. Indeed, they are the most active policy entrepreneurs in the European Union and are the invariable source or channel of directives. However, nation-states at domestic level shape the agenda by establishing the general framing document (by way of a White Paper) for proposed legislation to which other actors react, and this document generally remains intact, with minor amendments. However, a Commission proposal, often inspired by a member state, can be mauled out of all recognition (sometimes by other states) as it lumbers its way through the complex processes of consultation. Finally, part of the agenda of the EU is shaped outside the arena of Brussels by member states (notably Germany and France) striking deals in diplomatic negotiations. These deals affect not only history-making decisions, but traditional sectoral policies. For instance, the important Company Accounts Directive of 1978 was carefully prepared by the Germans, who assiduously visited other national capitals before placing the proposal on the EU agenda (Siedentopf and Ziller 1988: 29).

The institutional organisational density, complexity and fluidity of Brussels. Brussels is a decisional maze which encompasses the independent organisation of the Community as well as the intergovernmental bodies which interact through a complex web of *ad hoc* and permanent committees, subcommittees and working groups. These committees are largely responsible for the mass of micro-level sectoral decisions (which are then formally accepted by the competent authority) and they are interwoven with a set of overlapping bargaining networks. Brussels is truly an overcrowded policy arena. It is also an arena full of latecomers (the Court of Accounts goes back only to 1975 and European agencies continue to be created (Majone 1998)), and where authority relations are sometimes ill-defined (for example, between the institutions of political co-operation and of COREPER and between regulatory bodies such as Eurofed, the European Environment Agency, the Agency for Pharmaceutical Products, and the corresponding Directorates-General) and fluid. Power may shift between Council and Commission, and with the development of the Union, Parliament may become a more significant player (Cassese and della Cananea 1992; Lequesne 1993). In the same policy sector authority may switch between different bodies (Swinbank 1989) or may be transferred to a new body such as an *ad hoc* working party or an official task force created by COREPER. The influence of the Presidency of the Commission and of certain Directorates-General (notably ex DG IV, now DG Competition) has waxed and waned according to the policy climate and the personality of the incumbents.

The complexity and fluidity of procedures, particularly since the Single Europe Act and Maastricht. The complexity may be seen in the decision-making procedures of the Commission, which sometimes acts collegially, sometimes individually, and, on occasions, by a group of Commissioners. The constant procedural changes include the co-operation procedure which has drawn the Parliament into the early stages of some policy processes, the extension of the use of QMV and an increase in the number of specific procedures (for economic, monetary and foreign affairs, for justice, and for internal affairs). If one combines the various voting methods of the Council with the different forms of participation by the Parliament, it is possible to detect no fewer than twenty-five distinct *formal* procedures for making decisions in the EU (with many more informal differences). Now, the power of institutions clearly varies according to the procedures invoked, and different decision rules generate the need for different co-ordinating mechanisms and styles. They also engender different outcomes: unanimity rules slowed down the adoption of regulatory and distributional policies by the respective sectoral councils, while QMV accelerated the pace of acceptance of the harmonising directives for the open market (Pollack 1994: 140–1).

In this absence of a stable and generalised system of decision-making, the institution to be targeted by national co-ordinators differs according to the sector and the issue (Ziller 1993: 243), and perhaps even the individual nation. To complicate matters further, there are unwritten codes concerning the use of the national veto, and the understanding that significant minorities cannot be ignored or overruled.

The essential requirement of coalition-building, which is much more difficult than at the domestic level. In the unstable policy environment of Brussels, alliance-building is unpredictable and time-consuming. This is not to deny that some coalitions may be emerging – north versus south (the so-called Club Med countries) as one of the consequences of successive enlargements; free-marketeers versus *dirigistes* and protectionists (on issues such as the liberalisation of civil aviation, energy and telecommunications, or state aid to ailing national enterprises); budget expanders versus budget restrictors (Guerivière 1992). Yet the cleavages which shape the coalitions are often cross-cutting, and run *within* national delegations. Thus, Agriculture Ministers have a tendency to oppose their own national Finance Ministers. Furthermore, patterns of domestic alliance-building are not always reproduced in Brussels. For instance, the German Transport Ministry does not share its British counterpart's sympathy for the national road-users lobby. Unstable coalitions are, therefore, inevitable in a world of sectoral segmentation, of log-rolling within and across sectors, of issue-linking, of side payments and of package dealing (Héritier 1999). The (often necessary) opacity of some coalition-building is also a source of difficulty for co-ordinators, since it gives rise to information barriers (Weber and Wiesmeth 1991). These problems are compounded when the deals are struck outside Brussels through traditional diplomatic channels.

The weakness or the absence of certain official channels of co-ordination which are present at the national level. At the national level, unofficial channels – of co-ordination policy networks, political parties, professional networks, personalised clans – often compensate for weak official networks. This is much less the case in Brussels. Unofficial channels, in the form of nationally organised networks that link the various institutions of the Union do exist in Brussels. But they are often ill-structured and unreliable. Moreover, path dependency and referential frameworks which reduce the scope of required co-ordination and which provide systemic ballast and predictability are also weak in some sectors of EU policy, especially as the Union expands its range of policy concerns. Furthermore, effective political parties and settled sectoral professional networks – powerful agents of co-ordination – are weaker and more divided in Brussels. Professional organisations tend to be less well-organised on a Europe-wide basis and may have very different ideas about best practice. Indeed, it might be argued that the problem of distinctive and even competing sectoral logics and cultures is exacerbated at EU level (Bellier 1994; Scharpf 1988).

The problem of administrative mismatch. This problem exists at three levels. First, a particular item on the EU agenda may be co-ordinated by different national ministries shaped by different needs and cultures – insurance policy is generally dealt with by the DTI in Britain but by the Finance Ministry in France (Siedentopf and Ziller 1988: 28–9). There is some evidence of countries altering ministerial structures to conform to the pattern of Brussels DGs, but this has not yet gone far (Mueller 2000). Second, the structure and the functioning of the administration of Brussels bear all the hallmarks of a multinational mongrel, having absorbed or been directly influenced by the practices of several states. Parts of it inevitably fit badly with the administrative organisation and culture of certain member states (Bodiguel 1995; Dubouis 1975; Rideau 1987; Jamar and Wessels 1985; Cassese and Franchini 1994). Finally, there is the problem of the divorce between, on the one hand, the initiatory, agenda-setting and formalisation stages of Brussels decision-making, and, on the other, the process of implementation. The problem exists particularly in Brussels because the Commission is entirely dependent, for implementation, on member states which themselves suffer from implementation problems: the policy chain is thus lengthened among weak links.

The difference in the range and type of skills, styles and resources required to co-ordinate at national and at EU level: some skills and resources may be similar (legal, technical, administrative and linguistic expertise is an obvious example), but co-ordinating in the quagmire of Brussels may also call for a type of co-ordination which not only is different from that prevalent at national level but may even be in conflict with it. This is a point which is explored at greater length in the following section.

The instruments of co-ordination

Domestic co-ordination of EU policy involves more than negotiating with one's own side to reconcile internal differences, to clarify objectives and priorities and to discuss strategies and tactics (Metcalfe 1987: 277). It also requires negotiating with shifting constellations of actors over very different issues at very different levels. And it involves the transmission to the country's representatives in Brussels of a reasonably coherent version of the negotiated compromises.

Four major conclusions emerge from a study of the domestic instruments of European policy co-ordination:

- major political and constitutional EU issues are increasingly dealt with by the heads of government aided by the Foreign Minister and the Finance Minister;
- the formal link between the domestic capital and Brussels is now generally assured either by the country's Foreign Affairs Ministry or by its Finance or Economics Ministry – or by both;
- most ministries in all member states have adjusted their internal organisations to the requirements of European policy-making;
- in spite of some emulation and convergence, the nature of domestic co-ordination of European affairs varies widely across the member states. There are marked differences in the ambitions of co-ordination and in the instruments used at the domestic level.

(Kassim *et al.* 2000)

Highly politicised and major constitutional issues at EU level are co-ordinated at core executive level, generally by the head of government in close consultation with the Foreign Minister and the Finance Minister. In France, it has generally been the President who has dictated major policy ambitions. It was President de Gaulle who fathered the Fouchet Plan and the Luxemburg compromise, and who blocked enlargement in 1964 and 1967. It was his successor, Pompidou, who lifted the French veto on enlargement, and it was Giscard d'Estaing who took the French decision on direct elections to the European Parliament, and who powerfully contributed to the creation of the European Council. The Socialist government's decision to remain in the EMS was taken by François Mitterrand, who also played a key role in resolving the problem of the British budgetary contribution. His hand could be seen in most of the major constitutional developments in the EU in the 1980s. During the first period of *cohabitation* Mitterrand had to share power with Prime Minister Chirac (who installed a diplomatic cell at Matignon), and during his terminal illness at the end of the second period of *cohabitation*, his influence in European affairs was largely symbolic.

Successive German Chancellors have also had a major constitutional role in the construction of Europe – from the early influence of Adenauer to the more recent roles of Schmidt and Kohl in the creation of the European Council, the launching and consolidation of monetary union and in the 'relaunching of the EC' in the 1980s. Less glorious, but no less significant, has been the role of British Prime Ministers, who have frequently imposed their wishes on a hapless and unhappy Foreign Office. Equally, there is little doubt that Gonzales and Papandreou defined the main lines of their countries' responses to major high-politics decisions in the EU.

It should be noted, however, that the Prime Minister is not always free to pursue his or her own agenda. This is most notably the case in The Netherlands and Denmark (Peterson 2000), where all ministers enjoy equal autonomy and status, and in Belgium, where the Prime Minister has frequently to contend with the conflicting and competing demands of the representatives of Flanders and Wallonia. In most countries, heads of government have to co-operate closely, on major EU constitutional issues, with their Foreign Ministers and their Finance Ministers – a lesson that even Prime Minister Thatcher was reluctantly obliged to learn.

The second major conclusion is that, increasingly, the co-ordinating link between the domestic capital and Brussels is being formally assumed by the Foreign Ministry. Throughout Europe, attempts are being made by member states to transmit a reasonably coherent message to their representatives in Brussels. This has involved the administrative reorganisation of several Foreign Ministries. Thus, in May 1993, the German Foreign Ministry created a new division which merged the co-ordinating tasks of previously separate units. Nevertheless, the precise nature of the co-ordinating link provided by the Foreign Ministry differs across countries: in some countries it attempts to co-ordinate policies before transmitting them to Brussels, while in others – notably Britain and France – it tends to convey policies co-ordinated by other bodies (in which it is represented). It should also be noted that in several countries – Germany and Greece, for example – there are competing co-ordinating channels, generally in the form of the Finance or Economic Affairs ministry, although the Foreign Affairs ministries tend to be winning in these internal struggles.

Finally, the increasing trend towards centralising the link to Brussels does not preclude the widespread practice of direct linkage between sectoral ministries and their counterparts in Brussels. Some empirical evidence demonstrates that the central co-ordinators often are not even aware of the connections between the sectoral ministries and their counterparts in Brussels, and hence have no opportunity for co-ordination (Mueller 2000). Indeed, paradoxically, both centralised co-ordination and the countervailing phenomenon of sectoral segmentation (each a response to the other) appear to be on the increase.

The accelerating adjustments to European policy-making *within* each ministry provide the third major conclusion (Le Vigan 1990; 1988). This phenomenon is the inevitable reaction to the deepening and widening of the scope of EU policy-making. Each member state has witnessed a proliferation of internal co-ordinating bodies as well as of horizontal mechanisms to link each ministry with others: very few ministries now do not harbour at least one division or section devoted to interdepartmental co-ordination. Those ministries most immersed in EU affairs often have several co-ordinating mechanisms. Thus, the French Economy Ministry has a bureau in the Budget Division which liaises with the Ministry of Agriculture, the *cellules* in the Treasury Division which grapple with the consequences of the EMS and with its articulation with national monetary policy, and the DREE (*direction des relations économiques extérieures*), which monitors economic developments in other member states. The French Foreign Office also has three co-ordinating bodies: the *service de coopération économique*, the *bureau de droit communautaire*, and the *sous-direction de l'Europe occidental*, which is responsible for European political co-operation. Of course, this proliferation of co-ordinating mechanisms merely raises the question: who co-ordinates the co-ordinators? And this leads to the fourth major conclusion – that the nature of domestic co-ordinating instruments varies widely across the member states of the Union.

A frenzy of institutional experimentation and innovation characterises the sphere of EU co-ordination, as each country seeks to improve its effectiveness (Wallace and Wallace

1983; Page and Wouters 1995; Chiti 1992; Oberdorff 1992; Battini 1993; Cassese and Franchini 1994; Kassim *et al.* 2000). However, in spite of some evidence of institutional emulation and convergence (the creation of ministries or junior ministries of European Affairs (Burban 1971), of interdepartmental committees with like-sounding titles), variety is still the dominant feature of national co-ordination. This variety is determined by the interplay of four major factors: formal organisations and procedures; internal informal networks; internal politico-administrative style and culture; and the pattern of ambitions, resources and constraints.

Naturally, each country has a mix of official vertical and horizontal mechanisms, although the resort to, and the authority of these mechanisms differ widely. Among the better-known, and generally admired mechanisms of vertical co-ordination are the European Secretariat attached to the Cabinet Office in Britain, and the SGCI (*secrétariat général du comité interministériel pour les questions de co-opération économique européenne*) in France (Metcalfe and Zapico-Goñi 1991). These mechanisms have been emulated by many later arrivals to the European Union, albeit generally more in form than in any substantive capacity to generate effective co-ordination (Spanou 2000).

The task of managing EU policy in Britain is entrusted to one key ministerial committee, European Questions (OPD(E)), which is chaired by the Foreign Secretary, to its shadowing official committee (EQ(S)) and to the European Secretariat of the Cabinet Office. The latter is the permanent core of core executive co-ordinating activity. Established even before British entry into the EC, the European Secretariat is charged with constant overall policy co-ordination. It ensures that 'there is a policy', that consistency with wider policy goals is maintained, and that policies are implemented (Bender 1991). It also centralises and transmits all relevant documents, studies the potential impact of particular policies, and prepares for European Council meetings. As the centre of a set of tentacular and overlapping networks, the European Secretariat has proved itself highly competent in reacting quickly to emergencies, in providing an overarching framework for departments and in disseminating information quickly and widely (Mazey 1992; 1994; Edwards 1992). In the pursuit of its co-ordinating goals the European Secretariat convenes some two hundred interdepartmental meetings a year, and organises a weekly meeting with the UKREP from Brussels.

The much-respected French system of co-ordination centres on the SGCI, which has normally been attached to the Prime Minister's office (it spent only a very brief spell under the control of the Ministry for European Affairs). A body of some 120 officials, it performs many of the duties of its British counterpart, informing all relevant ministries and the Council of State of proposals of the European Commission, inviting preparatory studies of potential problems of harmonisation with national law, and, since 1986, ensuring the transition of EU directives into national law (Lequesne 1993; Carnelutti 1988; Guyomarch 1993).

A third example of a highly structured and centralised system is that of Denmark, with its cabinet subcommittee chaired by the Prime Minister. It meets weekly, working in tandem with a committee of senior officials who are chaired by the head of the Foreign Economic Affairs Ministry. The task of this latter committee is to co-ordinate the detailed work of the ministries (Laffan 1983). The Danish Foreign Affairs Ministry, in line with British, French and Swedish practice, is responsible for establishing a centralised link to the Permanent Representation in Brussels. The Danish system has the additional dimension of having to involve an active parliamentary committee in the discussions (Peterson 2000).

Elsewhere in Europe, centralisation gives way to fragmentation, with considerable variety in the extent and pattern of that fragmentation. Some countries rely essentially on two ministries – the Foreign Office and the Economics Ministry – to try to co-ordinate aspects of their European policies. This is the case in Germany, Ireland and Greece, although there is some tendency toward Foreign Affairs taking the leading role. In other countries – Spain, Luxemburg and Portugal – the Foreign Office has overall political responsibility for EU affairs. In many countries a lead ministry, that which is most involved in the relevant policy, is often charged with general co-ordination. In truth, in all these countries, there is a mix of these three solutions: Foreign Office for some purposes, bicephalous, or lead ministries for others (see Dinan 1986; Laffan 1983; Burns and Salmon 1977 on the Irish example). In all cases, however, the major means of co-ordination is a set of interdepartmental committees – the horizontal compensating for the imperfect vertical forms of co-ordination. Thus, the German Federal Republic often confers co-ordinating responsibility on the ministry most involved in a policy, but co-ordination also takes place in the weekly sessions organised by the Economics Ministry (Department E (Europe), which has the role of ensuring the two-way transmission between Bonn and the German Permanent Representative in Brussels) and by the Foreign Office and an occasionally assertive Chancellor's office.

In Spain, the Foreign Affairs Ministry, through a Junior Minister for European Affairs, enjoys overall political responsibility for EU affairs. The latter chairs two important inter-departmental bodies – the Interdepartmental Commission for Economic Affairs related to European Integration and the Delegated Commission for Economic Affairs. However, there are other committees charged with EU policy co-ordination and which escape the control of the Foreign Affairs Ministry (Moderne 1986; Acebes 1994; Burgoyne-Larsen 1995). In similar vein, the creation in Italy of a Department attached to the Prime Minister's office and given the task of co-ordinating European policy did not lead to the dismantling of the numerous interdepartmental commissions and committees charged with the same responsibility (Battini 1993; Chiti 1992: 403).

In The Netherlands, all Ministers enjoy the same constitutional status and autonomy. The country lacks, therefore, the top-down co-ordination exercised through the arbitration of a Prime Minister as well as a body, such as the British European Secretariat or the French SGCI. It thus relies on general co-ordinating activity through the Foreign Ministry and the Economics Ministry, and, occasionally, the Prime Minister's Office. Yet most co-ordination takes place through bargained compromises in the horizontally organised form of an official and unofficial nature (Van den Bos 1991; Andeweg 2000).

We should not exaggerate the distinction between centralised and fragmented systems. In France, for example, the SGCI is pivotal in some respects, but it may not be as powerful or as centralising as its friends contend or its enemies fear (Spence 1993: 55). It shares part of its general policy co-ordinating role with the Ministry of the Economy, the Foreign Office and the Ministry for European Affairs, and its role as monitor of legal implementation of EU law with the *Secrétariat Général du Gouvernement*. There are numerous examples of ministries resisting the centralising embrace of the SGCI: hence the succession of circulars sent by Prime Ministers (starting with Debré, including Rocard and ending recently with Balladur) insisting that departments had to refer European matters to the SGCI. Hence, too, the constant need for arbitration at Matignon among departments which refuse the authority of the SGCI. Furthermore, as in Britain, the practice of leaving co-ordination to a lead ministry is widespread. Similarly, in Britain, the major co-ordinating organ, the European Secretariat, may lie at the heart of co-ordinating activity, but high politics, such as GATT negotiations, constitutional reform at EU level or

European political co-operation, is managed more directly by the Prime Minister, by the Foreign Office or by cabinet committees, the most senior of which is the Overseas and Defence Committee, chaired by the Prime Minister and serviced by the Cabinet Secretariat. Its subcommittee – Overseas and Defence (Europe) – is chaired by the Foreign Secretary and serviced by the European Secretariat.

In Britain and France, moreover, a great deal of European policy of low political salience and involving little interdepartmental interaction tends to be dealt with in heavily segmented fashion by individual ministries or by *ad hoc* interdepartmental committees (Armstrong and Bulmer 1996). Finally, in all three centralised cases – Britain, France and Denmark – there is abundant evidence of many direct links between sectoral ministries and Brussels (Siedentopf and Ziller 1988: 63). At this level, attempts at centralised control, or even information-sharing, may break down in the face of links with policy experts from other countries and from the EU.

Conversely, the degree of official fragmentation in countries such as The Netherlands and Germany should be kept in perspective. The Dutch have made some tentative moves to improve co-ordination through the Directorate-General for Economic co-operation and Integration and through the Foreign Office (its Junior Ministry for European Affairs chairs CoCo and CoCoHan, two co-ordinating interdepartmental committees). Since January 1992 new instruments have been created, and the Foreign Office is now called upon to prepare a three-monthly implementation review for Parliament. In Germany, the Chancellor's office keeps a constant eye on major European issues, and conflicts between ministries are discussed in the monthly meetings of the *Ausschuss der Europa-Staatssekretäre*, a committee of state secretaries responsible for European affairs. It is chaired by a Junior Minister in the Foreign Office and comprises representatives of that ministry as well as those from the Economics, the Finance and the Agricultural Ministries, from the German Permanent Representation in Brussels, the State Secretary in the Chancellor's office responsible for European Affairs, and those State Secretaries whose departmental issues are under discussion. Moreover, a committee, which meets every Tuesday, examines the agenda of COREPER, and *ad hoc* meetings of officials may be convened to discuss specific issues. Other countries which lack a centralising co-ordinating body are not totally devoid of co-ordinating mechanisms. The Irish, for example, have created a committee of senior civil servants with a general co-ordinating role. In Italy, the Foreign Office has slowly assumed some ascendancy over the formal structures of co-ordination, through its Directorates-General for Economic Affairs and for Political Affairs (the latter deals with foreign policy and EU constitutional matters). Furthermore, since 1987, the prestigious Interdepartmental Committee for Economic Planning (CIPE) has been charged with providing the guidelines for the country's overall economic strategy, with improving the instruments for the rapid spending of EU funds allocated to Italy, and with monitoring the translation of EU directives into domestic law. These tasks require close co-operation with CIPI (industrial policy) and CIPES (external trade), two other important interdepartmental committees. However, in Italy, as in Germany, The Netherlands, Ireland and most other member states, developments designed to improve the machinery of co-ordination do not amount to anything approaching the British, French or Danish situations.

In exploring the instruments of co-ordination it is, of course, important to probe behind the official façade by considering actual practice: thus, as Van den Bos has pointed out, the formal equality of Dutch Ministers in EU policy-making masks the fact that some Ministers are clearly more equal than others. Furthermore, we need to analyse the role of unofficial networks of co-ordination as well as the politico-administrative environment and culture in which the official system is embedded. By doing so, it is possible to detect several different scenarios:

The British (and to some degree Swedish) scenario, in which a centralised official system is underpinned by an equally centralised and integrative politico-administrative culture (Dunleavy and Rhodes 1990);

The French scenario, in which an official centralised system is both further centralised by constant resort to the arbitration of Matignon and the Elysée as well as increasingly fragmented as the result of the confrontational styles and strong centripetal forces within the French administration – forces which surfaced in the early battle for control of the SGCI (Claisse 1992; Gerbet 1969: 202; Debbasch 1991: 132; Lequesne 1993: 45);

The Spanish scenario, in which a reasonably structured system is hampered by internal conflicts, notably amongst the *cuerpos*, which, like the *grands corps* in France, vie for supremacy in new sectors (Gomez Fuentes 1986);

The Irish and Dutch scenarios, in which officially fragmented systems have generated unofficial channels or networks to ensure a respectable degree of coherence in defining the national interest (Van den Bos 1991);

The German, Italian and Belgian scenarios, in which attempts at improving the fragmented machinery of co-ordination fall foul of persistent and deeply entrenched department rivalries. In these countries – and others such as Greece, The Netherlands and France – there is the traditional rivalry between the Foreign Affairs Ministry and the Economics or Finance Ministry. In Germany, European policy remains ill co-ordinated among large and disparate groups which are jealous of their autonomy, and it can be disrupted by tensions between the Chancellor's office, the Foreign Office and the Economics Ministry (Bulmer 1986; Hesse and Goetz 1992; Huelshoff 1993; Wessels and Regelsberger 1988). Italian government is 'government by department' (Hine 1995: 58), and traditional turf battles are exacerbated in EU policy co-ordination by the exigencies of coalition politics, of party politics and of personal enmities (Ronzitti 1987; Franchini 1990).

Belgium presents an extreme example of official fragmentation being compounded by the prevailing politico-administrative environment and culture. In European affairs, officials of the External Economic and Social Policy Committee (which is attached to the Prime Minister's office and which is dominated by officials from the Economics Ministry) have to compete with those from the Foreign Office who consider the EU as one of their *chasses gardées* (Ziller 1993: 63–4; 228). Still, the two major communities in Belgium (Flemish and Walloon) have virtually equal status in EU matters and can block action if they disagree with the central government position (Karremans 2000).

As at the national level, co-ordination in Brussels takes both an official and an unofficial form and it is shaped by politico-administrative culture and by policy style. Unlike at the national level, formal co-ordination in Brussels is similar for all member states. Each state is represented by a Permanent Representation, headed by an Ambassador who invariably hails from the diplomatic corps. The Permanent Representation is serviced, in the main, by national officials on secondment. The expanding scope of EU activity has led to a corresponding increase in the number and variety of such officials. Initially dominated by diplomats, Finance Ministry and Agricultural Ministry officials, each Permanent Representation has acquired specialists to shadow the increasing number of policy sectors, with those specialists coming from the functional ministries. The size of representation varies from the surprisingly modest to the barely adequate. During a state's presidency of the Council, membership tends to expand, roughly doubling in size in recent cases.

The first task of the Permanent Representation is to inform the national capital of possible or impending EU legislation. This requires sensitive antennae and an effective information-gathering and transmission service. Second, the Permanent Representation has the task of defining the national position in Brussels, and of presenting it in acceptable form and at the appropriate moment. A failure to present an issue in a desirable form may result in its transfer to the non-decision-making category (Peters 1994: 12). Likewise, mobilising the wrong resources may be costly – as the reputedly efficient French and British have sometimes painfully learnt (Dumez and Jeanemaître 1992: 16–19). Presenting a clear message is relatively easy when the Permanent Representation receives one from its Foreign Office, which, in turn, is presenting a position formulated in a centralised agency. This is the case for Britain, France and Denmark, where an official of the Permanent Representation regularly attends meetings of the national co-ordinating body. However, even these countries have the problem, which is acute for member states, of contending with issues which are of national concern but which are negotiated directly between individual ministries or interests and Commission officials.

The Permanent Representation also negotiates the national position. It works essentially through COREPER and its elaborate committee structure, which has the task of preparing the meetings of the Council of Ministers and which is the locus of brokering major legislative deals. It is also entrusted with managing its country's dealings with all the other institutions of the EU. Most officials of the Permanent Representations spend their time in the working groups of the Council, reporting back to their national co-ordinating bodies, or to ministries, details of relevant proposals. They also have the often unenviable task of translating national instructions into bargainable positions within the working groups. On the whole, officials of the Permanent Representations enjoy some discretion in settling technical matters, but leave political issues to the COREPER or to the full Council.

A Permanent Representation has a further important general brief in managing its country's business in Brussels: that of sensitising a whole range of EU institutions to the policy stances and constraints of its country. It hopes, thereby, to influence the agenda-shaping of the Union. Finally, the Permanent Representations have the task of reporting back to the appropriate national bodies on the decisions made in Brussels and on the repercussions of those decisions for national law.

The co-ordinating activities of the Permanent Representations are, therefore, of a generalised and of a specific nature, and are structured around a two-way system of transmission between Brussels and the member state and also within the black box of Brussels decision-making: it is the deliverer of messages it has only partly formulated and may even disapprove – a singularly uncomfortable position on occasions.

The role of unofficial co-ordinating channels is as important in Brussels as at the domestic level. In the pursuit of their objectives, Permanent Representations can often (although by no means always, since some national officials 'go native' and resist intergovernmental pressures (Michelmann 1978: 482–3)), count on the co-operation of their compatriots who staff key institutions of the Union – the consultative, management and regulatory committees and subcommittees which proliferate at all levels, the expert groups and work groups, the Directorates-General and the *Cabinets* (enclaves composed of the nationality of the Director-General) (Kassim and Wright 1991). Increasing attention is also being paid by some Permanent Representations to the parliamentary groups.

Some Permanent Representations also undertake the task (although unofficial) of assisting national interests to negotiate the maze of Brussels, and to be an entry for businesses and interest groups into that policy-making system. Again, the Permanent Representations undertake this task with varying degrees of zeal. UKREP is alleged to know the nature of almost all British interests involved in EU activity in Brussels and to seek to identify all these actors, while the representations of some member countries are said to be amazed when discovering the range of activity of their national organisations.

Member states have always been concerned to maintain a permanent presence along the critical pathways of the policy process, particularly in the early drafting phase of legislation, and especially in areas of national concern (agriculture for Ireland and Greece, fisheries for Spain, competition policy for the United Kingdom) (Siotis 1964). Indeed, they keep a keen eye on all important appointments within the Commission in order to protect their (unofficial and unwritten) 'quota'. Brussels decision-making is thus characterised by the existence of both official networks and ill-structured and loosely-functioning *administrations parallèles*, unofficial channels which provide access to the Commission. The Union's bureaucratic system is shot through with national officials and influences. There is, for example, an Italian 'Mafia' and a quite effective Spanish network. There is little doubt that a strategically placed and sympathetic national official can greatly ease the task of a member state. Thus, during the 1989–92 CAP negotiations, French officials were favoured by the presence of many of their compatriots in ex DG VI, now DG Agriculture (Le Theule and Litvan 1993: 771).

The differences in the style of co-ordination of European policy at national level are mirrored in Brussels. Thus, when UKREP receives a text from the Commission, it immediately reports to London and relevant embassies on its operational consequences and proffers precise advice. This is not the case with most other Permanent Representations, including that of France. In truth, UKREP is an efficient and tightly knit body which closely liaises with London, and it is strategically constrained by that factor, especially as instructions from London are those of the government as a whole. Concessions by UKREP in Brussels may, therefore, constitute the unpicking of a compromise that had been bitterly fought over in Whitehall. German, Irish and French officials, like their British counterparts, enjoy little strategic latitude but are afforded some tactical discretion.

By way of contrast, officials from Belgium, Italy and Luxemburg appear to work within relatively loose policy frameworks defined by their respective capitals (Nugent 1992: 414–15; Rutten 1992), while those from The Netherlands appear to have to work with a combination of vaguely formulated principles and ideas on some issues and precise instructions in some sectors (Van den Bos 1991). There is another reflection of the domestic position: the degree of homogeneity achieved by the Permanent Representations in presenting their country's position. Thus, in sharp contrast with the British, who generally stifle interdepartmental rivalries in Brussels, the Germans and Spanish occasionally parade them (as is evident in the occasional battles between officials from Agriculture, from Finance and from the Foreign Office). These differences can be functional at times, allowing these countries to negotiate along parallel lines to strike the best bargain.

Co-ordinating capacity: some concluding remarks

Any analysis of European Union policy co-ordination at domestic level must raise the questions of its *effectiveness*. However, raising the issue of effectiveness triggers further complex questions: for instance, is a centralised system inherently more effective than a fragmented one? In some senses, the answer must be that centralisation is effective. The British system, for example, ensures that 'there is a policy' which is binding on domestic actors, which is coherent and consistent with wider policy objectives, and which is clearly transmitted to UKREP in Brussels.

Although most discussion of co-ordination begins with an assumption that centralisation is effective, a centralised system may be dysfunctional in several ways. In the first place, the centre may be divided (the case in France during the first period of *cohabitation* between 1986 and 1988) or paralysed (as during the Pompidou illness at the end of his presidency, or in Belgium at almost any time) or inept (the case of Prime Minister Major over voting rights in 1994). Second, the negotiation and transmission of a tight domestic compromise may bind the hands of the country's negotiations in Brussels, where flexibility is often desirable (hence the tensions between the SGCI and the French Permanent Representation during a set of negotiations in 1996). Third, loose and horizontally organised but negotiated compromises may be messy and time-consuming, but they may also ensure a better implementation record because the agents of implementation have participated in the decision-making process. Fourth, the degree of centralisation is no guarantee of the *quality* of the decisions, which depend on resources such as adequate personnel, internal cohesion, sufficient time to deal with business, expertise (in technical sectoral matters, in languages, in European Union law and procedures). And while the political skills and leverage record on resources of the three centralising countries is generally good (although there is certainly a problem of internal cohesion and of time for the SGCI), it is clear that other member states enjoy at least some of the above resources. Thus, countries such as The Netherlands and even Italy, where the technical expertise of Foreign Office officials is singularly lacking (Hine 1995: 62), together with Britain, France and Denmark, have each a small network of EU experts who rotate between domestic and EU-level co-ordinating bodies, who reduce the formal density of the policy arena and who may even foster a certain team spirit in the pursuit of national interests (Hayes-Renshaw *et al.* 1989: 127; Van den Bos 1991).

But effectiveness must be judged not only according to the nature and resources of formal and informal co-ordinating mechanisms. It must be related to the nature of the issue – whether it is constitutional and political or simply bureaucratic and technical, or whether it is urgent and reactive or merely routinised. It may also be related to the requirements of EU domestic policy-making. It is, therefore, possible to evaluate effectiveness according to a number of states' capacities:

To anticipate new EU legislation and its impact at the national level. Almost all countries (particularly those of Southern Europe) are weak in this respect, with the possible exceptions of Denmark and Britain (where, for example, the 1996 IGC triggered the creation by the European Secretariat of a reflection group). Even the much-vaunted French system is seen as wanting in its anticipatory ability: during the prolonged CAP negotiations of the early 1990s the French delegation *a surtout découvert les problèmes au fur et à mesure qu'ils se présentaient* (Le Theule and Litvan 1993: 755). This weakness of the French system led to the creation by Edith Cresson, in January 1993, of *groupes d'études et de mobilisation*, but the experiment proved to be but a further addition to that Prime

Minister's long list of failures. There is some evidence that governments are increasingly aware that anticipation is now an important policy weapon. Thus, the Dutch established, in 1989, an interdepartmental group, the BNC, to review new European Commission proposals and their consequences for national policies and law. The Finnish Parliament also has established a Futures Committee that examines, among other things, European policy futures.

To shape the EU policy agenda and to tap the resources available in Brussels – two activities which demand somewhat different skills. The British and the Germans are considered to be good downstream lobbyists for economic matters, the French for cultural affairs and the Spanish and Greeks for agricultural issues. Success in shaping the agenda depends on presenting a technically sound dossier, at the right time, within the referential framework of the EU and ideally garbed in a legitimising pro-EU discourse, to the country's representatives in Brussels.

Smoothly and quickly to translate European legislation into national law. The patchy record of some member states, as seen in regularly published league tables, may be attributed to a set of factors including the extent of the adjustment required and the inertia or ineptitude of officials. Defects in the co-ordinating machinery may also be a factor in transposition of law (Knill and Lenschow 1997). Without doubt, efforts have been made by several guilty countries (notably France, The Netherlands, Italy and Spain) to improve their legal implementation performance (Hine 1995; Carnelutti 1988).

To implement and monitor European legislation at street level. This is a much under-researched area. While the major source of slippage may lie in the institutional design or in the resistance or lack of resources (budgetary and expertise) of those entrusted with the task (Aguilar Fernandez 1994; Georgiou 1994), it is clear that there are problems of co-ordination. Interestingly, the highly centralised French system, dominated by Parisian-based members of the *grands corps*, may be insensitive to problems of practical implementation (Claisse 1992: 179) while the diffused and negotiated co-ordinating style of the Germans may facilitate such implementation (Hesse 1991).

If we examine the factors which shape domestic co-ordinating capacity, we need to explore the extent of the adjustment required by EU policies: EU legislation may be the formal recognition of national practices or may be entirely novel and require major reforms. Pollution control illustrates this point admirably (Sbragia 1996). Clearly, the factors which determine the state's capacity for co-ordination are size, nature and degree of fragmentation of the state machine, its tendency towards sectoralisation, professional specialisation, bureaucratic turf-defending, and its interdepartmental and inter-corps rivalries. As noted above, there are striking contrasts between the situations among the member states. We need also very carefully to consider the extent of its functional and territorial penetration. The factors which determine a country's co-ordinating capacity at the EU level include some of the above factors, but also comprise the following:

Political clout, which is linked to size. However, the factor of size may be negated or diluted by political ineptitude (the case of Britain on occasions) or by self-restraint (the case for a long period of Germany, and for obvious historical reasons (Bulmer and Paterson 1989: 95–117))

Constitutional congruence – the extent to which a country's policy synchronises with the logic of the Union's basic constitutional principles or aspirations (Bulmer 1992). The relative success of the British in their pursuit of sectoral liberalisation springs from its match with the logic of the open market. In some areas, such as telecommunications, Britain has 'not merely opened the gate but provided ammunition for the EU to attack other fortresses'. Yet, constitutional congruence is no guarantee of quick success. Plans to liberalise the EU's energy markets, backed by Britain, Germany and the Commission, have been blocked in the Energy Council for several years because of the French government's opposition to competition in the area of energy distribution to customers (*Financial Times*, 6 February 1996). The fitful and painfully slow pace of liberalisation in the air transport sector provides another example of the capacity of protectionist countries (some very badly co-ordinated) to slow down a constitutionally congruent policy.

Existing policy congruence – the extent to which proposals are respectful of the *acquis communautaire*, or are not attempting to unbundle policies based on previous complex bargains. Problems are compounded if the proposals engender negative or zero-sum consequences – as the well-oiled and determined British co-ordinating machine was to discover over budget contributions.

Policy climate congruence – the degree to which a proposal is in harmony with the prevailing climate in Brussels. Thus, the air of budgetary crisis in 1984 and 1988 facilitated the reform of CAP, while the 1980s favoured market-creating and market-consolidating policies as well as providing a propitious terrain for the pro-integrationist demands of the Commission–French–German troika. The climate after the Maastricht ratification difficulties has been much less conducive to pro-integration initiatives, and has shifted the balance of power within the Union.

Administrative congruence – the extent of the match between the administrative procedures and style of a country and the procedures and 'emergent policy style' at EU level (Mazey and Richardson 1993). Thus, the open, flexible, co-operative, pragmatic and consensus-building style of the Germans, Dutch and Swedes may be ill-suited to formulating overall steering strategies (the apparent strength of the British and the French), but is well suited to the building of coalitions, which is the basis of much successful EU policy-making, particularly when a country is occupying the Presidency. Nor have the German deficiencies prevented it from playing a major role in shaping the constitutional destiny of the Union. Conversely, the elitist, centralising and confrontational style of the French, so evident in the interdepartmental committees at home, may be very counterproductive – as was clear in the failure of the French to prevail in the controversial de Havilland affair, the reform of CAP in 1990, the importation of Japanese cars in 1991, and the reform of the Common Fisheries Policy in 1993 (Muller 1992: 23–4).

At both national and EU level, a country's capacity to co-ordinate is naturally affected by the pattern of domestic constraints – judicial, industrial, institutional and political. Clearly, the mix, extent and nature of constraints vary widely, even if we restrict our analysis to the political level. Thus, if parliaments are generally weak in constraining governments – there are exceptions, notably in Denmark (with its highly professional and politicised EU Committee) and Austria (Laffan 1983: 57; Ronzitti 1987: 38–44). Similarly, majority parties or ruling coalitions are rarely an obstacle for governments, although in

Italy, The Netherlands, Finland and Germany, coalition politics seriously weaken the capacity to centralise co-ordination (Van den Bos 1991; Bulmer and Paterson 1989: 115; Bulmer and Paterson 1988; Hine 1995). Coalitions may exist within a single party, and in Britain the hapless Major government constantly shifted its EU policy to try and accommodate the irreconcilable objectives of its own backbenchers. Similarly, subnational constraints in formulating EU policies are not a problem in countries such as Britain, France, Denmark, Portugal and The Netherlands, but are significant in Spain and, more especially, in Belgium. They may also become more important in Germany, as the Länder try to claw back some of the powers allegedly lost through EU policy-making. Intergovernmental relations are much more important at the implementation phase: ignoring local governments may lead to problems of compliance.

Finally, the effectiveness of co-ordination cannot be divorced from the aspirations and objectives of the member states (Nugent 1992: 413–14). It is all too readily assumed that all member states share the British and Danish, and to some degree Swedish, characteristics of suspicion towards the EU and of sustained greed towards its resources – twin characteristics that require a constant and global co-ordinating function. Nor is every country as obsessed with managing sectoral spillovers or externalities. It may be perfectly legitimate to reproach the French for frequently failing to set specific EU policies into a larger national referential framework, since they have the pretension of doing so (Le Theule and Litvan 1993: 783). But for member states with more modest ambitions the criticism would be invalid. As also noted above, the policy activism of countries varies according to type (with the Germans and the French keen constitutional reformers) and sector (the British push a pro-competition, while the Germans are keen environmentalists and the Swedes press social issues and the question of free access to information. In short, the effectiveness of a country's domestic EU co-ordinating capacity must be judged according to the issue, the policy type, the policy requirements and the policy objectives. Merely to examine the machinery of co-ordination is to confuse the means and the outcomes.

A number of more general conclusions may be drawn from this brief study. The first is that, given all the difficulties of co-ordination, what is surprising is the amount that appears to take place. Second, while co-ordination may be important in some respects, its absence does not appear to be disruptive or dysfunctional. Indeed, third, lack of co-ordination or inadequate co-ordination may be functional, and not only in ensuring latitude at the bargaining table, but also particularly for those countries which bear the highest costs in terms of policy adjustment, since legal compliance or street-level implementation may be phased in a more prolonged and politically palatable way. Poor national co-ordination may even be functional for the EU itself, since it does facilitate interstate bargaining, while policy slippage due to weak implementation co-ordination may be yet another price the Union has to pay for support.

Note

1   This is similar to the argument of Robert Putnam (1988) concerning 'two level games' in international politics.

References

Acebes, Angel Martin (1994) 'Adattamenti organizzativi e funzionali dell'amministrazione spagnola nel processo di integrazione europea', in Y. Meny and V. Wright, *La riforma amministrativa in Europa*, Bologna: il Mulino.

Aguilar Fernandez, Susana (1994) 'Convergence in Environmental Policy? The Resilience of National Institutional Designs in Spain and Germany', *Journal of Public Policy* 14/1: 39–56.

Andeweg, R. (2000) 'The Netherlands', in H. Kassim, A. Menon, B. G. Peters and V. Wright (eds), *Coordinating European Policies: The National Dimension*, Oxford: Oxford University Press.

Armstrong, Kenneth and Bulmer, Simon (1996) 'The United Kingdom', in D. Rometsch and W. Wessels (eds), *The European Union and Member States: Towards Institutional Fusion?*, Manchester: Manchester University Press.

Battini, Stefano (1993) 'L'influence de l'intégration européenne' *Revue française d'administration publique* 67.

Bellier, Irene (1994) 'La Commission Européene: Hauts fonctionnaires et "Culture du Management"', *Revue française d'administration publique* 70: 253–62.

Bender, B. G. (1991) 'Whitehall, Central Government and 1992', *Public Policy and Administration* 6/1: 13–20.

Bodiguel, Jean-Luc (1995) 'The Civil Service and the European Union' *International Review of Aministrative Sciences* 6/3: 433–53.

Bulmer, Simon (1986) *The Domestic Structure of European Community Policy-Making in West Germany*, New York: Garland.

Bulmer, Simon (1992) 'Completing the European Community's Internal Market: The Regulatory Implications for the Federal Republic of Germany', in Kenneth Dyson (ed.), *The Politics of German Regulation*, Aldershot: Dartmouth, pp. 53–78.

Bulmer, Simon and Paterson, William (1987) *The Federal Republic of Germany and the European Communities*, London: HarperCollins.

Bulmer, Simon and Paterson, William (1988) 'European Policy-Making', in W. Wessels and E. Regelsberger (eds), *The Federal Republic of Germany and the EC: The Presidency and Beyond*, Bonn: Europa, Union Verlag, pp. 231–68.

Bulmer, Simon and Paterson, William (1989) 'West Germany's Role in Europe: "Man-Mountain" or "Semi-Gulliver"', *Journal of Common Market Studies* 28/2: 95–117.

Burban, J. (1971) 'La création de ministres des Affaires Européennes au sein du gouvernement des Etats membres de la communauté', *Revue du Marché Commun* 147: 355–8.

Burgoyne-Larsen, L. (1995) *L'Espagne et la Communauté Européenne*, Brussels: Editions de l'Université de Bruxelles.

Burns, B. and Salmon, T. (1977) 'Policy-making Coordination in Ireland on European Community Issues', *Journal of Common Market Studies* 15/4: 272–87.

Carnelutti, A. (1988) 'L'Administration française face à la Règle Communautaire', *Revue française d'administration publique* 40.

Cassese, S. and della Cananea, G. (1992) 'The Commission of the European Economic Community: The Administrative Ramifications of its Political Development (1957–1967)', in Erk Volkmar Heyen, *Yearbook of European Administrative History: Early European Community Administration*, Baden-Baden: Nomos Verlagsgesellschaft, pp. 75–94.

Cassese, S. and Franchini, C. (1994) *L'amministrazione pubblica italiana*, Bologna: il Mulino.

Chiti, Mario P. (1990) 'Il coordinamento delle politiche comunitarie e la riforma degli apparati di governo', Associazione per gli studi e le ricerche parlamentari, no. 1, pp. 235–54.

Chiti, Mario P. (1992) 'Implicazioni Amministrative della integrazione europea', *Rivista Italiana di Diritto Pubblico Comunitario* 2/4.

Claisse, A. (1992) 'L'adaptation de l'administration française à la construction européenne (1948–1969), in Erk Volkmar Heyen, *Yearbook of European Administrative History: Early European Community Administration*, Baden-Baden: Nomos Verlagsgesellschaft, pp. 165–80.

Claisse, A. (1994) 'L'obiettivo della modernizzazione amministrativa in Francia: riconciliare Stato e società', in Y. Meny and V. Wright (eds), *La Riforma Amministrativa in Europa*, Bologna: il Mulino, pp. 71–110.

Conrad, Yves (1992) 'L'administration belge face à la construction européenne (1952–1967). Une première orientation historique', in Erk Volkmar Heyen, *Yearbook of European Administrative*

History: Early European Community Administration, Baden-Baden: Nomos Verlagsgesellschaft, pp. 223–37.

Cram, L. (1993) 'Calling the Tune Without Paying the Piper? Social Policy Regulation: The Role of the Commission in the European Community Social Policy', *Policy and Politics* 21/1: 135–46.

Debbasch, C. (1988) *National Administrations and European Integration*, Paris.

Debbasch, C. (1991) 'L'influence du processus d'intégration communautaire sur les administrations nationales', in *L'Europe et le Droit*, Paris: Dalloz.

Dinan, Desmond (1986) 'Political-Economic Linkage and Bureaucratic Rivalry: A Case Study of Ireland in the EEC', *Administration* 34/4: 434–54.

Dinan, Desmond (1994) *Ever Closer Union?*, Basingstoke: Macmillan.

Dror, Y. (1975) 'From Management Sciences to Policy Sciences', in M. J. White *et al.* (eds), *Management and Policy Science in American Government*, Lexington, MA: Heath, ch. 13.

Dubouis, L. (1975) 'L'influence française sur la fonction publique communautaire', in *La France et les Communautés européennes*, Paris: LGDJ, pp. 501–7.

Dumez, H. and Jeanemaître, A. (1992) 'La France, l'Europe et la concurrence: enseignements de l'Affaire A.T.R. – de Havilland', *Commentaire* 57: 16–19.

Dunleavy, P. and Rhodes, R. A. W. (1990) 'Core Executive Studies in Britain', *Public Administration* 68: 3–28.

Dyson, Kenneth (ed.) (1992) *The Politics of German Regulation*, Aldershot: Dartmouth.

Edwards, G. (1992) 'Central Government', in S. George (ed.), *Britain and the European Community: The Politics of Semi-detachment*, Oxford: Oxford University Press, pp. 64–70.

Franchini, Claudio (1990) *Amministrazione Italiana ed Amministrazione Comunitaria*, Rome: Edi. Press.

Georgiou, George A. (1994) 'The Responsiveness of the Greek Administration System to European Prospects', *International Review of Administrative Sciences* 60: 131–44.

Gerbet, Pierre (1969) 'La préparation de la décision communautaire au niveau national français', in Gerbet and D. Pepy (eds), *La décision dans les Communautés européennes*, Lyon.

Goetz, Klaus (1995) 'National Governance and European Integration: Intergovernmental Relations in Germany', *Journal of Common Market Studies* 33/1: 92–116.

Gomez Fuentes, A. (1986) *Asi cambiara España: la batalla del Mercado Comun*, Barcelona: Plaza & Janes.

Grant, Wyn (1993) 'Pressure Groups and the European Community: An Overview', in Sonia Mazey and Jeremy Richardson (eds), *Lobbying in the European Community*, Oxford: Oxford University Press, pp. 27–46.

Guerivière, Jean de la (1992) *Voyage à l'intérieur de l'Eurocratie*, Paris.

Guyomarch, Alain (1993) 'The European Effect: Improving French Policy Coordination', *Staatswissenschaften und Staatspraxis* 4/3: 455–78.

Hay, R. (1989) *The European Commission and the Administration of the Community*, Brussels: Official Publishers of the European Commission.

Hayes-Renshaw, F., Lesquesne, C. and Mayor Lopez, P. (1989) 'The Permanent Representation of the Member States to the European Communities', *Journal of Common Market Studies* 26/2: 119–37.

Héritier, A. (1999) *Policy-making and Diversity in Europe*, Cambridge: Cambridge University Press.

Hesse, Joachim Jens (1991) 'West German Federalism: Effects, Outputs and Implications for European Integration', Discussion Paper no. 3, Oxford: Centre for European Studies, Nuffield College.

Hesse, Joachim Jens and Goetz, Klaus H. (1992) 'Early Administrative Adjustment to the European Communities: The Case of the Federal Republic of Germany', in Erk Volkmar Heyen, *Yearbook of European Administrative History: Early European Community Administration*, Baden-Baden: Nomos Verlagsgesellschaft, pp. 181–206.

Heyen, Erk Volkmar (1992) *Yearbook of European Administrative History: Early European Community Administration*, Baden-Baden: Nomos Verlagsgesellschaft.

Hine, David (1995) 'Italy and Europe: The Italian Presidency and the Domestic Management of European Community', in R. Leonardi and F. Anderlini (eds), *Italian Politics: A Review*, vol. 6, London: Pinter, pp. 50–68.

Hix, S. (1998) 'The Study of the European Union II: The New Governance Agenda and its Rival', *Journal of European Public Policy* 5: 38–65.

Huelshoff, Andreas (1993) *From the Federal Republic to Deutschland*, Colorado: Westview Press.

Hurrell, Andrew and Menon, Anand (1996) 'Politics Like Any Other? Comparative Politics, International Relations and the Study of the EU', *West European Politics* 19/2: 386–402.

Jacquel, J. P. (1994) 'Le labyrinth décisionnel', *Pouvoirs* 69.

Jamar, J. and Wessels, W. (1985) *Community Bureaucracy at the Crossroads*, Bruges.

Karremans, B. (2000) 'Belgium', in H. Kassim, A. Menon, B. G. Peters and V. Wright (eds), *Coordinating European Policies: The National Dimension*, Oxford: Oxford University Press.

Kassim, Hussein and Wright, Vincent (1991) 'The Role of National Administrations in the Decision-making Processes of the European Community', *Revista trimestrale di diritto pubblico* 3: 832–50.

Kassim, Hussein, Menon, Anand, Peters, B. Guy and Wright, Vincent (2000) *Coordinating European Policies: The Brussels Dimension*, Oxford: Oxford University Press.

Knill, Christoph and Lenschow, Andrea (1997) *Coping with Europe: The Impact of British and German Administration on the Implementation of EU Environmental Policy*, Florence: European University Institute.

Laffan, Brigid (1983) 'Ireland and Denmark in the European Community: Political and Administrative Aspects', *Administration* 29/1: 43–62.

Lequesne, Christian (1993) *Paris-Bruxelles: Comment se fait la politique européenne de la France*, PFNSP.

Ludlow, Peter (1993) 'The UK Presidency: A view from Brussels', *Journal of Common Market Studies* 31/2: 246–60.

McLaughlin, A. M., Jordan, G. and Maloney, W. A. (1992) 'Policy-making in Agriculture: Primary Policy Community or Specialist Policy Communities', Working Paper Series, no. 5, University of Aberdeen: British Interest Group Project.

Mahieu, Marie-Paule (1969) 'La préparation de la décision communautaire au niveau national belge', in P. Gerbet and D. Pepy (eds), *La Décision dans les Communautés européennes*, Brussels: Presses Universitaires.

Majone, G. (1998) 'Non-Majoritarian Institutions and European Integration', unpublished paper, Graduate School of Public and International Affairs, University of Pittsburgh.

Mazey, Sonia (1992) 'The Adjustment of the British Administration to the European Challenge', unpublished paper, July.

Mazey, Sonia and Richardson, Jeremy (eds) (1993) *Lobbying in the European Community*, Oxford: Oxford University Press.

Menon, A. (2000) 'France', in H. Kassim, B. G. Peters and V. Wright, *Policy Coordination in the European Union: The National Dimension*, Oxford: Oxford University Press.

Meny, Yves, Muller, Pierre and Quermonne, Jean-Louis (eds) (1996) *Adjusting to Europe: The Impact of the European Union on National Institutions and Policies*, London: Routledge.

Metcalfe, Les (1987) 'Comparing National Policy Coordination: Do the Differences Matter?', paper presented at the Erenstein Colloquium, Maastricht, European Institute of Public Administration.

Metcalfe, Les and Zapico-Goñi, E. (1991) 'Action or Reaction?', in *European Policy Making*, London.

Michelmann, Hans J. (1978) 'Multinational Staffing and Organisational Functioning in the Commission of the European Communities', *International Organisation* 3/2: 477–96.

Moderne, Franck (1986) 'L'Administration espagnole et l'intégration européenne', in *Annuaire Européen d'Administration Publique*, vol. 9, Paris: CNRS, pp. 137–55.

Mueller, W. (2000) 'Austria', in H. Kassim, B. G. Peters, A. Menon and V. Wright (eds), *Policy Coordination in the European Union: The Brussels Dimension*, Oxford: Oxford University Press.

Muller, Pierre (ed.) (1992) *L'administration française est-elle en crise?*, Paris: L'Harmattan.

Nugent, Neil (1992) *The Government and Politics of the European Community*, London: Macmillan Education Ltd.

Oberdorff, Henri (1992) 'L'administration face aux enjeux de la construction communautaire', in P. Muller (ed.), *L'administration française est-elle en crise?*, Paris: L'Harmattan, pp. 129–45.

Page, Edward C. and Wouters, Linda (1995) 'The Europeanisation of the National Bureaucracies?', in Jon Pierre (ed.), *Bureaucracy and the Modern State*, Aldershot: Elgar, pp. 185–204.

Paterson, W. and Whilson, C. (1987) *Government and the Chemical Industry: A Comparative Study of Britain and West Germany*, Oxford: Clarendon Press.

Peters, Guy A. (1994) 'Agenda Setting in the European Community', *Journal of European Public Policy* 1/1: 9–26.

Peterson, John (1991) 'Technology Policy in Europe: Explaining the Framework Programme and Eureka in Theory and Practice', *Journal of Common Market Studies* 29/3: 269–90.

Peterson, John (1992) 'The European Technology Community: Policy Networks in a Supranational Setting', in D. Marsh and R. Rhodes (eds), *Policy Networks in British Government*, Oxford: Clarendon Press.

Peterson, T. (2000) 'Denmark', in H. Kassim, B. G. Peters, A. Menon and V. Wright (eds), *Policy Coordination in the European Union: The Brussels Dimension*, Oxford: Oxford University Press.

Pollack, Mark A. (1994) 'Creeping Competence: The Expanding Agenda of the European Community', *Journal of Public Policy* 14/2: 95–145.

Putnam, R. D. (1988) 'Diplomacy and Domestic Politics', *International Organization* 42: 427–60.

Rideau, Joel (1987) 'Le système communautaire et le modèle européen d'administration public', in *Annuaire Européen d'Administration Publique*, vol. 10.

Ronzitti, Natalino (1987) 'European Policy Formulation in the Italian Administrative System', *The International Spectator* 22/4: 207–14.

Rutten, Charles (1992) 'Au coeur du processus de décision européen: le COREPER', *Revue française d'Administration Publique* 63.

Sandholtz, W. and Zysman, J. (1989), 'Recasting the European Bargain', *World Politics* 42: 95–128.

Sbragia, A. (1994) 'From Nation State to Member State', in P. M. Lutzeler (ed.), *Europe After Maastricht*, Providence, RI: Berghahn.

Sbragia, A. (1996) 'Environmental Policy: The "Push–Pull" of Environmental Policy', in Helen Wallace and William Wallace (eds), *Policy-Making in the European Union*, Oxford: Oxford University Press.

Scharpf, Fritz W. (1988) 'The Joint Decision Trap: Lessons from German Federalism and European Integration', *Public Administration* 66: 239–78.

Schmidt, Vivien A. (1995) 'Democracy at Risk? The Impact of European Integration on National Patterns of Policymaking', paper presented for the fourth biennial International Conference of the European Community Studies Association, Charleston, South Carolina, 11–14 May.

Schmidt, Vivien A. (1996) 'The Impact of European Integration on Domestic Political Economic Policymaking Institutions: The Cases of France, Great Britain and Italy', unpublished paper.

Selznick, Philip (1957) *Leadership in Administration: A Sociological Interpretation*, Evanston, IL: Row & Peterson.

Siedentopf, Heinrich and Ziller, Jacques (eds) (1988) *Making European Politics Work*, vol. 1: *Comparative Syntheses*, London: European Institute of Public Administration/Sage.

Siedentopf, Heinrich and Ziller, Jacques (1988) *Making European Politics Work: The Implementation of Community Law by the Member States*, London: Sage.

Siotis, J. (1964) 'Some Problems of European Secretariats', *Journal of Common Market Studies* 2: 226–48.

Snyder, F. (1990) *New Direction in EC Law*, London: Weidenfeld & Nicolson.

Spanou, Calliope (2000) 'Greece', in H. Kassim, B. G. Peters and V. Wright (eds), *Coordination of European Union Policy: The National Dimension*, Oxford: Oxford University Press.

Spence, D. (1993) 'The Role of the National Civil Service in European Lobbying: The British Case', in S. Mazey and J. Richardson, *Lobbying in the European Community*, Oxford: Oxford University Press.

Sutherland, Peter (1993) 'Progress to European Union: A Challenge for the Public Service', *Administration* 41/2: 108–12.

Swinbank, Alan (1989) 'The CAP and the Politics of European Decision-Making', *Journal of Common Market Studies* 27/14: 303–22.

Le Theule, François-Gilles and Litvan, David (1993) 'La réforme de la PAC: Analyse d'une négociation communautaire', *Revue française de sciences politiques* 43/4–6: 755–87.

Van den Bos, Jan M. (1991) *Dutch EC Policy-making: A Model Guided Approach to Coordination and Negotiation*, thesis, Amsterdam.

Le Vigan, Thomas (1988) 'L'administration et la construction européenne' *Revue française d'administration publique* 48.

Le Vigan, Thomas (1990) 'Les finances et Bruxelles', *Pouvoirs* 53: 73–88.

Wallace, H. and Wallace, W. (1983) *Policy-making in the European Community*, Chichester: Wiley.

Weber, Shlomo and Wiesmeth, Hans (1991) 'Issue Linkage in the European Community', *Journal of Common Market Studies* 28/2: 255–67.

Wessels, Wolfgang and Regelsberger, E. (eds) (1988) *The Federal Republic of Germany and the EC: The Presidency and Beyond*, Bonn: Europa Union Verlag.

Wright, Vincent (1994) 'Reshaping the State: The Implications for Public Administration' in W. C. Muller and V. Wright (eds), *The State in Western Europe: Retreat or Redefinition?*, London: Frank Cass, pp. 102–37.

Ziller, Jacques (1993) *Administrations comparées*, Paris: Montchrétien.

Chapter 9

The Court of Justice and the European policy process

DANIEL WINCOTT

Introduction

Processes of negotiation and mutual adjustment are the focus of much scholarship that adopts a 'policy perspective'. This perspective questions the ability of actors to achieve a synoptic overview of a policy problem on both organisational and cognitive grounds. As a consequence the scope for rational policymaking is strictly limited. Instead, the contingencies of the construction of policy 'problems' and 'solutions' (and how they are brought together) are emphasised. Even once a policy has been 'made', actors face further radical difficulties in attempting to implement it. A focus on the independent and/or constitutive influence of ideas and knowledge has provided a fruitful prospectus for much recent policy analytic research. In the first edition of this book I applied a policy perspective to the European Court of Justice (ECJ) and Community law. I continue to believe that this perspective is particularly appropriate for analysing European integration, the development of European Community law and the Court of Justice (as an actor).

Looking back, four main themes emerge from the earlier chapter. First, I distinguished the process of constitutionalising Community law from the impact of the Court in particular substantive policy areas. Second, and relatedly, I argued that the EC's legal system did 'make a difference' to European integration and policymaking, but that the difference it had made historically was conditional and contingent, a situation likely to continue into the future. Third, I suggested that close consideration of its legal system was necessary in order to understand the strengths and weaknesses of the implementation of EU policy. The EU's 'implementation gap', smaller than that of most international organisations and larger than most states, reflects the character of its legal system, 'more' than international law, without constituting a distinct system of domestic law. Finally, I stressed the weak autonomous coercive powers of the Community and its legal order.

All four of these points remain pertinent. If anything, the distinction between 'constitutional' issues and the Court's policy impact became more important during the 1990s. Particularly since the Maastricht Treaty, the Court is not as bold in relation to substantive policy developments. Nevertheless, as far as the 'constitutional framework' of law is concerned, the Court remains innovative. The Court is particularly assiduous in developing the federal prerogatives of EC law in the area of enforcement and implementation (see, for example, Case C-194/94 *CIA Security International* [1996] ECR I-2201, analysed in Weatherill 2000).

In other words, the still developing 'legal-constitutional' character of the EC/EU and the issue of implementation remain closely entwined with one another. On the other hand, future enlargement of the Union will stretch the EC Court and legal system, perhaps even to breaking point. As *one* Court co-ordinating a wide range of substantive issues and a Community of potentially much enlarged geographical scope, it faces considerable organisational difficulty in the future. Moreover, Community and national law(s) in Europe are increasingly mutually dependent. Until recently, this dependence may have resulted in fruitful symbiosis and co-evolution. Whether this balance can be maintained in an enlarged Union remains an open question, in my view (Wincott 2000 provides an extended discussion).

The process of constitutionalisation – the design of a comparatively effective (non-state) legal order – is where the Court can be regarded as most successful in pursuing a 'policy'. Yet we shall see that recent research on sex equality law – a key substantive site in which the 'Constitution' was constructed – calls into question the view that the Court's approach was 'courageous and coherent' (Kilpatrick 1998, the quote is a gloss on Dauses

1985). Presented with several opportunities to develop the EC 'constitution', the 'Court either did not want them or did not understand them', Kilpatrick argues (1998: 149). The process of construction of the European Constitution may have been less rational and coherent than is usually thought. As a consequence, EC law may be a much more flimsy structure than most politicians, lawyers and analysts believe (for a discussion, see Wincott 2000).

Political debate in the UK remains largely mired in discussion of the Court as hero or villain. The best scholarly analysis has moved beyond perspectives of this sort (see particularly the contributions in Slaughter *et al.* 1997). According to some earlier analyses the Court has played a, or perhaps even *the*, crucial role in the integration process, acting as 'the principal motor for the integration of Europe' (Mancini, cited in Volcansek 1992: 109). Some studies suggested that the Court is 'an unsung hero' of the 'unexpected twist' by which, in the face of the scepticism of most political science and international relations theory, the European Community became 'something far more than an international organisation of independent sovereigns' (Burley and Mattli 1993: 41).

On the other hand, some analysts continue to argue strongly that the Court has little or no independent influence. The most vociferous such scholar claims that the Court is an obedient agent of its 'principals' – the member states (Moravcsik 1995). Others have suggested that the ECJ reflects the interests of dominant member states (Garrett 1992). These scholars have claimed that the Court is incapable of 'imposing' a policy that was not within the set of relatively well-defined member state preferences (Garrett and Weingast 1993).

Adopting a position somewhere between these extremes, I argue that the Court should not be viewed as an imposing and wholly independent institution that is 'forcing' (as Volcansek claims of economic integration, 1992: 109) or has 'engineered' (Burley and Mattli 1993: 44 on 'legal integration') integration. But neither should the role of the Court be minimised. It has become increasingly the case that the Court operates within a complex and changing strategic and structural context. While the Court has certainly made a key contribution to the development of these structures, it cannot control them. The image of the Court with which I operate sketches it as one actor among many in the European policy process.

This chapter will be divided into three further sections. In the first of these sections the role of the Court in the process of constitutionalising the Treaty of Rome and in the general development of the Community's legal system will be examined. The second section will consider the role of the Court of Justice in the making of substantive Community policy by examining developments in a number of sectors. The final section presents an extended conclusion. In it I develop an assessment of the contribution of the Court to the European policy process and evaluate the developing field of political science analysis of the Court.

The 'constitutional' role of the Court

The 'constitutionalisation' of the Treaty of Rome refers to the transformation of Community law from a system of conventional international law, which in principle imposes direct obligations on only states, to a new form of law, much more like the internal law of a state. The constitutionalising of the Treaty addressed the main problem of legal policy faced by the Court, ensuring the effectiveness of Community law. It has sought to solve, or at least manage, this problem by giving Community law rights directly to individuals, particularly rights of redress against governments which fail to live up to their Community obligations. As a result, Community law is much more effectively implemented than conventional international law. Nevertheless, it remains true that the Community suffers from an 'implementation gap' which is wider than that in most national systems, probably because it still relies to a considerable extent on the good faith of the states to enact Community rules into their national legal systems.

The constitutionalisation of the Treaty of Rome is usually presented as though decisions of the European Court by themselves transformed the Treaty into the European constitution. In a gloss on Eric Stein's important argument (Stein 1981), Burley and Mattli partially imported this legal understanding into the political science literature by suggesting that:

> By their own account, now confirmed by both scholars and politicians, the thirteen judges quietly working in Luxembourg managed to transform the Treaty of Rome ... into a constitution.
>
> (Burley and Mattli 1993: 43–4)

By contrast with most legal analyses, Burley and Mattli emphasise the manner in which other interests were drawn into the process of integration. However, they seem to attribute an overweening influence to the Court, at least in the sphere of what they call 'legal integration', which, whatever else it encompasses, certainly includes the constitutionalising process. In particular, they describe legal integration as 'engineered' by the Court (Burley and Mattli 1993: 44). Thus, their account does not emphasise the relational or negotiated character of the development of the European constitution sufficiently. By contrast Weiler analyses the relationship between the Court and national governments, courts and the legal profession as one of partnership in 'a dialogue or "multilogue"' (1993: 419, see also 1994). The other actors are the Court's 'interlocutors' (Weiler 1993: 418–33, see also the discussion in Slaughter *et al.* 1997).

Direct effect

The notion that Community law might have a 'direct effect' in the legal orders of the member states is not present in the Treaty of Rome, although one form of Community secondary legislation – the Regulation – is 'directly applicable'. Thus the attribution of direct effects to (certain) provisions of the Treaty of Rome was a piece of judicial activism. Direct effect means that individuals can rely on Community laws as such, without a requirement for national implementing legislation. The ECJ initially established the principle of direct effect in relation to a limited category of articles of the EEC Treaty, but soon extended it to a wider range of Treaty articles and eventually to many categories of Community secondary legislation, including some directives.

Ultimately the issue of whether a provision of Community law can have direct effect comes down to two issues: whether it is capable of being ruled upon by a court, and whether national courts would be prepared to accept it. Pierre Pescatore, a former judge of the ECJ, has argued that the issue of direct effect

> boil[s] down to a question of justiciability. A rule can have direct effect whenever its characteristics are such that it is capable of judicial adjudication, account being taken both of its legal characteristics and of the ascertainment of the facts on which the application of each particular rule has to rely. This means that 'direct effect' of Community rules in the last analysis depends less on the intrinsic qualities of the rules concerned than ... on the assumption that

they [national judges] take these attitudes in a spirit of goodwill and with a constructive mind. … To this extent, direct effect appears to be in a way 'l'art du possible'.

(Pescatore 1983: 176–7)

The development of direct effect began with the *Van Gend* case (26/62 [1963] ECR 1), in which the Court made clear the radical basis of the doctrine. It claimed that the Community represented a 'new legal order', and that the 'States had limited their sovereign rights' (Case 26/62 *Van Gend* [1963] ECR 1 at 12) by becoming members of the Community. On this basis and 'independently of the legislation of Member States, Community law therefore not only imposes obligations on individuals but is also intended to confer upon them rights which become part of their legal heritage' (Case 26/62 *Van Gend* [1963] ECR 1 at 12). Subsequently the ECJ extended the principle of direct effect to apply to positive obligations contained in Treaty provisions as well as the prohibitions, and to cover relationships between individuals as well as those between an individual and the state (i.e. direct effect could be 'horizontal' as well as 'vertical').

Surprisingly, the initial development of the direct effect of Treaty provisions was more or less uncontested by the member states. Despite the fact that some states objected to the idea of direct effect in the proceedings of the *Van Gend* case, after the Court took its decision the member states accepted it without further ado, perhaps because the practical impact of this doctrine initially seemed relatively minor. It is more difficult for member states to avoid implementing directly effective Treaty provisions, embodying policies to which they were already committed in principle (see Weiler 1993: 430, for a discussion of the importance of the low visibility of Court decisions during the early phase of integration).

If the attribution of direct effect to Treaty provisions began the transformation of EC law, its extension to some categories of Community secondary legislation fundamentally altered the Community policy process. The extension of the direct effect principle to directives, the most widely used form of secondary legislation, was particularly important. On the face of it a directive leaves member states a good deal of discretion concerning the achievement of the general objectives they set out, which might have made it difficult to ensure that member states were implementing them adequately. However, if a directive could have direct effect then this problem is more or less removed. Even if a member state failed to implement the directive, or failed to implement it adequately, individuals could rely on it as law.

The Court developed the notion of the direct effect of directives gradually. Initially, in *Grad* v. *Finanzamt Traunstein* (Case 9/70 [1970] ECR 825) the Court argued that a combination of several forms of Community legislation (Directives and Decisions) could produce direct effects. In subsequent cases the Court provided further hints that some directives might be directly effective (see Case 79/72 *Commission* v. *Italian Republic Re Forestry Reproductive Material* [1973] ECR 667). Eventually in *Van Duyn* (Case 41/74 [1974] ECR 1337), the ECJ argued that a directive, on its own, could produce direct effects. The Court justified this development partly because it would improve the effectiveness of Community law – a political, rather than legal, argument. In addition, the Court suggested that it would be incompatible with the binding effect of directives to argue that in principle they could *not* have direct effects. Finally the Court implied that the existence of Article 234 (former Article 177), which allows national courts to ask the ECJ to interpret matters of Community law, suggested that directives might have direct effect.

The justifications provided by the Court for attributing direct effect to directives in *Van Duyn* were widely disputed, both academically and by national judiciaries (see Weatherill and Beaumont 1993: 296–301, 323–5; Wincott 1995b). In *Ratti* (Case 148/78 [1979] ECR

1629) the Court provided a stronger argument in favour of the proposition that some directives should be capable of producing direct effects. In particular, the Court suggested that member states should not be able to benefit from their own failure to fulfil their Community obligations.

As subsequently became clear (Case 152/84 *Marshall* [1986] ECR 723) this argument could only justify the direct effectiveness of directives in cases against the state (vertical direct effect), which left an inconsistency in the application of Community law. This inconsistency resulted in a stream of cases in which the ECJ was confronted with having to attempt to define what the extent of the state might be (see, for example, Weatherill and Beaumont 1993: 299–300 for discussion). It may also have led to the Court using Article 10 (former Article 5) of the Treaty of Rome creatively, to draw national courts further into the business of applying Community law, as we shall see below (see also Maher 1994).

Supremacy

The supremacy principle is a logical corollary of direct effect. Which set of rules should govern if a directly effective Community law contradicted provisions of national law? The ECJ presented its resolution to this issue soon after *Van Gend*, in the *Costa* case (6/64 [1964] ECR 585). It ruled that in the event of a conflict national law should give way to Community law. In other words, the Court declared that EC law was supreme over domestic law, despite the fact that the Treaty of Rome did not contain a supremacy clause. The doctrine of supremacy was not received with the equanimity that had been displayed towards the initial statement of direct effect. Instead a lengthy negotiation took place between the European Court and national courts, particularly in Italy, Germany and France, over the issue of supremacy (see Wincott 1995b for a discussion of this process).

One of the most symbolically significant aspects of this negotiation concerned the issue of human rights protection. If Community law is supreme over all national law, it must even take precedence over protection of human rights in national constitutions. Since the Treaty of Rome contained no provisions protecting human rights, a risk existed that supreme Community law might violate constitutionally protected national human rights. To guard against this possibility the German and Italian constitutional courts reserved the right to review Community law against their national human rights standards, which amounted to a limitation to the principle of supremacy. In consequence, partly in order to protect the principle of supremacy, and under considerable pressure particularly from the German courts, the ECJ departed from its previous refusal to read human rights into the Treaty. In a dramatic example of judicial activism, it 'created' human rights protection as a fundamental principle of Community law. Ironically, the European Court subsequently turned this difficulty to its advantage and developed a body of case law on human rights, which allowed it to add considerable *gravitas* and legitimacy to its claim that the Treaty of Rome should be regarded as a constitution.

Although it took a considerable time for supremacy to be accepted in the legal systems of all the member states, for practical purposes this principle is now established. Nevertheless, difficulties surrounding the relationship of the EC and national legal orders do emerge periodically. The German Constitutional Court's (*Bundesverfassungsgericht*) ruling on the Maastricht Treaty (Judgement of 12 October 1993 CMLR [1994] 1) is a case in point. The German Court expressed a 'quite flat (and renewed) denial of the absolute supremacy of Community law and its supreme judicial organ' (Herdegen 1994: 239).

Community law and national law

The relationship between the ECJ and national courts has been based mainly on Article 234 (former Article 177) of the Treaty of Rome, although more recently Article 10 (former Article 5) has come to play a larger role, as we shall see. Under Article 234 (former Article 177) the ECJ interprets Community law for national courts when a national court refers a question of Community law raised in a case before it. The judgement in the particular case is left to the national court. Article 10 (former Article 5) contains a 'loyalty clause' which says that member states must take appropriate measures to ensure the fulfilment of their Treaty obligations. In the 1980s the ECJ began to argue that this provision requires national courts to ensure that legislatures and executives meet their responsibilities under Community law.

Article 234 (former Article 177) has come to play a central part in the legal life of the Community, probably providing more of the case load of the Court than any other method of access to it. It is also the main way in which individuals have gained access to Community law. The alternative would have been to allow individuals to have direct access to the European Court, perhaps by means of Article 230 (former Article 173). The ECJ rejected this option. It might have increased the burden on the ECJ while at the same time making Community law much less accessible to the general public. Other methods of ensuring that the member states implement Community rules adequately rely on other member states or the Commission taking a particular state to Court (using Articles 226 and 227 – former Articles 169 and 170). Although the Commission has prosecuted member states for failing to implement Community laws properly, inevitably the Commission cannot scrutinise the detail of national law in the way that a multiplicity of self-interested domestic actors would. In addition, it is politically difficult for the Commission and the member states to sue one another.

Several commentators suggest that Article 234 (former Article 177) was included more or less as an afterthought (Burley and Mattli 1993; Weiler 1991), implying that Articles 226 and 227 (formerly 169 and 170) were indeed the main mechanisms for the enforcement of Community law in the member states. Others argue that the similarity of Article 234 (former Article 177) to various national provisions makes it improbable that those who drafted the Treaty failed to understand 'the immense potential of such provisions' (Cappelletti 1987: 13). It is clear, however, that the Court of Justice was eager to develop the use of Article 234 (former Article 177), and used judicial and extra-judicial means to do so (Rasmussen 1986). From the late 1960s onwards, the ECJ made every effort to educate national judges in the use of Article 234 (former Article 177), including hosting seminars and conferences in Luxemburg. In addition the ECJ aided national courts by reinterpreting inappropriate questions, which were often asked, in such a way as to allow it to make a ruling (Mancini 1989: 606).

In co-operation with national courts, some analysts argue, the ECJ has transformed 'Article 234 (former Article 177) into a tool whereby private individuals can challenge their national legislation for incompatibility with Community law' (Mancini 1989: 606; see also Hartley 1986). This transformation was achieved despite the wording of the Article, and the formal refusal of the Court to review national laws under it. In a remarkably candid discussion Federico Mancini, an ECJ Judge, argued that the Court was paying 'lip service to the language of the Treaty'. He carried on to claim that 'having clarified the meaning of the relevant Community measure, the Court usually went on to indicate to what extent a *certain type* of national legislation can be regarded as compatible with that measure. The national judge is thus led hand in hand as far as the door; crossing the threshold is his [sic] job, but now a job no harder than child's play' (Mancini 1989: 606).

During the 1980s the Court began to interpret Article 10 (former Article 5), as binding on all the organs of the state, in their internal relations with one another. Thus, national courts were given a duty to ensure that their legislatures and executives meet their Community obligations. Thus the judicial review capacity of national courts, to judge national laws against a Community standard, increased. This development partially resolved the inconsistency left in Community law as a result of directives having only vertical, not horizontal, direct effect.

In the *Von Colson* (Case 14/83 [1984] ECR 1891) and *Marleasing* (Case C-106/89 [1989] ECR I-4135) rulings, the Court argued that national courts should interpret domestic law, whatever its apparent meaning, in a manner consistent with Community law. It seems that national courts should now interpret national law so as to 'implement' Community law even if no national legislation exists on the relevant issue (Maher 1994: 231). The ECJ developed the use of Article 10 (former Article 5) further in the *Francovich* case (C-6&9/90 [1993] CMLR 66). In this case the ECJ decided that the national court could award damages to an individual against the national government, where loss has been suffered in consequence of non-implementation of a directive.

The Court's decision in *CIA Security International* (Case C-194/94 [1996] ECR I-2201) suggests that it remains radical in the post-Maastricht period, at least in relation to the structure and enforcement of Community law. According to Directive 83/189/EEC national authorities are obliged to notify the Commission of their intention to issue (technical) standards and regulations, so that the Commission could check their compatibility with the internal market. According to the prevailing procedures and explicit terms of the directive, the Commission could take a member state to Court if it implemented a regulation without (adequate) notification. However, this *post hoc* procedure could allow serious damage to the structure of the internal market. It would take considerable time for the Commission to identify regulations in breach of internal market rules and take legal proceedings against the state concerned. As early as 1986 the Commission made clear its view that regulations which a member state had not notified should be unenforceable. This view met with considerable resistance from several states and some other European institutions. It was seen as an unacceptable encroachment by the Commission into the EC legal process and perhaps also of the Community system into national legal procedures.

The Court's decision, in 1996, to accept the Commission's view had consequences in two main areas. The first is 'constitutional'; the decision represents a doctrinally innovative strengthening of the legal structure of the EC. The EC legal system was stronger because its enforcement/implementation capacity was substantially increased. The default position was transformed. Previously a reactive Commission responded to national regulation. Now national regulations are assumed to be unenforceable unless they have the Commission's sanction. The onus is on national authorities to notify the EC of their intention to regulate (Weatherill 2000 develops a persuasive argument concerning the scope of ECJ activism revealed by this case).

As ever, of course, the Court's 'constitutional' decisions take place in a particular policy context. In a period where the ECJ is widely perceived to be more cautious than previously, it is worth noting that this strengthening of EC law occurred in the core area of the internal market, not at the fringes of Community law. The particular policy consequence is that the internal market is made more robust. This case shows *both* that the Community institutions remain seriously engaged in developing and entrenching the internal market *and* that such activity remains necessary. The market system requires constant political and legal vigilance as well as regular regulatory updating. While increasing the reach of the EC system in relation to the internal market, this case also indicates just how much regulatory scope the member states still have *vis-à-vis* the internal market (and particularly how much they have had until recently).

Enlargement and the Treaty of Nice

Over time the role of the Court of Justice has altered as a result of changes in its context as well as it own activism. As the substantive scope of the Community has grown and it has increased in size geographically, the organisational capacity of the Court of Justice to maintain a coherent and uniform body of law has been stretched, even with the aid, since 1988, of the Court of First Instance. The development of the Community continues. Such innovations as the Charter of Fundamental Rights discussed at Nice are likely to further elaborate, and perhaps complicate the judicial function further (especially, but not exclusively, if the Charter should become formally legally binding). The prospect of a further enlargement of the European Union to include 20+ states, which have neither previous experience of the operation of the Community (legal) system, nor, arguably, domestic legal systems that are as securely entrenched as those of the existing members, begs serious questions about the future of the Community legal order. Various suggestions have been made about how the Community legal system might be changed to improve its current operation and meet the challenges it is likely to face in the future. One forum within which these issues were considered was provided by the Nice IGC (on which see Arnull 2001). In general, the IGC followed the Courts themselves in eschewing the option of differentiating the legal system territorially, for example by creating regional courts, instead allowing a further development of functional specialisation within it.

The Nice Treaty (available only in draft at the time of writing) extends the role of the Court of First Instance by allowing it to hear preliminary references. As we have seen, such references to the Court of Justice have played a key role in the historical development and current operation of the Community legal system. The extension of this system to the CFI in Article 225, paragraph 3 (with the possibility of appeal to the ECJ) marks a potential significant increase in its status and influence. indirectly this reform may increase the degree of functional specialisation within the Community legal system, by raising the status of the specialised CFI. Other proposed changes include the possibility of creating Judicial Panels for some types of case, such as disputes between the Community and its servants. The members of Judicial Panels will be appointed by the Council on the same terms as currently apply for appointment to the CFI. They will be 'attached to the CFI', which, as a consequence will no longer really be a Court of First Instance. At Nice the member states seem to have deferred a decision on the precise form of judicial institution desirable to handle intellectual property cases. The Commission had proposed the creation of a Community Intellectual Property Court. The Nice Treaty produced a less ambitious result, while acknowledging that some institutional innovation would be required to handle this growing area of law. Currently it seems likely that a Judicial Panel on Intellectual Property will be created.

In the light of enlargement, the Court faces issues of collegiality somewhat similar to the much-debated question of the size and make-up of the College of Commissioners. At Nice no decision was taken to restrict the number of judges. There will still be a judge from each country. Instead, the rules on formations – 'Chambers' – within which the Court sits were altered. The precise form of these changes should make it possible for the Court to retain collegiality, although the new Grand Chamber may prove difficult to organise (for the technical reason that it must generally include each of the Presidents of the five-Judge Chambers).

The changes agreed at Nice generally represent sensible and gradual alterations of the operation of the Community legal structure, but they only seem to deal with the most recent enlargement. The question of whether they are enough to face the considerable challenge to the Community legal order of the next enlargement remains unanswered. Aside from a French proposal that the full Court should not exceed 15 Judges even after the next enlargement, little attention seems to have been paid to the implications of future enlargement for the operation of the Community legal system.

The Court and the European constitution

The process of constitutionalising the Treaty of Rome is notable for a number of interrelated reasons. These include the incremental strategy of doctrinal development adopted by the Court, the importance attached to ensuring that member states implement Community legislation adequately and the relational character of the constitutionalisation process. Although the constitutionalising process has resulted in individuals being given rights directly by Community law, the motivation for these developments seems to have been to bring pressure to bear on the member states by opening them up to prosecution. The constitutionalising process has been largely a political negotiation between courts and lawyers. In the area of substantive policy-making a larger range of interests and groups can be drawn into the integration process, as we shall see.

The Court in the European policy process

The Court of Justice has played an important part in substantive policy development in Europe. However, we shall see that to understand its contribution, the Court's rulings need to be placed in the context of the wider legislative and policy process in the Community, where they do not always have the impact which seems to have been intended by the Court. The Court can be boldest when its rulings are likely to be supported by some significant social or economic group and is most influential when its rulings feed into the Community legislative process.

Free movement of goods

The policy of the free movement of goods is central to economic integration in Europe. It is an area where the Court might be expected to have had a major influence. However, even the *Cassis de Dijon* judgement (120/78 [1979] ECR 649), which is famous for launching the internal market programme, is less influential than is often thought. In legal terms the radical interpretation of the internal market occurred in the *Dassonville* ruling (8/74 [1974] ECR 837) (Alter and Meunier-Aitsahalia 1994; Wincott 1995b; Volcansek 1992 also discusses this case). *Dassonville* rendered illegal all trading rules which might 'actually or potentially, directly or indirectly' impede intra-Community trade. The *Cassis* decision actually restricted the scope of the basic *Dassonville* rule, by allowing several justifications for the restriction of trade. The fact that *Dassonville* is not as well known as

Cassis, despite the greater legal significance of the earlier case, illustrates the extent to which the context of a ruling dominates its content.

Cassis did introduce the principle that alcoholic drinks lawfully marketed in one member state should be allowed to circulate freely throughout the Community. However, the slogan 'mutual recognition', which became an emblem of the internal market programme, did not appear in *Cassis*. This expression, which has its origins in the Treaty of Rome, was applied to the free movement of goods in the debates which followed the *Cassis* ruling.

The real significance of the *Cassis* case is the legislative use made of it by the Commission (Alter and Meunier-Aitsahalia 1994; Wincott 1995a; Armstrong 1995; Armstrong and Bulmer 1998). Alter and Meunier-Aitsahalia (1994) have argued that the Commission went well beyond the meaning of the Court's judgement in attempting to relaunch the integration process. Moreover, they argue, agreement on the desirability of mutual recognition developed as a result of a process of political mobilisation and bargaining by the Commission, states and interest groups which occurred well after the Court's *Cassis* judgement.

The free movement of goods policy, as well as being a site of important pro-integration jurisprudence, has also provided evidence of the Court being unable to control its environment and eventually retreating from a radical pro-integration position under pressure which resulted from self-interested litigation by private interests. A striking example of the disruptive influence of strategic litigation on the integration process is the 'saga' of Sunday trading (Rawlings 1993). Various UK retailers, particularly those specialising in DIY, attempted to use Community law to provide a basis for trading on Sunday, which was then banned by rather ramshackle legislation in England and Wales. The UK politics of reforming this legislation was complicated because it cut across conventional political cleavages. In the ruling Conservative Party the issue pitted free marketeers against proponents of traditional religious and family values. As a result it proved difficult to find a consensus in favour of either rolling back the *de facto* increase in trading on Sunday or a fully liberalised solution.

A number of retailers sought to bypass the national political debate by means of an appeal to Community law on free movement, so the Court of Justice was drawn into the 'saga'. Specialist legal teams evolved both for the retailers and for the local authorities which prosecuted them. The Court's judgement has been described as 'delphic' in places (Rawlings 1993: 317, referring to the *Torfaen* case (145/88 [1990] 1 CMLR 337). It was reluctant to be drawn into the detail of the case and left it to the national court to decide whether the 'restrictive effect' of the Sunday trading rules on the free movement of goods exceeded 'the effects intrinsic to trade rules' (cited in Rawlings 1993: 317). Both sides claimed victory after this decision, the general impact of which was to sow confusion in the English legal system.

In the end, the English legislation was altered, and Sunday trading was (partially) liberalised, as a result of a general political and legal campaign, of which the Euro-litigation was only one part. Indeed, the main 'use' of the European litigation for those campaigning for the right to trade on Sunday was to cause chaos in the English law, thereby forcing the government to legislate to clarify the situation. This use of Community law places the European Court in a difficult position. As one commentator has suggested, the ECJ's part in the Sunday trading 'saga' 'may do great damage to the reputation of Community law inside and among member states' (Rawlings 1993: 335).

Moreover, it probably contributed to the Court subsequently seeming to retreat from its very wide-ranging *Dassonville* interpretation of Article 28 (former Article 30) on the free movement of goods in the *Keck* judgement (Keck and Mithouard Cases C-267, C-268/91 [1993] ECR I-609).

Gender equality

Article 141 (former Article 119) of the Treaty of Rome committed the member states to implement equal pay for women and men by the end of 1962. The historical record shows that this deadline for implementation fell by the way, as did many subsequent ones during the 1960s. Even by the mid-1970s Article 141 (former Article 119) was effectively un-implemented. Despite regular pressure from the Commission, the member states were unwilling to tackle the issue (Warner 1984). By the early 1970s, however, a number of influences favourable to the implementation of Article 141 (former Article 119) had developed. First, 'second wave' feminism gained ground across Europe and, second, the political leaders of the member states adopted an attitude more open to the development of European social policy.

However, these influences were not sufficient conditions for the passage of Community legislation on equality. Although the women's movement undoubtedly influenced the general climate of opinion in the member states and the Commission, the 'direct input' into the European policy process by women was small (Hoskyns 1986: 308). The evidence from other aspects of social policy suggests that although a number of pieces of social legislation were passed in the late 1970s, many of the proposals in the Commission's 1974 Social Action Programme failed to become law.

Judgements made by the Court of Justice made a crucial difference in raising the issue of equality on the Community's legislative agenda, and in putting pressure on the member states to pass proposed legislation. In the 'Defrenne' cases it was hinted (in 1970–71) and subsequently confirmed (1975–76) that Article 141 (former Article 119) of the Treaty of Rome was directly effective. In other words, by 1976, irrespective of existing national legislation, any woman (or man) who had been treated unequally in terms of pay could sue her employer. These cases had a strong impact on the legislative agenda by raising the idea that Article 141 (former Article 119) could be directly effective. They also altered the terms on which the member states participated in the legislative process.

It is worth noting that the Court did not move immediately to declare Article 141 (former Article 119) directly effective, never mind to produce an expansive interpretation of what 'equal pay' might mean. Instead, in the first Defrenne case (Case 80/70 *Defrenne* [1971] ECR 445) the Court did not consider the question of the direct effect in its judgement, despite the fact that the Advocate-General had raised the issue. Indeed the Advocate-General argued that Article 141 (former Article 119) did have direct effect. It was only in the second *Defrenne* case (Case 43/75 [1976] ECR 455) that the direct effect of Article 141 (former Article 119) was confirmed by the Court.

If the gradualism of the Court in relation to the confirmation or attribution of direct effect of Article 141 (former Article 119) shows a characteristic, and political, feature of its methods, the second *Defrenne* case involved one of the most dramatic presentations of the Court's political face. As a matter of legal principle, if Article 141 (former Article 119) was directly effective, its effect should date from the end of 1962, as the Court recognised in its judgement. However, in the face of considerable pressure from national governments, the Court inserted an extraordinary proviso that the judgement would have only a prospective effect, except for those individuals who already had cases before a court.

These cases again show the importance of having a determined litigant or group of litigants, prepared to return time and time again. Although no doubt buttressed by the general development of the women's movement, the determination of Defrenne's lawyers played a key role in the Court of Justice being able to develop its position on Article 141 (former Article 119). Without a batch of cases on the subject, the influence of the Court would have been much more limited (Hoskyns 1996).

Subsequently, the legislation passed in the 1970s became the subject of expansive interpretation by the Court of Justice. However, recent empirical research on this period has cast the role of the Court in a rather more sceptical light than before. Developing this revisionist view, Claire Kilpatrick provides a coruscating analysis of the ECJ's reaction to a range of sex equality cases sent from the UK. She suggests that the Court appeared 'extremely confused' in response to carefully constructed references from the UK and that, consequently, the English lawyers involved experienced 'crushing disappointment' (Kilpatrick 1998: 149).

During the 1980s the British Equal Opportunities Commission pursued a strategy of litigation that attempted to force an unresponsive national government to develop equal opportunities policies. While this strategy met with some success, it eventually provoked a dramatic political response, which augurs badly for the future influence of the Court. Several member states and a number of major pension companies objected to a potential development of the Court's case law on equality into the area of pension provision. They managed to get a protocol (known as the Barber protocol) attached to the Maastricht Treaty which amounted to a manipulation of the judicial process by politicians – a clear indication that the Community's legislators are prepared to restrict the judicial independence of the Court. 'The law' remains an important backdrop to policy development. Nevertheless, the recent emergence of policies aimed at 'mainstreaming gender' has been politically, not legally driven. 'Mainstreaming' policies seem to have filtered down to the EU from the UN (Pollack and Hafner-Burton 2000), rather than having originated in a politics of EC law.

Merger regulation

One of the most dramatic examples of the Court supporting the extension of Community competence has been in competition policy. The Commission has an unusually extensive administrative role in this policy area, which even includes a judicial component. Although on the face of it this might have marginalised the contribution of the Court, in fact it placed special importance on the particular ability of the Court to construct a position as legally legitimate.

As with the provisions of the Treaty of Rome on free movement of goods, the articles governing competition provide the basis and framework for a policy. Articles 81 and 82 (former Articles 85 and 86) contain the main substantive provisions, and regulate cartels and the abuse of a dominant position respectively, but neither mention merger control. More generally the nature and extent of the Community's competence remained to be spelled out. During the 1960s the Commission was not strongly concerned to develop a competence to regulate mergers, and indeed in 1966 it issued a memorandum specifically ruling out the use of Article 81 (former Article 85) to control mergers.

By the early 1970s, the Commission's general role in the regulation of competition had become fairly well established, and the Commission's interest in merger regulation began to grow. In 1972, in proceedings against Continental Can, the Commission attempted for the first time to use Article 82 (former Article 86) to control a merger. When this case was taken to the Court of Justice on appeal, the Court gave legal sanction to the principle that Article 82 (former Article 86) could be used to regulate mergers, although, characteristically, the specific case against Continental Can was dismissed (Case 6/72 [1973] ECR 215). Some nine months after the Court's ruling in February, the Commission brought forward a proposal for a merger regulation in October 1973. For a variety of reasons (not the least of which was the necessity for unanimity in competition legislation) this regulation was not passed by the Council of Ministers. Indeed, revised (and watered down) drafts of this regulation were re-presented to the Council during the 1970s and 80s, all of which failed to become law.

Even after *Continental Can*, Article 82 (Article 86) did not provide a legal framework which forced companies to refer proposed mergers to the Commission. However, in the late 1970s and early 1980s uncertainty about the existing rules and the prospects for legislation meant that the companies began to refer plans for mergers to the Commission (Bishop 1993: 300–1). This development, in combination with the emergence of the internal market programme, led big business to press for the development of a coherent Community regime for the regulation of mergers. Industry was particularly concerned that a 'one-stop shop' should be created, so that the parties to a merger did not have to clear the project with a range of national authorities as well as the Commission.

In 1987 the Court of Justice strongly increased the pressure for Community legislation on mergers. Its ruling in the *Philip Morris* case (joined cases 142/84 and 156/84 [1987] ECR 4487) altered the widely held understanding that Article 81 (former Article 85) could not be used to regulate mergers. In interpreting the article in this way the Court was contradicting the mood of the member states as expressed in their refusal to accept drafts of a merger regulation placed before them in 1982 and 1984. Arguably, the Court was able to make this move because of the emerging mood of support for Community-level merger control among industrialists. The Court's decision in this case strongly increased the concern about the incoherence of merger control in Western Europe. The magnification of the existing anxiety among industrialists strengthened their pressure for an EC regulation. In addition, this decision eroded the power (or sovereignty) of the member states, and weakened their will to resist Community-level legislation. Indeed, after the *Philip Morris* case, arguably the member states could actually regain some ability to limit the development of the Community merger control regime through participation. In this context it is worth noting that the substance of the regulation was further watered down between 1987 and 1989, when the Merger Control Regulation (Regulation 4064/89) was passed.

The Court and substantive policy

The Court's role in the making of substantive policy is often overstated. Certainly, the Court's ability unilaterally to make policy is limited. However, the Court can have a significant impact on policy, usually by influencing the legislative process (either at the Community or national levels). The Court can do this, for example, by issuing judgements which unsettle established practices and understandings (*Dassonville* and *Cassis*) and alter the balance of forces in a legislative process (*Philip Morris*). The Court is best able to make an expansive ruling when it can rely on some significant social or economic interest to support and legitimate its judgement, especially when a loose alignment of forces can come together to overcome the objections of particular member states. However, we have also seen that the use of Community law by private interests does not always produce results favourable for integration. As Community law continues to mature we can expect an ever wider range of interests to become aware of its potential, and to use Community law in ways which do not suit the ECJ.

Conclusion: the place and power of the Court in the European Community

The analysis presented here suggests that the Court of Justice does not have the capacity to force or engineer the process of integration in Europe. Nevertheless, the Court has made a substantial contribution to the integration process through its role in developing both the Community's legal system, and particular policy sectors. The influence of the Court has been attributed to a number of factors. These include the cleverness and political acumen of the judges, the normative power of the 'formalism' of the law (Weiler 1993; 1994) and the lack of attention paid to the Court during the early stages of the integration process (Stein 1981; Weiler 1994).

Structural characteristics of the Court and EC law engage the material interests of various groups in ways that are of particular interest. On one hand Burley and Mattli (1993) have developed a legal neo-functionalist theory according to which the material interests of individuals in general, and national judiciaries and academic and practising lawyers, were engaged by the Court to further the process of 'legal integration' in Europe. On the other, Stone Sweet and Caparoso argue that a 'virtuous circle' interaction of transnational exchange, transnational dispute resolution and the elaboration of supranational rules has created a system of supranational governance (1998).

Mancini, an ECJ judge of the 1980s and 1990s, attributed the success of the Court to its judges, or what he called 'the cleverness of my predecessors':

> If what makes a judge 'good' is his [sic] awareness of the constraints on judicial decision-making and the knowledge that rulings must be convincing in order to evoke obedience, the Luxembourg judges of the 1960s and the 1970s were obviously *very* good.
>
> (Mancini 1989: 605)

As time passes, this argument seems likely to be called into question (Kilpatrick 1998). It certainly downplays the extent of the difficulty the ECJ faced in persuading national judges to 'obey' them. Also, it directs attention away from the unconvincing character of crucial doctrinal developments, such as the attribution of direct effects to directives.

If the pure persuasive force of the arguments of ECJ judges cannot wholly explain their influence on the integration process, the normative power of the legal form, what Weiler has called 'the pull of formalism' (Weiler 1993: 423–4, 427), may have contributed to the states' acceptance of the Court's jurisprudence. Perhaps the 'cleverness' of judges has been in their ability to take up frankly political positions, while broadly retaining credibility as a legal, that is an apolitical, institution (Burley and Mattli 1993; Weiler 1993; 1994). However, the ability to retain legal credibility may have been mainly a result of factors beyond the control of the Court. The recent growth of controversy around the role of the Court certainly seems to owe more to changes in its environment, rather than any radicalisation of the Court (Weiler 1993; Wincott 1994).

The 'legal' character of its rulings helps to explain the Court's ideological influence. A number of scholars have argued that the Court has contributed crucial 'ideas' to the integration process (Alter and Meunier-Aitsahalia 1994; Garrett and Weingast 1993; Gerber 1994). Some of these analyses present these ideas as discrete inputs into the European policy process. However, sometimes ideas which seem to originate with the Court turn out to have been thought up elsewhere (Wincott 1995b; Gerber 1994). Moreover, it is very difficult, and often fruitless, to discover the origin of a particular 'idea'. Understanding the general structure of knowledge in the Community is more likely to produce useful insights. The construction of ideas as expert legal knowledge by the ECJ is an important characteristic of the Community.

National judiciaries may have been drawn into the integration process as a result of Community law offering them an opportunity to engage in increased judicial review of national legislation (Burley and Mattli 1993). Weiler has argued that

> [i]nstitutionally, for courts at all levels in all Member States, the constitutional architecture with the ECJ signature meant an overall strengthening of the judicial branch *vis à vis* the other branches of government.
>
> (Weiler 1993: 425)

On the other hand, some courts, and perhaps particularly higher courts, clearly feel that their national prerogatives are threatened by the ECJ, as the reaction of the German Constitutional Court to the Maastricht Treaty illustrates. Whatever the explanation, it is certainly true that the engagement of national courts in the Community project was crucial. By being presented to the people and governments of Europe partly through the medium of their own courts, Community law benefited from the legitimacy and coercive capacities of the national legal systems.

As far as the engagement of private interests in Community law is concerned, the Court may be more inclined to expansive judgements where a significant portion of the relevant population seems likely to support the new development. There is some evidence of this sort in the attribution of direct effect to Article 141 (former Article 119) or the use of Article 81 (former Article 85) to regulate mergers. Indeed, in both these areas the Court appears to have innovated gradually. This gradualism might have helped to test out the level of support it would be likely to receive. Particularly in the case of merger regulation, gradualism may have actually contributed to the generation of support for its position by slowly strengthening the capacity of the Community to regulate mergers.

However, we have also seen evidence, in the 'saga' of Sunday trading, of private interests using Community law in ways that seem to compromise the integration process rather than supporting it. This evidence suggests that European law has not been the 'domain' of an automatic process of neo-functional integration, nor has the European Court been in a position to control, or engineer, the uses made of Community law by private interests. To the extent that Community law may have disintegrative effect, the questions 'Why was it not used in this way earlier?' and 'Under what conditions is the integration process likely to be either supported or undermined by private interest litigation?' become crucial for future research. Stone Sweet and Caparoso's fascinating and convincing research only makes variation in the 'success' of the Court and differences in the 'depth' of the law (or its 'reach' into national systems and 'daily life' across Europe) in various domains the more intriguing.

The incremental character of the Court's approach to the development of both legal doctrines and Community policies has been strongly emphasised by the analysis here.

One legal analyst, aware of the constraints on the Court, characterised the style of the Court thus:

> A common tactic is to introduce a new doctrine gradually: in the first case that comes before it, the Court will establish the doctrine as a general principle but suggest that it is subject to various qualifications; the Court may even find some reason why it should not be applied to the particular facts of the case. The principle, however, is established. *If there are not too many protests*, it will be re-affirmed in later cases; the qualifications can then be whittled away and the full extent of the doctrine revealed.
>
> (Hartley 1988: 546, emphasis added)

This gives a nice flavour of the tactics of the Court, although it may attribute too much foresight to it. Hartley implies that the Court had the doctrine fully worked out initially, and subsequently implemented it gradually. On some occasions the Court may plan out the gradual introduction of a new doctrine, but on others the development of the Court's jurisprudence probably owes more to serendipity or 'learning by doing' than conscious planning.

The role of the Advocate-General has been of particular importance for this sort of development. The Advocate-General is an officer of the Court whose job is to consider the legal arguments made in a case, and perhaps to come to a provisional conclusion on it, but whose 'opinion' does not have a legally binding character. Advocates-General have often been able to 'sound out' new ideas in their opinions, without risking the good name of the Court as a whole.

The question of why it adopts an incremental approach goes to the heart of the nature of the Court. The explanation mainly lies with issues of legitimacy and power. The legitimacy of a court making a major contribution to the development of specific policies or the general legal character of a polity is questionable. The issue of legitimacy is particularly important in the context of the European integration, because the Community as a whole, including its legal system, is deficient in one of the defining characteristics of a state – the power of coercion. At times the Court may have been gradually implementing an internally predefined doctrine while at others it took advantage of opportunities produced by developments unfolding in its wider environment (some of which might partially be a product of its own activity). In either case the Court has had to persuade the individuals, states and Community institutions which make up the EC to obey its rulings, rather than being able to force them to do so. The weakness of the EC/EU's coercive power may help us to understand why the Court seems to have adopted an incremental approach.

The absence or weakness of coercive power in the Community also sheds some light on the peculiar character of the implementation of Community legislation. Increasingly, analysts of the European policy process are turning their attention to problems of implementation, which are generally regarded as severe, even judged by the reality of national standards rather than the traditionally assumed ideal of faultless translation of policy into practice. The development of the legal structure of the Community has been largely an attempt to improve the effectiveness of Community law, and by comparison with international organisations, Community implementation is remarkably effective. However, the Community remains profoundly dependent on the member states, in the form of national governments and judiciaries, which leads to wide variation in implementation across the member states.

If ever it was useful to view European Community law and the national law of member states as 'independent' of one another, this image is no longer helpful. As a consequence, the effectiveness of 'European' law depends on mutual trust. Actors in each member state must trust that European rules are being implemented effectively in the 'national' legal orders of all other states.

Overall, the Court of Justice has made contributions in two main areas of European integration. First, it has played a leading role in the development of the Community's legal system. For all its faults, this system is the main feature which distinguishes the Community from conventional international organisations. Perhaps the most significant aspect of this contribution is the fact that it dramatically increases the likelihood that laws passed by the Community will be implemented at national level. The development of the Community's legal system, and particularly the doctrines of direct effect and supremacy, also increased the capacity of the Court to influence substantive policy-making in Europe. In general, however, it would be misleading to attribute the development of substantive policies wholly to the Court. In fact, the Court has been most effective when its rulings have altered the balance of power in the policy-making process so as to facilitate the passage of legislation which might otherwise have failed to become law. The interaction of the Court with other institutions (Wincott 1995a) and interests in the development of the Community legal system and policy process is a crucial characteristic of European integration.

References

Alter, K. and Meunier-Aitsahalia, S. (1994) 'Judicial Politics in the European Community: European Integration and the Pathbreaking *Cassis de Dijon* Decision', *Comparative Political Studies* 26/4.

Armstrong, K. (1995) 'Regulating the Free Movement of Goods: Institutions and Institutional Change', in G. More and J. Shaw (eds), *The New Legal Dynamics of European Union*, Oxford: Clarendon Press.

Armstrong, K. and Bulmer, S. (1998) *The Governance of the Single European Market*, Manchester: Manchester University Press.

Arnull, A. (2001) 'Modernising the Community Courts', unpublished paper, University of Birmingham, February.

Barnard, C. (1995) 'A European Litigation Strategy: The Case of the EOC', in G. More and J. Shaw (eds), *The New Legal Dynamics of European Union* Oxford: Clarendon Press.

Bishop, M. (1993) ' "European or National?" The Community's New Merger Regulation', in M. Bishop and J. Kay (eds), *European Mergers and Merger Policy*, Oxford: Oxford University Press.

Bulmer, S. (1994) 'Institutions and Policy Change in the European Communities: The case of Merger Control', *Public Administration* 72/3.

Burley, A.-M. and Mattli, W. (1993) 'Europe Before the Court: A Political Theory of Legal Integration', *International Organization* 47/1.

Cappelletti, M. (1987) 'Is the European Court of Justice "Running Wild"?', *European Law Review* 12/1.

Dauses, M. (1985) 'The Protection of Fundamental Rights in the Community Legal Order', *European Law Review* 10.

Garrett, G. (1992) 'International Cooperation and Institutional Choice: The European Community's Internal Market', *International Organization* 46/2.

Garrett, G. and Weingast, B. (1993) 'Ideas, Interests and Institutions: Constructing the EC's Internal Market', in J. Goldstein and R. Keohane (eds), *Ideas and Foreign Policy*, Ithica, NY: Cornell University Press.

Gerber, D. (1994) 'The Transformation of European Community Competition Law?', *Harvard International Law Journal* 35/1.

Hartley, T. (1986) 'Federalism, Courts and Legal Systems: The Emerging Constitution of the European Community', *American Journal of Comparative Law* 34.

Hartley, T. (1988) *The Foundations of European Community Law*, Oxford: Clarendon Press.

Herdegen, M. (1994) 'Maastricht and the German Constitutional Court: Constitutional Restraint for an "Ever Closer Union"', *Common Market Law Review* 31.

Hoskyns, C. (1986) 'Women, European Law and Transnational Politics', *International Journal of the Sociology of Law* 14.

Hoskyns, C. (1994) 'Gender Issues in International Relations: The Case of the European Community', *Review of International Studies* 20.

Hoskyns, C. (1996) *Integrating Gender: Women, Law and Politics in the European Union*, London: Verso.

Kilpatrick, C. (1998) 'Community or Communities of Courts in European Integration? Sex Equality Dialogues between the UK Courts and the ECJ', *European Law Journal* 4.

Maher, I. (1994) 'National Courts and European Community Courts', *Legal Studies* 14/2.

Mancini, G. (1989) 'The Making of a Constitution for Europe', *Common Market Law Review* 26.

Mazey, S. (1988) 'European Community Action on Behalf of Women: The Limits of Legislation', *Journal of Common Market Studies* 27/1.

Moravcsik, A. (1995) 'Liberal Intergovernmentalism and Integration: A Rejoinder', *Journal of Common Market Studies* 33/4.

Pescatore, P. (1983) 'The Doctrine of "Direct Effect": An Infant Disease of Community Law', *European Law Review* 8.

Pollack, M. and Hafner-Burton, E. (2000) 'Mainstreaming Gender in the European Union', paper prepared for presentation at the 12th Biennial Conference of Europeanists, Chicago, Palmer House Hilton, 30 March–2 April.

Rasmussen, H. (1986) *On Law and Policy in the European Court of Justice*, Dordrecht: Martinus Nijhoff.

Rawlings, R. (1993) 'The Eurolaw Game: Some Deductions from a Saga', *Journal of Law and Society* 20/3.

Sandholtz, W. and Stone Sweet, A. (eds) (1998) *European Integration and Supranational Governance*, Oxford: Oxford University Press.

Shapiro, M. (1980) 'Comparative Law and Comparative Politics', *Southern California Law Review* 53.

Slaughter, A.-M., Stone Sweet, A. and Weiler, J. H. H. (eds) (1997) *The European Courts and National Courts: Doctrine and Interpretation*, Oxford: Hart.

Stein, E. (1981) 'Lawyers, Judges and the Making of a Transnational Constitution', *American Journal of International Law* 75/1.

Stone Sweet, A. and Caparoso, J. (1998) 'From Free Trade to Supranational Polity: The European Court and Integration', in W. Sandholtz and A. Stone Sweet (eds), *European Integration and Supranational Governance*, Oxford: Oxford University Press.

Volcansek, M. (1992) 'The European Court of Justice: Supranational Policy-Making', *West European Politics* 15/3.

Warner, H. (1984) 'EC Social Policy in Practice: Community Action on behalf of Women and its Impact in the Member States', *Journal of Common Market Studies* 23/2.

Weatherill, S. (2000) 'A Case Study in Judicial Activism in the 1990s: The Status Before National Courts of Measures Wrongfully Un-Notified to the Commission', in D. O'Keeffe (ed.), *Liber Amicorum Gordon Slynn*, Kluwer Law International.

Weatherill, S. and Beaumont, P. (1993) *EC Law*, London: Penguin.

Weiler, J. H. H. (1991) 'The Transformation of Europe', *Yale Law Journal* 100/8.

Weiler, J. H. H. (1993) 'Journey to an Unknown Destination: A Retrospective and Prospective of the European Court of Justice in the Arena of Political Integration', *Journal of Common Market Studies* 31/4.

Weiler, J. H. H. (1994) 'A Quiet Revolution: The European Court of Justice and its Interlocutors', *Comparative Political Studies* 26/4.

Wincott, D. (1994) 'Is the Treaty of Maastricht an Adequate "Constitution" for the European Union?', *Public Administration* 72/4.

Wincott, D. (1995a) 'Institutional Interaction and European Integration: Towards an "Everyday" Critique of Liberal Intergovernmentalism', *Journal of Common Market Studies* 33/4.

Wincott, D. (1995b) 'The Role of Law or the Rule of the Court of Justice: An Institutional Account of Judicial Politics in the European Community', *Journal of European Public Policy* 2/4.

Wincott, D. (2000) 'A Community of Law? "European" Law and Judicial Politics: The Court of Justice and Beyond', *Government and Opposition* 35/1.

Part III

CHANNELS OF REPRESENTATION

Chapter 10

European elections and the European voter

Mark Franklin

Elections in a democracy are supposed to perform the functions of holding governments accountable and representing voters' interests, thus legitimising the exercise of power. Elections to the European Parliament fail to perform these functions. Since the Treaty of Union (often known as the Maastricht Treaty after the town where it was signed) came into force in November 1993, the European Parliament has had a role to play in selecting the President of the European Commission. Nevertheless, European elections do not set in motion a process of government formation in the same way as do national elections in the member states. Moreover, policies proposed by parties and candidates in European elections rarely have much European content. Instead they relate to the national political arena and are generally specific to particular countries. Parties use these elections as opportunities to test their standing with the public in terms of their domestic political agendas. But national governments do not stand or fall by European election results either, so the choices of voters have no immediately obvious repercussions on policy at either level. In the circumstances it is perhaps not surprising that many citizens of the European Union fail to take these elections seriously, and turnout is generally low – often even lower than at regional and local elections, which everywhere are less important than national elections. The low level of public participation in European elections in turn raises questions in some minds about the legitimacy of the European Union.

But the fact that European elections have no consequences for government formation at the national or European levels, and no discernible effect on the conduct of European affairs, does not mean that they have no effects. Indeed the very failure of European elections to legitimate the exercise of European power has consequences for the future of the European Union, and European elections do have many consequences – most of them unanticipated and many of them unfortunate – for the politics of member states. They also determine the composition of the European Parliament (even if voters do not focus on this aspect of their votes) which in turn can have implications for policy-making, especially with the new co-decision-making powers of the European Parliament following the Treaty of Union and Treaty of Amsterdam.

In this chapter we will not concern ourselves with the consequences of European elections for policy since this would require a focus on EU policy-making rather than on EU elections. Instead we will describe some of the effects that European elections have had on the politics of member states, and evaluate their role in creating a 'crisis of legitimacy' for the European union. But first we need to describe the nature of these elections.

The European electoral process

Elections to the European Parliament were first conducted in the (then) nine members of the (then) European Economic Community in June 1979, and were repeated in June of every fifth year thereafter. Greece held its first European elections in 1981, adding its representatives to the Parliament already elected in 1979; Portugal and Spain did the same in 1987, adding their representatives to the Parliament of 1984–89; Austria, Finland and Sweden followed the same path in 1995, adding their representatives to the Parliament of 1994–99. By 1999, therefore, ten countries had participated in five European elections, twelve countries had participated in four, and fifteen countries had participated in two – 64 elections altogether – quite enough for us to be able to grasp the process involved in the different countries and to reach some fairly firm conclusions about consequences.

While we can speak broadly of Europe-wide elections, there are significant variations in the way in which these elections are conducted in member states. Most strikingly, they are not all conducted on the same day. Some European countries traditionally go to the polls on Sundays while others have favoured mid-week voting. So European elections have been held on a Thursday in Denmark, Britain, Ireland, The Netherlands and Spain, but on the following Sunday elsewhere. Although this difference in timing has potentially important consequences (similar to the consequences of polls closing in California after outcomes have been announced in New York) in fact it matters little because the contests are so different in different countries that the outcome in one country can hold little interest for those voting anywhere else. Another difference between countries is the electoral system employed. Except in the British Isles, list-system proportional representation has been universal since 1979, but in England, Scotland and Wales (until and including the election of 1994) plurality voting was used (first past the post, with single-member districts); while in Ireland and Northern Ireland a Single Transferable Vote system continues to be employed, similar to that used in Ireland in national elections (Northern Ireland uses the British system for national elections). Again these differences would have potential consequences for the nature of the representational process in the European Union if European elections contributed to any such process. As it is, far more important than these differences between countries are the differences between the system employed in any particular country for European elections and that employed for national elections in the same country.

As already mentioned, Northern Ireland (and now Britain too) has a quite different electoral system for European than for national elections. In other countries the system may be superficially similar in both types of election, but there are always differences in practice – sometimes quite subtle ones. Except in The Netherlands, which effectively has only a single constituency for national elections, the number of constituencies into which the electorate is divided is always fewer in European elections (78 in Britain until 1994, five in Italy, four in Ireland, two in Belgium, and one each in Denmark, France, Greece, Luxemburg, Portugal and Spain). In Germany the two-vote system used for national elections is changed in European elections to a single-vote system, with the same single constituency as is used for second votes in national elections. Fewer constituencies makes it easier for a party to run candidates throughout the country, and this benefits smaller parties. On the other hand, except in Germany (which enforces the same 5% threshold in European as in national elections), the number of votes required to get any candidate elected is always greater in European elections (much greater in The Netherlands), which has the contrary effect – disadvantaging small parties. To the extent that small parties are advantaged or disadvantaged in European elections this can have important consequences for national politics if European elections themselves are taken as indicators of strength in the national political arena.

Although the European Parliament contains party 'groups' that sit together and co-operate in legislative matters, these groups are hardly relevant to the electoral process. In some countries the European Parliamentary group affiliation is mentioned on campaign literature (in Ireland, for example, Fine Gael campaigns as part of the social democratic People's Party of Europe) but this does not appear to be salient to voters. Transnational party activity was probably most extensive at the first elections in 1979, when EC funds were available for such activities, but voters appear to have paid little attention even then. There was little perception of the result of the election in transnational terms. Blumler and Fox, in their study of the 1979 European elections (1982) revealed that about 50% of voters admitted they had no idea which party grouping had been most successful in Europe as a whole, and that even among voters who claimed to have some idea there was considerable diversity of opinion (cf. Marsh and Franklin 1996).

Only in Denmark are there parties that campaign specifically on European issues (one is against Danish membership in the EU and the other is against any further moves towards closer union), and European elections in Denmark do have a distinctively European flavour (Worre 1993; 1996); but this simply emphasises the lack of European flavour to these elections elsewhere. In other countries it is rare for a European issue to intrude on a European election campaign, although Franklin and Curtice (1996) have shown that in 1989 attitudes to the Social Charter had measurable consequences for the outcome of the election in Britain (Franklin and Curtice argue that the issue was 'domesticated' in terms of national political discourse). The same thing appears to have happened again in Britain in 1999, and this process might serve as a model for the way in which European issues could in time come to have more impact in other countries; but, to the extent that this happens, the consequences of European elections for domestic politics will become even more unpredictable than they are at present (see below).

European elections and the national political arena

The apparent lack of any distinctively European character to European elections led commentators to focus initially on the manner in which these elections reflect national political processes. Reif and Schmitt (1980) coined the term 'second-order national election' to stress the similarity between European elections and local and regional elections, where voting patterns also tend to reflect national political trends (see also Reif 1984; 1985). The most important characteristic of second-order national elections is that there is less at stake than in first-order elections. This is why turnout is expected to be lower. It is also why European election outcomes are expected to reflect the balance of political forces in the national political arena.

But this early focus on the way in which European elections reflect national political forces left a great deal unexplained. In particular, while turnout in European elections was everywhere lower than in national elections, there were also major differences between turnout in successive European elections held in the same country. Moreover, the connection between support for government parties in European and national elections is closer when European elections are compared to subsequent national elections than when they are compared to previous national elections (Marsh and Franklin 1996; Marsh 1998), suggesting that any causal connection might actually run the other way than was initially supposed.

Partly because of these findings, recent research has started to focus on how European elections affect the national political arena in member countries of the European Union. Most importantly, the very fact that these elections can be used as 'markers' for the standing of national parties in the national political arena gives them an importance as catalysts of change in that arena. It is well-established that European electoral success played a role in the rise of the National Front in France and was important to the early success of the German Greens. Reif (1984) notes that government coalitions may be strained by adverse results, and gives illustrations. However, the nature of these effects and their importance depends on when they occur in the national electoral cycle (van der Eijk, Oppenhuis and Franklin 1994; Oppenhuis, van der Eijk and Franklin 1996).

Since European elections are held at the same time in all participating countries but national elections are not, it follows that European elections occur at different times relative to national elections in different countries (and in the same country at different European elections). Sometimes the European elections will occur shortly after a national election, sometimes only after the elapse of a number of months or years, and sometimes they will occur in the shadow of national elections that are known (or felt) to be imminent. Evidently the value of European elections as markers for what would happen in a national election held at the same time as (or instead of) the European election will depend on how soon a national election will be held. If a national election was recent, then the value of a European election outcome as a marker will be minimal: a better marker already exists in the shape of the recent national result. On the other hand, if some considerable time has elapsed since the most recent national election (and especially if another national election is imminent) then the importance of European elections as markers is evidently much greater. We will see that the position in the electoral cycle at which a European election occurs matters for the choices made by voters and for the consequences of the election for national politics, as well as for the level of turnout in the election itself.

Only in Denmark can European elections not be employed as markers for the standing of national parties. This is because the two Euro-sceptical parties in that country compete only in European elections. Because they receive a significant share of the vote, which is taken from other parties in proportions that are hard to compute with any accuracy, these elections do not have an outcome that is readily interpreted in national terms. Politicians and commentators in Denmark cannot easily tell what would have been the outcome of a national election held at the same time as (or instead of) the European election, and so Danish domestic politics are insulated from the consequences of European elections as nowhere else in the EU.

European elections and the study of voting behaviour

Because European elections have no apparent European content (except in Denmark) and no consequences for policy-making in the European arena that are discernible to voters, the political behaviour displayed at European elections is the behaviour of individuals in relation to their national political arenas; but because national political power is not at issue in these elections, it is a study of national electoral processes uncontaminated (except in a few important instances) by the intrusion of political concerns that might dominate particular national elections. Consequently, European elections present themselves as unique laboratories for a truly comparative study of why people vote and why they vote the way they do.

The most important feature of this laboratory is that it permits us to measure the effects of contextual variables that are necessarily invariant in any particular national election. These contextual variables include the nature of the electoral system, whether compulsory voting is in effect, the timing of elections (Sunday or weekday), and other institutional factors that are different in different countries of the European Union. They also include social and political factors that not only vary as between countries but can also change (perhaps slowly) over time even in particular countries. Such factors include educational level (the most widely validated influence determining the likelihood that individuals will vote), extent of unionisation (generally supposed to promote voting by social groups that would otherwise have low participation – see Verba *et al.* 1979; Parry *et al.* 1990), and the strength of linkages between social groups and political parties (class or cleavage voting, see Powell 1980; 1986). They also include the number of parties (one indicator of the adequacy of choices available), their distribution in terms of size (and hence their likelihood of wielding government power) and the extent to which citizens appear satisfied with the choices on offer (van der Eijk and Oppenhuis 1991; cf. Sartori 1994). Even more importantly, European elections, by falling at different times in the national political calendar, differ in their importance to voters for reasons explained above.

Over and above these contextual differences is one additional way in which European elections differ from each other: some of them occur concurrently with national elections (this happened eleven times between 1979 and 1999). Our ability to treat this circumstance as a contextual variable along with other contextual variables permits us to validate our analyses of the extent to which voters behave differently in European elections than they would in national elections that were otherwise identical.

The characteristics outlined above are quite numerous, but we have 64 elections conducted in different countries since 1979 that differ in terms of these variables – more elections than variables by a considerable margin, especially as it turns out that most of the listed factors have no influence on the outcomes of European elections. To the extent that these factors account for the different outcomes we observe, we will know that these outcomes are not the result of idiosyncratic peculiarities of individual countries but are simply the consequence of the political, social and institutional setting within which the elections are held. Indeed, it appears that the peculiarities of European elections can very largely be explained in such terms.

Turnout variations

One of the most evident differences between European and national elections has always been the low turnout recorded in European elections. Many commentators have suggested that low turnout indicates lack of legitimacy for the EC/EU, since citizens appear by their failure to vote to be withholding their support for European institutions. Table 10.1 shows that Britain and Denmark, the two most Euro-sceptical members of the EU, have often been the countries with lowest turnout in European elections.

Indeed, two early studies of individual-level voting choice found a connection between attitudes to Europe and propensity to vote (Inglehart and Rabier 1989; Blumler and Fox 1982). More recent studies, however, have found this relationship to be spurious (Niedemeier 1990; van der Eijk and Schmitt (1991); Schmitt and Mannheimer 1991; Marsh and Franklin 1996) – the result of failing to control for other variables – and Table 10.1 does show that turnout in the by no means Euro-sceptical Netherlands has averaged even less than in Denmark. If individual-level analyses fail to find effects on turnout from attitudes to Europe, then presumably we should seek explanations for the low aggregate level of turnout in The Netherlands and Britain from among the contextual features of European elections listed earlier.

One additional contextual feature that we have not yet mentioned has been widely noted in the literature: the first European election ever held in each country (in 1995 in Austria, Finland and Sweden, in 1987 in Portugal and Spain, in 1981 in Greece, and in 1979 elsewhere) saw generally higher levels of turnout than later elections. The exceptions are Belgium, Denmark, Britain, Greece and Luxemburg; but in ten other countries the inauguration of European elections evidently generated a level of interest that could not be sustained. Indeed, apart from a temporary plateau from 1984 to 1989, the decline in turnout over the course of five European elections appears continuous, fuelling concerns about a democratic deficit in the conduct of EU affairs.

These concerns are probably misplaced. There is certainly a democratic deficit in the governance of the European Union (van der Eijk and Franklin, with Johan Ackaert *et al.* 1996: ch. 21), and the low turnout in European elections is certainly due to the fact that European elections do not provide European voters with meaningful choices that would

Table 10.1 Turnout (%) in European elections by country, 1979–99*

	Election year					Average
	79	84	89	94	99	79–99
Austria				67.7[c]	49.0 :	58.3
Belgium	90.1	91.2	90.3	90.2	85.0 :	90.4
Denmark	47.8	52.4	47.4	52.9	50.4 :	50.2
Finland				60.3[c]	30.1 :	45.2
France	60.7	56.7	48.8	52.7	47.0 :	53.2
Germany	65.7	56.8	62.3	60.0	45.2 :	58.0
Great Britain	32.3	32.6	36.6	36.1	24.0[d] :	32.1
Greece	78.6[a]	77.2	80.1	71.2	83.2 :	77.3
Ireland	63.6	47.6	65.9	44.0	48.6 :	54.3
Italy	84.9	83.4	81.4	74.8	70.8 :	79.0
Luxemburg	88.9	88.8	96.2	88.5	85.8 :	89.6
Netherlands	58.1	50.6	48.8	35.6	29.9 :	44.6
Portugal		72.4[b]	51.1	35.5	40.4 :	49.8
Spain		68.9[b]	54.7	59.6	64.6 :	61.9
Sweden				41.6[c]	38.3 :	40.0
EU Average*	67.1	64.9	63.6	58.9	56.0	62.1
N	10	12	12	15	15 :	64

Notes:
* All countries weighted equally.
a Greece's first election was held in 1981. Because it is generally recognised that turnout in Greece is underestimated, each of the figures for turnout in that country is corrected on the basis of analysis conducted in van der Eijk and Franklin, with Johan Ackaert et al. (1996).
b The first election for Portugal and Spain was held in 1987.
c The first election for Austria, Finland and Sweden was held in 1995.
d Britain for the first time employed a PR List system in the election of 1999.

give them a real say in the future direction of European policy-making (van der Eijk and Franklin, with Johan Ackaert *et al.* 1996: ch. 19). However, the decline in the average level of turnout across the EU as a whole in successive elections to the European Parliament is not a sign that this deficit is increasing. Rather it is primarily an artefact of the accession to the EU of new countries with characteristics that are different from those of the original member countries, and the evolution of these countries from first-time participants to seasoned (perhaps 'disillusioned' would be a better word) members. This can most easily be explained in the context of an analysis of the determinants of turnout in European Parliament elections.

When countries are coded on the basis of contextual features, and these features are used to try to explain differences in turnout from country to country and election to election, one important variable is time until the next national election which, at the date of writing, is unknown for most members of the 1999 European Parliament. For these cases

Table 10.2 Effects on turnout of contextual factors

VARIABLE	B	SE	SIGF
(CONSTANT)	55.38	2.39	.0001
Compulsory voting in country	33.06	2.52	.0001
Years to next national election	−3.27	−0.81	.0002
First EP election held in country	8.20	2.61	.0026
Adjusted variance explained	0.80		
N	64		

we have estimated the time to the next national election on the basis of the average from past electoral cycles. Over all elections held since direct elections to the European Parliament were inaugurated in 1979, our ability to explain the large variations in turnout shown in Table 10.1 above is impressive. Table 10.2 reports the effects on turnout of those variables whose effects prove significant in multivariate perspective. Taken together, three variables explain 80% of the country-to-country turnout variations, and come within 5% of accounting for most of the 64 values of turnout recorded in these elections. Only Britain and (more recently) Sweden show turnout that is always below what would have been expected on the basis of their characteristics (by averages of 14 and 10%). At the other end of the scale, Spain and Germany have averaged 11 and 7% more than expected. No other country's turnout diverges significantly (in the statistical sense) from what would be predicted on the basis of characteristics listed in Table 10.2. So the variations in turnout that we saw in Table 10.1 can be largely explained by the divergent contexts within which European elections take place (for a more detailed assessment of the sources of turnout variation see Franklin, van der Eijk and Oppenhuis 1996; Franklin 2000).

The most powerful predictors of turnout at European elections are compulsory voting, the length of time yet to elapse before the next national election, and whether the election was the first election to the European Parliament ever held in the country concerned. Countries with compulsory voting on average see turnout that is 33% higher than those in which voting is strictly voluntary; turnout is generally lower by over 3% for each year that is still to elapse before the next national election; and the first EP election in each country saw turnout higher by 8.2% on average than later elections.

It is well-known that compulsory voting raises turnout. The surprise is to find it having so great an effect; but the reason is that turnout in EP elections would otherwise be very low. In low-turnout elections, compulsory voting shows its power to greatest advantage (Franklin 1999). This fact alone explains much of the decline in turnout over the 20 years of European Parliament elections, because the countries taking part in the elections of 1999 are very different countries from those that took part in the elections of 1979. In the first elections, almost half the countries taking part (four out of nine) did so under conditions of compulsory voting. Today there are still four countries with compulsory voting, but these are now four out of fifteen – only just over a quarter. Because of the large effect of compulsory voting, this drop of 18% in the proportion of countries with this characteristic would lead us to expect a drop of almost 6% in turnout as a pure mathematical consequence (18% of 33%). Moreover, in 1979 all countries were eligible for the 8.2% first-election turnout boost, whereas in 1999 there were no countries taking part in an EP election for the very first time. These two effects cannot simply be added (because of the large number of countries which, in 1979, did not receive the first-time turnout boost), but together they go a long way towards accounting in a rather prosaic fashion for the overall decline in turnout since 1979.

Of course, Table 10.2 shows that individual countries have seen big changes in turnout that cannot be accounted for by these two factors. From this perspective, more interesting is the 3% per year effect of time until the next national election. As already mentioned, European elections gain a surrogate importance from their role as barometers of the standing of national parties. Evidently this role is more important as national elections approach; but again the surprise is to find so great an effect. In a country with five-year parliaments, position in the electoral cycle could make a 15% difference to European election turnout (5 times 3%). With four-year parliaments, position in the electoral cycle could make a 12% difference. Given the largely random position of European elections within national election cycles (except for Luxemburg, which has always held both elections on the same day), this one factor explains much of the variation seen in Table 10.1 from election to election within particular countries. Indeed the huge falls in turnout seen in Germany in 1999 and in The Netherlands in 1994 are quite understandable when one recalls that those particular EP elections were held shortly after national elections in those countries, whereas the previous European Parliament elections in both countries were held just before national elections. Indeed, over the EU as a whole, we would have expected a fall in turnout of 1.8% (seven twelfths of 3%) in 1999 simply because of the fact that in that year, on average, EP elections were held seven months earlier in the electoral cycles of member countries than had been the case for earlier EP elections.

So while the fact of low turnout at European Parliament elections is a matter for some concern, the apparent decline in EP turnout is not. Indeed, when we correct for the factors listed in Table 10.2, turnout actually appears to have increased after 1979 to a peak about 6 points higher in 1989 and then to have fallen off in 1994 – a fall that continued in 1999 to a point about level with the 1979 starting position. This movement might be random (the changes each year are not statistically significant) but it is possible that there are other things that move turnout, apart from the factors we have been discussing. If so, those other things appear to create fluctuating turnout levels rather than a steady decline (see Franklin 2000, for a more detailed discussion of these matters).

But even if turnout has remained pretty close to the level we should have expected, other analyses indicate that the extent to which turnout can be explained by contextual factors has declined. Until 1994, Sunday voting was a significant predictor of turnout, as was the proportionality of the electoral system; but when we include the elections of 1999 these variables cease to discriminate significantly between higher and lower turnout countries. Moreover, when we add the seventeen post-1994 cases (three for new entrants who held their first European elections in 1995 and fifteen for the countries that participated in the 1999 European elections) the loss of Sunday voting and proportionality as predictors leads explained variance to fall from 85 to 80% – an increase of a third in unexplained variance.

What seems to be happening is that, with the passage of time, those voters who do turn out at elections to the European Parliament are behaving in a manner that is less and less structured by their national political contexts. We will see further evidence of this when we look at the rate at which those who do vote choose different parties than they would have done in a national election – a rate that has been rising continuously over the three elections for which we have appropriate survey data (see Table 10.3).

Results of European elections

The outcomes of European elections in terms of party choice differ much less from what would have occurred in concurrent national elections than does turnout. Nevertheless, some parties do gain and some parties do lose compared to what would have occurred had the elections been general elections – often by as much as 6% of total votes. These gains and losses occur for two reasons. Some parties gain (lose) from the fact that they are more (less) successful in getting their normal supporters to the polls. The low turnout in European elections helps (hurts) some more than others. Other parties gain (lose) because they are supported (abandoned) in European elections by voters who in national elections would have voted differently. For some parties these two processes cancel out, leaving them with about the same level of support that they would have enjoyed in national elections; for others the two processes reinforce each other, leading to quite dramatic divergences from national election outcomes. However, by far the greater of the two effects is the effect of people voting differently which is generally more than twice as great as the turnout effect, and can involve more than 40% of those voting (at the 1994 and 1999 elections in France and Denmark, and at the 1999 election in Italy), as shown in Table 10.3. Note, however, that this total amount of what has been called 'quasi-switching' (van der Eijk, Franklin *et al.* 1996) involves a great many contrary movements that cancel out in aggregate, leaving net effects of much lower magnitude (seldom more than 6%, see above).

The consequence of this behaviour by voters is very different for different parties. To a large party, the loss of 6% may be chastening but not disastrous. To a small party, the loss of 6% could amount to decimation. Thus in 1989 the British Conservatives lost about 3% compared to what they would have expected to get in a general election, while the Liberal Democrats lost some 4%. But while to the Conservatives this was just a rather poor showing, to the Liberal Democrats it amounted to a virtual halving of the vote they would have received had the election been a national general election (Franklin and Curtice 1996). Meanwhile, the British Green Party benefitted by 6.6%, virtually doubling the vote it would have received in a national election.

The example of the British Liberal Democrats notwithstanding, most losses in European elections are suffered by large parties and most gains are enjoyed by small parties. This appears not to be because of the desire of voters to punish government parties (opposition parties also lose if they are large) but purely a result of the fact that political power is not at stake in European elections. It turns out that (when political power seems to be at stake) an important influence on voting choice is party size: other things being equal, voters prefer to support a party that has a better chance of putting its policies into practice. Evidently this question is not at issue in a European election, and so large parties fail to get the bonus that they would have been accorded in a national election (van der Eijk, Oppenhuis and Franklin 1994; van der Eijk, Franklin and Oppenhuis 1996) – a bonus that appears to be worth about 5% of the vote to a party that enjoys the support of 40–50% of the electorate. But while small parties gain in European elections compared to their performance in national elections, such gains are not apportioned evenly among small parties. Moreover, which particular small parties gain depends very largely on the location of the European elections in the domestic electoral cycle. Just as in the case of turnout, people behave differently when a national election is imminent than when one has recently occurred.

The critical difference appears to be the attention paid to the outcome by politicians and commentators. We have indicated that, in the immediate aftermath of a national

Table 10.3 Those voting differently than they would have voted in national elections, as a percentage of those voting in the European elections, 1989–99*

Country	1989	1994	1999
Austria	–	–	22.4
Belgium	12.6	18.5	10.9
Denmark	35.4	42.9	45.4
Finland	–	–	26.3
France	27.2	40.8	41.1
Germany	11.8	14.2	23.2
Great Britain	13.0	16.0	32.6
Greece	8.1	12.4	18.6
Ireland	28.7	23.8	34.4
Italy	19.7	20.7	49.6
Luxemburg	15.0	14.3	9.6
Netherlands	12.4	19.6	28.6
Portugal	9.7	12.7	10.2
Spain	22.2	12.5	17.9
Sweden	–	–	30.1
EU average	14.4	16.6	26.7

* At the time of writing, the necessary matching of European and national parties for the election of 1999 had not yet been finalised, so figures for 1999 are provisional.

election, a European election outcome is of no great interest. A better marker of the standing of parties in the national arena already exists. These are also the elections in which the largest transfer of votes from large to small parties takes place, and the small parties that benefit are on the whole moderate parties of the center. It is as though, freed from concerns about governing the country, voters in such elections could 'vote with the heart'. These are the elections in which voting is apparently most sincere, in contrast to national elections themselves, when voters 'vote with the head', taking into account the strategic situation in which large parties are more likely to get their policies enacted.

As the national electoral cycle advances, however, and the next national election comes closer, two things happen to affect the behaviour of voters should a European election take place. The first is that the marker set by the previous national election has become obsolete, so that party leaders and commentators look to the European election as a relevant measure of the standing of parties. The second is that, with the approach of a national election, party leaders are motivated to take account of any messages they receive from the electorate in order to improve their chances when the national election comes. This is the circumstance in which protest voting appears most prevalent, since this is when extreme parties do best. Clearly voters do not suppose that their votes will cause such parties to gain office; but they evidently hope that the parties they normally support will take note of the protest and adapt their policies accordingly. Borrowing a phrase from the lexicon of British football hooligans, we have called this behaviour 'voting with the boot' (van der Eijk, Oppenhuis and Franklin 1994; Oppenhuis, van der Eijk and Franklin

1996). Votes for far right parties in France and Germany in 1989 should be seen in this light, as should votes for Green parties in several countries.

The striking thing about these findings, both those relating to turnout and those relating to party choice, is the apparent sophistication of the voting act. In the shadow of a forthcoming national election up to 15% more people will take the opportunity to give their parties a piece of their mind than in the immediate aftermath of a national election; and the message that is sent in such circumstances is quite different from the message sent at a national election or in the aftermath of one. At the individual level, the evidence of rationality is even greater (van der Eijk, Franklin *et al.* 1996).

Of more concern, however, is another manifestation of rationality. In elections to the European Parliament, voters are increasingly casting their votes without reference to features that would have governed their behaviour in national elections. The reason why electoral proportionality is supposed to affect turnout is because the incentive to vote is greater if voters are assured that their votes will not be wasted. Given that proportionality of the electoral system had, by 1999, ceased to discriminate significantly between low and high turnout countries, it seems voters are becoming aware that their votes in these elections have no value in the conventional sense. The same implication flows from the fact that voters are more and more likely to vote for different parties in European than in national elections. Other analyses (not shown) indicate that the effect on turnout of time until the next election is going up. These changes imply that voters are feeling increasingly free to leave behind their normal party loyalties when they vote in European Parliament elections.

In itself this would be no bad thing. Indeed, if this meant that voters were turning their attention to European matters at European elections then the change would be a good thing. In fact what is more likely is that voters are increasingly taking advantage of the opportunity to behave differently than at national elections, voting with the heart or with the boot rather than with the head, and making it more and more problematic to interpret the results of European elections as markers for parties' standing. To the extent that this leads national parties to make poor policy choices, the perverse effects of European elections for national politics – the subject of the next section – can only increase.

Consequences for national politics

The consequences of European elections for national politics are of three kinds. In the first place national parties may be led to take various actions as a result of extrapolating the outcome to a national election situation. Sometimes a government party may be led to call an early national election, as in Spain in 1989, to capitalise on the popularity they see themselves enjoying (del Castillo 1996). Sometimes such a party may be led to adapt its policies, as in Germany in the same year (when a much harsher policy towards Eastern European migration was briefly adopted) in order to defuse the apparent appeal of an extreme party (Schmitt 1996). These reactions may or may not have the effect that the party intended, depending on how accurately the European election outcome reflected the true situation in the national political arena; but there will always be a tendency for miscalculations to occur exactly in proportion to the extent of the interest taken in the European election outcome: to the extent that party leaders and commentators take notice, voters behave differently than they would have done had national power been truly at stake (which is different again from how they would have behaved had no-one been paying attention).

This mismatch between the use of the indicator and the accuracy of the indicator might appear perverse, but it is a natural result of the different objectives and perceptions of voters and politicians. Because real national power is not at stake, voters expect no repercussions from voting one way rather than another; so, when politicians indicate that they are paying attention to the outcome, voters suddenly find themselves in an unaccustomed position of power. They can send a message of displeasure without the risk of electing a party that is untried or dangerous.

The second type of consequence is more insidious. European election outcomes differ from the outcomes that would occur in national elections for more reasons than that voters behave differently than politicians expect. Small parties are often advantaged for technical reasons as well, having to do with differences in the electoral system under which European elections are held. For both these reasons a party system can progressively break down under the impact of successive European elections, as appears to be happening in France (Cayrole and Ysmal 1996) and perhaps also in Germany (Schmitt 1996).

The third type of consequence results more directly from the fact that European elections are not employed as opportunities to put forward or oppose policies related to the European arena. Keeping such policies off the national agenda seems to be a preoccupation of national politicians, for reasons too complex to be discussed here (see Franklin, van der Eijk and Marsh 1996). Occasionally, however, such issues break through to become salient in national terms. When this happens, the results can be quite devastating for individual parties or leaders (as in the case of Mrs Thatcher, following the European elections of 1989). European elections would be the proper venue for such matters to be discussed, if only such elections could be fought by different parties than fight national elections; but this only happens in one country, Denmark. In that country national politics are insulated from the effects of European elections. Precisely because they are not fought by the same parties as fight national elections, European elections cannot be used as markers even while they can be used to give an airing to real European issues. Elsewhere, European elections constitute something of a sword of Damocles that national parties hang over their heads, apparently unknowingly, because of the potential that European issues have for splitting national parties into pro- and anti-European factions (Franklin, van der Eijk and Marsh 1996).

Decoupling European elections from the national political arena would remove this uncertainty, and would also mitigate the other two consequences summarised above, since all three arise from the use of these elections as markers for what would happen in national elections. Mitigating their effects on national politics would be good enough reason to reform the way in which European elections are conducted; but there are even better reasons when one considers these elections from a European perspective.

Consequences for the future of the European Union

Proper democratic representation and accountability are associated with the notion of free elections. However, in order for elections to fulfil these functions, a number of conditions must be met which are not necessarily provided by the simple institution of elections *per se*. The logic of democratic elections presupposes that the political verdict of electorates can be construed as emanating from the political preferences of voters – preferences that are relevant to the decision-making arena concerned. If this condition is met, elections can be considered simultaneously (1) to legitimise power allocated by the elections (and therefore also to legitimise policies which may be devised with this power), (2) to exert electoral control by holding officeholders accountable and (3) to represent groups of citizens and their interests in the political process (thus showing sensitivity to their concerns). In order for elections to function in these ways, electorates must have some awareness of the political stance and record in the arena under consideration of those who are contending for their votes (Franklin and van der Eijk 1996).

It is evident that these conditions are lacking in the present-day European Union. Voters have on the whole never been encouraged to develop preferences for different European policies that would permit them to choose among candidates and parties in a European election in such a way as to legitimate and control the exercise of power at the European level. Indeed, candidates and parties seldom put forward policies that differ in regard to Europe, and frequently do not put forward policies of any relevance at all to European matters. By failing to take the opportunity to present voters with meaningful choices, party leaders also miss the chance to educate them about European affairs. This failure is primarily due to the fact that the parties that select candidates and put forward policies at European elections are not European parties but national parties, and these parties generally treat European elections as opportunities to test their own relative popularity in the national arena. Naturally, national elections offer even less of a forum for discussion of European matters. So neither in their choice of national leaders who compose the Council of Ministers nor in their choice of Members of the European Parliament who hold the Commissioners accountable are voters given the opportunity to have any input into the conduct of European affairs. As Bogdanor has stated (1989: 214), 'Elections, if they are to be meaningful, must fundamentally allow for choice', but national party systems provide 'an artificial superstructure unable to articulate the wishes of the electorate'. There are reasons why politicians maintain this 'artificial superstructure' – reasons that may not be easily overcome (Franklin, van der Eijk and Marsh 1996) – but the consequence is that input into the European decision-making process is restricted to individuals and groups who have non-electoral routes (for example interest group lobbying) for making their desires known.

This lack of proper democratic accountability and control in European affairs is a grave problem, potentially amounting to a crisis of legitimacy for the European Union. How this crisis will manifest itself cannot be anticipated, but the ratification process for the Treaty of European Union signalled a warning that should not have been ignored (Dinan 1994: 290–1).

Members of the European Parliament (as well as many professional observers of European integration) diagnose a democratic deficit in European representative institutions. To their eyes, this deficit often appears in terms of a lack of power on the part of the European Parliament to assert itself in relation to the Commission and (particularly) the Council of Ministers. In fact, it should be evident from a reading of this chapter that the democratic deficit felt by Members of the European Parliament actually results from the fact that European elections are fought primarily on the basis of national political concerns, rather than on problems relevant to the European arena. It is true that the European Parliament lacks certain powers (in comparison with modern-day national parliaments); but what it lacks most is not power but a mandate to use that power in any particular manner. It lacks that mandate because of the way in which European elections are conducted. Lacking a succession of mandates to develop Europe in any particular way, the European Union and its predecessor entities were built by national governments with little input by their citizenry, on the basis of what has been called a 'permissive consensus' regarding successive moves towards European unity (Inglehart 1971).

The consequence of this permissive consensus has been to free national parties from the need to coherently address and articulate European policy concerns – often a difficult matter for parties whose origins lie in the aggregation of quite other sorts of interests and concerns. Instead of defending their participation in European regulatory decision-making on the grounds of fulfilling an electoral mandate, ruling parties have consistently defended such actions on the grounds that they have done their best to protect national interests, thus casting European politics as a zero-sum game between the member states, and undermining their efforts in other spheres to stress the positive-sum aspects of European integration. Sometimes, of course, their 'best' is not enough, and unpopular consequences seem to flow from European developments. Governments are then tempted to blame 'Europe' for these consequences. But to the extent that governments succeed in this, they merely cause themselves to appear impotent to influence events in Brussels, displacing the crisis of legitimacy from the European to the national arena (Franklin and van der Eijk 1996).

In this manner, the permissive consensus appears to be eroding, faster in some countries than in others. A variety of developments have increased the salience and visibility of European policies to individual citizens. In the absence of well-established alternatives regarding the substantive direction of such policies, leading to a debate within each country (or over Europe as a whole) regarding what type of European Union the people want to live in, criticism might well move from a focus on 'what Europe' to 'whether Europe'. This would yield unpredictable consequences for European political systems, as amply demonstrated by the Danish and the French referenda regarding the Maastricht treaty and Mr Major's difficulties with the British Conservative Party when that treaty came to be ratified. It also puts into question the very future of the European project.

The proper place for debates of this kind would be in the context of European election campaigns, but European elections have never been used for such a purpose. Possible means of stimulating such debates are discussed at length in the final chapter of van der Eijk and Franklin with Ackaert *et al.* (1996); but the first step is to recognise the potential consequences of a continued failure to conduct meaningful European elections.

References

Blumler, J. and Fox, A. (1982) *The European Voter: Popular Responses to the First European Community Elections*, London: Policy Studies Institute.

Bogdanor, V. (1989) 'Direct Elections, Representative Democracy and European Integration', *Electoral Studies* 8: 205–16.

Castillo, P. del (1996) 'Spain: A Dress Rehearsal', in van der Eijk and Franklin with Ackaert *et al.* (1996).

Cayroll, R. and Ysmal, C. (1996) 'France: The Midwife Came to Call', in van der Eijk and Franklin with Ackaert *et al.* (1996).

Dinan, D. (1994) *Ever Closer Union? An Introduction to the European Community*, London: Macmillan.

Eijk, C. van der, Franklin, M. and Oppenhuis, E. (1996) 'The Strategic Context: Voting Choice', in van der Eijk and Franklin with Ackaert *et al.* (1996).

Eijk, C. van der and Franklin, M., with Ackaert, J. (1996) *Choosing Europe? The European Electorate and National Politics in the Face of Union*, Ann Arbor: University of Michigan Press.

Eijk, C. van der and Oppenhuis, E. (1991) 'European Parties' Performance in Electoral Competition', *European Journal of Political Research* 19: 55–80.

Eijk, C. van der, Oppenhuis, E. and Franklin, M. (1994) 'Consulting the Oracle: The Consequences of

Treating European Elections as "Markers" of Domestic Political Developments', Madrid: European Consortium for Political Research.

Eijk, C. van der and Schmitt, H. (1991) 'The Role of the Eurobarometer in the Study of European Elections and the Development of Comparative Electoral Research', in Karlheinz Reif and Ronald Inglehart (eds), *Eurobarometer: The Dynamics of European Opinion*, London: Macmillan.

Franklin, M. (1999) 'Electoral Engineering and Cross-National Turnout Differences: What Role for Compulsory Voting?' *British Journal of Political Science* 29: 205–16.

Franklin, M. (2000) 'More Means Less: The Consequences of Successive Enlargements of the European Union for Turnout at European Parliament Elections', paper prepared for the annual meeting of the American Political Science Association, Washington DC, August.

Franklin, M. and Curtice, J. (1996) 'Britain: Opening Pandora's Box', in van der Eijk and Franklin with Ackaert *et al.* (1996).

Franklin, M. and van der Eijk, C. (1996) 'The Problem: Representation and Democracy in the European Union', in van der Eijk and Franklin with Ackaert *et al.* (1996).

Franklin, M., van der Eijk, C. and Marsh, M. (1996) 'Conclusions: The Electoral Connection and the Democratic Deficit', in van der Eijk and Franklin with Ackaert *et al.* (1996).

Franklin, M., van der Eijk, C. and Oppenhuis, E. (1995) 'The Motivational Basis of Turnout in European Elections, 1979–1994: The Case of Britain', in C. Rallings, D. Farrell, D. Broughton and D. Denver (eds), *British Elections and Parties Yearbook 1995*, London: Frank Cass.

Franklin, M., van der Eijk, C. and Oppenhuis, E. (1996) 'The Systemic Context: Turnout', in van der Eijk and Franklin with Ackaert *et al.* (1996).

Inglehart, R. (1971) 'Public Opinion and European Integration', in L. Lindberg and S. Scheingold (eds), *European Integration*, Cambridge, MA: Harvard University Press, pp. 160–91.

Inglehart, R. and Rabier, J. (1989) 'Europe Elects a Parliament', *Government and Opposition* 14/4: 479–505.

Marsh, M. (1998) 'Testing the Second-Order Election Model after Four European Elections', *British Journal of Political Science* 28: 591–608.

Marsh, M. and Franklin, M. (1996) 'Understanding European Elections, 1979–1994', in van der Eijk and Franklin with Ackaert *et al.* (1996).

Niedemeier, O. (1990) 'Turnout in the European Elections', *Electoral Studies* 9/1: 45–50.

Oppenhuis, E., van der Eijk, C. and Franklin, M. (1996) 'The Party Context: Outcomes', in van der Eijk and Franklin with Ackaert *et al.* (1996).

Parry, G., Moiser, G. and Day, N. (1990) *Political Participation and Democracy in Britain*, Cambridge: Cambridge University Press.

Powell, B. (1980) 'Voter Turnout in Thirty Democracies: Partisan, Legal and Socio-Economic Influences', in R. Rose (ed.), *Electoral Participation: A Comparative Analysis*, Beverly Hills: Sage.

Powell, B. (1986) 'American Voter Turnout in Comparative Perspective', *American Political Science Review* 80: 17–43.

Reif, K. (1984) 'National Electoral Cycles and European Elections', *Electoral Studies* 3/3: 244–55.

Reif, K. (1985) 'Ten Second-Order National Elections', in K. Reif (ed.), *Ten European Elections*, Aldershot: Gower, pp. 1–36.

Reif, K. and Schmitt, H. (1980) 'Nine Second-Order National Elections: A Conceptual Framework For The Analysis Of European Election Results', *European Journal of Political Research* 8/1: 3–44.

Sartori, G. (1994) *Comparative Constitutional Engineering: An Inquiry into Structures, Incentives, and Outcomes*, New York; New York University Press.

Schmitt, H. (1996) 'Germany: A Bored Electorate', in van der Eijk and Franklin with Ackaert *et al.* (1996).

Schmitt, H. and Mannheimer, R. (1991) 'About Voting and Non-voting in the European Elections of June 1989', *European Journal of Political Research* 19/1: 31–54.

Verba, S., Nie, N. and Kim, J. (1979) *Participation and Political Equality: A Seven Nation Comparison*, Cambridge: Cambridge University Press.

Worre, T. (1993) 'Denmark and the European Union', in B. Thomesen (ed.), *The Odd Man Out? Denmark and European Integration 1948–1992*, Odense: Odense University Press.

Worre, T. (1996) 'Denmark: Second Order Containment', in van der Eijk and Franklin with Ackaert *et al.* (1996).

Chapter 11

Interest groups and EU policy-making

Organisational logic and venue shopping

SONIA MAZEY AND JEREMY RICHARDSON

Introduction: three assumptions

Our central thesis is that once the EC/EU began to develop into a significant venue or arena for public policy-making in Europe, a certain trajectory of institutionalised interaction between the EC/EU and interest groups was likely. We base this prediction on three theoretical assumptions.

- First, that *bureaucracies have a tendency to construct stable and manageable relationships with interest groups in each policy domain as a means of securing some kind of 'negotiated order' or stable environment.*
- Second, that *interest groups generally exhibit a preference for state bureaucracies as a venue for informing themselves about and influencing public policy.*
- Third, that *interest groups will seek to exploit new opportunity structures or venues as a means of maximising their capacity to shape public policy to their own advantage.*

We suggest that different types of actors have associated behavioural patterns – or at least exhibit *procedural ambitions* (Richardson and Jordan 1979) which condition and structure their behaviour in the real world. Moreover, as many of these procedural ambitions are deeply embedded in the political cultures of the majority of the fifteen member states, it should be no surprise to see the gradual emergence of a 'European policy style' emphasising group intermediation (Mazey and Richardson 1995: 337–59).

The European Commission as a bureaucracy: the art of strategic group politics

Our theoretical starting point is bureaucracy and the particular behavioural traits that modern bureaucracies exhibit. In his classic study of bureaucracies, Anthony Downs formulated many hypotheses concerning bureaucratic behaviour. Two of his central hypotheses are especially relevant to a discussion of Commission/group relations. He assumed *rational behaviour* on the part of bureaucrats – 'they act in the most efficient manner possible given their limited capabilities and the cost of information' (Downs 1967: 2). He also hypothesised that 'Every organization's social functions strongly influence its internal structure and behaviour, and vice versa' (Downs 1967: 2). If we apply these two hypotheses to the Commission (which certainly has limited resources and an especially great need for information from across the fifteen member states), we can assume that it will structure itself in ways that facilitate efficient policy formulation – its 'social function' under the Treaty of Rome. We can also assume that it will adopt behavioural patterns that maximise its ability to interpret the external world so as to facilitate efficient policy formulation. If we regard the Commission as a relatively new or *adolescent* bureaucracy (Mazey and Richardson 1995), then another of Downs's observations seems valuable – namely that the 'generation of … external support is particularly crucial for a new bureau'. He suggests that a new bureau's survival strategy includes continually demonstrating that its services are worthwhile to some group with influence over sufficient resources to keep it alive (Downs 1967: 7). Initially, the external sources of support are said to be 'weak, scattered and not accustomed to relations with the bureau. The latter must therefore rapidly organise so that its services become very valuable to the users' (Downs 1967: 7–8). Once the users of the bureau's services get used to the gains they secure from it 'and *have developed routinised relations with it*', the bureau then can rely on a degree of inertia to maintain the external support (Downs 1967: 8, emphasis added). This rather clientelistic relationship itself leads to *institutionalisation* in the form of rule-making, he predicts. Thus, 'many of the decisions of bureaux covered by *formalized rules* involve interactions with people outside the bureau' (Downs 1967: 60, emphasis added). In the case of the Commission, it has developed sets of informal and formal 'rules' which emphasise the key role that consultation with interest groups plays in policy-making. As Lehmbruch suggests, this relationship with the bureau's external environment can often be quite proactive. He notes that 'in critical junctures state bureaucracies have often played an important formative part of their own' (Lehmbruch, cited in Mazey and Richardson 1993: 253). Thus, 'interactions of governmental bureaucracies with associations or other corporate economic actors seem to be of crucial importance in linking the macro- and meso-levels and result in the emergence of network configurations which will eventually become instutionalized' (ibid.). Thus, from what we know about bureaucracies generally, we might predict the emergence of 'normal' interest groups politics in the EU.

All of these hypotheses and observations seem to fit the Commission perfectly. It has acted rationally as a 'purposeful opportunist' (Klein and O'Higgins 1985; Cram 1994) in expanding its policy domains and creating new ones (extending its 'territoriality' in Downs's terms). It has also practised the art of 'strategic group politics' – the capacity of a policy-maker to 'regulate their interactions with outside constituencies in a way that fulfils their strategic objectives' (Peterson 1992: 612). In particular, it has recognised the utility of interest groups as sources of (a) information, (b) support and (c) legitimacy in its key policy-making roles. Finally, like all 'state' bureaucracies, it has recognised that *institutionalising* consultation (Mazey and Richardson 2001) with interests is a classic form of *risk reduction*. By seating the appropriate stakeholders at the appropriate seats, bureaucrats both reduce likely resistance to their policy proposals at other venues and avoid the blame for subsequent policy failures or fiascos (Henderson 1977). Moreover, in the context of the EC/EU, the need to construct complex advocacy coalitions (Sabatier 1988; 1998) in favour of policy innovation is especially pressing for the Commission. Faced with intense institutional competition, it has every incentive to seek and nurture allies who can be active in other European and national policy-making venues.

Interest groups: exploiting multiple venues and allocating resources rationally

From what we know about interest groups in Western democracies, we can expect them to seek to establish close relations with state bureaucracies and regulatory agencies. Interest groups are capable of allocating resources rationally as between possible lobbying targets – be they institutions (see Coen 1997; 1998; Bennett 1997; 1999) or individual legislators (Snyder 1991). Indeed, the often symbiotic (and in some systems corporatist) relationships between state bureaucracies and groups in a joint venture of consensus building is a characteristic of the policy styles of many Western European states in most of the post-war decades (Richardson 1982). Empirical studies of interest groups often reveal marked preferences for the bureaucratic venue as a means of influencing public policy decisions. Within the EU, groups were quick to recognise the formal and informal powers of the Commission as an agenda-setter. They know, as Hull observed, that the Commission official sitting at his or her desk with the blank sheet of paper is a target worth cultivating (Hull 1993). Lobbying resources allocated to this early stage of EU agenda-setting are likely to produce greater returns than resources allocated to lobbying later in the policy process. Similarly, groups know that the rational allocation of lobbying is not just about influencing or changing public policy – it is also about minimising their surprises. Hence, *knowing* what is going on may be just as important to an adaptive interest organisation, as trying to *influence* what is going on. In that sense, participation in the institutions of intermediation (including the whole range of European institutions) is perfectly rational even if no policy pay-off results. Finally, the increasing technical content of policy and the 'unpacking' of broad policy problems into more manageable, low-salience, technical issues, so familiar in Western democracies, further increases the incentive for groups to form 'policy partnerships' with Commission bureaucrats in (preferably) closed policy-making structures. This process facilitates continuous trade-offs in a system of 'mutual exchange' (Jordan and Richardson 1982). Groups and the Commission thus have an especially acute, mutual interest in trying to form stable policy communities and policy networks over time.

Making policy communities and networks work can be difficult, however, even at the national level (Richardson 2000). Many *exogenous* factors intervene – including new ideas or 'frames' (Schön and Rein 1994); the structure of institutions; the arrival of new interests in a policy area; and the sheer numbers of interests to be accommodated. The EU is a classic example of the appearance of a new opportunity structure (Kitschelt 1986) whose emergence has brought the possibility of a different stakeholder bias in terms of institutional power (Lindblom 1977; Dahl 1982; McAdam 1996). Thus, our third hypothesis, reflecting the work of social movement theorists and interest group analysts alike, is that interest groups will seek to exploit (and sometimes create) new opportunity structures, or venues, which they believe will maximise their chances of public policy pay-offs. Research on opportunity structures has sought to show how changes in some aspects of a political system create new possibilities for collective action (McAdam *et al.* 1996: 17). Compared with most of the member states (the federal and judicialised German polity being a clear exception perhaps), the EC/EU as a polity presents an American-style plethora of opportunity structures to which interest groups can go. The creation of the EC/EU has, therefore, created a quite new opportunity for what Baumgartner and Jones term 'venue shopping' by national and cross-national interest group actors in Europe (not all of whom, of course, are 'European').

Venue shopping is part of the explanation for the (undisputed) growth in EC/EU-level interest group formation and lobbying outlined below. As Baumgartner and Jones suggest, political actors are capable of strategic action by employing a dual strategy as follows:

> On the one hand they try to control the prevailing image of the policy problem through the use of rhetoric, symbols and policy analysis. On the other hand, they try to alter the roster of participants who are involved in the issue by seeking out the most favourable venue for consideration of these issues.
>
> (Baumgartner and Jones 1991: 1045)

Although Baumgartner and Jones developed the 'venue shopping' thesis from their study of nuclear energy politics in the USA, the relevance of the thesis to the EU is clear. It too is a system of multiple access points created by institutionalised multi-level governance. We believe that the creation of a maturing system of interest group intermediation at the European level has both transformed national policy-making systems and fundamentally changed the roster of actors who constitute the power elites in Europe.

This transformation is due to the simple fact that national governments have, for whatever reasons, ceded sovereignty over large areas of public policy-making to the EC/EU level. Once public policy was made at the supranational level, groups were bound to allocate increasing amounts of lobbying resources to that level. Moreover, the very involvement of interest groups in transnational settings, such as the EC/EU, in turn contributed to a further reduction of national sovereignty, whether or not states (individually or collectively) see such a development as in their interest. Thus, in their study of activists beyond borders Keck and Sikkink argue that 'by thus blurring boundaries between a state's relations with its own nationals and the recourse both citizens and states have to the international systems, advocacy networks are helping to transform the practice of national sovereignty' (Keck and Sikkink 1998: 1–2). Though their study focuses on a particular type of transnational actor (such as environmental, human rights and women's groups), much the same conclusions could be reached by studying the behaviour of more conventional groups, such as firms (for example see Coen 1997; 1998) in the EC/EU. A central theme in the Keck and Sikkink thesis, and in ours, is the autonomy from states which transnational action can deliver to activists and interest groups. As Keck and Sikkink suggest, the 'two-level game' metaphor developed by Putnam (Putnam 1988) is useful in pointing out the role played by domestic interests in shaping national preferences. Putnam sees 'international relations as a two-way street, in which political entrepreneurs bring international influence to bear on domestic politics at the same time that domestic politics shapes their international positions' (Keck and Sikkink 1998: 4). This is precisely our argument in the case of the EC/EU as an 'international system'. It is incredibly open and permeable to interest group lobbying compared with even the most pluralistic member states. As one Commission official put it to us, 'the Commission is the most open organisation I've ever worked in. I've worked in national administrations, the regulators, the supervisors, and never before have I worked in an organisation like the Commission where *anyone* can call us' (Interview DG XV, 9 July 1999).

The permeability of the Commission, and other EU venues such as the European Parliament (EP) and European Court of Justice (ECJ), to interest groups weakens the ability of states to control and steer national interest groups and, indeed, to control their national policy agendas. Insofar as groups become 'activists beyond borders', to borrow Keck and Sikkink's terminology, they both weaken the power of states in the process of transnational governance and may become an independent source of integration. If our assertion is correct, it is a challenge to the intergovernmentalist position that 'the primary source of integration lies in the interests of the states themselves and the relative power that each brings to Brussels' (Moravcsik 1991: 75). More specifically, it is a challenge to the view that 'the unique institutional structure of the EC is acceptable to national governments only insofar as it strengthens, rather than weakens, their control over domestic affairs, permitting them to attain goals otherwise unachievable' (Moravcsik 1993: 507). The difference between our position and those of classic intergovernmentalists is that we agree with Keck and Sikkink that interest groups can act independently of states and their help, to shape international policy agendas and outcomes. Thus, we do not accept that 'above all, the primary political instrument by which individuals and groups in civil society seek to influence international negotiations is the nation-state, which acts externally as a unity and rational actor on behalf of its constituents' (Moravcsik 1998: 22). Our thesis is that the national preference formation process is certainly 'shaped through contention among domestic political groups' (Moravcsik 1998: 22) as intergovernmentalists argue, but that domestic groups are increasingly engaged independently at the supranational level and see that level as a venue where they can pursue their own goals.

In practice, it is important to remember, first, that European integration is not just about grand bargains or high politics – increasingly it is about technical regulations and also policy change via soft law. Second, we need to be cautious in perceiving interest groups to be national – multinational companies, for example, are difficult to categorise as national interests, so are environmental and women's groups. Third, we should bear in mind the subtleties of the EU agenda-setting process – the intergovernmental phase of EU policy-making (which is clearly a crucial stage in the process) may be preceded by an agenda-setting process in which national governments are not always the predominant actors. Fourth, account needs to be taken of inequalities in the degree of information which different types of actors possess regarding EU policy initiatives – interest groups may well be better informed than national governments and may be disinclined to share information with them.

The rational and independent exploitation of new EC/EU structures by interest groups exists alongside a less tangible process of identification with the new Euro-level structures in which these interests participate – especially if the structures deliver valuable policy pay-offs. Transnational lobbying, particularly as it becomes institutionalised in the EU, can have long-lasting effects on the perceptions and behaviours of actors. The newly created institutional structures can be shaped as 'meaningful objects of identification' (Breton 1995: 40). Following Breton's analysis, some kind of path dependency in the EC/EU might therefore be postulated. Transnational organisation expands in virtually all domains. The expanding scope and diversity of players is accompanied by increased institutionalisation; the critical institutions are those established for collective decision-making, mobilisation of resources, circulation of information, co-ordination of activities and control of free-riders. The corresponding ideologies are those that legitimate particular institutional arrangements; the experience of interdependence in turn tends to generate a 'community fate' identity, a pragmatic solidarity (drawn from Breton 1995: 40–2). A good example of this pragmatic solidarity is provided by the controversial plan, from the Commission itself, to relinquish its near forty-year monopoly on anti-trust policing by returning some powers back to the member states. Designed as a means of reducing the Commission's own workload, the proposal met with opposition from both firms and consumers. The European employers association, UNICE, suggested modernising the substantive and procedural rules rather than 'opt for the risky approval of a full decentralisation (to the Member States)' (*European Voice* 30 September/6 October 1999: 21).

We see, therefore, a similar phenomenon in the European policy-making process and in the long-established traditions of national policy-making in Western Europe – namely a high degree of interest group integration into the policy process, based upon the twin 'logics' of organisation and negotiation. This development appears to be taking place at the two main levels in the Euro policy process – at the European level itself and within the existing national states. Indeed, the importance of Euro-lobbying at both of these levels (and at the regional level too for some issues) raises an important paradox – namely that the gradual shift in the locus of power to the European level in many policy sectors has caused both a proliferation of lobbying at the supranational level and an intensification of lobbying at the national level. We return to this paradox later but meanwhile note Spence's interesting suggestion that national officials who participate in the Euro-policy process are *'lobbied lobbyists'* – they are simultaneously subjected to influence and called upon to exercise it (Spence 1993: 48). Discussing the British civil service in the context of the Euro-lobbying system, he notes that 'whereas a lobbyist knows that in the context of national legislation, Whitehall is the prime focus of law-making, in the European context the British civil servant is but one of many points of access in the decision-making process' (Spence 1993: 48). Here, Spence highlights a central feature of the Euro-lobbying system. It is essentially a multi-arena, multi-level, decision-making system, in which all actors *necessarily* participate in a complex series of what Tsebelis termed 'nested games' (Tsebelis 1990). This makes it especially difficult to make really reliable and robust generalisations about the distribution of power between the different policy actors or stakeholders in the EU policy process which can apply to both grand bargains and routinised policy-making. However, one generalisation seems to be well founded and based on solid empirical evidence – the number and range of interest groups active at the European level has increased enormously over the history of the EU. It is to the trajectory of this mobilisation that we now turn.

The emergence of a European interest group system: from under-supply to over-supply of representation?

One of the earliest systematic studies of the emergence of a European interest group system was Kirchner's analysis of interest group formation, published in 1980 (Kirchner 1980a). He quotes Meynaud and Sidjanski's earlier study of European pressure groups which found that many of these groupings established themselves at the Community level in response to the formation of a new centre of decision-making and as a result of advantages expected from Community action (Kirchner 1980a: 96–7). Sidjanski's study suggests that some of the groups were formed as the EEC's own institutions were formed, others when it became clear that the EEC's regulatory powers could actually affect different interests in society (Sidjanski 1970: 402). Sidjanski also noted a phenomenon common in all developed political systems – that public bureaucrats often assist the emergence and creation of groups, reflecting the functional 'logic' which we suggested earlier. In other words, if a European interest group system did not exist, the Commission would have to invent it as an essential building block of a European policy-making system. For example, Mazey suggests that, since the late 1970s, 'the Commission has also fostered the development of transnational women's networks and set up European networks of "experts" to monitor and advise on various aspects of equality policy. This *constituency mobilisation strategy* is consistent with theories of bureaucratic expansion and neo-functionalist models of European integration' (Mazey 1995: 606, emphasis added). A similar phenomenon was identified by Cowles, who describes the role of the Commission in the setting up of the European Round Table (ERT), representing some of the largest companies within the EU. She records that 'the first list of potential industry members was drawn up in 1982 in the Commission's Berlaymont building by Volvo and Commission staff' (Cowles 1997: 504). (The ERT eventually played a major role in the emergence of the Single European Act (SEA) and the creation of the 1992 single market programme.)

Kirchner notes that yet another phenomenon familiar from studies of national interest groups systems was evident in the early years of the Union – namely that groups beget yet more groups. Once one set of interests is mobilised and organised to influence decision-makers, those interests in society who have not yet organised will see the need to do so; if they do not, they are leaving policy space exclusively occupied by rival interests. Interest group mobilisation is at least a means of 'risk avoidance' in the manner first suggested by David Truman in 1950. In an attempt to defend pluralism in the USA (surely, now the defining characteristic of the EU interest group system), he argued that over time interest group power would tend to reach some kind of equilibrium. This was partly because society was full of what he termed 'potential groups' which, when threatened by the successes of those interests already organised, would themselves become organised to defend their own interest (Truman 1951: 31). The mobilisation of trade unions at the European level seems a classic example of this phenomenon. In his study of trade unions as pressure groups in the EC, Kirchner suggests that European trade union interest group organisations emerged because of a perceived threat from already organised business groups (Kirchner 1977: 28). This process has continued. As he notes, 'the threats posed by expanding multinational corporations and the opportunity for involvement in meaningful policy development with such regional organisations as the EC, the Council of Europe, EFTA and OECD, have all contributed to new transnational organisations and more ambitious trade union goals (Kirchner 1980b: 132). A similar risk-avoidance 'insurance' strategy has been noted even for powerful multinational companies. McLaughlin and Jordan (drawing on McLaughlin's study of the lobbying activities of the European motor industry) suggest that a 'negative incentive' is at work for firms when deciding whether or not to join the relevant European association for their industry. If a firm does not join, the Euro-associations may produce 'unwelcome group decisions' (McLaughlin and Jordan 1993: 155). The danger of *not* participating in a European association is that the Commission (formally emphasising, as it does, the importance of Euro-associations in its consultation procedures) might take the Euro-association's view as the definitive view of the industry as a whole, to the detriment of the non-participating firm. These 'counterstrike' or risk-avoidance strategies may go some way to explaining the seemingly endless increase in interest group mobilisation at the European level. Rather like a rolling snowball, lobbying creates more lobbying.

It would be quite wrong, however, to explain the emergence of a European interest group system solely in these defensive terms. As Kirchner notes in the case of trade unions, there were also perceived *positive* benefits from European-level organisation. He suggests that one of the aims of the trade unions in mobilising at the Euro-level 'is to promote, at the European level, the interests which become increasingly difficult to achieve at the national level' (Kirchner 1980b: 132). We believe that, increasingly, this is a major motivation underpinning the continuation and development of the EU interest group system, consistent with neo-functionalist theory, i.e. groups increasingly see positive benefits from Euro-level solutions. This is particularly the case for groups concerned with trans-frontier problems, such as environmental groups and even companies bearing heavy costs due to the proliferation of different national regulations. At a more theoretical level, Stone Sweet and Sandholtz posit a demand/supply model of European integration, rather similar to Deutsch's transaction theory (Stone Sweet and Sandholtz 1998; Deutsch 1957). Thus, they see the Community's rules for organisations as favouring 'economic actors with a stake in cross-border transactions (trade, investment, production, distribution). Rising levels of transnational exchange trigger processes that generate movement toward increased supranational governance' (Stone Sweet and Sandholtz 1998: 2). Essentially, transnational interests demand more Euro-level regulation as it facilitates efficient (and increased) transnational exchange, and European-level institutions – such as the Commission and the ECJ – are ready suppliers of these new regulations. Kirchner's data implies that the development of the EU and the development of the EU interest group system went hand in hand. Sectional groups (i.e. those groups representing a particular section or functional category of society and based on their members' occupational roles or professions) outnumbered promotional groups (groups seeking to promote specific causes or values, such as environmentalists) by two to one in this period. His general conclusion is that 'there is a linkage between the extent to which Community policies exist in a given sector and the degree of co-operation and integration reached by European interest groups in that sector' (Kirchner 1980a: 115).

The story since 1980 has been one of rapid acceleration of Euro-interest group formation. By 1985, Butt Philip was reporting that 'almost five hundred Europe-wide pressure groups now devote their resources to influencing decisions taken by the EC' (Butt Philip 1985: 1). In addition to the proliferation of Euro-groups, (encouraged by the Commission) he noted that 'some national pressure groups and industrial corporations have also appointed several representatives or agents in Brussels to circulate among the diplomatic, bureaucratic and representative elites' (Butt Philip 1985: 1). In a key passage, he argued that:

> In general, pressure groups have come to recognise the importance of protecting and promoting their interest in the European Community by means of suitable Community wide organisations.
>
> (Butt Philip 1985: 8)

However, he suggested two important qualifications to this general trend of the emergence of a Euro-level interest group system. First, he recognised that the continued importance of national governments in the Council of Ministers 'may mean that pressure groups prefer to supplement their national representations by means of direct approaches to Community institutions – rather than substitute international representations for national action. If this should prove to be the rule then little will have been achieved for the integration within the Community as a whole of interests which cross national frontiers' (Butt Philip 1985: 8). Second, he prophesied that 'we should not expect much increase in the number of such [Euro] groups in the future' (Butt Philip 1985: 88).

Although it would have been difficult to know this at that time, there is now reason to believe that both observations have been overtaken by subsequent events. If we take the numbers issue first, clearly the rate of formation of Euro-associations has slowed down. As, by definition, they are sectoral or trans-sectoral level organisations, at some point pretty well all sectors will have their own Euro-association. We suspect that this is almost the case today, but in 1986 Grote found rather more Euro-groups than had Butt Philip – 654 in fact (Greenwood, Grote and Ronit 1992: 1). By February 2000, the Secretary-General's list of non-profitmaking interest groups included some 800 groups. The growth in other types of Euro-level representation seems to have been almost exponential. Thus, in 1992, the Commission estimated that there were no less than 3,000 'special interest groups of varying types in Brussels, with up to 10,000 employees working in the lobbying sector' (Commission 1992: 4), and that over 200 firms had direct representation in Brussels, with, in addition, approximately 100 lobbying consultancy firms. It is difficult to gauge how reliable this information is or, indeed, how active in the *lobbying* process all of these groups and individuals are. Aspinwall and Greenwood (1998: 2) consider the Commission's figure to be something of an overestimate. Undoubtedly, many Euro-groups will be small-scale operations – mere 'listening posts' whose function is to simply gather information on funding opportunities or new EU-level policy initiatives. However, it is also possible to argue that the true size of the Brussels-level lobbying industry could actually be *higher* that the Commission's estimate, if the census were to include all of those individuals who visit Brussels in order to lobby, but who are not based in Brussels. Our guess is that the number of people who fly into Brussels on a regular basis, but who are not based in Brussels, runs into many thousands. This, no doubt, explains why there are no fewer than twenty-two flights per day from London to Brussels as, ant-like, British interest groups (and government officials) beat a path to the EU institutions in Brussels. By February 2000, the Secretary-General's list of non-profitmaking interest groups included some 800 groups, divided into eleven categories as follows:

Regions, towns, rural life
Trade unions and employers' federations
Political interests
Consumer organisations
Animal welfare, nature and environmental organisations
Conservation and development
Welfare and social interests
Religion
Human rights
SMEs
Miscellaneous

(http: //europa.eu.int/comm/secretariat_general/sgc/lobbies/)

Data on the formation of Euro-associations collected by Greenwood *et al.* (1999: 129) show that two-thirds of their sample of Euro-associations were formed before 1980. Our hypothesis is that the rate of formation of new Euro-associations will in future be quite slow. Most significant interests in Europe have by now formed a Euro-association. The existence of a Liaison Committee of Podiatrists of the European Union suggests that there are few interests yet to be organised at the Euro-level! In any case, Euro-associations are often thought to be rather sluggish policy actors, due to the complex and slow process of consensus-building within many of them. Also they are often said to be under-resourced, especially in terms of the technical expertise which is often the currency of influence. Greenwood *et al.*, however, suggest that Euro-associations are rather better resourced than conventional wisdom suggests. They report that 'over half (56% – 230) of all Euro groups have at least 3 employees' (Greenwood *et al.* 1999: 130). While no doubt true, this leaves 44% with fewer than 3 employees – hardly an indicator of a robust pillar on which the Commission (or European Parliament) could build a stable and manageable system of interest group intermediation. In practice, it is probably unusual to find examples of Commission officials relying solely on Euro-associations in the consultation process. Our own interviews suggest that officials habitually go directly to the source of technical expertise on which the Euro-associations themselves usually draw. Even though 'consult the Euro-associations' is certainly a 'rule' which the Commission follows, there are other, more important, informal rules such as ensuring that proposals are technically robust and that all of the stakeholders have been mobilised. For example, one Commission official confided that he had found it necessary to make direct contact with people who work in the financial markets and had, therefore, set up a 'Market Practitioners' Group'. He wanted to contact people 'whose bread and butter it was to work in the markets, who might come across the problems we identified in their day-to-day practices'. He admitted that this caused 'a lot of bad blood with the federations because we end up bypassing them' (Interview DG XV, 9 July 1999).

Whatever the Commission might wish, however, the individual members of Euro-associations (such as national associations and individual firms) increasingly spread their lobbying resources in a risk avoidance strategy. Like other organisations, interest groups have a learning capacity. Brussels might be a policy-making maze, but groups learn their way round it. They cannot be corralled into working exclusively via Euro-groups, even if the Commission wished it. For example, there appears to be a proliferation of *ad hoc* coalitions focusing on single-issue politics (Coen 1997; Pijnenburg 1998) and definitely an increase in direct Euro-lobbying by firms (Coen 1997; 1998). The more complex the multi-venue Euro-policy game becomes, the greater the need for flexibility and manoeuvrability by interest groups if they are to create policy win situations. Concentrating resources on one type of (federal or confederal) organ of representation is a very risky strategy and likely to fail. Creating *ad hoc* coalitions (often between groups who might oppose each other on different issues) is a sensible strategy, particularly when multiple opportunity structures (each having a different institutional bias) present themselves. Rational action demands direct lobbying in multiple venues. The problem for both the Commission and the Euro-associations is that direct lobbying is not conducive to the creation of the type of intermediation on which a corporatist or neo-corporatist system could be built. Promiscuity, rather than monogamy, is the more rational interest group behaviour.

Promiscuity, institutionalisation and venue shopping

The EU policy system – characterised by uncertain agendas, shifting networks and coalitions, and unstable procedural rules – encourages interest groups (and other actors) to behave promiscuously. However, all actors recognise that, although promiscuity might be inevitable, it has its costs. Hence there are attempts to institutionalise promiscuity, especially by the Commission. Thus the Commission has not only been a 'purposeful opportunist' in terms of policy expansion. It has also been opportunistic in creating new institutions as a means of locking diverse interests into the *ongoing* process of Europeanisation (Mazey and Richardson 2001). It has been a strategic actor in constructing constellations of stakeholders concerned with each of the Commission's policy sectors. It is important to stress that each institutional innovation is linked to a broad *organisational culture* which has become embedded in most parts of the Commission. This culture is clearly outlined in the Commission's 1992 definitive publication *An Open and Structured Dialogue* (Commission 1992) and further developed in publications subsequent to the Cardiff European Council of 15/16 June 1998. The latter document stressed the need to bring the Union nearer to its citizens by making it more transparent, more understandable and closer to everyday life. In practice this has meant an even greater emphasis on interest group accommodation by the Commission.

In its December 1992 document the Commission had argued that it 'has always been an institution open to outside input. The Commission believes this process to be fundamental to the development of its policies. It is in the Commission's own interest to maintain open access since interest groups can provide the services with technical information and constructive advice' (Commission 1992: 1). More recently, the Commission has created a website devoted to its relations with interest groups reflecting its 'wish to create a single site reserved for the working tools that enable officials to promote the participation of socio-economic circles and the representatives of civil society in the legislative process' (see Commission Europa website at http: //europa.eu.int/comm/sg/sgc/lobbies/en/index_htm#top). The *functional logic* of consultation is at the fore of these statements as is the determination to further extend the consultative process. The Commission's 'procedural ambition' to seek out and institutionalise interests is absolutely clear. Its current statement on the value of consultation states:

> The Commission has always been an institution open to input from special interest groups. The Commission believes this process to be fundamental to the development of sound and workable policies. This dialogue has proved valuable to both the Commission and to interested outside parties. The Commission acknowledges the need for such outside input, welcomes it and intends to build further on this practice in future. To this end the Commission is taking a series of measures intended to broaden participation in the preparation of its decisions.

> *Minimum Requirements for a Code of Conduct Between the Commission and Special Interest Groups*
> (http://europa.eu.int/comm/sg/sgc/lobbies/en/communication/)

In practice, this procedural ambition is itself a recipe for promiscuity in terms of relations between the Commission and interest groups. The more the Commission stresses openness and consultation, the more new groups will come to Brussels. The more groups there are in Brussels, the more groups will want to come to Brussels. The intensity and scope of lobbying has itself become a problem in need of regulation of some kind, and both the Commission and the EP have investigated this possibility (for a comprehensive review, see Greenwood 1997: 80–100; and Preston 1998: 222–32). In practice, the usual difficulties have arisen and it would be wrong to suggest that even a basic, legally based regulatory system has emerged. However, some very basic written rules, in the form of guidelines and voluntary codes of practice, exist. In reality, these are supplementary to some rather important informal, but unwritten, rules and norms which facilitate exchange among individuals.

As Greenwood demonstrates, attempts to formulate agreed formal written rules governing lobbying have not had a happy history. For example, it took the European Parliament some seven years to agree, finally in 1996, a set of rules governing lobbying (Greenwood 1997: 96). Moreover, different EU institutions face different problems posed by interest groups and have differing strategic motivations in constructing norms and rules. The Commission, as we have suggested earlier, has been greatly concerned to maintain its culture of open consultations with as wide a constituency of groups as might emerge or, indeed, can be mobilised. If anything, the Commission's strategic objective seems to be to expand the range and diversity of groups consulted. On the other hand, the Parliament has been attacked for corrupt relations with groups and has therefore sought to clean up its image. Whereas institutionalising relations with groups has been dysfunctional to the legitimacy of the Parliament, it has enhanced the legitimacy of the Commission. At least until recently, the Commission was less under attack for corruption than for its 'nannying' policy style and capacity for policy errors. Thus, the imperatives for regulating relations with groups were quite different for the two institutions. Above all, the Commission needs to demonstrate two things. First, it must try to ensure that its proposals are technically robust and workable in the fifteen different and dense 'policy hinterlands' of the member states (Mazey 1998). Second, it must strengthen its legitimacy as an institution and for each of its policy proposals. To pursue an *exclusive* rather than an inclusive policy towards interest groups would not be conducive to either objective. Consulting as many stakeholders as you can find is rational in terms of gaining the best information and knowledge. It is also a good way of avoiding the dangers of asymmetric information supplied by lobbyists. (For a discussion of lobbying and asymmetric information, see Potters and Van Windern 1992.) The need for a more balanced institutionalisation of interest group intermediation is reflected in the Commission's encouragement of NGOs. Thus, in 1997 it adopted a communication *Promoting the Role of Voluntary Organisations and Foundations in Europe* (Commission 1997). This document recognised that NGOs needed to be consulted more widely and systematically. The increasing institutionalisation of NGO–Commission relations is also reflected in the considerable financial support the former receive from the Commission. The Commission recognises that relying on producer groups for advice, however technical and accurate it might be, is a risky business in terms of legitimacy. Even if the broadening of consultations produces no new (or usable) information, it does strengthen the Commission's position in inter-institutional battles. Sometimes the receipt of information can be as important as the information itself. Thus, as Potters and Van Windern suggest, 'it need not be the *content* of the message as such that transmits information, but merely the *fact* that a message has been received' (Potters and Van Windern 1992: 286). For example, when the Environment Council failed to adopt a Common Position on a text from the Council in December 1998, the Commissioner responsible complained that the delay was unnecessary as 'industry had been consulted all along' (see http://europa.eu.int/comm/dg11/press/bio99108–1.htm). In practice the Commission has been anxious to avoid anything that would deter groups from approaching the Commission or participating in its policy-making processes.

As we suggested earlier, the functional logic for a bureaucracy to behave in this way is compelling. In addition, the Commission needs to get ever closer to groups as it knows that groups have other, attractive, EU venues where they can influence the policy process. For example, increasingly, the European Parliament has secured for itself a greater role in the EU policy process, via the series of grand bargains to which Moravcsik (1998) refers. On the EP see Bergman and Raunio in this volume. As a result of this shift in the balance of power between EU institutions (and the continuing uncertainty of how the latest institutional bargain works in each particular case), the EP has moved up the rank order of lobbying targets, depending on the issue at hand.

It has been conventional wisdom to argue that the European Parliament is an inherently weak institution and therefore a relatively unattractive opportunity structure for interest groups. (Interestingly, similar remarks are often made about several EU member states' national parliaments.) Yet, important qualifications to this analysis are needed. First, the EP has, for a very long time (and long before the recent increases in its powers) attracted a great deal of lobbying activity – so much so, in fact, that the question of regulating lobbying has been a key issue within the EP for several years (as suggested above). There are three obvious explanations for this apparent inconsistency. First, groups, as rational actors, recognise that the EU policy process demands a multi-track lobbying strategy – a 'belt and braces' approach to lobbying. Expressing a preference for one opportunity structure over another does not preclude some lobbying of less favoured structures. Second, it seems likely that the EP attracts a disproportionate amount of lobbying from certain types of groups (environmentalists, women, consumers, animal rights) who, historically, may not have enjoyed such easy access to the Commission and/or national governments. Third, the EP's power in the EU policy process varies across policy sectors both because of the Treaties and because of the internal political dynamics of different policy sectors. Where there are effective EP committees, and legislative power is shared between the Council and the Parliament under co-decision, such as in the environmental field, lobbying of the EP is likely to be more intense.

Moreover, the expansion of the EP's legislative role since 1986 has changed the calculation of the logic of influence by groups. A key development in recent years has thus been the elevation of the EP in its importance as a lobbying target for groups (for data see Kohler-Koch 1997). As Kohler-Koch suggests, 'reflecting the new role of the EP as an important institution in the European decision-making process, the Parliamentarians are becoming a decisive target group for lobbyists, and lobbyists have to cope with the institutional structure, the procedures, and the policy style within the Parliament' (Kohler-Koch 1997: 10). Indeed, her research suggests that interest groups and the Parliament can sometimes be effective 'advocacy coalitions' in the EU policy process, albeit sometimes coalitions of the weak. As she argues, changes in the Parliament's role, and in its relationship with groups, seem to be shifting the EP in the direction of a US Congress-type legislature. For example, there has been a proliferation of EP 'intergroups' (of which there are now approximately sixty) – informal meetings of MEPs to discuss policy issues. As one lobbyist has reported, intergroups such as the Pharmaceutical Intergroup are often the target of interest groups (Porter 1998: 4). Two other lobbyists have argued that the increased role for the EP has 'wrested power from other institutions of the EU and especially from closed negotiations between governments and officials in Brussels' and this development is 'good for commercial and other interests' (Earnshaw and Wood 1998: 10). Typically, the public hearings of the EP's committees attract the relevant stakeholders, all interested in pressing their view on the Parliament. For example, the Committee on External Relations held public hearings on 'The European Union and the Agenda of the WTO Millennium Round' on 22 March 1999. Interests such as OXFAM; Greenpeace; ETUC (European Trade Union Confederation); COPA (Comité des organisations professionnelles agricoles de l'Union Européenne); ERT (European Round Table of Industrialists); and FERA (Fédération européen des réalisateurs audiovisuals) all made presentations as part of their attempts to influence the 'framing' of the EP's position. Thus, although relatively little research has been undertaken on the relationship between lobbies and the EP, we can conclude that the latter is now an important opportunity structure. As such, it has further increased the complexity of the Brussels lobbying game. Few interests now dare risk leaving the parliamentary arena to their opponents and, hence, parliamentary hearings attract the full melange of stakeholders. Thus, Wessels has produced data showing that there are probably some 67,000 contacts between the EP and interest groups annually (Wessels 1999: 109). Following Kohler-Koch, he concludes that 'the more the EP becomes a veto-player, the more attention it receives' (Wessels 1999: 109). Similarly, Grant notes that business interests have realised that more attention needs to be paid to the EP, citing the example of the chemical industry's Euro-association, CEFIC, which appointed a full-time EP liaison officer in 1990 (Grant 2000: 118).

The crucial attention which interest groups pay to the EP is a direct reflection of its power as an institution. Similarly, the ECJ's attractiveness as a venue relates to its position in the EU's institutional hierarchy. Here, again, we see the EU interest intermediation system exhibiting some familiar features. In those political systems which accord the judiciary a major role in the interpretation of legal and constitutional arrangements, recourse to the courts has long been a standard 'lobbying' strategy. For example, much of the progress gained by black groups in the USA (and by newer 'movements' such as the anti-nuclear energy movement) has been achieved through the Supreme Court and other courts in the US political system. This is in great contrast to Britain, for example, where judicial institutions have, traditionally, not been seen as a major opportunity structure by interest groups. In the EU, however, once the ECJ had acquired for itself a major role in the EU policy process it was inevitable that interest groups would pay it a lot of attention and allocate resources to influencing Court rulings. (On the ECJ see Wincott in this volume.) In practice, the ECJ has emerged as a perfect example of the working of the 'venue shopping' theory of Baumgartner and Jones, cited earlier. When groups fail to gain satisfaction at the national level, the Commission, EP or Council of Ministers, they have the option – albeit a costly one – of bringing cases (usually in the form of test cases, backed by groups) before the Court, or of persuading the Commission to bring a case before the Court.

Women's and environmental groups (and also trade unions) have been adept in securing favourable ECJ decisions which have been extremely important in prompting policy change. For example, Mazey argues that the EU generally has been an important venue for women's groups and that the ECJ, in particular, has been a very important opportunity structure or venue in supporting the plight of working women and forcing national policy change (Mazey 1998: 136). In the environmental field, Cichowski has reached similar conclusions. She argues that the ECJ has played an important role in the creation of supranational norms which fuel the integration process, often in opposition to the preferences of member states. Private litigants (individuals and interest groups) have played an integral role in this process (Cichowski 1998). These interest groups are, of course, not exclusively environmental groups, but include business groups who, for example, seek to prevent 'tough' national environmental laws from being used to undermine the principles of free and unrestricted trade enshrined in the SEA. At a more general level, Stone Sweet and Brunell have portrayed the Court as a 'supplying' institution – supplying integrative decisions in response to the demands of transnational actors such as businesses and individuals ... who need European rules and those who are advantaged by European law and practices compared with national law and practices (Stone Sweet and Brunell 1998: 72). Dehousse also argues that the expansion of EU competence, particularly in the areas of environmental and social policies, has prompted much greater use of the ECJ by individuals and groups, who perceive the ECJ as an ally (Dehousse 1998).

An intergovernmental theorist would argue that, in theory, the Council of Ministers should be the main European-level opportunity structure to be targeted by interest groups. Yet, it is the least *directly* accessible of all EU institutions. As with Cabinets in Western democracies, lobbying has to be rather indirect. However, as Hayes-Renshaw and Wallace suggest, although groups 'have no formalised relationship with the Council, their influencing efforts pervade the atmosphere in which the Council works' (Hayes-Renshaw and Wallace 1997: 22).

There are three main channels of indirect lobbying of the Council. First, interest groups routinely lobby the national delegations in Brussels, i.e. those national officials who are members of the so-called Permanent Representations based in Brussels. These officials participate in the Council working groups, of which there are approximately 200 (Van Schendelen 1998: 6) and prepare the ground for meetings of the Committee of Permanent Representatives (COREPER) and the ministerial Councils. Where possible, these officials try to reach consensus and compromise between their respective national governments, leaving only the most contentious points to be resolved when the ambassadors meet in COREPER I and II (or, ultimately, the ministers in the Council meetings).

As the national representatives (i.e. the ambassadors and deputy ambassadors to the EU) in COREPER play such a key role in the Council process (some 80% of legislative proposals are adopted at COREPER level), national groups make sure that they lobby 'their' national officials, who (the interest groups hope) will then ensure that their views are represented in the COREPER meetings – hence the description of members of

COREPER as the 'lobbied lobbyists' (Spence 1993: 48). Euro-groups and those national associations and firms who really understand the importance of intergovernmentalism in EU policy-making also lobby a range of national delegations in Brussels – particularly of those member states who are known to hold strong positions on any given policy issue. In addition, it appears that 'explanatory material' from lobbyists is sometimes circulated within the Council Secretariat (Hayes-Renshaw and Wallace 1997: 22).

A second indirect means of lobbying Council is for interest groups to lobby members of the many Council working groups. Rather like COREPER, this form of institution-alised 'issue processing' presents opportunities for detailed, technical arguments to be presented and for national representatives to be won over. The working groups are a sort of boiler-house of European integration. Composed of national officials 'congregating in their thousands every working day in Brussels, they (constitute) the backbone of the European system of integration … they are performing the vital and frequently time-consuming technical groundwork for what will eventually become a piece of European legislation or policy' (Hayes-Renshaw and Wallace 1997: 98). Thus, for example, if a Council working group on vehicle pollution is meeting and contains a civil servant from the Swedish government, the civil servant will certainly have been lobbied by Volvo and Saab and will be fully aware of the ways in which the Swedish motor vehicle industry might be affected by any proposed EU legislation. Occasionally, interest groups may secure representation on Council working groups if one of their officials is 'deemed' by a national government to be a civil servant for those purposes.

The third and most obvious means of influencing the Council is, of course, directly via national governments. Several authors see national governments as, in fact, the *main* opportunity structure for interest groups, not just as a means of influencing the Council but as the key opportunity structure through which groups can influence the EU policy process as a whole. For example, Grant has long been sceptical of the thesis that Brussels is the most effective lobbying arena (Grant 2000: 106–15). Similarly, Greenwood describes the 'national route' as the 'tried and tested ground for many organised interests' (Greenwood 1997: 32). The national level 'is where established policy networks operate which can equally well be used for the purposes of EU representation as they can for the governance of domestic affairs' (Greenwood 1997: 32). Wessels also argues that 'a European route of interest intermediation is clearly not dominant' (Wessels 1999: 117). Bennett's survey data on the lobbying strategies of British business associations confirms this view of interest group behaviour. He found that the national route was the preferred Euro-lobbying strategy of the majority of associations (except federations). He, too, argues that this is perfectly rational: '[T]he preference for this route can be explained by its relative cheapness and its continuity of use of traditional channels of information and exchange that have developed from the period before European economic integration' (Bennett 1997: 85).

Clearly, the importance of national governments as an opportunity structure varies according to the policy issue, the type of interest group, the time, and the nature of the national government itself. On the latter, Aspinwall and Greenwood suggest that 'in hier-archical, state dominated systems, interests tend not to develop transnational (EU level) strategies as readily as in more open, liberal polities' (Aspinwall and Greenwood 1998: 22). In the French case, Kassim has argued that interest groups are having to loosen their ties and dependency on the French state in order to increase their own influence in the EU (Kassim 1997: 179). He sees this as a consequence of the weakening (in the EU arena) of even the traditionally strong EU states such as France – what he calls the 'dissipation of the national'. Elsewhere, we have argued that the extension of qualified majority voting in the Council is bound to erode still further the traditional ties between interest groups and national governments and force interests to develop strategies independent of 'their' governments. Even when an interest group and a national government are on the same side (often not a reasonable assumption), the group cannot rely on a national government to be able to deliver under QMV (Mazey and Richardson 1997: 212). Moreover, as cross-sectoral trade-offs between member states are not uncommon in last-minute bargaining, a national government may choose to 'dump' an interest group in favour of some other policy goal.

Conclusion: the politics of uncertainty

In their analysis of the origins of the Single Market, Sandholtz and Zysman suggest that the 1992 movement was characterised by uncertainty – 'neither the pay-off from nor the preferences for any strategy were or are yet clear' (Sandholtz and Zysman 1989: 107). We conclude on this note of uncertainty. It is an affliction suffered by all players in the EU policy process. In such situations those policy actors possessing certain 'decisional' and 'attitudinal' attributes may have particular advantages in constructing 'win' situations in a series of nested games. Two such attributes might be, first, the development of a long-term view of Europe and its place in the globalisation process, and, second, an ability to change preferences readily in response to changing circumstances. At least *some* European interest groups appear to possess these attributes: for example the large multi-national companies do, indeed, take a European and global view; they may also have a more flexible decision-making process and preference-formation processes than, say, member states, or those interest groups exclusively 'anchored' in national interest group systems. As Heinz *et al.* suggest in their study of US interest groups, 'interest representation involves learning. A group's understanding of its interests may change as a result of improved analysis or reflection on past experience' (Heinz *et al.* 1993: 392). Much more research is needed, but it seems reasonable to hypothesise that organisations such as multinationals and interest groups such as Greenpeace, Friends of the Earth (FOE) and Worldwide Fund for Nature (WWF) are probably less constrained in their lobbying strategies and have more flexible preference-formation processes than, for example, governments.

If, as Heinz *et al.* suggest, uncertainty begets uncertainty, it would be rational for all interest groups wishing to influence the European policy process to avoid becoming locked into any one set of relationships (e.g. with 'their' national government) or into any one 'advocacy coalition' (Sabatier 1988) or any one policy community or policy network. Thus, in one of the few detailed comparative studies of national variations in policy networks and their effect on Euro-lobbying, Josselin, comparing British and French policy networks in the financial services sector, concluded that domestic policy networks

> in which private actors retained relative autonomy fuelled in part by distrust and the need for information, appeared to be better suited to the pursuit of multiple [lobbying] targets; conversely, vertical, state-dominated structures would not encourage the development of active strategies of transnational linkages on the part of non-governmental organisations.
>
> (Josselin 1996)

British sectoral actors, who were 'less tied to a strict policy structure than the French, were better able to exploit the multi-access lobbying system of the EU' (Josselin 1996). Thus, we conclude by suggesting that lobbying in the EU is likely to remain pluralistic, unpredictable and favouring those actors who can mobilise ideas and knowledge in order to 'massage' the 'framing' of public policies, who can manage a series of multi-level and shifting coalitions, and who can reformulate their preferences rapidly and consistent with the long-term goals of their organisation. The practical reality of the EU interest group intermediation system is that more and more groups participate in more and more institutions of intermediation. However, we do not suggest that these institutions are necessarily stable or, indeed, neutral. All institutions have a bias and create winners and losers. The central paradox is that institutionalisation and promiscuity go hand in hand. In a sense, institutionalisation is an attempt to constrain promiscuity. The fact that there are so many different venues for lobbying mean that the EU is an inherently *disjointed* policy process. Deals done at one institutional site can get undone at another. At best, therefore, we might see a process of serial institutionalisation of group intermediation in each EC/EU venue, leaving problematic the ambition for joined-up governance in the European Union.

Acknowledgements

This chapter draws on our previous and forthcoming published work on lobbying in the European Union, especially the following: Sonia Mazey and Jeremy Richardson (1998), 'Interests', in Laura Cram, Desmond Dinan and Neill Nugent (eds), *Developments in the European Union*, Basingstoke: Macmillan, pp. 105–29; Sonia Mazey and Jeremy Richardson (2001), 'Institutionalising Promiscuity: Commission/Interest Group Relations in the EU', in N. Fligstein, W. Sandholtz and A. Stone Sweet (eds), *The Institutionalisation of Europe*, Oxford: Oxford University Press; Sonia Mazey and Jeremy Richardson (2001), 'The European Commission and the Lobby: Reconciling Openness and Effective Policy Making', in Geoffrey Edwards and David Spence (eds), *The European Commission*, 3rd edn London: Catermill; Jeremy Richardson (2000), 'Policy Making in the EU: Familiar Ambitions in Unfamiliar Settings?', in Anand Menon and Vincent Wright (eds), *From Nation States to Europe: Festschrift in Honour of Jack Hayward*, Oxford: Oxford University Press; Jeremy Richardson (2000) 'Government, Interest Groups and Policy Change', *Political Studies* 48/5.

References

Aspinwall, M. and Greenwood, J. (1998) 'Conceptualising Collective Action in the European Union: An Introduction' in J. Greenwood and M. Aspinwall (eds), *Collective Action in the European Union: Interests and the New Politics of Associability*. London: Routledge, pp. 1–30.

Baumgartner, F. and Jones, B. (1991) 'Agenda Dynamics and Instability in American Politics', *Journal of Politics* 53/4: 1044–73.

Bennett, R. (1997) 'The Impact of European Integration on Business Associations: The UK Case', *West European Politics* 20/3: 6–90.

Bennett, R. (1999) 'Business Routes of Influence in Brussels: Exploring the Choice of Direct Representation', *Political Studies* 47: 240–57.

Breton, R. (1995) 'Identification in Transnational Political Communities', in K. Knop, S. Ostry, R. Simeon and K. Swinton (eds), *Rethinking Federalism: Citizens, Markets, and Governments in a Changing World*, Vancouver: University of British Columbia Press, pp. 40–58.

Butt Philip, A. (1985) *Pressure Groups in the European Community*. London: University Association for Contemporary European Studies (UACES).

Cichowski, R. (1998) 'Constrained Court or Autonomous Policy-maker? The European Court of Justice and Integration', *Journal of European Public Policy* 5/3: 387–405.

Coen, D. (1997) 'The Evolution of the Large Firm as a Political Actor in the European Union', *Journal of European Public Policy* 4/1: 91–108.

Coen, D. (1998) 'The European Business Interest and the Nation-State: Large-Firm Lobbying in the European Union and Member States', *Journal of Public Policy* 18/1: 75–100.

Commission of the European Communities (1992) *An Open and Structured Dialogue*, SEC (1992) 2272 final, Brussels: European Commission.

Commission of the European Communities (1997) *Promoting the Role of Voluntary Organisations and Foundations in Europe*, Luxemburg: Office for Official Publications of the European Communities (ISBN 92–828–1613–3).

Cowles, M. Green (1997) 'Organizing Industrial Coalitions: A Challenge for the Future?', in H. Wallace and A. Young (eds), *Participation and Policy-Making in the European Union*, Oxford: Clarendon Press, pp. 116–40.

Cram, L. (1994) 'The European Commission as a Multi-Organisation: Social Policy and IT Policy in the EU', *Journal of European Public Policy* 1/1: 195–218.

Dahl, R. (1982) *Dilemmas of Pluralist Democracy*, London: Yale University Press.

Dehousse, R. (1998) *The European Court of Justice*, Basingstoke: Macmillan.

Deutsch, K. (1957) *Political Community at the Internatioal Level: Problems of Definition and Management*, Garden City: Doubleday.

Downs, A. (1967) *Inside Bureaucracy*, Boston: Little, Brown.

Earnshaw, D. and Wood, J. (1998) 'Winning in Brussels', *The Public Affairs Newsletter*, July.

Grant, W. (1989) *Pressure Groups, Politics and Democracy in Britain*, London: Philip Allen.

Grant, W. (2000) *Pressure Groups in British Politics*, Basingstoke, Macmillan.

Greenwood, J. (1997) *Representing Interests in the European Union*, Basingstoke: Macmillan.

Greenwood, J., Grote, J. and Ronit, K. (1992) 'Introduction: Organized Interests and the Transnational Dimension', in J. Greenwood, J. Grote and K. Ronit, *Organized Interests in the European Community*, London: Sage, pp. 1–41.

Greenwood, J., Strangward, L. and Stancich, L. (1999) 'The Capacities of Euro Groups in the Integration Process', *Political Studies* 47: 127–38.

Hayes-Renshaw, F. and Wallace, H. (1997) *The Council of Ministers*, London: Macmillan.

Heinz, J. P., Laumann, E. O., Nelson, R. L., Salisbury, R. H. (1993) *The Hollow Core: Private Interests in National Policy Making*, Cambridge, MA: Harvard University Press.

Henderson, P. E. (1977) 'Two British Errors: Their Probable Size and Some Possible Lessons', *Economic Papers* 29/2: 159–205.

Hull, R. (1993) 'Lobbying in Brussels: A View from Within', in S. Mazey and J. Richardson (eds), *Lobbying in the European Community*, Oxford: Oxford University Press, pp. 82–92.

Jordan, G. and Richardson, J. (1982) 'The British Policy Style or the Logic of Negotiation?', in J. Richardson (ed.), *Policy Styles in Western Europe*, London: George Allen and Unwin, pp. 80–110.

Josselin, D. (1996) 'Domestic Policy Networks and European Negotiations: Evidence from British and French Financial Services', *Journal of European Public Policy* 3/3: 297–317.

Kassim, H. (1997) 'French Autonomy and the European Union', *Modern and Contemporary France* 5/2: 167–80.

Keck, M. E, and Sikkink, K. (1998) *Activists Beyond Borders*, Ithaca: Cornell University Press.

Kirchner, E. (1977) *Trade Unions as Pressure Groups in the European Community*, Farnborough: Saxon House.

Kirchner, E. (1980a) 'International Trade Union Collaboration and the Prospect for European Industrial Relations', *West European Politics* 3/1: 124–37.

Kirchner, E. (1980b) 'Interest Group Behaviour at the Community Level', in L. Hurwitz (ed.), *Contemporary Perspectives on European Integration*, London: Aldwich.

Kitschelt, H. P. (1986) 'Political Opportunity Structures and Political Protest: Anti-nuclear Movements in Four Democracies', *British Journal of Political Science* 16/1: 57–85.

Klein, R. and O'Higgins, M. (1985) 'Social Policy After Incrementalism', in Klein and O'Higgins (eds), *The Future of Welfare*, Oxford: Blackwell.

Kohler-Koch, B. (1997) 'Organised Interests in the EU and the European Parliament', paper presented to the International Political Science Association XVIII Congress, Seoul, 17–21 August 1997.

Lindblom, C. (1977) *Politics and Markets*, New York: Basic Books.

McAdam, D. (1996) 'Conceptual Origins, Current Problems, Future Directions', in D. McAdam, J. McCarthy and M. Zald (eds), *Comparative Perspectives on Social Movements: Political Opportunities, Mobilizing Structures, and Cultural Framings*, Cambridge: Cambridge University Press, pp. 23–40.

McAdam, D., McCarthy, J. and Zald, M. (1996) 'Introduction: Opportunities, Mobilizing Structures and Framing Processes: Towards a Synthetic, Comparative Perspective on Social Movements', in D. McAdam, J. McCarthy and M. Zald (eds), *Comparative Perspectives on Social Movements: Political Opportunities, Mobilizing Structures and Cultural Framings*, Cambridge: Cambridge University Press, pp. 1–22.

McLaughlin, A. and Jordan, G. (1993) 'The Rationality of Lobbying in Europe: Why are Euro-groups so Numerous and so Weak? Some Evidence from the Car Industry', in S. Mazey and J. Richardson (eds), *Lobbying in the EC*, Oxford: Oxford University Press, pp. 27–46.

Mazey, S. (1995) 'The Development of EU Equality Policies: Bureaucratic Expansion on Behalf of Woman?', *Public Administration* 73/4: 591–609.

Mazey, S. (1998) 'The European Union and Women's Rights: From the Europeanisation of National Agendas to the Nationalisation of a European Agenda?', *Journal of European Public Policy* 5/1: 131–52.

Mazey, S. and Richardson, J. (eds) (1993) *Lobbying in the European Community*, Oxford: Oxford University Press.

Mazey, S. and Richardson, J. (1995) 'Promiscuous Policymaking: The European Policy Style?', in C. Rhodes and S. Mazey (eds), *The State of the European Union*, vol. 3: *Building a European Polity?* Boulder: Lynne Rienner, pp. 337–59.

Mazey, S. and Richardson, J. (1997) 'Policy Framing: Interest Groups and the Lead up to the 1996 Inter-Governmental Conference', *West European Politics* 20/3: 111–33.

Mazey, S. and Richardson, J. (2001) 'Institutionalising Promiscuity: Commission/Interest Group Relations in the EU', in N. Fligstein, W. Sandholtz and A. Stone Sweet (eds), *The Institutionalisation of Europe*, Oxford: Oxford University Press.

Moravcsik, A. (1991) 'Negotiating the Single European Act: National Interests and Conventional Statecraft in the European Community', *International Organisation* 45: 19–56.

Moravcsik, A. (1993) 'Preferences and Power in the European Community: A Liberal Intergovernmentalist Approach', *Journal of Common Market Studies* 31: 473–524.

Moravcsik, A. (1998) *The Choice for Europe: Social Purpose and State Power from Messina to Maastricht*, London: UCL Press.

Peterson, M. A. (1992) 'The Presidency and Organized Interests: White House Patterns of Interest Group Liaison', *American Political Science Review* 86/3: 612–25.

Pijnenburg, B. (1998) 'EC Lobbying by ad hoc Coalitions: An Exploratory Case Study', *Journal of European Public Policy* 5/2: 303–21.

Porter, M. (1998) 'Intergroups and Interest Representation in the EU', *ELIR Newsletter* 4/1: 4–5.

Potters, J. and Van Windern, F. (1992) 'Lobbying and Asymmetric Information', *Public Choice* 74: 269–92.

Preston, M. E. (1998) 'The European Commission and Special Interest Groups', in P.-H. Claeys, C. Gobin, I. Smets and P. Winand (eds), *Lobbyisme, Pluralisme et Intégration Européenne*, Brussels: Presses Interuniversitaires Européennes, pp. 222–32.

Putnam, R. (1988) 'Diplomacy and the Logic of Two-level Games', *International Organisation* 42: 427–60.

Richardson, J. (ed.) (1982) *Policy Styles in Western Europe*, London: George Allen and Unwin.

Richardson, J. (2000) 'Government, Interest Groups and Policy Change', *Political Studies* 48/5.

Richardson, J. J. and Jordan, A. G. (1979) *Governing Under Pressure*, Oxford: Martin Robertson.

Sabatier, P. A. (1988) 'An Advocacy Coalition Framework of Policy Change and the Role of Policy-oriented Learning Therein', *Policy Sciences* 21: 129–68.

Sabatier, P. (1998) 'The Advocacy Coalition Framework: Revisions and Relevance for Europe, *Journal of European Public Policy* 5/1: 98–130.

Sandholtz, W. and Zysman, J. (1989) '1992: Recasting the European Bargain', *World Politics* 42/1: 95–128.

Schön, D. A. and Rein, M. (1994) *Frame Reflection: Toward the Resolution of Intractable Policy Controversies*, New York: Basic Books.

Sidjanski, D. (1970) 'Pressure Groups and the European Economic Community', in C. Cosgrove and K. Twitchett (eds), *The New International Actors: The United Nations and the European Economic Community*, London: Macmillan, pp. 222–36.

Snyder, J. M., Jr (1991) 'On Buying Legislators', *Economics and Politics* 3/2: 95–109.

Spence, D. (1993) 'The Role of the National Civil Service in European Lobbying: The British Case', in

S. Mazey and J. Richardson (eds), *Lobbying in the European Community*, Oxford: Oxford University Press, pp. 47–73.

Stone Sweet, A. and Brunell, T. (1998) 'The European Court and the National Courts: A Statistical Analysis of Preliminary References, 1961–95', *Journal of European Public Policy* 5/1: 69–97.

Stone Sweet, A. and Sandholtz, W. (1998) 'Integration, Supranational Governance, and the Institutionalisation of the European Polity', in W. Sandholtz and A. Stone Sweet (eds), *European Integration and Supranational Governance*, Oxford: Oxford University Press, pp. 2–26.

Truman, D. (1951) *The Governmental Process: Political Interests and Public Opinion*, New York: Knopf.

Tsebelis, G. (1990) *Nested Games: Rational Choice in Comparative Politics*, Berkeley: University of California Press.

Van Schendelen, M. P. C. M. (1998) 'Prolegomena to EU Committees as Influential Policymakers', in M. P. C. M. Van Schendelen (ed.), *EU Committees as Influential Policymakers*, Aldershot: Ashgate, pp. 3–22.

Wessels, B. (1999) 'European Parliament and Interest Groups', in R. Katz and B. Wessels (eds), *The European Parliament, the National Parliaments, and European Integration*, Oxford: Oxford University Press, pp. 105–28.

Chapter 12

Bypassing the nation-state?

Regions and the EU policy process

MICHAEL KEATING AND LIESBET HOOGHE

Introduction

European integration and regionalism have both altered the architecture of the Western European political order, creating new spaces above and below the nation-state. Their combined effects have created new forms of politics and a complex of three-level interactions. Much has been written on the Europe of the regions (Anderson 1991; Petschen 1993), which some observers think, or hope, will rival or even displace the Europe of states. Others have discerned new forms of 'multi-level governance' (Jachtenfuchs and Kohler-Koch 1995; Marks 1992; 1993; Marks, Hooghe and Blank 1996; Scharpf 1994; 1999) or third-level politics (Bullman 1994; Jeffrey 1996). In this chapter we examine the emergence of the region in the context of the state and of the European Union. Then we look at the links between regions and the EU and the influence of regions in EU policy-making. We find that, rather than a new and ordered territorial hierarchy, authority is diffused across multiple territorial levels. Policy-making continues to be centred primarily on the state, but national governments increasingly share decision-making with European and regional actors.

Regions and regionalism in Western Europe

The emergence of the region, like that of the EU itself, is a response to functional, political and institutional developments which have had varied impacts in different places. Functionalist analyses stress the links between territory and economic change and the rediscovery of the region as the motor of economic development (Storper 1997; Scott 1998). Together with the decline of national diversionary regional policies and planning, this has led to an emphasis on endogenous development and self-help and to increased competition among regions for investment, markets and technology (Keating 1998). This analysis is taken to extremes by observers like Ohmae (1995), who sees regions engaged in a struggle for economic advantage to the exclusion of all other policy considerations. In fact, regions are defined not merely by economics but also by culture and history, which define their boundaries and shape social relations within them. Regions are also the outcome of political leadership and competition. In some parts of Europe territory has become a significant political cleavage and regions have emerged as political spaces, sustaining a debate about the common interest and sustaining a distinct political agenda. Regions have also emerged as institutions, an intermediate level of government between states and municipalities, but taking very different forms, from the fully-fledged federalism of Germany, Belgium and Austria, to the weak, administrative regionalism of Italy and France. This has produced a very heterogeneous pattern across Europe, according to whether the various meanings of the region coincide or not, and to the degree of institutionalisation of regional government. In some places, like Scotland or Catalonia, the economic, cultural and political regions (or rather stateless nations) coincide and are endowed with important institutions with legislative and administrative competences. Some of the other Spanish autonomous communities and many of the German Länder have a much weaker sense of political and cultural identity, although still possessing autonomous institutions. French regions were designed to suppress rather than encourage political and cultural identity and, like Italian regions, rarely constitute political spaces or a primary reference point for political debate. In some of the smaller states and in England there are no elected regional governments at all and, at best, a system of functionally specific agencies for economic development. In some cases, the most important level for economic, social and political mobilisation is not the region but the city; this is generally so in France.

As a polity, the region has much in common with the EU itself. It is complex, patchily institutionalised and contested. Arenas and actors vary across policy areas and policy-making is organised through networks, which may be functionally or territorially based. As in Europe (Hooghe and Marks 1999), there is a constant struggle between those who see the region as primarily an economic entity, driven by competitive market considerations locked in a neo-mercantilist competition for economic advantage, and those who favour a stronger social dimension (Keating 1998). As in the European Union, concerns of economic competitiveness have usually trumped questions regarding the region as a basis for social solidarity. In a few regions, strong regional governments are able to impose coherence on the array of local actors and define a common territorial interest. In other regions, development coalitions have emerged to promote a vision of the region's place in European and global markets but without an overall social project. Yet other regions are a political no man's land, fought over by rival political and social interests, often with different territorial bases.

Regions and European integration

European integration has further enhanced the importance of regions, in the political and economic domains, and produced a new dynamic. In the economic domain, the opening of markets has produced a new territorial hierarchy. At one time, it was thought that integration would concentrate development in the central regions of the 'golden triangle' to produce a new centre–periphery cleavage, but it is clear now that matters are more complex. Some French economists replaced the analogy of the golden triangle with that of the 'blue banana' and others have favoured the analogy of the mosaic, with pockets of underdevelopment even in the booming regions. There is, however, a broad, if not universal, consensus that market integration is still likely to exacerbate territorial disparities (Molle et al. 1980; Keeble et al. 1988; Camagni 1992; Steinle 1992; Begg and Mayes 1993; Commission 1991; 1999; André et al. 1989). Unlike nation-states, the EU has no automatic compensation mechanism through fiscal equalisation and large universal spending programmes financed by general taxation (Mackay 1993). The needs of national competitiveness together with EU rules also prevent states from intervening to correct these disparities through diversionary policies. EU competition policy may disadvantage marginal regions, through preventing cross-subsidisation of communications services and opening public procurement (Fullarton and Gillespie 1988). Other EU policies, including agriculture and research spending, also tend to benefit the more developed regions (Strijker and de Veer 1988; Cheshire et al. 1991; Grote 1992; Commission 1996). The single-market programme has further disarmed national governments, while economic and monetary union has removed their ability to manipulate exchange rates and interest rates or to run budget deficits, all instruments used for regional as well as national purposes.

Politically, European integration has also served to enhance the salience of regions. Competencies transferred to the EU include matters in which regions have a direct interest. There have been two types of reaction at the regional level. A rejectionist regionalism opposes European integration fearing a further loss of democratic control, more remote government and the triumph of market principles. This reaction was common in many regions in the 1970s and is still visible in Scandinavia. A second type of regionalism seeks to use Europe as a source of political and economic resources, if necessary against the state itself. Most obviously this involves economic development issues, but Europe has also been seen as a source of support for minority cultures and languages threatened within large states (Cardús 1991; de Witte 1992). Hence regional interests have sought new mechanisms to get into the European policy game.

More generally, Europe has provided a new arena for the expression of regional and minority nationalist aspirations. Some minority nationalist movements note that European integration has reduced the cost of national independence, and propose simply to join the list of member states; this is the case of the Scottish National Party and some Basque nationalists. Others want to replace the existing Union with a federation of regions and small nations, abolishing the existing states; this is the policy of the Welsh nationalist party Plaid Cymru and of many Basque nationalists. Others again are more pragmatic, seeing in Europe an arena in which their nationalist aspirations can be expressed and legitimised, while seeking to exert influence at whatever points are available; this is the case of the Catalan governing alliance, *Convergència i Unió* (CiU).

Europeanisation and regionalisation are occurring at a time of profound change in the functions and working of the European state. Factors include the rise of neo-liberal ideology, the advance of markets and deregulation, and the strengthening of civil society in systems formerly dominated by strong states. The classic nation-state was the locus of sovereignty and ultimate authority and the basis for governing institutions. It was the arena for public policy-making. It was the framework for economic activity and 'national economies'; the basis of cultural and political identity; a system of representation and legitimisation of decisions; and a forum within which economic competitiveness and social integration could be reconciled. These processes are increasingly divorced as economic change escapes the control of states; policy-making retreats into complex networks which do not correspond to formal institutions; and new and rediscovered forms of identity emerge at the subnational and even the supranational level.

European integration and regionalism are Janus-faced phenomena. On the one hand, they contribute to this process of disaggregation of state functions. On the other hand, they also represent attempts to create new political arenas to try and recapture control over state functions. The shape of these arenas will condition the politics that is possible within them, hence a series of conflicts over the character of the European Union: the social versus the market vision; the unitary versus the federalist vision; and the role of regions. In the next section, we examine the channels by which regional interests have sought to influence Europe. Then we examine how the European Union has itself sought to use regions in pursuit of its own policy objectives. The result has been a dynamic interplay of interests at three levels, among regions, the EU and nation states. This has spawned a considerable literature examining the ways in which regions can influence policy in the EU (Balme 1996; Bullman 1994; Hooghe 1996; Jeffrey 1996; Jones and Keating 1995; Keating and Jones 1985; Le Galès and Lequesne 1997).

Channels of access

Formulating an interest

Regions, as emphasised above, are not merely actors but also political arenas, containing a plurality of interests. Their first problem in seeking access to European decision-making is formulating a regional interest. In some cases, such as the German Länder, the Belgian regions or the Austrian Länder, strong regional governments are able to formulate a regional interest, given legitimacy by democratic election. In others, such as the French regions, regional governments are institutionally weak and rivalled by powerful political figures rooted in the cities and departments as well as in a territorial bureaucracy of the central state. Some states have no regional governments at all.

A number of regions have a capacity to mobilise territorial lobbies encompassing both governmental and private actors. Despite the lack of elected institutions before 1999, Scotland has shown a consistent ability to mobilise a territorial lobby encompassing business, trade unions, municipal governments, religious and other social leaders, and the deconcentrated arms of the central bureaucracy itself (Midwinter *et al.* 1991). In the historical Spanish regions of Catalonia, the Basque Country and Galicia, regional governments are able to draw upon a sense of historical identity to legitimise a regional interest, though with varied results. In some French regions, powerful notables are able to mobilise a lobby around themselves, despite the fragmentation of the system of political representation, with its three levels of subnational government. In the case of the regions of England, there are as yet no regional governments and the capacity to organise lobbies within civil society is rather low. Italian regional governments have traditionally been institutionally weak, dominated by national political parties and poorly linked to civil society; this has undermined their ability to formulate a regional interest.

There are some interests common to regions within the EU. These include institutional matters, the design of partnerships in policy implementation and the general principle of subsidiarity and its interpretation. There are also common interests in inter-regional co-operation and cross-border initiatives. Yet regions are also in competition with each other, to attract public funding and private investment, and to shape EU policies to suit their particular interests. So there is a constant tension between promotion of regionalism in general, and the pursuit of regions' individual concerns. Regions have a multiplicity of channels for the pursuit of these collective and individual matters, of varying efficacy depending on the subject to be pursued and the political context. There is not, nor can there be, a single mode of representation of 'regional' interests in the EU.

Access via the national government

The most important channel of influence is via national governments. Generally, the more effectively regional interests are integrated into the national policy-making system, the better they will be looked after in Brussels. The strongest mechanism is provided by Article 203, originally introduced in the Maastricht Treaty, which allows a state to be represented by a minister of a subnational government in the Council of Ministers. This clause, which stipulates that representatives must have ministerial status, was designed for federal states like Austria, Germany and Belgium or federalising ones like Spain and the UK, and not for countries with administrative regions like France. It does not, it must be emphasised, allow regions to represent themselves at the Council of Ministers. A regional minister appearing there represents the state, and there needs to be a prior agreement among the regions and the state as to what their interest is. The clause has been used in Germany, Belgium and Austria, but in rather different ways. In the German case, the Länder negotiate an agreement through the Bundesrat, and one of them then represents the common position. The Belgian regions, communities and federal government have laid down by special law detailed arrangements on federal–subnational representation and decision-making in Council of Ministers machinery. Each level represents the Belgian position and casts the vote in matters exclusively under its own jurisdiction, while both are involved in matters of joint competence, with one taking the lead. In contrast to the German collective approach, Belgian regions and communities minimise the need for prior agreement by taking turns in assuming the lead responsibility for the Councils on matters within their jurisdiction. The distinction between the collective and the individual approach rests upon fundamentally different premises. The German approach accepts that regions are the third level in a multi-layered European polity and that they are ultimately nested in a national arena. The Belgian approach minimises the national mould. Europe is seen as a polity with multiple actors at multiple levels who interact directly with European institutions on matters within their competencies.

Regions may also be involved in the process of treaty revision, to secure their own rights. As a condition of the ratification of the Maastricht Treaty in the Bundesrat, the Länder obtained a provision that the Bundesrat would have to approve all further transfers of sovereignty, even those that do not impinge on Länder competencies. In Belgium, treaty changes need the approval not only of the Senate, which is the federal chamber but, where regional competencies are involved, of each regional and community assembly separately.

The devolution legislation for Scotland allows Scottish ministers to form part of the UK delegation in the Council of Ministers. This is an extension of the old system whereby Scottish Office ministers participated as part of the UK government. It is not anticipated that Scotland could pursue an interest distinct from that of the central government, and it is hard to see the arrangement lasting were the two levels of government controlled by different political parties (such as the pro-European Scottish nationalists and the anti-European Conservatives). There is also provision for participation by Northern Ireland ministers, but the most interesting stipulation there is for co-operation with the Republic of Ireland on European matters.

Elsewhere, regions have only a consultative role in European matters. In Spain, the central government consults the autonomous communities through sectoral conferences, including one specifically on European affairs, but the impact of these is very uneven. In their pact with the incoming Partido Popular government in 1996, the Catalans and Basques secured the appointment of an observer from the autonomous communities in the Spanish Permanent Representation and some participation in working groups preparing the Spanish negotiating position. Italian regions have some input through the six-monthly meetings of the Standing Conference on State–Regional Relations.

France provides another model of influence via the national state, through its integrated bureaucracy which links local and national policy-making, and the cumulation of mandates, by which politicians may simultaneously hold national and local office. To some degree, this unitary system with territorial influence has been extended to the EU (Balme 1995). A powerful politician like Valéry Giscard d'Estaing, former president of the republic, member of the European Parliament and president of the regional council of Auvergne, was able to pull strings at various levels at the same time. This system is highly uneven in its incidence. While the presence of local politicians in the national parliament provides a powerful institutional defence for the system of local government in France, there is no powerful lobby for the defence of these institutional interests in Europe.

Individual regional interests may also be projected through national governments by partisan links. This is particularly important in southern Europe. Finding itself in a minority following the 1993 general elections, the Spanish socialist central government negotiated a pact with the Catalan CiU; this was repeated by the Partido Popular after the 1996 elections, and continued after the 2000 elections, even though the Partido Popular obtained this time a comfortable absolute majority. This provides access to national policy-making and thence to Europe. In Belgium too, regional interests have access to the federal government through party networks.

Direct access: subnational offices

Recent years have seen a spectacular growth in direct links with the EU. These take a variety of forms. Regional and local governments make frequent visits to Brussels to lobby Commission officials, and they often engage the services of consultants to help them make a case and find their way through the bureaucracy. Many have opened permanent offices in Brussels. In the fifteen years to 2000, the number of these grew from just two to 150 (Marks, Salk, Ray and Nielsen 1996; McLeod 1999). The type of subnational office varies considerably across Europe. For countries with a strong tier of regional government, regional governments dominate representation in Brussels. Thus one finds every German *Land*, all three Belgian regions and all Austrian *Länder* represented in Brussels along with most Spanish autonomous communities. In countries with a weaker regional tier, representation usually consists of a mixture of local and regional units. In France, most offices represent regions, but several *départements* also have offices. In the United Kingdom, local authorities, regional quangos, regional enterprise organisations, national local authority organisations, universities and elected regional assemblies fund offices representing individual local authorities, regional groupings of local authorities and a national local authority organisation, alongside offices representing the North of England, Northern Ireland, Scotland, and Wales.

The status of these offices differs considerably. Some are public–private consortia concerned with economic issues, while others are political representatives of the regional government. Catalonia has maintained the public–private formula with the Patronat Català Pro-Europa, while the Basque government has chosen to establish a direct political presence. Scotland has both forms, Scotland Europa, founded in 1992 as a platform for Scottish interests, and Scotland House, the representative of the new Scottish Executive. The legal status of the offices also differs according to domestic law. Spanish and Italian regions had to go to court to challenge national bans on opening Brussels offices and the French regions had to tread carefully around the constitution. The German federal government only recognised the Länder offices in 1993. Particular sensitivity is aroused by ventures across national borders; the Italian government long resisted a proposal for a joint office between the region of Alto-Adige and its Austrian neighbour Tyrol. On the other hand, crossborder joint lobbying in Brussels is specifically encouraged in the Northern Ireland peace agreements as a way of defusing conflict.

These offices are sometimes represented as forms of direct representation in EU decision-making, yet the Commission is tied by regulations in deciding on matters like the allocation of regional funds, while political decision-making is in the hands of the Council of Ministers and the European Parliament. The offices really serve two more subtle roles. In the first place, they provide information to regions on upcoming initiatives, allowing them to lobby their national governments; and they provide information and regional viewpoints to Commission officials, who are otherwise dependent on national governments for information. In the second place, they serve a symbolic role in projecting regions and regional politicians in the European arena and presenting them as participants in the policy process. This allows regional politicians to take credit for EU initiatives and particularly for funding that they would have received in any case under existing regulations. The open bureaucracy of the Commission encourages lobbying, while the opacity of the political decision-making process and the funding regulations allows a whole variety of actors to take credit for the outcomes.

Regional lobbies are rarely powerful on their own in Brussels. Where they can work with a national government, they can achieve more. They may also be effective when linked with powerful sectoral interests, such as a major corporation based in the region, or a sector with links into the Commission directorates. The best examples are in Germany, where sectoral interests are often linked into the system of territorial government in the *Länder*.

European-wide lobbies

Several organisations lobby for regions as a whole at European level. The International Union of Local Authorities and the Council of Communes and Regions of Europe are both wider in scope than the Community and have been closely associated with the Council of Europe, which they persuaded to establish a Permanent Conference of Local and Regional Authorities in 1957. In 1986, they opened a joint office to deal with the EC. In 1985, the Council (later Assembly) of European Regions was launched, with 107 members including eleven Swiss cantons. It has pressed for involvement of regions in European decision-making, for the principle of subsidiarity, and for institutional changes. Other regional organisations seeking to influence policy-making in Brussels are the Conference of Peripheral Maritime Regions; the Association of European Frontier Regions; Working Group of Traditional Industrial Regions; and a number of transnational frontier organisations.

Consultative mechanisms: Committee of the Regions

The establishment of formal rights of consultation with the Community owed a great deal to the pressure of the European Parliament, which in the course of the reforms of the regional fund stressed the need for greater involvement of regions. In 1988, the Commission created a Consultative Council of Regional and Local Authorities with consultative rights over the formulation and implementation of regional policies as well as the regional implications of other Community policies. Its forty-two members were appointed by the Commission on the joint nomination of the Assembly of European Regions, the International Union of Local Authorities and the Council of Regions and Communes of Europe. The Maastricht treaty replaced this with a stronger Committee of the Regions, which the Commission, the Council of Ministers and, since the Amsterdam Treaty, the Parliament are obliged to consult. It has the same status and powers as the Economic and Social Committee, with which it was initially organisationally linked, although its scope is slightly narrower. It can also issue opinions on its own initiative and forward these to the Commission and Council. More ardent regionalists had hoped for a regionally based second chamber of the European Parliament or even of the Council of Ministers; what they got was a great deal less. In addition to its purely consultative status, several factors weaken the Committee (Farrows and McCarthy 1997). Its membership is decided by national governments, some of which, like France, have exercised strong control, while others, including Belgium, Germany and Spain, have left the matter to regions themselves. National politics are also felt in the allocation of committee chairs and memberships and even the allocation of own-initiative opinions by national quotas. The committee includes not just regions but municipal representatives, with different institutional interests. From the outset, it was highly politicised, not so much on a right–left basis as on a north–south one. The marginalisation of northern European representatives, especially the German Länder, is likely to reduce its influence and to lead those regions to seek other outlets. Finally, the Committee has the task of representing regions as a whole, which may limit it to institutional matters where a common interest can be discerned, though even here the regional–local division may cause problems.

The Commission and the regions

Traffic between regional interests and the EU is not one-way. The Commission has itself played an important role in mobilising regional interests, establishing new networks and creating a dialogue among regions, states and itself. The main stimulus for this has been the EU's regional policy, now subsumed under the structural funds. These now account for a third of the EU budget, less than agricultural spending but far more than any other item. Elsewhere (Hooghe and Keating 1994) we have explained the development of regional and structural policy as the product of converging logics. A policy logic, whose guardian is the Commission, combines with a political and distributive logic, located in the Council of Ministers and intergovernmental negotiations. The policy logic for EU regional policy is similar to that for national regional policies of the 1960s and 1970s. It is a mechanism for rectifying the territorial disparities produced by market integration and for achieving allocative efficiency; it is a social compensation for losers in the process of economic restructuring; and it is a device to legitimise the European project in regions where support might otherwise be lacking. The political logic is the need to redistribute resources among member states. Initially, this meant compensating Britain for its disproportionately large net contribution to the Community budget in the 1970s. Later, the policy was extended to compensate the southern European countries for the effects of the single market programme and EMU. These different logics produced conflicts between the Commission and member states from the inauguration of the European Regional Development Fund (ERDF) in 1975 (Mawson et al. 1985). In order to gain the consent of member states, the ERDF was divided into fixed national quotas; all regions that were eligible under national regional policies were eligible for ERDF funding. Funds were administered by national governments, who almost invariably refused to treat them as additional to national spending but rather as a reimbursement to themselves for their own regional policy spending. Consequently, the policy was a way of dressing up an interstate transfer mechanism as a European policy.

Over the years, the Commission has sought to increase its own influence over the framing and implementation of the policy, to convert it to a genuine instrument of regional policy, and to ensure that spending is additional to national spending programmes. From the late 1980s, it also sought to co-opt regional interests as partners in designing and implementing programmes. This has produced a three-level contest for control of the policy instrument, among the Commission, member states and regions themselves. In 1988, there was a major reform, again guided by both political and policy logics. The political logic was provided by the need to compensate the countries of southern Europe and Ireland for the adoption of the single market programme measures in the period to 1993. The policy logic was the Commission's desire to convert the ERDF and other structural funds into a genuine policy. The funds doubled and the three main ones, the ERDF, the European Social Fund (ESF) and the Guidance Section of the European Agricultural Guidance and Guarantee Fund (EAGGF) were brought together (Armstrong 1995). Five objectives were laid down, three of which are regional in nature. For the first time, the Commission drew up its own map of eligible areas, using Community-wide criteria. Funds were disbursed only to projects within approved Community Support Frameworks (CSFs), apart from 9%, which was reserved for Community Initiatives sponsored by the Commission. CSFs were negotiated between the Commission and member states, with the involvement of regions themselves. Within these, the negotiators framed programmes of action while partnerships involving Commission representatives, national governments, and representatives from the regions were responsible for administering them. Additionality was laid down as a general principle, so that spending would be over and above national spending. The whole policy was guided by the notion of subsidiarity, with the greatest possible involvement of regional and local interests and the social partners in the world of business, labour and voluntary groups. The regulations prescribed an integrated approach to regional development: as this links spatial policy to technology, environmental policy, education, public procurement and competition policy, it should bring regions into contact with a range of EU policies and directorates. The Commission, in line with contemporary thinking on development policy, also sought to move from infrastructure to human capital, productive investment and indigenous development. This too implies a more active and participative role for regional actors of various sorts.

These changes potentially paved the way for greater regional involvement in policy-making and for stronger direct links between the Commission and regional interests. To a significant extent, this has happened (Hooghe 1996). Those states without regional structures have been obliged to create them, or at least a substitute for them, in order to be eligible for funds. This is the case in Greece, Ireland and even Sweden. There has been a great deal of political mobilisation around the funds. Some English regions have even constituted lobbies in the absence of regional governments, in order to face the European challenge (Burch and Holliday 1993). The belief that there is a pot of gold in Brussels is one reason for the explosion of regional lobbying and offices in the EU capital. Regional actors have been brought into contact with Commission officials, and its thinking on development policy has diffused through the mechanism of partnership.

Yet the effect on territorial relations should not be overstated. For one thing, the Commission itself does not have a consistent definition of what a region is. Its NUTS table (Nomenclature of Territorial Units for Statistics) consists of three levels, each of which is an aggregation of national administrative units. Nor does it limit itself to regional authorities, however defined. Sometimes its initiatives involve municipal governments, others are aimed at the private sector or local action groups within civil society. The Commission's objective following its policy logic is to get programmes going, to spend the funds in the most effective way possible, and to involve whatever partners are appropriate for the task at hand.

National governments have also found their way back into the act and from the high point of 1988 there has been considerable re-nationalisation of the policy field. While the Commission has succeeded in concentrating funds on the neediest regions, it still has to make sure that everyone gets something in order to keep national governments on side. Even the new Nordic members, although net contributors to the EU budget, received a piece of the structural policy in 1995, through a new Objective 6 aimed at areas of sparse population. While there are officially no national quotas, there was an understanding that Britain, for example, would get a large share of the funds for industrial areas, while France would do well in the rural category. The map of eligible areas was in practice negotiated between states and the Commission, a practice that was formalised in 1993. Community Support frameworks (CSFs) are nationally based and negotiated bilaterally with the Commission. In the 1993 changes, states could submit instead a single document including their overall development plan and the individual applications for assistance rather than having to have the former approved first. Partnership in the CSFs is decided by member states and this too was formalised in 1993, though the Commission has sought to make partnership as inclusive as possible.

The 1999 revision, which sets the rules for the period 2000–06, builds upon the two alterations of 1993. It reinforces a very broad, indeed representative, definition of partnership by specifying that, in addition to the Commission and the national government, regional and local governments, economic and social partners and other relevant bodies should be included. When designating the most representative partners, national governments should 'take account of the need to promote equality between men and women, as well as sustainable development' (Article 8.1, Council Regulation (EC) No. 1260/1999 of 21/06/99). But the more consequential alteration – under the denominator of 'decentralisation' – may very well be that the new rules lay down a separation of roles for subnational, national and supranational partners. The Commission's main task under the 1999 rules is to ensure that policy-making expresses EU strategic priorities, and so it requires the Commission to participate primarily at the beginning and end of the programme stage. The national government, from its side, is responsible for setting up a domestic two-tier structure of supervisory management authorities and programme-specific monitoring committees. Each monitoring committee 'shall draw up its own rules of procedure within the institutional, legal and financial framework of the Member State concerned' (Article 35.2, Council Regulation (EC) No. 1260/1999 of 21/06/99). This effectively decentralises implementation and ongoing management back to the national arena. The original political ambition of the 1988 reform was to replace twelve or fifteen different national models for setting priorities and spending EU money by one European mould (Hooghe 1996; 1998). The 1999 revision is more modest: it seeks to implement common cohesion priorities in a relatively loose EU mould that allows for nationally specific partnerships. These new rules weaken subnational authorities' claim for direct access to European decision-making, and they make it more difficult for the Commission to interact directly with regions or municipalities against the will of national governments.

Even though the 1999 cohesion policy rules may be less region-friendly than those of 1988, the size of the cohesion budget remains an important lever for subnational mobilisation. The 1988 and 1993 revisions saw the budget for cohesion policy doubled twice. The agenda 2000 negotiations, concluded in March 1999, did not produce another major increase. The budget was kept virtually constant at 213 billion euro for the seven-year period of 2000–06: 195 billion euro for the structural funds and 18 billion for the cohesion fund. This is equivalent to approximately one-third of the EU budget (36% in 2000, declining to 32.6% in 2006), or 0.41% of EU GDP in 2000 (declining to 0.31% in 2006) in 1999 figures. These funds are now divided across three objectives, instead of the original five: objective one for regions with a GDP below 75% of the EU average; a new objective two for economic and social adjustment in areas with structural difficulties (industrial, urban, rural or fisheries); and a new non-regional objective three, which targets issues of education, training and employment. This amount of money provides the European Union with considerable financial leverage to affect national territorial relations.

The retreat from interventionist regional policy since 1988 reflects general political pressures to contain the role and power of the Commission. But it also stems from a concern within the Commission that an active role was too costly in time and resources and ineffective in control; regional funds featured in the mismanagement scandals that erupted in the late 1990s (Hooghe 1998). So, while structural policy has stimulated increased regional activity, this has followed distinctly national lines. Where regional governments have a strong institutional position in the domestic arena, they have become important actors. Where they are weak domestically, states have largely retained their central role concerning links to the Commission and control of regional policy implementation. At one extreme are the Belgian regions, which deal directly with the Commission on the designation of eligible areas, the allocation of the funds, negotiation of the contracts and implementation. The German Länder are also deeply involved, through the mechanisms of co-operative federalism. Individual Länder participate in the design and implementation of CSFs, through the Joint Tasks Framework *Gemeinschaftsaufgabe* (Anderson 1996). At the other extreme are Ireland and Portugal, which lack an elected regional tier of government, as well as Greece, with an elected though extremely weak regional level. At the urging of the Commission, even in those inhospitable settings, local actors have become more involved, though the changes fall well short of undermining the state's gatekeeping role (Laffan 1996; Ioakimidis 1996; Reese and Holmes 1995; Yannopoulos and Featherstone 1995). In France and the UK (outside Scotland and Wales) there has, paradoxically, been some increased centralisation since the 1988 reforms, as the structural funds have become financially significant and politically more salient (Balme 1995; Jones and Keating 1995; Balme and Jouve 1996).

The portion of the structural funds budget available for Community initiatives could potentially be an important instrument to establish links between Commission and regions, because the Commission has considerable discretion in these. Local, regional or group interests can lobby the Commission to launch an initiative aimed at them, independently of their national governments. For example, the Rechar initiative originated in the collaboration between Bruce Millan, Commissioner for Regional Policy, and a coalition of British local governments from coal-mining areas (McAleavey 1993). However, the Commission's role has been scaled back considerably over the past two reforms. In 1993, its role in determining around 9% of the entire budget for structural funding was constrained by the creation of an oversight body made up of national representatives, with the power to reject a Community initiative drawn up by the Commission. In 1999, the budget was reduced to 5.35%, but more importantly, the Commission lost its discretionary power to create initiatives in the course of the programming period. The number of Community initiatives is now fixed, falling from thirteen in 1999 to four from 2000 onwards: Interreg (cross-border, transnational and interregional co-operation), Leader (rural development), Urban (urban innovation) and Equal (exclusion from the labour market). The Commission retains considerable discretion over some funds (less than 1% of each fund's working budget) earmarked for innovative actions and technical assistance.

Overall, the institutional machinery of partnership, oiled by a considerable budget, has strengthened features of multi-level governance (Ansell *et al.* 1997; Hooghe 1998). In a 1999 report, the Commission concludes that 'as an institution, the delivery system developed for the structural funds is characterised by multi-level governance, i.e. the Commission, national governments and regional and local authorities are formally autonomous, but there is a high level of shared responsibility at each stage of the decision-making process. The relationship between these is, accordingly, one of partnership and negotiation, rather than being a hierarchical one' (Commission 1999: 143) This challenges state-centric governance in that European institutions set general rules, regions participate in making decisions, and the three parties are in a relationship of mutual dependency rather than hierarchy. But this partnership has never applied evenly across all phases of decision-making. It has traditionally been strongest in the implementation stage of structural programming, but weak in the strategic planning stages. Under the 1999 rules, which strengthened the Commission's powers in planning, the Commission may be able to put more pressure on national governments to involve subnational authorities in this stage, but that may come at the expense of partnership during the implementation. It is possible, then, that – on the whole – the 1999 rules will weaken partnership as a tool for regional mobilisation. With the new rules encouraging more partners (not only subnational authorities), greater adjustment to national practices, and greater separation of responsibilities, partnership rules may no longer provide regional authorities an unconditional entitlement to participate in EU decision-making.

Conclusion

Regionalism and European integration have changed the national state in important ways. It is difficult, however, to isolate these from other factors pointing in the same direction – the internationalisation of markets; capital mobility; the rise of transnational corporations; and neo-liberal ideology. Territorial politics in the European Union is complex. We have not seen the rise of a homogeneous regional tier of government in the EU. Instead, variety in forms of territorial mobilisation has persisted: historic nations; large provincial regions; units in federal or quasi-federal states; cities and city-regions. Regions also differ in their social and political constitution. In some cases, the region can be identified with a structure of government; in others, civil society or private groups are more important in defining and carrying forward a regional interest.

We have not seen the rise of a new territorial hierarchy. The national state has not been bypassed in favour of a Europe of the regions. The national state remains the primary actor in the EU. This does not mean, however, that policy-making in this field can be explained simply by interstate bargaining. The intergovernmental perspective on EU policy-making presents national politics as a closed, domestic game, where the national interest is formulated before being taken to the EU, where a second game commences, characterised by intergovernmental bargaining (Moravcsik 1993). In fact, national politics is penetrated by European influences (Muller 1994), through law, bureaucratic contacts, political exchange, the role of the Commission in agenda-setting and, to a greater or lesser extent according to the state, through regional influences. So we are witnessing both a Europeanisation and a regionalisation of national policy-making.

The aspiration to see regions recognised as a 'third level' (Bullman 1994; Jeffrey 1996) within the EU has been partially satisfied. Both the institutionalisation of the regions and the interest of the Commission in an active and interventionist role peaked around the early 1990s, and since then there has been consolidation. Regions have continued to seek a role in Europe, but access and influence are unevenly distributed. The regions that are best equipped institutionally and that have the best access to their national governments are advantaged in the new setting. They also tend to be the most economically and technologically advanced. EU initiatives through the structural funds have attempted to offset these advantages for resource-rich regions by concentrating resources on the poorer regions and encouraging partnership and administrative modernisation, especially in southern Europe. As we have seen, these efforts have been partially successful. Furthermore, the practice of multi-level governance seems now entrenched in European policy-making: the previously dyadic relationship between European institutions and national governments has been transformed into a three-way one – among regions, national states and European actors. Keeping the 'second' relationship going enables each party in the triad to retain strategic autonomy (Ansell *et al.* 1997). Regions, even in southern Europe, are unlikely to be blocked from access by their national governments.

Two new challenges to cohesion and the role of regions are posed by the single currency and enlargement (Keating and Pintarits 1998). If the single currency is extended to the whole of the EU, this could pose further territorial strains as less competitive regions can no longer rely on national currency devaluations to sustain them in the single market. One response to this would be to move to a system of fiscal federalism, with automatic transfers to depressed regions. Another would be a huge increase in cohesion spending. Neither is likely in the foreseeable future. Regions must therefore adapt themselves to the new conditions of competition, a process which is likely to be conflictual and difficult. If Europe cannot respond with more resources and concessions, this might lead the poor regions to abandon their recent pro-Europeanism and align themselves once again with the opposition. If the single currency continues with only some member states participating, this could create strains within non-participating states as their more dynamic regions or those with strong autonomist aspirations seek to join. If the single currency fails altogether, this might lead to a renationalisation of spatial policy with states reasserting control over their spatial economies. Enlargement could produce similar strains as, for example, the western regions of Poland sought tighter integration into Europe, while the eastern regions preferred greater national protection. Expansion to the east will also bring in more needy regions, which will not, given current political conditions, be financed as generously as the southern countries and Ireland were in the 1990s. Indeed, the anticipated enlargement was one factor in the most recent reform of the structural funds and the scaling-down of the ambitions for EU spatial policy. What all these scenarios have in common, however, is that the future of regions and of European integration will remain closely linked to each other.

References

Anderson, J. (1991) 'Sceptical Reflections on a Europe of the Regions: Britain, Germany and the ERDF', *Journal of Public Policy* 10/4: 417–47.

Anderson, J. (1996) 'Germany and the Structural Funds', in L. Hooghe (ed.), *Cohesion Policy and European Integration: Building Multilevel Governance*, Oxford: Oxford University Press.

André, C., Drevet, J.-F. and Landaburu, E. (1989) 'Regional Consequences of the Internal Market', *Contemporary European Affairs* 1/1–2: 205–14.

Ansell, C., Parsons, C. and Darden, K. (1997) 'Dual Networks in European Regional Development Policy', *Journal of Common Market Studies* 35: 347–75.

Armstrong, W. H. (1995) 'The Role and Evolution of European Community Regional Policy', in B. Jones and M. Keating (eds), *The European Union and the Regions*, Oxford: Clarendon.

Balme, R. (1995) 'French Regionalization and European Integration: Territorial Adaptation and

Change in a Unitary State', in B. Jones and M. Keating (eds), *The European Union and the Regions*, Oxford: Clarendon.

Balme, R. (ed.) (1996) *Les politiques du néo-régionalisme*, Paris: Economica.

Balme, R. and Jouve, B. (1996) 'Building the Regional State: Europe and Territorial Organisation in France', in Liesbet Hooghe (ed.), *Cohesion Policy and European Integration*, Oxford: Oxford University Press, pp. 219–55.

Begg, I. and Mayes, D. (1993) 'Cohesion, Convergence and Economic and Monetary Union in Europe', *Regional Studies* 27/2: 149–65.

Bullman, U. (ed.) (1994) *Die Politik der dritten Ebene*, Baden Baden: NOMOS.

Burch, M. and Holliday, I. (1993) 'Institutional Emergence: The Case of the North West Region of England', *Regional Politics and Policy* 3/2: 29–50.

Camagni, R. (1992) 'Development Scenarios and Policy Guidelines for the Lagging Regions in the 1990s', *Regional Studies* 26/4: 361–74.

Cappelin, R. and Molle, W. (1988) 'The Co-ordination Problem in Theory and Practice', in W. Molle and R. Cappellin (eds), *Regional Impact of Community Policies in Europe*, Aldershot: Avebury.

Cardús, S. (1991) 'Identidad cultural, legitimidad politica e interés económico', in *Construir Europa. Catalunya*, Madrid: Encuentro.

Cheshire, P., Camagni, R., Gaudemar, J.-P. and Cuadrado Roura, J. (1991) '1957 to 1992: Moving toward a Europe of Regions and Regional Policy', in L. Rodwin and H. Sazanami (eds), *Industrial Change and Regional Economic Transformation: The Experience of Western Europe*, London: HarperCollins.

Commission of the European Communities (1991) *Les Régions dans les Années 90. Quatrième rapport périodique sur la situation et l'évolution socio-économique des régions de la Communauté*, Luxemburg: Office for Official Publications of the European Communities.

Commission of the European Communities (1993) *Community Structural Funds, 1994–99. Regulations and Commentary*, Luxemburg: Office for Official Publications of the European Communities.

Commission of the European Communities (1996) *First Report on Economic and Social Cohesion 1996* (preliminary edition), Luxemburg: Office for Official Publications of the European Communities.

Commission of the European Community (1999) *Sixth Periodic Report on the Social and Economic Situation and Development of the Regions of the EU*, Brussels: Commission of the European Communities.

De Rynck, S. (1996) 'Europe and Cohesion Policy in the Flemish Region', in L. Hooghe (ed.), *Cohesion Policy and European Integration: Building Multilevel Governance*, Oxford: Oxford University Press.

Desideri, C. (1995) 'Italian Regions in the European Community' in B. Jones and M. Keating (eds), *The European Union and the Regions*, Oxford: Clarendon.

de Witte, B. (1992) 'Surviving in Babel? Language Rights and European Integration', *Israel Yearbook on Human Rights* 21: 103–26.

Farrows, M. and McCarthy, R. (1997) 'Opinion Formulation and Impact in the Committee of the Regions', *Regional and Federal Studies* 7/1: 23–49.

Fullarton, B. and Gillespie, A. (1988) 'Transport and Telecommunications', in W. Molle and R. Cappelin (eds), *Regional Impact of Community Policies in Europe*, Aldershot: Gower.

Grote, J. (1992) 'Diseconomies in Space: Traditional Sectoral Policies of the EC, the European Technology Community and their Effects of Regional Disparities', *Regional Politics and Policy* 2/1–2: 14–46.

Hooghe, L. (1995) 'Belgian Federalism and European Integration', in B. Jones and M. Keating (eds), *The European Union and the Regions*, Oxford: Clarendon.

Hooghe, L. (ed.) (1996) *Cohesion Policy and European Integration: Building Multi-level Governance*, Oxford: Oxford University Press.

Hooghe, L. (1998) 'EU Cohesion Policy and Competing Models of European Capitalism', *Journal of Common Market Studies* 36/4: 457–77.

Hooghe, L. and Keating, M. (1994) 'The Politics of European Union Regional Policy', *Journal of European Public Policy* 1/3: 367–93.

Hooghe, L. and Marks, G. (1999) 'The Making of a Polity: The Struggle Over European Integration', in Herbert Kitschelt, Peter Lange, Gary Marks and John Stephens (eds), *Continuity and Change in Contemporary Capitalism*, Cambridge: Cambridge University Press, pp. 70–97.

Ioakimidis, P. K. (1996) 'EU Cohesion Policy in Greece: The Tension between Bureaucratic Centralism and Regionalism', in L. Hooghe (ed.), *Cohesion Policy and European Integration: Building Multilevel Governance*, Oxford: Oxford University Press.

Jachtenfuchs, M. and Kohler-Koch, B. (1995) 'Regieren im dynamischen Mehrebenensystem', in Markus Jachtenfuchs and Beate Kohler-Koch (eds), *Europäische Integration*, Opladen: Leske & Budrich, pp. 15–44.

Jeffrey, C. (1996) *The Regional Dimension of the European Union: Towards a Third Level in Europe?* London: Frank Cass.

Jones, B. and Keating, M. (eds) (1995) *The European Union and the Regions*, Oxford: Clarendon.

Keating, M. (1988) *State and Regional Nationalism, Territorial Politics and the European State*, Hemel Hempstead: Harvester Wheatsheaf.

Keating, M. (1995) 'Regions and Regionalism in the European Union', *International Journal of Public Administration* 18/10.

Keating, M. (1998) *The New Regionalism in Western Europe: Territorial Restructuring and Political Change*, Aldershot: Edward Elgar.

Keating, M. and Jones, B. (eds) (1985) *Regions in the European Community*, Oxford: Clarendon.

Keating, M. and Pintarits, S. (1998) 'Europe and the Regions: Past, Present and Future', *Comparative Social Research* 17: 33–63.

Keeble, D., Offord, J. and Walker, S. (1988) *Peripheral Regions in a Community of Twelve Member States*, Luxembourg: Office of Publications of the European Communities.

Laffan, B. (1996) 'Ireland, a Region without Regions: The Odd Man Out?' in L. Hooghe (ed.), *Cohesion Policy and European Integration: Building Multilevel Governance*, Oxford: Oxford University Press.

Le Galès, P. and Lequesne, Ch. (eds) (1997) *Les paradoxes des régions en Europe*, Paris: Editions La Découverte.

Mackay, R. R. (1993) 'A Europe of the Regions: A Role for Non-market Forces?', *Regional Studies* 27/5: 419–31.

Marks, G. (1992) 'Structural Policy in the European Community', in A. Sbragia (ed.), *Euro-Politics*, Washington: Brookings Institution.

Marks, G. (1993) 'Structural Policy and Multi-level Governance in the European Community', in A. Cafruny and G. Rosenthal (eds), *The State of the European Community: The Maastricht Debates and Beyond*, Boulder: University of Colorado Press, pp. 391–410.

Marks, G., Hooghe, L. and Blank, K. (1996) 'European Integration since the 1980s: State-Centric versus Multi-Level Governance', *Journal of Common Market Studies* 34/4: 341–78.

Marks, G., Salk, J., Ray, L. and Nielsen, F. (1996) 'Conflict, Cracks and Conflicts: Regional Mobilization in the European Union', *Comparative Political Studies* 29/2: 164–92.

Mawson, J., Martins, M. and Gibney, J. (1985) 'The Development of European Community Regional Policy', in M. Keating and B. Jones (eds), *Regions in the European Community*, Oxford: Clarendon.

McAleavey, P. (1993) 'The Politics of European Regional Development Policy: The EC Commission's Rechar Initiative and the Concept of Additionality', *Regional Politics and Policy* 3/2: 88–107.

McLeod, A. (1999) 'Regional Participation in EU Affairs: Lessons for Scotland from Austria, Germany and Spain', paper prepared for and published by *Scotland Europa*, Brussels.

Midwinter, A., Keating, M. and Mitchell, J. (1991) *Politics and Public Policy in Scotland*, London: Macmillan.

Molle, W., van Holst, A. and Smit, H. (1980) *Regional Disparity and Economic Development in the European Community*, Farnborough: Saxon House.

Morata, F. (1995) 'Spanish Regions in the European Community', in B. Jones and M. Keating (eds), *The European Union and the Regions*, Oxford: Clarendon.

Moravcsik, A. (1993) 'Preferences and Power in the European Community: A Liberal Intergovernmentalist Approach', *Journal of Common Market Studies* 31/4: 473–524.

Muller, P. (1994) 'Les mutations des politiques publiques européennes', *Pouvoirs* 69: 63–76.

Nevin, E. T. (1990) 'Regional Policy', in A. M. El-Agraa (ed.), *The Economics of the European Community*, 3rd edn, New York: Philip Allan.

Ohmae, Kenichi (1995) *The End of the Nation State: The Rise of Regional Economies*, New York: Free Press.

Petschen, S. (1993) *La Europa de las regiones*, Barcelona: Generalitat de Catalunya.

Putnam, R. (1993) *Making Democracy Work: Civic Traditions in Modern Italy*, Princeton: Princeton University Press.

Reese, N. and Holmes, M. (1995) 'Regions within a Region: The Paradox of the Republic of Ireland', in B. Jones and M. Keating (eds), *The European Union and the Regions*, Oxford: Clarendon.

Scharpf, F. (1994) 'Community and Autonomy: Multi-Level Policy-Making in the European Union', *Journal of European Public Policy* 1/2: 219–42.

Scharpf, F. (1999) *Governing in Europe: Effective and Democratic?* Oxford: Oxford University Press.

Scott, A. (1998) *Regions and the World Economy: The Coming Shape of Global Production, Competition, and Political Order*, Oxford: Oxford University Press.

Shackleton, M. (1991) 'The European Community between Three Ways of Life: A Cultural Analysis', *Journal of Common Market Studies* 24/6: 575–601.

Steinle, W. J. (1992) 'Regional Competitiveness and the Single European Market', *Regional Studies* 26/4: 307–18.

Storper, Michael (1997) *The Regional World: Territorial Development in a Global Economy*, New York and London: Guildford.

Strijker, D. and de Veer, J. (1988) 'Agriculture', in W. Molle and R. Cappellin (eds), *Regional Impact of Community Policies in Europe*, Aldershot: Avebury.

Tsoukalis, L. (1991) *The New European Economy: The Politics and Economics of Integration*, Oxford: Oxford University Press.

Vickerman, R. W. (1992) *The Single European Market: Prospects for Economic Integration*, New York: St Martin's Press.

Yannopoulos, G. and Featherstone, K. (1995) 'The European Community and Greece: Integration and the Challenge to Centralism', in B. Jones and M. Keating (eds), *The European Union and the Regions*, Oxford: Clarendon.

Part IV

A SUPRANATIONAL STATE?

Chapter 13

Enlarging the European Union

The short-term success of incrementalism and depoliticisation

GERDA FALKNER AND MICHAEL NENTWICH

Introduction

For a long time, the participation of ever more states in the process of European integration was of interest almost exclusively to a few 'widening experts'. Only during the 1990s, did the process of widening and its implications for the European Union (EU) policy-making process became of central interest for most, if not all, scientific and political observers of the European Union. This corresponds to the acceleration of the enlargement process, since the 1950s and 1960s saw only the six original member states participating in the integration enterprise. The first doubling of participants occurred between 1973 and 1985, and this number did not increase until the inclusion of some of the European Free Trade Area (EFTA) countries (Austria, Finland and Sweden) ten years later. Yet, within another ten years, from 1995, the EU's membership could have increased by two-fifths to include 26 members..

Membership negotiations are now under way with twelve applicants: since March 1998 with the 'first wave' countries – Poland, Hungary, Czech Republic, Estonia, Slovenia, Cyprus; and since mid-February 2000 with the 'second group' – consisting of Romania, Bulgaria, Lithuania, Latvia, Slovakia and Malta. With the former group, the 'final' chapters were opened in 2000 (with some other chapters already being 'provisionally closed'). With the second group, negotiations start – as they usually do – with those parts of the *acquis* which are considered easiest. At the Helsinki European Council of December 1999, it was decided that members of the second group may, according to the 'regatta' approach, catch up with some of the first.

This will depend on the annual individual country reports which assess the progress the candidate countries have made in meeting the so-called Copenhagen criteria (European Council 1993). According to the latter, membership requires that the country has

- achieved stability of institutions guaranteeing democracy, the rule of law, human rights and respect for and protection of minorities;
- a functioning market economy as well as the capacity to cope with competitive pressures and market forces within the Union; and
- the ability to take on the obligations of membership, including adherence to the aims of political, economic and monetary Union.

It is important to note that both political and economic criteria are included in this catalogue. The duality of financial and political interests is actually present on both sides of the EU border. The respective weights differ from country to country (both among the members and among the applicants) and shift over time. Since the dismantling of economic borders is already well advanced by now (although there are sectors excluded under the Europe Agreements),[1] and since the economic models so far indicate that eastern enlargement seems to be a 'win–win' game for both sides (Breuss 1999: 32)[2], it seems that issues of political stability and democracy gain in importance.[3]

The most pressing problems of each of the applicants according to the 1999 evaluation are assembled in Table 13.1 of the Annexe. Comparing the issues listed there, one can see that some show up more frequently (e.g. administrative reform, justice and the protection of minorities) whereas others are rather specific (e.g. the political Copenhagen criteria). The Commission detects in all countries problems with the functioning of the market economy structure, at least in certain fields. Shortcomings thus identified are usually included in the annually updated 'Partnerships for Accession', which have as a goal to set out in detail and explain, for each of the countries concerned, the fields and sectors in which, according to the EU, these countries must make priority efforts to prepare for membership.

At the time of writing, it is impossible to say if the applicants' target dates for joining the EU 'mystery train' will hold (see Table 13.2), although some seem rather unrealistic. There is still no EU decision on when to admit new members. The IGC 2000 adopted, however, a Declaration on the future of the Union (no. 23 annexed to the Treaty of Nice) which states that with the ratification of this Treaty all the institutional changes necessary for enlargement will have been completed. In its 2000 progress report, the European Commission is still confident of being able to conclude negotiations with the most advanced candidate countries in 2002 (European Commission 2000b). The Commissioner for enlargement, Günter Verheugen, explained that this does not rule out an earlier decision, but that three conditions will need to be met: the necessary financial resources must be available (a condition which Verheugen considers is satisfied with Agenda 2000; but see below), the results of the EU institutional reform must be operational (i.e. ratification completed), and the accession negotiations must be concluded with the applicants in question. Usually well-informed sources conclude that the ratification process for the first accession treaties could thus begin in 2003. 'Given the usual length of time needed for Member State ratification, the first accessions could take place in 2004 at the earliest' (*Europe*, 11/12/1999).

Confronted with literally hundreds of publications on one or the other aspect of the process of EU enlargement, and with fast real-world developments while this text goes to press, this chapter can only address some basic issues and refer to the most central books and a few important articles. The first section will discuss an empirical paradox involved in EU enlargement: the obvious development of the original European Communities into a Union with important supranational features and ever more policy clout has by no means discouraged aspirant member states. Why is it that more and more states are willing to give up much of their otherwise cherished national sovereignty by joining this Union, knowing that even more sovereignty will be eroded over time? The second section addresses the major challenges the EU has to face before actually widening any further, concerning financial and institutional issues as well as internal and external boundaries. The third section will discuss implicit and explicit EU enlargement strategies of past and present times. It will argue that there is a danger that the incrementalist and de-politicised character of the recent enlargement (non-)discussions are successful only in the short term while actually being rather dangerous in the longer run.

Join the rolling mystery train!

Viewed from a distance and over time, the EU can be seen as the centre of a galaxy. For many years it seemed as if some of the surrounding groups of states moved quite independently and sometimes in the opposite direction. They belonged to the communist (Central and Eastern European Countries – CEEC), authoritarian (Spain, Portugal, Greece) or neutral 'third way' world (Austria, Finland, Sweden, Switzerland). In the event, their trajectories have converged, and further 'repositionings' are likely. However, significant developments have also occurred within the Union itself, making it a 'moving target' for the outside world. Thus, over time, not only does the nature of the aspirant states change, but also the EC/EU itself has evolved into a different kind of political system to which new member states need to be accommodated.

When the United Kingdom, Ireland, Denmark and Norway applied for membership in 1961, the European Economic Community (EEC) was still in the first of three transitory phases during the introduction of its common market. When the negotiations were completed in 1972,[4] the EEC had reached its final stage and achieved a customs union. Even if supranational features, explicitly provided for in the EEC Treaty (notably qualified majority voting), had hardly come into play in the aftermath of the 1965/66 'crisis of the empty chair' and the so-called Luxemburg Compromise, the European Court of Justice (ECJ) had meanwhile developed its doctrines of direct effect and supremacy of EC law (ECJ judgements Van Gend 1963; Costa/ENEL 1964). They significantly contributed to the supranational quality of the EC's legal order – a factor not clearly envisaged by the founding fathers.

While the main ambitions of the first additional member states, Great Britain, Ireland, and Denmark,[5] had been economic (Laurent 1994: 126), the subsequent three southern applicants, Greece (1975) and Spain and Portugal (1977), desired membership for more overtly political reasons. These (then) recently democratised states were included in the Communities, despite their comparatively less-developed capitalist economies, for the purpose of keeping them democratic and non-communist (Wallace 1989). Clearly, however, their specific economic interests subsequently influenced the further development of the Union; this mainly concerned the financing of new EC policies. Soon after joining the Union in 1981, Greece made the accession of Spain and Portugal (finally achieved on 1 January 1986) conditional upon the setting up of 'Integrated Mediterranean Programmes', whose task was to fight regional disparities within the EC (Nicholson and East 1987: 201). And when the first major reform package of the Rome Treaties, the Single European Act, was negotiated in 1985–86, the less-developed EC economies achieved a significant transfer of money via the structural funds, in order to cover the expected costs to them of the internal market. Similarly, the Cohesion Fund was introduced by the Maastricht Treaty, which set up a timetable for Economic and Monetary Union (EMU) among the EC members in 1992.

The negotiations on this new 'constitution' for the EU (1991–92) were, even then, followed with lively interest by the majority of the EFTA member states,[6] who had to wait for another repositioning of the 'moving target' EC before membership negotiations were started with them. On the eve of the various EFTA applications, the EC's decision had been to deepen significantly before widening subsequently. Because the Internal Market Programme proved to be attractive to non-members as well, Commission President Delors, in early 1989, offered to the EFTAns a new kind of structured partnership, based on wider market integration as well as on common decision-making and administrative institutions. Thus, the establishment of the 'European Economic Area' (EEA) might dampen the immediate membership ambitions although, in the event, it did not meet the EFTA members' expectations.[7]

Austria was first among the group to apply officially for membership in 1989 (Schneider 1994; Falkner 1995). When the end of the Soviet Union had significantly altered the broader international arena and also partly influenced their national economies, Sweden, Finland, Switzerland and Norway applied in 1991–92. Eventually, the EC decided that negotiations with the EFTA applicants could begin after the signing, but before the actual implementation, of the Maastricht Treaty. The Union's internal difficulties – particularly economic recession, and the ratification problems of the Treaty on European Union (TEU) – seem to have made an externally oriented initiative politically attractive and opportune. For some of the new members, the Union had again developed to a significant extent between their application and their final admittance to the club in January 1995. Again, deepening did not seem to make membership less attractive to aspirant member states.

One significant development was the increased stress on correct implementation of EC law. In its Francovich ruling 1991, the ECJ introduced liability of the member states for damage resulting from incorrect or non-implementation of directives. Furthermore, the Maastricht Treaty provided for fines against governments which do not follow an ECJ ruling (now Article 228 TEC). Thus, the new members of 1995 had to accept not only more, but also more binding rules. The association that they joined had a much stricter set of club rules! The post-Maastricht Union had a strongly increased supranational character with features such as a Union citizenship, increased powers for the European Parliament (EP), and the independent European Central Bank overseeing EMU.

To date, there is still little sign of the 'moving target' slowing down. The Amsterdam Treaty[8] (in force since 1 May 1999) once again brought significant policy innovations. In particular, it integrated the Schengen agreement, set up a common visa policy, made employment policy co-ordination a European competence, and also reinforced the foreign and defence policy structures and competencies. In short, it extended the Union's area of activity beyond anything known so far in economic integration. On the basis of the Amsterdam Treaty reforms, but mainly driven by external and national developments, the EU has recently developed into much more of a political union than before. In the words of German Chancellor Schröder, the EU is now even a 'community of values' (*Europe*, 13/12/1999). While this must be understood partly as political rhetoric, it is not without foundation.

A development in this direction can be seen, first, in the relation between the EU and its member states. The sanctions of fourteen member states against Austria, after a centre-right government including the Freiheitliche Partei Österreich (FPÖ) (until spring 2000 chaired by Jörg Haider) came into office, indicate that the EU now wants to go much further in the direction of controlling national politics (even at the level of government formation) than ever before. At the level of policies, the EU increasingly touches even those realms which are (*de jure* or *de facto*) beyond its regulative activities under the present Treaties. This is often done via new governance mechanisms such as peer pressure, benchmarking and the like. Further 'soft steering' happens by formulating EU guidelines and having the member states report on an annual basis. The EU's recent intervention in additional policy areas which were hitherto managed at the national level only happens occasionally on the basis of an explicit and specific Treaty (see for example the Amsterdam employment chapter). Other examples come under the cover of economic policy goals. A prominent case in point is the annual economic policy guidelines. The Commission's report on the implementation of the 1999 guidelines, for example, urged Germany to take steps towards a far-reaching reform of its social security and pension systems. The Commission furthermore involved itself in the French debate on whether to use additional funds from higher than expected growth rates to cut taxes or to lower the deficit, by pressing for the second option (*Financial Times*, 9/3/2000). In any case, EU involvement in formerly purely internal member state affairs nowadays goes far beyond what was practice when Austria, Finland and Sweden joined the EU in 1995.

The new quality of political union is, second, expressed in the relationship between the EU, on the one hand, and applicant as well as third countries, on the other. Earlier pre-accession processes and relationships so far based on association agreements only included multiple contacts but did not impose an EU model on the applicant countries, at least not before joining. Nowadays, adaptive pressure on national politics and state structures in those countries which want to become members in the future is enormous. The EU clearly wants to exert the largest possible influence and will not accept applicants before they, for example, abolish the death penalty, have free press and party systems, reform their administrations according to EU standards, promote social and civic dialogue, control their external borders regarding immigration, and protect minorities within their frontiers. The latter point is an obvious example where widening will lead to further deepening, since there are to date no common rules on minority protection among the EU-15 (on processes of 'internalisation', see Friis and Murphy 1999b). In addition to the striking argument of potential membership, EU instruments employed with a view to influencing external political systems are diplomatic[9] and financial.[10]

The Treaty of Nice not only includes institutional reforms but also some further steps towards political union (e.g. fundamental rights, common foreign and security policy). It is to be expected, however, that no applicant state will be ready to fundamentally reconsider membership on the basis of the changes envisaged. Once again, the increasingly supranational and constantly changing character of the European integration enterprise seems not to harm prospective new members' ambitions to jump on the moving train. Indeed, ever more European countries are interested in joining – leaving Norway, Switzerland, Iceland and Liechtenstein as 'deviant' cases (see Annexe, Table 13.2). Apart from the applications of Cyprus and Malta (both pending since 1990) and Turkey (the 1987 membership application had until 1999 been set aside following an unfavourable Commission opinion in 1989 (see Redmond 1993) but was revived late 1999), it is the former members of the Eastern bloc who now have an urgent wish to join the Union. It is worth noting that until 1988 the USSR and its eastern European allies did not even formally recognise the EC (Laursen 1993: 222). Yet several 'reform states' decided very quickly after their transition to pluralist democracy that they are ready to relinquish much of their newly gained political sovereignty in order to become Union members (see Table 13.2). Even the Ukraine,[11] Armenia, Azerbaijan and Georgia (Wolter 1999: 33) have expressed the wish to join at least in the long run. All this despite the fact that the east Europeans are seeking to enter a substantially more integrated Union from a lower economic base than has been the case in previous enlargements (Preston 1995: 459).

Clearly, the fact that so many additional candidates want to take over such far-reaching duties is partly the result of much-debated economic and security considerations (for the detailed specification of which there is no space here). However, there are also political aspects to be taken into account. Contradicting the suggestion that European integration is a zero-sum game (i.e. if the Union gains in political influence, the member governments necessarily lose an equivalent amount), researchers have focused increasingly on European integration as a reaction to general economic and political trends, providing rather beneficial effects for national polities. This is particularly true for governments and their administrations as opposed to other actors (which is one reason why EU membership is not an unchallenged option anywhere). The west European states have reached a new stage of development, in which they can no longer independently meet increased welfare provision due to increased internationalisation of economies. Thus, joint management of regional and global interdependence becomes increasingly attractive (see for example Wessels' 'fusion thesis' (1992)).

Also, the EU has been seen as providing the governments with a tactical advantage *vis-à-vis* other national actors. The Union can be viewed as an additional arena for action, allowing them to strategically employ both the European and the national environments in order to increase their action capacity in a 'two-level game' (Putnam 1988) or 'nested game' (Tsebelis 1990). Thus, powerful interest groups at the national level can sometimes be circumvented via the EU channel (Grande 1996). One well-known example of this phenomenon was that the Austrian membership application in part reflected the leading politicians' impression that only with the EC internal market as a 'whip in the window'

(Schneider 1990: 102; Falkner 2000) could the existing structure of economic protectionism be dissolved in the face of a variety of vested interests embedded in Austrian politics. Also, the 'mantle of the EC adds legitimacy and credibility to Member State initiatives' (Moravcsik 1993: 515). This is probably even more relevant in most of the reform countries, whose governments still have to establish both trust in the newly created pluralist political systems and respect of their rule of law. If the belief in political traditions and a country's own political elite is weak, being embedded in a larger political system may add significantly to the stability of the national political system by providing legitimacy (Rupp 1995: 7). What appears as a benefit to many, if not all, EU governments might, therefore, be a special membership incentive for the Central and Eastern European Countries' (CEEC) political leaders.

However, before more members are admitted, the EU and the applicants still have to find agreement on a number of delicate issues, among them notably financial and institutional ones.

Open questions and major challenges

Financial issues

Even given that eastern enlargement appears to be a 'win–win' game in economic terms (see above), the financial issue nevertheless touches the fundament of European integration: 'At the economic core of the integration model is a balance between attaining economic efficiency through competition and free trade on the one hand and mitigating the effects of rapid adjustment to economic change on the other' (Smith and Wallace 1994: 433). While the EFTA widening not only increased the potential gains from the enlarged common market, but even improved the Union's budgetary performance, any of the likely further widenings would have had adverse effects in the second respect, at least, under status quo conditions. This is why a reform of the EU budget was considered indispensable (for a background analysis of the 'budget and enlargement' issue, see Nicolaides 1999).

To this effect, the 'Agenda 2000' was adopted at the Berlin European Council in March 1999. This shorthand label describes the reform of the EU's major spending policies and of the financial means to fund them, effected in the most complex of all EU package deals so far. It included a financial framework fixing the medium-term financial limits within which the annual budgets for the Union will be drawn up for the period 2000–06, six draft regulations reforming the EU Structural and Cohesion Funds, eight draft regulations reforming the arable crops, beef, veal and milk production sectors, including modifications to Common Agricultural Policy (CAP) financing, direct support schemes and rural development regulations, amendments to the financing of trans-European networks, and three regulations on co-ordinating the pre-accession strategy and establishing two new pre-accession instruments on agriculture and structural policies (for details see Galloway 1999).

This hypercomplex task had to be fulfilled under the conditions of stable budgetary thresholds (the net contributors were very clear on this) and of reluctance of those member states mainly benefiting from the agricultural and structural funds that their share of the cake be diminished. To satisfy the demands of the first group, the Commission suggested in Agenda 2000 accommodating new member states[12] within the existing budget ceiling of 1.27% of the EU's GNP.[13] To obtain the agreement of those member states who mainly benefit from the EU structural funds, a separation between expenditure for EU-15, on the one hand, and the amount earmarked for enlargement, on the other hand, was approved in the financial perspectives 2000 to 2006. 'In order to underline the fact that enlargement posed no risk for current spending in EU-15, the Berlin European Council conclusions expressly provided that in the event of any development of actual expenditure as a consequence of enlargement proving likely to exceed the ceiling on payment appropriations, the financial commitments for EU-15 agreed in the financial perspective will have to be respected' (Galloway 1999: 19).

Considering that Agenda 2000 managed very significant reforms of the structural funds policy (geographical concentration of means, more efficient administration, only three basic goals instead of seven; Wulf-Mathies 1999) and CAP (lower intervention prices, partly compensated by direct transfers; Jessen 1999), one might think that budgetary issues are no longer on the list of major challenges related to EU enlargement. However, it seems that both reforms did not go far enough to pre-empt serious conflict in forthcoming membership and budgetary negotiations. For the Cohesion and Structural Funds, concentration of assistance could have gone further, and it is still an open question if current beneficiaries will accept the lower GDP thresholds, which seem necessary if new and much poorer countries join and if the budget is not increased significantly. CAP reform was a less ambitious reform than initially proposed. While forthcoming World Trade Organisation negotiations will create further pressures to cut intervention prices, including the CEECs (as they demand) in the scheme of direct compensation payments granted to current EU farmers seems overly costly to some Council delegations.

While these important issues still need to be tackled in the frame of further changes to the EU's agricultural and structural policies, fundamental reform in the institutional field was postponed in the Amsterdam Intergovernmental Conference and brought to an end with the Treaty of Nice.

Institutional challenges of enlargement

Given the size of the USA, there can be little doubt that a political system of between twenty and thirty members is workable. It is more realistic to suggest, therefore, that the specific working conditions of a Union of fifteen-plus member states, rather than the size *per se*, will be decisive in terms of the success of an enlarged EU. Regardless of the striking imbalances in size and population of the single states, the US manages the accommodation of diversity via a bicameral system, with equal representation in the Senate (two members per state irrespective of unequal sizes) and representation according to population size in the Congress. Within the EU, a comparable political system should be able to handle any foreseeable increase in membership without drastically reducing efficiency and policy innovation. If one were to include the existing and the probably soon associated countries, the Union would still have only about half as many states as the USA. Yet, there is so far no federal commitment comparable to the American approach.

Therefore, the forthcoming EU enlargement presents a major challenge from the institutional perspective – in addition to being a special case and, in some respects, a qualitative leap. First, unlike previous enlargement rounds, the EU is not negotiating with up to three (or four) candidates any more, but with twelve (or thirteen). Setting aside the view that not all of the prospective members will join the Union at the same time, the number of EU member states is about to almost double in a very short period of time (from fifteen to twenty-seven). Second, for the first time in its history, the EU is about to change from a mainly Western European enterprise to a truly pan-European institution. Similar to the USA, the EU will cover a large proportion of 'its' continent. Third, and again in contrast to previous enlargements, the EU is not a purely, or very predominantly, economic entity any more, but a highly integrated political actor (see above).

In 2000, another intergovernmental conference (IGC) took place in order to deal with the so-called 'left-overs' from Amsterdam (cf. for example Neunreither and Wiener 2000; Griller *et al.* 2000; European Council 1999; ICRI 1999) and to negotiate on the institutional adaptations needed to prepare for this much wider membership. These are the most important institutional and procedural issues (in the wider sense) and how the Treaty of Nice solved them:

1 *The number of members in the various institutions.* Obviously, near-doubling again the number of member states to twenty-seven means a considerable strain on the institutions, originally designed for only six members. While it seemed practical in the past to simply apply the original rules more or less mechanically when searching for new figures, this strategy when applied to the forthcoming Eastern enlargement would arguably lead to a complete deadlock of the institutions. On the basis of twelve new member states and without changing the rules, we would have, for example, a Commission with thirty-two members and a Parliament with over 850 members (MEPs). The negotiators of the Amsterdam Treaty already addressed the issue in Protocol no. 11, by envisaging the IGC 2000 settling the issue of the size of the college of Commissioners, amended Article 189 TEC through the insertion of a new second paragraph fixing the maximum number of MEPs at 700, and stipulated 'appropriate representation of the peoples of the States brought together in the Community' whenever a change in the number of MEPs might be required in the future, i.e. in case of enlargement (Article 190 para. 2 TEC). Several options existed for both respecting the upper limit and ensuring 'appropriate representation' (note that the Treaty does not require 'strict proportionality' and thus provides some room for the smallest countries to have a larger number of MEPs than otherwise computed). In any event, all options would lead to a sharp increase in the number of German MEPs, while the middle-range countries would lose up to ten seats each (cf. Griller *et al.* 2000: 285ff.). The negotiators of the Treaty of Nice opted to increase the maximum number of seats to 732 and to interpret the formula of appropriate representation rather generously, thus continuing to heavily under-represent the larger countries, in particular Germany, and giving the smallest countries at least six seats each.

In the case of the size of the Commission, too, several strategies have been debated (European Commission 2000a: 13ff.). One option would have been to surrender the principle that each member state should have at least one national in the college and to set up a system of rotation which would treat all member states strictly equally on the basis of a pre-set order; another would have been only to take away the right of the five largest countries to nominate two nationals, but would restructure the relationships between the various members of the Commission in order to ensure efficient decision-making in such a large body. The IGC 2000 has decided to defer again imposing an exact ceiling on the number of Commission members. From 2005 onwards, the bigger countries will lose their second Commissioner. As soon as the Union reaches 27 member states, there will be fewer Commissioners than states. The Council will decide unanimously on how many exactly and on a fair system of rotation, bearing in mind that all member states will be treated on an equal footing and that each Commission must satisfactorily reflect the different demographic and geographic characteristics of the member states. The powers of the Commission President have been increased considerably concerning the internal organisation and the allocation of portfolios during the term of office; s/he will also be able to demand a Commissioner's resignation, subject to the Commission's approval.

Also under scrutiny were the size of and relationship between the two European Courts given the expected increase in workload in an enlarged Union as well as the numbers of the Economic and Social Committee, of the Committee of the Regions and the Court of Auditors.

2   *The effectiveness of the decision-making procedures.* While the IGC 2000 also addressed the further extension of the co-decision procedure and other measures to make the Treaty framework more coherent in terms of the legislative procedures, the main issue to be tackled with respect to enlargement was the danger of frequent and persistent stalemate in those still numerous areas of Union policy where there is a requirement of unanimity in the Council of Ministers. During 2000, it seemed that there was growing consensus that, first, unanimity needs to be limited in an enlarged Union and, second, there will be some categories of decisions 'for which serious and lasting reasons warrant making an exception to the general rule of qualified-majority voting' (European Commission 2000a: 22ff.). These are essentially those of a 'constitutional' type (for example, uniform electoral procedure, Statute of the European Central Bank), though decisions in the fields of tax and social security, not related to the proper functioning of the internal market, were frequently mentioned. Though extending the qualified majority vote in a number of cases, the Treaty of Nice falls short of lifting the burden of unanimity in a large number of policies.

The other hotly debated issue with regard to the Council's decision-making procedures in the wake of enlargement was how to adapt the weighting of the votes. Extrapolation of the current system would lead to a regular decline in the representativeness of a qualified majority decision in population terms with – in an extreme case – the theoretical possibility of a qualified 'majority' decision taken by a 'minority' in terms of population (for a detailed analysis, see Kerremans 1998; and European Parliament 1999). The options considered were, on the one hand, increasing the relative weight of the votes of the most populous member states (this is commonly referred to as 're-weighting') and redefining altogether what is meant by 'qualified majority'. In a complex compromise, the IGC 2000 opted for a system of 'double' majority: the number of votes allocated to each member state will be lifted while increasing the share of the larger countries over-proportionally. Furthermore, the threshold for a qualified majority vote will be lifted. Any Council member may request verification that the qualified majority represents at least 62% of the total EU population. If this condition is not met, the decision is not adopted.

3   *The internal organisation of the institutions.* Resizing the institutions and streamlining the formal decision-making procedures is only one important step towards making the EU institutions capable of coping with enlargement. The other aspect is the internal organisation of the institutions. We have already dealt with the Commission above (1), since preserving a high number of Commissioners ultimately needs internal reform. The Commission has already presented a comprehensive programme of administrative reforms, in particular with regard to financial and personnel management (European Commission 2000c). Also the Council is preparing major reforms, based on a special report by its Secretary-General in March 1999, which may include, among other things, a separation between the Foreign Affairs Council and a new co-ordinating General

Affairs Council, as well as a reduction of all other Council formations in order to improve coherence (European Council 1999: Annexe III).

4   *The future of closer co-operation within the EU framework.* It would be even more difficult to deepen integration in an enlarged, less homogenous Union that consists both of latecomers having a hard time digesting economic reform and of well-advanced and long-standing members heading for integrationist benefits beyond economics. Reconciling 'deepening' and 'widening' therefore was one rationale of the Amsterdam Treaty framework for enabling a coalition of member states to go ahead and co-operate more closely, thereby realising what has been discussed widely under the heading 'multi-speed Europe' (Articles 43 and 45 TEU and Article 11 TEC). In essence, the Amsterdam Treaty asks for a unanimous decision to allow a group of states to work together more closely, for a majority of member states joining the group and for strict respect for the *acquis communautaire*. The new provisions had only been in force for a couple of months when the IGC 2000 started, and there was no single attempt to make closer co-operation work (which may be a sign in itself). There was a consensus that the conditions to be met would not be workable in a Union of twenty-seven. In the perspective of enlargement, the Treaty of Nice comprehensively overhauled the respective provision. The minimum number of member states required to establish enhanced co-operation is lowered (eight instead of a majority of states); the veto possibility in the framework of the first and third pillars has been removed; and in the area of common foreign and security policy, closer co-operation may be established for the implementation of joint actions or common positions.

5   *The diversity of working languages.* So far, the number of official languages of the Union has increased with each enlargement according to the number of additional official languages of the new member states. It now stands at eleven, while, over the course of time, English and French (and, partly, German) have turned out to be the working languages in most institutions. In an EU of twenty-seven, another ten languages would have to be added. Already at this stage, translating official documents into all eleven official languages and providing simultaneous translation services, at least for the major meetings, accounts for a considerable proportion of the EU budget. Owing to the non-linear increase of possible one-to-one relations between languages (with twenty-one languages there are 210 language pairs) and the restricted possibility of translating via intermediary languages, this is a serious problem. It could be tackled either by restricting the number of official languages or by introducing a sort of language hierarchy. The latter could mean that not all documents would be translated into all languages, and an official status would be given to the present (or a slightly increased number of) working languages for all meetings. The Treaty of Nice did not address this issue.

Which boundaries?

Apart from institutional issues, the EU will need to tackle some questions of fundamental principle in the near future, most notably on its external and internal boundaries.

First, should the Union be enlarged until it finally covers all of geographic Europe, which is usually considered to stretch from the Atlantic to the Ural Mountains? More specifically, should all countries become members which are at least in part 'European' in the geographical sense – considering that Turkey has already been accorded official applicant status since December 1999? If so, an EU with fifteen plus twenty-seven members is looming. This includes for example the Ukraine and the states succeeding former Yugoslavia. Russia is admittedly both a qualitative and quantitative leap, due to its sheer size and population, but if Europe ends at the Ural Mountains and if Turkey is acceptable in principle, it is difficult to see why Russia should be discriminated against if, one day, it were to apply for EU membership. The Commission has rightly stressed that the 'EU's relationship with Russia, as with the Ukraine, is fundamental, and will shape the destiny of the European continent' (European Commission 1999: V.2).[14] Even if the basic decision is in favour of remaining open to widest possible membership (and even more so, if not), tailor-made models of closer co-operation with all European states (and their neighbours) need to be developed if the EU wants to promote peace, human rights and political and, finally, economic development in this region without delay.

Since the EU's explicit basic goals and principles, such as bringing down economic borders, progressively harmonising and improving living and working conditions, and respecting the principles of democracy and human rights, are thought to be of general validity, it is hard to argue that some states should be excluded (at least, as long as they are 'European'), in particular since such an attitude is likely to strengthen those endogenous political forces which are out of step with 'European' values (militaristic, fundamentalist, and the like).

Not closing the door to membership, furthermore, has the benefit of allowing the EU to exert an influence on (pre-)applicant states and hence to export its above-mentioned model of politics and economy. As the Commission states in the case of former Yugoslavia and Albania, 'the EU can best contribute to stability in the region by drawing it closer to the perspective of full integration into its structures' (European Commission 1999: V.2). To this effect, the Commission suggests further developing accession criteria to include notably mutual recognition of each other's borders, proper treatment of national minorities and participation in a regional organisation of free trade and economic co-operation.

While giving countries in political and economic transition the chance to perceive themselves as 'pre-ins' instead of as outsiders of the European 'family' and support for the spread of democracy, human rights and economic prosperity is a strong argument in favour of not putting any stop to further (conditional) EU enlargement, many fear that the development of an 'ever closer Union' would be impeded if too many and too diverse members have to agree. The second major issue will therefore be internal 'frontiers', in the wider sense of a differentiation between groups of member states in an EU-27+. This could be tackled by a fundamental reform of the Treaty's flexibility provisions, although many think that adequate solutions need to go further. Most prominently, Jacques Delors recently relaunched the idea of a 'confederation of European countries' (*Europe*, 3/1/2000: 4). In his view, an avant-garde (always open for the rest to join in later) should even 'have their own institutions, to avoid any confusion' (*Europe*, 10/1/2000: 3). A 'union within the union' (and hence still outside the EU framework in the proper sense) is thus on the horizon, at least at the level of rhetoric. However, those who want to go much further than what the EU now represents are in a minority. Therefore, it seems realistic to expect that the EU will rather pursue its incremental path, albeit with a different practical enlargement strategy than in former times.

Handling the tide: past and present Union strategy

Since the 1951 Paris Treaty on the European Coal and Steel Community (see Article 98), the EC had been open to an expanded membership. Initially, this was subject only to the condition that applicants be 'European'. It was the 1997 Amsterdam Treaty (see Art. 49 TEU) which added as further membership conditions the criteria mentioned in Article 6.1 TEU, i.e. the principles of liberty, democracy, respect for human rights and fundamental freedoms, and the rule of law ('principles which are common to the Member States').

Past experiences show that widening has not been a politically easy task. This applies as much to the Union's handling of negotiations for membership as to the adaptation needed by the new member states. In all cases, enlargement, 'defined as joining and truly adhering to the integrated conditions of the member states, has been a painfully slow and internally combative process' (Laurent 1994: 128; and see Tovias 1995, on Spain). This is true despite the fact that since the first Mediterranean widening, the new entrants have regularly had prior bilateral trade agreements with the Union. Thus, the Greek Association Agreement with the EC was signed in 1961, with a provision for incorporation into the EC when the progress of its economy allowed Greece to fully assume the obligations involved. During the military regime of 1967–74, however, the Association Agreement was virtually suspended. Immediately after having been elected, civilian Prime Minister Karamanlis stated that Greece wanted to become an EC member, and in June 1975 the formal application was submitted. The European Commission opinion on Greek membership emphasised the economic problems that an accession might imply for Greece as well as for the EC, and suggested a pre-accession period of unspecified duration. However, the Council unanimously rejected this document and opened negotiations on Greek accession in July 1976 (for details of this widening, see Seers and Vaitsos 1986; Tsoukalis 1981).

In addition, Portugal and Spain had concluded bilateral trade agreements with the EC long before their accession, but the application of those agreements was again hampered by the authoritarian political circumstances in the two states. Their membership negotiations, officially started by October 1978 and February 1979 respectively, were the longest conducted by the EC until the late 1990s. The major stumbling blocks were internal EC problems with the financing of new EC policies ('Integrated Mediterranean Programmes') and the long-term budget crisis. The United Kingdom insisted on rebates to offset its still disproportionate contributions, as well as on increased budgetary discipline. Curtailment of agricultural spending seemed indispensable – and a general relaunch of the Communities desirable. Those issues could not be resolved until the 1984 Fontainebleau meeting of the European Council, when the official date was also set for Spanish and Portuguese accession.

Before the recent EFTA widening, the EC had, for the first time, made the conclusion of an intergovernmental conference reforming the Union a necessary condition for further enlargement. It wanted to fully implement the Internal Market Programme and set the pace for EMU before accommodating new entrants. The negotiations on this third EC widening round were significantly eased by the fact that the EEA agreement had already transferred sizeable parts of the EC's economic *acquis* to the EFTA states. Furthermore, there was a strong political will to include those wealthy and stable democracies, and thus an innovative negotiation tactic was chosen: for the first time, only the General Affairs Council (and not the more specialised Councils) negotiated with each of the four applicants (Granelli 1994). Despite the fact that the 1993–94 enlargement negotiations involved a large number of applicants, they were the least problematic and most rapid, and the agreed transition periods are shorter than previously (Cameron 1995: 33). It seems that what the Council had rejected in the Greek case, i.e. longer pre-accession periods and an early rapprochement to the *acquis communautaire*, has since shown beneficial effects in the EFTA enlargement round (EFTA–EC free trade since the 1970s; EEA since 1994) – and will thus be applied systematically in the future.[15]

Confronted with the changing geopolitical situation and increased interest in membership during the late 1980s, the Union initially reacted by concluding trade and co-operation agreements, and by organising programmes for economic assistance (and increasingly also for political reform), such as PHARE for the CEECs, TACIS for the ex-Soviet republics and MEDEA for the Mediterranean countries. In August 1990, the Commission proposed moving to associated status with the so-called 'Europe Agreements' (on association agreements generally, see Phinnemore 1999). By early 2000, ten such treaties exist with Hungary, Poland, the Czech and Slovak Republics, Bulgaria, Romania, Slovenia, Lithuania, Estonia and Latvia. The Europe Agreements aim at gradually establishing free trade by asymmetric[16] abolition of tariffs within ten years. Parallel to further economic aspects, such as restricted free movement of services and common competition rules, some political and cultural co-operation has also been established through common institutions. However, since the 'Europe association' formula provided *de facto* only very limited new opportunities both economically (it seems to have favoured EU interests over-proportionally) and politically,[17] and since it fell short of concise ideas on a sound European architecture, a certain 'EEA effect' (Smith and Wallace 1994: 431) has been produced: disappointed associates head towards full membership even faster.

This very phenomenon was to present a problem to the EU, since accepting prospective CEEC membership represented a major political decision which the Union was neither fit (consider, for instance, that incremental decision-making corresponds to the EU's 6-monthly summitry) nor willing (consider the different national positions on when and whom to admit) to take in haste. In fact, it only managed to take this decision at all by (1) breaking it down into minor bits and pieces and (2) depoliticising it:

1 *Deconstructing the major decision* on whether and when former members were to be accepted into a lot of minor decisions fits, in principle, very well with the EU's structure. According to Friis and Murphy (1999a), 'the process of governance through negotiations creates an inbuilt tendency to postpone decisions until the very last minute or until crisis occurs'.[18] One can indeed follow the half-yearly summitry and trace developments in the regular European Council Presidency Conclusions. A nice example of the piecemeal process of allowing the applicant states, albeit subject to various conditions, to become members after all is the way in which this was first indicated in an indirect form only. The Edinburgh December 1992 summit mentioned a Commission report 'in order to prepare the associate countries for accession' (EC Bulletin 12/1992). The following June, 1993, the Copenhagen European Council formally accepted membership of all applicants, but (implicitly) in the distant future only. Therefore, the piecemeal decision process of widening by no means stopped at Copenhagen (and it still continues, in fact). Further bits and pieces of the fundamental decision centred on the identity of the applicants and the commencement date for negotiations, whether a small or a larger group should be involved, and if their entry should be pursued according to a 'regatta' – i.e. individual entry dates – or a 'group' approach (for details, see Friis and Murphy 1999a; Friis 1998b; 1998a; Mayhew 1998).

The prime advantage of the step-by-step approach[19] was to make the overall decision on what the EU of the next millennium should look like more easily digestible for the governments. The downside was, however, that delaying clear answers as to the conditions and, most importantly, the date of possible inclusion of the applicants frustrated the latter. It somewhat weakened the stance of those politicians and public opinion leaders who promoted adaptation to the 'EU model' at the expense of nationalist, militarist and populist patterns. Finally, it contributed to a rise of EU-scepticism in CEEC public opinion polls (for most recent data, see the Annexe, Table 13.3).

2   *Evading political debates* has occurred at two levels, between the governments and within the member states. At the EU level, where the members of national governments come together, the enlargement issue clearly had to be not just addressed but negotiated. The specific evasion modus was therefore – after agreeing on some basic political and economic conditions in Copenhagen 1993 – framing the terms of the partial debates (see above) in non-political terms. Initially, the CEEC were treated as part of the EU's foreign relations. The EU offered traditional trade and co-operation agreements instead of developing innovative measures (Friis and Murphy 1999a: 218f.). After these early agreements had proved 'inadequate and transitory', the focus shifted to financial assistance (PHARE and European Bank for Reconstruction and Development (EBRD), see Sedelmeier and Wallace 1996: 362ff.). The negotiations on the later Europe Agreements still addressed the CEEC as an 'external' problem, plus they were conducted by the EC in 'a typical political economy mode of trade negotiations' (Sedelmeier and Wallace 1996: 371). Finally, during recent years, the Commission framed the issue with whom to open negotiations as 'an objective, apolitical exercise'. What was on the table was not a political decision. All the Commission and the member states had to do was to embark on a 'natural differentiation among the applicants for a variety of historical, political and economic reasons – letting the facts do the hard work, so to speak (Hans van den Broek, *Financial Times* 18/7/1997)' (Friis 1998b).

At the national levels, the strategy was to keep further EU enlargement out of the public debate. This was, most importantly, the case during recent electoral campaigns. The potential danger of this strategy was and is great: the topic of whether and how Eastern enlargement should be approached was left to opposition parties. In some member states, populists (such as Jörg Haider and his FPÖ in Austria) made ready use of this 'opportunity' to gain votes by raising fears of immigration and potential job losses. Concerns about the impact of competition from low-wage economies and about the possible influx of cheap labour are now widespread, although rarely articulated officially, in most EU member states. There are some good counter-arguments, but they are so far mainly expressed in the Commission[20] and expert reports[21] and are waiting not simply to be communicated but actually discussed with the wider public (for an academic discussion of costs and benefits of enlargement, see for example Mayhew 1998: ch. 7). In the longer run, eliminating major decisions such as this one from the agenda of public debate may not only endanger enlargement (which has ultimately to be approved by all member states) but furthermore destabilise the political systems of individual member states, and consequently the EU and the continent of Europe as a whole.

In short: incrementalism and evasion of political debates on one of the most pressing geopolitical issues of the twenty-first century actually appear as the most prominent features of the contemporary (implicit) strategy on EU widening. While the former already has a clearly visible downside, the latter might, in the long run, lead to a rebuilding of frontiers and even destabilise the current EU members.

Tables[22]

Table 13.1 Major problems as underlined by the Commission in the regular report 1999 on progress towards accession by each of the candidate countries[1]

Bulgaria	justice (judicial procedures, pre-trial detention, training of judges); corruption; protection of minorities (Roma); trafficking of human beings; conditions in prisons; functioning market economy; capacity to cope with competitive pressure and market forces within the Union
Cyprus	overall problem of the status of Cyprus as a divided island; economic structural reforms in certain fields
Czech Republic	parliament (rights of opposition, legislative procedures); reform of administration; justice (training of judges, overload of the courts, independence of the judiciary, no supreme administrative court, fight against organised crime and economic crime); corruption; protection of minorities (Roma); economic structural reforms in certain fields
Estonia	reform of administration; justice (adjustment on EU law, training of judges, overload of the courts, co-operation between police, prosecutors and judges); corruption; conditions in prisons; protection of minorities (language law); economic structural reforms in certain fields
Hungary	parliament (representation of minorities); justice (judicial procedures); corruption; protection of minorities (Roma); conditions in prisons; economic structural reforms in certain fields
Latvia	reform of administration; justice (overload of the courts, pre-trial detention); corruption; protection of minorities (language law); economic structural reforms in certain fields
Lithuania	justice (judicial procedures); corruption; functioning of market economy; capacity to cope with competitive pressure and market forces within the Union
Malta	reform of administration; justice (judicial procedures, execution of rulings); economic structural reforms in certain fields
Poland	justice (administrative capacity, judicial procedures, provision of access to the courts, training of judges); corruption; economic structural reforms in certain fields
Romania	legislative procedures; reform of administration; justice (training of judges, adjustment on EU law); corruption; child care; protection of minorities (Roma); functioning market economy; capacity to cope with competitive pressure and market forces within the Union
Slovakia	reform of administration; justice (independence of the judiciary); corruption; trafficking of human beings; asylum legislation; protection of minorities (Roma); functioning of market economy
Slovenia	legislative procedures; reform of administration; justice (judicial procedures); economic structural reforms in certain fields
Turkey	political Copenhagen criteria (stable institutions guaranteeing democracy, the rule of law, human rights and the protection of minorities); justice (emergency courts system, training of judges, witness protection, creation of a Penal Code, abolition of the death penalty); the military has important influence through the National Security Council; human rights, political rights; protection of minorities (Kurds); functioning of market economy; economic structural reforms in certain fields

Note:
1 European Commission 1999. Owing to discrepancies between the individual reports and the highly specific situation in each of the applicant states, it is not possible to offer a more direct comparison in brief.

Table 13.2 Associations and applications[1]

	Association agreement signed	Association agreement enters into force	Membership application	Start of negotiations[2]	Accession[3]	Desired date of accession
Denmark			11.05.1967[4]	30.06.1970	01.01.1973	
Great Britain			10.05.1967[5]	30.06.1970	01.01.1973	
Ireland			10.05.1967[6]	30.06.1970	01.01.1973	
Greece	09.07.1961	01.11.1962	12.06.1975	27.07.1976	01.01.1981	
Portugal			28.03.1977	17.10.1978	01.01.1986	
Spain			28.07.1977	05.02.1979	01.01.1986	
Former GDR					03.10.1990	
Austria	02.05.1992	01.01.1994	17.07.1989	01.02.1993	01.01.1995	
Finland	02.05.1992	01.01.1994	18.03.1992	01.02.1993	01.01.1995	
Sweden	02.05.1992	01.01.1994	01.07.1991[7]	01.02.1993	01.01.1995	
Cyprus	19.12.1972	01.06.1973	04.07.1990	30.03.1998		2003[8]
Czech Republic	04.10.1993	01.02.1995	17.01.1996	30.03.1998		2003[8]
Estonia	12.06.1995	01.02.1998	24.11.1995	30.03.1998		2003[8]
Hungary	16.12.1991	01.02.1994	31.03.1994	30.03.1998		2003[8]
Poland	16.12.1991	01.02.1994	05.04.1994	30.03.1998		2003[8]
Slovenia	10.06.1996	01.02.1999	10.06.1996	30.03.1998		2003[8]
Bulgaria	08.03.1993	01.02.1995	14.12.1995	15.02.2000		2006[9]
Latvia	12.06.1995	01.02.1998	13.10.1995	15.02.2000		2004[9]
Lithuania	12.06.1995	01.02.1998	08.12.1995	15.02.2000		2004[10]
Malta	05.12.1970	01.04.1971	16.07.1990[11]	15.02.2000		2003[9]
Romania	01.02.1993	01.02.1995	22.06.1995	15.02.2000		2007[12]
Slovakia	04.10.1993	01.02.1995	27.06.1995	15.02.2000		2004[13]
Turkey	12.09.1963	01.12.1964	14.04.1987			2010/15[14]
Norway	02.05.1992	01.01.1994	25.11.1992[15]	05.04.1993		
Switzerland	02.05.1992	——	26.05.1992			
Iceland	02.05.1992	01.01.1994				
Liechtenstein	02.05.1992	01.05.1995				
Croatia						2005[16]
Georgia						2039[17]
Moldova						long-term goal[18]

Notes:
1   Data from Phinnemore 1999.
2   Data for the start of the negotiations on accession of the actual candidate countries from *Handelsblatt*, 16/02/2000; data for the actual member states from Spiesberger 1998.
3   Data from Matern and Schultz 1997, as are data of the membership application of Denmark, Ireland, Portugal, Spain, the United Kingdom and Slovakia.
4   Denmark had already applied on 10/08/1961.
5   Great Britain had already applied on 09/08/1961.
6   Ireland had already applied on 31/07/1961.
7   Sweden had already applied on 28/07/1967.
8   *Financial Times*, 15/02/2000.
9   *Handelsblatt*, 16/02/2000.
10   *Financial Times*, 14/03/2000.
11   Malta reactivated the application on 10/08/1998 after having frozen it in October 1996.
12   *Handelsblatt*, 08/02/2000.
13   *Handelsblatt*, 21/01/2000.
14   *Agence Europe* No. 7668, 03/03/2000.
15   Norway had already applied on two previous occasions (30/04/1962 and 21/07/1967), Phinnemore 1999; on 25/09/1972 and 27–28/11/1994 it held negative referendums, Matern and Schultz 1997.
16   *Financial Times*, 18/02/2000.
17   Wolter 1999.
18   *Agence Europe* No. 7642, 27/01/2000.

Table 13.3 Public opinion and enlargement[1]

	Internal support for membership[2]	Support for enlargement (EU 15)	Highest support 1998	Lowest support 1998
Bulgaria	57%	39%	GR, S: 56%	A: 17%
Cyprus		45%	GR: 89%	B: 34%
Czech Republic	49%	45%	S: 69%	B: 30%
Estonia	35%	39%	SCAND: > 70%	A, B: < 30%
Hungary	56%	50%	DK: 69%	B: 30%
Latvia	40%	39%	DK: 77%	B: 26%
Lithuania	40%	38%	DK: 77%	B: 23%
Malta		52%	GR: 72%	B: 39%
Poland	63%	47%	DK: 76%	A: 24%
Romania	71%	37%	GR: 58%	A: 15%
Slovakia	62%	40%		
Slovenia	57%	36%	S: 54%	B: 23%
The 12	53%[3]	42%		
Turkey		29%	E: 45%	GR: 13%

Notes:
1   Data for all states except Turkey from Europäische Kommission 1998; data for Turkey from Europäische Kommission 1999. The countries mentioned are Austria (A), Belgium (B), Denmark (DK), Greece (GR), Spain (E), Sweden (S), and the Scandinavian countries (SCAND).
2   Data on internal support from European Commission 1998.
3   The 12 without Cyprus and Malta.

Table 13.4 Key data 1998 on EU-15 and (potential) candidate countries[1]

	Surface area[2]	Population[3]	GDP per capita[4]	Public deficit/ surplus[5]	Economic growth rate[6]	Inflation rate[7]
EU-15	3,191	374,888	100	−1.5	3.3	1.3
Bulgaria	111	8,230	23	−0.3	−12.7	22.3
Cyprus	9.2	663	78	−0.9	2.8	2.2
Czech Republic	79	10,290	60	−2.2	1.6	10.7
Estonia	45	1,446	36	2.6	1.8	10.5
Hungary	93	10,092	49	−5.4	12.6	14.3
Latvia	65	2,439	27	1.8	3.1	4.7
Lithuania	65	3,701	31	−0.7	7.0	5.1
Malta	0.3	378	——[8]	−7.7	0.7	2.4
Poland	313	38,667	39	−2.6	4.8	11.8
Romania	238	22,489	27	−3.5	−17.0	59.1
Slovakia	49	5,393	46	−4.4	3.6	6.7
Slovenia	20	1,978	68	−1.5	3.7	7.9
Turkey	775	63,451	37	−7.2	1.3	84.6
Albania	29	3,324				
Belarus	208	10,267				
Bosnia-Herzegovina	51	2,346				
Croatia	57	4,768				
Georgia	70	5,427				
Iceland	103	271				
Liechtenstein	0.16	31				
Macedonia	26	1,997				
Moldova	34	4,312				
Norway	324	4,404				
Russian Federation	17,075	147,307				
Switzerland	41	7,088				
Ukraine	604	50,698				
Yugoslavia	102	10,614				

Notes:
1 Data from Eurostat 1999; data for Albania, Belarus, Bosnia-Herzegovina, Croatia, Georgia, Iceland, Liechtenstein, Macedonia, Moldova, Norway, Russian Federation, Switzerland, Ukraine and Yugoslavia from M. Baratta (ed.) (2000) *Der Fischer Weltalmanach 2000*, Frankfurt/M: Fischer.
2 Total area in 1,000 km[2].
3 Total population in 1,000s.
4 GDP per capita in PPS (purchasing power standards), EU = 100.
5 General government deficit/surplus compared to GDP in %, data for Bulgaria, Czech Republic, Estonia, Hungary, Latvia, Lithuania, Poland, Slovakia and Slovenia from 1997, data for Malta and Romania from 1996, and data for Cyprus from 1995.
6 Growth rate of industrial production in %.
7 Inflation rate in %.
8 No data available.

Notes

1   The opening of the Iron Curtain, the GATT Uruguay Round and the Europe Agreements between the applicants and the EU (see below) already led to considerable advances in trade liberalisation. Joining the Customs Union will not alter much, since differences in external duties and tariffs will have been adapted by the time of accession. Recent economic studies came to the conclusion that the trade potential of East–West trade is already exhausted (Breuss 1999: 11). It may however be that EU membership will have further trade creation effects (ibid.). In contrast to trade liberalisation, enlargement would presumably have considerable impact on the flow of foreign direct investment into the new members and of migrants into the old members. Furthermore, as discussed below (p. 266), participation of the CEECs in the structural policies will have a major economic impact for both groups of countries.

2   It is interesting to note that the same author, based on a comprehensive comparison of the existing model simulations, points at a number of shortcomings of these models, such as the non-incorporation of factor movements or the both theoretically and politically complex question of finding out which EU incumbent will be a winner and which one a loser (ibid.: 35).

3   In the wider context of recent developments, it is of interest to note a recent publication which argues that the role of economics in European integration (as opposed to political goals) has actually been much smaller from the start than is usually assumed (Kamppeter 2000).

4   This delay was due to the French veto of the British application in 1961, which brought all four membership applications to a temporary halt.

5   After a negative referendum, Norway did not become a member but stayed within the 'nonsupranational' European Free Trade Area (EFTA).

6   On the EFTA applications and negotiations, see Wallace 1991; Michalski and Wallace 1992; Luif 1994; *Journal of Common Market Studies* 3 1995.

7   This was mainly because the EC, contrary to initial expectations, did not give up its decision-making autonomy. This meant that only EC law, decided upon by the Union members exclusively, could (by unanimous decision) develop into EEA law. Furthermore, the judicial system initially agreed upon was declared incompatible with the Treaty of Rome by the EC Court of Justice, so that the proposed common EEA Court had to be dropped. In short, the final say on the interpretation of EC (and, as the two are normally identical, *de facto* also EEA) law lies with the EC court. The Union is thus clearly a somewhat hegemonic actor within the EEA. In economic terms, the EEA constitutes an improved free trade area (with exemptions such as agricultural goods), but no customs union (Schwok 1991).

8   On details of the Amsterdam reforms, see for example Dinan 1999; Griller *et al.* 2000; for explanatory approaches on this Intergovernmental Conference (IGC), see for example Christiansen and Jørgensen 1999; Moravcsik and Nicolaïdis 1999; Pollack 1999; Sverdrup 1999.

9   For example visiting not only the Turkish government but also representatives of the social partners there, human rights organisations and Kurds (*Europe*, 11/3/2000); EU-Commissioner Patten even visited the Yugoslav subrepublic Montenegro, which strives for greater independence from Milosevic in Belgrade (*FTD*, 3/3/2000).

10   The EU supports democratisation and economic reforms not only in the pre-accession countries (see below), but even in places such as Russia (the TACIS programme was even refocused on democratic objectives in early 2000, *Europe*, 26/1/2000) and Montenegro (by 65 million euro 1998–2000, *Europe*, 11/3/2000). Another example of promoting compatible political and societal structures is the 'Action Plan to promote social and civil dialogue in south eastern Europe', elaborated by the European Training Foundation, within the framework of preparing the region for accession (600,000 euro for one year; *Europe*, 25 and 27/1/2000).

11   The co-operation agreements signed with Russia and the Ukraine in June 1994 do not – in contrast to the Europe agreements with the candidate states – contain any provisions mentioning possible future membership.

12   The working assumption used by the Commission in its proposals was that six new members would join the Union in 2002.

13   'The financial perspective has been drawn up to accommodate the full cost of enlargement until 2006, along with a significant increase in the pre-accession strategy, while also substantially increasing the margins for unforeseen expenditure under the own resources ceiling fixed at 1.27% of the EU's GNP' (Galloway 1999).

14   To date, the EU co-operates with Russia and the Ukraine on the basis of Partnership and Co-operation Agreements (which exist with almost all Newly Independent Republics) and of 'Common Strategies' (a new CFSP instrument introduced in the Amsterdam Treaty).

15   The German Democratic Republic was treated as a special case when it entered the FRG on 3 October 1990. (For the course of events and an analysis of the background to the East German EC entry, see Kohler-Koch 1991.)

16   The Union proceeds somewhat faster than its associates; for more detail, see Jaks 1993; Randzio-Plath and Friedmann 1994.

17   For criticism on the Europe agreements, see for example Phinnemore 1999, Grabbe and Hughes 1998, Smith 1998, Senior Nello 1998.

18   Adrienne Héritier describes making a decision small and sneaking it on to the policy agenda as another 'mode of "innovation by stealth" against the resistance of important actors. The responsibility for a large-scale decision is split up over a period of time into a number of small, innocuous decisions, each of which has a lock-in effect and which, in consequence, weakens the opposition to the former' (Héritier 1999).

19   Sedelmeier and Wallace (1996: 365) mention there being differences over an appropriate strategy not only among the governments (see also e.g. Friis and Murphy 1999a) but also within the Commission.

20   'The enlargement process is vital to securing political stability, democracy and respect for human rights on the European continent as a whole. It creates opportunities for growth, investment and prosperity which will benefit not only current and future Member States of the EU but also the wider international community. (...) Enlargement will also enhance the international community's ability to manage trans-national issues such as environmental pollution, the fight against organised crime and corruption and illegal trafficking.' (European Commission 1999).

21   'Enlargement, on the right terms, could provide a major boost to the EU's global competitiveness; in many respects, the reforms required to adjust to enlargement complement those demanded in response to global pressures. The costs of enlarging slowly, or imposing heavy regulatory burdens on the developing economies of new entrants, are likely to be higher: their growth will be held back, pressures to emigrate westwards will be intensified, and political tensions will rise, placing strains on new democracies. Political courage and leadership is required to explain to EU publics both the unavoidable costs of change, and the benefits to be gained from enlargement for the future prosperity, stability and security of Europe as a whole.' (Amato and Batt 1999)

22   We would like to thank Myriam Nauerz for her excellent research assistance!

References

Amato, G. and Batt, J. (1999) *The Long-term Implications of EU Enlargement: The Nature of the New Border. Final Report of the Reflection Group*, FSU European Commission. Florence, European University Institute, Robert Schuman Centre for Advanced Studies. Online http://www.iue.it/RSC/News.htm.

Breuss, F. (1999) *Costs and Benefits of EU Enlargement in Model Simulations*, IEF Working Papers 33, Research Institute of European Affairs, Vienna. Online http://fgr.wu-wien.ac.at/institut/ef/wp/WP33.pdf (June).

Cameron, F. (1995) 'Keynote Article: The European Union and the Fourth Enlargement', in N. Nugent (ed.), *The European Union 1994*, Oxford: Blackwell.

Christiansen, T. and Jørgensen, K. E. (1999) 'The Amsterdam Process: A Structurationist Perspective on EU Treaty Reform', *European Integration Online Papers* 3/1: Online http://eiop.or.at/eiop/texte/1999 001a.htm.

Dinan, D. (1999) 'Treaty Change in the European Union: The Amsterdam Experience', in L.

Cram, D. Dinan and N. Nugent (eds), *Developments in the European Union*, London: Macmillan.

Europäische Kommission (1998) *Eurobarometer. Die öffentliche Meinung in der Europäischen Union*. Brussels, European Commission. 50. Online http://www.europa.eu.int/comm/dg10/epo/eb.html.

Europäische Kommission (1999) *Eurobarometer. Die öffentliche Meinung in der Europäischen Union*. Brussels, European Commission. 51. Online http://www.europa.eu.int/comm/dg10/epo/eb.html.

European Commission (1998) *Central and Eastern Eurobarometer*. Brussels, European Commission. 8. Online http://www.europa.eu.int/comm/dg10/epo/ceeb.html.

European Commission (1999) *Regular Report from the Commission on Progress towards Accession by Each of the Candidate Countries*. 2. Online http://europa.eu.int/comm/enlargement/report_10_99/intro /index.htm (13 October).

European Commission (2000a) *Commission Opinion Adapting the Institutions to Make a Success of Enlargement* COM (2000) 34 (26 January).

European Commission (2000b) *Regular Report from the Commission on Progress towards Accession by each of the candidate countries*. Online. Available http://europa.eu.int/comm/enlargement/report_11_00/index.htm (2000-11-08).

European Commission (2000c) *White Paper Reforming the Commission* COM (2000) 200 (1 March).

European Council (1993) *Presidency Conclusions Copenhagen European Council* (21–2 June) BullEC 6/93.

European Council (1999) *Presidency Conclusions Helsinki European Council* (10–11 December).

European Parliament (Committee on Institutional Affairs) (1999) *Report on the Decision-making Process in the Council in an Enlarged Europe* (Rapporteur: J.-L. Bourlanges) PE 229.066/fin./A4-0049/99 (28 January).

Eurostat (1999) *EU Enlargement: Key Data on Candidate Countries*, Memo (October).

Falkner, G. (1995) 'Österreich und die europäische Einigung', in R. Sieder, H. Steinert and E. Tálos (eds), *Österreich 1945–1995*, Vienna: Verlag für Gesellschaftskritik.

Falkner, G. (2000) 'How Pervasive are Euro-Politics? Effects of EU Membership on a New Member State', *Journal of Common Market Studies* 38/2: 223–50.

Friis, L. (1998a) 'Approaching the "Third Half" of EU Grand Bargaining: The Post-negotiation Phase of the "Europe Agreement Game"', *Journal of European Public Policy* 5/2: 322–38.

Friis, L. (1998b) '"The End of the Beginning" of Eastern Enlargement: Luxembourg Summit and Agenda-Setting', *European Integration Online Papers* 2/7: Online http://eiop.or.at/eiop/texte/1998 007a.htm.

Friis, L. and Murphy, A. (1999a) 'The European Union and Central and Eastern Europe: Governance and Boundaries', *Journal of Common Market Studies* 37/2: 211–32.

Friis, L. and Murphy, A. (1999b) 'Negotiating in a Time of Crisis: The EU's Response to the Military Conflict in Kosovo', colloquium 'The European Union as a Negotiated Order' (22–3 October), Loughborough University.

Galloway, D. (1999) 'Keynote Article: *Agenda 2000* – Packaging the Deal', in G. Edwards and G. Wiessala (eds), *The European Union: Annual Review 1998/1999 of the Journal of Common Market Studies*, Oxford: Blackwell.

Grabbe, H. and Hughes, K. (1998) 'The Impact of Enlargement on EU Trade and Industrial Policy', in J. Redmond and G. G. Rosenthal (eds), *The Expanding European Union: Past, Present, Future*, Boulder, CO: Lynne Rienner.

Grande, E. (1996) 'The State and Interest Groups in a Framework of Multi-level Decision-making: The Case of the European Union', *Journal of European Public Policy* 3/3: 318–38.

Granelli, F. (1994) 'The Accession Negotiations', UACES Conference 'The 1995 Enlargement of the EU: Austria, Sweden, Finland and Norway?' (2 December), London.

Griller, S., Droutsas, D., Falkner, G., Forgó, K. and Nentwich, M. (2000) *The Treaty of Amsterdam: Facts, Analysis, Prospects*, Vienna: Springer.

Groupe de Réflexion (2000) *Rapport sur l'avenir du système juridictionnel des Communautés européennes*, European Commission. Online http://europa.eu.int/en/comm/sj/homesjen.htm (January).

Héritier, A. (1999) *Policy-Making and Diversity in Europe: Escape From Deadlock*, Cambridge: Cambridge University Press.

ICRI (1999) *Advancing the Union*, The Independent Commission for the Reform of the Institutions and Procedures of the Union, London. Online http://www.icri.org.uk/ (November).

Jaks, J. (1993) 'The EC and Central and Eastern Europe', in S. S. Andersen and K. A. Eliassen (eds), *Making Policy in Europe: The Europeification of National Policy-making*, London: Sage.

Jessen, C. (1999) 'Agenda 2000: Das Reformpaket von Berlin, ein Erfolg für Gesamteuropa', *Integration* 22/3: 167–75.

Kamppeter, W. (2000) *Lessons of European Integration*, Analyseeinheit Internationale Politik, Bonn: Friedrich Ebert Stiftung.

Kerremans, B. (1998) 'The Political and Institutional Consequences of Widening: Capacity and Control in an Enlarged Council', in P.-H. Laurent and M. Maresceau (eds), *The State of the European Union*, vol. 4: *Deepening and Widening*, Oxford/New York: Oxford University Press.

Kohler-Koch, B. (1991) 'Die Politik der Integration der DDR in die EG', in B. Kohler-Koch (ed.), *Die Osterweiterung der EG*, Baden-Baden: Nomos.

Laurent, P.-H. (1994) 'Widening Europe: The Dilemmas of Community Success', *Annals (AAPSS)* 531: 124–40.

Laursen, F. (1993) 'The EC in Europe's Future Economic and Political Architecture', in S. S. Andersen and K. A. Eliassen (eds), *Making Policy in Europe: The Europeification of National Policy-making*, London: Sage.

Luif, P. (1994) 'Die Beitrittswerber: Grundlegendes zu den Verhandlungen der EFTA-Staaten um Mitgliedschaft bei der EG/EU', *Österreichische Zeitschrift für Politikwissenschaft* 1: 21–36.

Matern, M. and Schultz, M. (1997) 'Zeittafel der europäischen Integration', in W. Weidenfeld and W. Wessels (eds), *Europa von A–Z: Taschenbuch der europäischen Integration*, Bonn: Europa Union Verlag.

Mayhew, A. (1998) *Recreating Europe: The European Union's Policy towards Central and Eastern Europe*, Cambridge: Cambridge University Press.

Michalski, A. and Wallace, H. (1992) *The European Community: The Challenge of Enlargement*, London: Royal Institute of International Affairs.

Moravcsik, A. (1993) 'Preferences and Power in the European Community: A Liberal Intergovernmentalist Approach', *Journal of Common Market Studies* 31/4: 473–523.

Moravcsik, A. and Nicolaïdis, K. (1999) 'Explaining the Treaty of Amsterdam: Interests, Influence, Institutions', *Journal of Common Market Studies* 37/1: 59–85.

Neunreither, K. and Wiener, A. (eds) (2000) *European Integration After Amsterdam: Institutional Dynamics and Prospects for Democracy*, Oxford/New York: Oxford University Press.

Nicholson, F. and East, R. (1987) *From the Six to the Twelve: The Enlargement of the European Communities*, London/New York: Longman.

Nicolaides, P. (1999) 'The Economics of Enlarging the European Union: Policy Reform versus Transfers', *Intereconomics* 1: 3–9.

Phinnemore, D. (1999) *Association: Stepping-Stone or Alternative to EU-Membership*, Contemporary European Studies 6, Sheffield: Sheffield Academic Press.

Pollack, M. A. (1999) 'Delegation, Agency and Agenda Setting in the Treaty of Amsterdam', *European Integration Online Papers* 3/6: Online http://eiop.or.at/eiop/texte/1999-006a.htm.

Preston, C. (1995) 'Obstacles to EU Enlargement: The Classical Community Method and the Prospects for a Wider Europe', *Journal of Common Market Studies* 33/3: 451–63.

Putnam, R. D. (1988) 'Diplomacy and Domestic Politics', *International Organisation* 42/3: 427–661.

Randzio-Plath, C. and Friedmann, B. (1994) *Unternehmen Osteuropa – eine Herausforderung für die Europäische Gemeinschaft: Zur Notwendigkeit einer EG-Ostpolitik*, Baden-Baden: Nomos.

Redmond, J. (1993) *The Next Mediterranean Enlargement of the European Community: Turkey, Cyprus and Malta?*, Aldershot: Dartmouth.

Rupp, M. A. (1995) 'The European Union and the Challenge of Eastern Enlargement', Second Pan-European Conference in International Relations, Paris (13–16 September).

Schneider, H. (1990) *Alleingang nach Brüssel, Österreichs EG-Politik*, Europäische Schriften 66, Bonn.

Schneider, H. (1994) 'Gerader Weg zum klaren Ziel? Die Republik Österreich auf dem Weg in die Europäische Union', *Österreichische Zeitschrift für Politikwissenschaft* 1: 5–21.

Schwok, R. (1991) 'EC–EFTA Relations', in L. Hurwitz and C. Lequesne (eds), *The State of the European Community*, Boulder, CO: Lynne Rienner/Longman.

Sedelmeier, U. and Wallace, H. (1996) 'Policies towards Central and Eastern Europe', in H. Wallace and W. Wallace (eds), *Policy-Making in the European Union*, Oxford: Oxford University Press.

Seers, D. and Vaitsos, C. (eds) (1986) *The Second Enlargement of the EEC: The Integration of Unequal Partners*, Basingstoke: Macmillan.

Senior Nello, S. (1998) 'The European Union and Central-East Europe: Background to the Enlargement Question', in R. Dehousse (ed.), *An Ever Larger Union? The Eastern Enlargement in Perspective*, Baden-Baden: Nomos.

Smith, A. (1998) 'Integration into the Single Market', in R. Dehousse (ed.), *An Ever Larger Union? The Eastern Enlargement in Perspective*, Baden-Baden: Nomos.

Smith, A. and Wallace, H. (1994) 'The European Union: Towards a Policy for Europe', *International Affairs* 3: 429–44.

Spiesberger, M. (1998) 'Übergangsregime zur Abfederung von Differenzen bei EG/EU-Beitritt', *Österreichische Zeitschrift für Politikwissenschaft* 4: 407–24.

Sverdrup, U. (1999) 'Precedents and Present Events in the European Union: An Institutional Perspective on Treaty Reform', in K. Neunreither and A. Wiener (eds), *European Integration: Institutional Dynamics and Prospects for Democracy After Amsterdam*, London: Oxford University Press. (Previous version: Online http://www.sv.uio.no/arena/publications/wp98_21.htm.)

Tovias, A. (1995) 'Spain in the European Community', in R. Gillespie, F. Rodrigo and J. Story (eds), *Democratic Spain Reshaping External Relations in a Changing World*, London: Routledge.

Tsebelis, G. (1990) *Nested Games: Rational Choice in Comparative Politics*, Berkeley and Los Angeles: University of California Press.

Tsoukalis, L. (1981) *The European Community and the Mediterranean Enlargement*, London, Allen & Unwin.

Wallace, H. (1989) *Widening and Deepening: The European Community and the New European Agenda*, London: Royal Institute of International Affairs.

Wallace, H. (ed.) (1991) *The Wider Western Europe: Reshaping the EC*, London: Pinter.

Wessels, W. (1992) 'Staat und (westeuropäische) Integration. Die Fusionsthese', *Politische Vierteljahresschrift* 33, special issue 23: 36–61.

Wolter, D. (1999) 'Die Kaukasus-Politik der Europäischen Union', *Aus Politik und Zeitgeschichte* 42: 32–9.

Wulf-Mathies, M. (1999) 'Agenda 2000 und die Reform der Europäischen Struktur- und Regionalpolitik. Die Neurorientierung an Beschäftigungs- und Wachstumspolitik macht Deutschland zum Gewinner der Reform', *WSI Mitteilungen* 6: 362–71.

Chapter 14

The EU as an international actor

MICHAEL SMITH

Introduction

From the beginning, the European Communities and now the EU have had to exist in a changing international context; indeed, many treatments of the history of European integration place great weight on the international dimension of both the foundation and the development of the phenomenon (Story 1993; Wallace 1990; Pinder 1991a). The EU, as will be shown in more detail later in this chapter, is also a major presence in the contemporary global arena. It is thus not surprising that there should have been consistent and growing attention to the international 'credentials' of the EC and then the EU.

To state this position, though, is to beg a central question. Although the EU is a major component of the contemporary world arena, just what is its status, role and impact? At one end of the spectrum, there are those who can discern a progression in the EU towards full-fledged international 'actorness', comparable to that of the national states that comprise the major concentrations of power in world politics. But such views have to wrestle with the inconvenient fact that the EU is not a 'state' in the accepted international meaning of the term, although it undoubtedly demonstrates some 'statelike' features. Notwithstanding its ability to act in the economic and diplomatic fields, the EU has been slow to develop a coherent security policy or even the beginnings of a European-level defence policy (Hill 1990; 1993; 1995; Smith 1994; Cameron 1999).

Thwarted in the search for an EU version of statehood, others have attempted to define the EU as a growing and increasingly structured 'presence' in the international arena, with its own forms of international behaviour and influence, and most significantly an important place in the foreign policies of other international actors, whether they be states or non-state groupings (Allen and Smith 1990; 1998). Thus, the EU cannot be avoided by national foreign policy-makers, nor can it be bypassed by international organisations such as the United Nations. This approach has its undoubted advantages, not least that of finessing the issue of statehood, but it also begs major questions. Perhaps most importantly, it raises the issue of relations between the EU's 'presence' and the persistence of the essentially national powers of the EU's member states themselves (Hill 1995).

Whatever the position taken on the EU's claims to 'actorness' or 'presence' in the international arena, the analyst must take into account two crucial aspects of the EU's international existence. First, the EU is not simply an 'actor' or a 'presence' but also a *process*; a set of complex institutions, roles and rules which structure the activities of the EU itself and those of other internationally significant groupings with which it comes into contact. Second, the EU as 'actor', 'presence' and process exists today in a world which has *changed* greatly, not to say fundamentally, since the foundation of the ECSC, the Treaty of Rome or even the Single European Act.

Between 1997 and 1999, it might be argued, a number of these pressures converged to provide a new impetus for the development of the EU's international 'actorness'. While the Treaty of Amsterdam (1997) was widely perceived to have fallen short of its aims in a number of areas, it did make some significant revisions to the CFSP. It gave the European Council responsibility for the framing of 'common strategies' to guide foreign ministers; it regularised the budgetary situation of CFSP; it established a Policy Planning Unit to provide the beginnings of an intelligence and planning capability; and it provided for the appointment of a 'high representative' to act as the figurehead for CFSP. These detailed changes were given new focus by the emergence during 1998 and 1999 of important new initiatives designed to formalise a 'defence policy' element in the CFSP, and by the drive by the British and French governments in particular to add muscle to the EU's security and defence activities. By the end of 2000, agreement had been reached on the creation of a 60,000-strong Rapid Reaction Force (RRF) and on further consolidation of a Common European Security and Defence Policy (CESDP). The question remained, however, how far these initiatives would go and how much they would change the EU's operations in specific international arenas (Cameron 1999: chs 8–9).

Two central questions thus act as the focus for this chapter. First, what is the evidence that the EU is moving towards full-fledged 'actorness' in the international arena, adding new focus and impact to its established presence and processes? Second, what role does the EU play in the new Europe and the new world of the twenty-first century, and how does that role reflect the unique status of the EU? On the basis of the discussion of these two areas, the chapter also attempts to project the possible future development of the EU's international role.

The structure of the chapter reflects the agenda set out above. First, it deals with the foundations, both institutional and political, of the EU's international role and impact. Second, it assesses the pattern of issues, interactions and relationships that constitute the substance of the EU's international life; and finally, it evaluates the models available to describe and explain the EU's international policy-making.

The foundations

As already noted, the EU derives much of its international role and impact from the foundations on which it is built. Perhaps the most obvious, yet also problematical, of these foundations is the EU's international 'weight'. In particular, the fact that the EU accounts for a large proportion of the world's economic activity, and is the world's champion trader, creates an inevitable focus on the extent to which and the ways in which the weight is translated into international outcomes. The difficulty, as Chris Hill has ably pointed out, is that there is a 'capability–expectations gap': to put it bluntly, the EU does not deliver consistently on the raw material given to it by the economic prosperity and muscle of the system it has developed. By implication, the conversion of muscle into meaningful action is deficient (Hill 1993; 1998). This theme will be developed further later in the chapter, but at this stage it leads directly into a discussion of the institutions and the politics of EU external policy-making.

The EU's international role rests explicitly on the constitutional base established in the treaties, but that base is neither comprehensive nor unambiguous. It is least unambiguous in the area of the Common Commercial Policy and the EU's international trade policies. Article 113 of the Treaty of Rome (now Article 133 in the Consolidated Treaties) gave the European Economic Community the responsibility for conducting the trade relations of the Community with the rest of the world, and from it has grown a complex web of both institutions and relationships. In important ways, the CCP was inevitable given the establishment of the customs union and the Common External Tariff; the need to manage the external trade relations of the Community, and to conduct relations with international partners, was a logical outcome of the establishment of the customs union, and the acquisition of international competence was one of the first items on the Commission's agenda (Smith 1997).

During the 1950s, 1960s and 1970s, therefore, the EEC developed a complicated network of international agreements, and came to play an important role in the development of the world trading system. The Commission was recognised as the voice of the EEC in the conduct of international trade negotiations, and the enlargement of the Community during the 1970s further increased the range and scope of its international economic involvement. But this was a partial international role at best: the Community and the Commission had competence in trade negotiations, but even in this area there was a division of powers between the Commission and the Council of Ministers. When the Commission negotiated, it was on the basis of a mandate from the Council and with the close attention of what became known as the '113 Committee' of national trade officials. Although other aspects of international economic relations such as monetary policy and investment were in many respects crucial to the development of the Community, they were not the subject of Community-level policy-making. Even the establishment of the European Monetary System in the late 1970s did not extend Community competence fully into this area, since the system was effectively operated by the central banks of the member states (Tsoukalis 1997).

If the initial competence of the Community was limited in the field of international economic policy, it was almost non-existent in the field of what some would call 'real' foreign policy: the 'high politics' of diplomacy, defence and security. What emerged in this area during the 1970s was not a Community policy, but a series of mechanisms through which the national foreign policies of the EC's members could be more closely co-ordinated. By the end of the 1970s, this had evolved into the framework known as European Political Co-operation (EPC), which effectively acted as a procedural device for the management of common interests. To be sure, EPC was backed up by facilities for the exchange of information and for the active co-ordination of diplomatic activity either in national capitals or in the framework of international organisations such as the Conference on Security and Co-operation in Europe (CSCE). But the member states had not yielded any of their formal freedom of action to the Community, and they retained the right to pursue purely national policies at the same time as participating in the EPC mechanism (Allen *et al.* 1982; Hill 1983).

This meant that by the early 1980s, there was only a patchy and partial basis for the development of the EC's international role. There were areas of intense and continuous activity, for example in the conduct of trade policy; there were areas of intense but temporary activity, such as those centred around the energy crises of the 1970s or the issue of economic sanctions as Soviet–American tensions waxed and waned; but in many areas including the politics of national security, the national policy mechanisms of EC members remained almost untouched.

During the 1980s, however, there were important changes both in the international conditions and in the institutional base for EC international policy-making. At the international level, it became apparent more and more that the separation of 'economic' and 'political' or 'security' issues was artificial. Indeed, many of the most pressing international problems were intractable precisely because of the ways in which the economic, the political and the security elements were intertwined and interdependent. Not only this, but in the world political economy itself there was an increasing awareness of the issues arising from technological change and shifts in competitive advantage (Stubbs and Underhill 1999; Smith and Woolcock 1993).

At the Community level, one response to the latter development was the Single Market Programme. It is possible to see the Commission White Paper of 1985 and the subsequent legislative programme simply as a process dealing with the internal economic activity of the EC, but it was apparent to many from the outset that this was also a programme designed to enhance the international presence and impact of the EC and its economic groupings. This implied a major increase in the international activity of the Community, not only to ensure that the single market was effectively integrated with the international economic framework but also to defuse the often suspicious reactions of economic partners and rivals such as the United States or Japan (Redmond 1992; Hufbauer 1990; Ishikawa 1989; Smith and Woolcock 1993).

The Single Market Programme thus carried with it important implications for the international role of the Community and the Commission, arising from the increasing interpenetration of the domestic and the international economies, and from the established institutional base for Community action. Alongside this, though, went crucial developments in the area of 'high politics', which gave the Community and its members both the incentive and some of the instruments to develop policy in new domains. One such development, already noted, was the linkage between economic and security aims in the world arena, at its most obvious in the use of economic sanctions against (for example) the Iranians, the USSR and South Africa. In these cases, however much the member states might have wished to act on a national basis, they could not do so effectively because of the concentration of commercial policy powers at the Community level (Pijpers *et al.* 1988; Allen and Pijpers 1984; Nuttall 1992).

Another set of significant international policy developments arose from the further evolution of EPC. During the 1980s, a process which remained resolutely intergovernmental was given further definition and a more formal institutional framework. The London Report of 1981 established more effective mechanisms for crisis consultation and for continuity of co-ordination between successive Presidencies of the Council of Ministers, and there were further refinements of the communications and information networks which had emerged in the 1970s. The process remained limited, though, by the fact that certain members of the Community did not want to be involved in security issues at the Community level, and by the conflicting pressures set up by crisis situations. In the case of the Falklands War of 1982, for example, the initial solidarity of the Community in imposing sanctions and working through the UN was eroded by the reluctance of the Irish and the Italians to remain committed as war approached; in the case of sanctions against South Africa, the British themselves were the key defectors and doubters (Pijpers *et al.* 1988; Nuttall 1992).

Nonetheless, the development of EPC during the early 1980s created growing pressures for further formalisation, without going so far as to incorporate the process fully into the Community framework. The result was Title III of the Single European Act, which for the first time created a treaty base – albeit an explicitly intergovernmental one – for the EPC mechanisms. The SEA formalised the 'troika' through which successive Council presidencies ensured continuity, and it established a permanent though small EPC secretariat. It even went so far as to introduce the word 'security' into the EPC framework, although there was a firm restriction to the 'political aspects' of security issues.

By the late 1980s, then, the framework for EC international policy consisted effectively of two strands: the Community strand as applied through the CCP and its instruments, and elaborated by the external impact of the Single Market; the intergovernmental strand as exemplified in Title III of the SEA and the EPC mechanisms. At the same time, there was an increasing consciousness of the artificiality of distinctions between 'high' and 'low' politics, or between economics and security. The lesson was borne in with unprecedented force by the events of 1989 in Europe, with the fall of the Berlin Wall and the subsequent more or less peaceful revolutions in central and Eastern European countries. Not only this, but the interlinking of economic, political and security issues in the 'new Europe' seemed to create new roles and responsibilities for the Community in ways which approximated to 'real' foreign policy. Thus the Community and the Commission were given responsibility for co-ordinating Western assistance to central and eastern Europe and then to Russia through the so-called G-24 grouping. For the advocates of Community foreign policy, the wind seemed set fair: the Community was a major participant and pole of attraction in the 'new Europe', and no single member of the EC could hope to play an independent foreign policy role (Wallace 1990; Pinder 1991b; Allen and Smith 1991–92).

It was in this context that the Maastricht Treaty on European Union attacked the issues of the 'second pillar' or foreign and security policy. Indeed, it was because of this context that the EC's members felt the need to go beyond the limits of intergovernmental co-operation so far established and to develop new mechanisms for foreign policy co-ordination. While the external commercial policy powers of the Community were hardly altered by the TEU, the provisions on a common foreign and security policy (CFSP) in the treaty broke new ground both in terms of substance and in terms of the organisational framework. The treaty declared the members' determination to establish a common foreign and security policy, which would lead in time to a common defence policy and even to a common defence (by implication, a military community to stand alongside the economic one in the framework of the Union). The existing Western European Union was defined as the defence arm of the Union, with provision for a growing together of the two organisations and a definitive review of their relations in the 1996 IGC (Norgaard *et al.* 1993; Rummel 1992; Forster and Wallace 1996; Regelsberger *et al.* 1997).

To support this set of aims and intentions, the TEU established new procedures. The Commission was given a (non-exclusive) right of initiative in the CFSP field, while the intergovernmental character of the framework was preserved by the guiding role of the European Council and the continued location of the primary operational responsibilities with the Council of Ministers. For the first time, voting procedures including majority voting were introduced to the domain of foreign policy, although there were strong safeguards for national positions. The common diplomatic positions generated by the EPC mechanism were supplemented by potential 'joint actions' within agreed limits, raising a number of issues about resourcing and the role of the Commission in implementing foreign policy decisions (Norgaard *et al.* 1993; Rummel 1992; Laursen and Vanhoonacker 1992; Regelsberger *et al.* 1997; Cameron 1999: chs 2–4).

As noted earlier in the chapter, the Treaty of Amsterdam in many ways continued the processes set in motion by the TEU. Indeed, since the TEU only entered into force in late 1993, the CFSP provisions had had little time to develop before they were once again subject to review. In addition to the procedural innovations summarised earlier – 'common strategies', the budgetary provisions, the Planning Unit and the 'high representative' – Amsterdam also introduced general provisions for 'flexibility', and for an extension of Qualified Majority Voting (QMV), whereby those member states wishing to move more rapidly, or to take more muscular action, might hope not to be impeded by the others. The Treaty also introduced into the CFSP the so-called 'Petersberg tasks' relating to humanitarian intervention and peace-keeping activities, and foreshadowed the eventual absorption of the WEU into the Union. These measures were not insignificant; indeed, they could form a basis for creative exploitation of the potential in the CFSP, as long as the political will was to be found. But it is open to question whether in themselves they resolved the 'unstable compromise' hammered together at Maastricht in 1991 (Forster and Wallace 1996; Cameron 1999: ch. 5). As noted earlier, the development during 1999 and 2000 of the Common European Security and Defence Policy did not resolve the issues: the Treaty of Nice, which concluded the Intergovernmental Conference of 2000, made no major institutional changes, although it did establish a Political and Security Committee to oversee crisis management operations.

Later parts of the chapter will deal with the practical impact of these CFSP provisions, but at this stage a review of the position reached in the TEU (and as modified at Amsterdam and Nice) is in order. Three interim conclusions are apparent. In the first place, the longstanding foundations of the EC's external policy powers in the field of trade and related areas continued to flourish, reinforced by the impact of the single market programme and the intensification of international economic interdependence. For example, at the same time as the TEU was adding new areas through the CFSP, the Commission on behalf of the Community was negotiating the Uruguay Round of trade agreements under the GATT, one of the most complex and far-reaching sets of international negotiations since 1945; it had developed a complex web of international economic agreements, and a powerful set of economic weapons with which to pursue external policy objectives. With the establishment of the World Trade Organisation in 1995, the EU and its member states became founding members of a major new international institution, and the evidence was that this led to a renewed impetus in EU commercial policy, conducted predominantly through the European Community and the Commission (Smith and Woolcock 1999).

Second, the 'civilian power' of the Community had been supplemented through intergovernmental channels by the increasingly 'high politics' of EPC and then the CFSP. Not only this, but in a number of cases it had been demonstrated that the Community and its powers were essential to the successful pursuit of diplomatic objectives in the area of 'high politics'. The SEA, the TEU, the Amsterdam Treaty and the Treaty of Nice had all focused on the need for 'consistency' between the economic and the foreign policy activities of the Community and then the Union – a logical consequence of the increasing linkages between economics and security and the politicisation of economic issues.

Finally, although this may appear to have been an inexorable advance towards the construction of an integrated Union foreign policy, and thus the achievement of full international 'actorness' on the part of the Union, there were a number of reasons to be cautious in making such judgements. The CFSP and CESDP remained intergovernmental, albeit much more effectively institutionalised than the original EPC framework. Member states might recognise the logic of fuller EU responsibilities for foreign policy, but certainly in the case of the major members they would be reluctant to give up the core elements of sovereignty and national security. And perhaps above all, the fluid and potentially dangerous situation in the 'new Europe' was always capable of placing severe strains on the co-ordination mechanisms available even under the TEU and Amsterdam. With this, it is appropriate to turn to the substance of EU international activities.

The substance of policy

Implicit in the preceding discussion has been the assumption that the EU is continuously and heavily involved in the international arena. Indeed, from this involvement arise many of the paradoxes of EU international action, including the 'capability–expectations gap' referred to in the previous section of the chapter. In order to arrive at a more precise description of the EU's international connections, and to explore the ways in which they affect policy-making, this part of the chapter examines four aspects of the problem. First, it evaluates the *agendas* on which the EU's international activities are focused. Second, it identifies the *arenas* within which the EU is involved. Third, it looks at the *relationships* that are central to the EU's international existence. Finally, it reviews the *levels* at which EU actions are shaped and take place, and provides some brief examples of the implications of multi-level policy-making. While these four aspects are separated here for analytical pruposes, in reality they are often closely – indeed, inextricably – linked. The final section of the chapter will attempt to bring them together in an examination of modes of EU policy-making.

Agendas

The earlier discussion has touched at many points on one of the key features of the EU's international activity: the fact that it is centred on a number of interconnected and often highly complex agendas. As the Community and then the Union have developed, the relevant agendas for EU attention and action have broadened and become more difficult to manage, raising the question of the Union's capacity to handle all of the resulting issues at the European level.

The longest-established agenda for action at the European level is that of trade and commercial relations. As the EU has evolved, it has spawned an extensive set of international trade and aid agreements, which some have described as a 'pyramid of privilege'. The extent and complexity of this network reflect the centrality of the trade and aid agenda to the EU; after all, this was the original *raison d'être* of the EEC, and the focus of the earliest common policy efforts of the Community in the international field. Thus today, the Union finds itself deeply and continuously engaged in international trade negotiations, either on a bilateral basis, or on an inter-regional basis, or in the context of the General Agreement on Tariffs and Trade (GATT). At the same time, it deals with less developed countries, particularly those of the African, Caribbean and Pacific grouping (ACP) in the framework of the Lomé Agreements. During the 1990s, a novel trade and aid agenda emerged, centred on the development and stabilisation needs of the former Soviet bloc – both central and eastern Europe and the former Soviet Union itself (Edwards and Regelsberger 1990; Hine 1985; Pinder 1991b; Piening 1997; Dent 1997).

Trade, aid and commercial agreements are thus at the core of the EU's international agenda. As the growth of international interdependence and interpenetration has proceeded during the 1980s and 1990s, this traditional focus has been joined by another: the links between markets and regulatory structures within and outside the EU. The Single Market Programme was launched in a different world from that of the Treaty of Rome or the CAP – a world in which the seemingly 'domestic' concerns of market regulation, standards-setting and competition policies were becoming the stuff of international politics. As a result, over the past decade, the EC and then the EU have had to develop new structures and procedures to deal with such matters as public procurement and market access at the international level (Woolcock 1992; Harrison 1994; Hocking and Smith 1997; Smith 1999).

Much of the traditional and the novel in the economic sphere can be seen as the logical development of the original concept of the common market, with the need to act at the international level closely connected with the internal agenda of European integration. As noted earlier, though, there had also been a shift towards European-level action in the areas of diplomacy and security. This agenda was for a long time separated from the more central economic and commercial EU agendas, but as time has gone on it has become increasingly difficult to maintain the distance between matters of economic welfare and matters of national or European security. From the mid-1970s on, the Community and then the Union have had to wrestle with the ways in which the old 'civilian' agenda has not only been transformed in itself by the impact of interdependence but has also become intertwined with the 'high politics' of peace and security. This inter-twining has become especially apparent in the aftermath of the collapse of the USSR; not only has the geopolitical division of Europe disappeared, but so also has the functional division in the EU between civilian and security agendas (Laffan *et al.* 2000: ch. 3). No clearer example of this could be found than in the events and processes surrounding the development of the 'European defence identity' during 1998 and 1999. While the formal institutionalisation process revolved around successive political 'summits', first between the British and the French at St Malo in the autumn of 1998, then in the European Councils of Cologne and Helsinki during 1999 and finally the Nice European Council of December 2000, there was also a move during the same period to set up a European Aerospace and Defence Corporation, to express the growing feeling that the EU's defence industries should consolidate and integrate.

Arenas

The position is further complicated by the increasing linkages between the arenas in which the EU is involved. As suggested above, the Cold War division of Europe and the enforced separation of East and West gave a particular definition to the international activity of the EC. Not only was the Community seen as 'civilian', it was also 'Western' in its orientation, an integral part of the transatlantic system centred on NATO, the GATT, the Organisation for Economic Co-operation and Development (OECD) and other institu-tions. This set of strong institutional affiliations largely defined the arena of EC activity. Alongside it went the still strong links to former colonial possessions of the EC members, from which grew the agreements clustered around the Lomé system established in the 1970s. The EC's arena of action, its main reference point for any sort of international identity, was the Western system and in particular the economic structure built around the North Atlantic area (Allen and Smith 1991–92; Smith and Woolcock 1993; Story 1993).

Just as the policy agenda for the EU has been transformed, so has the arena for its interna-tional actions. While the long-established institutional arrangements have not disappeared, they are implanted in a radically changed context, and have been joined by a number of novel arrangements reflecting the needs of the post-Cold War world. Many of these new arrange-ments reflect the linkages between agendas already noted: for example, the influence of the Organisation on Security and Co-operation in Europe with its focus on non-military as well as military aspects of security, or the role of the European Bank for Reconstruction and Development in the political and economic stabilisation of the 'new Europe'. The EU finds itself not only in a transformed world arena, but also in a newly institutionalised and rapidly developing European order, and this is a challenge to international action (Allen and Smith 1991–92; Smith and Woolcock 1993; Carlsnaes and Smith 1994; Laffan *et al.* 2000).

The challenge is complicated further by two sets of contradictions, which surround and penetrate the arenas for EU action. First, there is the coexistence of new and developing institutions with persistent disorder and conflict. This contradiction is most clearly seen in the conflicts that erupted in the former Yugoslavia during the 1990s. Although there was no shortage of institutions with roles and responsibilities, one of which was the EU itself, they were challenged and often defeated by the mercurial and combustible array of contending forces with an interest in chaos and destruction. A second set of contradictions surrounds the EU's role in the world political economy, where the coexisting forces of glob-alisation and regionalisation have given rise to major policy dilemmas and problems of management. The result of these contradictions is a complex, multilayered and often apparently uncontrollable set of policy arenas, in which the EU is not the only body subject to challenge (Laffan *et al.* 2000: chs 3–4).

Relationships

The challenge of the new, though, does not mean that all of the old has disappeared. In particular, certain relationships are central to the international policies of the EU. The most intense, highly developed and longest-established is that with the USA. Together, the EU and the USA account for nearly half of the world economy, and their relationship is both extensive and rich. It is one from which both parties benefit considerably, and in which the balance of economic advantage is relatively even. Not only this, but the EU–US relationship is implanted in the broader security relationship expressed through NATO and other institutions (Smith and Woolcock 1993; Peterson 1996; Featherstone and Ginsberg 1996; Frellesen and Ginsberg 1994; Guay 1999).

Given the intensity of the interdependence between the two partners, it is not at all surprising that there will be a continuous flow of disputes between them, particularly in areas of important trade or financial competition. Thus the relationship in the 1990s was beset by disputes over agricultural trade, over the openness of the Single Market to US financial and other institutions, and over politically symbolic high-technology projects such as the European Airbus. The point is that while challenging, such issues are conducted on the whole in the co-operative mode, with the intention of resolving differences and building new procedures. This aim was first expressed in the Transatlantic Declaration of November 1990, which spawned a set of specialist working groups and other forms of co-operation on significant issues (Frellesen and Ginsberg 1994). It was followed in the mid- and late 1990s by the New Transatlantic Agenda of 1995 and the Transatlantic Economic Partnership of 1998 (Smith 1998a).

The end of the Cold War put a new complexion on important aspects of EU–US relations. On the one hand, it found the EU anxious to develop new international roles in the development of the 'new Europe', often in areas where the USA found it difficult to respond. On the other, it became apparent that the role of the EU in high politics and security has severe limitations; there are still areas in which and ways in which only the USA has the capacity to act, particularly where this implies the rapid mobilisation of major military assets (as in former Yugoslavia). Although the Maastricht agreements established the CFSP, and recognised the growing linkage between the EU and the Western European Union in the evolution of security policy, this did not and could not make it the equal of the USA in theatres of active military conflict (Smith and Woolcock 1994; Allen and Smith 1998). As noted earlier in the chapter, during 1998–2000 there were apparently fundamental shifts in the EU's ability to muster a 'hard security' capability, with plans to set up a 60,000-strong EU Rapid Reaction Force. Significantly, the US government expressed reservations about both the feasibility and the appropriateness of this enterprise.

The relationship between the EU and the USA has thus been and will continue to be a central policy concern. Less comprehensive, but no less sensitive at times, has been the relationship with Japan, and alongside it those with China and the Asia-Pacific region. In the case of Japan, the texture of the relationship is primarily that of economic interdependence and economic competition, with the Japanese enjoying a considerable credit balance in the areas of trade and financial services. Thus, the EU has found itself dealing with the Japanese on a succession of more or less serious trade disputes, most notably in the areas of automobiles and consumer electronics. Although the early 1990s produced an EU–Japan

Declaration modelled after the Transatlantic Declaration, the effective scope of collaboration between the two partners remained significantly less ambitious and intensive. Partly this is a reflection of history, partly it reflects the relative distance and lack of complementarity between the two entities; nonetheless, there is a growing need to organise the relations between the two. With China, the EU during the 1990s experienced a rapidly growing relationship, but one bedevilled by trade disputes as the Chinese expanded their overseas trade, and by lingering tensions over human rights. At the same time, the EU made significant efforts to establish inter-regional contacts with the countries of Southeast Asia, through agreements with the members of the Association of South-East Asian Nations (ASEAN), and to bring together all of its Asia-Pacific partners in the Asia–Europe Meetings (ASEM), the first of which was held in 1996 (Smith 1998b; Maull *et al.* 1998; Dent 1999).

It has already been suggested that a key component of EU international activity in the 1990s was the need to deal with the 'new Europe'. This is not simply a matter of coping with the fallout from the collapse of the USSR; the European landscape was in many ways being transformed before 1989, and the development of new networks of relations was a growing concern of the EC throughout the 1980s. Essentially, there were two main focuses to this activity. First, there was the intensification of relations with the former members of the European Free Trade Association (EFTA), first through the negotiation of the European Economic Area agreement (EEA) and then through the formal incorporation of Austria, Finland and Sweden as EU members in 1995. The details of this process can be found in Chapter 13, but it is important to register here the ways in which this led during the late 1980s and early 1990s to a new set of developments in EU external relations. On the other hand, there was the establishment and intensification of relations with the countries of the former Soviet bloc, either on the basis of 'arm's length' relationships based on trade and assistance or (as in the case of the 'Visegrad countries') on the basis of increasingly close linkages and eventual membership of the Union itself (Pinder 1991b; Carlsnaes and Smith 1994; Wallace 1991; Smith K. 1999; Henderson 1999). Assuming that a significant 'eastern enlargement' would take place during the early years of the new millennium, this would lead to a further reorientation of both the economic and the political–security aspects of EU external policies, particularly as a result of the new 'geopolitics' and 'geoeconomics' implied by a shift to the east and to a common border with the former Soviet Union.

For the EU's international activities and policies, the overall impact of these changes in agendas, arenas and relationships has been profound. While the Cold War years were far from simple, they at least made it possible for EC leaders to focus on 'civilian' activities and to operate within a well-defined set of institutional and political arrangements. A combination of factors ranging from the Single Market Programme through the collapse of the USSR to the transformation of the global economy has made redundant a number of the longstanding assumptions on which the EC's international role was founded. This has meant a series of unavoidable challenges both for EU policy-makers and for the EU's institutions (Wallace 1990; Keohane *et al.* 1993; Story 1993; Laffan *et al.* 2000).

Levels

Not the least of these challenges has been that of dealing with the implications of multi-level politics and diplomacy. The EU has found in a number of contexts that it has to reconcile its own often limited capacity to act with the needs and demands of international institutions, major political and trading partners, and not least its own member states and their governments. Two examples will suffice to demonstrate this set of interlocking dilemmas.

First, in the area of traditional EC/EU action, there is the experience of the negotiations in the GATT Uruguay Round, which began in 1986 and came to a climax in the later part of 1993. Over a seven-year period, the EC and then the EU had to project its trade policy competence into new areas, meeting competition and conflicting demands from the USA, developing countries and a range of agricultural interests. At the same time, the Single Market Programme went from conception to completion, thus radically changing the perception of the EC as an international economic force. Not only this, but the divergent interests of EC members were underlined by the demands of the international negotiation process, and fed back into it often with widespread and potentially damaging implications (Smith and Woolcock 1993; Smith 1994; Woolcock and Hodges 1996). During the later 1990s, as noted earlier, the EU developed an active role in the WTO, but it was often possible to discern the same kinds of cross-cutting pressures at work in the formulation and implementation of EU policies (Smith 1999).

A second and very different example is provided by the EU's involvement in the conflicts in former Yugoslavia – from the independence of Croatia and Slovenia in 1991, through the Bosnian conflict of 1992–95 to the Kosovo crisis of 1999. In this most dangerous series of post-Cold War conflicts, the assumption at the outset was that the EU would have a special role and responsibility, not least because the USA proved unwilling to become directly engaged. A number of often tragic dilemmas ensued for the EU and its members. First, there was the problem of the recognition of Slovenia, Croatia and finally Bosnia-Herzegovina, in which the tensions between EU members were apparent throughout. Then, there was the problem of dealing with the escalation of the conflict, particularly in Bosnia – a conflict which exposed to the full the lack of military muscle behind the EU's position, and the overlapping concerns and competences of the UN, the EU and other organisations such as the CSCE. Third, there was the issue of stabilisation and the creation of safe areas for the ravaged population of Bosnia – a task to which the EU was in many respects peripheral, and in which the interaction of the UN and NATO came to play a central part. While playing a dogged and persistent diplomatic role, backed up by economic sanctions, the EU inevitably found it difficult if not impossible to go beyond exhortation and indirect pressure (Nuttall 1994; Zucconi 1996). By the time the Kosovo crisis became acute in 1999, expectations of EU action were understandably modest, and indeed, the EU itself played no significant role in the military campaign. On the other hand, the Union was able to take a positive lead in post-war reconstruction, and mounted an important long-term initiative in the shape of the Stability Pact for the Balkans, which coupled short-term stabilisation measures with the long-term prospect of EU membership for some if not all of the region's regimes.

The conclusion here is not that the EU succeeded or failed in either the GATT/WTO context or former Yugoslavia. The point is to show the ways in which during the 1990s, the EU was faced with profoundly challenging tasks in the international field. The evolution both of the world economy and of the post-Cold War international order created opportunities for a more expansive and ambitious EU role, but it also raised questions about the extent to which the EU policy process was capable of defining and pursuing appropriate and effective international action (Allen and Smith 1991–92; 1998). Those questions are the starting point for the next section.

Modes of international policy-making in the EU

From the preceding discussion, it should be clear that the EU has important roles to play in the contemporary international arena. Chris Hill (1993; 1998) has identified both a number of functions the EC and the EU have played in the international system up to the late 1990s and a number of potential future roles or functions.

In the past, the EC performed the roles of regional stabiliser in Western Europe; co-manager of world trade; a principal voice for the developed world in relations with the less developed countries; and provider of a second Western voice in international diplomacy. For the future, Hill discerns a number of conceivable roles: a replacement for the USSR in the global balance of power; a regional pacifier; a global intervenor; a mediator of conflicts; a bridge between the rich and the poor; and a joint supervisor of the world economy.

But to list these past and possible future roles is to raise a number of questions, which Hill has encapsulated in the notion of the 'capability–expectations gap' (see above). They testify to the ways in which the EU has become part of the international landscape, but they tell us relatively little about the ways in which the EU can shape or pursue its policies within the broad framework of possibilities generated by the development both of the Union and of the international system.

In this part of the chapter, it is suggested that one crucial element in the resolution of this problem is the study of *modes of EU international policy-making*. From the evidence produced so far, three such modes of policy can be identified and will be examined here:

- First, there is what can be termed *Community policy-making*: the development of the instruments and processes typical of the European Community and of its role in the world political economy.
- Second, there is what can be described as *Union policy-making*: the policy processes generated by the interaction of member governments and European institutions in the context of the Treaties and their practical application.
- Finally, there is the style of policy which can best be described as *negotiated order*: the response of both Community and Union to the multilayered political and economic environment in which they are implanted, and the outcome of the complex exchange relationships in which the member states and other actors are involved.

All three of these policy modes are affected and focused by a number of key dilemmas and assumptions, which have been ably evaluated by Hill and other analysts. They have to cope with the problem of *competence and consistency* within the EU, and the matching of institutional means to appropriate and agreed purposes. They must deal with the *intersection of economic, political and security issues* in the contemporary international arena. They confront the test of *multilayered policy-making and a multiplicity of policy actors* which is characteristic of the contemporary European and international milieu. And finally, they face the need to account for the *proliferation of institutions and instruments* which is equally central to the management of international policies in the new millennium.

Community policy-making

The longest-established and most highly developed form of EU policy process in the international sphere is that of *Community policy-making*. This is the policy mode encapsulated in the Common Commercial Policy and other parts of the Treaty of Rome dealing with the negotiation and conclusion of international agreements. The key elements of this policy mode are thus the concept of Community competence expressed through the Commission, and the development of policy instruments at the European level. They reach their highest level of development in the Community's role with respect to the GATT and the WTO, and in the use of policy instruments such as anti-dumping regulations. More recently, they have been extended into areas such as the international regulation of competition and the international co-ordination of policies in such areas as standards-setting or public procurement. In many ways, as it can be seen from these examples, the policy style is an external expression of internal Community powers and concerns. As such, it forms the core of the Community's claims to international 'actorness'.

It might be thought that in this policy mode, the development of internal Community competence would inexorably be reflected in the extension of its exclusive international competence. In fact, and significantly for those who see the EU as an international actor in the making, there are distinct variations both in the coverage of the process and in the extent to which it can be halted or reversed. Two examples will illustrate the point. First, the negotiation and conclusion of international agreements by the Community through the Commission remains crucially dependent on agreement between the member states in the Council of Ministers. For GATT/WTO negotiations, they give the mandate to the Commission and it is they who finally conclude the agreements after the involvement of the European Parliament and the Commission. Second, and in a related area, it has been the view of the Court of Justice that even the trade policy powers of the Community exercised through the Commission are limited. To be specific, areas of trade negotiation going beyond traditional trade in goods are the joint responsibility of the Community and the member states (so-called 'mixed agreements'). The Court's opinion, delivered in November 1994, clearly implied a set of boundaries to the Common Commercial Policy which had not been suspected previously, and which led to a series of tensions in the policy-making process during the later 1990s (Smith and Woolcock 1999; Meunier and Nicolaidis 1999).

Union policy-making

Community policy-making is thus a crucial but incomplete model for the conduct of the EU's international business. Alongside it there has developed what is termed here *Union policy-making*. The keynote of this mode of policy-making is the intensive and continuous co-ordination of national policies, rather than the application of agreed common policies. Central to its development is the evolution of EPC and then the establishment of the CFSP, but these are not the only examples. In this policy mode, the Commission is not the exclusive bearer of the Community mandate: rather, it is fully associated with the process and a vital source of information, advice and initiatives alongside the national governments.

It is clear that this mode of international policy-making falls close to the intergovernmental mode of general EU policy-making. But there are important, not to say crucial, differences. In particular, the role of the Commission as an active and continuous participant, and a vital facilitator of action, is distinctive; indeed, in some areas such as the imposition of sanctions or the provision of humanitarian or technical assistance, the Commission and the Community can be the only possible implementers of policy.

One dramatic example of this came in the Bosnian conflict, where during 1994 the EU installed an administrator to run the city of Mostar. This 'pro-consul' had wide-ranging powers, including that of derogating from the Bosnian Constitution. While the administrator was put in place through the CFSP, the infrastructure for the office and the financial resources were to an important extent provided through the Commission and the Community budget. A complex form of words expressed the equally complex reality: the policy was to be implemented by 'the member states of the EU working within the framework of the Union and in close association with the European Commission'. This appears to demonstrate that Union policy-making, far from marking a retreat to intergovernmentalism, marks a new departure and a creative way of bringing the various EU institutions and the member governments together. Other early joint actions in South Africa and in Russia (in each case primarily the monitoring of elections) were less dramatic but raised the same issues and possibilities. As noted above, the ways in which the EU operated during the Kosovo crisis of 1999 also raised the prospect of linkages between Union membership and regional stabilisation in a novel way.

International policy as negotiated order

Such developments give support to a third mode of international policy-making in the EU; indeed, the three modes being examined here represent coexisting tendencies rather than competing and mutually exclusive models. Given the complex institutional relationships and processes of exchange between Community, member governments and other actors in the Union's international policy process, it could be argued that the EU in its international activities constitutes an evolving *negotiated order*. Within the administrative, institutional and political structures established over the life of the Community and the EU, there is a constant, rule-governed process of negotiation between actors which produces policy positions and international policy outcomes. Process is as important as outcome, and it is thus inappropriate to apply to the EU the concepts of statehood or foreign policy which are typical of conventional international relations models and approaches (Allen and Smith 1990; Smith 1994; Elgström and Smith 2000).

It is important to note that this perspective on the international policy process in the EU coincides with new patterns of analysis for the global arena more generally, which stress precisely the multi-level, institutionalised and rule-governed behaviour to which attention has been drawn in this chapter (Hocking and Smith 1997: chs 1–2). In the more strictly EU context, such an approach leads in a number of directions. First, it draws attention to the ways in which 'Community policy-making' as outlined above is itself a focus for negotiation and exchange between a number of actors. To give but one example, the new Commission installed in 1999 had within it at least six Commissioners with substantial international policy responsibilities, and the process of allocating these responsibilities had been a source of considerable negotiation and conflict during most of the later 1990s. The appointment of Chris Patten as a kind of 'lead Commissioner' for external policies, and the development of consolidated co-ordination mechanisms not only between the Commissioners concerned but also between Patten and the 'high representative' for CFSP, Javier Solana, symbolised a major effort to ensure consistency among the various channels of EU external policy in conditions of complex policy-making.

A second feature of EU international policy-making which is captured by a 'negotiated order' focus is that in many cases the EU's international activities are undertaken in a multi-level negotiation context. The example of the GATT Uruguay Round cited earlier in this chapter is perhaps the most significant recent instance of the ways in which negotiations within the GATT, within the Commission, within and between the EU institutions and the member states all came together to provide a potent mix of overlapping and often irreconcilable claims. There are, though, many other instances of such relationships: the EU–US partnership, the attempts through negotiation to consolidate the post-Cold War European order, the negotiations attending the accession of new members.

In this view, then, the EU's international positions and actions are both the product of an institutionalised negotiation process and frequently part of such a process in the international arena. As such, they epitomise many features of the changing world political economy in the twenty-first century, but they also focus them in a very distinctive way. A key area of policy analysis for the foreseeable future will be the ways in which this situation plays out for the post-Nice EU, in particular in the context of the 'new Europe'.

Conclusion: towards an EU foreign policy?

This chapter started by examining briefly the debates which have centred around the EU's credentials as an international actor, and by suggesting the significance of the developments that have taken place in the EU's international involvement. Often, the debates and the significance are placed into the context of a broader debate about statehood, foreign policy and the EU's approximation to the conventional model of both. The argument in this chapter has tested both the substantive basis for claims about the EU's international significance and the broader conceptual claims made by those who foresee the emergence of a 'foreign policy' conducted by the Union or its representatives.

The general conclusions from the argument are threefold:

First, that the EC and now the EU have long-established and material foundations for their presence and impact in the international arena. These foundations are the reflection of the economic and political weight of the EU, of its institutional capacity and of the ways in which it has enlarged its tasks and roles in the changing world arena. But they are not monolithic, nor do they suppress the claims or the prerogatives of the member states. Indeed, as the EU has entered new areas of activity, it has occasionally seemed to reach the limits of its capacity to lay claim to the new territory on which it finds itself.

Second, that the substance of EU international policy betrays not only the value placed on the EU both by its members and by others as an international role-player, but also the limitations imposed by the ways in which the EU is constrained in its mobilisation of resources. While this is particularly apparent in the area of international security policy, there is no shortage of other examples to illustrate the 'capability–expectations gap' in the EU's international existence.

Third, that one way of taking further an appreciation of the distinctive nature of EU international policy is to focus on modes of policy-making. There is no single mode of such policy-making, and therein lies part of the unique character of the European construction. There are elements of 'Community policy-making', of 'Union policy-making' and of 'negotiated order' in all aspects of the EU's international policy. The challenge lies in interpreting the circumstances in which and the conditions in which they interact to produce distinctive mixes of policy.

There is therefore no definitive answer to the question 'Does the EU have a foreign policy?': rather there is a series of increasingly well-focused questions about the nature of

EU international action and the foundations on which it is based, which will constitute a major research agenda for the future.

References

Allen, D. and Pijpers, A. (1984) *European Foreign Policy Making and the Arab–Israeli Dispute*, The Hague: Nijhoff.

Allen, D., Rummel, R. and Wessels, W. (1982) *European Political Cooperation: Towards a Foreign Policy for Western Europe?*, London: Butterworth.

Allen, D. and Smith, M. (1990) 'Western Europe's Presence in the Contemporary International Arena', *Review of International Studies* 16/1: 19–39.

Allen, D. and Smith, M. (1991–92) 'The European Community in the New Europe: Bearing the Burden of Change', *International Journal* 47/1: 1–28.

Allen, D. and Smith, M. (1998) 'The European Union's Security Presence: Barrier, Facilitator or Manager?', in C. Rhodes (ed.), *The European Union in the World Community*, Boulder, CO: Lynne Rienner.

Cameron, F. (1999) *The Foreign and Security Policy of the European Union: Past, Present and Future*, Sheffield: Sheffield Academic Press.

Carlsnaes, W. and Smith, S. (eds) (1994) *European Foreign Policy: The EC and Changing Perspective in Europe*, London: Sage.

Dent, C. (1997) *The European Economy: The Global Context*, London: Routledge.

Dent, C. (1999) *The European Union and East Asia: An Economic Relationship*, London: Routledge.

Edwards, G. and Regelsberger, E. (eds) (1990) *Europe's Global Links: The European Community and Inter-regional Cooperation*, London: Pinter.

Elgström, O. and Smith, M. (eds) (2000) *Negotiation and Policy-Making in the European Union: Processes, System and Order*, Special Issue of the *Journal of European Public Policy* 7/5 (December).

Featherstone, K. and Ginsberg, R. (1996) *The United States and the European Community in the 1990s: Partners in Transition*, 2nd edn, London: Macmillan; New York: St Martin's Press.

Forster, A. and Wallace, W. (1996) 'Common Foreign and Security Policy: A New Policy or Just a New Name?' in H. Wallace and W. Wallace (eds), *Policy-Making in the European Union*, Oxford: Oxford University Press.

Frellesen, T. and Ginsberg, R. (1994) *EU–US Foreign Policy Cooperation in the 1990s: Elements of Partnership*, Brussels: Centre for European Policy Studies.

Guay, T. (1999) *The European Union and the United States: The Political Economy of a Relationship*, Sheffield: Sheffield Academic Press.

Harrison, G. (ed.) (1994) *Europe and the United States: Competition and Cooperation in the 1990s*, Armonk, NY: Sharpe.

Henderson, K. (ed.) (1999) *Back to Europe: Central and Eastern Europe and the European Union*, London: UCL Press.

Hill, C. (ed.) (1983) *National Foreign Policies and European Political Cooperation*, London: George Allen and Unwin.

Hill, C. (1990) 'European Foreign Policy: Power Bloc, Civilian Model – or Flop?' in R. Rummel (ed.), *The Evolution of an International Actor: Western Europe's new Assertiveness*. Boulder, CO: Westview Press.

Hill, C. (1993) 'The Capability–Expectations Gap, or Conceptualising Europe's International Role', *Journal of Common Market Studies* 31/3: 305–28.

Hill, C. (ed.) (1995) *The Actors in European Political Cooperation*, London: Routledge.

Hill, C. (1998) 'Closing the Capabilities–Expectations Gap?' in J. Peterson and H. Sjursen (eds), *A Common Foreign Policy for Europe? Competing Visions of the CFSP*, London: Routledge, pp. 18–38.

Hine, R. (1985) *The Political Economy of European Trade*, Brighton: Harvester Wheatsheaf.

Hocking, B. and Smith, M. (1997) *Beyond Foreign Economic Policy: The United States, the Single European Market and a Changing World Economy*, London: Cassell/Pinter.

Hufbauer, G. (ed.) (1990) *Europe 1992: An American Perspective*, Washington, DC: Brookings Institution.

Ishikawa, K. (1989) *Japan and the Challenge of Europe 1992*, London: Pinter/Royal Institute of International Affairs.

Keohane, R., Nye, J. and Hoffmann, S. (eds) (1993) *After the Cold War: International Institutions and State Strategies in Europe, 1989–1991*, Cambridge, MA: Harvard University Press.

Laffan, B., O'Donnell, R. and Smith, M. (2000) *Europe's Experimental Union: Rethinking Integration*, London: Routledge.

Laursen, F. and Vanhoonacker, S. (eds) (1992) *The Intergovernmental Conference on Political Union: Institutional Reforms, New Policies and International Identity of the European Community*, Maastricht: European Institute of Public Administration.

Maull, H., Segal, G. and Wanandi, J. (eds) (1998) *Europe and the Asia-Pacific*, London: Routledge.

Meunier, S. and Nicolaidis, K. (1999) 'Who Speaks for Europe? The Delegation of Trade Authority in the EU', *Journal of Common Market Studies* 37/3: 477–502.

Norgaard, O., Pedersen, T. and Petersen, N. (eds) (1993) *The European Community in World Politics*, London: Pinter.

Nuttall, S. (1992) *European Political Cooperation*, Oxford: Clarendon Press.

Nuttall, S. (1994) 'The EC and Yugoslavia – deus ex machina or machina sine deo?' in N. Nugent (ed.), *The European Union 1993: Annual Review of Activities*, Oxford: Blackwell: 11–26.

Peterson, J. (1996) *Europe and America in the 1990s: Prospects for Partnership*, 2nd edn, London: Routledge.

Piening, C. (1997) *Global Europe: The European Union in World Affairs*, Boulder, CO: Lynne Rienner.

Pijpers, A., Regelsberger, E. and Wessels, W. (eds) (1988) *European Political Cooperation in the 1980s: A Common Foreign Policy for Western Europe?*, Dordrecht: Nijhoff.

Pinder, J. (1991a) *European Community: The Building of a Union*, Oxford: Oxford University Press.

Pinder, J. (1991b) *The European Community and Eastern Europe*, London: Royal Institute of International Affairs/Pinter Publishers.

Redmond, J. (ed.) (1992) *The External Relations of the European Community: The International Response to 1992*, London: Macmillan.

Regelsberger, E., de Schoutheete de Tervarent, P. and Wessels, W. (eds) (1997) *Foreign Policy of the European Union: from EPC to CFSP and Beyond*, Boulder, CO: Lynne Rienner.

Rummel, R. (ed.) (1992) *Toward Political Union: Planning a Common Foreign and Security Policy in the European Community*, Boulder, CO: Westview Press.

Smith, K. (1999) *The Making of EU Foreign Policy: The Case of Eastern Europe*, London: Macmillan.

Smith, M. (1994) 'The European Union, Foreign Economic Policy and a Changing World Arena', *Journal of European Public Policy* 1/2: 283–302.

Smith, M. (1997) 'The Commission and External Relations', in D. Spence and G. Edwards (eds), *The European Commission*, 2nd edn, London: Cartermill.

Smith, M. (1998a) 'Competitive Cooperation and EU–US Relations: Can the EU be a Strategic Partner for the US in the World Political Economy?' *Journal of European Public Policy* 5/4: 561–77.

Smith, M. (1998b) 'The European Union and the Asia-Pacific', in A. McGrew and C. Brook (eds), *Asia-Pacific in the New World Order*, London: Routledge.

Smith, M. (1999) 'The European Union', in B. Hocking and S. McGuire (eds), *Trade Politics: International, Domestic and Regional Perspectives*, London: Routledge.

Smith, M. and Woolcock, S. (1993) *The United States and the European Community in a Transformed World*, London: Royal Institute of International Affairs/Pinter.

Smith, M. and Woolcock, S. (1994) 'Learning to Cooperate: The Clinton Administration and the European Union', *International Affairs* 70/3: 459–76.

Smith, M. and Woolcock, S. (1999) 'European Commercial Policy: A Leadership Role in the New Millennium?' *European Foreign Affairs Review* 4/4: 439–62.

Story, J. (ed.) (1993) *The New Europe: Politics, Government and Society since 1945*, Oxford: Blackwell.

Stubbs, R. and Underhill, G. (eds) (1999) *Political Economy and the Changing Global Order*, 2nd edn, Toronto: Oxford University Press.

Tsoukalis, L. (1997) *The New European Economy Revisited*, Oxford: Oxford University Press.

Wallace, H. (ed.) (1991) *The Wider Western Europe: Reshaping the EC/EFTA Relationship*, London: Royal Institute of International Affairs/Pinter.

Wallace, W. (1990) *The Transformation of Western Europe*, London: Royal Institute of International Affairs/Pinter.

Woolcock, S. (1992) *Market Access Issues in EC/US Trade Relations: Trading Partners or Trading Blows?* London: Royal Institute of International Affairs/Pinter.

Woolcock, S. and Hodges, M. (1996) 'EU Policy in the Uruguay Round', in H. Wallace and W. Wallace (eds), *Policy-Making in the European Union*, Oxford: Oxford University Press.

Zucconi, M. (1996) 'The European Union in the Former Yugoslavia', in A. Chayes and A. H. Chayes (eds), *Preventing Conflict in the Post-Communist World: Mobilizing International and Regional Organizations*. Washington, DC: Brookings Institution.

European regulation

Mark Thatcher

The 1980s and 1990s saw a rapid and sustained expansion of regulation in Europe. Monopolies were ended, replaced by rules governing competition; informal methods of decision-making were overtaken by formal rules; new regulatory bodies were established. Regulatory reforms were undertaken in many policy domains ranging from industrial sectors such as energy, telecommunications and financial services to horizontal policies applicable across sectors such as competition, the environment, equal opportunities and employment conditions.

A central feature of regulatory growth in Europe has been the expansion of EC regulation.[1] The EC's central policy activity is regulation rather than distribution or redistribution: its expenditure, revenues and staffing have remained small compared to those of national governments. In contrast, its regulatory role grew and grew in the 1980s and 1990s. It extended its activities into new policy areas and deepened its role in its existing policy domains. Aided by the doctrine of legal supremacy of Community law, it became a prominent source of regulation. The Commission became an important participant in regulatory decisions, including politically charged ones such as ending long-established monopolies, mergers and takeovers and state aids. The European Court of Justice (ECJ) and EC law were called upon by litigants in regulatory disputes.

This chapter examines the development of EC regulation. Many factors have contributed to EC regulation, which itself has been very diverse in forms and across policy domains. Hence the chapter adopts a broad 'actor-centred institutionalist' framework (cf. Scharpf 1997): EC regulatory growth has been the result of interactions between purposeful actors (the Commission, national governments, interest groups and courts) who have pursued their interests within the EC's institutional framework, which has provided incentives, allowed expansion to take place and offered constraints. That institutional framework has been altered, but relatively rarely, while the interests of the actors have evolved over time under the influence of the dynamics of European integration, technological and economic changes and new ideas. Thus the chapter analyses the interests, strategies and interactions of key actors and the institutional framework of regulation. It does so by looking at five themes: the forms of EC regulation and its growth; the factors responsible for expansion; the constraints and problems of that growth; reforms of EC regulation; the impacts of EC regulation.

EC regulation: forms and growth

Several different definitions of 'regulation' exist (Mitnick 1980: ch. 1; Ogus 1994: ch. 1). Economists usually emphasise rules to correct market failures (cf. Gaitsos and Seabright 1989), whereas political scientists and sociologists have broader conceptions that include rules governing state activity and can extend to all forms of social control and influence (Baldwin and Cave 1999: 2; cf. Wilks 1996; Majone 1996). Its 'central meaning' (Selznick 1985) is 'sustained and focused control by a public agency over activities that are valued by the community'. Control through regulation involves rules, although these can vary from the formal (for instance, formal legislation) to informal norms. Here, the focus is on EC rules, be these formal or less so, and regardless of whether they are directed at correcting market failures.

EC regulation covers the spectrum from legislation to informal norms of behaviour. The EC can issue binding legal acts. The most fundamental are Treaty Articles; they define the competencies and policy domains of the EC. However, the majority of EC regulation is in the form of secondary legislation – regulations, directives and decisions. Regulations, and some Treaty Articles and directives, are directly effective and hence can be used by litigants in national courts; in addition, the doctrine of 'indirect effect' allows EC law to influence national law. The EC has also used non-binding forms of regulation, often called 'soft law', which include recommendations, resolutions, declarations. Finally, the EC exercises regulatory influence by activities such as benchmarking and attempts to spread 'best practice', studies, conferences, networks and encouragement of reform and European integration. These can aid the development of European norms and standards of behaviour.

EC regulatory activities have expanded far beyond those existing in 1958 in terms of legal competencies, legislation and policy fields. The EC's initial focus was on creating a free trade area through removing barriers to trade ('negative' integration), in particular tariff barriers. Thereafter, EC action extended to non-tariff barriers to trade, from product standards to bans on monopolies and restrictive rules on the supply of activities ranging from telecommunications to financial services. The EC has engaged in re-regulation, corresponding to 'positive integration', setting rules governing competition and 'harmonisation' or minimal standards. By 2000, EC regulation covered 'horizontal' matters such as competition, free movement, gender discrimination, environmental protection, health and safety and consumer protection. It also comprised more focused, 'vertical' fields such as sectoral regulation for public utilities, agriculture, pharmaceuticals, financial services and professional services. Numbers also indicate the expansion of EC regulation. In 1970, there were 20 directives and 46 regulations; by 1980, the figures were up to 50 directives and 113 regulations; by the 1990s, these had risen dramatically, reaching 118 directives and 281 regulations in 1990 and 169 directives and 1,316 regulations in 1999.

While the overall picture is of EC regulatory growth, the speed, timing and extent of EC regulation have varied across policy domains (cf. Kassim and Menon 1996; Stravridis *et al.* 1997). The most detailed EC regulation has been in economic regulation, especially on competition. Even here, however, there have been cross-sectoral differences – for example, telecommunications have seen more detailed and earlier regulation than electricity (Schmidt 1997; Thatcher 2001). In other fields, EC action has been more recent and remains less developed, particularly those involving re-regulation – for instance, food safety and labelling or privacy. Nevertheless, there are now fewer and fewer areas of policy that lack an EC regulatory presence.

The process of EC regulatory expansion has taken place through several related channels. Regulatory powers and competencies have been explicitly given to the EC by member states via Treaties as the EC's policy domains have been progressively extended (cf. Fligstein and McNichol 1998). Under the 1958 Treaty of Rome, the EC's core powers mostly concerned building a free-trade area – removing restrictions on the free movement of goods, persons, services and capital. The focus was on tariff barriers and competition, although there were rare exceptions such as equal pay for equal work for men and women (Article 141[119]). The 1980s and 1990s saw member states provide further regulatory areas and powers to EC institutions via new Treaties. Moreover, the power of individual member states to veto directives and regulations was gradually reduced, thanks to the extension of qualified majority voting. The Single European Act added explicit sectoral fields, including the health and safety of workers, environmental protection, research and development and economic and social cohesion. Crucially, it introduced qualified majority voting for certain fields; the most notable (under Article 95 [100A]) was used for the internal market programme ('1992'). The Maastricht Treaty provided further explicit policy fields for EC regulation, notably consumer protection, public health and education. It also included social regulations, albeit in a separate Social Protocol that applied to all member states except Britain. Moreover, it widened the scope of qualified majority voting to areas such as consumer protection, the environment and some parts of social policy. Its most significant provision was to allow economic and monetary union, with a single currency and the establishment of the European Central Bank. The 1997 Amsterdam Treaty continued the expansion of EC competencies in social policy, the environment and employment.

Acting under Treaty Articles, the greatest direct source of increased EC regulation has been through programmes and secondary legislation (directives and regulations) agreed by the Council of Ministers and, in the 1990s, also the European Parliament. The most trumpeted extension, after the initial foundation of the EC, was the Internal Market Programme ('1992' – Commission 1985). This involved 300 legislative proposals to remove trade barriers within the EC through opening up markets, removing non-tariff barriers and setting EC standards. However, in many other fields, the expansion of EC regulation has taken place through gradual accretion over time – seen, for example, in social policy, environmental protection or employment. Passing secondary legislation has been made easier by the extension of qualified majority voting, and its volume rose sharply after the Single European Act (Fligstein and McNichol 1998).

Another, vital form of EC regulatory expansion arose from European Court of Justice decisions (cf. Stone Sweet and Caporaso 1998). An important example was Article 30, which prohibits member states from introducing quantitative restrictions on imports from other member states or measures having 'equivalent effect'. The ECJ stated (in the Dassonville case of 1974 – ECJ 1974) that 'all trading rules enacted by member states which are capable of hindering, actually or potentially, intra-Community trade' were covered. It therefore greatly extended the EC's powers to cover a host of national rules that, regardless of intention or even current effects, could reduce trade among member states. Another example concerns Article 86[90], which forbids member states from introducing or maintaining measures contrary to the Treaty, and in particular, Articles concerned with fair competition, for 'public undertakings' or enterprises given 'special and exclusive rights' (for example, monopolies); Article 86[90](3) empowers the Commission to issue directives to enforce this. Until the late 1980s, the Article was barely used, as it appeared not to apply to sectors in which national legislation established monopolies, especially those 'in the public interest', such as for the public utilities. Yet legal opinion evolved in the 1980s, and the Commission passed directives to liberalise the telecommunications sector under Article 86[90](3); when challenged, the Commission's directives were upheld by the ECJ (ECJ 1991 and 1992).

Although EC regulation has been extended, few new EC regulatory organisations have been created by Treaty (the major exception being the European Central Bank). Nor have EC powers been delegated to regulatory agencies: only ten agencies have been created (for example, the European Agency for the Evaluation of Medicinal Products and the European Environment Agency), and they have few powers, relying heavily on national bodies (Dehousse 1997; Kreher 1997). One major reason has been legal restrictions on delegation of Commission rule-making powers (under the Meroni doctrine – ECJ 1958]. Another, however, is that national governments and the Commission have not wished to give up powers. Moreover, they have built up an alternative system, namely 'committees' composed of national and Commission officials. There were estimated to be at least 1,500 committees by the mid-1990s, of which 410 were 'comitology committees' established under secondary legislation to undertake a variety of advisory, managerial and rule-making functions in its application (Wessels 1998; Vos 1997). Most EC regulation takes place through EC legislation that is applied by member states, either because it is directly effective or, more often, via transposition into domestic law. The Commission participates in passing secondary legislation and then oversees its implementation by national authorities; the main exception concerns competition policy, part of which it also enforces. Therefore national officials are intimately involved in passing most EC regulatory legislation, in advising, managing and making detailed rules through committees, and then in implementing it.

The pressures for EC regulatory expansion

Several related factors have driven the expansion of EC regulatory activity, which can be grouped under six headings: the role of the Commission; the ECJ and the EC's legal framework; decisions by national governments; national regulatory inadequacies; interest groups and increased transnational trade; the dynamics of EC policy-making. Assessing the balance of importance among these factors, and especially the weight of supranational actors (the Commission and ECJ), transnational trade and decisions by national governments, relates closely to general debates on European integration – particularly those between intergovernmentalism and neo-functionalism (cf. Sandholtz and Stone Sweet 1998; Moravcsik 1993). The relative importance of the different factors have also varied from one policy domain to another, reflecting many factors, such as differences in Commission powers and resources, ECJ case law, Treaty Articles, the position of national governments, exposure to transnational trade, interests and the extent of domestic regulatory inadequacies.

Commission activism

The Commission has been a central actor in EC regulatory expansion, putting forward new ideas, pressing for action and proposing specific measures. At times, it has launched headline-catching ambitious initiatives; the '1992 programme' for the internal market was the most prominent example. More generally, however, it has taken a less public but perhaps more effective strategy involving incremental steps and persistence even in the face of inertia and opposition by member states. The Commission has tended to follow a long process of garnering support before acting – for example, holding conferences and workshops with experts and interested groups, issuing Green Papers, commissioning studies and seeking to accommodate different points of view. It has then made specific legislative proposals and been able to offer a direction for regulation, with opponents left facing considerable momentum and a well-developed agenda. Thus, for example, in telecommunications, the Commission made very limited proposals in the period 1979–84, which were barely recognised by the Council (it merely passed non-binding Recommendations a few years later), then issued a Green Paper (Commission 1987) that attracted wide support, followed by proposals for limited reforms that led to directives in the late 1980s and early 1990s; only in the mid-1990s did the Commission turn to liberalising the entire telecommunications sector (Thatcher 2001). Merger control also illustrates Commission patience and persistence: discussion of empowering the Commission to vet large cross-border mergers began in 1973, and eventually led to the 1989 Merger Regulation which covered notification and approval of mergers (Cini and McGowan 1998).

Similar stories of the Commission continuing its efforts until circumstances were propitious can be told in many other fields, such as the environment, occupational safety, social policy or gender discrimination (cf. Eichener 1997; Richardson 1994; Wendon 1998; Mazey 1995).

The Commission has been able to utilise its legal monopoly over secondary legislative proposals, together with great influence as an 'agenda-setter' at the centre of many European networks (Peterson 1997; cf. Peters 1994). Within the Commission, different Directorates-General (DGs) compete with each other for prestige and territory, creating further pressures for action; for example, in the late 1980s, DG IV (the competition Directorate) was spurred into activity as its rival, DG III (at that time, both industry and internal market) used the 1992 Programme to expand its role. Perhaps most important of all, the Commission has been able to wait, taking time to place new ideas of increased EC regulation in the European policy space, testing out the balance of forces, gradually creating a climate of opinion and coalition supportive of its ideas, refining those ideas to match the balance of forces and, finally, making proposals at suitable times, or simply repeating them until accepted.

Yet the Commission has not been able to expand EC regulation on its own. Rather, it has also needed the support or at least acquiescence of other actors, particularly the ECJ and member states.

The EC legal framework and the ECJ

The EC's legal framework provides considerable incentives for regulatory activity, rather than distribution or redistribution. Most EC powers under the Treaties are to make rules rather than impose taxes or spend monies. The ECJ's decisions that directives could be directly effective also made passing such secondary legislation an attractive and relatively easy method of EC action, especially in combination with the doctrine of the supremacy of EC law. Moreover, the ECJ has frequently supported the expansion of EC competencies and regulation, taking a broad view of the scope of EC powers and legislation. Thus, for example, the ECJ has offered wide interpretations of equal payment legislation in a series of cases under Article 119 (equal pay for equal work), and other directives on equal pay for work of equal value (Directive 75/119), equal treatment in employment (Directive 76/207) and equal treatment in social security matters (Directive 97/7) (Stone Sweet and Caporaso 1998: 121–7; cf. Mazey 1995). The Court took a broad view of payment and discrimination, so that it interpreted Article 119 to mean equal pay for work of equal value, found that discrimination could be indirect and included pensions and retirement ages, even though these had been excluded from the directives. It has played a key role in the expansion of many other areas of EC regulation, from competition policy to the environment (cf. Stone Sweet and Caparoso 1998; Weiler 1991; Bulmer 1998; Gerber 1994; Cichowski 1998).

ECJ rulings have not only strengthened EC regulatory capacities, but also created incentives for secondary legislation. The best-known example is the Cassis de Dijon case (ECJ 1979): the ECJ ruled that goods legally produced in one member state, according to its rules and regulations, could be sold in other member states. 'In the absence of common rules', it was for individual member states to set their own rules, but other member states could not impose national restrictions that hindered trade (being caught by Article 30) except under limited circumstances (set out in Article 36, including, for instance, public morality, public policy or health and safety). A similar case occurred in merger control.

Since 1973, the Commission had been pressing for a merger regulation that would allow it to vet mergers between companies; member states failed to pass the regulation. However, ECJ rulings, notably in the Philip Morris case (ECJ 1987), that Article 81[85](1), which prohibits anti-competitive agreements, applied to mergers and takeovers, spurred national governments to act.

Such rulings gave member states good reasons to pass EC secondary legislation, in order to avoid uncertainty and also to play a part in the detail of regulation rather than merely following judicial decisions (cf. Bulmer 1998). The jurisprudence of the Dassonville and Cassis cases produced great impetus for legislation to set standards, since otherwise member states would have to accept the standards of other member states, over which they had no control, and/or justify restrictions in a possible flood of court cases, causing uncertainty and damage to trade. They were followed by the internal market programme and the 'new approach' to harmonisation and standardisation. In similar fashion, the Philip Morris case was rapidly followed by the 1989 Merger Regulation (Council 1990) that required mergers over certain thresholds to be vetted in advance by the Commission (Cini and McGowan 1998).

National governments

National governments have accepted increased EC regulation and, indeed, have sometimes embraced it, applying considerable political will to do so. They have provided increasingly wide regulatory powers to the EC under successive Treaties, extending the explicit legal ambit of EC activities. When faced with insistent opposition from a small minority (often Britain), they have found ways to circumvent it – for example, through the Social Protocol to the Maastricht Treaty signed by all member states except Britain. Moreover, they have made passing secondary regulatory legislation easier by extending qualified majority voting and restricting the requirement of unanimity in the Council of Ministers, in the Single European Act and later Treaties; individual member states have found themselves obliged to compromise and trade.

National governments have also accepted initiatives at the EC level to introduce regulation into new fields. Even as early as 1962, they passed Regulation 17 (Council 1962), whereby the Commission implemented competition law, including acting against anti-competitive agreements and abuse of a dominant position and granting exemptions under Article 81 [85](3). Later, they welcomed the 1992 programme and accepted EC Directives for environmental protection in the 1970s and 1980s. Even in an area such as social policy, apparently far removed from ending barriers to trade, they accepted EC regulatory action (Rhodes 1995). At times, member states have even used broad Articles to extend the EC's regulatory activities. In particular, Article 308 [235] operated as a 'catch-all' provision, as it allowed the EC action that is necessary to attain EC objectives but for which powers were not provided for explicitly in the Treaty; it was used to initiate EC regulation in several fields, including social security for migrants, the environment, and equal treatment in employment. Later on, explicit Treaty Articles followed, in effect ratifying the EC's entry into new areas.

There have been many reasons for which national governments have accepted or welcomed increased EC regulation – gains from trade, the desire for European integration, adaptation to transnational pressures, 'passing the buck' for regulatory decisions that faced powerful domestic opposition, to name but a few factors. A general analysis is that they were able to engage in a 'two-level game' (Putnam 1988; Evans *et al.* 1993) whereby they could pursue their domestic interests at the EC level. Of particular note for regulation, however, is that member states were able to maintain continuing participation in the detailed development of EC regulation, notably through regulatory and other committees (Vos 1997).

Nevertheless, acceptance of increased EC regulation by national governments has not been entirely voluntary or unpressured. The context of regulation has altered: in addition to EC institutions (the Commission and ECJ), governments have been faced with increasing inadequacies of purely national regulation and pressures by interest groups for regulatory reform.

National regulatory inadequacies

National policy-makers have turned to EC regulation when faced with difficulties in domestic regulatory arrangements. Such difficulties have arisen from two sources: greater interdependence among EC member states; and lack of credibility and effectiveness of existing institutions. The EC has offered a mechanism to establish rules that member states can accept more easily in the knowledge that other member states are placed under the same rules, making cheating and gaining regulatory advantages more difficult. It has also allowed delegation of powers away from inadequate national regulators. In both cases, EC regulation can offer benefits that are unavailable from purely domestic regulation.

International prisoners' dilemmas are one example of the pressures to engage in supranational regulation (Gaitsos and Seabright 1989). These may arise from 'regulatory externalities' in which the decisions of national regulators have effects on other EC member states; the clearest example is pollution, where discharges in one country affect other countries (for example, waste in the North Sea or air pollution in border areas). The benefits of regulatory decisions in one member state (for instance, higher pollution standards) may be negated by those in another, leaving the first with higher costs. National regulators may also engage in strategic behaviour, whereby some or all of the costs of their decisions are borne by other nations, yet co-operation would provide benefits for all; one example is that member states compete in increasing state subsidies to non-viable firms, negating their effects and using resources that could be better used for other purposes. In theory, national regulators could co-operate to capture potential gains from co-ordinated action, but in practice, co-operation faces information and transaction costs, arising, for example, from cheating, enforcement, discretion, differing cultures and organisational barriers to trading national gains and losses across policy fields (cf. Majone 1996: ch. 4). EC regulation allows co-operation and co-ordination to capture externalities – for example by setting common rules for state aid, pollution or standards – and by acting as a credible supranational arbitrator and enforcer.

The EC may also have greater credibility than national regulators, lowering the costs of regulation (for example, enforcement costs) and increasing benefits (Majone 2000). This is particularly true of domains with large, powerful domestic interests and/or in member states with poor records of regulatory enforcement (such as Italy or Greece). Hence, for example, the EC may be better placed to regulate the anti-competitive behaviour or pollution discharges of large firms than domestic regulators, who face powerful political pressures and may be 'captured' by particular interests; monetary regulation offers another example, since the ECB may have greater anti-inflation credibility than national central banks in states such as Italy, offering better inflation expectations and allowing lower interest rates for a given inflation outcome.

Interest groups and transnational trade

Interest groups such as firms, trade unions and pressure groups in areas such as the environment or gender equality have sought increased EC regulation. They have done so at the EC level, especially as the Brussels bureaucracy is remarkably permeable and open to lobbying (Mazey and Richardson 1993), and also at the national level. Frequently such activity has been linked to the growth of transnational trade, which has provided important incentives for EC integration (cf. Sandholtz and Stone Sweet 1998).

Internationalising firms (sometimes in conjunction with national associations and governments) have urged EC action to open up closed domestic markets and to establish a single set of predictable rules across the EC (Coen 1998). Thus, for example, companies such as BT and large City institutions, supported by the supposedly 'Euro-sceptical' British governments of the 1980s and 1990s, urged EC measures to liberalise areas such as financial services, airlines or telecommunications (cf. Hayward 1995). Conversely, firms facing 'dumping' or 'unfairly' subsidised foreign competitors (industries such as consumer electronics, steel or coal) have sought EC protection. Extra-European influences can also play their role – the development of rival standards, the development of large foreign markets that offer rival suppliers economies of scale or non-EC regulatory pressures. In response, European firms and policy-makers have turned to EC regulation to create Europe-wide standards and markets and to represent European interests in trade negotiations and battles, in areas such as High Definition Television and food safety standards. Domestic interest groups also seek EC regulation when frustrated by domestic politics – thus, when faced with years of hostile Conservative governments in the 1980s and 1990s, British trade unions discovered the virtues of Brussels in seeking increased worker rights.

The dynamics of EC policy-making

Dynamic patterns of interaction between actors, especially national governments and the Commission, have fuelled EC regulatory expansion. Member states are frequently in competition with each other: they seek to 'export' their regulatory model to the EC level, as this provides domestic companies with competitive advantages and requires little national adaptation. In the EC, there are often important first-mover advantages, notably in defining problems and setting agendas (Héritier 1996; Peters 1994). At the same time, the Commission plays a central role as a gatekeeper, due to its position at the centre of many European networks and its monopoly over legislative proposals. Member states therefore have an incentive to act quickly and offer nationally advantageous ideas for EC regulation to the Commission, before other countries enter the field and offer their own agendas and suggestions. The Commission is unlikely to accept proposals that reduce its powers and competencies. The result is a dynamic towards increased EC regulation, based on member states suggesting EC action. Examples can be found in many policy areas, from pollution control to telecommunications or electricity, as national policy-makers vie for the ear of the Commission and influence over EC regulatory development.

The interaction between negative and positive integration offers another dynamic that sustains EC regulatory growth. Attempts to end non-tariff barriers creates strong forces for EC re-regulation, since national standards and norms can and often do operate as non-tariff barriers. Moreover, they raise the problem of standards: if no EC standards are set and if member states are obliged to allow entry of products regardless of domestic standards, there are dangers of 'races to the bottom', as firms in EC countries with lower and less costly standards enjoy competitive advantages leading to the progressive reduction of standards (Dehousse 1992). Moreover, as markets are opened up, firms seek certainty about standards in order to plan ahead and compete effectively. Hence the internal market and liberalisation of markets such as telecommunications have seen both the removal of non-tariff barriers to trade and the development of EC regulatory standards. A key change came in standard-setting in the mid-1980s. As part of the dynamic between negative and positive integration, the EC altered its approach to standard-setting. Until then, the EC had attempted to issue detailed Community-wide standards. This largely failed, as it required consensus and desire by member states. In the mid-1980s, following the Cassis de Dijon judgement and as part of the internal market programme, the Community therefore turned to its 'new approach': harmonisation would be limited to certain 'essential requirements', mostly concerning health and safety; there would be mutual recognition of national standards; EC standards would be established, notably by using private standard-setting organisations (e.g. the European Telecommunications Standards Institute), which would be presumed to meet the 'essential requirements', but would be voluntary, since suppliers could adopt any standards that fulfilled the essential requirements (Commission 1985; Pelkmans 1987). The 'new approach' made standard-setting easier and allowed the EC to gradually expand its re-regulatory roles.

Limits on EC regulation

In analysing EC regulation, it is too easy to lose sight of the real limits on its growth and significance: increased activity is only one indicator of importance, and the expansion of EC regulation must be analysed in the context of its impact on member states. Closer examination reveals several factors that constrain the EC.

Veto points and the power of member states

There are many 'veto points' in the EC's decision-making processes that allow key actors, particularly member states, to block, hinder or delay EC regulation. Treaty amendments to provide the EC with new powers are slow and require approval by all member states. Passing secondary legislation, the key means of EC regulation, is now mostly covered by the co-decision procedure that gives powers to three actors (the Commission, Council and European Parliament), each with its own interests. The comitology process, a central method of moving from general principles and aims to specific EC requirements, involves national officials (cf. Vos 1997). The Commission itself is a collegial body, headed by the appointees of national governments (although the Amsterdam Treaty slightly strengthens the President). Regulatory decisions, including 'technical' ones in a highly juridicised environment such as the application of competition policy, must be approved by the College of Commissioners, leading to intense and often highly politicised battles (McGowan and Cini 1999). Individual Commissioners must therefore build alliances within the College and must watch carefully the reactions of national governments.

The resources of the Commission

Although the scope of EC regulation and the amount of legislation have expanded, the Commission remains a small organisation with limited constrained material resources. It has very few staff and low expenditure, especially relative to national bureaucracies and large firms. Even DG IV, responsible for policing and sometimes enforcing competition policy, has a tiny staff (approximately 400) relative to the breadth and importance of its tasks. Yet producing regulation is frequently difficult, and highly technical. The Commission therefore has to be very selective in where to attempt to regulate. Moreover, it relies heavily on other actors for information and expertise – including national governments and regulators, firms and interest groups. National officials play a key role in the preparation of legislative proposals (including through COREPER) and then, after directives have been passed, in fleshing out 'technical' matters through the comitology system. Staffing is constantly a problem, and many officials in Brussels are in fact seconded national officials and experts.

Implementation

Closely linked to lack of Commission resources is the fact that most EC legislation is broad, and offers only a framework for decision-making within member states. Directives are only binding as to their objectives and not their means. Almost all implementation is undertaken by national regulators. The major exception is competition policy, which the Commission enforces and where only it can issue exemptions to anti-competitive agreements (Article 81[85]) and has to be notified and vet mergers over certain thresholds (under the 1989 Merger Regulation). Even here, however, the Commission has recently proposed that national authorities and courts would become responsible for all notification and exemptions (Commission 1999a).

These features provide member states with much discretion in implementing EC regulation. They also make effective enforcement by the EC difficult. There can be considerable gaps between EC rules and their operation in practice. The Commission lacks resources to pursue all member states over implementation, even if it so wished. Moreover, infringement proceedings are slow and difficult. Private litigants within member states can play a part, but legal action is frequently financially costly, damaging to relationships with national actors and unlikely to offer swift results that may be required in fast-moving markets. The result is that even within policy fields with a fairly high degree of EC regulation such as the utilities, considerable national variations continue (Coen and Thatcher 1999).

Existing national regulation and regulators

The decentralised nature of most EC regulation makes the national level very important for regulation in practice. National institutions such as public ownership or the existence and powers of independent agencies, influence decision-making (Thatcher 1999). Legally, the EC cannot require changes in ownership (under Article 295[222]). Yet ownership can affect the impact of EC regulation; for example, public ownership of commercial enterprises poses significant difficulties over matters such as distinguishing state aid and new capital injections and can create incentives for governments to favour state-owned companies. Structural regulation (ie. creating competitive market structures) is generally more effective than conduct regulation, which faces difficulties such as information asymmetries and effective sanctions. However, the EC has been unable to break up large oligopolistic or monopolistic suppliers – even in markets subject to considerable EC regulation, powerful national champions such as BT, France Télécom, Deutsche Telekom, British Airways, EdF and Lufthanser continue to enjoy dominance in domestic telecommunications, electricity or airline markets. EC structural intervention has been largely confined to occasions of takeovers and mergers, and even on these, its requirements have been limited to the disposal of limited parts of businesses (for instance, AGF–Alliance in 1998 or Total–Fina in 1999). Member states retain great freedom over the organisational features of national regulatory authorities, as EC requirements are often limited; hence, for instance, in utilities regulation EC directives typically demand that national regulatory authorities be organisationally separate from suppliers and that they must act fairly and transparently, but add little detail about decision-making procedures and processes and do not insist that they be independent of elected politicians. Thus considerable variation in national regulation remains, even when EC regulation opens up markets – seen in electricity or telecommunications (Eberlein 1999; Thatcher 1995; 1999). Finally, EC regulation meets obstacles of well-established national relationships, policies and norms that remain important, even in areas of long-standing and/or detailed EC regulation. Thus, for instance, national regulators continue to encourage and actively aid mergers and takeovers designed to keep out foreign entrants; such moves have been seen in the late 1990s in sectors such as French or Spanish banking or the distribution of licences for GSM mobile telecommunications to selected groups.

Interest groups

The EC is highly dependent on interest groups – to persuade national policy-makers to accept its regulation, for information, for expertise and for monitoring implementation and challenging non-compliance (if necessary through litigation). Its scope to regulate in the face of well-organised hostile interests is therefore limited. This holds true even in competition policy, where the Commission offers informal guidance and negotiates with firms to obtain agreements, seeking to avoid lengthy legal proceedings that will take up time and resources; thus, for example, in 1998, 539 out of 581 cases opened by DG IV under competition Treaty Articles were closed through its 'informal procedures' (Commission 1998; cf. Wilks and McGowan 1996; McGowan and Cini 1999).

International regulation

The 1990s have seen the expansion of international regulation, notably the GATT and WTO. International trade negotiations may have strengthened EC regulation, as the Commission frequently represented the EC, as member states were obliged to co-operate with it due to shared competencies and as the Community sought to maximise its influence by establishing common positions. However, EC regulation is now subject to the WTO and decisions that affect international trade are liable to challenge under WTO rules. As a result, much of EC regulation, from food health and safety rules to product standards or EC content requirements, is open to attack; this process has already begun, often led by US multinationals and public officials, seen recently in disputes over genetically modified food.

The legitimacy of EC regulation

EC regulation suffers from significant problems of legitimacy. Under the first pillar of the EU, the EC has supranational competencies, and hence can impose regulation on unwilling member states. Yet passing legislation is shared between the Commission, the Council of Ministers and the European Parliament, with the ECJ playing a crucial role. The constitutional basis of the EC is therefore hybrid between elected (directly or indirectly) and non-majoritarian bodies. The use of non-majoritarian institutions is not fatal for legitimacy, which can be derived from other sources, such as 'fair' and open procedures, multiple controls, expertise, independence from 'interests' (including elected ones) and efficiency (cf. Majone 1999; 2000; Héritier 1999; Horeth 1999). However, these mechanisms may hinder decision-making. Moreover, EC decision-making procedures appear opaque – for example, debates within the Council and the Commission are not published, there is no overall code of conduct on how regulatory decisions should be made and the comitology system is closed and largely private. Lines of accountability are multiple and unclear, especially after the strengthening of the European Parliament's powers under the Maastricht and Amsterdam Treaties – the Commission answers to both it and the Council. Due to its limited resources and the power of national interests at all stages of regulation, the Commission's expertise, effectiveness and independence are open to severe questioning. Such problems rise rapidly to the surface whenever controversial decisions are taken that involve powerful national interests, as evidenced in the BSE crisis or regulation of state aids.

Reform of EC regulation

The problems and limits of EC regulation have led to attempts at reform, although thus far, changes have been limited. There has been discussion of establishing independent EC regulatory agencies that would be responsible for leading implementation and enforcement – for example, a European cartel office and a European telecommunications regulator; these could be entirely free-standing 'federal' bodies or composed of national regulators. Such ideas have found support, notably among large companies; they appear to offer advantages in terms of greater clarity, procedural legitimacy and accountability (Coen and Doyle 1999; Majone 2000). Yet proposals have met opposition and have not been implemented. One reason is the legal doctrine of Meroni, which limits delegation of Commission powers to non-Commission bodies, thus requiring Treaty amendments. More formidable obstacles have emerged from within the Commission, anxious about loss of powers, and from national governments who fear losing the influence they enjoy over the Commission, and via national implementation of EC regulation. Insofar as new regulatory bodies have been established, such as the European environment agency or the European agency for the evaluation of medical products, the Commission has only delegated executive functions, but has kept oversight and rule-making powers.

The alternative path has been greater co-ordination of national regulators. The process has begun, through regular meetings of national regulators, often aided by the Commission, and 'advisory' documents issued by the Commission. Greater co-ordination would involve formalising such arrangements in a 'network model' of European regulation (Coen and Doyle 1999). Improved implementation would result from peer pressure, consensus-building and exchange of information. Hence, for instance, current Commission proposals in telecommunications involve setting up a formal committee of member states and the Commission, and separately, a High Level Communication group of national regulatory authorities, with the Commission acting as secretariat (Commission 1999b). A 'network' model would not openly reduce the powers of member states, nor require Treaty amendments; nevertheless, it would fail to deal with problems of transparency and clarity of allocation of responsibilities.

A third path would be to reduce the enforcement role of the Commission and devolve more responsibilities (and rights) to regulators, interested parties and the courts in member states. The Commission's few implementation powers would be ended – for example, in competition policy (Commission 1999a). If national regulators failed to implement and enforce EC regulation correctly, interested parties could instigate litigation in national courts, with the ECJ as ultimate guardian of the supremacy of Community law. The Commission would propose legislation and provide information, aiding parties to decide whether EC regulation was being correctly followed. The system would be an extension of the current devolved approach to regulation, would place costs of enforcement on private parties who often have appropriate resources and would follow the logic of subsidiarity (incorporated in the Maastricht Treaty). Nonetheless, it would place heavy reliance on litigation and national courts, with dangers of delay, variations across member states and collusion between regulatees and national regulators.

The impacts of EC regulation

Regulatory development has been occurring at both the EC and national levels, together with the WTO in more recent years. Hence assessing the impacts of EC regulation within member states is far from easy. The impacts of EC have varied, both from one sector to another and among member states. At one extreme, in certain sectors there has been little EC regulation, and/or EC measures had already been introduced by some member states so that the EC was following rather than leading; in addition, EC rules may not have been implemented in practice, their impact being more apparent than real. At the other extreme, EC regulation has caused major repercussions in markets, institutions and strategies in member states, with claims of a move towards a 'European regulatory state' (McGowan and Wallace 1996). Moreover, the EC has only been one force for regulatory change. Nonetheless, certain impacts of EC regulation can be sketched.

Domestic markets have been increasingly liberalised and opened to competition. The EC has contributed to ending tariff and non-tariff barriers. It has also aided the ending of legal monopolies lying at the heart of states, such as telecommunications, energy and railways. Progress towards competitive markets has involved a two-stage process: altering the rules governing competition; ensuring effective competition in practice. Change has been uneven and often slow, but EC requirements have offered momentum, particularly for the first stage.

Internationalisation of European national markets – both suppliers and purchasers – has accompanied liberalisation. Foreign suppliers (European and subsidiaries of non-European firms) have entered previously closed national markets or expanded their market shares, in sectors ranging from the utilities or financial services to manufactured goods. Firms, especially large ones, have internationalised through cross-border mergers and takeovers that have often been aimed at becoming European-wide suppliers – from banking and insurance mergers to cars and pharmaceuticals. EC regulation is not solely responsible for internationalisation, but it has encouraged it, both directly by opening up markets, and indirectly by influencing expectations that firms need to expand across national borders in Europe.

Publicly owned enterprises have found themselves under increased pressure, in part because of EC regulation (cf. Hayward 1995). They have lost many of their legal monopolies. Coverage of losses by national governments has been subject to scrutiny as state aid by the Commission. The results have been lengthy and embarrassing investigations (eg. Air France) or even the Commission requiring privatisation as the counterpart of state aid (seen in negotiations over the Italian state holding IRI in the early 1990s or the sale of Crédit Lyonnais). National governments have been able to use the EC to justify privatisations sought for other objectives (the sale of Telecom Italia or part of France Télécom offer vivid illustrations – Thatcher 1995; 1999); even those favouring public ownership, such as the Jospin government after 1997, have argued that, 'reluctantly', they needed to privatise in order to meet EC pressures.

The EC has contributed to challenging well-established regulatory relationships within member states. Closed and cosy relationships between 'national champions', governments and other actors, such as trade unions, have been disturbed. EC regulation has provided new entrants with weapons to attack existing arrangements; one instructive example is offered in Italy, where a new entrant, Omnitel, used EC law and the support of the Commission to claw back a 750 billion lire levy imposed on it (but not on Telecom Italia) for a mobile telecommunications licence. The EC has also contributed to the increasing juridification of regulation. Its legal requirements have made regulation more technical and legal; they have limited the room for manoeuvre for national policy-makers. Matters such as licensing, tariffs, takeovers and public procurement, which were previously settled in private negotiations among selected participants, have become more open, more amenable to challenge, and involve new actors, including competing foreign and domestic firms.

Conclusion

EC regulation has grown, expanding from removal of tariffs to dealing with non-tariff barriers and introducing Community re-regulatory standards and rules. Its development has been the product of the interaction between the Commission, ECJ, national governments and officials, and interest groups, within an institutional framework that has increasingly aided the broadening of EC activity. At the same time, EC regulation faces significant constraints and limits, especially in implementation and enforcement. Its development has led to a multi-tiered regulatory system in Europe, with regulation being produced and/or implemented at several levels – EC, national and international. The outcomes of the regulatory system therefore involve complex interactions among the different levels.

Acknowledgement

The author gratefully acknowledges ESRC grant L216252007 within the Future Governance Programme and also the LSE Centre for the Analysis of Risk and Regulation.

Note

1   References are to the European Community, since almost all regulation discussed here falls under the EC pillar of the EU.

References

Baldwin, R. and Cave, M. (1999) *Understanding Regulation*, Oxford: Oxford University Press.
Bulmer, S. J. (1998) 'New Institutionalism and the Governance of the Single European Market', *Journal of European Public Policy* 5/3: 365–86.
Cichowski, R. (1998) 'Integrating the Environment: The European Court and the Construction of Supranational Policy', *Journal of European Public Policy* 5/3: 387–405.
Cini, M. and McGowan, L. (1998) *Competition Policy in the European Union*, London: Macmillan.
Coen, D. (1998) 'The European Business Interest and the Nation State: Large-Firm Lobbying in the European Union and Member States', *Journal of Public Policy* 18/1: 75–100.
Coen, D. and Doyle, C. (2000) 'Designing Economic Regulatory Institutions for European Network Industries', *Current Politics and Economics of Europe* 6/4: 83–106.
Coen, D. and Thatcher, M. (2000) *Regulating European Utilities*, special issue, *Current Politics and Economics of Europe* 9/4.
Commission of the European Communities (1985) *Completing the Internal Market: White Paper from the Commission to the European Council*, Luxemburg: Office for Official Publications of the European Communities.
Commission of the European Communities (1987) *Towards a Dynamic European Economy: Green Paper on the Development of the Common Market for Telecommunications Services and Equipment* (COM (87) 290), Brussels: Commission of the European Communities.
Commission of the European Communities (1998) *Annual Report on Competition Policy*, Brussels: Commission of the European Communities.
Commission of the European Communities (1999a) *White Paper on Modernization of the Rules Implementing Articles 85 and 86* (COM (99) (87)), Brussels: Commission of the European Communities.
Commission of the European Communities (1999b) *The 1999 Communications Review: Towards a New Framework for Electronic Communications Infrastructure and Associated Services*, Brussels: Commission of the European Communities.
Council of the European Communities (1962) *Council Regulation 17/62*, 1962 O.J. 204.
Council of the European Communities (1990) *Council Regulation 4064/89*, 1990 O.J. L257 14 (corrected version of 1989 O.J. L395 1).
Dehousse, R. (1992) 'Integration v. Regulation? On the Dynamics of Regulation in the European Community', *Journal of Common Market Studies* 30/4: 383–402.
Dehousse, R. (1997) 'Regulation by Networks in the European Community: The Role of European Agencies', *Journal of European Public Policy* 4/2: 246–61.
Eberlein, B. (2000) 'Configurations of Economic Regulation in the European Union: The Case of Electricity in Comparative Perspective', *Current Politics and Economics of Europe*, 9/4: 31–51.
ECJ (1958) Case 9/56, Meroni v. High Authority, [1958] ECR 133.
ECJ (1974) Case 8/74, Procureur du Roi v. Dassonville [1974] ECR 837.
ECJ (1979) Case 120/78, Rewe [1979] ECR 649. [Cassis de Dijon].
ECJ (1987) Case 156/84 [1987] ECR 4487.
ECJ (1991) Case 202/88 French Republic v. Commission [1991] ECR I-1223.
ECJ (1992) Joined Cases C-271/90, C-281/90 and C-289/90 Spain, France, Belgium and Italy v. Commission [1992] ECR I-5833.
Eichener, V. (1997) 'Effective European Problem-Solving: Lessons from the Regulation of Occupational Safety and Environmental Protection', *Journal of European Public Policy* 4/4: 591–608.
Evans, P., Jacobson, H. and Putnam, R. (eds) (1993) *Double-Edged Diplomacy: International Bargaining and Domestic Politics*, Berkeley, CA: University of California Press.
Fligstein, N. and McNichol, J. (1998) 'The Institutional Terrain of the European Union', in W. Sandholtz and A. Stone Sweet (eds), *European Integration and Supranational Governance*, Oxford: Oxford University Press.
Gaitsos, K. and Seabright, P. (1989) 'Regulation in the European Community', *Oxford Review of Economic Policy* 5/2: 37–60.
Gerber, D. J. (1994) 'The Transformation of European Community Competition Law?', *Harvard International Law Review* 35/1: 97–147.
Hayward, J. E. S. (ed.) (1995) *Industrial Enterprise and European Integration*, Oxford: Oxford University Press.

Héritier, A. (1996) 'The Accommodation of Diversity in European Policy Making and its Outcomes: Regulatory Policy as a Patchwork', *Journal of European Public Policy* 3/2: 149–67.

Héritier, A. (1999) 'Elements of Democratic Legitimation in Europe: An Alternative Perspective', *Journal of European Public Policy* 6/2: 269–82.

Horeth, M. (1999) 'No Way Out for the Beast? The Unsolved Legitimacy Problem of European Governance', *Journal of European Public Policy* 6/2: 249–68.

Kassim, H. and Menon, A. (eds) (1996) *European Industrial Policy*, London: Routledge.

Kreher, A. (1997) 'Agencies in the European Community: A Step towards Administrative Integration in Europe', *Journal of European Public Policy* 4/2: 225–45.

McGowan, F. and Wallace, H. (1996) 'Towards a European Regulatory State', *Journal of European Public Policy* 3/4: 560–76.

McGowan, L. and Cini, M. (1999) 'Discretion and Politization in EU Competition Policy: The Case of Merger Control', *Governance* 12/2: 175–200.

Majone, G. (ed.) (1996) *Regulating Europe*, London: Routledge.

Majone, G. (1999) 'The Regulatory State and Its Legitimacy Problems', *West European Politics* 22/1: 1–24.

Majone, G. (2000) 'The Credibility Crisis of Community Regulation', *Journal of Common Market Studies* 38/2: 273–302.

Mazey, S. (1995) 'The Development of EU Equality Policies: Bureaucratic Expansion on behalf of Women', *Public Administration* 73/4: 591–609.

Mazey, S. and Richardson, J. (eds) (1993) *Lobbying in the European Community*, Oxford: Oxford University Press.

Mitnick, B. (1980) *The Political Economy of Regulation*, New York: Columbia University Press.

Moravcsik, A. (1993) 'Preferences and Power in the European Community: A Liberal Intergovernmentalist Approach', *Journal of Common Market Studies* 31/4: 473–524.

Ogus, A. I. (1994) *Regulation: Legal Form and Economic Theory*, Oxford: Clarendon.

Pelkmans, J. (1987) 'The New Approach to Technical Harmonisation and Standardisation', *Journal of Common Market Studies* 25/3: 249–69.

Peters, B. G. (1994) 'Agenda-Setting in the European Community', *Journal of European Public Policy* 1/1: 9–26.

Peterson, J. (1997) 'States, Societies and the European Union', *West European Politics* 20/4: 1–23.

Putnam, R. D. (1988) 'Diplomacy and Domestic Politics: The Logic of Two-Level Games', *International Organisation* 42/3: 427–60.

Rhodes, M. (1995) 'A Regulatory Conundrum: Industrial Relations and the Social Dimension', in S. Liebfried and P. Pierson (eds), *European Social Policy*, Washington: Brookings Institution.

Richardson, J. (1994) 'EU Water Policy: Uncertain Agendas, Shifting Networks and Complex Coalitions', *Environmental Politics* 3/4: 139–67.

Sandholtz, W. and Stone Sweet, A. (eds) (1998) *European Integration and Supranational Governance*, Oxford: Oxford University Press.

Scharpf, F. W. (1997) *Games Real Actors Play*, Boulder, CO: Westview Press.

Schmidt, S. K. (1997) 'Sterile Debates and Dubious Generalisations: European Integration Theory Tested by Telecommunications and Electricity', *Journal of Public Policy* 16/3: 233–71.

Selznick, P. (1985) 'Focusing Organizational Research on Regulation', in R. Noll (ed.), *Regulatory Policy and the Social Sciences*, Berkeley, CA: University of California Press.

Stone Sweet, A. and Caporaso, J. A. (1998) 'From Free Trade to Supranational Polity: The European Court and Integration', in W. Sandholtz and A. Stone Sweet (eds), *European Integration and Supranational Governance*, Oxford: Oxford University Press.

Stravridis, E., Mossialos, E., Morgan, R. and Machin, H. (eds) (1997) *New Challenges to the European Union*, Aldershot: Dartmouth.

Thatcher, M. (1995) 'Regulatory Reform and Internationalization in Telecommunications', in J. E. S. Hayward (ed.), *Industrial Enterprise and European Integration*, Oxford: Oxford University Press.

Thatcher, M. (1999) *The Politics of Telecommunications*, Oxford: Oxford University Press.

Thatcher, M. (2001) 'The Commission and National Governments as Partners: EC Regulatory Expansion in Telecommunications 1979–2000', *Journal of European Public Policy* (forthcoming)

Vos, E. (1997) 'The Rise of Committees', *European Law Journal* 3/3: 210–29.

Weiler, J. (1991) 'The Transformation of Europe', *Yale Law Journal* 100: 2403-83.

Wendon, B. (1998) 'The Commission as Image-Venue Entrepreneur in EU Social Policy', *Journal of European Public Policy* 5/2: 339–53.

Wessels, W. (1998) 'Comitology: Fusion in Action: Politico-Administrative Trends in the EU System', *Journal of European Public Policy* 5/2: 209–34.

Wilks, S. (1996) 'Regulatory Compliance and Capitalist Diversity in Europe', *Journal of European Public Policy* 3/4: 536–59.

Wilks, S. and McGowan, L. (1996) 'Competition Policy in the European Union', in B. Doern and S. Wilks (eds), *Comparative Competition Policy: National Institutions in a Global Market*, Oxford: Oxford University Press.

Chapter 16

European Monetary Union

Developments, implications and prospects

Valerio Lintner

Introduction

The establishment of a full monetary union among twelve or more EU states in 2002 represents an historical development of real significance, perhaps a key turning point in European economic and political development. The nation-states that emerged from the Second World War as discrete economic and political entities, the 'Europe of the nations', are on the very verge of transferring important aspects of their systems of economic (and perhaps eventually political) governance to the supranational European level. Apart from the implications that this is having and will continue to have on the very fundamental issue of macroeconomic management, it will also further accelerate the development of a truly integrated and interdependent economy within the European economic space, which the EU has defined.

But why has this occurred, what are the underlying implications of EMU, and have we chosen an appropriate model on which to base the European monetary union? These are the questions that this chapter seeks to address. Thus we begin the chapter by outlining the rationale for EMU as well as its potential costs from a theoretical perspective. In the light of this we then examine succinctly the main phases in the development of monetary integration in the EC and the EU, concentrating naturally on the Maastricht model and how it developed into what we have now. We then briefly examine the extent to which this is appropriate to the needs of the EU and its citizens at the beginning of the new century, and we offer a few suggestions for development in the future.

Like most developments in European integration, EMU has both an economic and a political dimension. The view taken here is that an understanding of both of these dimensions is essential to any really fruitful analysis of the topic. Reality is, after all, essentially interdisciplinary. In this chapter we focus, however, on the economic, since it is in this field that the implications of EMU are most important, in the short run if not in the long run. Similarly the study of EMU is rooted in positive analysis, but it also involves a normative element: the type of economy and society we want to develop in Europe will to an extent determine the nature of the EMU we favour, and indeed whether we favour EMU in Europe at all.

The implications of EMU

Monetary union is of course most obviously associated with the replacement of national currencies with a single currency, and this is the model that has been adopted by the EU. However, a monetary union could in principle take a number of forms, including the introduction of a parallel currency alongside national currencies, or even a system of irrevocably fixed exchange rates for national currencies supplemented by total convertibility of these currencies.[1] The currency would realistically also have to operate within the confines of a reasonably complete single market. The really significant aspect of a monetary union, however, is that it has far-reaching implications for the conduct of economic policy in general, and monetary and fiscal policies in particular, since it involves these being determined and conducted to a large extent at the supranational level. The necessity for this to happen arises from the fact that a monetary union would be very problematic if not impossible at an acceptable economic and political cost without a considerable degree of economic convergence among EU states. This in turn is impossible to achieve without a commensurate amount of joint policy-making and implementation. If one does not have an appropriate level of convergence, then it is likely that the union will lead to the better-off areas benefiting at the expense of poorer participants. Broadly speaking, more competitive countries will tend to attract economic activity and employment at the expense of areas that are less well off. Without a monetary union, countries might hope to bridge competitiveness gaps by devaluation, since this reduces the price of exports in foreign markets and increases the price of imports in domestic markets. In the absence of different currencies, there can of course be no devaluation. Without devaluation, differences in competitiveness must be balanced either by falls in living standards, if labour markets are flexible and permit wages to fall in response to a decline in the demand for labour, or by unemployment. This may be supplemented, to the extent that labour is mobile, by migration as workers follow the geographical distribution of jobs, and a decline in the level of economic activity and thus in material prosperity in uncompetitive regions and countries.[2] All in all the costs of the monetary union will tend to fall disproportionately on weaker areas in such a scenario.[3]

It is important to note that there are different definitions of what should constitute convergence. As we shall see, the Maastricht model of EMU adopted a definition which is based almost exclusively on financial variables. It may be argued that this definition is an excessively narrow one, and that it would be more appropriate to include 'real' variables such as the level of employment, social variables and living standards in the definition of what constitutes convergence. The inclusion of real variables in the definition of convergence would imply different economic policy targets and would therefore significantly alter the type of policies adopted by the EU in the economic arena.

Whatever the definition of convergence one adopts, however, this will not materialise unless appropriate common policies are pursued by the participants in the monetary union. In the case of the EU this has involved centralising the conduct of monetary policy, which is now conducted by the European Central Bank (ECB) and the European System of Central Banks (ESCB). EMU will also have a huge impact on fiscal policy in EU countries. Most notably, the Stability Pact which forms part of the 'Maastricht model' of EMU entails public finances operating under constraints that are determined at the supranational level.

There are strong theoretical and practical arguments to suggest that some form of EMU, although not necessarily one based on the Maastricht model, is fundamentally desirable. EMU offers the possibility of increasing the effectiveness of economic policy-making in the context of the decreasing national control over macroeconomic policy that has resulted from globalisation, and in particular from the emergence of powerful, deregulated international capital markets. In other words, EMU represents a necessary response on the part of European nation-states to the process of globalisation. The experience of the 1992 ERM crisis, of the first Mitterrand presidency in France of 1981–83 (see below), the inability of the UK Conservative government to control the money supply in the early 1980s, and even the experience of the Labour government with the IMF in the 1970s, provide evidence of the declining macroeconomic sovereignty of individual, medium-sized nation-states. If global capitalism is increasingly out of democratic control, then EMU and the centralisation of macroeconomic policy-making that goes with it, offer the possibility at least of recapturing some of this lost control on a 'unity is strength' principle – enhancing economic sovereignty of nations through a process of pooling. The euro block unquestionably is a powerful actor on the international economic stage and affords its participants collective policy options not open to individual states. However, one question that arises in this context is whether the EU is the appropriate grouping of states for such a response to globalisation.

In addition, EMU might also offer vulnerable states the advantage of adopting some of the stability and credibility that has been enjoyed by Germany and others over recent years, thus instantly providing a credible anchor for the domestic economy. EMU also offers a number of other potential advantages mainly associated with making the common market work more effectively. EMU reduces transaction costs as well as uncertainty and risk for trade and capital movements. It will also increase the 'transparency of prices' since all values and prices will eventually be denominated in the same currency, which should make economic decisions more rational. It will in future years also afford participants the benefits, up to now predominantly enjoyed by US citizens, of possessing a major international currency. It could be argued, however, that the issue of national economic (and political) sovereignty is paramount in this context. Is EMU likely to reduce individual states' control over their own economies and economic policies, or might it have the opposite effect of increasing control over economic policy through a process of pooling? In order to ascertain this we need to discuss the extent to which the ability to conduct an independent economic policy at the national level in fact currently exists. After all, one cannot surrender what one does not possess in the first place. Needless to say this is a controversial area which throws up many issues that are not testable from a rigidly empirical point of view,[4] but there is compelling evidence of the limited economic sovereignty now available to small and medium-sized European nation-states in the contemporary scenario. The experience of Italy and the UK during the ERM crisis of September 1992 represents a particularly good case study of the limits of national sovereignty. It should be remembered that during the period between the UK's entry into the ERM in October 1990[5] and its ejection from the mechanism on 16 September 1992 there was almost complete consensus in the UK on the desirability of ERM membership: this was the central anchor of the government's economic policy, it was supported by the official opposition, the Liberal Democrat Party, the CBI and the TUC. Furthermore, the full weight of the UK government's exchange market and macroeconomic policy levers and of the additional means of intervention provided by the EU were employed to attempt to keep sterling within the ERM. In Italy the situation was very similar, ERM membership and participation in EMU being a matter of almost universal consensus. All this was to no avail in the face of the power of deregulated global capital markets. It should furthermore be noted that this crisis was not merely the result of currency speculation, as was claimed in the media at the time. The investments of the UK financial services industry alone are roughly equivalent to 100% of the country's GDP, and a mere 5% shift of these holdings out of sterling would effectively neutralise the whole of the UK's foreign exchange reserves – the front line means of intervention to support the currency. Even in the absence of speculation, prudent portfolio adjustment alone can thus affect the government's ability to control the economy and pursue its economic objectives. It is important to note that these issues of economic sovereignty fundamentally involve issues of democracy, for loss of economic sovereignty to international capital markets means that citizens are deprived of the possibility of having their choices on economic policy implemented. Capital markets are of course not democratically accountable.

On the other hand, critics of EMU have argued that participation in the project and the consequent transfer of policy-making powers to the supranational level does involve the erosion of national economic sovereignty, and does therefore involve important costs for the participants. This argument is based on a belief in the effectiveness of the residual economic powers still retained by nation-states. Other critics also point out that the proposed EMU might increase regional disparities, that it is costly to implement, and that it is certain to carry substantial risks, especially in its initial stages. For those who oppose

EMU, however, the question is essentially a political one based on a view of the desirability and effectiveness of the contemporary nation-state to deal with its own economic destiny. A balanced conclusion may be that the potential problems with EMU are likely to be outweighed by the counter arguments discussed above, and some form of monetary union in the EU is basically necessary and desirable.

The development of EMU: from Werner to Maastricht

This section seeks to trace the development of the monetary integration process up to the emergence of the Maastricht Treaty, and to discuss some of the factors that have driven the process. Many of these are equally applicable to subsequent developments. The latter point is naturally an important issue, which is also naturally a matter of some debate. A good starting point here is Dyson (1994), who has identified a number of 'structural' explanations for the development of EMU, many of which could equally be applied to the process of integration as a whole:

1   The 'global structuralist' explanation developed largely by Susan Strange (1988) and other proponents of international political economy. This emphasises the way in which EMU is a response to developments in the world economy, and in particular globalisation and the policies and actions of the USA.

2   The 'statecraft' explanation (Milward *et al.* 1993), which emphasises the need for European nation-states to be economically strong in order to preserve and enhance their own political power. Thus EMU offers the possibility for states to achieve economic outcomes which would otherwise be beyond them, acting individually.

3   The 'intergovernmental bargaining' explanation (Moravcsik 1991), which is in many ways similar to the Milward approach, but which sees monetary integration as a response to the failure of purely domestic strategies in the area.

4   The 'neo-functionalist' explanation, which is based on the concept of *spillover* (Haas 1958). This starts from the assumption that integration in one policy area has secondary effects, which then provide the rationale for development in other areas. Thus the EU's single market programme provided the impetus for EMU.

5   The 'neo-federalist' explanation (Pinder 1991), which emphasises vision and federalist ideology as the motive forces behind EMU.

6   The 'transaction costs' explanation (Williamson 1985), a purely economic approach which emphasises the way in which monetary integration reduces transaction costs and thus acts as a means of enhancing economic welfare.

7   The 'path dependency' explanation (Arthur 1988), which regards the process of European integration and of EMU as a 'self-reinforcing mechanism' which is driven by 'path dependence'. The major actors are propelled by the increasing returns provided by a chosen path, thereby locking themselves into a particular model of EMU to the exclusion of other, perhaps even superior, models. Incremental change then occurs within the chosen path.

All these structural explanations 'share a common focus on external factors that constrain actors within the EMU policy process to behave in certain ways … each reveals a different facet of European monetary integration' (Dyson 1994: 314). Dyson himself tends towards what he calls a 'dynamic process' approach, which is sensitive to the institutional setting, but which places greater stress on 'the fragile and fluid character of European monetary integration', paying more attention to the role of the individual actors involved. It will be of interest to analyse what light, if any, these various explanations may shed on the developments discussed later in this chapter.

The EU's progress towards monetary integration took place in three broad phases. Historically, monetary integration was not envisaged by the Treaty of Rome and was thus never an explicit objective of the EC. The issue first appeared on the European agenda at the Hague summit in 1969, partly as a strategy aimed at restoring stability after the political unrest in France in May 1968. The debate at the time centred on the extent to which Europe was in fact an 'optimum currency area',[6] and on the best strategy for constructing a monetary union. On the latter issue, there were two points of view, which came to be referred to as the 'economist' approach and the 'monetarist' position (nothing to do with Milton Friedman). The former, mainly supported by the Dutch and the Germans in the Schiller Plan, favoured a gradualist approach to EMU, involving the promotion of harmonisation and convergence in order to prepare the ground for the single currency. The latter, canvassed by the Commission, France and Belgium in the Barre Plan, supported a 'shock theory' approach, involving the introduction of fixed exchange rates as a *fait accompli*, leaving countries to adjust to these ex-post.

The outcome was predictably a compromise between the two proposals, in the shape of the Werner Plan of 1970, most of which was adopted by the Council of Ministers in March 1971 and which came into effect in March 1972. This provided for some efforts to harmonise economic policies, but also created the 'snake in the tunnel' system of fixed exchange rates. The 'snake' consisted of fixing the exchange rates between the ten participants (the original six plus Britain, Denmark and Ireland, who were in the process of joining the then EEC) within bands of $+-2.25\%$. The 'tunnel' involved fixing the parity of the snake currencies against the dollar and other world currencies within the 4.5% bands established in the Smithsonian Agreements of December 1971. The overall objective was a 'monetary union by 1980'. Needless to say the plan failed, collapsing in the wake of the disarray which followed the 1974 oil crisis. Fundamentally, European nation-states were unwilling to subordinate their own interests to those of European integration. Thus sterling left the fixed exchange rate system in June 1972, Italy in February 1973, France in January 1974 and again in March 1976, and EMU collapsed.

After the Werner Plan, the impetus towards monetary integration was revived in 1977 by Roy Jenkins. The EMS was agreed at the Bremen and Copenhagen Councils of 1978, and came into existence in March 1979. The EMS consisted of two features. First, the European Currency Unit (ECU), which was the potential European parallel currency and the fulcrum of the ERM. The ECU was based on a weighted basket of all the currencies involved. The second aspect of the EMS was the Exchange Rate Mechanism (ERM), which attempted to fix the exchange rates between the participating countries and between these currencies and the ECU, originally within a band of $+-2.25\%$ and $+-6\%$ for weaker currencies such as the lira and sterling. Following the sterling crisis of 1992, the bands became $+-15\%$, begging the question of whether the ERM had survived at all. There was thus a 'snake', but this time no 'tunnel', since the European currencies involved could float *vis-à-vis* the dollar, the yen and other world currencies. The mechanism for maintaining exchange rates within the system consisted of agreements for supportive central bank intervention in foreign exchange markets, a (limited) reserve pooling obligation, and a (largely unused) divergence indicator. These agreements were backed up by measures designed to promote policy convergence and were a limited redistributive mechanism.

There were few hopes for the EMS at the time of its launch, and it experienced significant instability in its early years. However, to many people's surprise it survived the storm of the early 1980s and provided the anchor for the development of the European economy in the later years of the decade. In practice, the ERM promoted exchange stability in Western Europe. There were only eleven realignments (twelve if one includes the exit of sterling and the lira in late 1992) altogether, and none at all between January 1987 and September 1992. On the other hand, currencies such as sterling, that were outside the ERM experienced considerably greater instability. The EMS also probably contributed to lower and increasingly convergent rates of inflation in Europe, although it should be noted that price stability was also facilitated by the neo-liberal consensus on economic policy during this period. Finally, the ECU became established to an extent as a private-sector currency in the course of the 1980s.

It is true that the EMS suffered from the UK's refusal to join the ERM (although sterling was always part of the ECU basket) until 'the time was right' in October 1990, and (arguably) by excessive reliance on German leadership. Nevertheless, it paved the way for what was to follow, for the very success of the EMS provided the stimulus in the late 1980s for the debate on how the system should develop. The Commission's response to this debate was to set up the Delors Committee, which produced the Delors Report in April 1989, calling for a full monetary union to be set up in three stages. This Report spawned two Intergovernmental Conferences (IGCs), one of which was on the subject of political union, which had not originally been on the agenda. The IGCs in turn prompted the Maastricht Treaty, which constitutes the third and current phase of the monetary integration process in the EU.

The 'Maastricht model' of EMU

We now turn to an examination of the model that has been chosen by the EU for its monetary union, which we refer to as the 'Maastricht model'. This consists of the EMU provisions of the Maastricht Treaty, as well as the set of agreements and arrangements that have been agreed since then, the most important of which is the Stability Pact on fiscal policy. The proposals for EMU contained in the Treaty of European Union arose, as we have seen, from proposals contained in the Report of the Delors Committee in April 1989, which had been established to examine the way forward for the EMS. They have remained largely unaffected by the Treaty of Amsterdam in 1997 and the Nice Treaty signed by Heads of Government in December 2000. The specific Maastricht proposals and timetable are summarised below.

First of all, EMU was to be achieved in three stages. Stage 1 was to consist of the completion of the single market, increased co-ordination and co-operation in the economic and monetary fields, a strengthening of the EMS, an extended role for the European Currency Unit (ECU), and an enhanced profile for the Committee of Governors of EU members' central banks. This stage began in 1990 and should have been completed by January 1993. In fact it was thrown into disarray by the currency crisis of late 1992 (see above). Stage 2 involved the preparations for the single currency: all members were to be included in the narrow band of the ERM, and the European Monetary Institute (EMI) was to be set up to promote the co-ordination necessary for EMU. This stage began in January 1994, but turmoil in the ERM meant that it was arguably never really completed. Finally, Stage 3 consists of complete monetary union, with the introduction of what has now been named the euro as the single currency for the EU, or most of it. A specific agenda was developed for this, with deadlines and convergence criteria to be met.

The timetable for Stage 3 was complicated. If, by December 1996, and if the Council of Finance Ministers decided by a qualified majority that a critical mass of seven states (six with the UK opt-out) had met the convergence criteria, then a date would be set for intro-ducing the euro in qualifying states. Failing this, by December 1997 there should be the start of an automatic process leading to complete monetary union among a minimum of five states by January 1999. Additionally, 1998 was to see the start of the creation of the European Central Bank (ECB), which replaces the transitional European Monetary Institute (EMI) and is the independent issuer of currency, and of the European System of Central Banks (ESCB), the independent body responsible for the conduct of monetary policy and foreign exchange operations. National central banks had all to become inde-pendent by this time. The Maastricht convergence criteria consisted of:

1   a maximum annual budget deficit of 3% of GDP;
2   a maximum total public sector debt of 60% of GDP;
3   no realignments within the ERM;
4   a rate of inflation not more than 1.5% above the average of the three lowest inflation countries in the year before decision, this rate to be judged as 'sustainable';
5   long-term (government bond) interest rates to be no more than 2% above the average of those in the three lowest-rate countries.

The Maastricht proposals can be seen as being halfway between the 'gradualist' and 'shock' theory approaches to EMU discussed above which have dominated the debate within the EU on how best to achieve EMU: there are provisions for promoting a certain type of convergence between EU countries, but there is also a very definite and tight timetable within Maastricht. The driving force behind EMU may be (partly) economic, but the establishment of EMU under Maastricht involves a definite political choice. Britain under the Major government negotiated an 'opt-out' from the Monetary Union provisions of Maastricht. Since 1997 the rhetoric of the Blair government has been infinitely more positive, but the decision to join has been put off until the next parliament. There are plausible economic reasons for this delay in joining, including the famous lack of synchronicity between the economic cycles of the UK and those of other EU states, and the advantages of avoiding early problems with the new arrangements. There are also dangers, such as being excluded from the formulation of the 'rules of the game' for EMU, as well as the effects on sterling of remaining outside. In the short run the latter might result in an overvalued exchange rate for sterling, which may be regarded as a safe hedge against the uncertainties involved in the launch of the euro. Nevertheless, one suspects the real motivation is political. The British Labour government must nurture some uncer-tainties about whether it can actually win the promised referendum on UK entry into EMU without a sustained campaign of persuasion. An early entry decision would also probably have dominated the parliamentary agenda, crowding out legislation in other areas.[7]

Implementation of the Maastricht proposals was far from smooth. The 1992 currency crisis had blown apart the ERM. In addition, convergence proved to be very difficult to achieve, especially in the context of German unification and the recession in the European economy during the early 1990s. German unification meant high continental interest rates which in turn exacerbated the European recession. The consequent downturn in economic activity resulted in falls in tax receipts and increased expenditure on welfare. Meeting strict public debt and borrowing criteria meant bringing further deflationary bias into economies by means of tax increases and severe cuts in public spending, which in turn further exacerbated the recession. Even then, some creative public sector accounting and a wide interpretation of the public debt rules were required for some states to qualify for EMU. The net result was record European unemployment levels of 17 million in 1997.

In order to complete the model for EMU, the original Maastricht proposals were supplemented by a number of agreements, the most notable of which is the Stability and Growth Pact, which seeks to control post-EMU fiscal policy by projecting the Maastricht fiscal criteria into the future. The essential features of the Stability Pact were agreed at the Dublin Summit of December 1996, and it was included in the Amsterdam Treaty of 1997. The Pact aims to ensure fiscal rectitude in EMU by codifying the 'excessive deficit procedure' outlined in the Maastricht Treaty. Countries are free to conduct their own fiscal policy, but national budgets are to be controlled by limiting government borrowing to the Maastricht level of 3% of GDP per annum, with a maximum public debt of 60% of GDP. Countries are free to spend more, but have to raise taxes to do so, *de facto* severely limiting public spending in the context of the free movement of labour and capital. There are quasi-automatic fines for those countries that deviate from this position. Furthermore, the potential restrictions on national fiscal stances are exacerbated by the 'gross' definition of debt in Maastricht, which ignores all assets in calculating government balance sheets. The stability pact does include some escape clauses for severe recession, but national governments will have to aim for balanced budgets in the long run.

Despite the difficulties, the EMU project was kept on course by a substantial amount of political will, no doubt reinforced by the amount of personal, political capital invested in it by the major political actors. At the time of writing the project has been launched and is heading full steam for the complete introduction of the euro in 2002 in the twelve countries that have so far joined EMU. While a recent Danish referendum on immediate EMU membership failed narrowly, the situation in Britain and Sweden remains uncertain.

With EMU in place, it is incumbent on us to examine the appropriateness of the Maastricht model to the achievement of a successful and inclusive EMU which meets the needs of the European economy into the future. Arguably the Maastricht model suffers from a number of fundamental flaws, which have resulted in considerable costs up to now and which might pose serious problems in the future. The problems associated with the 'Maastricht' model are discussed below.

First, the convergence criteria are very narrow in their coverage. They are clearly the product of the economic orthodoxy of the 1980s and early 1990s, and are largely based on the neo-liberal tenets of free markets and control over inflation as the main objective of economic policy, to be achieved by tight monetary and fiscal policies. The convergence criteria are exclusively financial, to the exclusion of real variables such as the level of employment, social factors or regional disparities. Furthermore, the intention is to project these criteria into the future by making them the basis for the operation of EMU. This would seem to reflect a rather partial and incomplete definition of convergence.

In addition, the convergence criteria have had a deflationary effect on the European economy. It has been argued above that, along with German unification, they exacerbated the recession of the early 1990s and that they are partially responsible for the high current level of European unemployment. As such, the convergence criteria have resulted in economic hardship and political fallout in most EU countries. This has arguably increased the degree of exclusion and marginalisation in some regions of the EU.

Secondly, the proposed structures and operation of EMU are arguably excessively rigid. The ECB has been given the exclusive objective of keeping inflation low, regardless of the effect on employment and social variables (Article 3b). This is regarded as essential to the successful establishment of the euro as a bona fide and strong currency accepted and trusted internationally, but it might impart a further deflationary bias on the European economy after EMU. In addition, there is provision, via the Stability Pact, for tight controls over fiscal policy within EMU. National governments in time of recession will be forced to cut public debt in order to keep within the limits, and this will increase the severity of economic downswings. This may suit some countries such as Italy, Greece and the UK, eager to establish new reputations for financial rectitude, but it will also constrain policies in areas such as job creation.

A third significant limitation of the Maastricht Model is that there is little provision within EMU for redistribution. As we have seen, this is desirable if not necessary in order to compensate the areas and groups of people that are likely to lose out from the process. There are also potential technical problems involved here. A redistribution mechanism is likely to be required in the future in order to facilitate transfers between states in order to deal with asymmetric shocks in a zone in which there can only be one interest rate. An example might be an increase in the price of oil which would benefit the UK as a producer, but would be detrimental to other EU countries. The MacDougall report (1977) suggested that a budget of 7% of Community GDP would be needed to eliminate 40% of existing inequalities at the time of the Werner Plan. The existing budget of the EU amounts to a mere 1.27% of EU GDP, and even the proposal of a modest increase to 1.38% was rejected at the Edinburgh summit. More recently, Currie (1997) has suggested that a budget of 2% of GDP might suffice for EMU, provided that it was entirely dedicated to redistribution and not to financing policies such as the CAP. This would permit redistribution of 20% at the margin between EMU members.

Finally, the Maastricht model throws up concerns about the democratic accountability of economic policy, since the Maastricht Treaty and the Stability Pact make very little provision for such democratic control. A key issue in EMU is how the objectives of economic policy are determined between member countries. This in turn opens up a debate on the nature of economic policy-making. There is a view that economic policy is a purely technical issue. This implies that the objectives of economic policy are given and unchangeable and economic policy can be conducted by 'experts' working within the monetary union's economic institutions. In such a situation there is no need for political involvement in the process. This is largely the position adopted in the Maastricht Treaty, which envisages an independent European Central Bank (ECB), run by 'experts' and modelled on the Bundesbank, which is not under political control and has fixed objectives such as low inflation (Article 3b) enshrined in its statute. An alternative position is that the conduct of economic policy involves political choices and the nature of these choices may change over time. This would imply the need for some political and democratic input into the process of economic policy-making. Ultimately there are few, if any, examples in history of a single currency existing without some form of government to support it. Similar conclusions may be drawn from the Stability Pact, which constrains fiscal policy within tight parameters and to an extent removes the choice of fiscal stance from democratic control. Thus in January 2001, Ireland faced pressure from the European Commission over its expansionary budget plans which, the Commission argued, were inconsistent with the EU's call for budgetary restraint. A few weeks later, the EU Finance Ministers took a major step in the history of EMU in telling Ireland that it should take steps to bring its 2001 budget into line with EU economic guidelines. Also, it was reported that the three-year budget plans of the twelve EU members would in future be subject to much tighter scrutiny, after criticisms of the 1999 and 2000 reviews from the ECB, MEPs and financial markets (see European Voice 18/01/01). The issue here is whether the provisions in the Maastricht model are desirable for a European economy which is currently characterised by unemployment, for they imply an inability to gear economic policy to tackling unemployment and social problems, as well as to dealing with asymmetric shocks. Moreover, path dependency means that the structures of EMU will be very difficult to change in the short run. For example, in order to change the statute of the ECB would require unanimity in the Council of Ministers, as well as considerable legal change. Changing the statute would certainly require a longer timespan than at the national level, leaving the structures of EMU open to the criticism of inflexibility.

Conclusions

We have discussed the nature, implications and development of EMU and some of the factors that have driven the process forward. We have also analysed the fundamental characteristics of the model that has been chosen for EMU. It may be argued that there are doubts and potential dangers surrounding the Maastricht model both as a democratic entity and as the basis for a successful EMU. It is important in this context to suggest alternative ways forward which might form part of a reform agenda designed to influence the future development of the EMU. A model for a more democratic EMU, more appropriate for the needs of the European economy and of European citizens into the next millennium, might begin with the introduction of real as well as financial criteria for convergence. These might include unemployment, regional variables, and social variables. At the very least this would focus attention on the standards of living and the quality of life of all parts of the European population, and force monetary policy-makers to take these into account.

Additionally, greater macroeconomic flexibility might be desirable, in the form both of greater flexibility in setting macroeconomic targets within the existing EMU, to take account of differing local conditions, and of a more flexible ERM in the transition period for new entrants. The former would include greater flexibility for national budgets than is at present envisaged in the Stability and Growth Pact. From a technical perspective, this would help to accommodate asymmetric shocks. From a democratic point of view, it would help to accommodate regional preferences in the macroeconomic policy mix, and it would also be of help in tackling specifically regional social problems. A more flexible ERM would reduce the potential costs of transition and render them more manageable. This might be of particular importance in view of the imminent Eastern enlargement of the EU which will inevitably involve absorbing economies which are at substantially different levels of economic development to existing member states.

Furthermore, the development of a credible redistribution mechanism will be of importance. Increasing redistribution would entail both reducing expenditure on the CAP very significantly and increasing the size of the overall EU budget, both of which are problematic, but probably essential in order to create and maintain a workable EMU in the long run.

There is also a view that some control over speculative capital movements may be desirable. Over the last few years it has been assumed that the operational difficulties involved might in practice render this impossible. From a neo-liberal economic perspective such a mechanism is of course anathema. Recently, however, in the context of the problems in the Far East and elsewhere, this orthodoxy has been questioned by, among others, the Chief Economist of the World Bank. There is provision for some degree of control of short-term capital movements within Maastricht. It is certainly the case that any increased influence by the EU over the operation of capital markets is likely to increase democratic control over the conduct of economic policy, to the extent that it would constrain the ability of these markets to subvert democratically expressed preferences in economic policy.

Finally, greater political influence over the ECB might be appropriate. This is clearly a very delicate issue, for credibility with international capital markets must also be established by the new EMU, and of course the current wisdom is that central banks should be as independent as possible. Nevertheless, the issue requires some thought for the reasons outlined above, i.e. for democratic reasons and because an exclusive emphasis on the control of inflation is not an appropriate approach to the conduct of economic policy in an era of high unemployment. A first question that arises here is the overall form that any democratic control might take. There is clearly a highly technical side to economic policy-making, and direct political control of the main levers of economic policy may prove technically inefficient, and could also result in a substantial loss in the credibility of EU economic policy *vis-à-vis* international capital markets. A reasonable compromise might be found in the 'New Zealand' model, which has been adopted in the UK, wherein the inflation objectives to be achieved are set by democratically elected authorities, while the Bank is left to implement a monetary policy designed to achieve them.

Even if one accepts the desirability of greater democratic control of the ECB, the fundamental issue which is immediately encountered concerns the means by which this might be achieved. This of course involves issues and principles which go far wider than even EMU, concerning the basic democratic nature of the EU and its institutions. It is therefore beyond the scope of this chapter. Nevertheless, the more obvious models which might be adopted to enhance democratic control over the ECB would include placing the ECB under direct control by the European Parliament and/or the European Council, increasing political representation on the ECB executive, and making the deliberations and processes of the ECB's executive more open.[8]

It is difficult to judge what the future may hold. Within the present international economic scenario of globalisation and powerful, deregulated international capital markets it is difficult to envisage an ECB which is not to some extent independent. At the risk of appearing to adopt an excessively Anglo-Saxon perspective, it may be that on balance the best and most realistic way forward might well consist of adopting a variant of the UK/New Zealand model in which the objectives of economic policy are determined by elected politicians, probably through the Council of Ministers (principally ECOFIN and the 'summits'), while the implementation of these objectives is left to the 'experts' who run the ECB. The European Parliament will undoubtedly have a role to play in the determination of economic objectives, as well as in monitoring the performance of the ECB. There would seem to be considerable scope for introducing greater flexibility in the area of fiscal policy, within well-defined limits. We shall see.

Notes

1   This scenario might call into question the real irrevocability of the monetary union. It also involves a forfeit of some important advantages of a single currency.
2   This may jeopardise the very creation of the monetary union, since potential losers from the process would of course be reluctant to join in the first place.
3   For a fuller treatment of the theory of monetary union see, for example, Lintner and Church 2000; Lintner and Mazey 1991; Lintner 1997 and 1998; Edye and Lintner 1996; and DeGrauwe 1996.
4   For a full treatment of the issue of national sovereignty see Brouwer *et al.* 1994; Newman 1996; Strange 1996; and Milward *et al.* 1993.
5   The Conservative government had always refused to join the ERM until the 'time is right'. The irony is, however, that they eventually joined at the time of German unification – it would be difficult to imagine a worse time to join, given that German unification led to higher interest rates than would otherwise have been appropriate, exacerbating or even partially causing the European recession of the early 1990s.
6   An area in which it is possible and beneficial to have fixed exchange rates, see Mundell 1961.
7   For a very readable account of the history and development of the UK's relationship with the EEC/EC/EU, see Young 1998.
8   For a fuller treatment of EMU reform, see Lintner 2000.

References

Arthur W. (1988) *Self-Reinforcing Mechanisms in Economics*, in P. Anderson, K. Arrow and D. Pines (eds), *The Economy as an Evolving Complex System*, Redwood City: Addison-Wesley.

Brouwer, F., Lintner V. and Newman, M. (eds) (1994) *Economic Policy and the European Union*, London: Federal Trust.

Church, C. and Phinnemore, D. (1994) *European Union and European Community*, London: Harvester Wheatsheaf.

Commission of the European Communities (1977) *Report of the Study Group on the Role of Public Finance in European Integration*, Economic and Financial Series no. 13, vols 1 and 2 (The MacDougall Report).

Currie, D. (1997) *The Pros and Cons of EMU*, London: HM Treasury.

DeGrauwe, P. (1996) *The Economics of Monetary Integration*, 2nd edn, Oxford: Oxford University Press.

Dyson, K. (1994) *Elusive Union*, London: Longman.

Edye, D. M. and Lintner, V. (1996) *Contemporary Europe: Economics, Politics and Society*, London: Prentice-Hall.

Haas, E. (1958) *The Uniting of Europe*, Oxford: Oxford University Press.

Lintner, V. (1997) '*Monetary Integration in the EU: Issues and Prospects*, in V. Symes, C. Levy and J. Littlewood (eds), *The Future of Europe: Problems and Issues for the Twenty-First Century*, Basingstoke: Macmillan.

Lintner, V. (1998) *Alternative Paths to Monetary Union*, UNL European Dossier 45, London: University of North London.

Lintner, V. (2000) 'Controlling EMU', in C. Hoskins and M. Newman (eds), *Democracy and the EU*, Manchester: Manchester University Press.

Lintner, V. and Church, C. (2000) *The European Union: Economic and Political Aspects*, London: McGraw-Hill.

Lintner, V. and Mazey, S. (1991) *The European Community: Economic and Political Aspects*, London: McGraw-Hill.

Milward, A., Lynch, F., Romero, F., Ranieri, R. and Sorensen, V. (1993) *The Frontier of National Sovereignty*, London: Routledge.

Moravcsik, A. (1991) *Negotiating the Single European Act*, in R. Keohane and S. Hoffmann (eds), *The New European Community*, Oxford: Westview Press.

Mundell, R. (1961) 'A Theory of Optimum Currency Areas', *American Economic Review* 51: 657–65.

Newman, M. (1996) *Democracy, Sovereignty and the European Union*, London: Hurst.

Newman, M. (1997) 'Democracy and the European Union', in V. Symes, C. Levy and J. Littlewood (eds), *The Future of Europe: Problems and Issues for the Twenty-First Century*, Basingstoke: Macmillan.

Pinder, J. (1991) *European Community: The Building of a Union*, Oxford: Oxford University Press.

Strange, S. (1988) *States and Markets*, London: Pinter.

Strange, S. (1996) *The Retreat of the State*, Cambridge: Cambridge University Press.

Symes, V., Levy, C. and Littlewood, J. (eds) (1997) *The Future of Europe: Problems and Issues for the Twenty-First Century*, Basingstoke: Macmillan.

Williamson, O. (1985) *The Economic Institutions of Capitalism: Firms, Markets, Relational Contracting*, London: Free Press.

Young, H. (1998) *This Blessed Plot: Britain and Europe From Churchill to Blair*, Basingstoke: Macmillan.

Chapter 17

Implementing EU[1] public policy

DIONYSSIS DIMITRAKOPOULOS
AND JEREMY RICHARDSON

> Implementation and enforcement has been a growing focus of attention in the European Union, both because of the problems of uneven implementation by the member states, and the recognition that compliance problems can arise even in countries which have relatively strict laws and procedures.
>
> (October 1996, Commission communication to the Council of the European Union and the European Parliament on implementing Community environmental law)

What is implementation?

Implementation as a complex and multifaceted process

Implementation is the complex process of putting a policy into practice by a variety of mechanisms and procedures involving a wide and diverse range of actors. Indeed it is the stage of the policy process where the underlying theories of policy decisions, the choice of policy instruments and the resources allocated during the formulation process are tested against reality. Implementation theorists are generally quite pessimistic about its likely outcomes. The subtitle of Pressman and Wildavsky's classic study of implementation (Pressman and Wildavsky 1973) illustrates this pessimism: 'How Great Expectations in Washington are Dashed in Oakland; or Why It's Amazing that Federal Programs Work At All'. They defined implementation as 'the ability to forge subsequent links in the causal chain so as to obtain the desired results' (Pressman and Wildavsky 1973: xv). On paper this may seem easily achievable, but, as they discovered, in practice it is not. This is partly due to the large number of 'decision points' implementation has to go through and the 'clearances' necessary for its success. A decision point is reached when 'an act of agreement has to be registered for the programme to continue ... Each instance in which a separate participant is required to give his consent is called a clearance' (Pressman and Wildavsky 1973: xvi).

The fact that much implementation theory has emanated from a federal state (that is the United States) is not a coincidence. The division of powers between different levels of government is a recipe for implementation problems. In a federal state many actors participate in the implementation of federal programmes at the federal, state and local levels, thus increasing the number of decision points and the likelihood of ineffective implementation. From what we know about implementation in federal states, we would predict problems for a multi-level system of governance such as the EU. However, complexity is not simply the result of the sheer number of decision points and clearances involved. Even in simple implementation chains, implementers do not necessarily share the policymakers' objectives (Mazmanian and Sabatier 1983: 34–5). They may even have a totally different point of view. Co-ordinating actors in a way that promotes the successful implementation of a programme, therefore, can be a task of Herculean proportions.

Implementation is a *process*. Its results take many forms. Conceptually, one can distinguish between implementation *output* and *outcome* (Lane 1983: 24). Indeed, implementation theory has stressed the fact that 'implementation performance should be divorced from its consequences, programmatic performance' (see Goggin 1986: 330). For example, while implementers of EU environmental policy may take all the necessary procedural and substantive measures stipulated in the relevant legal texts (output), environmental protection may not be enhanced because the 'theory' underlying the policy was flawed. In the case of training programmes, although a programme may effectively increase the skills (output) of a given target group in the short term, it may be unable to have a lasting effect on unemployment (outcome).

In the next section of this chapter we shall see that implementation is particularly diffi-cult in the EU where it entails the transposition of EU law into national legislation before any 'real' street-level implementation can take place. This is so because directives[2] can only produce their full effects after their transposition into national legislation since, in theory, they only specify the objectives to be achieved. This adds to the complexity of the process because it both increases the number of decision points involved and also provides a window of opportunity for national governments to 'erode' the original objec-tives of EU policies.

Objectivity, culture and the elusive pursuit of perfection

One should not conclude that unsuccessful implementation is inevitable only because of its complexity and the number of actors involved therein. The implementation process presents opportunities to re-fight battles lost in the policy formulation stage. Thus, imple-mentation frequently fails because of the conflicting interests involved in it. Bardach (1977: 85) rightly stated that 'implementation is the continuation of politics by other means'. Indeed, those defeated in the formulation stage may have an opportunity either to minimise losses or to totally defeat their opponents' objectives by undermining or eroding implementation. Culture also plays a significant role in both successful and failed imple-mentation. For example, some participants find it extremely hard (or even impossible) to act against a law even when either they disagree with it or it goes against their interests. Thus there can be a 'culture of compliance'. In contrast, others simply do not care about ignoring or breaking laws. The combination of all these factors explains why so far no polity can claim to have a perfect implementation record. There will always be slippage and implementation gaps, or even failure, and the EU is no exception.

Drawing upon the concept of 'perfect administration' introduced by Hood in his study of the limits of administration (Hood 1976) and other implementation theorists like Pressman and Wildavsky, Gunn has produced a list of ten conditions necessary for the achievement of perfect implementation (Gunn 1978: 170–5).

1   *The circumstances external to the implementing agency must not impose crippling constraints.* Given that implementation takes place in the real world, physical or even political obstacles may arise. For example, unusual weather patterns may undermine efforts to reduce the level of ozone depletion, or world trade may undermine European industries, as in the steel and computer sectors.

2   *Adequate time and sufficient resources must be made available to the programme.* This is a problem typically observed in the EU. The increasingly technical nature of the problems tackled by the EU (e.g. the BSE crisis) leads to increasing reliance on technical expertise in the implementation stage. Some member states possess it, others do not. The latter find it increasingly difficult to implement EU policy. The allocation of financial resources is particularly contentious. EU regional policy is partly based on the principle that EU spending is matched by national funds. This is by no means easy or unproblematic in a period of increased budgetary discipline (see for example Morgan 2000).

3   *The required combination of resources must be actually available.* For example, the EU co-finances major public works of European interest, but national authorities may lack the technical expertise to ensure they are planned and built properly.

4   *The policy to be implemented must be based upon a valid theory of cause and effect.* For example, increasing the skills of long-term unemployed people (e.g. through training schemes funded by the EU) will not help them find a job, if the skills they acquire are outdated. Many resources can be mobilised, but sometimes they are wasted. Thus, the European Court of Auditors discovered that, according to scientific research, the UK's selective cull scheme devised to help eradicate the effects of BSE in cattle will have only a marginal impact as it has been impossible to trace 65,000 of the animals concerned (Court of Auditors 1998a: 46).

5   *The relationship between cause and effect must be direct and there must be few, if any, intervening links.* Even if the policy contains a valid theory of cause and effect, it may fail because of the sheer number of the links one has to forge during implementation. For example, ensuring successful implementation of the EU equality policy means that the causal chain to be forged must reach each individual workplace. Similarly, EU regional policy involves a large number of (subnational) private and public actors (Morgan 2000).

6   *Dependency relationships between implementing agencies must be minimal.* Various parts of an implementation structure may have more than just a 'say' in implementation. Their agreement may be a precondition for successful implementation. Formally, national implementing authorities in the EU do not have the right to veto EU policy-making decisions when EU law is implemented, as EU law is supreme. In practice, however, no national politico-administrative system implements all EU policies with the same degree of zeal. This can lead to 'symbolic' implementation such as that envisaged by the British government in 1996 with regard to the directive on the 48-hour working week which it had fiercely opposed in the Council of Ministers (White 1996). Alternatively, there can be even outright rejection of a specific policy decision, like that of France against lifting the EU embargo on British beef exports (*Le Monde*, 9 December 1999).

7   *There must be complete understanding of and agreement on objectives throughout the implementation process.* Ideally, if this condition were to be fulfilled, the same individuals would define the national position, negotiate at the EU level, transpose EU law into national legislation and implement it at street-level. Although the Commission makes great efforts to consult as wide a range of actors as possible in the formulation stage, it can never include everyone who might be involved in implementation. Thus, in loosely coupled implementation structures like the EU (Peters 1997: 188; Dimitrakopoulos 1997: ch. 2) there is plenty of room for genuine misunderstandings and even outright cheating. Furthermore, the example of the 48-hour working week directive illustrates that disputes, in this case between the UK on the one hand and the 14 member states and the European Commission on the other, over the meaning or the legal basis of particular EU legislation and, subsequently, its field of application, is certainly not unknown in the EU.

8   *Tasks must be fully specified in the correct sequence.* The EU R&D Framework
    Programme comprises very specific roles for each of the participants (national
    administrations, host institutions, firms and researchers) in each and every part of
    the implementation process, including control procedures and penalties. Hence, there
    is little room for misunderstandings or cheating.

9   *There must be perfect communication and co-ordination between participants.* A
    single chain of command like that of an army (Hood 1976: 6) would minimise the
    chances for communication or co-ordination problems in implementation, but it does
    not exist in the EU. The multilingual, multicultural nature of the EU obviously pres-
    ents enormous problems and lots of opportunities for the distortion (accidentally or
    deliberately) of 'messages'. Equally, the existence of multi-level governance – a key
    characteristic of the EU polity – presents huge co-ordination challenges.

10 *Those in authority must be able to demand and obtain perfect compliance.* The exis-
    tence of powerful mechanisms (the European Commission, the European Court of
    Justice and, to a lesser extent, the European Court of Auditors) that promote compli-
    ance with decisions of the EU clearly distinguishes it from other international
    organisations. However, the situation is far from perfect given that (a) until recently
    member states faced no practical sanctions, such as fines, for not implementing deci-
    sions of the ECJ and (b) unlike relations within national polities, there are no formal
    hierarchical relations between the EU and the member states. Moreover, political real-
    ities loom large.

In the following section we will identify the actors involved in the EU implementation
process. There are, no doubt, other reasons, in addition to Gunn's, that prove why implementation is difficult, especially in the EU. However, we argue here that the sheer number
of actors involved in the EU implementation process, the fact that they are implementing
EU policy in unique national settings, and the complexities of co-ordinated action, are
possibly the most important constraints of all.

Implementation in the EU: who does what and how?

Variable institutional logics at the European level

There are basically two types of actors involved in the implementation process: public
authorities (European, national and subnational) and private actors (individuals, firms
and groups). However, not all of them are directly involved in 'street-level' implementation. The two main branches of formal legislative authority in the EU, namely the Council
of Ministers and the European Parliament, are two institutions at the beginning of the
long implementation chain. They are responsible for the formal adoption of EU policies.
Thus they make key initial choices which affect implementation. Although the link
between formulation and implementation may at first sight appear to be an indirect one, it
can have crucial repercussions upon effectiveness. Indeed, as Scharpf argued, the very
nature of the EU institutional configuration means that sub-optimal policies are easily
produced – the so-called joint-decision trap (Scharpf 1988). Thus Scharpf believes that
many EU policies will have inherent design faults. This is so because of the bargaining

process within the Council of Ministers and because the Council's 'intergovernmental' approach cannot always be reconciled with the European Parliament's more 'supranational' stance. Obviously, it is hard to argue that the intergovernmental and the supranational institutional logics are *necessarily* mutually exclusive, but conflicts between them are certainly not a good starting point in the quest for optimal policy formulation. It is often up to the European Commission as gatekeeper of the common interest to see if a viable implementable consensus between the many actors can be achieved.

Executive power, comitology and 'market order' at EU level

The European Commission is commonly depicted as the EU 'executive' body, although it was never meant to act exactly like a typical national executive institution. Thus, although the founding fathers had attributed to the Commission a clear role in monitoring implementation, national politico-administrative structures were given the responsibility to put into practice the policies agreed upon in Brussels. Executive tasks, that is the power to decide on detailed executive measures regarding EU policy, were initially the prerogative of the Council of Ministers. From the early 1960s the Council faced an incredible workload. Therefore it started delegating powers to a number of intergovernmental committees where the Commission was also represented. This practice first appeared in the agricultural sector, where various committees met in order to decide on detailed issues like prices for categories of products, after ministers had decided to establish the corresponding 'common market'. Thus the Council began to share its executive powers with the Commission via these committees as a result of functional pressures.

This phenomenon, named 'comitology' in EU jargon, grew so much in importance and size that calls for rationalisation led the Council of Ministers to adopt Decision 87/373/EEC in the aftermath of the Single European Act. Far from resolving the key issue of the conditions under which each type of committee would be used, however, this Decision merely reflected and in a sense 'codified'[3] the existing situation in terms of what the committees[4] did. Comitology is a system that reflects both the inability of the Council to face a huge workload and the need to ensure that once the Commission receives the power to adopt executive measures, it does not act in a manner that totally disregards national interests.

This 'danger' became more apparent as a result of a subtle but extremely important amendment of Article 145 of the Treaty that regulates the role of the Council in the EU policy process. Until the Single European Act this article ensured that the Council was the main executive institution of the then EC. The amendment agreed upon by the member states shifted the balance of executive power in favour of the Commission by making it the main executive institution. After the Single European Act, the Council can withhold executive powers only in special circumstances. As the delegation of executive powers to the Commission became the rule, the danger of the so-called 'runaway Eurocracy', that is Commission action totally disregarding national interests, has increased. Therefore, comitology came to be construed as an attempt of the member states to ensure that the Commission does not impose on them unwelcome burdens or limitations after policy has been formulated.

The definition of executive measures (e.g. the definition of criteria for funding under EU spending programmes adopted by the Council) is only one form of the Commission's participation in implementation. In the run-up to the establishment of the single market an increasing number of directives contained a clause obliging national authorities to send to the Commission draft legislative measures transposing EU legislation into national law *before* their formal adoption. Commission services check the compatibility of these measures with the spirit and the letter of the corresponding piece of EU legislation. The Commission is also responsible for

- direct implementation of competition policy, i.e. for ruling on state aid, mergers of EU-wide significance and abuses of dominant position in the single market; and
- the execution of the EU budgets.

The Commission, of course, has a major impact upon the implementation process by the means of its involvement in the policy formulation phase of the EU policy process. Thus, increasingly, it mobilises and institutionalises the participation of a very wide range of stakeholders, for each policy area or problem, in part because it recognises the practical value of the information which they can provide and the importance of getting them 'on board' for any proposals which might emerge.

At the other end of the policy process, the Commission has the power to *monitor* the implementation of EU policy. Indeed, it frequently receives complaints regarding the behaviour of public authorities and private firms during the implementation process. For example, competing firms denounce each other for using restrictive commercial practices, or they inform the Commission about the behaviour of public authorities that discriminate against them. Commission services examine these cases and commence a dialogue with the interested parties based on strict Treaty provisions. The Commission has the power either to impose fines on private firms or to take member states to the European Court of Justice for infringing EU legislation. Groups and individuals (such as environmentalists, women and consumers) often draw the attention of the Commission to implementation failure or slippage. Thus, in many respects they act as the 'eyes and ears' of the Commission – see below. Figure 17.1 illustrates why monitoring the implementation of policy is considered as one of the Commission's most significant functions.

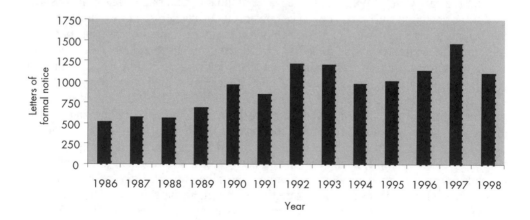

Figure 17.1 Letters of formal notice 1986–98

Source: Compiled by the authors, from Commission of the European Communities 1989; 1994; European Commission 1999.

Finally, specialised agencies (like the European Patent Office, the European Environmental Agency, the European Agency for the Evaluation of Medicinal Products, etc.) are an increasingly important public policy instrument in the EU (Majone 1996) with a potentially significant role in the implementation process. Although most of them – the exception being the European Agency for the Evaluation of Medicinal Products (EAEMP) – do not yet constitute fully-fledged executive bodies like the ones typically found in a number of member states (like, for example, the Health and Safety Executive in the UK), they mirror the increasingly technical nature of the issues dealt with by the EU and the willingness to de-politicise some policy decisions. Indeed, Previdi notes that the primary motive for the establishment of the EAEMP stemmed from the fact that only a small number of national governments had the technical capacity to adequately assess the safety of new medicinal products (Previdi 1997: 81).

The pivotal role of central governments

The role of national central governments in implementation is fourfold. First, they transpose most of EU law into national legislation by using the powers delegated to them by national parliaments. Indeed, in most cases national parliaments are unable to influence implementation through the process of transposition because the governments have extensive powers to transpose EU legislation through secondary legislation. Moreover, even when this is not the case and national constitutional provisions provide for the use of primary legislation, national governments typically have no problems obtaining the desired result from parliaments frequently dominated by executive-controlled majorities.

Second, central governments possess very considerable domestic powers and a variety of *tools* (Hood 1983) which they can use in order to perform their tasks. These tools are especially important in the implementation process where 'fixing' – i.e. corrective measures aiming to increase effectiveness (see Bardach 1977) is needed. Central governments provide, for example, human resources, funding, incentives, guidance and penalties. Thus, central governments are the key gatekeepers between the EU and nation-states and play a crucial role in the mediation process between what may be seen as supranational legislation and what Mazey (1998) calls the national policy hinterland. Their actions can encourage good implementation or can be downright obstructionist. For example, in 2000, the British government was forced to comply with an EU directive covering part-time workers. The government was forced to extend the scope of the directive under trade union pressure, although it was reported that 'many lawyers believe the UK government's redrafted regulations still fall well short of what is legally required to comply with the EU part-time work directive' (*Financial Times*, 4 July 2000, p. 14). Third, in some cases central governments implement EU policy directly, in those 'Europeanised' policy areas where they have direct responsibility within their national administrative systems. Finally, central governments alone are formally accountable for legal control of the implementation process. For example, if an awarding authority (e.g. a local council) fails to abide by EU rules on public procurement, the Commission takes up the issue with the central government of the member state in question rather than the said awarding authority. Moreover, we shall see that central governments can also be fined after the Treaty of Amsterdam if implementing bodies do not comply with judgements of the ECJ.

Subnational authorities and other executive bodies

Subnational authorities (i.e. regional and local authorities, depending on national constitutional arrangements) and executive regulatory bodies do a great deal of street-level implementation of EU policy. For example, regional and local authorities use structural funds disbursed by the EU; national health and safety regulatory agencies ensure the implementation of EU health and safety regulations at the workplace; environmental regulators enforce EU environmental laws; while national customs agencies implement the EU common commercial policy. Co-ordination between these bodies and central governments[5] is a crucial issue, because the different sets of actors might have very different perspectives on 'Brussels'. Thus, it might be argued that national governments have a better understanding of the reasons for the adoption of EU legislation via their role in the Council of Ministers. This is so

- either because they were the sole negotiators, so they have a better grasp of what the objectives of a policy are;
- or because of their better understanding of the EU policy process as a whole, which then enables them to have a clearer view of potential or actual infringements and the stance the Commission is likely to take. They are better able to judge what is necessary legally or possible politically.

On the other hand, this is not always the case. For example, national regulatory agencies, which are often independent of national governments, may have a much better understanding of how technical legislation came about and a much better understanding of its actual meaning. Their own staffs may well have been involved in the plethora of specialist committees, advisory bodies and professional networks set up by the Commission. For example, Swedish agencies tend to participate in Commission working groups, whereas departmental civil servants attend Council of Ministers working groups. Agency officers might also be more enthusiastic to see effective implementation as members of specialised epistemic communities. They can also be very critical of the EU, of course. The European Commission encourages co-operation between such agencies involved in the implementation of EU public policy. For example, the so-called IMPEL (EU Network for the Implementation and Enforcement of Environmental Law) was set up in 1992 and is an informal network that brings together representatives of the Commission and environmental authorities of the member states. Its objective is to generate the necessary impetus for the effective implementation of environmental legislation through the exchange of information and experience, and the development of consistent approaches in the transposition and implementation of EU environmental legislation (see European Commission 1998). So far, it has produced minimum criteria for inspections, a study of access to justice aiming to ensure the promotion of best practice, technical guidelines for regulatory bodies for a number of industries, and exchange programmes for inspectors. The Commission consults it with regard to implementation issues raised in draft EU legislation. Increasingly, regulatory agencies recognise the need to influence policy formulation. For example, the Office for Water Services (OFWAT) in the UK has argued for the need for greater consistency in the use of scientific information in the formulation stage and better analysis of costs and benefits (see Byatt 1996).

In addition to executive agencies, implementation involves subnational authorities too. The example of implementation of regional policy in Cantabria (Spain) is illustrative of the role of regional authorities. As the European Court of Auditors discovered, implementation of a regional development programme was delayed significantly in the mid-1990s due to the fact that the regional budget for 1994 was not adopted until March 1995, thus leading to the cancellation of the programme's 1994 tranche and the considerable reduction of the one scheduled for 1995 (Court of Auditors 1998b: 60).

The role of national and EU courts

National courts can exercise legal controls of implementation at the national level. However, this role is dependent upon the ability and willingness of the individuals, firms and groups concerned to bring national authorities to court. While ability can be determined objectively (i.e. one can or cannot afford legal costs), the willingness to take legal action also depends on subjective judgements (see for example Dimitrakopoulos 1997: ch. 8). For example, in some member states, companies avoid taking to court awarding agencies that may be violating EU public procurement rules because the companies do not want to enter into conflict with the agencies. This is why informal (as opposed to legal action) channels have been shaped both at the national and the EU level. Thus private actors frequently raise issues regarding implementation informally with national ministers and the European Commission before taking court action.

On the other hand, the European Court of Justice has developed a very significant jurisprudence on the rights and the obligations of national governments in the implementation process. The fundamental problem was that until the entry into force of the Maastricht Treaty, an important number of ECJ decisions were simply ignored by national authorities as no formal penalties were available to the Court. This, however, is beginning to change, as we shall see in the penultimate section of this chapter, as a more sanctions-based system has emerged. Finally, it is worth noting that in practice most of the action of the ECJ[6] and the involvement of the European Court of Auditors take place on a *post hoc* basis, i.e. after an infringement has actually occurred. However, in some cases the repercussions are still quite significant. For example, when the Court of Auditors discovered irregularities in the management of a major investment project implemented in Saxony-Anhalt (Germany), the corresponding items of expenditure had to be withdrawn (Court of Auditors 1998b: 61).

The empowerment of the individual and groups

So far, we have emphasised the role of institutions in the implementation process. However, the role of the individual and various associations representing interests both at the national and the European levels is crucial in implementation of EU policy. Their role is threefold. First, individuals, firms and groups implement EU policy directly. For example, in competition policy, firms merge, obtain state aid, etc., on the basis of EU legislation. In public procurement policy, firms bid for public contracts that must be awarded by public authorities and utilities on the basis of EU rules. Second, EU law (especially the jurisprudence of the European Court of Justice) has empowered them to take public authorities to court for failure to implement EU policy effectively or even seek financial compensation in cases of infringements by public authorities. Third, and more importantly, the development of the integration process has inevitably led to the establishment of informal links between the European Commission, on the one hand, and individuals and groups on the other. The latter seek to promote their interests when they feel these have been harmed by national authorities. In the Commission these interests see an impartial (and potentially sympathetic) public institution they can trust. The Commission, in turn, frequently uses 'tip-offs' of this kind in order to gather information on what is going on at member-state level and to exercise more control over implementation.[7] Complaints and 'tip-offs' are means of enabling the Commission to 're-steer' implementation. This constitutes a major difference between the EU and other international organisations, and enables the EU to erode some of the relative autonomy of national authorities in implementation. Having discussed the key actors, we now turn to a characterisation of the factors that affect implementation in the EU.

Characterising implementation in the EU

The implementation record of the EU is, naturally, imperfect. Broadly, this is due to six categories of factors:

- imperfect formulation of policy at EU level;
- imperfect legal transposition of EU legislation into national law;
- imperfect operationalisation of policy at the national level (deliberate or not) and deliberate obstruction at street level;
- institutional weakness;
- cultural characteristics of national implementation structures;
- imperfect monitoring of implementation.

The importance of the formulation or policy design stage: consensus-building as effective compliance?

Before discussing these factors, however, it is important to re-emphasise the importance of policy formulation to successful implementation. Thus, the formulation or policy design stage of the EU policy process is a key variable in determining implementation outcomes and outputs, as it is in all policy systems. First, as we indicated above, the different institutional logics underpinning, particularly, the Council of Ministers and the European Parliament can produce sub-optimal policy designs. This has become a typical feature of the EU polity. Although compromises ensure that more member states and other actors have a stake in the final outcome, inefficient 'fudges' arise to cover differences of view or interpretation which cannot be resolved in policy formulation (DTI 1993: 38). These unresolved problems are simply left to the implementation stage – a recipe for trouble later!

Second, formulation is important because each national representative in the Council tries to minimise the impact of EU policy by bringing it as close as possible to their country's existing policy in a given area. Each country desires a 'national home run' (see Héritier 1996) – that is the adoption by the EU of its own national policy framework. This is so because a 'home run' minimises that country's adjustment costs while it probably generates increased costs for others. This is especially significant in cases where national policy traditions are incompatible with each other and leads to what Héritier termed an EU 'regulatory patchwork' (see Héritier 1996). This comment about the importance of national policy traditions and the member states' efforts to project them at EU level concerns both the *content* and the *instruments* of a policy. Apart from a rather natural resistance of administrations to change, these policy traditions also reflect not just implementation styles but also quite different institutional arrangements. For example, regulating the British and the German financial industries may be a necessary and indeed a commonly agreed policy objective, but different methods and instruments may have to be used because there are substantial structural differences between the two industries. Furthermore, the extent of change introduced by EU policy is certainly a significant factor affecting implementation. Thus the degree of adjustment required is not consistent across nations or policy sectors. Its impact can be defined in terms of quality (i.e. effectiveness) or even time. For example, the European Court of Auditors discovered that implementation in Greece of some aspects of EU regional policy necessitated the adoption of twenty-one new legislative texts or regulations (Court of Auditors 1998b: 60). This has taken quite a lot of time although it could have been foreseen in the formulation stage.

The use of differentiated policy contents and instruments, which may be politically necessary as a response to the variety of institutional and social environments affected by proposed EU policy, raises the question of uniform and effective implementation. If *discretion* is granted to local implementers in an attempt to enable them to effectively apply general rules in specific cases, it is very likely to be used at the expense of uniformity. Thus, there is a constant tension between the need to reach a compromise in the policy formulation process in order to get member states to agree to policy change, and the need to ensure uniform implementation. Thus, specifying the right amount of discretion during formulation is by no means easy. More importantly, implementation theory alerts us to the need to use 'specific mandates' (see Montjoy and O'Toole 1979) – that is the opposite of discretion – in order to increase effectiveness. That kind of problem is certainly not unknown in the EU. For example, the Court of Auditors discovered that EU measures aiming to eliminate cattle deemed to pose a risk to public health have been undermined by the *discretionary decision* of Belgian authorities not to slaughter and destroy calves imported from the UK (Court of Auditors 1998a: 46). Clearly, in this case discretion has been utilised at the expense of effectiveness.

As we indicated earlier, the Commission, as the body formally responsible for policy formulation, is especially conscious of the need to anticipate implementation problems at the policy formulation and design phase.

Transposition of EU law

In theory, legal transposition is an opportunity for national governments to exercise their own discretion in the transformation of EU legislation into national law by choosing the appropriate *type of legal instrument* on the basis of their national constitutional provisions. In practice, however, there was a trend for increasingly technical and specific directives which had restricted this freedom during the 1980s and early 1990s. However, a counter-trend has emerged since then with the adoption of more 'framework directives'. Examined from an implementation perspective, this recent trend has led to three quite distinct but equally significant developments. First, some member states have simply copied EU legal texts into national legal instruments ('copy out' technique). This is not always simply an attempt to avoid having to interpret EU legislation. On the contrary, it is frequently the result of the detailed and technical nature of EU provisions. Second, national governments have tried to interpret the complex product of the negotiation process (formulation) into a set of more or less familiar concepts, rules and procedures that their administration is able to understand and act upon. Finally, interpretation can sometimes mean the introduction of provisions that were never meant to be part of a given EU policy (in effect 'over-implementation') or which constitute an attempt to dilute its effectiveness ('under-implementation'). Transposition is, however, only the first opportunity (certainly the easiest to detect from the Commission's point of view) for member states to limit losses that they may have incurred in the formulation stage. More serious and conscious attempts by member states to dilute or undermine EU policy implementation appear in the next sub-stage of the process, namely the actual operationalisation and delivery of policy.

Deliberate failure and cheating

This is the most difficult form of imperfect implementation to detect and punish. It takes a variety of forms, such as

- *tick the boxes implementation*, whereby implementation requirements are fulfilled only nominally and full compliance is reported;
- *fraud*, whereby recipients of subsidies capitalise on some co-ordination problems of the Commission or national authorities, or the ineffectiveness of detection mechanisms.

Deliberate failure occurs when:

- *national governments* reject a specific piece of EU legislation because they believe it contravenes other domestically determined overriding policy priorities (for example awarding public contracts to domestic producers in order to protect them from foreign competition);
- *national governments* manipulate, massage, or select implementation indicators in order to demonstrate 'compliance';
- *national pressure groups* opposed to a particular EU policy 'capture' key parts of the national politico-administrative structure, thus undermining implementation;
- *private actors* deliberately defy EU policy, for example by abusing their dominant position in the market in order to restrict competition, or simply by ignoring EU provisions such as safety or hygiene laws.

However, one should not place too much emphasis on 'cheating', at least with respect to the behaviour of national authorities, because of the EU consensual decision-making style. In long-run games, such as in the Council of Ministers, the short-run benefits of cheating might be outweighed by long-run costs due to erosion of reputation and trust. Players who cheat risk losing future influence over policy formulation. Also great effort is put (especially by the European Commission) into accommodating the interests of as many member states as possible in the formulation stage, thus trying to minimise the costs to the 'losers'[8] and so reduce the incentives to cheat. Cheating undoubtedly takes place. In the long run, however, every member state has a clear stake in implementation, albeit not one which is equally important in every policy area. Furthermore, it is long-established practice of the EU to accept the principle of derogations (more frequently claimed by southern member states) albeit for a limited period of time. Examples of this practice include the liberalisation of the electric energy market and public procurement, where more time has been given to southern member states to open up their domestic markets. This buys them some time, an important resource in public policy, but at the same time it enables the Commission to avoid the accusation that it imposes unpopular and costly policies on member states. Sometimes, however, states want things both ways. Thus they frequently use the EU as a scapegoat in the domestic political arena in order to avoid blame for tough policies which they wanted to introduce anyway. The convergence criteria for EMU are a classic example of this, reminding us that it is wrong to assume that national governments always wish to undermine implementation of EU policy. Sometimes, they are enthusiastic and admit it, sometimes they are enthusiastic and deny it, and sometimes they act to erode or even ignore it.

Institutional capabilities

Skocpol (1985: 16) has rightly argued that 'not infrequently, states do pursue goals ... that are beyond their reach'. In other words, irrespective of the quality of a policy they must implement, national politico-administrative structures have specific capabilities. Institutional capabilities are shaped by a variety of factors including lines of authority, the national civil service, funding, natural resources, technical expertise, etc. Comparative analysis of implementation in the EU is quite revealing in terms of the significance of institutional capabilities. Knill and Lenschow (1998: 602) argue that the responses of policy implementers to EU policy requirements are framed both historically and institutionally. They distinguish between factual and conceptual impediments stemming from domestic institutions. Discussing the transposition and practical implementation of EU environmental policy in the UK and Germany, they have demonstrated that when EU policy contradicts core (i.e. highly embedded) elements of domestic administrative arrangements, domestic institutions resist change, thus increasing the likelihood of ineffective implementation. By contrast, when EU requirements are compatible with existing institutional arrangements, the likelihood of effective implementation is higher.

There are other examples which underline the significance of institutional capabilities. The Court of Auditors has found that district offices in Lower Saxony were simply unable to curb swine fever because federal and regional services could not provide the necessary logistical support. In another example, the Court noted that only one member state producing olive oil had an operational cultivation register – albeit one lacking information – which was necessary for the assessment of production aid applications under the common agricultural policy (Court of Auditors 1996: 77, 86). Institutional capabilities do not depend only on the availability of resources, however. Setting priorities and acting upon them is a crucial element. Thus, typically, losers in interdepartmental battles over scarce resources attribute problematic outputs to an implementation structure's inability to prioritise in the correct manner (see for example Morgan 2000). Clearly, much depends on institutional capabilities, although good intentions and professionalism (i.e. cultural characteristics) can either exacerbate or resolve institutional problems.

Cultural characteristics

Different cultural characteristics mean that officials in some member states seem to care more about effective implementation of EU policy, even when it is incompatible with their national tradition (in terms of content or instruments) or it goes against their personal convictions. In broader terms, implementation problems in southern member states are frequently construed as the result of their political cultures. These are characterised by clientelism, patronage and disrespect for political and legal authority, thus contradicting the foundation upon which EU policies are based (see for example Pridham and Cini, quoted by Börzel 2000: 143). The argument runs that they already have a culture which has led to implementation problems (and failure) in the case of national laws and thus EU implementation problems are simply a continuation of national traditions. In contrast, some countries (Sweden being the classic example) appear to have a culture of compliance, especially when international agreements are concerned. Thus, cultural theory would predict significant cross-national variations in the implementation of EU laws.

However, one must be cautious when using this as the sole explanatory factor, as it would imply that some member states might have a perfect implementation record, simply because their political culture is different. In practice, even those member states which have an excellent record in transposition and street-level implementation (such as the UK, Holland and Denmark) find themselves before the ECJ on occasions (see European Commission 1999: 121–3). The notion of 'good' and 'bad' countries fails to take account of the richness and the complexity of implementation. Moreover, variations exist not only *between* states, but also *within* a state's implementation record in different policy areas, despite the persistence of domestic cultural characteristics. Also, national institutional factors not directly related to the implementation process can affect both the perception and the reality of implementation. For example, Britain's highly developed interest group system means that British groups are more active than others both in the EU policy formulation stage and in terms of 'whistle-blowing' to the Commission (Mazey and Richardson 1993: 19). The former increases the actual likelihood of better implementation, the latter creates an exaggerated impression of comparative failure.

Indeed, Börzel (2000) has demonstrated that the mobilisation of domestic groups is one factor that can contribute to the improvement of national implementation records. More importantly, she has argued convincingly that compliance varies *within* member states. Using a comparative approach, she developed a 'pull-and-push' model' which takes account of EU and domestic factors in the analysis of compliance with EU policy. In addition to the role of domestic actors, Börzel (2000: 148) underlined the importance of 'policy misfit', that is the extent to which EU policy causes pressure for adaptation at the national level, by arguing that the more EU policy generates demands for changes in domestic legal and administrative structures, the less likely compliance becomes. In sum, as the mobilisation of domestic actors and the extent of policy misfit vary within policies, implementation is 'patchy' within individual member states.

Imperfect monitoring

Finally, in a diverse environment like the EU, effectiveness clearly depends on monitoring. Haas rightly argues that 'information may affect political will by publicising state actions to potentially critical domestic and foreign audiences' (Haas 1998: 24–5). A policy's *target group* is usually the best monitoring mechanism. Target groups have a direct link with other market players and street-level policy implementers, unlike institutions such as the European Commission which actually rely on external sources of information. Naturally, attitudes and monitoring capacities of individuals, groups or firms vary across member states and policy areas. Not all can have a comprehensive view of implementation patterns and even if they do, they may be unable to act upon them because they do not possess the necessary resources. For example, the use of legal proceedings may take quite a lot of time and incur high costs, thus restricting the ability and the willingness of target groups to take corrective action. Furthermore, the action of target groups follows two different paths. On the one hand, action is frequently defined on the basis of national styles. Therefore, while target groups in some countries may choose to take public authorities or private actors to court, their counterparts in other member states may choose political channels of influence, e.g. by raising an issue with a minister. On the other hand, there are differences within policy areas in a given member state. Thus, Börzel (2000: 150–8) demonstrated that compliance with EU law at the national level depends on the priority accorded to an issue by domestic groups. Clearly, when priority is low, monitoring can be expected to be deficient.

Monitoring implementation cannot always be comprehensive. The implementation of EU regional policy by *public authorities* (i.e. the Commission and member states) has attracted criticism for concentrating excessively on financial progress thus giving little consideration to programme preparation, choice of projects, etc. (Court of Auditors 1998a: 67). This is not always the result of deliberate choices. In his classic *Administrative Behavior*, Herbert Simon demonstrated that 'administrators (and everyone else for that matter) take into account just a few of the factors of the situation regarded as most relevant and crucial. In particular, they deal with only a few problems at a time because limits on attention simply don't permit everything to be attended to at once' (Simon 1997: 119). Moreover, the *nature of the action* that is being monitored crucially affects the effectiveness of the monitoring mechanism. Indeed, Haas (1998: 26) has argued that verification is easier when the action that is being verified is large. However, the EU relies heavily on the *regulation of micro-behaviour*, i.e. the routine decisions and actions of state and non-state actors. This includes, for example, the implementation of health and safety regulations at the workplace, the regulation of industry, etc. These are policies that involve a large number of decision points and even the fitting of bathroom taps. Although the number and the nature of decision points varies from one policy area to another, monitoring action taken by public authorities cannot always cover every single aspect of a policy. Therefore, imperfect monitoring is hardly surprising, as monitoring costs are born by the member states, not the EU.

Thus, a combination of variable institutional logics and capabilities, formulation and transposition patterns, and cultural characteristics and attitudes, produce 'patchy' implementation patterns, a typical characteristic of federal polities. The increased awareness of implementation failure, and recognition of the need for effectiveness and uniformity, leads to increasing efforts, both at the European and the national level, to re-steer implementation.

'Re-steering' implementation in the European Union

The EU is an evolving polity. Thus, since its creation it has developed a number of mechanisms designed to improve its implementation record. These mechanisms are both informal and formal and constitute a combination of peer pressure, increased monitoring, persuasion and penalties, and policy re-formulation. First, the development of the single market project and the increasing significance of associated policies (environmental policy, consumer policy, etc.) has led to the establishment of a number of committees where representatives of member states and the European Commission discuss both implementation problems and issues regarding the development of EU action in a given policy area. Examples of these committees include the high-level committee of national single market co-ordinators which examines horizontal issues like the transposition of single market directives and the development of the single market score-board, and a similar committee discussing policy issues in the field of public procurement, etc.[9] In other cases comitology oversight extends to a wide range of implementation issues including post-transposition problems. Although these committees have no legal power to impose sanctions on individual member states, they are useful fora, where the Commission has the opportunity to raise, in a non-confrontational manner, issues regarding the behaviour of national implementing authorities, or even to 'air' its monitoring strategy. Individual member states clearly avoid raising issues against each other[10] (possibly because no-one is perfect), although a good implementation record is always a useful argument in the formulation stage, at both the technical and the political levels.

Second, since the early 1980s, the Commission has organised informal meetings in national capitals where issues regarding implementation are discussed in detail. The so-called *réunions-paquets*, unlike court procedures, bring together EU and national civil servants to discuss these issues in a non-confrontational manner. When this method fails, the Commission uses the legal powers assigned to it by the Treaty. In practice this entails the use of Article 226 (formerly Article 169) of the Treaty. As Figure 17.2 illustrates, the European Commission has tended to make increasing use of these powers over the years. If the velvet glove fails to work, there is always the iron fist!

The use of the monitoring powers has been combined with the growing involvement of target groups in the formulation stage. Apart from the obvious effect on the legitimacy of a policy, this has also helped the Commission to establish a sense of trust in its relations with these groups, thus turning them into a strategic asset in the implementation discussed above.

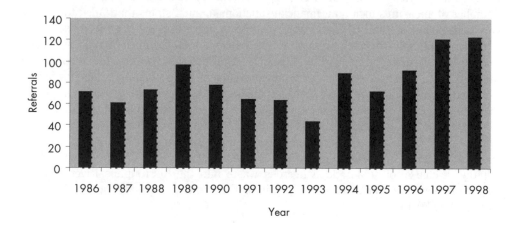

Figure 17.2 Infringement cases referred to the ECJ 1986–98

Source: Compiled by the authors, from Commission of the European Communities 1989; 1994; European Commission 1999.

Third, the judgement of the European Court of Justice in the now famous Francovich case (European Court of Justice 1991) introduced the *principle of state liability for violations of EU law*. The Court stated that compensation can be claimed by individuals when a member state has not implemented an EU directive if three conditions are met (see European Court of Justice 1991: para. 42):

- a directive must confer rights on individuals;
- these rights must be clearly identifiable in the directive;
- there must be a causal link between rights derived from the directive and losses suffered by the individual concerned.

The Court has further developed its jurisprudence on this issue throughout the 1990s, thus providing a key incentive for compliance, despite negative reactions from national governments and some hesitance demonstrated by some national courts (see Tallberg 2000: 110–11, 116–17).

Finally, the possibility of using EU-level sanctions exists, and it is a powerful incentive against less energetic attempts to implement EU policy effectively. For example, the Commission has repeatedly threatened Greek authorities that it would (and in at least one case has acted to) stop the flow of EU funds destined for major public works if they did not comply with EU rules on public procurement (Dimitrakopoulos 1997: ch. 8). Furthermore, for a long period judgements of the ECJ condemning member states for non-transposition or incorrect implementation of EU policy carried only moral weight. It was certainly not good to be seen as the 'black sheep' of the EU, as Italian and Greek authorities would testify, since this certainly had an impact upon a member state's political clout within the Union, but at the end of the day, it was difficult to see the *tangible* effect thereof. This has produced a quite disturbing record of ECJ judgements that remained unimplemented (see for example Commission of the European Communities 1994: 422–43).

The issue was placed on the agenda of the 1991 intergovernmental conference that produced the Treaty on European Union signed in Maastricht. The Commission proposed a number of measures including financial sanctions against states that failed to comply with judgements of the ECJ. National governments agreed on the need to render these judgements difficult (i.e. costly) to ignore. The outcome took the form of a Treaty-based procedure (under the modified Article 171/now Article 228) which entails the use of heavy fines against member states that ignore previous judgements condemning them for failure to implement EU policy. Whether this mechanism will have a positive and lasting effect upon the problem it is meant to address remains to be seen. Greek authorities found out in July 2000 that the political will exists in the EU to impose such fines in an effort to improve compliance with the judgements of the ECJ. In a landmark ruling of the ECJ, Greek authorities have been condemned to pay euro 20,000 a day as long as they don't halt the discharge of toxic and dangerous waste into the Kouroupitos River in Crete despite previous judgements of the ECJ obliging them to take corrective action (*Financial Times*, 4 July 2000).

Conclusion: imperfection is normal!

The EU implementation record is far from perfect, but this should not be a cause of surprise. The subtitle of Pressman and Wildavsky's book cited above captures the essence of the implementation process in the USA. The high hopes of the centre are often dashed on the rocks of the periphery. Similar factors to those identified in the USA explain implementation failure in the EU. First, implementation is a complex process necessitating effort, knowledge, time, money, human resources, penalties and incentives. Generating the right combination of resources at the right time and ensuring that they are available and properly used throughout the implementation process in fifteen member states is an extremely difficult endeavour which can become politically contentious. Second, implementation also depends on a number of institutions and other actors, their perceptions, interests and action. Each one operates on the basis of its own standard operating procedures and construes differently what is at stake. The ability of actors and their willingness to change in order to effectively implement EU policy depend on both endogenous and exogenous factors. Third, implementation is significantly shaped by choices made when a policy is formulated. The EU policy process is decidedly 'messy' (even 'garbage-can' politics) and is characterised by sub-optimal compromises. Moreover, actors cannot always judge what is at stake, and implementation problems cannot always be anticipated. However well-designed, each new policy is, to a degree, a leap in the dark. This increases the likelihood of ineffectiveness of the implementation stage.

Nevertheless, implementation is a really crucial and central test for the EU. Designing intelligent and appropriate policies means little if the capacity to implement them is lacking. Improving implementation has, however, become a key part of the EU agenda, and some important steps have been taken in the right direction. Just like every evolving polity, the EU as a whole, that is including its member states, is facing a strenuous and long process of learning how to do things effectively. The primary source of change is the need to provide a level playing field. The EU relies heavily on the regulation of the behaviour of public and private actors and knows 'free-riding' can still pay significant dividends to those who practice it. Not surprisingly, those actors who bear higher costs because they comply with EU legislation are becoming more active in pressing for better implementation in order to prevent free-riding. This is one reason why attempts to re-steer implementation in the EU coincided with increased competition stemming from the establishment of the Single European Market. There were two aspects to the creation of a level playing field – increased openness and increased attempts to prevent unfair implementation of agreed regulatory frameworks. However, detecting and punishing 'cheating' is neither the only nor the most significant reason why the EU must improve its implementation record. The EU has been successful in generating and maintaining peace in Europe. As one moves away from the Second World War, this is taken for granted. Younger generations are therefore more inclined to assess the EU on the basis of its ability to resolve daily problems. Support for a polity depends on its outputs. Thus, effectiveness has a direct impact on the legitimacy of the EU. The democratic deficit and the implementation deficit are linked.

Notes

1   Although we are using the generic term 'EU', we are actually not referring to justice and home affairs or the common foreign and security policy.
2   Unlike regulations, which are directly applicable, directives epitomise a sense of autonomy by allowing member states to use their own discretion for the choice of national measures for transposition, despite the common objectives enshrined in them.

3   It is important to note that the codification and formalisation of long-established practices is a typical characteristic of the process of integration. The development of the Common Foreign and Security Policy, which begun as an informal process (European Political Co-operation) in 1969 and then was formalised in 1986 and strengthened in subsequent Treaty revisions, is a classic example of this phenomenon.

4   There are three types of committees, namely *advisory*, *management* and *regulatory*. They differ in terms of how much freedom they leave to the Commission in the adoption of executive measures, advisory committees being the least limiting.

5   For a convincing account of the way in which the UK central government maintained its gate-keeping role, see Bache 1999.

6   The rest of the action of the ECJ concerns its dialogue with national courts with regard to the interpretation of EU law.

7   The British Department of Trade and Industry has established a unit that collects complaints regarding the implementation of single market legislation by other member states' authorities *vis-à-vis* British firms. These complaints are forwarded to the Commission for further handling.

8   The obvious side-effect is the 'fudge' that we discussed earlier.

9   It is worth noting that some of the members of these committees participate also in comitology committees.

10 The same attitude has been observed with regard to the use by member states of Article 170 of the Treaty of Rome (now Article 227), which provides for individual member states to take each other to the ECJ for failure to fulfil Treaty obligations.

References

Bache, Ian (1999) 'The Extended Gatekeeper: Central Government and the Implementation of EC Regional Policy in the UK', *Journal of European Public Policy* 6/1: 28–45.

Bardach, Eugene (1977) *The Implementation Game: What Happens after a Bill Becomes a Law*, Cambridge, MA: MIT Press.

Börzel, T. A. (2000) 'Why There Is No "Southern Problem": On Environmental Leaders and Laggards in the EU', *Journal of European Public Policy* 7/1: 141–62.

Byatt, I. (1996) 'The Impact of EC Directives on Water Customers in England and Wales', *Journal of European Public Policy* 3/4: 665–74.

Commission of the European Communities (1989) *Sixth Annual Report on Monitoring the Application of Community Law*, COM (89) 411 final, 21 December, Brussels.

Commission of the European Communities (1994) *Eleventh Annual Report on Monitoring the Application of Community Law*, COM 94 (500) final, 29 March, Brussels.

Council of the European Communities (1987) 'Council Decision 87/373/EEC of 13 July 1987 Laying Down the Procedures for the Exercise of Implementing Powers Conferred on the Commission', *Official Journal of the European Communities* L197, 18 July.

Court of Auditors (1996) 'Annual Report concerning the Financial Year 1995', *Official Journal of the European Communities* C340, 12 November.

Court of Auditors (1998a) 'Annual Report concerning the Financial Year 1997', *Official Journal of the European Communities* C349, 17 November.

Court of Auditors (1998b) 'Special Report No 16/98 on the Implementation of Appropriations for Structural Operations for the Programming Period 1994–1999', *Official Journal of the European Communities* C347, 16 November.

Dimitrakopoulos, D. (1997) 'Beyond Transposition: A Comparative Inquiry into the Implementation of European Public Policy', unpublished Ph.D. thesis, University of Hull.

DTI (1993) *Review of the Implementation and Enforcement of EC Law in the UK*, London: DTI.

European Commission (1998) *A Guide to the European Union Network for the Implementation and Enforcement of Environmental Law*, Luxemburg: Office for Official Publications of the European Communities.

European Commission (1999) *Sixteenth Annual Report on Monitoring the Application of Community Law*, COM (99) 301 final, 9 July. Online http://www.europa.eu.int/comm/secretariat_general/sgb/infringements/report_98en.htm.

European Court of Justice (1991) Francovich et al. *v.* Italy, joined cases C-6/90 and C-9/90, *European Court Reports*, p. 5357.

Goggin, M. (1986) 'The "too few cases/too many variables" problem in implementation research', *Western Political Quarterly* 39/2: 328–47.

Gunn, L. (1978) 'Why Is Implementation So Difficult?', *Management Services in Government* 33/4: 169–76.

Haas, P. (1998) 'Compliance with EU Directives: Insights from International Relations and Comparative Politics', *Journal of European Public Policy* 5/1: 17–37.

Héritier, A. (1996) 'The Accommodation of Diversity in European Policy-making and its Outcomes: Regulatory Policy as a Patchwork', *Journal of European Public Policy* 3/3: 149–67.

Hood, C. (1976) *The Limits of Administration*, London: Wiley.

Hood, C. (1983) *The Tools of Government*, London: Macmillan.

Knill, C. and Lenschow, A. (1998) 'Coping with Europe: The Impact of British and German Administrations on the Implementation of EU Environmental Policy', *Journal of European Public Policy* 5/4: 595–614.

Lane, Jan-Erik (1983) 'The Concept of Implementation', *Statsvetenskaplig Tidsskrift* 86: 17–40.

Le Monde (1999) 'La France maintient l'embargo, la "guerre du boeuf" reprend', 9 December. Online http://www.lemonde.fr/article/0,2320,34031,00.html.

Majone, G. (1996) 'The Future of Regulation in Europe', in G. Majone (ed.), *Regulating Europe*, London: Routledge.

Mazey, S. (1998) 'The European Union and Women's Rights: From the Europeanisation of National Agendas to the Nationalisation of a European Agenda?', *Journal of European Public Policy* 5/1: 131–52.

Mazey, S. and Richardson, J. (1993) 'Introduction: Transference of Power, Decision Rules and Rules of the Game', in S. Mazey and J. Richardson (eds), *Lobbying in the European Community*, Oxford: Oxford University Press.

Mazmanian, D. A. and Sabatier, P. A. (1983) *Implementation and Public Policy*, Glenview, IL: Scott, Foresman & Co.

Mendrinou, M. (1996) 'Non-compliance and the European Commission's Role in Integration', *Journal of European Public Policy* 3/1: 1–22.

Montjoy, R. and O'Toole, L. (1979) 'Toward a Theory of Policy Implementation: An Organizational Perspective', *Public Administration Review* 39/5: 465–76.

Morgan, O. (2000) 'How to Lose a Billion: Parsimony and Red Tape Mean UK Regions Miss Out on EU Aid', *The Observer*, 13 February, p. 2 (business section).

Pedler, R. and Schaefer, G. (eds) (1996) *Shaping European Law and Policy: The Role of Committees and Comitology in the Political Process*, Maastricht: European Institute of Public Administration.

Peters, B. G. (1997) 'The Commission and Implementation in the European Union: Is There an Implementation Deficit and Why?', in N. Nugent (ed.), *At the Heart of the Union: Studies of the European Commission*, London: Macmillan.

Pressman, J. and Wildavsky, A. (1973) *Implementation: How Great Expectations in Washington are Dashed in Oakland*, Berkeley: University of California Press.

Previdi, E. (1997) 'Making and Enforcing Regulatory Policy in the Single Market', in H. Wallace and A. Young (eds), *Participation and Policy-Making in the European Union*, Oxford: Clarendon Press.

Pridham, G. and Cini, M. (1994) 'Enforcing Environmental Standards in the European Union: Is There a Southern Problem?', in M. Faure, J. Vervaele and A. Weale (eds), *Environmental Standards in the EU in an Interdisciplinary Framework*, Antwerp: Maklu.

Sabatier, P. A. and Mazmanian, D. A. (1983) 'Policy Implementation', in S. Nagel (ed.), *Encyclopedia of Policy Studies*, New York: Marcel Dekker, pp. 143–69.

Scharpf, F. W. (1988) 'The Joint-Decision Trap: Lessons from German Federalism and European Integration', *Public Administration* 66/3: 239–78.

Siedentopf, H. and Ziller, J. (eds) (1988a) *Making European Policies Work: The Implementation of Community Legislation in the Member States*, vol. 1: *Comparative Syntheses*, London: Sage.

Siedentopf, H. and Ziller, J. (eds) (1988b) *Making European Policies Work/L'Europe des Administrations?*, vol. 2: *National Reports/Rapports nationaux*, Brussels/London: Bruylant/Sage.

Simon, H. (1997) *Administrative Behavior: A Study of Decision-Making Processes in Administrative Organizations*, 4th edn, New York: Free Press.

Skocpol, T. (1985) 'Bringing the State Back In: Strategies of Analysis in Current Research', in P. Evans, D. Rueschemeyer and T. Skocpol (eds), *Bringing the State Back In*, Cambridge: Cambridge University Press.

Tallberg, J. (2000) 'Supranational Influence in EU Enforcement: The ECJ and the Principle of State Liability', *Journal of European Public Policy* 7/1: 104–21.

White, M. (1996) 'Major Defiant on 48-hour Week', *The Guardian*, 12 November, pp. 1–3.

Chapter 18

Democracy and accountability in the EU

Michael Newman

It is now a conventional wisdom that fundamental problems of democracy and accountability in the EU originate from the early years of West European integration. For the European Community was constructed on the basis of a 'permissive consensus' within the six member states, with 'peace, prosperity and supranationalism' as its legitimating values (Weiler 1994).[1] European construction was seen as conducive to the stabilisation of liberal-democratic capitalism within Western Europe as a whole, but this was not coupled with any genuine attempt to incorporate democracy within the new institutions. Certainly, the Coal and Steel Community and the EEC included parliamentary assemblies, but as their members were nominated by the governments, this was no more than paying lip-service to democratic principles. Furthermore, there was comparatively little discussion of the key decisions within the parliaments of the six, and much less popular involvement. There was therefore weak authorisation for an innovation of historic importance and, to the extent that democracy and accountability operated, these were entirely on the basis of the domestic systems of the member states. Yet it was in this period that the policy-making system was constructed on the basis of an increasingly common market, on capitalist principles, with the European Court of Justice establishing the doctrines of direct effect and legal supremacy. This meant that there were increasing constraints on domestic autonomy, a particular kind of economic organisation was underpinned by supranational law, and a pattern of decision-making was introduced which strengthened governments in relation to those to whom they were theoretically accountable. Meanwhile the major economic interests developed effective ways of lobbying the Council and Commission, while less well-resourced groups were generally unable to operate on this level. Yet parliaments and electorates still tended to view the interactions between the member states as traditional relations between states in the international system.

The ending of the 'permissive consensus' was manifested in the crisis over the ratification of the Maastricht Treaty in 1992–93. But this was only the culmination of a gradual process which was brought about by a number of factors from the 1970s onwards: the accession of less *communautaire* states, which were uncomfortable with aspects of the *acquis*; the increasingly evident penetration of the Community into the domestic realm; economic recession; the growth of extremist and xenophobic parties; and the demands of the European Parliament (directly elected from 1979) for a stronger role in decision-making. But by now the policy process was well-established and the structural features incorporating the democratic and accountability deficits were embedded in it. Moreover, the attempt by governments to maintain control over key areas of policy had exacerbated the problems. The growing importance of the European Council and of secretive intergovernmental decision-making, in such areas as foreign and security policy and immigration control, had evaded the formal Community processes and reinforced the difficulties of domestic accountability. The subsequent formalisation of the procedures in the three-pillar structure in the Treaty of European Union (established at Maastricht and amended at Amsterdam) has maintained a situation in which the roles of the European Parliament and Court of Justice remain weaker in the second and third pillars (respectively, the Common Foreign and Security Policy and Justice and Home Affairs) than in the first pillar (the European Community). Hence, the problems of democratic control and accountability which exist at both European and national levels in relation to the first pillar are compounded in the second and third pillars. While it could be argued that external policies have traditionally also been subject to comparatively weak democratic control in most states, matters of justice and home affairs include key issues of liberty and human rights. The limitations of parliamentary and legal involvement in the third pillar are therefore matters of crucial concern in relation to democracy and accountability.

This is not to suggest that the position has remained static. Calls for the democratisation of the Community increased throughout the 1980s, resulting in a series of gradual changes. The Single European Act, which was implemented in 1987, went some way to meet the claims of the European Parliament (EP) that an enhancement in its legislative role would reduce the 'democratic deficit', and the Maastricht Treaty introduced further changes of this kind. The enunciation of the ambiguous doctrine of 'subsidiarity' in this treaty, with its emphasis on taking decisions as closely as possible to the citizen, also had potential democratic relevance. Moreover, the Amsterdam Treaty introduced further significant steps. First, it reduced and simplified the previously complex and numerous procedures of decision-making in which the EP is involved, and broadened the scope of the simplified co-decision procedure. Second, the Parliament was given the right of approval of the Commission president, while the Commission president's own role was also strengthened. This combined process defined clearer lines of accountability, which the EP used with dramatic effect in March 1999 when forcing the resignation of the Commission. Third, there was also a stronger commitment to transparency in decision-making. It was thus agreed that the minutes of Council meetings when acting in a legislative capacity, together with the votes and an explanation for them, would be made public, and that there would be a right of access to all Council, Commission and Parliament documents related to Union decision-making. In addition, the Amsterdam treaty introduced new articles in areas concerning human rights. It provided for new sanctions (ultimately including suspension of membership) against member states violating the principles of democracy and human rights, and the Court of Justice was also granted jurisdiction to ensure that the Community institutions respected fundamental rights as guaranteed by the European Court of Human Rights. Finally, provisions for legislation against racism (and other forms of discrimination) were included in the treaty. At the end of 1999 the Commission submitted draft anti-discrimination legislation to the Council (European Commission 1999), and a special convention began to work on proposals for a Charter of Fundamental Rights to be presented to the European Council by the end of 2000.

Yet there are fundamental problems with the steps towards democratisation taken by the Community thus far, for piecemeal changes have chipped away at the outer layers of the system without affecting its most basic characteristics. Moreover, there is a comparatively low level of interest and awareness of the EU as an economic, legal and political actor among the peoples of Europe, although its policies have an ever greater impact on their lives. In particular, the establishment of Economic and Monetary Union (EMU) at the beginning of 1999 has led to a further erosion of domestic autonomy. Nevertheless, this is not widely discussed, despite the fact that democratic control over the European Central Bank is extremely weak at both national and EU levels.

If the problems of democracy and accountability are deeply embedded in the structures and operation of the EU, the difficulties in effecting change are not only practical, but also theoretical. For it is not at all obvious how a democratic and accountable Union is even to be *conceptualised*. The first section therefore outlines some of the fundamental concepts and values on which this analysis is based. The next section then evaluates some of the approaches which have been adopted by the EU based on analogies from liberal democracy or the nation-state, while the third section evaluates alternative approaches which have departed from this analogy. The final section offers some positive suggestions for an approach to democratisation.

Democracy and accountability in theory

Democracy within an isolated autarchic community of one hundred people with equal amounts of property and educational attainment, an abundance of resources, and a high sense of involvement and solidarity is not too difficult to *imagine*, even if no such community exists or may ever have existed. Rousseau's conceptions in *The Social Contract* might be realised with the definition of a General Will in an Assembly in which all would participate in the legislative process. It is questionable how far there would be a problem of accountability in such a community. If the general assembly was the sole decision-making body, there would be no issue of accountability at all, since there would be no distinction between the governors and the governed. However, it is very probable that even a tiny community would sometimes delegate a small group to act on its behalf for some purposes, and the question of accountability would then be introduced. Procedures would be necessary so that the citizens as a whole could satisfy themselves that the group had acted prudently and in accordance with the purposes for which it had been established. This would perhaps involve a report to the General Assembly, which might submit questions, debate approval, amendment or rejection of the report, and impose sanctions (a censure motion, or dismissal from 'office') in the event of serious disapproval of the way in which the delegated group had carried out its tasks. Rousseau incorporated this idea of accountability into his theory. Arguing that all governments sought to perpetuate their power, he stipulated that the 'sovereign' (that is, the people) must always have the opportunity to ask, and vote on, two questions:

> The first should be 'Does it please the Sovereign to preserve the present form of government?' And the second: 'Does it please the people to leave the administration with those who are at present charged with it?'
>
> (Rousseau 1947: Bk 3, Ch. 18, p. 91)

This elucidates the relationship between the two concepts. Democracy is the more powerful and positive notion – that of a self-governing community *deciding* what should be done. Accountability has more to do with *controlling* those who are acting on its behalf. Yet once it has been recognised that it is necessary to have a division of function between the community as a whole and those delegated to carry out certain functions, accountability has a vital role within democracy. Unless the community has means of ensuring that those who have been authorised to act on its behalf have carried out the tasks with which they have been entrusted, democracy cannot operate. For in this case the delegated few would be able to substitute their own wishes for those of the community which they were purportedly serving.

Of course the EU is light years away from this fictional community. Instead of one hundred people, there are 350 million; instead of self-sufficiency there is constant commercial and financial interaction between economies; instead of equality of property and education, there are vast inequalities; instead of involvement and solidarity, there is widespread indifference and ignorance; and, in contrast to direct democracy and clear accountability, there is a Byzantine system of policy-making and, at best, a highly diffuse and weak form of accountability. However, while it is utopian to believe that democracy and accountability in the EU could ever operate as in a community of one hundred people, the *implications* of the concepts – self-government and control – remain constant. In other words, if democracy and accountability are to be enhanced in the EU, these basic principles, and the relationship between them, need to be applied in some way. But there is a further complication: the centrality of the liberal-democratic 'nation-state' in historical experience and conceptual dominance.

As Rousseau recognised, by the eighteenth century, European states were already too large and complex for the form of democracy he proposed to be practical, and the system that eventually became dominant owed far more to the liberal thought of Locke. Democracy operated indirectly through the periodic election of representatives to parliaments; and the strongest forms of accountability lay in the need for governments to secure the support of a parliamentary majority, and to be re-elected by the people. Other forms of accountability took place alongside these which were not necessarily democratic in character.[2] In particular, constitutions were often deliberately entrenched so as to make their amendment very difficult, thus limiting the power of elected governments and making them accountable to constitutional courts. But such constraints were justified with the claim that these guaranteed the overall operation of a system which was itself democratic, or that they protected fundamental rights. Over time, political parties also emerged as the major intermediary between an amorphous electorate and both parliament and government, and these formed a further key element in the linkage between democracy and accountability. Membership or electoral support for a party offered the theoretical prospect of sharing in the translation of a party programme into government policy, and the threat of withdrawing such support enhanced the accountability of the party to its supporters. There was one further element in the substitution of Locke for Rousseau in the development of the dominant form of democracy. Whereas Rousseau had seen approximate social and economic equality as a precondition for democracy, Locke justified the rights of unequal property ownership, and modern liberal democracy followed him in this.

The relationship between the theoretical claims of the system to be democratic and its operation in practice may be very questionable. More specifically, there are also serious problems about the effectiveness of accountability procedures with fragmented authorities, the trend towards the marketisation of services, and the volume of policy for which government may theoretically be held to account (Stewart *et al.* 1992). Recent trends towards personalised leadership on the one hand and complex relationships between bureaucracies and private agencies on the other have made it particularly difficult to locate responsibility for particular policies. Yet, despite its weaknesses, liberal democracy has now become so dominant that some of its basic features are inescapable in *any* viable conception of democracy. Such notions as freedom of information, opinion, expression and organisation, universal suffrage, a choice of political representatives, and a separation of powers, are thus necessary in any complex society. However, democratic systems include a cluster of *procedural* conditions and *substantive* values, and the relative importance of each of these is a matter of constant debate. The choices made between their relative importance, and the priorities in particular circumstances, are inevitably based in ideological frameworks. It is necessary to state the position taken here on three perpetual debates. The first tension is between *liberty* and *equality* and the emphasis here lies on greater equality. Second, as between *elitist* and *participatory* forms of democracy, the stress here is on participation. And, finally, on the question of *exclusiveness* and *inclusiveness*, the view taken is that a political system should be as inclusive as possible, valuing diversity.

The approach therefore draws on some of the concepts of democracy and accountability evident in Rousseau, but also incorporates ideas and institutions developed in liberal democracy, while adopting a particular set of priorities within the constellation of values embedded in it. However, there was one further key historical and conceptual development in the evolution of modern democracy: its territorial location within the 'nation-state'. Historically, the legitimation of states through the moulding of national consciousness and symbols was at least as strong as specifically democratic appeals, and conceptually it became difficult to dissociate democracy from the spatial form in which it had developed. But this means that the approach to democratising the EU has tended to be dominated by two predispositions: a view that regards the 'nation-state' as the only possible location for democracy and accountability; and a view which holds that liberal democracy is the model for the EU to emulate. As will be argued in the next section, such perspectives have not always been helpful.

Approaches to democratisation based on liberal democracy and the nation-state

The state-centrist view

Liberal democracy at the level of the 'nation-state' has one key advantage in comparison with the EU: the theory on which it is said to operate is easy to understand. The strongest claims about democracy and accountability operating through the electoral process are absorbed quite easily in early socialisation and political education. This provides a large part of the attraction for the state-centrist proposal for enhancing democracy and accountability. And this has particular relevance for states such as Britain and Sweden, which have had long traditions of liberal-democratic development, and political cultures emphasising their distinctiveness from 'Europe'.

Taking the territory of the 'nation-state' as the necessary location for liberal democracy, proponents of state-centrism have thus opposed all aspects of the EU which demarcate it from a traditional international agreement between states. These are regarded as threatening to liberal democracy within the state, and the solution is seen as the repatriation of policy until intergovernmentalism is restored. This involves an insistence on maintaining veto power in the Council, a weakening of the European Court of Justice, a strict limitation on Community competencies, governmental control over the Commission, and a rolling back of the power of the European Parliament. Currently such arguments are most commonly associated with the Right, but historically they have just as frequently been emphasised by the Left (albeit with different political, economic and social justifications), and this continues to be the case in Sweden (Gustavsson 2000). However, I would argue that the argument for thoroughgoing repatriation of policies, let alone withdrawal from the EU, is now anachronistic for the following reasons. First, the extent of integration and interdependence is so advanced that the repatriation of policy to the member states could only be secured with massive disruption and destabilisation in Europe. Second, many of the forces of globalisation which undermine the domestic autonomy of all but the strongest states would operate whether or not the EU existed. Third, any state which attempted a repatriation of policy by itself would almost certainly suffer as a result of the greater potential punitive power of the other member states: at the very least, it would find that it needed the EU more than the EU needed it. Finally, there are some normative arguments against state-centrism, even when it is not based explicitly on extreme nationalism and xenophobia. The EU has created some positive forms of transnational politics in a multi-ethnic, multi-lingual environment and has the potential to go further in this respect. Repatriation of policy would set back this project and, given the vast practical economic and political difficulties which would be involved, there is a strong probability that it would be accompanied by an intolerant nationalist rhetoric, whatever the original motivations for the policy.

Yet if this is no longer a viable or desirable option, it does not mean that insights derived from the perspective have no relevance for democracy and accountability. For state-centrists are justified in arguing that the process of European integration has reinforced executive dominance within 'nation-states' by institutionalising the ways in which governments and major lobbyists circumvent traditional forms of domestic authorisation and accountability. They are also right to stress the fact that the EU is an opaque system of institutions and processes which is inherently difficult to understand, let alone control.

Federalism

If the European 'nation-state' no longer seems viable as an autonomous location for democracy, there is a temptation to accept an argument at the other extreme. Because of the strength of the identification between a political system and the territorial state, many have found it compelling to view the EU as a kind of replacement for the latter. The EU is thus seen as a kind of state, albeit of a highly decentralised and federal kind. Of course, there has always been a federalist tradition among supporters of European integration, which has favoured the establishment of some kind of United States of Europe on normative grounds. But others have also accepted such arguments as an apparently pragmatic response to the processes of globalisation and integration which have allegedly rendered the 'nation-state' obsolescent. Indeed, it has often been suggested that the EU is already an embryonic federation, since it has a federal legal system, a single market (now reinforced by a single currency in most of its members), and supranational political institutions. On this argument, it appears to follow that the requirement is now to draw up an overall constitutional settlement which would openly define and limit the powers operating at each level within the EU system, so that clear forms of democracy and accountability could be established.

The fundamental problem with this suggestion is that the EU does not really resemble a federal state.[3] The governments, particularly of the larger and more powerful states, retain primacy in the policy-making process and exercise a range of powers in domestic and external policy which differ very considerably from those of regional governments within a federal state. It is true that there is considerable variation in the relationships between the state and sub-state tiers of government in federations and that some sub-state tiers in particular countries exercise very considerable powers (Fitzmaurice 1996). Nevertheless, federal systems have a hierarchical structure with the central state at the summit. In the EU, by contrast, the governments retain a vast array of domestic powers. Of perhaps still greater significance in comparison with the federal model, the stronger member states remain important international actors and, despite the aspirations of the Common Foreign and Security Policy, the bilateral relationships of individual states, particularly with the United States, are often of greater significance than those between the member states. It is true that some states are more willing to cede new powers to the EU, but in general the governments would be totally opposed to the wholesale transformation of the Community and they retain sufficient power to prevent this from happening. Indeed, the three-pillar structure of the Union appears to consolidate the power of the states.

The reconstruction of liberal democracy on a new territorial basis therefore seems highly unlikely for the foreseeable future. Yet, once again, rejection of the federalist project does not mean rejection of all the arguments on which the call is based. For it is true that EU law supersedes national law (in the way in which federal law 'trumps' state law in federal systems); and it is true that there is constant interaction between policy-makers at EU and member-state levels (often including sub-state levels), and that an ever-increasing number of decisions are taken co-operatively rather than by the member states alone. Federalists are therefore quite justified in suggesting both that there are democratic and accountability problems at EU level, and that some of the solutions must be sought in supranational and transnational terms.

Legitimacy and the 'nation-state' model

One way in which the Council and Commission have tended to react to the erosion of the 'permissive consensus' has been to seek legitimation through emulating the process of 'nation-state' construction. In other words, they have sought to counter democratic concerns by treating them as a crisis of *legitimacy* which might be reversed by enhancing the popularity of the Community (Beetham and Lord 1998). Some attempts to do so, like Jacques Delors' effort to construct a 'social dimension' to counterbalance the single market, resulted in some tangible benefits to ordinary people. But many of the initiatives have been largely symbolic efforts to recycle the rituals of national construction, for example, through a European anthem, flag and passport. A further development of this kind, with far greater potential importance, was the establishment of European Union citizenship, first introduced in the Maastricht Treaty. Since a precondition for acquiring this status was citizenship in a member state, and the majority of the rights of EU citizens had already been acquired in earlier phases of the integration process, the innovation was again largely symbolic. Moreover, while citizenship (at least of certain kinds) might be *related* to democracy, it is not necessarily democratic. This does not, of course, mean that the EU has never viewed greater democracy as a means to enhance legitimacy. But the search for legitimacy is not inherently democratic, and the pale imitations of the process of national construction may even have been counterproductive.[4]

The fundamental way in which the 'nation-state' has been the primary reference point in the quest for legitimation has been in the claim that its legitimacy rests on a sense of common identity. Because of 'we-feelings' towards the rest of the population within the state, we are, it is alleged, willing to accept 'our' state and its need for significant powers. However, the lessons drawn from this have not always been helpful in relation to the EU. The rather feeble attempts to construct a similar form of Union identity through symbols have largely failed.[5] But this ineffectiveness can then lead to negative conclusions about the possibility of democratic legitimacy at Union level, which may, in turn, be used to justify an argument that the EU itself must be confined to certain forms of regulation. As I will argue later, this conclusion is highly unsatisfactory on democratic grounds. But it is related to a confusion between legitimacy and democracy, and a misguided attempt to build the legitimacy of the EU on the model of national construction.

Drawing from the institutional model of liberal democracy

An alternative way of applying the historical and conceptual model of liberal democracy to the EU has been to assume that the *institutions* associated with the system within the state should play a similar role at EU level.

The European Parliament (EP) has been the central element in this assumption as it is the only body directly elected on a European basis. Ever since the first direct election, the EP has therefore been seen (and has certainly seen itself) as the main vehicle for the democratisation of the EU, and its powers have steadily increased. In general, MEPs have taken their role seriously and the Parliament as a whole has certainly become a far more important actor in the EU system as a whole. Nevertheless, there is room for considerable scepticism about the *extent* to which the EP has ameliorated the problems of democracy and accountability within the system, or can be expected to do so.

The first fundamental weaknesses in its position is its comparative remoteness from the concerns of its electorate, which is manifested both in the overwhelming salience of domestic issues in Euro-elections and in the constant decline in the turnout – from an average of 63% in 1979 to 49.4% in 1999.[6] While there are obviously differences between the member states, it is generally the case that neither the EP itself, nor the MEPs, are firmly embedded in the political consciousness of the population as a whole. Given this, it is difficult to maintain that the Parliament is a strong expression of European democracy. Its second weakness is the relative obscurity of its role in relationship to *government* – that is, the fact that governments are not formed from it and cannot be forced out of office by it. The two weaknesses are probably inextricably connected: that is, the European elec-torate would take more note of the Parliament if it had the power to bring down the Council. However, even if true, this does not advance the argument since the EP could not secure such power without the establishment of a federation. This does not mean that the EP is impotent in relation to the Council, for it has used its powers effectively to enhance its role in decision-making. Indeed, the attempt to strengthen its position in an ongoing bargaining relationship with the Council and the Commission has probably been the Parliament's main preoccupation. (Hoskyns and Lambert 2000). However, even if this is beneficial to the policy process, it does not establish a system of democratic accounta-bility.

One other institutional approach, which attempts to overcome the intractable difficul-ties in extricating the EU from this impasse, is to consider the possibilities of democratising the Commission. It was thus argued long ago that the EP did not have the potential to play the role ascribed to it, but that the EU institutional system was much closer to the American model of liberal democracy, in which there is a 'separation of insti-tutions, a separation of persons and a separation of powers' and 'no one institution can control the others' (Bogdanor 1986). Following the analogy, it was therefore suggested that the direct election of the Commissioners on alternative partisan programmes for the Community as a whole could stimulate popular interest in the system, promote a greater sense of division between 'government' and 'opposition' and provide the Commission with 'both a democratic base and a legitimacy which it presently lacks' (Bogdanor and Woodcock 1991). This may well be right, but it is again highly unlikely that the govern-ments will allow an alternative body, which has greater initiating power than the European Parliament, to claim a democratic mandate which would be far more 'European' than its own. Nor would the EP want a new rival to challenge its democratic legitimacy. An alternative would be for the Commission to be indirectly elected out of the majority party grouping in the EP. This would certainly appeal far more to the EP, but is only marginally more probable than a directly elected Commission. For the governments would still resist the challenge that this would present to their own democratic credentials at EU level, and would be reluctant to cede the power of appointment of the Commission to the EP. It is far more likely that both the nomination and accountability of the Commission will continue to be subject to bargaining between the Council and the Parliament. Again, such incremental changes might be helpful within the policy-making system, but would have little significant impact upon the problems of *democratic* accountability. For they would no doubt remain as imperceptible to the public as a whole as the piecemeal reforms in institutional relationships which have taken place since the mid-1980s.

And, more generally, it seems that institutional 'tinkering', based on analogies with the liberal-democratic model at state level, is unlikely to do much to reduce the democratic deficits at EU level. Yet alternative approaches are not necessarily any more helpful. The next section illustrates this.

Alternative approaches

Democratic 'outputs' and the argument for efficiency in decision-making

One reaction by the EU to concerns about democracy has been to treat the problem as one which can be remedied by greater *effectiveness and efficiency*. In a general sense, this has meant enhancing the powers and competencies of the EU so that it can compete more effectively in the world or make the single market a success. This may be regarded as a preoccupation with the 'output' side of the policy-making system (Kohler-Koch 1999), and it is possible that the EU could again rest on tacit consent (as in the period of 'permissive consensus') if it were able to provide sufficient demonstrable benefits to the member states and their populations. However, the same point could be made about any kind of political regime, for it is not a specifically democratic argument. Indeed, a concentration on outputs without improvements in democratic inputs – in terms of authorisation and accountability – can simply reinforce the problems. This has particular relevance to the efficiency argument in relation to the decision-making system within the Council.

If the EU were purely a co-operative arrangement between independent states, it would be expected that each of them would have one vote and a right of veto. In this case, it would also be possible for each government to be accountable to its domestic parliament and electorate for any decisions that it agreed. But because it is an entity with important aspects of supranational policy-making, there is some approximation between the number of votes wielded by each member state in the Council and the size of its popula-tion. Each enlargement has made decision-making more complex as a larger number of interests need to be accommodated and as more sceptical states join the club. Thus during the 1980s a greater use of majority voting in the Council was introduced so as to cope with the expansion of the Community from nine to twelve member states; in the Treaty of Amsterdam the flexibility clause was devised in an attempt to bypass the British veto; and in the Treaty of Nice in 2000 a re-weighting of votes in the Council, and a further increase in the use of majority voting, was negotiated in order to prepare for the next enlargement.[7]

It is true that *inefficiency* in decision-making can undermine a system of democracy, since a complete impasse could prevent the translation of a popular will into policy, leading to widespread alienation. However, improving efficiency within the Council obvi-ously complicates the process of domestic accountability whenever a government is out-voted or accepts a decision solely in the expectation of being out-voted. And the weighting of votes means that smaller states are more likely to find themselves in this position than larger ones. Yet the exact weighting of votes and the size of blocking minorities agreed at any time is the result of bargaining and alliances. All these outcomes have more to do with *realpolitik* than democratic arguments. Nevertheless, the attempt to enhance efficiency in decision-making (as part of the concern with outputs) can exacerbate the problem of democratic accountability.

Independent accountability

A second alternative approach departs from a conventional European liberal-democratic model as the basis for thinking about the issues of authorisation and accountability, and suggests that distinct forms of governance are necessary. In particular, it is argued that the 'nation-state' has high levels of welfare expenditure and that elements of redistribution are acceptable because of a shared identity. The EU has neither the available funds nor the democratic legitimacy for these kinds of policies. Instead it is far more suited to *regulation* than *redistribution*, and the appropriate agency is that of an independent body of experts established by the EU to oversee tasks entrusted to it (Majone 1996a).[8] Independence and accountability can be reconciled through various mechanisms, including statutory objectives for performance standards, reason-giving and transparency requirements facilitating judicial review and public participation, due process provisions to ensure fairness among the inevitable losers from regulatory decisions, and professionalism in order to withstand external interference and to reduce the risk of arbitrary use of agency discretion (Majone 1996a: 300, cited in Gustavsson 2000: 52). Indeed, Majone argues that this form of independence provides a stronger system of accountability than the conventional one, since it insulates the regulatory system from short-term political pressures and he thus envisages a future in which a 'web of networks of national and supranational regulatory institutions [are] held together by shared values and objectives, and by a common style of policy-making' (Majone 1996b: 276). Accountability in a regulatory system is thus recommended as a general approach in the EU, but the European Central Bank (ECB) is the most important example, and it is this which will be discussed here.

Although the approach stresses the specific characteristics of the EU, the argument is coupled with a critique of existing models of democracy at the level of the nation-state. In particular, it notes that governments have manipulated monetary policy for electoral advantage or to appease particular interest groups in society. Ensuring that the ECB is outside political control is therefore regarded as the best way of keeping it to its appointed tasks. However, this argument understates the politics of *any* form of economic policy and, in the particular case of EMU, fails to appreciate the implications for democracy and accountability of the current monetary guidelines and independence of the ECB. On its current basis, the most satisfactory verdict for EMU and the ECB could be to be judged positive by *results*: that is, if economic growth, competitiveness and prosperity in the EU *as a whole* appeared to improve, it might be argued that the monetary system was beneficial to the underpinning of the political and social structures. However, even if this outcome were to be realised, it could reinforce the inequalities between areas and social groups and, by removing existing levers of economic policy-making from the control of member states, it would make it far more difficult for them to counteract such tendencies. Moreover, the independence of the European Central Bank undermines any strong form of democratic authorisation or accountability for its policies at either domestic or EU level (Gustavsson 1999; Lintner 2000).

If these considerations are examined in relation to the rationale for this form of regulation, the conclusions appear highly paradoxical. The suggestion that the EU is not an appropriate body for redistributive policies is used to argue for independent agencies to become accountable for specific tasks entrusted to them. But the decisions of the ECB may lead to regressive redistribution in both a social and spatial sense. If so, this would suggest that the EU does not have the legitimacy for redistribution to *lessen* inequalities, but that no similar problems arise if its policies redistribute resources so as to *increase* them. Such conclusions are, in my view, unacceptable on democratic grounds. The fact that governments may have often abused monetary policy for political purposes, or that parliaments have generally been uninterested in the details of central banking decisions (Magnette 1999) are not justifications for effectively removing such areas of policy from traditional forms of democratic authorisation and accountability.

Policy-making by consensus and intra-elite accountability

The justification for accountability through entrusting independent agencies with particular tasks emphasises the weak democratic legitimacy of the EU as a reason for a distinct approach. A different argument for suggesting that traditional notions of liberal democracy are inappropriate focuses more on the specific policy-making process at European level. This, it is claimed, is based on the construction of a *consensus*, while much conventional thinking about democracy (perhaps particularly in Britain) is based on assumptions of *conflict* (Lord 1998: 94–5). Such notions, it is argued, have little relevance for the policy-making process in the EU. The government–opposition dichotomy does not apply and there is a very strong incentive for co-operative policy-making both within and between EU institutions. Votes take place only rarely within the Council and the main impact of qualified majority voting has been to facilitate the search for a consensus. Similarly, the need for the Parliament to secure an absolute majority of its component members, to exploit its legislative role to full effect, has also encouraged the two biggest groupings (the Party of European Socialists and the European People's Party) to co-operate, rather than to compete (Hix and Lord 1997). Furthermore, the co-decision legislative system means that the Council, Commission and EP have powerful inducements to conciliate one another to ensure that agreement is reached on proposals. The same pressures are at work in the elaborate committee system in which national and EU officials, and the key interest groups whom they consult, translate outline proposals into detailed legal instruments. Finally, the conflict model, based upon alternative parties articulating opposing views in society as a whole, is also inappropriate because of the comparative weakness of the transnational parties and the continuing dominance of national political consciousness among party members and voters. All this means that the EU policy-making process is based on a constant search for consensus, with the result that the initial ideas for legislation are re-formulated and amended by this ongoing 'conversation' between all the actors within this elaborate process. This, it has been suggested, provides effective forms of accountability (Héritier 1997; Joerges and Neyer 1997).

This consensus system is certainly at work within the EU. But it does not follow that this form of policy-making, with an array of officials, politicians and recognised interests scrutinising and amending proposals, is a substitute for more conventional notions of democracy and accountability. Moreover, the committee and comitology system remains singularly opaque, despite reforms in 1999 (Rhinhard 1999; Armstrong 2000). Neither the manner of appointment to the committees, nor the ways in which they operate, are transparent, and it is not clear that there are any clear channels for the control and scrutiny of their activities. Crises such as the BSE dispute expose the salience of committees in the policy-making process but, in general, they carry out a vast amount of work behind closed doors. As Chris Lord has put it:

> [T]he EU has developed an elaborate system of deliberation at *elite* level ... to include all kinds of actor types in mutual reflection and critiques. The Union is likewise characterised by often respectable levels of inter-elite accountability. As yet, however, the public is scarcely involved at all. At the risk of some frivolity, we might characterise it as democracy without the people.
>
> (Lord 1998: 129)

But the exclusion of 'the people' obviously also excludes ideas that might undermine the elite consensus on which policy is currently based. Certainly, any major disturbance caused by intruders into the 'private conversation' could threaten to bring back the noisy conflicts which have more often characterised domestic politics. However, the goals of democracy and accountability necessitate the inclusion of discordant voices. Their current absence does not demonstrate that the EU policy process is inevitably different from that of the member states in this respect – only that these characteristics are the result of confining the system largely to privileged actors and interests.

Towards enhanced democracy and accountability

How then might democracy be envisaged and enhanced in the EU? It is, I believe, helpful to view the Union as an entity which is simultaneously characterised by elements of fusion (Rometsch and Wessels 1996; Wessels 1997) and elements of separation (Chryssochoou 1998; Benz 1999). Given the continuing power of the member states, it is misleading simply to treat it as a polity characterised by 'multi-level governance' (Marks *et al.* 1996). Yet the extent of the interactions between the different levels of government and between transnational actors also makes it inappropriate to treat it as if any rigid demarcation between the EU and the states (or sub-state levels) was possible. This makes it far more difficult to conceptualise democracy than would be the case if either of the above characterisations – complete fusion or complete separation – was appropriate. There is one further complication: the fluidity of the contemporary world. Space and time have been compressed and there has been a fragmentation of traditional structures, solidarities and ideologies. Analysis of existing forms of governance and proposals for reform must therefore recognise the inadequacy of assumptions based on a static view (Lebessis and Paterson 1999; Bertrand *et al.* 1999).

Yet this necessary recognition of complexity and flux can also go too far when it ignores the fundamental continuities in the situation – above all, the concentration of economic and political power among elite groups in society. While much has changed, much stays the same and, in my view, it is only possible to envisage democratisation in the EU by attempting to apply traditional concepts in this confusing situation. It is at least possible to indicate an approach to the multiple dimensions of the problems based on the analysis in the previous sections and the ideas outlined in the first section.

First, I would suggest that the emphasis on institutional reform at EU level, which has so often dominated discussions of democracy and accountability, should play a subordinate role in the immediate future. This is not to say that further adjustments in the inter-institutional arrangements will never be necessary, but to argue that both experience and theory imply that they will not play a key role in enhancing democratisation at present. Second, it appears impossible to privilege any one level – either in territorial or functional terms – in the attempt to enhance democratisation and accountability. This means that it is necessary simultaneously to seek democratic reforms at local, regional, national and transnational levels. This is partly because non-accountable forms of power, which are often interconnected, exist at all levels. If governments and major economic and financial interests operate both nationally and transnationally, countervailing democratic power also needs to operate on both levels. But it must be acknowledged that contradictions may result from democratic demands at different levels. Certainly, this will not always be the case. For example, it is evident that both the EP and domestic parliaments have an interest in securing greater openness and transparency in the Council, and the Treaties of Maastricht and Amsterdam have encouraged a strengthening of the inter-parliamentary co-operation.[9] Yet there can sometimes be tensions and clashes between those seeking stronger forms of democracy and accountability at the different levels, and it is not possible (or even desirable) for those operating on one level to take account of all the others. This means that the process of democratisation must be a 'journey to an unknown destination' (Shonfield 1973). However, while this suggests that tidy forms of democratic governance in the EU as a whole will probably never be established, it does not necessarily mean that the contradictory pulls and pushes do not contribute to the overall process of democratisation. Thus when the Danish people rejected the Maastricht Treaty in June 1992 their motivations were overwhelmingly *national* in character. Nevertheless, the shock this caused to the leaders of the EU was conducive to the process of democratisation: indeed it was a catalyst for putting the relevant questions on the agenda.

The refusal to privilege particular levels in the quest for democratisation is closely related to a further element in this approach to the issues: a rejection of the assumption that the EU is always the appropriate body for the conduct of policy or that all policies should necessarily be 'Europeanised'. It was argued earlier that the wholesale repatriation of policies would be impracticable and destructive, but this is quite different from suggesting that it might sometimes be preferable to consolidate rather than to advance (Kohler-Koch 1999). Nor is democracy furthered by presenting voters and parliaments with complex package deals – as at Maastricht – and demanding that the only two alternatives are overall acceptance or rejection. But this begs the question of *how* this could be changed.

Arguing that the current trend in the EU is towards greater centralisation, and that the attempt to build indirect democracy into the system has failed, Heidrun Abromeit has proposed the injection of direct democracy by developing the use of referendums which would provide a veto power against decisions taken at EU level (Abromeit 1998). The objectives of these proposals are to heighten popular involvement, to ensure that policy is based on consent and to slow down the EU juggernaut. Such referendums would provide a form of participatory democracy, and their nature and frequency should help to counteract the well-known weaknesses of this form of direct democracy: in particular, manipulation by governments or voters giving their opinions on quite different questions from those that they are asked. However, this proposal is explicitly justified on the basis of a *negative* approach through the establishment of a new participatory veto system. It therefore emphasises control and accountability rather than active participation in policy-making. Other authors have suggested that this might be strengthened by applying the insights of the theory of *deliberative democracy* to the EU (Bohman and Rehg 1997; Gerstenberg 1997; Hoskyns 2000a; 2000b; Benz 1999). This focuses on the manner in which decisions are taken, emphasising the inclusion of diverse voices and the whole range of interests affected by policy. Given that the EU policy-making system is already based on deliberation, the task is therefore seen as one of injecting new voices from civil society into the major deliberative forums, and far greater transparency about key processes such as the comitology system. In this context, it is encouraging that such ideas have recently been advanced within the European Commission itself (Lebessis and Paterson 1999) and that the proposals for a Charter of Fundamental Rights in 2000 were drawn up by a Convention, including a far wider group of interests than is normal in the EU policy-making system.[10] Both direct and deliberative democracy are useful ways of enhancing participation.

The goal of inclusiveness cannot be addressed simply by viewing democracy and accountability in *quantitative* terms as the rule of the majority: it must also be seen in *qualitative* terms, so as to include the acceptance of fundamental rights for *all*. The policies of the EU now have an immense impact over the lives of millions of people, but its doctrine of rights has evolved in a piecemeal and incoherent manner, which has lagged behind the development of the Union as an economic force (Alston and Weiler 1999). The elaboration of a doctrine of fundamental rights at EU level, with clarity about monitoring and enforcement measures, would constitute a significant advance towards both democracy and accountability. It is particularly urgent to secure European-wide legislation against racism and other forms of discrimination and also to tackle human rights issues in relation to the Third Pillar. Of course, neither a charter of fundamental rights nor legislation can secure the establishment of an inclusive society, for political statements, even when backed by law, have only limited effect. Much of the responsibility would still lie at the level of the member states, some of which would no doubt go further than any general provision. Nevertheless, only the EU as a whole is able to define minimum standards for the area as a whole and it will be a significant qualitative advance if it does so.

Equality is the most remote democratic goal, particularly in view of the EU's current economic and monetary strategies, which circumscribe its approach to gender and wider social policies. It is possible to conceive of a form of EMU which would build social values into its operating mechanisms, but it would take an immense political transformation to bring this about in practice. With the decline of the traditional Left, and the redefinition of European social democracy, the forces pressing for socio-economic equality have also become substantially weaker in recent years. Yet it surely remains true that genuine political equality cannot exist in conditions of extreme socio-economic inequality? If so, the achievement of democracy and accountability in the EU will ultimately depend upon a revitalisation of the political forces which regard equality as the priority goal.

Notes

1 Some of the ideas and arguments in this chapter are developed more fully in Newman (1996) and Hoskyns and Newman (2000).

2 Lord (1998: 80–106) suggests that effective democratic accountability requires all of the following: administrative accountability of bureaucracies to political leaders; continuous parliamentary accountability of political leaders to democratic actors; electoral accountability based on a radical simplification of voter choice by democratic intermediaries, such as political parties, and on opportunities for the public to sanction their political leaders; and a system of judicial accountability through which citizens can bring power-holders to account if they seek to evade or distort the rules. He relates each of these to the EU in an excellent succinct analysis.

3 There are, of course, many theorists who disagree with this view. Some of the most persuasive arguments have been put by Joseph Weiler, who argues that there is, in effect, a constitution

which makes the Community a federal system, but that this has taken place without any explicit democratic authorisation. However, Weiler's legal and philosophical arguments do not seem to contradict the view expressed here that, in terms of power and political reality, the federal analogy is unhelpful.

4   Dictatorships also seek legitimacy and have sometimes done so partly by providing tangible benefits through the use of social policy.

5   Abromeit and Schmidt (1999) have presented a powerful argument to suggest that this form of legitimacy cannot be achieved by the EU.

6   It is true that there is also declining turnout in national elections in most countries, but this has limited relevance. Declining electoral turnout suggests that there are major problems in established liberal democracies, but there is an important difference between the situation in such systems and the EU. For the EU has not established democratic credentials and the Euro-elections constitute the sole visible aspect of democracy.

7   The relationship between increasing institutional efficiency and the potentially negative impact on issues of democracy was partially recognised in the report presented to the Commission (Dehaene *et al.* 1999) on 'The Institutional Implications of Enlargement'. But the solutions suggested did not address the fundamental problems.

8   Although Majone, the foremost theorist of this approach, has emphasised the distinctive characteristics of the EU, he has also argued that the tradition of regulation (rather than redistribution) has been embedded in the American system.

9   It is also notable that a protocol was added to the Treaty of Amsterdam to enable national parliaments to become more involved in EU affairs. This set a minimum of six weeks between the publication of a formal proposal by the Commission and its presentation to the Council, and stipulated that documentation sent to national parliaments would contain the date on which the proposed legislation was to be discussed by the Council.

10   There are also some difficulties in the approach: in particular, the mode of selection of the new actors and their relationship with society as a whole; and their need to ensure that they are not simply there to help legitimate decisions without playing a key role in the real policy-making process.

References

Abromeit, H. (1998) *Democracy in Europe: Legitimising Politics in a Non-State Polity*, New York/Oxford: Berghan Books.

Abromeit, H. and Schmidt, T. (1999) 'The Riddle of Borderless Democracy: On the Search of Transnational Demoi', paper presented at the conference of the IPSA Research Committee on European Unification, Brussels, 2–3 December 1999.

Alston, P. and Weiler, J. (1999) 'An "Ever Closer Union" in Need of a Human Rights Policy: The European Union and Human Rights', in P. Alston, M. Bustelo and J. Heenan (eds), *The EU and Human Rights*, Oxford: Oxford University Press.

Armstrong, K. (2000) *Regulation, Deregulation, Reregulation: The Paradoxes of European Governance*, London: Kogan Page/London European Research Centre.

Beetham, D. and Lord, C. (1998) *Legitimacy and the European Union*, London: Addison Wesley/Longman.

Benz, A. (1999) 'Compounded Democracy and Multi-Level Governance in the EU', paper presented at the conference of the IPSA Research Committee on European Unification, Brussels, 2–3 December 1999.

Bertrand, G., Michalski, A. and Pench, L. (1999) *Scenarios Europe 2010: Five Possible Futures for Europe*, Brussels: European Commission (Forward Studies Unit).

Bogdanor, V. (1986) 'The Future of the European Community: Two Models of Democracy', *Government and Opposition* 21/2: 161–76.

Bogdanor, V. and Woodcock, G. (1991) 'The European Community and Sovereignty', *Parliamentary Affairs* 44/4: 481–92.

Bohman, J. and Rehg, W. (eds) (1997) *Deliberative Democracy: Essays on Reason and Politics*, Cambridge, MA: MIT Press.

Chryssochoou, D. (1998) *Democracy in the European Union*, London/New York: Taurus.

Dehaene, J.-L., Simon, D. and von Weizsäcker, R. (1999) 'The Institutional Implications of Enlargement', Brussels: Report to the European Commission.

European Commission (1999) 'Proposal for a Council Directive Implementing the Principle of Equal Treatment between Persons Irrespective of Racial or Ethnic Origin', COM [1999] 566 final 99/0225 (CNS).

Fitzmaurice, J. (1996) *The Politics of Belgium: A Unique Federalism*, London: Hurst.

Gerstenberg, O. (1997) 'Law's Polyarchy: A Comment on Cohen and Sabel?' *European Law Journal* 3/4: 343–58.

Gustavsson, S. (1999) 'Monetary Union without Fiscal Union: A Politically Sustainable Asymmetry?' paper presented at the Research Conference of the Nordic Political Science Association, Uppsala, 19–21 August 1999.

Gustavsson, S. (2000) 'Reconciling Suprastatism and Accountability: A View from Sweden', in C. Hoskyns and M. Newman (eds), *Democratizing the European Union: Issues for the Twenty-First Century*, Manchester: Manchester University Press.

Héritier, A. (1997) 'Policy-Making by Subterfuge: Interest Accommodation, Innovation and Substitute Democratic Legitimation in Europe: Perspectives from Distinctive Policy Areas', *Journal of European Public Policy* 4/2: 171–89.

Hix, S. and Lord, C. (1997) *Political Parties in the European Union*, Houndmills/London: Macmillan.

Hoskyns, C. (2000a) 'Democratizing the EU: Evidence and Argument', in C. Hoskyns and M. Newman (eds), *Democratizing the European Union: Issues for the Twenty-First Century*, Manchester: Manchester University Press.

Hoskyns, C. (2000b) 'Deliberative Democracy and the European Union', paper presented at the PSA Conference, London, 10–13 April.

Hoskyns, C. and Lambert, J. (2000) 'How Democratic is the European Parliament?', in C. Hoskyns and M. Newman (eds), *Democratizing the European Union: Issues for the Twenty-First Century*, Manchester: Manchester University Press.

Hoskyns, C. and Newman, M. (eds) (2000) *Democratizing the European Union: Issues for the Twenty-First Century*, Manchester: Manchester University Press.

Joerges, C. and Neyer, J. (1997) 'Transforming Strategic Interaction into Deliberative Problem-Solving: European Comitology in the Foodstuffs Sector', *Journal of European Public Policy* 4/4: 609–25.

Kohler-Koch, B. (1999) 'Europe in Search of Legitimate Governance', paper presented at the conference of the IPSA Research Committee on European Unification, Brussels, 2–3 December.

Lebessis, N. and Paterson, J. (1999) *Improving the Effectiveness and Legitimacy of EU Governance: A Possible Reform Agenda for the Commission*, Brussels: European Commission (Forward Studies Unit).

Lintner, V. (2000) 'Controlling EMU', in C. Hoskyns and M. Newman (eds), *Democratizing the European Union: Issues for the Twenty-First Century*, Manchester: Manchester University Press.

Lord, C. (1998) *Democracy in the European Union*, Sheffield: Sheffield Academic Press/UACES.

Magnette, P. (1999) 'Can an Independent Organ be Held Accountable? The Emergent Parliamentary Control of the European Central Bank', paper presented at the conference of the IPSA Research Committee on European Unification, Brussels, 2–3 December.

Majone, G. (1996a) 'Regulatory Legitimacy', in G. Majone (ed.), *Regulating Europe*, London: Routledge.

Majone, G. (1996b) 'A European Regulatory State?', in J. Richardson (ed.), *European Union: Power and Policy-Making*, London: Routledge.

Marks, G., Hooghe, L. and Blank, K. (1996) 'European Integration from the 1980s: State-Centric vs Multi-Level Governance', *Journal of Common Market Studies* 34/3: 341–78.

Newman, M. (1996) *Democracy, Sovereignty and the European Union*, London: Hurst.

Rhinhard, M. (1999) 'Governing in Committees: An Analysis of the Democratic Legitimacy of the European Union Committee System', paper presented at the conference of the IPSA Research Committee on European Unification, Brussels, 2–3 December 1999.

Rometsch, D. and Wessels, W. (1996) (eds) *The European Union and Member States: Towards Institutional Fusion*, Manchester: Manchester University Press.

Rousseau, J.-J. (1947) *The Social Contract* , New York: Hafner.

Shonfield, A. (1973) *Europe: Journey to an Unknown Destination*, Harmondsworth: Penguin.
Stewart, J., Lewis, N. and Longley, D. (1992) *Accountability to the Public*, London: European Policy Forum.
Weiler, J. (1994) 'Fin de siècle Europe', in R. Dehousse (ed.), *Europe After Maastricht: An Ever Closer Union?*, Munich: Beck.
Weiler, J. (1999) *The Constitution of Europe*, Cambridge: Cambridge University Press.
Wessels, W. (1997) 'An Ever Closer Fusion? A Dynamic Macropolitical View on Integration Processes', *Journal of Common Market Studies* 35/2: 267–99.

Index

Note: page numbers in *italic* type refer to *tables*; page numbers followed by n refer to notes.